GIRLS
& SEX

PEGGY ORENSTEIN
GIRLS & SEX

NAVIGATING THE COMPLICATED
NEW LANDSCAPE

HARPER

An Imprint of HarperCollins*Publishers*

The names and identifying characteristics of certain individuals have been changed to protect their privacy.

HarperCollins books may be purchased for educational, business, or sales promotional use. For information, please e-mail the Special Markets Department at SPsales@harpercollins.com.

FIRST EDITION

Designed by Lisa Stokes

Library of Congress Cataloging-in-Publication Data has been applied for.

ISBN: 978-0-06-220972-6

16 17 18 19 20   OV/RRD   10 9 8 7 6 5 4 3 2 1

*For my one daughter, my eight nieces, my two nephews,
and all the girls and boys I've met along the way*

Contents

Contents

GIRLS
& SEX

Everything You Never Wanted to Know About Girls and Sex (but Really Need to Ask)

A few years ago I realized that my daughter wouldn't be a little girl much longer. She was headed toward adolescence, and honestly, it put me in a bit of a panic. Way back in preschool, when she was swanning around in her Cinderella gown, I took a deep dive into the princess industrial complex and came back convinced that its seemingly innocent pink-and-pretty culture was priming little girls for something more insidious later on. Well, "later on" was now coming at us like a Mack truck—a Mack truck whose driver was wearing five-inch heels and a micro-mini, and was checking her Instagram when she ought to have been looking at the road. I'd heard horror stories from friends with teenagers about how girls were treated in the so-called hookup culture; of girls coerced into sexting or victimized in social media scandals; of omnipresent porn.

I was supposed to be the expert at decoding the mixed messages of girlhood. I traveled the country schooling parents on the difference between sexualization and sexuality. "When little girls play at 'sexy' before they even understand the word," I'd tell them, "they learn that sex is a performance rather than a felt experience." True enough. But what about once they *did* understand the word?

It wasn't as if I had any answers. I, too, was just trying my best to raise a healthy daughter at a time when celebrities presented self-objectification as a source of strength, power, and independence; when looking desirable seemed a substitute for feeling desire; when *Fifty Shades of Grey*, with its neurasthenic lip-chewing heroine and creepy stalker billionaire, was being hailed as the ultimate feminine fantasy; when no woman under the age of forty appeared to have pubic hair. Sure, as a girl I wore out songs such as "Sexual Healing" and "Like a Virgin," but they were Disney Channel fodder compared to L'il Wayne's "bitch" whose "strict diet" in the song "Love Me" consists of nothing but "dick"; or Maroon 5's promise to hunt a woman down and eat her alive in "Animals." (In the video, lead singer Adam Levine stalks the object of his obsession while dressed as a butcher wielding a meat hook, then has sex with her in a blood-drenched finale.) It's enough to make me apologize to Tipper Gore for the way my friends and I mocked her in the '90s. Meanwhile, study after study has revealed a shocking prevalence of sexual assault on college campuses; the problem is so dire that the president of the United States (himself the father of two teen girls) has become involved.

Even as girls outnumbered boys in college, as they "leaned in" to achieve their academic and professional dreams, I had to wonder: Were we moving forward or backward? Did today's young women have more freedom than their mothers to shape their sexual encounters, more influence and more control within them? Were they better able to resist stigma, better equipped to explore joy? And if not, why not? Girls now live in a culture where, increasingly, unless both parties agree unequivocally to a sexual encounter, there is no consent—only "yes means yes." All well and good, but what happens *after* yes?

I NEEDED, AS a mom and a journalist, to find out the truth behind the headlines, what was real and what was hype. So I began interviewing girls: engaging in in-depth, hours-long conversations about their attitudes, expectations, and early experiences with the full range of physical intimacy. I recruited daughters of friends of friends (and the friends of those girls, and their friends, too); students of high school teachers I had met. I would ask professors on campuses I visited to send out an e-mail blast, inviting any girls interested in talking to me to get in touch. In the end, I interviewed more than seventy young women between the ages of fifteen and twenty, an age span during which most will become sexually active. (The average American has first intercourse at seventeen; by nineteen, three fourths of teens have had sex.) My focus remained on girls alone because, as a journalist, writing about young women has been a passion, a calling: I've been chronicling their lives for over twenty-five years. Girls, too, continue to live with unique contradictions as they make sexual choices: despite the seismic changes in expectations and opportunity, they're still subject to the same old double standard, the idea that a sexually active girl is a "slut," while a similar boy is a "player." Now, though, girls who abstain from sex, once thought of as the "good girls," are shamed as well, labeled "virgins" (which is not a good thing) or "prudes." As one high school senior said to me, "Usually the opposite of a negative is a positive, but in this case it's two negatives. So what are you supposed to do?"

I don't claim to reflect the experience of all young women. My interview subjects were either in college or college bound—I specifically wanted to talk to those who felt they had all options open to them, the ones who had most benefited from women's economic and political progress. They were also self-selected. That said, I cast my net broadly. The girls I met came from across the country, from large cities and small towns. They were Catholic, mainline Protestant, Evangelical, Jewish, and unaffiliated. Some of their parents were married, some were divorced; some lived in blended families, some in single-parent households. They came from politically conservative as well as liberal backgrounds, though most leaned somewhat toward the latter. The majority was white, but many were Asian American, Latina, African American, Arab American, or mixed race. About 10 percent identified as lesbian or bisexual, though most, particularly those still in high school, had not acted on their attraction to other girls. Two were physically disabled. While most came disproportionately from upper-middle-class families, there was some range of economic background—I interviewed girls from the East Side of Manhattan and the South Side of Chicago; girls whose parents managed hedge funds and those whose parents managed fast-food restaurants. To protect their privacy, I have changed all names and identifying details.

At first, I worried that girls wouldn't discuss such a personal subject with me. I needn't have. Wherever I went, I had more volunteers than I could handle. They were not just eager, they were *hungry* to talk. No adult had ever before inquired about their experience of sexuality: what they did, why they did it, how it felt, what they hoped for, what they regretted, what was fun. Often in interviews, I barely asked a question. The girls would just start talking, and before we knew it, hours had gone by. They told me how they felt about masturbation, about oral sex (both giving and receiving), about orgasm. They talked about toeing that line between virgin and slut. They told me about boys who were aggressive and boys who were caring; boys who abused them and boys who restored their faith in love. They admitted their attraction to other girls and their fears of parental rejection. They talked about the complicated terrain of the hookup culture, in which casual encounters precede (and may or may not lead to) emotional connection; now commonplace on college campuses, it was rapidly drifting down to high school. Fully half the girls had experienced something along a spectrum of coercion to rape. Those stories were agonizing; equally upsetting, only two had previously told another adult what had happened.

Even in consensual encounters, much of what the girls described was painful to hear. Perhaps that seems like nothing new, but that in itself is worth exploring. When so much has changed for girls in the public realm, why hasn't more—*much* more—changed in the private one? Can there be true equality in the classroom and the boardroom if there isn't in the bedroom? Back in 1995 the National Commission on Adolescent Sexual Health declared healthy sexual development a basic human right. Teen intimacy, it said, ought to be "consensual, non-exploitative, honest, pleasurable, and protected against unintended pregnancy and STDs." How is it, over two decades later, that we are so shamefully short of that goal?

Sara McClelland, a professor of psychology at the University of Michigan, writes about sexuality as a matter of "intimate justice," touching on fundamental issues of gender inequality, economic disparity, violence, bodily integrity, physical and mental health, self-efficacy, and power dynamics in our most personal relationships. She asks us to consider: Who has the right to engage in sexual behavior? Who has the right to enjoy it? Who is the primary beneficiary of the experience? Who feels deserving? How does each partner define "good enough?" Those are thorny questions when looking at female sexuality at any age, but particularly when considering girls' early, formative experience. Nonetheless, I was determined to ask them.

A number of the girls I met stayed in touch long after we spoke, e-mailing updates about new relationships or evolving beliefs. "I wanted to let you know that because of our conversation I've changed my major," one wrote. "I'm going to study health with a focus on gender and sexuality." Another, a high school junior, told me our discussion affected the questions she asked while touring college campuses. A third, a high school senior, confessed to her boyfriend that all her "orgasms" had been fake; yet another high-schooler told *her* boyfriend to stop pressuring her to climax; it was ruining sex. The interviews—with the young women themselves and with psychologists, sociologists, pediatricians, educators, journalists, and other experts—changed me, too, forced me to confront my biases, overcome discomfort, clarify my values. That, I believe, has made me a better parent, a better aunt, a better ally to all the young women, and the young men, in my life. I hope, after reading this book, you will feel the same way.

CHAPTER 1

Matilda Oh Is Not an Object—
Except When She Wants to Be

Camila Ortiz and Izzy Lang had heard it all before. They were seniors at a large California high school—with a campus of over 3,300 students—so this was their fourth September, their fourth "welcome back" assembly. They sat toward the rear of the auditorium, alternately daydreaming and chatting with friends as administrators droned on about the importance of attendance ("especially for you seniors"); the behaviors that could get you suspended; the warnings about cigarettes, alcohol, and weed. Then the dean of students addressed the girls in the crowd. "He was like, 'Ladies, when you go out you need to dress to respect yourself and respect your family,'" recalled Izzy. Blond and blue-eyed, she had a dimple in one cheek that deepened as she spoke. "'This isn't the place for your short shorts or your tank tops or your crop tops. You need to ask yourself: if your grandmother looks at you, will she be happy with what you're wearing?'"

Camila, whose left nostril was pierced with a subtle crystal stud, jumped in, her index finger wagging. "'You need to cover that up because you need to have respect for yourself.' *You need to respect yourself. You need to respect your family.* That idea was just . . . repeated and repeated. And then he went from that immediately into the slides defining sexual harassment. Like there was a connection. Like maybe if you don't 'respect yourself' by the way you dress you're going to get harassed, and that's your own fault because you wore the tank top."

Growing up in this very school system, Camila had learned the importance of challenging injustice, of being an "upstander." So she began to shout the dean's name. "Mr. Williams! Mr. Williams!" she yelled. He invited her to the front of the auditorium and handed her the mic. "Hi, I'm Camila," she said. "I'm a twelfth-grader and I think what you just said is not okay and is extremely sexist and promoting 'rape culture.' If I want to wear a tank top and shorts because it's hot, I should be able to do that and that has no correlation to how much 'respect' I hold for myself. What you're saying is just continuing this cycle of blaming the victim." The students in the auditorium cheered, and Camila handed back the mic.

"Thank you, Camila. I totally agree," Mr. Williams said as she walked back to her seat. Then he added, "But there's a time and a place for that type of clothing."

This was not the first earful I'd gotten about girls' provocative dress: from parents, from teachers, from administrators, from girls themselves. Parents went to battle over the skimpiness of shorts, the clingy V-necks, the tush-cupping yoga pants that showed "everything." *Why do girls have to dress like that?* moms asked, even as some wore similar outfits themselves. Principals tried to impose decorum, but ended up inciting rebellion. In suburban Chicago, eighth-graders picketed a proposed policy against leggings. High-schoolers in Utah took to the Internet when they discovered digitally raised necklines and sleeves added to female classmates' shirts in their yearbook photos.

Boys run afoul of dress codes when they flout authority: "hippies" defying the establishment, "thugs" in saggy pants. For girls, the issue is sex. Enforcing modesty is considered a way both to protect and to contain young women's sexuality; and they, by association, are charged with controlling young men's. After the assembly, the dean of attendance, who was female, stopped Camila in the hallway. "I totally get that you're trying to empower yourself," she told the girl, "but it's a bit distracting. You have male teachers, and there are male students."

"Maybe you shouldn't be hiring male teachers that are focused on staring at my boobs!" Camila shot back. The dean said they could continue the conversation later. "Later" never came.

That was three months ago, and Camila was still furious. "The truth is, it doesn't matter what I wear," she said. "Four out of five days going to school I will be catcalled, I will be stared at, I will be looked up and down, I will be touched. You just accept it as part of going to school. I can't help my body type, and it's super distracting to *me* to know that every time I get up to sharpen my pencil there's going to be a comment about my butt. That doesn't happen to guys. No guy has ever had to walk down the hall and had girls going, 'Hey, boy, your calves are looking great! Your calves are *hot*.'"

Camila is right. Addressing boys directly is the only way to challenge the assumption by some that girls' bodies exist for them to judge—and even touch—however and whenever they wish. The previous year at the girls' high school, a group of boys created an Instagram account to "expose" the campus THOTs, an acronym for That Ho Over There. (Every generation seems to invent a new *Scarlet Letter* word—*strumpet, hussy, tramp, slut, skank, ho*—with which to demonize girls' sexuality.) They down-loaded pictures from girls' Instagram or Twitter accounts (or snapped one in the hallways), captioning each with the girl's pur-ported sexual history. All the girls singled out were black or La-tina. Camila was one of them. "It was such a violation," she said. "Part of the caption was 'I dare you to go fuck her for a good time.' I had to go to school with that out there." When she lodged a formal complaint, she was placed in a room with four male school security guards who, she said, asked whether she had ac-tually performed the acts attributed to her on the site. Humili-ated, she let the matter drop. The Instagram account eventually petered out; the perpetrators were never caught.

Whether online or IRL ("in real life"), Camila's was hardly an isolated case. Another girl, a high school junior in nearby Marin County, California, who played varsity volleyball, told me how boys from the soccer team gathered in the bleachers to harass her teammates during practice, yelling things like "Nice gooch!"(urban dictionary slang for perineum) when the girls lunged to make a shot. (There are, incidentally, hundreds of close-up, rear-view photos of underage girls in volleyball shorts on the Internet.) A senior in San Francisco described how, within days of arriving at an elite summer journalism program she attended in Chicago, the boys created a "slut draft" (akin to a fantasy football league), ranking their female peers in order of "who they wanted to fuck."

"The girls were pissed off," she told me, "but we couldn't com-plain because of all the implications, right? If you complain and you're on the list, you're a prude. If you complain and you're not on it, you're ugly. If you complain about it being sexist, then you're a humorless feminist bitch and a lesbian."

I heard about a boy who, claiming to have "magic arms,"

would hug random girls in his New York City public school hallway and then announce his assessment of their bra size; about a high school boy who sauntered up to a stranger at a party in Saint Paul, Minnesota, and asked, "Can I touch your boobs?"; about boys at dances everywhere who, especially after a few (or more) drinks, felt free to "grind" against girls from behind, unbidden. Most girls had learned to gracefully disengage from such situations if uninterested. Boys rarely pursued. Several young women, though, said a dance partner had gone further, pushing aside their skirts and sliding a quick finger into their underwear. By college, girls attending a frat party may not make it to the dance floor at all unless they passed what one called the "pretty test" at the front door, where a designated brother "decides whether you are accepted or rejected, beautiful or ugly. He's the reason you better wear a crop top in subzero weather or you'll end up home alone eating microwave popcorn and calling your mom."

I'm going to say this once here, and then—because it is obvious—I will not repeat it in the course of this book: not all boys engage in such behavior, not by a long shot, and many young men are girls' staunchest allies. However, every girl I spoke with, *every single girl*—regardless of her class, ethnicity, or sexual orientation; regardless of what she wore, regardless of her appearance—had been harassed in middle school, high school, college, or, often, all three. Who, then, is truly at risk of being "distracted" at school?

At best, blaming girls' clothing for the thoughts and actions of boys is counterproductive. At worst, it's a short step from there to "she was asking for it." Yet, I also can't help but feel that girls such as Camila, who favors what she called "more so-called provocative" clothing, are missing something. Taking up the right to bare arms (and legs and cleavage and midriffs) as a feminist rallying cry strikes me as suspiciously Orwellian. I recall the simple litmus test for sexism proposed by British feminist Caitlin Moran, one that Camila unconsciously referenced: Are the guys doing it, too? "If they aren't," Moran wrote, "chances are you're dealing with what we strident feminists refer to as 'some total fucking bullshit.'"

So while only girls get catcalled, it's also true that only girls' fashions urge body consciousness at the very youngest ages. Target offers bikinis for infants. The Gap hawks "skinny jeans" for toddlers. Preschoolers worship Disney princesses, characters whose eyes are larger than their waists. No one is trying to convince eleven-year-old boys to wear itty-bitty booty shorts or bare their bellies in the middle of winter. As concerned as I am about the policing of girls' sexuality through clothing, I also worry about the incessant drumbeat of self-objectification: the pressure on young women to reduce their worth to their bodies and to see those bodies as a collection of parts that exist for others' pleasure; to continuously monitor their appearance; to perform rather than to feel sensuality. I recall a conversation I had with Deborah Tolman, a professor at Hunter College and perhaps the foremost expert on teenage girls' sexual desire. In her work, she said, girls had begun responding "to questions about how their bodies feel—questions about sexuality or arousal—by describing how they think they look. I have to remind them that looking good is *not* a feeling." Self-objectification has been associated with depression, reduced cognitive function, lower GPA, distorted body image, body monitoring, eating disorders, risky sexual behavior, and reduced sexual pleasure. In one study of eighth-graders, self-objectification accounted for half the differential in girls' reports of depression and more than two-thirds of the variance in their self-esteem. Another study linked girls' focus on appearance to heightened shame and anxiety about their bodies. A study of twelfth-graders connected self-objectification to more negative attitudes about sexuality, discomfort in talking about sex, and higher rates of sexual regret. Self-objectification has also been correlated with lower political efficacy: the idea that you can have an impact in the public forum, that you can bring about change.

Despite those risks, hypersexualization is ubiquitous, so visible as to be nearly invisible: it is the water in which girls swim, the air they breathe. Whatever else they might be—athletes, artists, scientists, musicians, newscasters, politicians—they learn that they must, as a female, first and foremost project sex appeal. Consider a report released by Princeton University in 2011 exploring the drop over the previous decade in public leadership positions held by female students. Among the reasons these über-elite young women gave for avoiding such roles was that being qualified was not enough. They needed to be "smart, driven, involved in many different activities (as are men), and, in addition, they are supposed to be pretty, sexy, thin, nice, and friendly." Or, as one alumna put it, women had to "do everything, do it well, and look 'hot' while doing it." A 2013 study at Boston College, meanwhile, found that female students were graduating with lower self-esteem than when they entered the school (boys' self-esteem rose). They, too, in part blamed "the pressure to look or dress a certain way." A sophomore in a survey at Duke that reached similar conclusions called the phenomenon "effortless perfection," the "expectation that one would be smart, accomplished, fit, beautiful, and popular, and that all this would happen without visible effort." No wonder they faltered.

"Hot," as journalist Ariel Levy wrote in her book, *Female Chauvinist Pigs*, is different from "beautiful" or "attractive." It is a commercialized, one-dimensional, infinitely replicated, and, frankly, unimaginative vision of sexiness, one that, when applied to women, can be reduced to two words: "fuckable and saleable." Levy says that "hotness" is specifically women's work, and nowhere was that more evident than on the 2015 *Vanity Fair* cover featuring Caitlyn Jenner, née Bruce. To announce her physical transition from male to female, the sixty-five-year-old appeared in a corset (from a store called Trashy Lingerie), breasts overflowing, lips glossed like an ingénue's. That image was often juxtaposed in the press with a picture of her as Bruce, hair lank with sweat, arms raised in triumph after winning Olympic gold. As a man, he used his body; as a woman, she displayed it. Certainly, it's no revelation that girls are held to a punishingly narrow, often surgically or digitally enhanced ideal of "sexy," and then labeled as "sluts" when they pursue it. What has changed is this: whereas earlier generations of media-literate, feminist-identified women saw their objectification as something to protest, today's often see it as a personal choice, something that can be taken on intentionally as an expression rather than an imposition of sexuality. And why wouldn't they, if "hot" has been portrayed as compulsory, a prerequisite to a woman's relevance, strength, and independence?

The girls I met talked about feeling both powerful and powerless while dressed in revealing clothing, using words like *liberating*, *bold*, *boss bitch*, and *desirable*, even as they expressed indignation over the constant public judgment of their bodies. They felt simultaneously that they actively chose a sexualized image—which was nobody's damned business but their own—*and* that they had no choice. "You want to stand out," one college sophomore told me. "You want to attract someone. So it's not just about being hot, but who can be the *hottest*. One of my friends has gotten to the point where she's practically naked at parties." Girls shifted between subject and object day by day, moment by moment, sometimes without intending to, sometimes unsure themselves of which they were. Camila, for instance, had worn a brand-new bustier top to school the previous day. "When I got dressed I was like, 'I feel super comfortable with myself,'" she said. "'I feel really hot and this is going to be a good day.' Then, as soon as I got to school, I felt like"—she snapped her fingers— "automatically I wasn't in control. People are staring at you, looking you up and down, saying things. I started second-guessing myself, thinking, 'I shouldn't have worn this shirt. It's too revealing, it's too tight.' It was dehumanizing." Listening to Camila, I was struck by the assertion that how "hot" she felt would determine the quality of her day; also that, midway through her story, she switched to the second person—as if she, like those around her, suddenly saw herself as an object.

I used to say, when speaking publicly on college campuses or to groups of parents, that one could disentangle sexualization from sexuality by remembering that the first is foisted on girls from the outside, the other cultivated from within. I'm no longer sure it's so simple. It may seem clearly unhealthy when a three-year-old insists on wearing high heels to preschool every day or a five-year-old asks if she's "sexy" or a seven-year-old begs for that padded bikini top from Abercrombie (an item that was pulled from the shelves after parental protest). But what about the sixteen-year-old who washes her boyfriend's car clad in a bikini top and Daisy Dukes? What about that strip aerobics class the college freshman is taking? And what about, you know, that *outfit*? As Sydney, a Bay Area high school senior sporting oversize geek-chic glasses, asked me, "Isn't there a difference between dressing slutty because you *don't* feel good about yourself, and you want validation, and dressing slutty because you *do* feel good about yourself and don't need validation?"

"Could be," I replied. "Explain how you know which is which."

Sydney gazed down at the chipped black polish on her nails and began flipping one of her silver rings from finger to finger and back again. "I can't," she said after a moment. "My whole life is an attempt to figure out what, in the core of myself, I actually like versus what I want to hear from other people, or wanting to look a certain way to get attention. And part of me feels cheated out of my own well-being because of that."

Girls do push back against the constraints of "hot," the contradictory message that it is mandatory yet also the justification for their harassment or assault. A spontaneous movement of "Slutwalks" exploded in 2011, after a Toronto policeman suggested that college women who wanted to avoid sexual assault shouldn't dress so provocatively. Infuriated, young women across the globe, many in fishnets and garters, hit the streets bearing signs reading such things as "My Dress Is Not a Yes!" and "My Ass Is Not an Excuse for Assault!" At the other end of the spectrum, Generation Y made news both by growing out their armpit hair and rejecting the torture device commonly known as thong underwear (some in favor of "granny pants" with "Feminist" stamped across the rump), proving they could be sexy without pandering to "hot." On a more personal level, one of the young women I met, an art student, told me that, tired of the "costume" that girls were expected to don at college parties, she was opting for a different one, showing up dressed as a sparkly unicorn. "I feel liberated," she told me. "It's still kind of body-conscious, and there is a lot of makeup involved, but I'm also fully covered. And I'm one-of-a-kind."

Hot or Not: Social Media and the New "Body Product"

Girls did not always organize their thinking about themselves around the physical. Before World War I, self-improvement meant being *less* self-involved, *less* vain: helping others, focusing on schoolwork, becoming better read, and cultivating empathy. Author Joan Jacobs Brumberg highlighted this change in her book *The Body Project* by comparing the New Year's resolutions of girls at the end of the nineteenth and twentieth centuries:

"Resolved," wrote a girl in 1892, "to think before speaking. To work seriously. To be self-restrained in conversations and actions. Not to let my thoughts wander. To be dignified. Interest myself more in others."

And one hundred years later:

"I will try to make myself better in any way I possibly can. . . . I will lose weight, get new lenses, already got new haircut, good makeup, new clothes and accessories."

Brumberg's book was published in the late 1990s, a good decade before social media took off. With the advent of MySpace, then Facebook, then Twitter, Instagram, Snapchat, Tumblr, Tinder, YikYak, and—mark my words—some social media–linked microchip that they'll soon implant in all our heads, the body has become even more entrenched as the ultimate expression of the female self, evolving from "project" to consciously marketed "product." There are myriad ways social media can be fun, creative, connective, political. They can be a lifeline for kids who feel different from their peers, particularly LGBTQ teens, providing them with crucial support and community. They have also reinforced the relentless externalization of girls' sense of self. There is evidence that the more concerned a girl is about her appearance, weight, and body image, the more likely she is to consult the magic mirror of her social media profile, and vice versa: the more she checks her profile, the more concerned she becomes about appearance, weight, and body image. Comments on girls' pages, too, tend to focus disproportionately on looks, and even more than in the real world, that becomes a measure of friendship, self-image, and self-worth.

In a windowless basement office on a private midwestern college campus, Sarah, a first-semester sophomore, stood in front of me with the toes of one foot pointed forward, one knee slightly bent, to demonstrate the "leg bevel"—a pose pioneered by showgirls but which is now standard in girls' social media photos. "It slims your body more than if you stand normally," she explained. Sarah grew up in Atlanta, where she attended a small Christian high school. She had dyed blond hair that hung to her shoulders, blue eyes, and carefully applied makeup—foundation, eye shadow, lipstick. "People will"—she stopped and laughed self-consciously—"this is so stupid, but people will learn the ways to pose in pictures so they'll look good on Facebook or Instagram. I mean, I do it. A hand on your hip—that makes you look thinner, too. Or, whichever side you part your hair on, the other side would be your 'better' side, so I try to face this way in photos." She turned her right cheek toward me and continued. "I edit little blemishes out and fix the lighting. And if you watch things like *America's Next Top Model*, you learn to 'find your light.' Things like that."

Teens have always been acutely aware of how they are seen by their peers. Social media amps up that self-consciousness: rather than experimenting among a small group of people they actually know, they now lay out their thoughts, photos, tastes, and activities (as well as their lapses in judgment) for immediate approval or censure by their 947 BFFs, many of whom are relative strangers. The result, according to Adriana Manago, a researcher at the Children's Digital Media Center in Los Angeles who studies college students' behavior on social media, is that young people have begun talking about the self as a brand rather than something to be developed from within. Their "friends" become an audience to be sought after and maintained. Ninety-two percent of teens go online daily, including 24 percent who are online "almost constantly." Nearly three-quarters use two or more social networking sites. Also, especially on photo-sharing sites such as Instagram, girls are more active than boys, who are more likely to be gamers. "You use your experience to create an image," Matilda Oh, a high school senior in San Francisco told me, "with the ultimate goal being to show that you're desirable and attractive and wanted and liked." Every young woman, she said, knows that she will "get ten times as many 'likes' by posting a picture of yourself in a bikini than you would if you were wearing a snow jacket." Yet, just as in the real world, girls must be careful to come off as "hot" yet not "slutty," sexually confident but not "thirsty." In one study of 1,500 Facebook profiles, college-age women judged other girls' profiles far more harshly than they did boys', criticizing those who had "too many" friends, shared "too much" information, showed "too much" skin in photos, name checked their boyfriends "too often," posted "too many" status updates. This despite the fact that 1,499 of the profiles aspired to the same "ideal": a girl who, through status updates, glamour shots, and skin-bearing selfies, depicted herself as "fun" and "carefree"; who had lots of attractive friends, went to lots of parties, and was interested mostly in romance, pop culture, and shopping. You could easily get trashed, then, for the very thing you needed to do to court approval.

It doesn't take much to become a target. "You can totally

get stigmatized," agreed Sarah. "I knew a girl who only Insta-grammed selfies. Every single picture was a selfie. And people talked about it. It made her seem like she either had no friends or was too into herself. There are so many ways to be judged. And of course you're afraid that the judgments you pass against others will be passed against you. It's not something you ever talk about, though. You just try to listen to what people say and kind of learn those unwritten rules. Like, don't change your profile picture too much. Don't post statuses about everything you're doing. Don't have too many pictures of yourself."

In 2013 *selfie* was named the "international word of the year" by Oxford Dictionaries. Anyone with a Facebook or Instagram account probably has posted a few, but no one matches the self-chronicling output of adolescent girls (interestingly, after age forty, men become the more dominant selfie posters—perhaps in midlife, women unconsciously render themselves invisible). The portraits can be a giddy assertion of pride for young women, a claim staked for the right to take up public space. "If you write off the endless stream of posts as image-conscious narcissism," Rachel Simmons, author of *Odd Girl Out*, has written, "you'll miss the chance to watch girls practice promoting themselves—a skill that boys are otherwise given more permission to develop, and which serves them later on when they negotiate for raises and promotions."

Personally, I love flipping through posts by the girls I know (my nieces, my friends' kids, the girls I interview), seeing them in front of national monuments or on graduation day or clown-ing around with friends. That doesn't, however, allay my con-cern that selfies can impose another tyranny on girls, another imperative to dish up their bodies for inspection by others and themselves, another way in which their value is reduced to the superficial, flattened, measured by visibility. As one girl said to me, "It's like cell phones, Facebook—all of it comes back to the issue of: Am I pretty? How many friends do I have? How do my profile pictures look? Let me stalk *myself*."

The girls I met, again, were not passive; they were not victims of social media. They were acutely literate, often avidly feminist. They actively engaged in contemporary culture even as they struggled with the meaning and impact of that engagement. Nearly two-thirds of teen girls in one large-scale survey did feel that selfies boosted their confidence. So there's that. But about half also said that photos posted of them by *others* (presumably less mindful of their best angles) have the potential to make them feel bad. Body dissatisfaction seems less driven by the actual time young women spent on social media than by how much of that time they spend sharing and viewing photos; the more they look at others' pictures, whether close friends or distant peers, the more unhappy they become about their own appearance. Little wonder, then, that there has been a proliferation of "selfie surgery apps," which allow a user to shrink her nose, whiten her teeth, broaden her smile. Actual plastic surgery among those under thirty is on the rise, too. In 2011 there was a 71 percent increase in the number of high school girls obtaining chin implants specifically because they wanted to look better in prom selfies. One of every three members surveyed by the American Academy of Facial Plastic and Reconstructive Surgery in 2013 said that their patients sought their services to look better in selfies.

Posting pictures of yourself—even lots and lots of pictures of yourself—while eating cereal or shopping for a prom dress or hanging with your besties is one thing. What really worries parents is the selfie's evil cousin: the sext. *Do not*, we tell our daughters, absolutely *do not* send anyone sexually explicit messages or, God forbid, a nude or seminude photo. The Internet is forever, we say. Snapchat doesn't prevent screenshots that can be redistributed in an instant and used as weapons (witness the rise of "revenge porn": explicit images posted online without the victim's consent, often following a breakup). In truth, it's hard to know exactly how common "sexting" is among teens. In surveys, between 15 and 48 percent (depending on the age of the children asked and how "sexting" is defined) say they have sent or received an explicit text or photo. What is clear, though, is that the practice is not gender neutral. While equal numbers of boys and girls may sext voluntarily, girls are twice as likely to be among those who were pressured, coerced, blackmailed, or threatened into it—fully half of teen sexting in one large-scale survey fell into those categories. That's particularly disturbing, since coercion into sexting appears to cause more long-term anxiety, depression, and trauma than coercion into real-life sex. Among the girls I met, the badgering to send nude photos could be incessant, beginning in middle school. One girl described how, in eighth grade, a male classmate threatened (in a text) to commit suicide if she didn't send him a picture of her breasts. She told her parents, while a friend of hers he also targeted complied. Sometimes the pressure was mixed with girls' own desire to please, to provoke, or to be affirmed as hot. They sexted photos to boyfriends to prove their trust, or to boys whose interest they hoped to attract. (Boys did this, too, but girls typically considered it aggressive and "gross.") One girl told me that there had been an "epidemic" of classmates at her private Jewish middle school who flashed their breasts at boys while video chatting. The boys began taking screenshots and posting them online.

"Did the girls want that to happen?" I asked.

"No," she said. "But it did." By high school, the girls had "grown out of it," but the boys had not. "I would video chat with boys, and they'd be like, 'Come on! Flash me! Flash me!' I wouldn't do it, but they'd be very persistent. They'd say, 'Just do it. I promise I won't take a picture.' And if you really like the guy, you think maybe he'll like you back. . . . There were boys who had whole folders of pictures. Like trophies."

Some girls considered sexting and sexy video chatting a way to experiment with sex safely (at least as they saw it). "I would do really graphic sexting over IM in middle and high school," a freshman at a mid-Atlantic college told me, "or do stripteases on Skype. I wasn't ready to lose my virginity, but I loved being the bad girl." She didn't worry that her recipients might share her performances; she believed she could use her body to intimidate as well as entice. "I'm six feet tall," she said. "I'm not this dainty little thing. I was like, if you pass this around you will not have balls anymore. I will *hurt* you. So I felt in control."

Are selfies empowering or oppressive? Is sexting harmful or harmless? Is that skirt an assertion of sexuality or an exploitation of it? Try this: looking up at the ceiling, raise your hand over your head and trace a clockwise circle with your index finger. Continue to trace the circle while slowly lowering your arm so that your finger is at eye level. Now, still tracing, lower your arm further until it's at your waist. Look down at the circle. Which direction is it spinning? Although it would seem impossible, the circle moves clockwise and counterclockwise at the same time. Management consultants use that "both/and" concept to break down rigid "either/or" thinking. Deborah Tolman has suggested that it's equally useful when considering young women's complicated relationships to their bodies, their sexuality, and sexualization. That's the challenge to both parents and girls themselves: whether you're discussing dress codes, social media, or the influence of pop culture, there is rarely a clear-cut truth.

Parts Is Parts

2014 was "all about that bass," the lyrics to Meghan Trainor's wildly popular confection themselves riddled with both/and contradiction. The song ostensibly celebrated the body positive, rejecting the "stick-figure silicone Barbie doll" ideal. Yet it contained a Trojan horse: not only did Trainor take a gratuitous swipe at "skinny bitches" (followed by a coy "No, I'm just playing"), but she also reassured young women that "boys, they like a little more booty to hold at night." So, sure it's fine to be curvier—as long as guys still think you're hot.

Trainor was kind of late to the party, though: the "bass" was already in ascendance, metamorphosing from a Sir Mix-A-Lot novelty song to a JLo trademark, to a national obsession. On the cover of her single "Anaconda," Nicki Minaj squatted, back to the camera, her knees splayed, revealing a prodigious (and, rumor has it, surgically enhanced) posterior. The art for Lady Gaga's single "Do What You Want" featured a be-thonged upthrust rear. (The chorus of the song itself, a duet with alleged child rapist R. Kelly, is "Do what you want, what you want with my body.") During her On the Run tour, Beyoncé appeared in a Givenchy-designed bodysuit with cutouts that showed off her naked buns. The cover of the 2014 *Sports Illustrated Swimsuit Issue* portrayed yet another rear view: three topless supermodels gazing playfully over their shoulders as they offer their near-bare bum cheeks for readers' inspection. Later that year, Lopez rereleased her trend-launching hit "Booty" with a new, far more explicit video, featuring "Pu$$y" rapper Iggy Azalea. And Kim Kardashian notoriously tried to "break the Internet" with a *Paper* magazine cover shot of her bounteous (and, again, possibly augmented) derrière, slick with baby oil.

And there's more! Jen Selter, a fitness model dubbed the Belfie Queen—that's "butt selfie"—has over 7 million Instagram oglers and earns as much as sixty thousand dollars for sponsored posts. For the more ordinary mortals, an eighty-dollar gizmo called a "belfie stick," designed to help capture that perfect rear angle, sold out immediately online and, at this writing, had a months-long waiting list. Between 2012 and 2013 the number of "Brazilian butt lifts" performed in the United States, in which fat is transferred from another part of the body to the rear, jumped 16 percent. For those short the ten thousand dollars required for that procedure, sales of twenty-two-dollar Booty Pop panties—think padded bra for the bum—were up in November 2014 nearly 50 percent from the same period a year earlier; the company subsequently introduced a new, larger product, with 25 percent more foam.

Maybe it was just the butt's turn: After all, how many more hours could women while away obsessing over their stomachs, breasts, hips, upper arms, necks, and faces? How many more cosmetic procedures could they undergo? Something had to fill the breach. Truly, you'd think that after buying into the horror of the "thigh gap," women would resist being defined by yet another body part, particularly this one. As Amy Schumer rapped in "Milk, Milk, Lemonade," her brilliant send-up of the booty craze, we're "talkin' 'bout my fudge machine." The girls I met, though, didn't see it that way. Matilda Oh suggested I was hypocritical for dismissing Nicki Minaj as self-objectifying in "Anaconda" but hailing Lena Dunham as subversive for playing Ping-Pong topless on *Girls*. But Dunham wasn't trying to be hot. Quite the opposite: she is dough-bellied and soft-chinned, with natural, lopsided breasts. Her "bass" is perhaps a little *profundo*. In other words, she looks like an average American woman. She uses her body to shatter taboos against showing the imperfectly ordinary, to challenge our pneumatic, implant-propelled expectations. "Nicki Minaj is challenging, too," Matilda countered. Minaj cast off shame, rejected the male-generated shackles of "respectable" female sexual behavior, refused to see the behind—especially when it's large, especially when it's attached to a woman of color—as "dirty." "People always gripe about Nicki Minaj's butt," Matilda said, "but I think it's kind of 'damned if you do, damned if you don't.' If you emphasize it, you could potentially normalize black bodies in the mainstream, but you'll also be accused of 'objectifying' yourself. If you don't do it, though, you are arguably participating in a culture of body shame. So how is a woman of color supposed to 'take control of her sexuality' or be 'body-positive' without it being construed as internalized fetishization?"

Is Minaj's butt transgressive? What about Gaga's? What about those *Sports Illustrated* swimsuit models'? How can one tell which of these images is defiant and which is complicit; which liberates and which limits; which undermines standards of beauty and which creates new ones? Can they do both simultaneously? "I love Beyoncé," a freshman at a West Coast college told me. "She's one of my idols. She's, like, a queen. But I wonder, if she wasn't beautiful, if people didn't think she was so sexy, would she be able to make the feminist points she makes?"

Feminist scholar bell hooks, who kicked the Beyhive in 2014 when she called Beyoncé a "terrorist, especially in terms of her impact on young girls," has suggested that the fascination with the butt is nothing more than the latest way to reduce a woman to a body part: the latest PG-13 stand-in for "the pussy." The obsession is no different, no more subversive, and no more "empowering" to women than the fetishization of the breast or the wet, open mouth. As with those pop culture memes, she said, it raises the basic question: "Who possesses and who has rights to the female body?"

Young fans such as Matilda argue that the stars themselves do. Female artists, they insist, are taking control (or at least are being marketed as taking control) of a hypersexualized industry that too often exploits women. Yes, these women may be products, but they are also *producers*. The decision to twerk onstage, or twirl on a poll, or dance in one's drawers around a fully clothed man, or to pose nude on the cover of a magazine is now a woman's alone: rather than capitulating, they are actually reclaiming their sexuality. Yet those performers still work within a system that, for the most part, demands women look and present their bodies in a particular way in order to be heard, in order to be seen, in order to work. Successfully manipulating that system to their advantage by, say, nominally reimagining the same old strip club clichés may get them rich, it may get them famous, but it shouldn't be confused with creating actual change. Artists such as Gaga or Rihanna or Beyoncé or Miley or Nicki or Iggy or Kesha or Katy or Selena may not be puppets, but they aren't necessarily sheroes, either. They're shrewd strategists, spinning commodified sexuality as a choice, one that may be profitable but is no less constraining, ultimately, either to female artists or to regular girls. So the question is not whether pop divas are expressing or exploiting their sexuality so much as why the choices for women remain so narrow, why the fastest route to the top as a woman in a sexist entertainment world (just as for ordinary girls on social media) is to package your sexuality, preferably in the most extreme, attention-getting way possible.

The Twerk Seen 'Round the World

Miley Cyrus's face floated against the back wall of Oakland's Oracle Arena, a cross between a humongous selfie and the disembodied head from *The Wizard of Oz*. An eye winked, the lips pursed and stretched. A pink tongue unfurled, and suddenly the real Miley, dressed in a red, spangly two-piece leotard with bird feather shoulders, stepped out, arms aloft, and slid onto the stage. As she launched into the opening lines of her song "SMS (Bangerz)," tens of thousands of girls (and a few boys) screamed and held up flashing iPhones, the latter-day version of waving cigarette lighters. It was February 2014, about six months since Miley buried her Disney image forever with what has been called "the twerk seen 'round the world."

For those who may have recently migrated from Pluto, Miley sparked international outrage with her performance at the 2013 MTV Video Music Awards, first mimicking anilingus on a black female backup dancer (who inexplicably had a giant stuffed teddy bear strapped to her back) and then stripping down to plastic, skin-colored skivvies and vibrating her butt, or "twerking," against Robin Thicke's crotch as the two performed his controversial hit, "Blurred Lines." She also employed a foam finger, the kind fans typically brandish at sporting events, in ways that, once witnessed, could never be unseen. Throughout, there was that freakish wagging tongue, which now rivals KISS's Gene Simmons's in notoriety. The performance sparked predictable hand-wringing by both conservative pundits and feminists. (No less than Sinead O'Connor, who once shredded a picture of the Pope on live TV while singing the word *evil*, urged Miley "not to let the music industry make a prostitute of you.") Then came a backlash, led largely by young women, accusing both groups of "slut-shaming" Miley for "expressing her sexuality." Miley was also attacked as racist for appropriating aspects of black "ratchet" culture to boost her bad-girl cred and using her voluptuous backup dancers' bodies as props. None of it mattered. By the next morning Miley's singles had secured the top two spots on iTunes. The *Bangerz* album, released about six weeks later, debuted at number one on the *Billboard* charts.

This was not my first Miley concert. Five years earlier I'd attended her Wonder World tour, also at the Oracle Arena, where she shocked a crowd of tweenie-bopper *Hannah Montana* fans by grinding on the boys in the band while clad in leather short shorts and a cleavage-baring vest. This time around it seemed those little girls (or their mothers) had gotten the memo: they were nowhere in sight. Or maybe they were here; they were simply older now, as was Miley. Before the show, the halls of the arena were jammed with young women in their late teens and early twenties sporting Miley's pigtail bun hairstyle from the VMAs. Some wore crop tops emblazoned with the word *twerk* in six-inch-high capital letters. A number of them carried foam fingers. A few had found knock-offs of the furry teddy-bear-faced lingerie teddy that Miley had worn before stripping at the awards, with its winking eye and chops-licking tongue. ("Miley Cyrus costume" had been the second most popular search on Google that Halloween, with those teddies selling for around ninety dollars a pop.) One girl waltzed by clad in a flesh-toned bra and panties, and while that might not in itself have raised eyebrows, the two middle-aged adults trailing her with cameras, paparazzi-style (presumably her parents), turned more than a few heads. There was lots of midriff on parade, a lot of leg, a lot of stilettos. The smell of weed permeated the air.

I planted myself near a concession stand, where no fewer than thirty girls over the course of about fifteen minutes asked me to snap their picture beside a life-size poster of Cyrus displaying her famous tongue. A few made "duck lips" or "faux surprise" face—*I'm fun! I'm ironic!*—but most imitated their idol. I asked one girl, a nineteen-year-old named Emilia, to explain the appeal of the pose. "I guess it's to say, 'I don't care,'" she said.

"You don't care about what?"

She shrugged. "I just *don't care!*"

A twenty-one-year-old women's studies major from San Francisco State University stood nearby dressed in a black-and-white striped romper, her hair wound into pigtail buns, a slash of red lipstick on her mouth. "I like Miley because she is just herself," she explained. "I loved *Hannah Montana.* I've seen every episode. But I'm grown up now, and so is Miley. She needed to break free and show that she wasn't the Disney star anymore." The girl looked around the hallway. "And she did."

"She is the epitome of perfection," enthused her friend. "And she's *not* going to fit into any cultural ideal. Everyone tells you who you're supposed to be as a girl, but Miley? She is just who she is."

The show itself was a kaleidoscope of quasi-psychedelic images. A caricatured animated Miley (conceived by *Ren and Stimpy* creator John Kricfalusi), bug-eyed and buck-toothed, with huge, flopping butt cheeks, cavorted on-screen as the real-life version performed with those plush stuffed dancing bears, pinching and palpating more backup dancers. A giant bed disgorged dancers of both sexes, who joined Miley in a mock orgy. She simulated intercourse with a "little person," pantomimed fellatio on a dancer dressed as Abraham Lincoln ("party in the USA!"). She urged her audience to make out with each other, drawling, "The more tongue, the better. The *dirtier*, the better." The "nastiest" couples, she said, would be projected onto Jumbotrons flanking the stage. ("Girl on girl is *always* appreciated," she said with a smirk.)

The show was unquestionably graphic but not especially erotic. The images and actions were too random, too devoid of larger meaning or purpose. They were just so much flotsam and jetsam seemingly thrown out to stimulate reaction—*any* reaction. *Look, a thirty-foot cat! Miley in a cannabis body suit! Miley getting off on the hood of a car! Miley astride a giant, airborne hot dog!* Cyrus, her pixie-cut hair dyed platinum, was thinner than she'd been five years before, with no curve to her hips or breasts. She looked surprisingly androgynous, an R-rated Cathy Rigby, a tripped-out Peter Pan. Watching her, I recalled Ariel Levy's observation that Paris Hilton was the perfect celebrity for a time when interest in the *appearance* of sexiness had surpassed interest in the existence of sexual pleasure. In Hilton's famed sex tapes, she looks excited only when posing for the camera; during the actual sex, she seems bored, even taking a phone call in the midst of intercourse. Today's "raunch culture," Levy wrote, is not liberating or progressive, not about "opening our minds to the possibilities and mysteries of sexuality." There's a disconnect between its representation of "hotness" and sex itself. Even Hilton, Levy pointed out, has said, "My boyfriends always tell me I'm not sexual. Sexy, but not sexual."

Maybe Miley provides a release for her fans, an escape from respectability, a vision, however compromised, of a girl who doesn't dither over whether anyone (parents, other entertainers, the media) thinks she is "too slutty." The crotch slapping, the butt shaking, the crude talk, the simulated sex acts—all gave the illusion of sexual freedom, the illusion of rebellion, the illusion of defiance, the illusion that she "doesn't care." But of course Miley *does* care. As someone trying to maintain her status as a celebrity, as a chart topper, she cares very, very much. I keep coming back to her because I find her not unique, but the opposite: she's a human Rorschach, a lint trap of images and ideas about mainstream, middle-class girlhood. When she was fifteen, that meant wearing a "purity ring" and vowing to be a virgin until marriage; at twenty-three, it meant performing mechanistic, mock sex acts on a dwarf while dressed in a racy leotard emblazoned with pictures of money—and calling that liberation. Perpetually striving to mix the perfect cocktail in her cultural blender, she both reflects and rejects what a young woman needs to do to maintain celebrity, to snag attention, to be noticed, to be "liked"—all without seeming to try. And isn't that what every girl is struggling to do, writ very, very large?

In the middle of the show, Miley took a break from singing to address the audience. "How the fuck are you?" she bellowed. Then she turned around, lifted her iPhone high over her head, stuck out her tongue, snapped a selfie with the crowd as backdrop, and posted it immediately to Instagram. She was, it seemed, just like them.

Pop Goes the Porn

"I'm very sensitive about porn," said Alyson Lee, tugging nervously at her dark, purple-streaked hair. Alyson was nineteen, a sophomore at a mid-Atlantic college. She'd grown up in what she called a "culturally conservative" Chinese family in a Los Angeles suburb made up almost entirely of immigrant parents and first-generation kids like her. She studied how Americans are supposed to act and feel, especially about sex and romance, by watching *Grey's Anatomy*. "So now," she said, "I have the very typical, liberal college woman point of view."

One that includes ambivalence about porn. Alyson has had two serious boyfriends—one in her senior year of high school, one as a freshman in college—and both told her the same thing: "Of course I watch porn: every teenage boy does."

"I'm not one of those people who think that porn is wrong and morally terrible and disgusting," Alyson explained. "But it makes me feel super insecure. Like, am I not good enough? I'm definitely not as hot as a porn star. And I'm not going to do the things porn stars do. Both guys were really reassuring that it wasn't about me, and I knew logically there was no connection between them watching porn and some flaw of mine. But it stayed in my head."

If, as bell hooks suggested, pop culture portrayals of women beg the question "Who has access to the female body?" the answer may ultimately be found in the ever-broadening influence of porn. That is, after all, the source of the arched backs, the wet open mouths, the ever-expanding breasts and butts, the stripper poles, the twerking, and the simulated sex acts. That is the source of women's sexuality as a performance for men.

The Internet has made porn more prevalent and accessible than at any time in history, especially to teens. As with pop culture, that has spurred an escalation in explicitness, a need to push the boundaries to maintain an easily distracted audience. Mirroring (and raising further questions about) the mainstream culture's "booty" trend, in one large-scale study of sexual behavior and aggression in best-selling porn, anal sex was depicted in over half of the videos surveyed, always as easy, clean, and pleasurable to women; 41 percent of videos also included "ass to mouth," in which, immediately after removing his penis from a woman's anus, he places it in her mouth. Scenes of "bukake" sex (multiple men ejaculating on one woman's face), "facial abuse" (oral sex aimed at making a woman vomit), triple penetration, and penetration by multiple penises in a single orifice are also on the rise. I'm going to go out on a limb here and say that in real life those practices wouldn't feel good to most women. Watching natural-looking people engaging in sex that is consensual, mutually pleasurable, and realistic may not be harmful—heck, it might be a good idea—but the occasional feminist porn site aside, that is not what the $97 billion global porn industry is shilling. Its producers have only one goal: to get men off hard and fast for profit. The most efficient way to do so appears to be by eroticizing the degradation of women. In the study of behaviors in popular porn, nearly 90 percent of 304 random scenes contained physical aggression toward women, while close to half contained verbal humiliation. The victims nearly always responded neutrally or with pleasure. More insidiously, women would sometimes initially resist abuse, begging their partners to stop; when that didn't happen, they acquiesced and began to enjoy the activity, regardless of how painful or debasing it was. The reality is, as one eighteen-year-old pursuing a porn career told documentary filmmakers Jill Bauer and Ronna Gradus, "I'm supposed to be having sex with guys I would never have sex with, and saying things I would never say. There is nothing sexually arousing. You're just processed meat."

Media has been called a "super peer," dictating all manner of behavioral "scripts" to young people, including those for sexual encounters: expectations, desires, norms. In one era, they learn that you don't kiss until the third date; in another, they learn that sex precedes an exclusive relationship. Bryant Paul, a professor of telecommunications at Indiana University Bloomington who studies "scripting theory," explained, "I'll ask students, 'Think about how you learned what to do at your first college party. You'd never been to one, but you knew you were supposed to gather around the keg. You knew that couples would go off to someone's room.' And they'll say, 'Yeah, from *American Pie* and all those movies.' So where are they learning their sexual socialization, especially in terms of more explicit behaviors? You'd be foolish not to think they're getting ideas from porn. Young people are not *tabulae rasae*. They have a sense of right and wrong. But if they're repeatedly exposed to certain themes, they are more likely to pick them up, to internalize them and have them become part of their sexual scripts. So when you see consistent depictions of women with multiple partners and women being used as sex objects for males, and there's no counterweight argument going on there . . ." He trailed off, leaving the obvious conclusion unspoken.

Over 40 percent of children ages ten to seventeen have been exposed to porn online, many accidentally. By college, according to a survey of more than eight hundred students titled "Generation XXX," 90 percent of men and a third of women had viewed porn during the preceding year. On one hand, the girls I met knew that porn was about as realistic as pro wrestling, but that didn't stop them from consulting it as a guide. Honestly? It pains me to hear that the scatological fetish video *Two Girls, One Cup* was, for some, their first exposure to sex. Even if what they watch is utterly vanilla, they're still learning that women's sexuality exists for the benefit of men. So it worried me to hear an eleventh-grader confide, "I watch porn because I'm a virgin and I want to figure out how sex works"; or when another high-schooler explained that she "watched it to learn how to give head"; or when a freshman in college told me, "There are some advantages: before watching porn, I didn't know girls could squirt."

There is some indication that porn has a liberalizing effect: heterosexual male users, for instance, are more likely than peers to approve of same-sex marriage. On the other hand, they're also less likely to support affirmative action for women. Among teenage boys, regular porn use has been correlated with seeing sex as purely physical and regarding girls as "play things." Porn users are also more likely than their peers to measure their masculinity, social status, and self-worth by their ability to score with "hot" women (which may explain that disproportionate pressure girls report to text boys naked photos of themselves as well as the plots of most Seth Rogen films). Male *and* female college students who report recent porn use have been repeatedly found to be more likely than others to believe "rape myths": that only strangers commit sexual assault or that the victim "asked for it" by drinking too much or wearing "slutty" clothing or by going to a club alone. Perhaps because it depicts aggression as sexy, porn also seems to desensitize women to potential violence: female porn users are less likely than others to intervene when seeing another woman being threatened or assaulted and are slower to recognize when they're in danger themselves.

Boys (both in high school and college), not surprisingly, use porn more regularly than girls. Slightly less than half of male college students use it weekly; only 3 percent of females do. Given that frequent consumers of porn are more likely to consider its depictions of sex realistic, this can skew expectations in the bedroom. "I do think porn changes how guys view sex," mused Alyson Lee. "Especially with my first boyfriend. He had no experience. He thought it would happen like in porn, that I'd be ready a lot faster and he could just, you know, *pound*."

"They think they're supposed to do this hammer-in-and-out thing and that's what girls like," agreed a sophomore at a California college. "They don't realize, 'Dude, that does *not feel good.*' It's all they know. It's what they see. If you're just hooking up with someone, like a one-time thing or whatever, you just *pretend* it feels good."

In her prescient book *Pornified*, Pamela Paul found that women had begun feeling competitive with porn stars, worried that unless they put on their own show to maintain a partner's interest, they would lose him to the Internet. They believed that the unnatural thinness, inflated breasts, and overfilled lips of those surgical cyborgs were distorting men's standards of beauty, eroding women's own body image, increasing their self-consciousness. "Porn has terrible effects on what young women are supposed to look like, particularly during sex," said Leslie Bell, a psychotherapist and author of *Hard to Get: Twenty-Something Women and the Paradox of Sexual Freedom*. "There's this idea that someone is going to be evaluating your appearance not only outside of the bedroom, which was true before, but also during sex, that your body has to look a certain way then. It seems very pressured and shame-inducing, because bodies don't look like that naturally." You'd need self-esteem of steel to remain immune.

The girls I met sometimes disconnected from their bodies during sex, watching and evaluating their encounters like spectators. "I'll be hooking up with some guy who's really hot," confided a high school senior in Northern California, "and we'll be snuggling and grinding and touching and it's cool. Then things get heavier and all of a sudden my mind shifts and I'm not a real person: it's like, *This is me performing. This is me acting.* It's like,

How well am I doing? Like, *This is a hard position, but don't shake.* And I'm thinking, *What would 'she' do? 'She' would go down on him.'* And I don't even know who it is I'm playing, who that 'she' actually is. It's some fantasy girl, I guess, maybe the girl from porn."

JON MARTELLO IS a simple guy, a New Jersey native who cares about "my body, my pad, my ride, my family, my church, my guys, my girls, my porn," not necessarily in that order. The protagonist of the film *Don Jon*, played by Joseph Gordon-Levitt (who also wrote and directed), Jon Martello got his womanizing nickname by "pulling" a different girl every weekend. No single partner, though, can compare to the bounty he finds online. "All the bullshit fades away," he says in a voice-over, "and the only thing in the world is those tits . . . dat ass . . . the blow job . . . the cowboy, the doggie, the money shot and that's it, I don't gotta say anything, I don't gotta do anything. I just fucking lose myself."

During one of Jon's after-Mass Sunday dinners at his parents' house, where the TV inevitably blares in the background, an ad for Carl's Jr. comes on. The camera lingers as Nina Agdal, a *Sports Illustrated* swimsuit model, rubs oil onto her glistening, bikini-clad body. She arches like a cat on hands and knees on a beach, hair flowing, and then sits, legs splayed, and takes a big, juicy bite of a codfish sandwich. Don's mother looks away, fiddles with an earring. His sister, whose back is to the TV, doesn't even glance up from her cell phone. Don and his father, wearing identical white tank tops, stare at the screen wearing identical slack-jawed expressions. In an interview about that scene, Gordon-Levitt commented, "What I'm saying is whether it's rated X or 'approved by the FCC for a general viewing audience,' the message is the same."

He's right. You don't need to log in to PornHub to absorb its scripts; they're embedded in the mainstream. And the impact of that garden-variety, "pornified" media on young people—from *Maxim* magazine to Dolce & Gabbana couture ads to *Gossip Girl* to multiplayer online games to infinite music videos—is indistinguishable from actual porn. The average teenager is exposed to nearly fourteen thousand references to sex each year on television; 70 percent of prime-time TV now contains sexual content. College men who play violent, sexualized video games are more likely than their peers to see women as sex objects as well as to be more accepting of rape myths, more tolerant of sexual harassment, and to consider women less competent. College women who, in experiments, played the virtual game *Second Life* using a sexualized avatar were more likely to self-objectify *off*line than those who played with a nonsexualized avatar and, again, were more likely to hold false beliefs about rape and rape victims. (Seeing yourself as an object apparently leads you to view other women that way as well.) Meanwhile, in a study of middle and high school girls, those who were shown sexualized pictures of female athletes subsequently scored higher on measures of self-objectification than those who saw the same athletes engaged in, you know, actual athletics. Young women who consume more objectifying media also report more willingness to engage in sexualized behavior, such as taking a pole dancing class or entering a wet T-shirt contest, and to find those activities empowering. They're more likely to justify sexualization, and less likely to protest against it. In other words, as Rachel Calogero, a psychologist at the University of Kent in England, has written, "Objects don't object."

The sex in TV and movies can be simultaneously explicit and evasive. Sex, particularly noncommitted sex, is typically presented as fun and advisable; rarely is it awkward or silly or challenging or messy or actively negotiated or preceded by discussion of contraception and disease protection. There's always plenty of room in the backseat of those limousines, and nary a pothole in the road. Of course there are exceptions: *Glee* in its early seasons deftly portrayed issues surrounding teen pregnancy, sex and disability, homosexuality, bisexuality, first intercourse, fat and slut shaming, and the nature of love. *Orange Is the New Black*, which was beloved by many of the girls I met, brought unprecedented gender and sexual diversity to TV. The sex in Lena Dunham's work is radically raw. One of the most realistic (if depressing) scenes ever filmed may be found in her 2010 release, *Tiny Furniture*. In it Aura, a newly minted college graduate played by Dunham, finally gets together with the object of her affection, a loutish chef at the restaurant where she works. A typical Hollywood version of such an encounter—which takes place outside at night, in a metal tube on a loading dock while both partners are mostly clothed—would've been sleek and effortless, the woman instantly orgasmic. In Dunham's hands, it went something like this: they kissed for ten seconds; he unzipped his fly and wordlessly shoved her head downward; he told her to "suck harder," cursed her incessantly ringing phone, and then scuttled around her body to enter her doggie style; he pounded into her until he ejaculated, which took less than a minute; he never once looked at her face. Aura's expression shifted from aroused to confused, to slightly disappointed, to resigned. Afterward, he bid her good-bye while checking his texts. The scene is hard to watch without cringing—it's poignant, it's agonizing, it's embarrassing, and it's real.

Young women grow up in a porn-saturated, image-centered, commercialized culture in which "empowerment" is just a feeling, consumption trumps connection, "hot" is an imperative, fame is the ultimate achievement, and the quickest way for a woman to get ahead is to serve up her body before someone else does. If Paris Hilton synthesized the zeitgeist ten years ago, it may be her former bestie, Kim Kardashian, who embodies it now. Kardashian is the Horatio Alger of the selfie set, pulling herself up by her bra straps and parlaying exhibitionism and a genius for self-promotion into an impressive eighty-five-million-dollar empire. Like Hilton, Kardashian came to prominence via a sex tape in a deal that, rumor has it, was brokered by her mother. She, too, seems strangely bored by the on-screen acts in that tape, chewing gum throughout. Still, the notoriety generated by the did-she-or-didn't-she-leak-it-on-purpose speculation was enough to pique the E! network's interest in a reality show. *Keeping Up with the Kardashians* (*KUWTK*) premiered in 2007. Soon after, Kim posed for *Playboy*, encouraged on *KUWTK* by her mother. By 2008 she was the world's most googled celebrity. Kardashian's personal brand would eventually extend to boutiques, fitness videos, clothing lines, skin care products, perfumes, a best-selling video game, and more. She wrangled eighteen million dollars in endorsements and broadcast rights for her 2011 wedding to pro basketball player Kris Humphries (the marriage lasted seventy-two days, prompting rumors that it had been a publicity stunt). By 2015 she was thirty-third on the *Forbes* list of the World's Highest Paid Celebrities. At this writing, she has more than forty-four million Instagram followers (she follows only ninety-six people herself) and has unseated Beyoncé as the site's most followed person. Kardashian reportedly earns up to twenty-five thousand dollars per sponsored tweet and an average of one hundred thousand dollars for personal appearances. Her aforementioned full moon on the cover of *Paper*, while it didn't "break the Internet," generated nearly sixteen million page views within thirty hours. She's now married to one of the foremost hip-hop artists on the planet—in an ode to their love, he penned a touching lyric about knowing she could be his "spouse, girl," "when I impregnated your mouth, girl"—and, together they have a daughter, North West, currently a toddler. I wonder how they'll react to *her* first sex tape.

Kardashian's A-list ascent has been a perfect storm of social media and pop and porn cultures, her celebrity not a result of talent, achievement, or skill but of the relentless pursuit of attention: she is famous for being #famous. Curiously, the adjective most used about Kim by her fans (besides *hot*) is *relatable*. She seems authentic to them even though they know that her "reality" is entirely artificial: staged, edited, curated, cross-promoted, co-branded, augmented, and enhanced. Perhaps more than anyone, she has mastered the body "product": figured out how, as a woman, to harness the contradictory demands of the media landscape and to do it for her own enormous profit. Again, this can be read as empowerment—if your definition includes perpetuating shopworn stereotypes about women. Girls point to her style, her work ethic, and her wealth—aren't those admirable qualities? Yet, as the blog *Sociological Images* pointed out after Kardashian's wax figure was installed in Madame Tussauds, Kim's true contribution has been an ingenious "patriarchal bargain": her acceptance of roles and rules that disadvantage women in exchange for whatever power she can wrest from them. It's difficult to see how Kardashian's success expands options for anyone but herself. (Okay, it helped her sisters.) It's feminism defined by "I've Got Mine," underscored by the winking title of her 2015 book, *Selfish*. Even Tina Brown, the former *Vanity Fair* editor who virtually invented high-low journalism, was concerned that a 2014

Vogue cover positioned Kim as "aspirational" to young women. Those aspirations, Brown wrote, "now have very little to do with any notion of excellence, either of character or of comportment. Our hopes have gotten so cheesy that even the cheese is ersatz."

If the script handed down by our hypersexualized culture expanded the vision of "sexy" to include a broad range of physical size and ability, skin shade, gender identity, sexual preference, age; if it taught girls that how their bodies feel to them is more important than how they look to others; if it reminded them that neither value nor "empowerment" are contingent on the size of their boobs, belly, or ass; if it emphasized that they are entitled to ethical, reciprocal, mutually pleasurable sexual encounters; then maybe, *maybe* I'd embrace it. The body as product, however, is not the same as the body as subject. Nor is learning to be sexually desirable the same as exploring your own desire: your wants, your needs, your capacity for joy, for passion, for intimacy, for ecstasy. It's not surprising that girls feel powerful when they feel "hot": it's presented to them over and over as a precondition for success in any realm. But the truth is that "hot" refracts sexuality through a dehumanized prism regardless of who is "in control." "Hot" demands that certain women project perpetual sexual availability while denying others any sexuality at all. "Hot" tells girls that appearing sexually confident is more important than possessing knowledge of their own bodies. Because of that, as often as not, that confidence that "hot" confers comes off with their clothes.

CHAPTER 2

Are We Having Fun Yet?

A latte can be a great prop, kind of like a cigarette in a 1940s noir movie. Giving it a stir, taking a thoughtful sip, offers you time to gather yourself, which can be pretty vital when a virtual stranger, one who is basically old enough to be your mother, asks you point blank how often you masturbate, whether you've ever had an orgasm, or to describe your last sexual encounter with a partner. In fact, it gives the stranger asking the questions something to focus on as well, because, let me tell you, launching into a discussion of blow jobs with someone you've just met, someone young enough to be your daughter, can feel just a smidge uncomfortable. So I was relieved that Sam, eighteen, a senior at a California high school, had chosen to meet me on the patio of her favorite café, even if we were sitting next to a couple of middle-aged guys in Dockers and button-downs who were clearly shocked by our conversation. Sam was tall and full-figured, with golden skin and dark, loose curls that flowed nearly to the middle of her back. Her mother, a middle school math teacher, was African American; her father, whom she had rarely seen since her parents split, was white. Her mom had re-married a man from Samoa about five years ago; Sam calls him Dad. "I knew about romance and all that from an early age be-cause I'd meet my mom's boyfriends," Sam told me. "And when I went through puberty, she had books around."

I asked Sam whether her mother had explained to her about periods and reproduction. She nodded. What about masturba-tion? She laughed. "No," she said. The location of her clitoris? She laughed again. What about orgasm? She shook her head. "My parents are liberal," she said. "And they'll talk about sex gen-erally, or joke about it. We'll watch *South Park* or talk about the disfigurement of girls in the Middle East. But when it comes to *me*, it's a little more iffy. Then it's more like a conservative house-hold, where we don't talk directly. If I approached them, they'd be open to discussing it, but it's hard for them to bring up and it's hard for me to bring up."

Like most of the girls I met, Sam was both curious about sex and resourceful, so she did her own research on the subject, looking up on the Internet whatever she didn't know—through Google searches such as "how to give a blow job," or by checking out porn ("just to see how things fit together," she said). And, of course, she learned from doing. "Freshman year in high school was when everything became a reality," she recalled. "Sex, drink-ing, all of that. That's when you weren't just watching it on TV anymore. But we weren't *really* partying yet. It was mostly for ap-pearance. Like, you'd go to some park on the weekend and take a shot and sort of pretend you were drunk. And you'd hook up with some guy and maybe go to second or third base."

I stopped Sam right there. The terrain of relationships and sexual intimacy had changed since I was a girl. Along with it, there was a whole new vocabulary that both tripped me up and, as I'm someone passionate about words, fascinated me: *Talking*, for instance, did not mean conversation, but was a synonym for what, in an earlier era, would've been called "seeing" someone. As in "We're not serious, Mom. We're just talking." (It seemed a particularly ironic choice for today's teens, given their preference for connecting via text over actual conversation.) "Hooking up," a phrase that has inspired a full-scale media panic about the morals of a new generation, could mean anything from kissing to intercourse. Its ambiguity was the source of perpetual misunderstanding not only between girls and adults but among peers: *hooking up* was so vague a term that they could never be quite sure what their friends were up to. *Catching feelings* meant developing an emotional attachment and was, for many girls, something to protect against when hooking up, just as they would guard against catching herpes or chlamydia. A boy being "all cute" meant he may have "caught feelings" since he was behaving in a caring, thoughtful way toward a girl—what I would have called "romantic." *Dating*, though never a word much used beyond sixth grade, was the *last* step on the path toward a relationship, coming well after "hooking up" and "exclusive hooking up." Girls sometimes referred to their genitals as "my junk," and the phrase "making love" prompted gagging sounds. I couldn't help but notice that much of this new lexicon was devoid of terms not only connoting intimacy, but also indicating joy or pleasure.

So what, I asked Sam, was today's version of "the bases"?

She took a long swig of her latte. "Well, first base would be kissing," she said. "Second base would be a hand job for a guy and fingering the girl."

I raised my eyebrows. Already it seemed to me that a few steps had been skipped.

"And third base would be oral."

"Both ways?" I asked.

Sam laughed again and shook her head. "For the *guy*," she said. "Girls don't get oral sex. No. Not unless you're in a long-term relationship."

"Wait," I said. "Back up. I don't actually recall oral sex as being a base at all."

Sam shrugged. "That's a difference between my generation and yours," she said. "For us, oral sex is not a big deal. Everyone does it."

Why Do You Think They Call It a Blow "Job"?

There has been a lot of anxiety over the past couple of decades about teens and oral sex. Much of it can be traced back to the late 1990s, to a *New York Times* report that among middle-class teens, oral sex—and by "oral sex," it meant fellatio—not only was becoming ubiquitous, but that they were engaging in it far earlier and more casually than teens' busy (read: neglectful) working parents realized. One health educator was quoted as saying, "'Do you spit or do you swallow?' is a typical seventh-grade question."

Two years later, the *Washington Post* covered a parent meeting called by middle school counselors in Arlington, Virginia, a town of "elegant brick homes, leafy sycamores and stone walls"—again, code for white and middle class—to discuss the fellatio craze among thirteen-year-old girls. The reporter linked that incident to a wider regional trend, based largely on "student grapevine"–generated claims of girls who had dropped to their knees during study hall or at the back of a school bus.

Girls' bodies have always been vectors for a society's larger trepidations about women's roles. It was likely no coincidence, then, that those early blow job scandals surfaced just as oral sex was making front-page news for another reason: the country was gripped by an obsession with a certain blue Gap frock and a cigar that was by no means just a cigar. President Bill Clinton's alleged dalliance with Monica Lewinsky, a White House intern less than half his age, dominated the headlines, sending mortified parents leaping from the couch to twist the radio dial or grab the TV remote when the latest reports aired. Most famously, in January 1998, Clinton testified under oath that "I did not have sex with that woman, Miss Lewinsky." A few months later, when DNA from his semen was discovered on the fabled dress that she had squirreled away as a memento of their tryst—and, might I say, *ick*—he insisted that he had not perjured himself because their relationship involved only *oral* sex. Suddenly, people across the nation were hotly debating whether mouth-to-genital contact was, indeed, "sex." If it wasn't, what exactly was it? And how were Americans supposed to explain the president's hairsplitting to their children?

Oral sex had only recently become a standard part of Americans' erotic repertoire. Historically, both fellatio and cunnilingus were considered *more* intimate than intercourse, acts to be engaged in only after marriage, if at all. In 1994, just a few years before the Clinton affair broke, *Sex in America*, the most definitive survey at that time to be released on this country's sexual practices, found that while only a minority of women over fifty had *ever* performed fellatio, among women under thirty-five, three quarters had done so. (Most men, whatever their age, said they had been both providers and recipients of oral sex.) The rise in going down among straight couples, the authors wrote, was the biggest sexual change of the twentieth century. By 2014 oral sex was so common as to be unremarkable: as one researcher

49

quipped, the number of Americans who thought Barack Obama was Muslim was larger than those who had never given or received oral sex.

But the notion that the practice was aging downward, that among teens it was becoming more common and less meaningful than intercourse, was most definitely a new phenomenon, one that caught not only parents but also researchers off-guard. There was very little hard data to back those early journalistic claims. Oral sex practices of minors had been considered unfundable in academia; even if one could get the money, what parent would allow their child to be questioned on the subject? More generally, there was a presumption among conservative politicians that talking to teens about any form of sex, even in the name of research, was tantamount to handing them an instruction manual. Because of that, vital information about kids' sexual behaviors, including disease transmission, went virtually unstudied.

By 2000 the Clinton presidency was winding down, but the blow job panic had just begun. A new story in the *New York Times* declared that sixth-graders were now, basically, treating fellatio like a handshake with the mouth. According to one Long Island child psychologist, girls that age would tell him earnestly that they expected to wait until marriage for intercourse, yet had already given head *fifty or sixty times*. "It's like a goodnight kiss to them," he claimed, "how they say good-bye after a date." The director of the Parenting Institute at New York University, meanwhile, predicted that soon a "substantial" number of kids would be having intercourse by middle school. "It's already happening," he told the *Times*. (That was not true: according to the Centers for Disease Control and Prevention, in most states rates of intercourse among middle schoolers were dropping.) An article in the now-defunct *Talk* magazine blamed dual-career "parents who were afraid to parent" for an epidemic of oral sex among seventh-graders—again acting out larger anxieties about women, in this case working mothers, through concerns about unsupervised, wayward girls.

It was Oprah, however—isn't it always Oprah?—who sounded the loudest alarm. In 2003 she invited onto her show a reporter for *O Magazine* who had interviewed fifty girls about their sexual practices. "Hold on to your underwear for this one," the writer said, before revealing her ultimate stunner: the rainbow party. In this version of *Girls Gone Wild*, young women barely past their Barbie phase were donning different shades of lipstick, then fellating groups of boys in turns, leaving behind a "rainbow" of makeup on each penis. The girl whose color hit farthest down was declared the "winner."

Well, what parent wouldn't freak out? Children were having indiscriminate sex (or indiscriminate not-sex) everywhere! Under the table at bar mitzvahs! Behind the monkey bars during recess! No one, least of all Oprah, seemed to question the actual logistics of any of this. Exactly *how* were girls managing to complete multiple, random sex acts during the school day without an adult's notice? Were thirteen-year-old boys really up to fifteen public blow jobs in the space of a few hours? Wouldn't any rainbow effect be rinsed off or at least indelibly smudged by each subsequent partner? A 2004 NBC News/*People* survey taken shortly after the rainbow party story broke found that, in truth, less than one half of 1 percent of children ages thirteen to sixteen said they'd attended an oral sex party. Although that's not zero, it's hardly rampant.

So, no, children were not having orgies. That said, the seed from which the "rainbow party" myth sprouted did come from somewhere: oral sex has become relatively commonplace among teens. By the end of ninth grade, nearly one in five children has engaged in oral sex; by age eighteen, about two thirds have, with white and more affluent teens indulging more than others. Pinning that change on Bill Clinton or the sexual revolution or parental permissiveness, however, would be simplistic—and incorrect. Right-wing influence on sex education has played an equal, if not greater role. Federally mandated abstinence-only programs, which began in the early 1980s, not only reinforced that intercourse was the line in the sand of chastity, but also, using the threat of AIDS as justification, hammered home the idea that it might well kill you. Oral sex, then, was the obvious workaround. I doubt, though, that social conservatives would consider it a victory that, across a range of studies, college students who identify as religious are even more likely than others to say oral sex is not "sex," or that over a third of teenagers included it in their definition of "abstinence" (nearly a quarter included anal sex), or that roughly 70 percent agreed that someone who engages in oral sex is still a virgin.

I wondered, though: If teens didn't consider oral sex to be "sex," how did they perceive it? What did it mean to girls to give or receive oral sex? Did they enjoy it? Tolerate it? Expect it? One evening, shortly after her graduation from a suburban Chicago high school, a young woman named Ruby allowed me to join her and four of her friends for a chat. We met in Ruby's bedroom, one wall of which she'd painted midnight blue. Leggings, T-shirts, and skirts tumbled out of half-open dresser drawers. The girls sprawled on the floor, across the bed, on a beanbag chair.

When I asked about oral sex, a girl named Devon shook her head. "That's not a thing anymore," she said, waving a hand dismissively.

"So what is it, then?" I asked.

Devon shrugged. "It's nothing."

"Well, it's not that it's *nothing*," added Rachel.

"It's not *sex*," Devon countered.

"It's like a step past making out with someone," said Ruby. "It's a way of hooking up. A way to have gone farther without it being seen as any big deal."

"And it doesn't have the repercussions that vaginal sex does," Rachel added. "You're not losing your virginity, you can't get pregnant, you can't get STDs. So it's safer."

That, unfortunately, is not entirely true—though, again, because oral sex is ignored by parents and educators, there is a widespread belief among teens that it is risk free. The result is that while their rates of intercourse and pregnancy have dropped over the past thirty years, their rates of sexually transmitted diseases have not. Teens and young adults account for half of all new STD diagnoses annually and the majority among women. The new popularity of oral sex has been linked to rising rates of Type 1 herpes and gonorrhea (a disease that, about a decade ago, researchers thought was on the verge of eradication). Avoiding STDs, though, isn't really why girls engage in oral sex. The number one reason they do it, according to a study of high schoolers, is to improve their relationships. (Nearly a quarter of girls said this, compared to about 5 percent of boys.) What, though, did "improving a relationship" mean exactly, especially since so many also told me that oral sex, at least where fellatio was concerned, was a way to emotionally distance themselves from their partners, protect against the overinvestment they feared would come with intercourse. For years, psychologists have warned that girls learn to suppress their own feelings in order to avoid conflict, to preserve the peace in friendships and romantic partnerships. Was performing fellatio another version of that? Whether they hoped to attract a boy's interest, sustain it, or placate him, it seemed their partner's happiness was their main concern. Boys, incidentally, far and away, said that the number one reason they engaged in oral sex was for physical pleasure.

For both sexes, but particularly for girls, giving oral sex was also seen as a path to popularity. Intercourse could bring stigma, turn you into a "slut"; fellatio, at least under certain circumstances, conferred the right sort of reputation. "Oral sex is like money or some kind of currency," Sam explained. "It's how you make friends with the popular guys. And it's how you rack up points for hooking up with someone without actually having sex, so you can say, 'I hooked up with this person and that person,' and increase your social status. I guess it's more impersonal than sex, so people are like, 'It's not a big deal.'"

I may be of a different generation, but, frankly, it's hard for me to consider a penis in my mouth as "impersonal." Beyond that, I was concerned about the dynamics around oral sex: the morass of obligations, pressures, and judgments leveled at girls; the calculus and compromises they made to curry favor with boys while remaining emotionally, socially, and even physically "safe"; the lack of reciprocity or physical pleasure they described, or expected.

One afternoon in San Francisco's Golden Gate Park, I met Anna, a freshman at a small West Coast college. Anna had grown up in a politically liberal family and attended progressive private schools through twelfth grade. She wore skinny jeans with lace-up boots and had recently pierced the small flap of cartilage in front of her ear canal with a silver hoop; her long, wavy brown hair was swept to one side. "Sometimes," she told me, "a girl will give a guy a blow job at the end of the night because she doesn't want to have sex with him and he expects to be satisfied. So if I want him to leave and I don't want anything to happen . . ." She trailed off, leaving me to imagine the rest.

There was so much to unpack in that short statement: why a young man should *expect* to be sexually satisfied; why a girl not only isn't outraged, but considers it her obligation to comply; why she doesn't think a blow job constitutes "anything happening"; the pressure young women face in any personal relationship to put others' needs before their own; the potential justification of assault with a chaser of self-blame. "It goes back to girls feeling guilty," Anna said. "If you go to a guy's room and are hooking up with him, you feel bad leaving him without pleasing him in some way. But, you know, it's unfair. I don't think he feels badly for you."

In their research on high school girls and oral sex, April Burns, a professor of psychology at City University of New York, and her colleagues found that girls thought of fellatio kind of like homework: a chore to get done, a skill to master, one on which they expected to be evaluated, possibly publicly. As with schoolwork, they worried about failing or performing poorly—earning the equivalent of low marks. Although they took satisfaction in a task well done, the pleasure they described was never physical, never located in their own bodies. They were both dispassionate and nonpassionate about oral sex—socialized, the researchers concluded, to see themselves as "learners" in their encounters rather than "yearners."

The concern with pleasing, as opposed to pleasure, was pervasive among the girls I met, especially among high schoolers, who were just starting sexual experimentation. They often felt, for instance, that once they'd said yes to intercourse with a partner, they could never say no again, whether or not they were "in the mood." "I remember sort of hating it," said Lily, now a sophomore at a West Coast public university, about her sexual relationship with a high school boyfriend. "I wanted to please him, but it felt sometimes like we couldn't have a normal conversation because he was so distracted by wanting to have sex. And I couldn't really think of a *reason* to refuse"—not wanting to didn't seem adequate. "Sometimes I felt like I was just a receptacle for his hormones."

Those media-fueled sex panics tend to prey on parental fears about girls' promiscuity or victimization; the backlash dismisses both as overblown. Rarely does anyone ask the girls themselves what they think, what they gain from or enjoy about their experiences. Sam mentioned social status. Lily talked about pleasing a boyfriend. Gretchen, a seventeen-year-old classmate of Sam's, said she enjoyed the thrill, however short-lived, in having power over a boy. "I've gone down on four guys now. I don't even know, really, why I do it." She paused, chewing contemplatively on her lower lip. "I guess I like that feeling of 'Ha! You can't get this from anyone else. I am in control here!' You knew they *really, really* wanted it and you could be like, 'No! No!' and then they'd be like, 'Please! Please!' Because they were so desperate. That part's kind of fun. But it's definitely not the physical side of it, because that's so gross and it really hurts my throat. I mean, it's sort of fun getting in the rhythm of it. But it's never *fun* fun."

Performing oral sex could make girls feel like the more active partner in an encounter. By contrast, they described cunnilingus and intercourse as passive, like something that was being done *to* them, leaving them vulnerable. Those empowered feelings about fellatio, though, coexisted with their opposites: a lack of control, pressure to comply, the unspoken threat of danger. Sam commented that while her male peers had been warned not to coerce girls into intercourse, pushing for oral was fair game. Because of that, while she had "plenty of guy friends," she preferred not to be alone with them (which would, it seems, be an obstacle to true friendship). "In my social world, if you're hanging out alone with a guy, the usual expectation is that you're going to hook up with him," she explained. "And if you decide not to, he might try to pressure you. So I'll hang out with a guy at school, but I would *never* go to his house or to a movie or do anything that could be construed as more than 'just friends' unless I wanted that to happen. It's not that they'd force themselves on you; it's that there would be *pressure*. There would be *disappointment*. And there might be tension in our relationship if it didn't happen."

I want to be clear here. Sam was not a pushover, not a meek or mousy girl. She was an honor student, an editor on her school paper, a varsity tennis player. She identified as a feminist and casually bandied about terms such as *slut shaming, gender binary,* and *rape culture*. She was applying to top-tier colleges. She was an astute observer of her world. She was also, most definitely, immersed in it. Nearly all the girls I interviewed were bright, assertive, ambitious. If I had been interviewing them about their professional dreams or their attitudes toward leadership or their willingness to compete with boys in the classroom, I might have walked away inspired. A sophomore at an Ivy League college, a lacrosse player whose mother was a partner in a large law firm, bragged to me about the "strong women" in her family. "My grandmother is a firecracker at eighty-eight, and my mom is crazy, and my sister and I are going to be as crazy as they are," she said. "In my family, you have to have a personality and be loud. That's how we interact. It's like a form of feminine power and knowing yourself."

Even so, she described how, at age thirteen, she slipped into a bedroom with her best friend's older brother, a ninth-grader on whom she'd had a longtime crush. Although she had never kissed a boy, never held hands, never had a boyfriend, somehow—she doesn't remember the details—she ended up going down on him. Afterward, he never mentioned the incident again, so neither did she. Her subsequent sexual experiences, a handful of casual hookups, haven't been much different. "It's always the same unspoken sequence," she said. "You make out, then he feels you up, then you give him head, and that's it. I think girls aren't taught to express their wants. We're these docile creatures that just learn to please."

"Wait a minute," I countered. "Didn't you just tell me about all the strong women role models in your family, about how you were loud and have a big personality and didn't take shit?"

"I know," she said. "I think I didn't realize . . ." She paused, trying to reconcile the contradiction. "I guess no one ever told me that the strong female image also applies to sex."

Discussions of sexual assault and consistent, enthusiastic consent are, thankfully, becoming more common on college and some high school campuses, yet if teens think of fellatio as not-sex (or not "anything"), if it's thought of as an entitlement or considered an appeasement, then both girls' right to say no and boys' obligation to respect that are compromised, and the lines between consent and coercion and assault risk becoming blurred. "You know," Anna mused, "in some ways giving head is a bigger deal than sex. Because it doesn't necessarily do anything for *me*. So it's like doing the person a favor because you love and care about them. And if it's someone you're dating, there's an expectation that he'll reciprocate. But in hookups, guys are typically really douchey about it. And there's pressure for the girl to do it. So it's about how comfortable you are resisting that pressure or not. It gets awkward to keep resisting."

Most young men do, of course, take no for an answer. Yet nearly every girl I spoke with had at least one experience with a boy who had tried, despite her clear refusal, to coerce or force her into oral sex: verbally, via repeated texts, or by physically planting his hands on her shoulders and pushing downward. A sophomore at a midwestern public university, for instance, told me she felt lucky that she'd never been sexually assaulted. A few minutes later she described going back to a boy's room after a party during her freshman year. They kissed for a while, and then he attempted the shoulder push. She said no, and he backed off, only to try again a few minutes later, and then once more shortly after that. When she refused for the third time, he blew up. "Fuck you, then. I'll find someone else," he said and shoved her out of his room. It was the middle of the night in February and her dorm was two miles away. She cried the whole way home.

Another young woman, a freshman at a New England college, told me that she performed oral sex for the first time shortly after her sixteenth birthday. It was not by choice. "It was the summer after sophomore year in high school," she recalled. "I'd been talking to this guy for a while; he seemed nice. We were in the back of his car kissing. He just . . . I don't know how it happened. I was high, and that was confusing. He was very aggressive. He wanted to have sex, and I was like, 'I don't think this is a good idea.' He was not accepting. He kept trying for sex. And I was like *no*. So he sort of forced oral sex. He pushed my shoulders. And I didn't know how to get out of it. I was mostly just shocked. It wasn't a good feeling. And it's lasted. I never liked the idea of oral sex again after that. I still don't."

Girls have long been made the gatekeepers of male desire, charged with containing it, diverting it, controlling it. Providing reliable release from it had now become their responsibility as well. Oral sex had become their compromise, a loophole, a strategy for carrying out that expectation with the minimum of physical, social, or emotional fuss. "It's almost like . . . *clean*, you know what I mean?" a junior at a New York City public high school told me. I didn't know what she meant, not really. "It's like . . ." she said, "it's like . . . it's what's expected of you."

Girls rarely mentioned manually stimulating a boy. If the goal was to remain detached and impersonal, I would've thought that would be the obvious choice. "No," said Ruby in Chicago. "A guy can do that himself. 'A hand job is a man job. A blow job is yo' job.' Guys will actually say that. 'Just give me a blow job if you're going to do anything.' "

Listening to stories of obligatory, sometimes coerced, usually one-sided oral sex, I began to wonder: What if, rather than blow jobs, guys were expecting girls to, say, fetch them lattes from Starbucks? Would the girls be so compliant?

Sam laughed when I asked her that. "Well, a latte costs money . . ."

"Okay," I said. "Pretend it was free. Let's say guys expected you to keep getting them cups of water from the kitchen whenever you were alone. Would you be so willing? And would you mind that they never offered to bring you one in return?"

Sam laughed again. "Well, I guess when you put it that way . . ."

As Anna said, reciprocity in casual encounters was never assumed. That was fine with some girls, even a relief; those like Anna, however, who enjoyed oral sex, were miffed. "It's just expected that the guy will get off," she complained, "and then maybe he will be like"—she dropped her voice into a low register and gestured halfheartedly toward my torso with her chin—" 'Oh, uh, do you want me to . . . ?' It's never like he'll do something for me and *maybe* I'll do something for him. It's like, *naturally* I'll do something and then he'll ask if I 'want' him to."

One young woman I met, a college freshman who was a self-described "nympho" (who had also, she said, spent every summer of her teens at "Jesus camp") told me that she no longer tolerated lack of reciprocity from her "randoms." "The worst experience I had was when I hooked up with this guy and he got me down to my bra and underwear and he's in his boxers. Normally the next thing would be the bra comes off. But the bra didn't come off. Instead, all of a sudden his boxers were off. And then he did this"—she pantomimed the shoulder push. "And I was like, 'Wait, just because my organs are inside and yours are outside I'm not going to get *anything* and you expect me to go down on you?' I was like, 'We are done. This is not going to happen.' It was incredibly awkward, though. I had to get him out of my room."

It's Sacred Down There. Also Icky.

When my daughter was a baby I read somewhere that, while labeling their infants' body parts ("here's your nose," "here are your toes"), parents typically include a boy's genitals (at the very least, "here's your pee-pee") but not a girl's. Leaving something unnamed makes it quite literally unspeakable: a void, an absence, a taboo. Nor does that silence change much as girls get older. Adolescent penises insist on recognition. Enter any high school and you'll see them scrawled everywhere: on lockers, on notebooks, on desks, on clipboards. Boys cannot seem to restrain themselves from drawing their sexual organs, loud and proud, on any blank surface. But whither the bushy vulva, the magnificent minge, the triangular twat?

Did I hear an "eww"? Exactly.

Even the most comprehensive sex education classes stick with a woman's internal parts—uteri, tubes, ovaries. Those classic diagrams of a woman's reproductive system, the ones shaped like the head of a steer, blur into a gray Y between the legs, as if the vulva and the labia, let alone the clitoris, don't exist. Imagine not clueing a twelve-year-old boy into the existence of his penis! And whereas males' puberty is characterized by ejaculation, masturbation, and the emergence of a near-unstoppable sex drive, females' is defined by . . . periods. And the possibility of unwanted pregnancy. Where is the discussion of girls' sexual development? When do we talk to girls about desire and pleasure? When do we explain the miraculous nuances of their anatomy? When do we address exploration, self-knowledge? No wonder boys' physical needs seem inevitable to teens while girls' are, at best, optional.

Few of the heterosexual young women I interviewed had ever had an orgasm with a partner, though most, from time to time, had faked it, taking their cues from the soundtrack of porn videos. Around a third masturbated regularly, which was, I was surprised to discover, about average. About half said they had never masturbated at all. It's hard to imagine adults would stand for such ignorance or lack of curiosity about any other body part. Most girls waved away my questions on masturbation, saying things such as "I have a boyfriend to do that" (though these were the same girls who'd never come with a partner). Beyond making them dependent on someone else for their pleasure, this was yet another inversion of what they said boys believed: that since they could masturbate on their own (it was a "man job"), they didn't require a partner for that. As for being on the receiving end of oral sex, girls tended to describe allowing (let alone *wanting*) a boy to head south as an intimate, emotional act requiring a deep level of trust. "I was in a relationship with a kid for a year where I had given him head," recalled Rachel in Chicago, "but I never felt comfortable for him to return the favor. Because . . . okay, this is weird to say, but a guy going down on you is more like a sacred thing. Like once you've done *that*, you really must be comfortable with the person, because it is not something that I'm just going to let you do."

"I'd rather have sex before I did that," Devon agreed.

"A guy is totally aware of what he looks like down there," Rachel continued, "but I don't know what they're seeing on me. I can't see it."

"Well," I said, "there are these things called mirrors . . ."

"Yeah," Rachel said dryly. "I'm not going to do that."

It's understandable that girls wouldn't let a partner go "down there" if they themselves were squeamish about their genitals. They worried that their vaginas were ugly, rank, unappealing. Again, not new concerns—I recall hiding a can of FDS "feminine deodorant spray" in the back of a desk drawer in junior high—but how is it that they still persist? Hadn't these girls heard of *The Vagina Monologues*? Erin, a senior at a San Francisco high school who was president of her school's feminist issues club, boasted that she was "really good" at giving oral sex to her boyfriend of a year, but when I asked how she felt about receiving it, she wrinkled her nose. "He doesn't go down on me," she said. "He doesn't want to. And I've never asked. Because . . ." She took a deep breath. "I don't like my vagina," she admitted. "I know that sucks. And I don't know why it should be so different, but I've internalized that idea.

"It's like that whole thing about queefing," she continued.

"Queefing?" I asked.

"Yeah," she said. "It's a fart with your vagina? There were these episodes on *South Park* about it, and now teenage boys have that as something they can say about girls, and girls know that boys have that, so you feel awkward." She sighed. "It's just, there's this whole comedic culture around making fun of female sexuality, you know? And it's super strong."

While queefing had blessedly escaped my notice, the overall rise of the word *vagina* as a punch line had not. Snarky references to women's nethers are the new *fag*—a way to denigrate masculinity, to ridicule or dominate an opponent. Even women use the word to signal that they're "cool with it," down with the bros. The implication is that *everyone* shares a secret distaste toward a lady's parts, or at least a sense that the word *vagina* itself is a goof (as opposed to *cunt*, which wouldn't be funny at all, and *pussy*, which as an insult has lost much of its anatomic specificity). So in the 2007 film *Knocked Up*, Jason Segel taunts a bearded Martin Starr by saying, "Your face look like a vagina." In *Forgetting Sarah Marshall*, Mila Kunis similarly slams Segel, when he hesitates before diving off a Hawaiian cliff: "I can see your vagina from here," she calls from the ocean below. "I can see your hoo-hah." Another female character, in the trailer for the Adam Sandler flop *That's My Boy*, heckles an ineffectual Andy Samberg with "Throw [the ball] you big vagina!" Off-screen, an essay on the website Thought Catalog titled "I'm a Feminist, but I Don't Eat Pussy" went viral in 2013. Among its pithy observations: that while vaginas "feel really good when your penis is inside of them" they are "objectively gross . . . covered in hair. They ooze and slime . . ." They are dirty, the male writer continues, and taste bad, and for women to expect oral sex "when you know the strain it puts on men, is selfish and, frankly, discriminatory." If that weren't enough to plunge the average young woman into a shame spiral, heartthrob actor Robert Pattinson, whose fame and fortune were forged from the erotic fantasies of teenage girls, breezily confessed to *Details* magazine, "I really hate vaginas. I'm allergic to vagina."

Sign me up for Team Jacob.

No wonder girls are insecure. Remember the shoulder push? The wordless gesture boys use to urge their partners downward? Young women had their own version, but it was a two-palmed shove *away* from the pelvis, a silent redirection to safer, if less erogenous, ground. Sam said that her ex-boyfriend, whom she had dated for a year, went down on her exactly twice during their relationship. Both times it was his idea. "It was not fun for me," she said. "I was not comfortable with it at all. I guess because I've never been comfortable with my parts down there. It's not something I find attractive. So I don't like the idea of someone else down there." To be fair, she said, he would "finger" her, but he had no idea what felt good; nor, since she had never masturbated, did she: even if she did know, she probably couldn't have said it out loud. Mostly, he just inserted a finger and sort of rummaged around.

Obviously, I wouldn't expect girls to be fully aware of their sexual needs or able to articulate them easily—many adult women can't do that even with long-term partners—but they are at a critical juncture in their development, learning foundational lessons about attraction, intimacy, arousal, sexual entitlement. Those early experiences can have a lasting impact on the understanding and enjoyment of their sexuality. So their aversion to their own genitals was disheartening. Watching girls squirm in response to my questions, I thought again about the images of female sexiness that assaulted them: Fergie's "London Bridge" going down, Miley swinging naked on a wrecking ball, Beyoncé dancing in her scanties around her suit-clad husband, Nicki giving Drake a lap dance (tweeting beforehand that she had just knocked back some "confidence juice"). The culture is littered with female body parts, with clothes and posturing that purportedly express sexual confidence. But who cares how "proud" you are of your body's appearance if you don't enjoy its responses? One sophomore in college showed me photos from her Instagram feed in which she was dressed for a party in a leopard-print crop top, a tiny skirt, and skyscraper heels. Later in our interview she admitted, "I don't enjoy getting oral sex. I am so in my head. All I think about is if I should tell him that it doesn't feel good or if he's getting tired or if he's even grossed out?"

Women's feelings about their genitals have been directly linked to their enjoyment of sex. College women in one study who were uncomfortable with their genitalia were not only less sexually satisfied and had fewer orgasms than others but were more likely to engage in risky behavior. (Boys were the opposite: those who felt *positively* about their penises were more likely to engage in risky sexual behavior.) Another study, of more than four hundred undergraduates, found that early engagement in fellatio led to feelings of inferiority and low self-worth among girls; by contrast, cunnilingus at the same young age was associated with greater self-awareness, sexual openness, and assertiveness. Young women who feel confident masturbating during sex, meanwhile, more than double their odds of orgasm in either hookups or relationships.

So how young girls feel about "down there" matters. It matters a lot.

The Psychological Clitoridectomy

Sex is probably not the first thing that jumps to mind when you think about Indiana. But it happens that the state university in

Bloomington is home to the Kinsey Institute, a center of research on sexual health founded by biologist Alfred Kinsey. I flew there one icy winter afternoon to meet Debby Herbenick, an associate professor at IU's School of Public Health. Herbenick, who is also a sex columnist and the author of books such as *Sex Made Easy*, was the very picture of the modern sexpert: in her late thirties, with long, dark hair and cocker spaniel eyes, and dressed in a chic houndstooth minidress with over-the-knee boots. Her own research is in an area called genital self-image: how people feel about their private parts. Over the past few years, she said, young women's genital self-image has been under siege, with more pressure on them than ever to see their vulvas as unacceptable in their natural state: "They need to shave them, decorate them, or otherwise groom before sex," she said. "There's this real sense of shame as a girl if you don't have your genitals prepared, a real sense that there is a possibility someone will judge them."

Most of the young women I met had shaved or waxed their pubic hair, all of it, since they were about fourteen. When I asked them why, the girls would initially say it wasn't something they'd ever questioned: they already shaved their legs and armpits, and they'd seen older girls who were bare, so it seemed the thing to do. They said hairlessness made them feel "cleaner" (mistakenly, as it turns out. Though it diminishes the risk of pubic lice, clear cutting creates a festive-sounding "happy culture" for most other STDs: without the shield of protective hair, for instance, the labia can become carpeted with genital warts). As with self-objectification, girls considered depilation a personal choice, something done "for oneself," for comfort, hygiene, practicality. Invariably, though, they would bring up another motivation: avoiding humiliation. Consider the trajectory of comments by Alexis, a sixteen-year-old at a public high school in Northern

California. "I didn't really think about it," she began. "One friend had an older sister who was doing it, so she started, and then we all did it. It was like a chain reaction.

"But then, I also heard these guys in class one day talking about a girl. Her shorts were low cut and when she'd raised her arms, her shirt had lifted up, and they were like, 'I could see pubic hair! Man, it was so gross!'"

Girls are already self-conscious about their (typically unnamed) pubic region; it doesn't take much to stoke that insecurity. Ruby, in Chicago, was one of the girls who said shaving made her feel "clean," especially during her period. But she, too, added, "I remember these boys telling stories about this girl who 'got around.' And guys would go down there to finger her, or whatever, and there would be hair, and they were appalled. So I just . . . I mean, guys act like they would be *disgusted* by it."

Herbenick said that in her college town, chalkboard displays outside local salons offered sales on "back-to-school waxes" in the fall; April brought similar specials on spring break Brazilians. "That's a pretty public reminder that you better look a certain way," she said. A few years ago, she had a female student confide that she'd started shaving after a boy announced—during one of Herbenick's class discussions—that he'd never seen pubic hair on a woman in real life, and if he came across it on a hookup partner, he'd walk out the door.

Full-frontal waxing—which is not only pricey but excruciating—was once the province of fetishists and, of course, porn stars. The first "Brazilian" salon (so named because its owners were from that country) in the United States opened in New York in 1987, but it was an episode of *Sex and the City* that took the practice mainstream. By 2006, trendsetter and the former Posh Spice Victoria Beckham declared that Brazilian waxes should be "compulsory" starting at fifteen. (Let's check back with her in 2026, shall we, when her daughter reaches that age.) There's no question that a bald vulva is smooth. Silky smooth. Baby smooth—some would say disturbingly so. Perhaps in the 1920s, when women first started shaving their legs and armpits, that, too, seemed creepily infantilizing, but now depilating those areas is a standard rite of passage for girls, an announcement, rather than a denial, of adult sexuality. That first wave of hair removal was driven by flapper fashions that displayed a woman's limbs; arms and legs were, for the first time, no longer part of the private realm. Today's pubic hair removal may indicate something similar: we have opened our most intimate parts to unprecedented scrutiny, evaluation, commodification. Largely as a result of the Brazilian trend, cosmetic labiaplasty, the clipping of the folds of skin surrounding the vulva, has skyrocketed: while still well behind nose and boob jobs, according to the American Society of Aesthetic Plastic Surgeons (ASAPS), there was a 44 percent rise in the procedure between 2012 and 2013—and a 64 percent jump the previous year. Labiaplasty is almost never related to sexual function or pleasure; it can actually impede both. Never mind: Dr. Michael Edwards, the ASAPS president in 2013, hailed the uptick as part of "an ever-evolving concept of beauty and self-confidence." The most sought-after look, incidentally, is called—are you ready?—the Barbie: a " 'clamshell'-type effect in which the outer labia appear fused, with no labia minora protruding." I trust I don't need to remind the reader that Barbie is (a) made of plastic and (b) *has no vagina*.

Herbenick invited me to sit in on the Human Sexuality class she was about to teach, one of the most popular courses on Indiana's campus. She was, on that day, delivering a lecture on gender disparities in sexual satisfaction. More than one hundred fifty students were already seated in the classroom when we arrived, nearly all of them female, most dressed in sweats, their hair pulled into haphazard ponytails. They listened raptly as Herbenick explained the vastly different language young men and young women use when describing "good sex." "Men are more likely to talk about pleasure, about orgasm," Herbenick said. "Women talk more about absence of pain. Thirty percent of female college students say they experience pain during their sexual encounters as opposed to five percent of men."

The rates of pain among women, she added, shoot up to 70 percent when anal sex is included. Until recently, anal sex was a relatively rare practice among young adults. But as it's become disproportionately common in porn—and the big payoff in R-rated fare such as *Kingsman* and *The To Do List*—it's also on the rise in real life. In 1992 only 16 percent of women aged eighteen to twenty-four said they had tried anal sex. Today 20 percent of women eighteen to nineteen have, and by ages twenty to twenty-four it's up to 40 percent. A 2014 study of heterosexuals sixteen to eighteen years old—and can we pause for a moment to consider just how young that is?—found that it was mainly boys who pushed for "fifth base," approaching it less as a form of intimacy with a partner (who they assumed would both need to be and *could* be coerced into it) than a competition with other boys. Girls were expected to endure the act, which they consistently reported as painful. Both sexes blamed that discomfort on the girls themselves, for being "naïve or flawed," unable to "relax." Deborah Tolman has bluntly called anal "the new oral." "Since all girls are now presumed to have oral sex in their repertoire," she said, "anal sex is becoming the new 'Will she do it or not?' behavior, the new 'Prove you love me.'" And still, she added, "girls' sexual pleasure is not part of the equation." According to Herbenick, the rise of anal sex places new pressures on young women to perform or else be labeled a prude. "It's a metaphor, a symbol in one concrete behavior for the lack of education about sex, the normalization of female pain, and the way what had once been stigmatized has, over the course of a decade, become expected. If you don't want to do it you're suddenly not good enough, you're frigid, you're missing out, you're not exploring your sexuality, you're not adventurous."

I recalled a conversation I'd had with Lily, the girl who was exasperated by her high school boyfriend's preoccupation with intercourse. He watched a lot of porn, too, she'd said, and was particularly game to try anal sex. She complied mostly because she wanted to please him. "The first time, we had to stop right away because I hated it," she said. "Later, he pressured me to do it again; he said that we hadn't actually done it before, since it was so short. At that point I guess I did it out of stubbornness. Like, *Okay,* fine. *I'll do it again and I still won't like it.*" She laughed. "Which clearly isn't very healthy."

In sexual encounters, girls, it seemed, were growing more accustomed to coercion and discomfort than, say, orgasm, afraid to say "no" lest they seem uptight. Consider that at every age three-quarters of men report regularly climaxing during partnered sex, while only about 29 percent of women do. Or that girls are four times more willing than boys to engage in sexual activity they don't like or want, particularly oral and anal sex. Women also, Herbenick said, use more negative language than men when describing *unsatisfying* sexual experiences. Again, they talked about pain. But they also talked about feeling degraded and depressed. Not a single man surveyed expressed similar feelings. According to Sara McClelland, who coined the term *intimate justice*, the whole notion of comparing women's and men's reports of "sexual satisfaction" assumes a common understanding of what the phrase means. Clearly, that's not the case. Not if, going into their encounters, women anticipate less pleasure and more pain than men. Among the college students McClelland studied, women tended to use their *partner's* physical pleasure as the yardstick for *their* satisfaction, saying things such as "If he's satisfied, then I'm sexually satisfied." For men, it was the opposite: the measure was their own orgasm. (Women's commitment to their partners' satisfaction, by the way, was independent of that person's gender, which may explain, in part, why girls are more likely to orgasm in same-sex encounters.) So when young women report sexual satisfaction levels equal to or greater than young men's—which they often do in research—that may be deceptive. If a girl goes into an encounter hoping it won't hurt, wanting to feel close to her partner, and expecting that *he* will have an orgasm, then she'll be satisfied if those criteria are met. There is nothing wrong with wanting to feel close to a partner or wanting him to be happy, but "absence of pain" is a pretty low bar for your own physical fulfillment. As an eighteen-year-old high school senior told me, "I understood before I started having sex what it meant for a guy to finish. You know it has to happen for sex to be over and for them to feel good. But I had no idea what it meant for a girl. Honestly? I still don't know. It's never addressed. So I've gone into it all without really understanding myself."

Listening to girls' litany of disembodied early experiences, it sometimes struck me that we'd performed the psychological equivalent of a clitoridectomy on our daughters: as if we believed, somehow, that by hiding the truth from them (that sex, including oral sex and masturbation, can and should feel fabulous) they won't find out, and so will stay "pure." What if the opposite were true: what if understanding one's physical responses, truly "expressing your sexuality" instead of just impersonating sexiness, could actually raise girls' expectations of intimate encounters? What if self-knowledge encouraged them to hold a higher standard for their experiences, both within and outside relationships? What does, or should, "sexually active" mean, anyway? Clearly, the classic definition is obsolete. It may be that we have to reconceptualize "sex" entirely, starting with virginity.

CHAPTER 3

Like a Virgin, Whatever That Is

Christina Navarro sat cross-legged on a pillow on the floor of her college cooperative, watching a YouTube video on her laptop. On the screen a forty-something woman named Pam Stenzel paced back and forth in front of a sign that read, "The High Cost of Free Love." She was dressed in a denim jacket and jeans, pontificating in a gravelly, I'm-down-with-the-kids voice about virginity. "If you're here today and you're a virgin," she said to a rapt audience of high schoolers, "*Good for you! GOOD FOR YOU!* You have something *so* special, *so* valuable it is worth *whatever it takes* to get to your marriage with no past, fear, or disease." The students cheered and applauded.

Stenzel is one of the nation's most renowned (or, depending on how you look at it, most notorious) abstinence-only educators, invited to the White House and the United Nations, a guest on programs such as *The Dr. Laura Show* and *Politically Incorrect with Bill Maher.* Allegedly the daughter of a rape victim who was adopted into a Christian home, she has dedicated her life to promoting chastity and exalting virgins. She earns as much as

$5,000 a gig; according to tax records, her company, Enlighten Communications, takes in around $240,000 a year.

I watched Christina watch the video, a look of amusement playing across her face. She was twenty, though looked and sounded several years younger, and a junior at a public university on the West Coast. The walls of the room in which we sat were painted a deep purple; Indian print bedspreads were tacked to the ceilings and covered the mattress. A plate with the remains of a vegetarian burrito lay on the floor by the door. If I didn't know better, I could've sworn I'd time-tripped back to 1980. Just last week, Christina told me, the residents of the house had engaged in a spirited debate (one that brought up nostalgia for my own college days) over whether women should be free to walk around topless in the common areas. "It sparked this long conversation about how women's breasts have been objectified and sexualized by the media," she said, "and how in our house we should be able to express our bodies and be safe." Naturally, the decision was ultimately determined by consensus.

Earnestly naked girls in cooperative student housing may seem a long way from Pam Stenzel's chastity rants, but Christina grew up in Colorado Springs, Colorado, one of the most conservative cities in America and home to so many fundamentalist Christian organizations that it has been dubbed the Evangelical Vatican. Christina herself was not raised in that tradition—she's Catholic—but the "sex education" she received at her small parochial school was essentially identical, encapsulated by one word: *don't*. Rather than a Health Class, human sexuality was covered in tenth-grade Theology. The curriculum consisted mostly of scary statistics about the inevitability of pregnancy and disease for those who engaged in premarital sex and of the perils of abortion. Students were directed to memorize Bible passages interpreted as condemning homosexuality and advocating chastity. Watching Stenzel's videos in that class was an annual event, Christina recalled, a kind of rite of passage among her classmates, similar to the way watching gruesome films of incinerated accident victims once was for those who took Driver's Ed. Stenzel, who is based about an hour away from Colorado Springs, even lectured in person at an assembly at Christina's school. She was greeted with the anticipation and hoopla of a rock star. Even at the time, Christina said, she suspected Stenzel's presentation was "biased," and a little cheesy, but she didn't necessarily consider it inaccurate. And she never questioned the value of remaining "pure" until marriage.

On-screen, Stenzel was still talking: "Once it's gone, it's gone," she warned. "It takes that long"—she snapped her fingers—"to throw it away. It takes a lot of integrity to wait."

There was more applause, and then the video ended. We were quiet for a moment. "Are you still planning to save yourself for marriage?" I asked Christina.

She laughed and shook her head. "Oh, no," she said. "It's too late for that."

Cashing in the "V Card"

Nearly two thirds of teenagers have intercourse at least once before college—the average age of virginity loss in this country, as I've said, is seventeen—and while most do so with a romantic partner, a sizable number of girls cash in what they call their V card with a friend or a guy they've only just met. Over half, both in national samples and among my own interviews, were drunk for the occasion. Most say they regret their experience and wish they'd waited—maybe not until marriage, but longer than they did.

In some ways, I was surprised that the girls I talked to still considered first intercourse such a milestone. Most of them had already been sexually active for several years at that point, but again, that's assuming you "count" oral sex (or anything other than intercourse) as "sexually active." One could argue that in the modern world, "virginity" as a symbol of sexual initiation is an outdated, meaningless concept. It never had actual medical basis anyway (many girls have no hymen or have torn it through exercise, masturbation, or with a tampon), nor even a fully agreed-upon social meaning: in her book *The Purity Myth*, for instance, Jessica Valenti writes about the notion of "secondary virginity," the idea that virginity can magically be reinstated even after intercourse if one subsequently commits to abstinence until marriage. While that allows purity advocates to embrace those who have "stumbled," it also shows how arbitrary the definition of "virginity" can be. I'm not suggesting that first intercourse is psychologically or physically insignificant. Not at all. But why do girls in particular still elevate this single act (which, among other things, is rarely initially pleasurable for them) to a status beyond all others? Why do they imagine this one form of sexual expression will be transformational, the magic line between innocence and experience, naïveté and knowing? How does this notion of "virginity" as a special category shape their sexual experience? How is it affecting their sexual development, their self-understanding, their enjoyment of sex, their physical and emotional communication with a partner?

On a mellow fall Sunday morning, I joined Christina again, this time with a group of her friends on the rooftop veranda of the co-op. The other girls listened wide-eyed as Christina talked about her background; they found her stories exotic and a little shocking. "It's so surprising to me," said Caitlin, pushing her purple Clark Kent glasses up the bridge of her pierced nose. "At my high school they gave out condoms for free. They handed out *lube!*"

Even Annie, a freckled girl who attended an all-girls Catholic school in Orange County, California, considered her upbringing to be liberal compared to Christina's. "In high school my teacher unwrapped a peppermint patty and put it on the floor," Annie recalled. "Then she asked if we would eat it. Of course we were all, 'Eww, no!' And she said, '*Exactly!* Once you're "open," nobody will want you!'"

The girls cracked up. "But, then," Annie added, "my mom was kind of a hippie. So she would tell me to forget all that. She'd say, 'It's really important to test-drive a car before you buy it; you don't just kick the wheels.'"

When Brooke was in middle school, her mother gave her a pile of old-school sex-positive books such as *Our Bodies, Ourselves.* ("They all had these totally seventies covers," she recalled. "It was hilarious!") As for Caitlin, whose public high school passed out free condoms, when she was fifteen her mom took her to a "woman-friendly" sex store to buy a vibrator. "She said, 'I think it's really important that you get in touch with your own body and sexuality before you start having sex with someone else.'"

Neither Caitlin nor Brooke ever imagined saving her virginity for marriage. Until meeting Christina, they'd never met anyone who'd even considered it. "I think my mother's exact words were 'Virginity is a patriarchal construct,'" Caitlin said, and laughed. She had intercourse for the first time at sixteen, with a boy whom she would date for the next three years. "I would have actually done it earlier, with a different guy, my sophomore year," she said, "but he never initiated it. And I'm glad. Because I would have. Not because I *wanted* to have sex with him, but because I wanted to please him and I wanted to feel important. When I finally did have sex, it was only two months into my relationship, but I felt like I *wanted* to. It was really empowering to be absolutely sure of that decision and to realize that I hadn't been ready before but now I definitely was."

Brooke's first intercourse was younger still, at fifteen. She had imagined it would happen with a boy she cared about—she never used the word *love*—in the kind of romantic, gauzy setting you'd find in a vintage Summer's Eve douche commercial: on the edge of a cliff with the Pacific Ocean crashing against the rocks below. "I was probably thinking more about what it would be like to remember it later than the act itself," she admitted. "Like, how it would sound as a story."

It didn't go quite that way: Neither Brooke nor her boyfriend of seven months had a car, for one thing, so there was no way to get to the beach. Plus, it was winter. Anyway, what if someone walked by and caught them? In the end, they lost their mutual virginity in a fairly mundane fashion: in his bunk bed during a weekend when his family was out of town. She brought the condoms, which she had spent ages choosing at a nearby Walgreens, and the lube; she also, for reasons she can't remember, brought over a batch of home-baked cookies. "The truth is, losing your virginity is about the least sexy sexual act there is," she said. "It's awkward, especially when losing it to another virgin. Putting on the condom is the opposite of smooth. Things don't seem like they're going to fit together. You don't know how much of your weight to put on the other person. It's a little sweaty. And it doesn't feel good." After a minute or so, they felt like they had "done it" enough to say they had (both to themselves and to their friends), so they just . . . stopped. "But, you know," Brooke added, "it was a very positive experience for me. We bonded over the awkwardness, and that was fun. And even though the sex was lackluster, I felt totally comfortable with the situation and with him, and I'm grateful for that." They slept together a few more times before breaking up; Brooke kept their first condom wrapper as a souvenir, inscribing it with the date she used it.

Both Brooke and Caitlin were relieved to have lost their virginity when and how they did: too many of their friends, they said, were panicked about unloading "it" before college and, as a result, had made hasty choices that led to unpleasant experiences. College had loomed as a deadline for most of the girls I spoke with: being tagged as a prude freshman year seemed a greater threat to them than being labeled a slut. Better to get it over with, have sex with *someone*, rather than risk being seen as an "inexperienced freak" or, worse, as "too ugly to fuck." In general, young people overestimate how many of their peers have had sex, how many times they've had sex, and how many partners they've had (not to mention whether any of that sex has felt good). One in four eighteen-year-olds hasn't had intercourse. However, unless they're religious, most don't advertise their status—some even lie about it. Christina, who as a college freshman still expected to remain abstinent until marriage, felt she had to perpetually defend that choice, putting it out there right away when she met a guy at a party, to avoid any pressure or assumption. "But if you think it through," said Brooke, "it's ridiculous what happens. I mean, you're seventeen, you're graduating high school, and you're so worried about going to college a virgin that you get drunk and have sex with some random guy. It's not like that prepares you for anything. It's not like it gives you all this experience or understanding of sex. People, myself included, talk like just doing the act changes you . . ."

"*Oh my God*!" Annie broke in. She'd had intercourse the first time last year, at age nineteen, with her longtime boyfriend. "I thought it would be this whole new world after I had sex the first time! I had learned at school and at church that when you find the 'right person' and you're really in love and you have sex, you will be transformed. Like, this veil would be lifted. But I didn't feel that way. I didn't feel like a new person. There were no birds chirping or bells ringing. And I thought, 'Oh my gosh, maybe it wasn't the right time after all, or maybe we didn't do it right.' I felt like I'd been sold a bill of goods."

In her book *Virginity Lost*, Laura Carpenter finds four ways young people relate to virginity, each, more or less, reflected in what these girls described to me. The first group believed virginity was like a gift: a precious expression of love, though one no longer connected to marriage. Like Annie, and to a degree like Brooke, "gifters" romanticized their first time—the person, the setting, the significance—wanting everything to be "perfect" and expecting sex to strengthen their relationships, deepen a partner's commitment. If the experience wasn't up to snuff, especially if they felt tricked or coerced into intercourse, they were devastated. Worse yet, the betrayal often left them feeling worthless, unable to assert themselves in future relationships. "Having given away her virginity to someone who clearly didn't appreciate it," Carpenter wrote of one such girl, "Julie felt diminished in value, so much so that she believed she was no longer special enough to refuse sex with less special men." The risk for "gifters," then, according to Carpenter, was that their experience, of virginity loss itself and beyond, was defined by their partners' reactions.

At the other end of the spectrum were those who treated virginity as a stigma, viewing it with mounting embarrassment and dismay as they neared high school graduation. They imagined first intercourse would be kind of like a reality show makeover, changing them instantly from duckling to swan, from child to adult. Relationships? Romance? Forget it. This group just wanted it *out of the way*. Although they tended to be more satisfied with the experience than those who saw virginity as a gift of love (largely because their expectations were so much lower), they were often disillusioned by how little actually changed for them in the aftermath.

Nearly a third of Carpenter's subjects, similar to Caitlin, saw virginity loss more as a process, a rite of passage: part of, but not the determining factor in, becoming an adult. They neither idealized virginity nor saw it as a burden; first intercourse was just a natural, inevitable step in growing up and exploring sexuality. They felt more in control of their choices than the other groups—especially over with whom they had sex and when. They also tended to have experimented extensively with at least one other partner before intercourse, and saw doing "everything but" as worthy in its own right. By contrast, those who considered virginity a gift saw "lesser" sex acts mostly as a way to measure their partners' trust and commitment; those who saw virginity as a millstone considered anything short of intercourse to be a letdown, a consolation prize.

Like most Americans today, the young people in these three groups did not expect to remain abstinent until marriage. At the same time, Carpenter found that a substantial minority of teens, which once would have included Christina, had gone resolutely the other way, becoming more committed to and more vocal about remaining chaste until their wedding night. For them, too, virginity was a "gift" to be shared with one true partner, but it was also something else: a way to honor God.

Waiting for the Prince

An attractive couple stepped out of a low-slung sports car at the entrance of the East Ridge Country Club in Shreveport, Louisiana. He dark-haired, in a tuxedo; she in what appeared to be a wedding dress: strapless, with a sparkling white bodice and yards of floor-length tulle. At second glance, though, I saw that something did not quite fit: there was a touch of gray at the man's temples. The woman was not actually a woman at all: she was a fourteen-year-old girl. These were not newlyweds; they were father and daughter, here for the seventh annual, tristate, Ark-La-Tex Purity Ball. Inside, other couples, similarly dressed, milled around a table laden with candy: pink and orange jelly beans and gum balls. Most of them were white, though there was a smattering of African Americans and a few Latinos. One group of daughters and dads (or other male "mentors," who were equally welcome) stood near curtains covered in twinkle lights. Some had already taken their seats at round tables decorated with candles and silk flowers. A few posed for commemorative photos of the evening, which, according to its online invitation, was "designed to equip and encourage young women seventh through twelfth grade to stay pure until marriage." For one hundred dollars a couple (plus fifty dollars each for any additional daughters), it continued, "this event allows fathers an opportunity to pledge themselves to love and protect their daughters. It also helps young women begin to realize the truth: that they are infinitely valuable princesses who are *'worth waiting for'*" (emphasis in original).

The world's first Purity Ball was organized in 1998, in Colorado Springs, the town where Christina grew up, by a pastor named Randy Wilson. As the father of seven children, five of them girls, Wilson believed it was his duty to "protect" his daughters' virginity. It's unclear how many such events are held each year—for a while, reports placed the number at fourteen hundred internationally, but that turned out to be hype. More accurate figures are hard to come by, especially because the balls, like any community event, wax and wane based on local interest and organizers' skills. Either way, they are an outgrowth of a larger "True Love Waits" movement launched by the Southern Baptist Convention in the mid-1990s. The first year of the campaign, more than 100,000 young people joined, signing a pledge to remain abstinent until marriage. By 2004 more than 2.5 million had pledged—1 in 6 American girls. Another campaign, Silver Ring Thing, which was until 2005 partially funded by the U.S. government, has held more than 1,000 events, using Christian rock, hip-hop, and a high-energy, club-like atmosphere as a draw; more than 50 were scheduled in the first half of 2015.

The ball I attended was somewhat unusual, in that although it focused on fathers and daughters, it was organized entirely by women. Its founder, Deb Brittan, was, when it began, a sexual health educator at a local Crisis Pregnancy Center, the kind of organization that steers women with unplanned pregnancies away from abortion and toward adoption or parenting. "My heart was and has always been that I want those baby girls to have the best sex," she told me as the partygoers tucked into a dinner of baked chicken breast and potatoes. "Obviously, when you look at statistics, it becomes *very evident* that the healthiest choice and the only guarantee of not getting a sexually transmitted disease or becoming three times more likely to attempt suicide is to look at a commitment to abstinence until marriage."

I made a note to myself to check that suicide figure: it wasn't wrong; it came from a 2003 study by the conservative Heritage Foundation. The link between sex and suicide, though, could hardly be called causal. Girls, for instance, are also more likely than boys to be bullied and stigmatized for sexual activity, which in itself puts them at risk of depression and suicide. So it may be the shaming of sexually active teens rather than sex itself that is the problem. It may also be that teens who are already depressed are more likely to engage in and subsequently regret sexual activity. Or it may be that teens' expectations of sex are media-driven and unrealistic; or that having first intercourse specifically while drunk puts a child at greater risk. Whatever the case, Brittan's job was to go into local public and private schools and, like Pam Stenzel, give students her version of the facts of life. "Whatever they choose after that is up to them," she told me. "But by the time I got done"—she winked and gave me a playful nudge with her elbow—"they couldn't say no one told them."

EARLIER THAT DAY, I had stopped by the country club to chat with some of the previous ball attendees, who return each year to help with the festivities. Several of them wore sweatshirts bearing the initials S.W.A.T., for "Sisters Walking Accountable Together," a club formed to support girls in vows of chastity. I had changed my own shirt three times before heading out the door. A loose-fitting scoop-necked sweater over a tank top suddenly seemed too revealing, especially since the sweater tended to slide around and show a bra strap. A cardigan over the same tank also seemed potentially immodest. I settled on a boat neck pullover, hoping it wouldn't be seen as too tight. These are not, I hasten to say, my typical thoughts as I dress in the morning, but somehow the Purity Ball's emphasis on "modesty" and "purity" made me feel more conscious of how my body and self-presentation might be judged by others than I had been since I was a teen.

In the daylight, the ballroom was relentlessly beige, its view a winter-drab golf course under a sodden sky. Several girls were tying pink tulle bows to chairs. Haylee, a high school senior, dressed in sweatpants and a S.W.A.T. sweatshirt, stood back to survey the effect, hands on her hips, brow furrowed. "I think it might be a little too 'Sweet Sixteen,'" she said.

"But that's how old the girls are!" another girl countered.

Haylee was, in many ways, like any of the girls I met: she was bright and articulate, excelled in school, was athletic. (She'd played soccer competitively since she was five years old and taught windsurfing in the summer.) She even attended what she called a "hipster, do what you want" liberal arts magnet school. On a chilly Saturday, she had wound her hair into a messy bun, and the red polish on her short nails was chipped. I asked if there were many other pledgers among her classmates. She snorted with laughter. "No," she said. "Actually it's very easy to be anything at my high school *except* for a Christian. People are very accepting of whatever gender you think you want to be. That's cool. And you can be whatever sexuality you want to be, too, *except* for pure. It's strange that way. Most people, when I talk about the Purity Ball are like, 'You are so judgmental.' And I say, 'You're being judgmental about me!'" As a result, she said, she has few friends at school, mostly hanging around a small group of like-minded athletes. For her, she said, the ball, which she first attended four years earlier, at age thirteen, had been a revelation. "I'd never really felt special the way the ball made me feel," she explained. "I didn't know I could love and be loved the way I can and do now."

Haylee had never had a boyfriend. "My school is two-thirds girls, and most of the guys are gay," she said cheerfully. If she did, though, she thinks she would draw the line at hand-holding.

Possibly a kiss, but nothing more. "I think it would be really cool not to have your first kiss until your wedding day," she said. Other girls around us agreed. One said she would never be alone in a room with a boy, not even a dark movie theater—"*Maybe* a two-person table at a restaurant," she allowed. Another girl limited hugs with her boyfriend to three seconds so, she said, "things wouldn't get stirred up."

Haylee and her friends seemed utterly sincere, totally confident in their convictions. If they remain so, though, they will be in the minority. According to Mark Regnerus, a sociologist at the University of Texas, nearly three-quarters of white evangelical teens disapprove of premarital sex, as opposed to half of mainline Protestants and a quarter of Jews. (Evangelical virgins, incidentally, are also the least likely to imagine that sex will feel good; Jews are most likely to cite pleasure as a reason to indulge.) Despite that, evangelicals are the *most* sexually active of those groups. They lose their virginity younger, at an average age of sixteen, and are less likely to protect against pregnancy or disease, perhaps due to a lack of education, or perhaps because preparing for intercourse would make their fall from grace appear premeditated.

Abstinence vows do have some impact, particularly among younger teens: according to sociologists Peter Bearman of Columbia University and Hannah Brückner of Yale, fifteen- and sixteen-year-old pledgers delay intercourse about eighteen months beyond their peers (though that's decidedly *not* "until marriage") and have fewer sexual partners. But the effect vanishes if more than 30 percent of those in a given community want in. Pledging has to feel special, like membership in an exclusive club. Hence, I suppose, the lure of abstinence swag: the rings, T-shirts, notebooks, wristbands, gimme caps, and other gewgaws that declare, "Don't Drink and Park," or "Keep Calm and Stay Pure," or simply, "True Love Waits."

So maybe it does, but not indefinitely and not for everything. Male pledgers are four times more likely to have anal sex than other young people, and pledgers of both sexes are six times more likely to engage in oral sex. What's more, by age eighteen, their resolve begins to crack; by their twenties, over 80 percent of pledgers either deny or have forgotten that they ever pledged at all. The only lesson that sticks is that they remain less likely to use contraception and drastically less likely to protect against disease. Having heard Pam Stenzel warn repeatedly that condoms are useless against infections and that taking birth control pills will leave a girl "sterile or dead," I guess I'm not surprised. Still, it's interesting that young adults retain the unsafe-sex messages of abstinence education even as they jettison the rest. The upshot is that pledgers have the same rates of STDs and pregnancy as the general population, even though they begin intercourse later and report fewer sexual partners overall. Nor is marriage fully protective: female pledgers married younger than other women, but even those who had never previously had intercourse (about 12 percent) tested positive for STDs at the same rates as married nonpledgers.

Folks such as Wilson and Stenzel like to say that waiting for your one true partner will make sex not only holier but hotter. The chemicals your brain releases during sex, they explain, will bond you to that one person, training you, Pavlov-style, to feel aroused and sensual whenever you are together. It's a romantic notion, but, again, it does not appear to be true. A 2014 study of young evangelical Christian men offered a more objective glimpse into the post-abstinent marriage bed. It turned out the men couldn't shake the idea that sex was "beastly" after the prohibition against it was lifted. They were surprised to find themselves still beset by temptation: pornography, masturbation, other women. What's more, back when they were single, they had the support of other abstinent men. Once wed, they found that talking to friends about sexual problems was considered a betrayal of one's wife, and they had no idea how to communicate with their spouses directly.

A young woman who had taken a virginity pledge in the Baptist Church at age ten told a similar story on the website xoJane. After marriage, she couldn't let go of the shame and guilt that had been drummed into her: "Sex felt dirty and wrong and sinful even though I was married and it was supposed to be okay now," she wrote. "Sometimes I cried myself to sleep because I wanted to like [sex], because it wasn't fair. I had done everything right. I took the pledge and stayed true to it. Where was the blessed marriage I was promised?" Meanwhile, a 2011 survey of more than 14,500 people revealed that those who had fallen away from religion were more sexually satisfied and felt less guilty about their sex lives than they had when they were believers.

AT THE BALL, the girls and their fathers rose from their tables, looked into one another's eyes, and exchanged vows. The girls committed themselves to purity. The men promised to "cover" their daughters, to lead, guide, and pray for them. The girls recited the following pledge: "Knowing that I'm worth waiting for, I make a commitment to God, myself, my family, my friends, my future husband, and my future children, to a lifetime of purity, including sexual purity, from this day, until the day I enter into a biblical marriage relationship." The couples then gathered at the back of the room. Each pair linked arms and, one by one, walked down the center of the dance floor, almost as if in a wedding. The fathers plucked silver tiaras from a basket and "crowned" their daughters; the girls then chose a white rose from a second basket.

Brittan introduced me to Dave, a divorced thirty-nine-year-old entrepreneur, who was there with his fourteen-year-old daughter. "As a dad, what I want for her is the best life she can possibly have," he told me. "And the truth is this: Whatever we do between the time we start becoming a young woman or man until we actually get married, whatever happens, whatever takes place in every relationship you have, whether it's physical, emotional, or mental—every experience you have you're going to bring that into a marriage. Purity can actually cut off at the root a lot of future pain. Instead of having to be healed of something, isn't it better not to get sick in the beginning? Who can argue against that?"

Dave should know, he continued. He faltered before his own marriage, something he regrets and blames, in part, for its ultimate failure. "I went off to college and was on my own," he said. "And I got off track. I did not surround myself with like-minded people. There was a lot of heartache and a lot of pain. That's why I think this is so flipping important. We get told all the time no one will be abstinent, there's no way they'll do it. Why? It's a choice." He pointed to his daughter, who was standing silently beside him, twirling her white rose. "If someone put a gun to her head every day and said if you lose your purity, I'll shoot you, I guarantee she wouldn't lose her purity. It's all about choice."

Dave did not, at least on the surface, hold a double standard. Abstinence, to him, was as important for males as females. He planned to serve as a role model to his children, remaining chaste until (or unless) he remarried. He expected "purity" from his sons as well. Again, his concern seemed less about sex than the pain wrought by emotional intimacy—pain that others may consider essential to personal growth, to developing mature ideas and expectations of relationships.

Listening to Dave, it occurred to me that the idea that purity would protect either him or his children from divorce—that practicing the skills of emotional or physical intimacy before marriage threatens rather than enhances a partnership—seemed as much a fairy tale as the fake crown he'd just placed on his daughter's head. I've been married nearly twenty-five years. Virginity, by the time of our wedding day long gone, was not something special or cherished my husband and I gave each other; our love and commitment were. That's true for all the long-term married couples I know; it was equally true of everyone I know who has divorced. What's more, if Dave really wanted his children to marry for keeps, he might want to start checking the real estate listings in liberal bastions such as New York, Boston, or San Francisco. Statistically, the strongest factor predicting higher divorce rates in any given county is its concentration of conservative or evangelical Protestants, in part because they marry and have children younger. Taboos against sexual experimentation and emotional intimacy may, then, boomerang on parents such as Dave, pushing their children to wed someone incompatible or before they're ready so they can have an openly physical relationship.

It's easy for those of us who think pledging is wacky to feel a little smug. Yet it occurred to me that these girls who were "virgins for God" weren't really so different from those who imagined virginity as a "gift" or even those who saw it as an embarrassment: they all believed that *one* sexual act would magically transform them—for better or for worse—and they all risked harm to their sexual and emotional development as a result. They all based their worth, calibrated their self-respect, and judged other girls' characters (tacitly or overtly) based on what was happening, or not happening, between their legs. And they all were still fundamentally defining themselves by their sexuality: by whether, when, where, with whom, and how many times they'd had intercourse.

By focusing on virginity, young people minimize (and often rush through) other forms of sexual expression, denying themselves the very opportunities for knowledge and experience that they seek. After all, moving slowly and intentionally with a partner is not only incredibly sensual, it's vital to learning, truly *learning*, about desire, pleasure, communication, mutuality, intimacy. That's ultimately far more life-altering than "achieving" intercourse. " 'Experience' is a stupid way of thinking about it," said Dennis Fortenberry, professor of pediatrics at the Indiana University School of Medicine and one of the foremost researchers on adolescent sexuality. "If you think of it as a *pool* of experiences of closeness, warmth, desire, attraction, arousal, touch, orgasm—all those are part of the possibilities of sexual learning. That's what young people should be doing. Learning about the incredibly nuanced thing we call sex that we assume will be part of their lives in different manifestations for the next sixty years or so. I don't think I'll see this in my lifetime, but what if we could even begin to think of actually saying to kids, 'Spend a year or two having oral-genital sex with people that you want to do that with and really get to know what that's about and then figure out what might follow.' "

I had walked into this ballroom unsettled, to say the least, by the white dresses, the wedding motif, the idea of fathers being made the guardians of girls' "sexual purity." The fathers were even given a Lucite-encased sixpence to keep as a symbol of their daughters' virtue, until the girls' wedding day (as in "something borrowed, something blue, and a silver sixpence in her shoe"). What could be more patriarchal, more regressive? At the same time, the sexualization so rampant in secular culture, which measures a woman's value first and foremost by how "hot" she is, is little better. I utterly, vehemently disagree with how they approach it, but like me, these parents only want what's best for their daughters; in their own way, they believe they're helping their girls combat modern pressures and degrading stereotypes. Brittan talked to me about the "pornography epidemic" and the importance of "empowering" young people to "navigate the assault of sexuality everywhere they go" so that they can make ethical, responsible, "healthy sexual choices." Like me, she believed that we should educate our children about sex "in a very direct way." It was all the same language, yet the intent was completely different. To me, purity and hypersexualization are flip sides of the same coin. I'd rather girls were taught that their sexual status, regardless of what it is, is not the measure of their personhood, their morality, their worth.

The dads and daughters, having completed the crowning ceremony and signed a "covenant" of purity, took to the floor for their "first dance," yet another ritual that mirrored a wedding. They looked so happy: the daughters basked in the attention of their fathers or mentors. I may not have agreed with the reason for the gathering, I may not have agreed with their message, but I did appreciate that fathers were communicating with their daughters at all, that they were taking time to deepen their bond with the girls: to create trust, to discuss ethics and values around sex. I interviewed more than seventy young women for this book: only two had ever had a substantive conversation about sex with their fathers. The rest just laughed when I raised the subject. Moms don't fare much better: even those who believe they've talked to their daughters about sex tend to overestimate the efficacy, openness, and comfort level of those discussions. Somehow, once parents stopped saying "don't," many didn't know what to say. So while it's easy to be appalled by the blatant sexism of Purity Ball dads—and yes, I absolutely was—I am equally appalled that the alternative to them seems to be total silence.

After a song or two, the dads drifted off the dance floor, while the girls kicked off their high heels. They jumped around in little scrums to "clean" pop songs such as Pharrell Williams's "Happy." As I slipped out the door, "Let It Go," the anthem from *Frozen*, came on. At the chorus, like young women everywhere, the girls flung their arms extravagantly wide and belted the words. The fathers looked on, smiling indulgently, apparently unaware that the point of the song—"No right, no wrong, no rules for me. I'm free!" and "That perfect girl is gone"—is that Elsa, the princess, is coming into her power, rejecting the restrictive, false morality that was imposed on her by her father, the king.

The Good-Person Checklist

Christina had known Brandon since kindergarten. They chased each other on the school playground, went to each other's birthday parties at the local skating rink. He won first prize in the middle school science fair, she took second. They shared their first kiss after the winter formal during their junior year. Over time, their physical intimacy deepened, but the specter of the Church was never far from her mind. "It was like, 'My boyfriend took off my shirt. What if other people find out?'" she recalled.

"Even now, I can logically talk myself out of those feelings, but it's all still there. There are degrees of shame and guilt that are probably permanently embedded in me. I wish that wasn't so. It haunts a lot of my actions." She paused thoughtfully. "But then, I don't know where the line is between how I was raised and what's just my personality. By nature, I'm a very cautious person."

Perhaps. Yet when I met Christina, she was planning a semester abroad in Botswana, which seemed pretty nervy to me. She'd also purposely chosen to attend a college that would challenge her long-held values, and sought housing that would push her even further. Christina's willingness to step so far out of the bubble of her upbringing—something that's hard for any young person to do regardless of her politics—struck me as admirable, even brave. She couldn't fully explain why she'd done it. It may have been because her parents weren't as conservative as her teachers. Christina's mother never contradicted the school's teaching on chastity, but she drew the line at its condemnation of homosexuality as a sin. "She just told me straight out, 'That's not true,'" Christina said. Beyond that, though, Christina always felt different from her peers. The other kids in her grade were white, and she resembled her Filipino father; she was the only Asian in the entire school. In middle school, boys teased her about the shape of her eyes, the color of her skin; it made her feel, even to this day, unattractive, undesirable. That sense of difference, of alienation, may have been enough to set her searching.

Christina expected her values to be tested when she entered college. "I knew I'd have to stick to my morals," she said. "If I didn't want to drink, I wasn't going to do that. If I didn't want to have sex with someone, I wasn't going to do that." Within a couple of months, though, she began to, as she called it, "loosen up": venturing out to parties, having a drink or two, making out with boys on the dance floor. "I guess I kind of did glamorize all that," she admitted. "I think I kind of envied the freedom of these girls who didn't have a lot of rules set up for them. I wanted to know what that felt like."

At one of those parties, early in the fall of her sophomore year, she met Ethan, a tall, gentle boy who, like her, was from a conservative community. They talked all evening, and found they enjoyed each other's company. At first she was hesitant to enter into a relationship, but within a month or so, they were dating exclusively, and by the end of October, they began having sex. "It was just very natural," Christina said. "I wanted to get to know him in that way, and he wanted to get to know me in that way. There was no pressure. It was totally my decision and all very partner-y."

Which is exactly how one would hope girls' experience of intercourse would be. Could that care and concern for a partner have been an unintended by-product of her conservative education? Was it simply because she was older than many girls at first intercourse? It's hard to say. Christina did credit her school with teaching an overarching ethic of kindness and respect for others—though apparently that didn't preclude people teasing her about her race. She also believed that since sex was off the table, boys in her class were forced, for the most part, to see girls as something other than sex objects. At the same time, that education left her especially insecure and ignorant about her body and its responses. "I didn't know *anything* before I got to college," she said. "I had no idea what a clitoris was. And there's still so much I don't know." Like what? I asked. "Well," she said slowly, "I worry about what's 'normal' in sex, but you can't ask because everyone is different. So I can't . . ." Christina trailed off. "I don't know. I don't know what's 'normal' for me. Like . . ." She hesitated again and then looked at me shyly. "Like is it normal never to have orgasms?"

Christina and Ethan were together for about six months. She never regretted losing her virginity with him, but once they broke up, she wondered, what now? "Am I going to be a person who only sleeps with people if I'm in a serious relationship? Do I want to make a rule that I'll go on a certain amount of dates with someone before I sleep with him? And if I do sleep with another person, that would bring my number to two. Do I care about that number?"

The "number" was a common source of concern among girls. Even those who felt that virginity was a vestige of another time wondered how many sexual partners was too many. (The "number," like virginity itself, included only intercourse—no one counted boys with whom, say, they'd had oral sex.) Losing their virginity in itself may not have tainted them, but was it possible to go too far? The stigma of the slut, the girl who was overly and overtly sexual, who allowed herself to be used, still held: their character could still be compromised, for themselves as well as others, by their sexual activity. "I guess I would feel icky if my number started to climb into the double digits," Brooke admitted. She glanced over at Christina, who was counting on her fingers, silently enumerating Brooke's lovers. "Stop that!" she snapped, laughing, and then grew serious. "I feel that sex is important. I don't want to have sex with people who don't mean something to me. And I'm not old enough yet to have had that many partners who do mean something."

Caitlin shook her head and pushed impatiently at her glasses. "I kind of don't feel that way," she said. "I feel like I could have sex with someone and it could mean nothing. I remember the first person I had sex with after the guy I'd been with for three years.

It was so surprising that it could feel . . . emotionally light, just fun and relaxed and easy.

"And what is that, anyway, to 'mean something'?" she continued. "Does it mean you have to love the person? Could it be about an out-of-body experience? Could it just be that this person was a good person and I appreciated how generous they were? Isn't that meaningful?"

Brooke shrugged, picking at her nail polish. "Maybe it's my own self-consciousness. For me, saying no is so hard under any circumstances, even to a favor for a friend. So I can see myself accidentally letting things escalate with someone I didn't want them to escalate with, and that wouldn't feel good to me. But I guess if I was turned on by someone who I wasn't into emotionally . . . I can't really imagine it, but that would be okay."

"It's such a relative thing," Christina mused. "Where I came from is so different than where you came from, so what sex means to me is so different. If a year ago I'd had sex with two people, I wouldn't have been okay with that. But now I am. So I think the 'meaningful' has to be a sliding definition both for each person and over time. And I think . . . I think I don't care anymore about someone's number. I mean, for safe sex, yes, but in terms of feeling like they're a morally better or worse person . . . I used to think the checklist of whether or not you were a good person was about 'are you drinking, are you smoking, are you having sex, are you loose in these ways'? That's not my checklist at all anymore. Because everyone has so much more depth and so many more dimensions than that.

"And I don't think I want to set lines for myself anymore, either," she added. "Because you'll be disappointed when you cross them. I have to trust myself to know what feels good and natural and what doesn't."

Caitlin was messing with Christina's computer and had cued up another Pam Stenzel video. This one was called "Definition of Sex." Stenzel was still pacing in front of the "High Cost of Free Love" sign, spieling like a Catskills *tummler*. She talked about a girl she'd met who'd had a "radical hysterectomy" at eighteen; her cervical cancer was diagnosed in ninth grade, caused by her contracting HPV in seventh. (While she warned, correctly, that condoms can't fully protect against HPV, Stenzel neglected to mention there is a vaccine, offered by pediatricians when children are eleven, that will. Nor did she mention that regular pap smears will effectively screen for abnormalities.) Then she began to talk once again about virginity. "I'm now going to give you the medical definition of 'sex,'" she said. (And right there a viewer should have been suspicious, since, as I've said, there actually isn't one.) "This is the medical line over which you can't step, and if you have ever stepped over this line, you have risked disease *and* you need to get tested, and don't you *DARE*! Don't you *DARE* tell anyone you're a virgin! Here is the line over which you can't step. Absolutely *no genital contact of any kind*. That's hand-to-genital, mouth-to-genital, genital-to-genital. Oral sex, which is mouth-to-genital, is sex. Hence the name 'oral sex.' And if you have had oral sex, you are not a virgin and don't you *dare* tell anyone you are."

The girls watching the video giggled and occasionally gasped in shock. Weirdly, though, I found myself agreeing with Stenzel, if not with her conclusions or her effort to shame and terrorize her audience. Our definition of "sex" is too narrow. I realize that it's idealistic to call for a dismantling of virginity for the sake of girls' health, but even questioning the implications of our assumptions about it has value. It is worth asking how putting this one act into a separate category is keeping girls (and boys) safer from disease, coercion, betrayal, assault; whether it gives them more control over their sexual experience; whether it encourages mutuality and caring; how it affects their perception of other kinds of sexual interactions; what it means for gay teens, who can have multiple sex partners without heterosexual intercourse. Again, this is not because that form of intercourse is no big deal, but because it's not the *only* big deal. I'd rather young people think of sex more horizontally, as Dennis Fortenberry suggested, as a way to explore intimacy and pleasure, than as this misguided vertical race to a goal. What if your first kiss were a form of virginity loss? The first time you had oral sex? What if it was first love? What if, as Jessica Valenti suggests in *The Purity Myth*, a girl didn't lose her virginity until she'd had her first orgasm with a partner?

Before leaving Christina and her friends, I asked how she would raise her own daughter if she had one. She pondered that for a moment. "There are huge holes in my sex education that I can't ignore," she finally said, "but at the risk of losing the other lessons that benefited me, I wouldn't wish to have done it differently. Still, I really want to have a more open discussion with my children. I can't quite imagine being at a level of saying, 'Okay, so this is what your clitoris is,' but then again, I'd want that for them if that would make them more comfortable in the world.

"I guess I would have to tell my daughter, 'It's totally your decision,'" she continued. "'It's whatever you feel comfortable with. But you have to be safe: there are these bad things that can happen in sex, but there are also benefits.' I would have to tell her, 'It's very much up to you and how you feel.' Because I think, in the end, it is the most personal of all decisions."

CHAPTER 4

Hookups and Hang-Ups

Holly, a sophomore at a private East Coast college, volunteered to talk to me for a specific reason. She wanted it known that some college girls, girls such as she, enjoyed the so-called hookup culture. "In books and articles they always say that if a girl sleeps around she'll get called a slut or that all girls only really want relationships," she said, sweeping her strawberry blond hair back over one shoulder. "Otherwise, it's just about how hookup culture is good for guys, and how they feel this sense of accomplishment when they've had sex with a number of girls. But I'll just put it out there: I feel accomplished after I have sex with someone that I wanted to have sex with. Last Thursday morning I woke up and apparently everyone in my sorority house knew I'd had sex because they'd heard the bed squeaking through the ceiling. And everyone goes, 'Holly! High five! You get it, girl!' I felt accomplished, just like a boy would. I felt like, 'I went out, I looked good, I showed myself off, and I got it last night. Good for me.'"

What's Sauce for the Gander

As with oral sex in the 1990s, discussions of the current "hookup culture" are fertile ground for good old-fashioned media-induced panics. The take-away from most reports tends to swing extreme: Hookups are terrible for girls! Hookups are liberating for girls! Girls are being victimized! Girls are going wild! Here is what they rarely say: young people are not, in fact, having more sex than they used to—at least, if you define sex by intercourse. The seismic tectonic shift in premarital sexual behavior really took place with the Baby Boom generation, according to Elizabeth Armstrong, a sociologist at the University of Michigan who, with her colleagues, has conducted the most comprehensive research on college student hookups. That was when the introduction of the Pill, the rise of the women's movement, and relaxed attitudes about supervision of "coeds" ignited the sexual revolution. Nor did today's young 'uns invent the concept of casual sex. What has changed, however, among college students and increasingly among high schoolers, is that when relationships do occur, instead of starting with a date, they often begin with noncommitted sexual contact. Rather than being a product of intimacy, then, sex has become its precursor, or sometimes its replacement. That's what is meant by the term *hookup culture.* "Casual sex was happening before in college," said Debby Herbenick at Indiana University's Kinsey Institute, "but there wasn't the sense that it's what you *should* be doing. It is now. I have students who say people should be able to have no emotions in sex, and if you can't, there's something wrong with you and you're missing out."

The word *hookup* itself, as I've said previously, is ambiguous, indicating anything from kissing to oral sex to intercourse to anal sex. To make things more confusing, there are different types of hookups: one-time hookups, repeated hookups, exclusive hookups, "friends with benefits." The only common thread is that there is no thread—or, more correctly, no *strings*: no emotional commitment, no promise by either partner of anything beyond the moment. According to the Online College Social Life Survey, which included some twenty thousand students at twenty-one universities, 72 percent of both male and female college students hook up at least once by senior year, with the average number of partners being seven. The behavior is most typical among affluent white heterosexuals and least common among African American women and Asian men. Twenty percent of college students hook up ten times or more by senior year; 40 percent hook up three times or fewer. Only a third of these hookups included intercourse; another third involved oral sex or some form of manual genital stimulation; the rest consisted of kissing and what my grandparents would have called "heavy petting." So it's not exactly the fall of Rome out there. Kids themselves tend to overestimate the sexual activity of their peers, again, perhaps driven by media "scripts"—from the 92 percent of songs on the *Billboard* charts that are about sex to movies such as *No Strings Attached* and *Friends with Benefits* to TV shows from *Pretty Little Liars* to *Vampire Diaries* to *Awkward* to *Grey's Anatomy* (Mindy Kaling, creator and star of *The Mindy Project*, has joked that her eponymous character has dated more men in a few seasons—making out with thirty of them—than she, the real Mindy, has in her entire life). There is also the rise of hookup apps such as Tinder, that portray millions of people as blithely bed hopping. But overstating the amount of sex going on is not young people's only perception-reality gap: when Herbenick anonymously polled the one hundred fifty students in the Human Sexuality class I had visited, over 70 percent of both sexes believed that their classmates solely sought hookups, while less than half believed others were interested in relationships. The truth is, nearly three-quarters of the boys and 80 percent of the girls said they'd prefer a date to a hookup, and nearly 80 percent of both sexes would like to be in a loving relationship within the next year.

Some girls, such as Holly, reported feeling affirmed by hook-ups, released from emotional responsibility for their partner, free to acknowledge straight-up lust. At the same time, the actual sex? *Meh.* Girls' physical satisfaction in hookups tends, once again, to be secondary, an afterthought. They are considerably less likely, for instance, to receive oral sex in casual encounters, and when they do, it's rarely to climax: only 17 percent of women reported orgasms in first hookups that included oral sex alone, as opposed to 60 percent whose most recent cunnilingus experience was in a relationship. (Men in hookups, incidentally, overestimate their partners' orgasms by a third to a half.) In hookups involving intercourse, 40 percent of women said they'd come (half the rate of men who did), as opposed to three-quarters in serious relationships. Orgasm may not be the only measure of sexual satisfaction—girls sometimes complained to me that the pressure from boyfriends to "achieve" climax stressed them out, especially when they were sexually inexperienced—but since young women are up to six times more likely to say they enjoyed an encounter (either in a relationship or a hookup) when they did come, neither is it irrelevant. Perhaps one could argue that it takes time for men to learn a female partner's body and responses, but it also requires interest—and basic respect. Young men routinely express far less of both for hookup partners than for girlfriends or even "friends with benefits." As one boy put it to Armstrong and her colleagues, "In a hookup, I don't give a shit." Women were equally invested in their partners' pleasure either way. That may partly explain why 82 percent of men said that the morning after a hookup, they were generally glad they'd done it, compared to 57 percent of women.

Even so, 57 percent is a lot of girls, enough to show pretty clearly that hookups neither are driven by nor benefit only boys. As the age of first marriage rose and the idea of finding one's husband during college became an anachronism, Armstrong and her colleagues found girls' willingness to devote time to relationships waned. With years of single life still ahead of them, many want to focus their energy on "self-development": pursuing academic, personal, and professional goals or hanging out with friends. Parents, too, have urged them to focus on ambition rather than romance. Hookups allow them to do all that while still enjoying an active sex life. Besides, how many times can you—or do you *want* to—fall in love? Hookup culture, then, acts as a kind of buffer, a placeholder until the time for more official adult partnerships begins. The girls I met often claimed to be too "busy" for relationships. On one hand, it was heartening to hear that their lives didn't revolve around men. Yet it was also hard to imagine a time when that "busyness" would abate—it would arguably become more intense after college, when they'd be career building or attending graduate school. What were they so busy doing, anyhow? It's not like they had to shop for food, prepare their own meals, or pick up their children at school. While I was all for broadening possibilities, the idea that romance and ambition were mutually exclusive troubled me. It sounded a bit too redolent of "you can't have it all," a phrase that blames individual women rather than structural inequities for our struggles at work and home.

"There's this idea now that identity is built independent of relationships, not within them," said Leslie Bell, the psychotherapist and author. "So only once you're 'complete' as an adult can you be in a relationship. It's an interesting shift from earlier academic thinking and folk wisdom—that women are naturally relationship-oriented and develop within them more than they do independent of them." Bell isn't opposed to hookups, but found that her own subjects, who were five or ten years older than mine, weren't having the experience of trying out love, intimacy, vulnerability, or self-advocacy with a partner. Their adulthood and independence were based on denying rather than expressing emotional connection through sexuality. "It's all about the importance of not getting played," she said. "Why isn't there much discussion about going through a bad love experience and learning from it? Why aren't there as many stories about the importance of taking risks even if you do end up feeling played? It's like a perversion of relatedness and interdependence—as though for women to participate in a relationship will always mean a loss of self."

Listening to Bell, I recalled a conversation I'd had with Mackenzie, a sophomore at a Bay Area high school dominated by hookup culture. She was going through a rocky patch when we met: her boyfriend of a year had just cheated on her, making out with another girl while drunk at a party, and she was conflicted over whether to break things off. She was often teary as we talked, describing ways she'd "lost herself" in their relationship. "I'm not saying that's all a negative thing, though," she added. "I've learned a lot about myself, too. I've learned that I have so much to me. I have a lot to give. Also I learned a lot about myself and vulnerability. I can love very deeply, and I think that's a good thing. I've learned a lot about my body, about my mind—just being with someone else, hearing their views on things, being intimate. I'm still learning. I'm learning what it's like to deal with heartbreak and someone you believed would never hurt you and he did. All of that."

On the college campuses I visited, hooking up was considered the ticket to a social life, to enjoyment, empowerment, even to a potential relationship. The girls who opted out, especially freshmen, could be left bored and lonely on a Saturday (or a Friday or a Tuesday) night. What fun was that? Their objections were usually not moral: they didn't think that girls who hooked up were "sloppy" or indiscriminate so much as that casual sex seemed emotionally hollow, potentially unsafe, and, sometimes, unhygienic. Becca, for instance, a freshman at an East Coast private school, had been nicknamed Grandma by her friends because she was often in bed by nine. She'd hooked up plenty of times when she was younger—making out with boys at the private Jewish middle school she attended, performing oral sex for the first time in ninth grade, losing her virginity at fifteen in a haze of weed and alcohol. Those experiences left her feeling lousy. Since early senior year, she'd had a steady boyfriend with whom she was in love; she remained committed to him even though he was at school in another state. "My friends have said, 'Bec, you shouldn't have a boyfriend when you're in college!'" she told me. "So, last night I went to a party and two separate people told me this sophomore guy wanted to fuck me. I was like, 'Great. He doesn't want to get to know me but he wants to *fuck* me?' I have found someone I genuinely love and I'm not going to let that go to hook up with random people. I mean, you want me to hook up with a bunch of guys and get mono? I don't understand." (Becca, it is worth mentioning, was the only girl I interviewed on her campus who was not sick with a nasty upper respiratory infection that students called the Sludge.) Similar to Sam, the high school girl who wouldn't spend time alone with her male friends, Becca

also felt that the hookup culture was an obstacle to platonic relationships. "Like, I was hanging out at a frat house recently after a
'darty' [daytime party]," she said. "Just hanging out and talking
to the guys, and one of the brothers was not shy in expressing his
confusion over why I would do that, since I wasn't hooking up
with anyone."

Sierra had her share of hookups in high school, too, but found
them similarly unfulfilling. A freshman in college when we met,
she'd been with her current boyfriend for nearly a year. "I used
to think the sexual stuff was how you got to the emotional connection," she said. "But that's not true. The emotional connection comes first. That's what has made the sex so good. The first
time we had sex, my subconscious was thinking, 'He's excited to
do this not just for the sake of doing it, but to be doing it with
me. To be doing it with someone he's going to end up loving.' He
cares about how I am feeling. He texts me in the morning: 'Good
morning! How are you today?' And if I text, 'I'm tired,' he texts
back, 'Great. But how *are* you today? Mentally? Are you stressed?
Are you happy? Are you sad?' It's knowing that we got to know
each other, to know what makes us pissed off or happy or sad. It's
that connection, that reassurance, that this isn't a 'hit and run.'
We live in the moment and love every second, but it is absolutely
the emotional connection before the sexual stuff that has made
it worth it."

At the other extreme, or so I initially thought, was a freshman
at a midwestern college who regaled me with tales of her sexual
swashbuckling for nearly two hours, telling me how she rejected
boys whose penis sizes "didn't meet my standards," or who were
too heavy ("I don't like fat guys," she said). Yet at the end of our
conversation, when I asked if there was anything she'd like to
add, she hesitated, and almost in a whisper said, "philophobia."

I looked at her questioningly. "It's the fear of falling in love or being in love," she explained. "I read about it in a book. Sometimes I feel that's why I never get into an actual relationship. It's so hard for me to have an emotional attachment to people. I don't want to get hurt. So I just go from guy to guy, putting a barrier between me and others to keep that from ever happening."

I don't want to idealize relationships. While some girls had found love and joy within them, others had experienced manipulation and devastation. Becca had undergone two depressive episodes after splitting up with high school boyfriends. Mackenzie cried until she vomited when she discovered her boyfriend's recent betrayal, and had hardly eaten in days. Her schoolwork was suffering, too. More than half of physical and sexual abuse of teen girls by a romantic partner happens within a relationship, and those experiences prime girls to be victimized again in young adulthood. One girl I spoke with described how her tenth-grade boyfriend slapped her and flung her into a fence when she threatened to break up with him. Another girl, a sophomore in college, hadn't realized she could be—and was—raped by her recent boyfriend. Encouraging girls to explore sexuality within mutually caring, emotionally connected relationships is one thing; *insisting* on it is another. That can turn sex into a commodity that girls barter for the "safety" of commitment, and implicitly condone the shaming of those who don't comply.

There was no consistent attitude toward either hookups or relationships among the girls I met. They all, however, had to negotiate the culture of casual sex, whether they participated in it or not. They all had to find comfortable ground in a culture that was simultaneously fun and antagonistic, carefree yet riddled with risk. The question to me, then, became less about whether hookups were "good" or "bad" for girls than about how to ensure reciprocity, respect, and agency regardless of the context of a sexual encounter. That meant understanding the contours of girls' new freedom as well as the constraints, both physical and psychological, that remained.

The Happy Hookup

Holly, a Spanish and psychology major, revised her definition of "slut" for the first time when she was sixteen. She grew up in a mostly white, affluent, liberal East Coast suburb and attended a progressive, all-girls high school. Her mom told her to wait until marriage to have sex, but in Health class she learned about birth control and practiced putting a condom on a rubber model of a penis. (Again, though, the location of the clitoris, masturbation, and female orgasm went unmentioned.) In tenth grade, some of her friends began performing oral sex on their boyfriends; within a year or so, they were having intercourse. "My opinion had very much been, 'It's only those skanky public school girls who are doing that sort of thing,'" Holly said. "But if my friends were having sex, it had to be okay, right? So I had to reevaluate. I thought, 'That's fine; they've been dating for a year. They've built trusting relationships.'"

Holly, however, stayed both chaste and sober: a "good girl" who imagined she'd save sex for a loving relationship and alcohol until age twenty-one. When she did imagine having a boyfriend, her fantasies hewed to the romantic rather than the sexual—beaches and sunsets were usually involved. She entered college, she said, "very pure," but campus life quickly changed her. Her fourth night at school, she made out at a party with a guy she barely knew. It was fun. A week after that, she gave the same guy a hand job, and he fondled her breasts. "It was a *huge* thing for me," she recalled. "I touched a boy's penis! He touched my boobs! I was slightly overwhelmed. Because three weeks before, I would have said no. But I wanted to be doing this, although nothing more than this." By early October, she had happily hooked up with two more guys, making out on the dance floor and going back to their rooms. "I almost feel like I wanted the opportunity," she said. "Because in high school I never had the opportunity to hook up with boys. And in college I have this endless opportunity to do it, so I felt like I could."

Holly met Connor, who lived on her floor, at a school football game, and the two bonded over their politics—which were more liberal than those of many of their peers—and a mutual passion for *The Daily Show*. They began texting, and one night Connor asked if Holly and her friends would take him to a frat party. Freshman year was tough for boys on campuses dominated by Greek life. In order to "preserve the ratio" of girls to boys at a party—keeping the odds in the hosts' favor—frats limited the number of unaffiliated males allowed in. So unless a freshman guy was accompanied by a large enough group of women (three, four, sometimes more), he risked being turned away.

Holly showed me a picture of herself on a recent night out that she'd posted to Instagram. She was dressed in what I came to think of as the sorority uniform: a tight black miniskirt, bare legs, crop top, and stilettos. Her hair was flat-ironed straight, and she wore red lipstick and dark eyeliner. She looked like a different person from the scrubbed-face girl before me. "There are few times that I feel more confident about my body than when I wear a crop top and my boobs are showing and my legs are showing and I'm wearing super high heels," she told me. "I never feel more liberated than then. I'm proud of my body, and I like to show it off."

That phrase, "proud of my body," continued to bedevil me. On one hand, I admired the young women's bravado, their willingness to be overtly on the prowl, their refusal to be shamed for how they did or didn't dress. At the same time, only certain bodies were allowed to be a source of "pride," to be seen as sexual, to deflect shame, and Holly's had not always been one of them. As a freshman, she was twenty-five pounds heavier than when we first met—she'd dieted and worked out all summer to lose the weight—and her wardrobe had been considerably more conservative. "I would never have worn anything skimpy because I wasn't happy with how I looked," she said. "Presenting myself in skimpy attire would have had a very negative impact on my mental state, because there would be those people, especially boys, who would say, 'She's fat and she should wear something else.'" It's understandable that Holly would feel good about showing off the "right" body—it's affirming to attract male approval and even female envy—but it's hard to see her outfits as "liberating" when the threat of ridicule always lurks. One of her sorority sisters, for instance, had recently gained weight. "It's not that she *couldn't* wear skimpy clothes," Holly said. "But she knows how she would feel if there were asshole-y boys who were like, 'She's a fat girl.'"

On most of the campuses I visited, Greek life (or houses where athletes lived) was the center of the hookup scene. The twenty-six sororities in the National Panhellenic Conference are voluntarily dry. So it is the frats that host, control entry to, and provide alcohol for most parties. Fraternity pledges typically chauffeur groups of girls from freshman dorms or sorority houses to events (though not necessarily home again) that can offer endless variations on a single concept: young women as prostitutes. Themes include "CEOs and business hos," "workout bros and yoga hos," "lifeguard bros and surfer hos," "GI Joes and army hos." Girls who liked to party shrugged off those slights (similar to the way they ignored degrading lyrics in a favorite song) as a form of "boys will be boys," unconnected to how most guys acted "in person." Frats got in trouble only when their sexism became even more egregious or was mixed with racism: the Phi Sigma Kappa chapter at California Polytechnic was investigated in 2013 by the school's administration for its "Colonial Bros and Nava-Hos" party. (No violations of university policies were found.) The Sigma Chi chapter at Harvard raised hackles with a similar bash, called "Conquistabros and Navajos." Meanwhile, the Duke chapter of Kappa Sigma was suspended in 2013 after news broke of its racist "Asia Prime" party, whose invitation began, "Herro Nice Duke Peopre!!" (Duke frats have made headlines repeatedly in the past few years for such antics as inviting "all potential slam pieces" to a "Plan-B Pregame" party and sending an e-mail to female classmates requesting they arrive at a Halloween party dressed "like a slutty nurse, a slutty doctor, a slutty school girl, or just total sluts.") The Delta Kappa Epsilon chapter at Yale was banned from campus in 2010 after brothers gathered near the freshmen dorms and chanted, "No means yes, yes means anal!" and "My name is Jack, I'm a necrophiliac, I fuck dead women and fill them with my semen." Students protested in 2012 after the same frat's Amherst chapter had a T-shirt printed up for its annual pig-roasting party depicting a woman clad in a bra and thong tied up and roasting on a spit, an apple jammed in her mouth, her sides bruised, and a pig standing beside her. Its caption read, "Roasting Fat Ones Since 1847." In 2014 the Texas Tech chapter of Phi Delta Theta had its charter revoked for displaying a banner that read, "No Means Yes, Yes Means Anal!" at a party, along with a "vagina sprinkler" that shot water at guests.

The members of all those houses, as in most of the Greek system, were primarily white and affluent; somehow they believed that racism and misogyny marked them as rebels rather than merely the latest recruits to an entrenched old guard.

Young women are tacitly expected to repay their hosts' generosity with sex, or at least the promise of its possibility. "Every girl knows that when you walk into a fraternity house, your most valuable asset is your sex appeal," a junior at a private East Coast college told me. "Everyone knows you have to imply you'll have sex with guys to get them to give you alcohol, drugs, rides, whatever. Everyone plays this game—and since at my school we're all overachievers, we do it really well!"

Girls who pledge sororities at Holly's school were required to attend frat parties at least four nights a week. (There were "ragers" every night but Monday.) Before the main event, they would "pregame" with a different frat, socializing and drinking for an hour or two. Holly would typically have three or four beers at those occasions and sometimes also a couple of shots. The girls would then be picked up by a second round of pledge rides and driven to the real party. "In some houses, basically you get there, go down to the basement, grind with a guy, and go back with him. Just that fast. But at my favorite house, I talk to my friends, we play drinking games, we dance a little, we go back and smoke a little. Sometimes I'll just dance with my sisters, and that's a good time. And grinding is fun, too. It's fun to have a guy holding on to you like that. You don't have to hook up—and anyway, there's more girls than guys at parties, so not everyone can. But it's often a big hookup scene."

When I added it up, Holly was regularly downing three to six (or more) drinks in an evening. For women, four qualifies as binge drinking. She didn't consider herself a heavy drinker, and likely her friends wouldn't, either. Alcohol is endemic to hookup culture. Hookups aren't just lubricated by drinking; they are *dependent* on it, in order to create what Lisa Wade, an associate professor of sociology at Occidental College, calls "compulsory carelessness." As a sophomore at an East Coast university told me, "It's like the girls I know live dual lives. From Sunday night to Thursday afternoon we're in the library all the time, working really hard. Then comes the weekend. We all rip back shots in our dorms before a frat's *pre*-party. Like four to eight shots in about a half hour. That's pretty normal. And then it's normal to wake up next to some guy and not remember how you got there."

Alcohol, according to Wade, is how students signal to one another that the sex they're having is meaningless. For her own research, she asked eighty-four freshmen to submit weekly journal entries over the course of a semester about sex and dating on campus. "They talked about having sex while sober in these reverent tones," she said, "like it was an amazing unicorn: it was 'meaningful' in a way that drunk sex is not." Drunkenness had replaced mutual attraction as the fuel for sexual interactions in college: "In a morning-after recap," Wade continued, "it is a reason in itself to have had sex."

As with intercourse, the proportion of young people who drink has actually dropped over the past decade, but the *amount* that girls in particular (and white girls specifically) drink on each occasion has not. A 2013 survey by the Centers for Disease Control and Prevention found that one out of four college women and one out of five high school girls had binged within the previous thirty days; they typically binged three times a month, downing an average of six drinks on each occasion. Other surveys have found that nearly two-thirds of college women and over 80 percent of men had episodes of binge drinking, and linked the practice with disordered eating—sometimes called "drunkorexia"—among girls who try to restrict food intake to reserve their calories for alcohol. Eighty-nine percent of college students get drunk before a random hookup, averaging four or more drinks each time. Three-quarters get drunk before hooking up with an acquaintance. They're most likely to be the most drunk when the encounter includes some form of penetration: oral, vaginal, or anal; they're also most likely to express regret after such experiences.

The girls I talked to often spoke of "going crazy" as an integral part of "the college experience"; they sounded like they were all quoting from the same travel brochure. I'm not sure when that phrase began to refer specifically to drunken partying. Although I recall a certain amount of alcohol and weed when I was at school, if someone had asked me to describe it, I would have said the "college experience" was more about redefining myself away from my family through intense late-night talks with friends, exposure to alternative music and film, finding my passions, falling in love. But according to a blistering exposé by Caitlin Flanagan in *The Atlantic*, as tuitions have skyrocketed, universities apparently need to convince "consumers" (their prospective students) that it's worth the staggering debt they'll take on to attend. What better enticement than to position higher education as not only edifying, but off-the-chain fun? "Every moment of the experience is sweetened," Flanagan wrote, "by the general understanding that with each kegger and rager . . . they are actively engaged in the most significant act of self-improvement available to an American young person: college!" That's a far cry from the original purpose of universities: to train young men for the ministry, a process that involved asceticism, temperance, and chastity.

When I asked why they didn't hook up sober, girls would laugh and say that would be *awkward*—their catchall word (along with *uncomfortable* and, sometimes, *weird*) for any unpleasant emotion. In this case, what seemed to unnerve them was not only having nothing on which to "blame" their behavior, but the idea of being fully emotionally, psychologically, and physically present in a sexual encounter. "Being sober makes it seem like you want to be in a relationship," one freshman told me. "It's really uncomfortable."

That first night Connor tagged along with Holly, they both got tipsy and kissed on the dance floor. The next day, they attended a football game together. Within a week, she had given him oral sex, something she'd never done before. "It was like, 'Whoa! Where did this come from?'" she said. "He didn't even ask. I was slightly alcohol-induced, and I was like, 'Okay, I'm just going to go for it.' And I thought, 'You know, this isn't too bad. Why was I making a big deal about it?'" She paused, considering. "That was the moment, I think, when I became a lot less uptight."

Looking back on it, Holly believed she was "too generous" with Connor—she wanted to make him "happy," but he didn't seem to return the sentiment. "There was one night I asked, 'Do you want to give me oral?'" she said. "He went down on me for about a half second. Then he said, 'I just can't do this. It grosses me out.'"

"I mean, I had a good time," she continued, "but it wouldn't be about *me*. My orgasm was never a given. It was not as important. It was not part of the deal."

Two weeks after their first hookup, Connor asked Holly to be his girlfriend. She was thrilled. He never pressured her to have intercourse, she said; he told her to just tell him when she was ready. A month later, she was. She thought it would be "like the movies: this magical and beautiful moment." She even decorated her room with Christmas lights for the occasion. Instead, it hurt. A lot. "I made him stop. We kissed for a little while and cuddled and were cute with each other. And then I said we could try again. It lasted a little longer, but it still hurt too much."

Intercourse may have been a disappointment for Holly, but it still felt like an accomplishment, a milestone. After Connor left, she strutted into a friend's room blasting the song "I Just Had Sex" on her iPod (a somewhat ironic choice, given that the lyrics—"I just had sex, / And it felt so good, / A woman let me put my penis inside of her"—describe a guy who is comically oblivious to his partner). "I was like, I feel *so cool*!" she said. "I feel like such a grown-up! And I had shared this special moment with a guy who I liked and trusted and who I had feelings for and who had feelings for me. Also, I was sober—that was very important to me. I was not going to have sex the first time drunk. I wanted to be able to *experience* it."

Connor broke up with her two days later.

This was a boy who had compared their relationship to his parents' (who had also begun dating each other the second month of freshman year). He had talked about how much he'd miss her over winter break, which was still over a month away. He had asked her to be his *girlfriend*. Holly was devastated. She left school two days early for the Thanksgiving break, needing to get away.

When her parents picked her up at the train station, her mom looked her up and down. "You lost your virginity," she said.

"I asked her how she knew," Holly told me. "And she said, 'Look at you. You're a mess! I hope that's a good lesson for you about not giving your body away to just anyone.'"

Girls' ideas and attitudes about sex are shaped by family, media, friends, and their own experience. Holly had followed the contemporary rules of female sexual respectability, done everything she believed was "right," and she was betrayed. She responded by giving up on love and commitment. She wanted to be "not *feeling-less*, exactly, but not in a relationship." Besides, she was busy: doing her schoolwork, pledging her sorority, going to parties. She still planned to reserve intercourse for a committed partner, whenever that might happen. "I felt like"—she stopped and corrected herself. "I *still* feel like it means something, that you're intimately connected and really like this person and you're showing affection."

Since she didn't have a boyfriend, Holly invited a male buddy from her dorm to her sorority's winter date party in February. They arrived already loaded—she'd had six shots at pregames. After the party, she went back to his room thinking they would make out, but she was still awfully drunk. So when he said she was beautiful and that he'd like to have sex with her, she thought, "Why not?"

A few minutes later, she felt as if she'd snapped out of a trance. "I thought, 'Holy shit! I'm having sex and I'm not supposed to be doing this unless I'm in a relationship.'" Holly panicked, telling the boy she needed to stop. He urged her to stay, but she jumped out of bed and threw on her dress. Still barefoot, holding her shoes, she flung open the door of his room to find a group of young men standing directly outside, listening in. She ran to a friend's room and cried.

"I was so upset with myself that I'd had sex outside of a relationship," Holly said. "Which I eventually got over. Now I don't care so much about that. I just care that I know the guy. But back then, in my head, I was a skank. I was one of those skanks who just has sex with people. I was a bad person."

Everyone's Slutty Friend

A picture of a kitten hung on one wall of Megan Massoud's room. Above her pillow was a poster from *Pulp Fiction*, the one in which Uma Thurman lies stomach-down on a bed, her stiletto-shod feet crossed at the ankles, a cigarette dangling from the fingers of one hand, a pistol flung casually near the other. Megan's desk was littered with half-drunk bottles of Coke Zero, open boxes of cookies, and several shot glasses. I picked my way through piles of clothes heaped on the floor, cleared a chair of some laundry, and sat down, resting my feet on a polka-dotted hassock.

Megan, a sophomore at a midwestern public university majoring in economics, was tiny (barely five feet tall), with enormous dark eyes, a quick smile, and flat-ironed dark hair that she would absentmindedly braid and unbraid as we spoke. Her mom, she said, was a "generic white woman." Her dad, who was Lebanese, gave her a pink lipstick-shaped canister of pepper spray just before her freshman year; Megan kept it out as a joke. "He thinks I'm a virgin," she said, laughing.

Megan pulled on a cropped orange tank top and a thigh-grazing skirt that hugged her butt and fit tight across the stomach. She examined herself in the mirror from the front, from the side, from the back. "Does my stomach look big in this?" she asked a friend, who was standing in the doorway. "Don't fuck with me."

"I'm not fucking with you," the friend said. "You look hot. Like the skinniest fucking bitch." Megan looked at herself again, dissatisfied. "I never think about what I eat until I get dressed for a party. Then I think I shouldn't have had that extra doughnut," she said.

As she continued to dress, Megan told me about the Gender Studies class she was taking this semester. "I had never noticed that guy models in ads are always doing something—playing a guitar or driving—and girl models are just . . ." She struck a classic pose: head tilted, chin down, hand on hip, a coy smile.

I laughed. "You do that really well," I said.

"I haven't taken a picture without the head tilt since I was six," she replied. "I don't know where I learned it."

She looked again at her stomach, again at her butt. She changed her shirt. She pulled off her skirt, tried on a different one, decided the first made her stomach look better, changed back. "In my gender class I'm all, 'That damned patriarchy,'" she said. "But at night it all goes to shit. The only thing I care about is: 'Does this skirt make my ass look good?'" She grabbed her cosmetics pouch and headed to the bathroom. Although she hates makeup, she said, it's part of attracting guys' attention, so she swiped on dark lipstick and some smoky, sparkly eye shadow. She smoothed her hair with two hands (a brush in one, a comb in the other), put on a pair of four-inch heels, and doused herself with perfume. "It makes me feel less self-conscious to wear the outfit and the heels," she said. "I feel kind of like I'm swaggering, like, 'Yes, I am the baddest bitch in this room.'" The evening was cold, but Megan didn't take a jacket. Nor did she carry a purse. She held her keys and school ID in one hand (later she would lose both) and tucked her phone and iPod into the waistband of her skirt, which was tight enough to hold them fast. She looked in the mirror one last time, turning to check her butt, and tugged down the hem of her skirt, a gesture she'd repeat every few minutes throughout the evening. She grabbed a bottle of vodka to share at pregames, and headed out the door. It was nearly ten o'clock. Her goal? "To get really drunk and make out with someone," she said cheerfully. "Because what's the point of a night if you aren't getting attention from guys?"

The stigma of "slut" didn't disappear with the rise of hookup culture. Its criteria just became ever more elusive. Girls routinely told me they hated the word, that they never used it, didn't "slut-shame" their classmates (though in truth, they often did). At the same time, they policed themselves. Some, like Holly, would continually revise, rather than discard, the definition of "skank" as their own behavior changed. Others, such as Megan, took "slut" on as a badge of honor, or at least tried to. "I'm the slutty friend," she told me gleefully when we'd first met. "I find it liberating. I love being the crazy one. If someone is going to judge me for what I do, then fine, judge me. I don't care. Fuck you if you think you're better than me just because you don't have sex that much. I feel bad for you if you don't have sex that much because sex is awesome. I'm not saying that every time I go out, I hook up with someone. That's definitely not the case. But it's more fun to not control myself. Not to worry how it will look. And in college, nobody gives a shit."

Like Holly, Megan described her behavior as "liberating," even as she struggled with its limits. During another conversation, she insisted, "I'm not a slut. Some people probably would consider me one, but I don't consider myself one because I don't carry myself like that. . . . When I think of a slut, I picture that girl who has the really thick black mascara and smoky eyes and wears two bras to push up her boobs." On another occasion, she told me, "I love being single," and a few minutes later confided, "No boys want to date the slut." Back and forth she went, between resisting and submitting to age-old ideas about girls' sexuality. Talking to Megan sometimes felt like watching someone trying to shore up a sand castle whose walls kept collapsing. Megan had less transcended limits than tried to legitimize herself within them, despite them. "I think," she told me at one point, "that every girl's goal is to be just slutty enough, where you're not a prude but you're not a whore. Yeah, you have your one-night stands. Yeah, you're experienced. But you're not sleeping with every guy in the fraternity. You're not making brothers 'Eskimo brothers'"—when two or more fraternity members have intercourse with the same girl. "Finding that balance is every college girl's dream, you know what I mean?"

Like Holly, Megan had her own agenda for our conversations: she, too, wanted an opportunity to make sense of a sexual history that had progressed quite differently from how she'd once expected. Also like Holly, she described herself as a "good girl" in high school—not even kissing a boy until she was seventeen, by which time she was eager to move forward. "I really wanted to get rid of my 'firsts' with a boyfriend," she said. "And all my friends had already kissed guys, already given blow jobs. I was behind." During four months of dating her first boyfriend, she "caught up," performing oral sex that was never reciprocated. "I didn't even think that was an option," she said. She lost her virginity the summer before college with another guy she was dating, though, she said, they were never "Facebook official." She was relieved to get first intercourse over with, and remembers the experience fondly.

Megan had masturbated since she was a young teen. She had no difficulty reaching orgasm on her own, but had never climaxed with a partner. "A lot of guys don't do enough foreplay," she explained. "They just get to sex really quickly. And then, after a while I get tired, and I know they're doing their best, so I just fake an orgasm to end it, and then I'm like 'Oh, that was *so* good.'" Most of the girls I talked to had faked an orgasm now and again; that seemed unfortunate, though not unusual. But according to *The Sex Lives of College Students*, the number who fake has been rising steadily, from less than half in 1990 to 70 percent today. That may at least in part explain the gulf between the proportion of boys who think their partner has come during an encounter and the percentage of girls who actually did. Girls feigned climax because they were bored, they were tired, they were in pain, they wanted the night to end. They were often, like Megan, protecting their partners' egos, or felt pressured to be perceived as enjoying sex even if they weren't—especially since pleasure was presumably the whole *point* of a hookup. They also faked because they didn't, or couldn't, ask for what they wanted in bed. A few were starting to question whether the practice was counterproductive. "I haven't really cared enough about the people I've been with to invest the time in training them in how my body works and what I like and don't like," a sophomore at an Ivy League college told me. "But now I'm going to put in the effort. Because I feel like I owe it to other girls to do them the favor of bringing these things to guys' consciousness. And why am I using my time like this if I'm not even going to enjoy it?"

Megan, like Holly, had her first college hookup within days of arriving on campus. The sex, she said, was "pretty terrible. He was the thrusting type, you know, jack-hammering me until I faked an orgasm, and then he went to sleep." Even so, she said, she continued hooking up with him semiregularly over the next two months. I asked her why she went back when the sex was so bad. She shrugged. "Sex is always good on one level," she said. "And whenever I get drunk, I hate going home alone. It's like, I need a boy or a burrito, you know?"

When we'd first met, midway through her sophomore year, Megan pulled out her period tracker app, where she had logged hookups that included intercourse. She'd had twelve partners, she said—though, if anyone asked, she reduced it to a more socially acceptable five. She preferred to remain "blissfully ignorant" of how many hookups had included only oral sex. "Giving a guy a blow job is something I don't really consider a big deal," she said. "Like, this one guy, when I go to his frat he'll say, 'Hey, Megan, do you want to come see my room?' And I'll give him a blow job and we'll make out. I told him, 'I like this casual thing we have going.' He's like, 'I know, me too.' I don't even have his phone number."

It was clear to me what he was getting out of that arrangement, I told Megan, but what was she getting? She shrugged. "I guess I could ask that every time I have sex. 'What am I getting out of it?' Guys tell me I'm really good at blow jobs, probably because I have a lot of practice. I really like kissing him. It's exciting, it's an adrenaline rush. And it's like, at least I'll have company. At least he'll appreciate me, even if it's for that fifteen minutes. I'll have someone to hang out with, and make out with, and make me feel special."

When the Fun Stops

Holly needed a guy. That's what one of her sorority sisters thought. So she asked her boyfriend to introduce Holly to his frat brother Robert. The four of them would go out to lunch, they'd go on double dates. Holly thought Robert was sweet, but she wasn't especially interested in him, either romantically or sexually. Still, simply by virtue of being thrown together so much, they got to know each other, and one night, at a party at his frat, they began making out on the dance floor. A little while later, she "found herself" in his room, doing "everything but intercourse." She had a wonderful time. "Oral sex both ways," she said, "which was a big deal for me." Robert walked her back to her dorm afterward. Even though she was hammered, she said he was a "gentleman and didn't take advantage of that and have sex with me."

The school year was winding down by then. She and Robert texted each other through finals, went for a couple of walks, made out. She had no interest in anything more; she was just enjoying his company. One night, after midnight, they snuck into an academic building and hooked up in a classroom. She'd had two beers, but said she wasn't particularly drunk. Neither was he. Again, they did "everything but intercourse," though this time it was mainly because he didn't have a condom. "Weirdly enough, I really wanted to have sex with him," Holly said—perhaps because he was the first guy who seemed authentically invested in her physical pleasure. "It was good that we didn't, though," she continued, "because I would have hated myself. I would've thought, 'Look, you've only started to get to know this guy. You need to know him better.'"

Over the summer, Holly tried to talk to her mom about birth control. She wanted to go on the Pill. "I told her it was safer in the social environment that I was in to have it, in case something happened. But she said, 'Well, you shouldn't want to be having sex. You're not in a relationship. You're nineteen years old.' And in my head I was thinking the opposite: 'I'm nineteen years old, I'm not in a relationship, and I *want* to be having sex!' She has no idea. If I told her what I've told you, she wouldn't let me come back to college. She'd say I was 'one of *those* girls.'"

Something else happened that summer, too. Holly had never before masturbated—it wasn't something she thought girls did. A few of her sorority sisters, as a joke, had given her a vibrator for her last birthday. One day, home alone and bored, she decided to give it a try, and she had her first orgasm. She spent the rest of the summer exploring her body. "It was cool!" she said. "I was able to learn all about myself without having to feel the awkwardness of trying to direct someone else." Girls often told me their first orgasm was transformative, whether they experienced it alone or with a partner. Why wouldn't it be, given their dearth of education on the subject? "The first time I had an orgasm I cried," one high school senior told me. "I *cried*! It was so powerful. I think it really helped me grow as a person."

Holly started her sophomore year with a new sexual standard. Still uninterested in a "serious" relationship but eager to experiment, she decided she would have intercourse only with someone she knew in a situation in which she felt safe. "Like, not in some weird room somewhere where you can't get help if you needed it," she said. Also, condoms were nonnegotiable. Then, one night, she did three shots at pregames and another three at a party. Then she had a "Jäger bomb," a shot of Jägermeister dropped into a beer. She followed that up with a Red Bull. Mixing energy drinks with alcohol leaves a person feeling deceptively sober—or "wide-awake drunk": college-age bar patrons who mix caffeine and alcohol, for example, leave drunker than their peers yet are four times more likely to believe they can drive. Maybe that's why Holly's sorority sisters, who are supposed to "look out" for one another, thought she seemed fine. Or maybe they were in no state themselves to notice. Either way, that drink was the last thing Holly remembered that night.

MEGAN WAS PLAYING beer pong at a low-key party just after winter break when a sophomore named Tyler began flirting with her. When her friends got ready to leave, around two in the morning, he asked Megan to stay.

"I'm not going to have sex with you," she told him.

"That's cool," he replied. "We'll just kiss and cuddle."

Megan's friend caught her eye one last time, silently double-checking her decision. Megan nodded. She wasn't too drunk, and she was having fun with Tyler.

They held hands and chatted as they walked back to his frat, getting to know each other. He seemed sweet. As soon as they got inside, though, his manner changed. He rushed her upstairs to his room and into his bed. They made out, and she started going down on him, but he kept pushing for intercourse. Megan said no. He pushed harder. Megan claimed not to have birth control, thinking that was a good, inoffensive excuse, one that wouldn't hurt his feelings. Instead, he grabbed a condom, held her down, and entered her. "I just kind of laid there," she said. "I thought maybe if I'm really shitty at sex, he'll just stop. At one point he asked if I wanted to take a shower together, and I was like, 'Well, we already had sex. What's the point in saying no now?' I just kept trying to make it better, to psych myself into thinking it wasn't what it was."

In the shower, Tyler kissed her roughly, then pushed her up against the tiles and began having sex with her from behind. She turned up the hot water tap all the way, hoping that would make him stop. It didn't. He switched to anal sex. "I told him he was hurting me, and he was like 'Oh, I'm sorry,' but then he'd keep going. His frat brothers actually came into the shower and saw us and laughed." She asked Tyler to stop twice more; finally he did. Not knowing what else to do, she spent the night. The next morning, when he dropped her off at her dorm, she told him, "Thanks, I had fun." She still doesn't know why she said that. A friend stopped by her room to find out how her night had gone.

"I think I was raped," Megan said.

THE CAMPUS PARTY scene can be exhilarating—if it weren't, no one would participate. But as Armstrong and her colleagues have pointed out, it also facilitates rape. Women, not men, wear body-baring outfits. Women, not men, relinquish turf and transportation. Women, as females and often as younger students, are expected to be "nice" and deferential to their male hosts. A "fun girl" wouldn't make a scene just because a guy grabbed her ass or held her down and grinded against her; she'd just find a way artfully and politely to disengage. "Fun girls" also drink freely—alcohol gives them license to be sexual, loosening inhibitions while anesthetizing against intimacy, embarrassment, or accountability. It can also undermine their ability to resist, remember, or feel entitled to report sexual assault. The manipulation of the party culture is both systematic and invisible, Armstrong writes, seemingly part of the continuum (if at the extreme edge) of acceptable "crazy" collegiate behavior. Since victims have a hard time convincing anyone, including themselves, that a crime has actually occurred, it is also generally consequence-free.

Holly woke the next morning with no idea where she was. There was a guy next to her in the bed, a senior she knew only by name and didn't remember seeing at the party. There was also a used condom on the floor.

"Do you remember what happened last night?" he asked.

She shook her head.

"We had sex," he said.

The boy lived several blocks off-campus, and claimed his car had broken down. So Holly, still dressed in the party clothes and high heels that had made her feel "proud of her body" the night before, made her way back to her sorority house alone. The so-called walk of shame is another aspect of hookup culture that calls out only young women's behavior, since boys often wear the same clothing at parties that they'd wear during the day. Sometimes girls borrow something from a sexual partner (though they may never have occasion to return it), but as Megan told me, "Everyone knows when you're in 'shacker clothes' and they'll heckle you when you cross campus, like, 'Ohhh! How was your night last night?'" Again, such harassment is typically leveled only at girls.

Holly spent the rest of the day in sweat pants, crying and watching TV while her roommate hugged her. That was just two weeks before we met. "I'm not going to let it ruin my life," she told me, her voice stalwart. "It's not something that defines me. It was just something that happened, and I can't get that drunk again."

While getting blackout drunk is never a good idea, and it seemed only natural for Holly to want to regain some sense of control, it troubled me that she placed all the blame on herself, on her drinking, rather than on the boy who took advantage of it. "I'd like to say he didn't know how drunk I was," she said. "But I don't know. My friend who is in an organization that fights rape on campus said that by definition I couldn't consent, so I was raped. And I almost . . ." she paused. "Not that I wish rape upon myself, but I hope I wasn't sitting there saying, 'Yeah, I want to have sex!' Because that would go against everything that I've said about not having sex with a random person." She shook her head and sighed. "I guess I'm fortunate that I don't remember."

I had no way of knowing, when I met them, that Megan was a rape victim or that Holly may have been. I didn't ask about nonconsensual sex in my recruitment e-mails, and it wasn't, they each said, what had motivated them to talk to me. A report by the Justice Department released at the end of 2014 found that, despite the growing national awareness of campus sexual assault, only an estimated 20 percent of college victims report the crime, a markedly lower rate than nonstudents the same age. They're inhibited by fear of reprisal, shame, self-blame, or the belief that reporting would only make things worse, especially given the historically low rate of campus assailants who are punished. Also by the deliberate muddying of consent that happens at parties. Mariah, a junior at a private university in the South, urged me not to demonize the Greek system. "I'm an intelligent woman," she said in an e-mail. "If all a sorority did for me was make me vulnerable to sexual assault and alcohol poisoning, I'd have bailed by now." She had made the dearest friends of her life among her sorority sisters, girls she described as "involved," "inspiring," and "brilliant." Yes, she said, the Greek system was "heteronormative" and riddled with racial and gender inequalities that needed to be addressed. "But I firmly believe," she wrote, "that sororities are, and can be, a wonderful experience, a vehicle for change, and a bastion of feminism on modern college campuses."

At the same time, though, she felt that she and her sisters were being "crushed" by a campus hookup culture in which drunken frat boys felt free to touch, kiss, or rub up against them without permission. ("You're supposed to swat them away like flies," she said.) Girls could quickly slip from feeling emboldened by sexiness to feeling objectified: like things to be used and consumed. Boys, too, could feel confused, uncertain: eager to fit in, yet struggling with assumptions about masculinity, sex, coercion, conquest. They could misinterpret mixed messages, or be too drunk themselves to realize a partner's state—both may wake up the morning after unsure of who they're with or what went on. "No one here knows what rape is," Mariah wrote, neither the boys nor the girls. "Would I know if I was raped? Maybe if it was a stranger in a dark alley, yeah, but otherwise, I'm not so sure."

I was surprised, then, to hear that Megan, at the urging of a campus therapist, had pressed charges against Tyler through her school's office of student ethics. The investigation took the entire second semester. Megan told her story repeatedly. Her friends gave statements about how much she'd changed since that night, growing depressed, unable to concentrate, how she dropped a class and was drinking more than usual. Tyler gave his version of events as well. When asked when, precisely, he believed Megan had given consent for intercourse, she recalled him saying, 'Well, she gave me a blow job. I pretty much call that consent.' " That had infuriated her. "I was giving him the blow job to end it, not to start something. I told him I did not want to have sex. I told him I did not have birth control. And he just hopped out of bed, put on a condom, and raped me."

What she suspects ultimately made her case was not so much what either she or Tyler had said, but that Tyler's own frat brothers turned on him, admitting that he could be aggressive, even violent; he had already been on probation for fighting. In the end, Tyler was suspended for a year and his credits for the semester nullified. Megan is pretty sure he won't be back, though she can't say whether he's learned anything from the experience. "After the hearing he said he was sorry I felt the way I did, but he never apologized," she said. "He never believed he'd done anything wrong." In fact, she confessed, *she* had to control herself from apologizing to *him*. "I hated him," she said, "but it was weird. I also wanted to give him a hug and tell him I was sorry for doing all this, for ruining his life."

DESPICABLE ME PLAYED on TV at an off-campus house as Megan and her friends poured pregame shots into candy-colored glasses. There were six girls and two boys, who were in town visiting from another school. They traded war stories about hangovers they'd had, the hazards of Everclear, and the crazy drinks they had tried: Jungle Juice, apple pie moonshine, vodka infused with cannabis or Skittles candy. Over the next hour, Megan and the other girls in the group would knock back four or five shots each. The boys would drink six. "We have a system," one of the boys told me. "Drink three shots, wait three minutes, drink two more shots, wait five minutes, one more shot and you're done." I asked what the wait was for. "So we can have time to see if we're too affected by it," he said, apparently in all seriousness.

In between drinks, the group chatted, texted friends, and posted selfies to Instagram, always looking carefully around to make sure no liquor was visible in the frame (all of them were underage). "It doesn't happen unless it happens on Instagram!" Megan told me, only half-joking. Each of them had a few stock expressions they could call up on command: a sexy chin drop, a "this is my friend and I love her" smile, an open-mouthed "aren't I crazy and having fun" face. The boys clowned around, striking the classic "sorority squat" pose. One of them checked his feed. "I only have one 'like,'" he complained. "By now I should have forty-seven!" They spent at least half their time together engrossed in their individual screens.

I doubt they realized how often they referenced gender, whether it was when a boy called a female high school classmate "all Christian during the day and slutty at night," or during a good-natured argument over which sex ultimately pays more for a frat party: the brothers, who buy all the liquor, or the girls, who have the "upkeep" of hair, nails, clothes, shoes, and makeup.

The girls reminded the boys that their cost wasn't only monetary. "Like, we have to remove our hair *everywhere*," one said.

"No razors below the neck for me," answered a boy, laughing.

"And okay," said another girl, "we have to walk in five-inch heels."

At that, the boys conceded. The girls had won, if you call that winning.

They talked, too, about the collateral damage of the party scene: a girl they knew who was bulimic; another who was in rehab; the frats that had been kicked off campus; the drunk boy who tried, with tragic results, to do a backflip off a bar.

The song "Blurred Lines" came up on the playlist, with its hooky, contentious chorus, "I know you want it, I know you want it." Megan bobbed her head in time to the beat, seemingly indifferent to the lyrics.

Surprisingly, Megan said, after the rape, her sex drive became even stronger. Like Holly, she didn't want a negative experience to define her or her college years. "I had lots of casual sex for a while. And it was good. I liked feeling giddy in the morning again instead of horrible, like when I left Tyler." But now, in the second semester of her sophomore year, she was growing weary of one-night stands. "I do get hurt feelings a lot," she said. "I set myself up for it. I know it's going to end without him texting. It does every time. Guys don't respect you after they have sex with you. That's just how it is. And that sucks. You do want that text, though. I mean just someone saying that was fun and we should hang out. If someone doesn't text me for three days afterward, I'm like, fuck you, but then if they text you suddenly on Saturday night and say, 'Hey, wanna come over?' you feel kind of obligated because you do want to see them and that's the only way."

Even though most girls and boys claim they're generally

happy with their last hookup, majorities of both also express having had, at some point, regret over casual sex. When they do, boys tend to feel remorse about "using" someone; girls feel bad about being "used." I commented to a sophomore at a private New England college that a text seemed a pretty low standard for common decency after a night in bed with someone. "And even *that* seems like such a concession to guys," she agreed. "Meanwhile, the girl has to sit and wait. And that is torturous. If you texted first, it would freak him out. On our campus, we only have one dining hall, so there's this whole thing of seeing him and he hasn't texted and, you know, 'Look me in the eye. I don't want to marry you.' Or maybe the boy next to you in Bio has seen your boobs and now wants nothing to do with you. So it's better not to hook up with people from your classes. You don't go for someone who lives on your floor. You keep your social self and your academic self detached."

Victims or Victors?

A week after her blackout, Holly hooked up again with Robert, the boy she'd started seeing at the end of the previous semester, and the two finally had sex. It was amazing. "I woke up the next morning happy that I had sex with someone I wasn't in a relationship with, who I know and like as a person, who is a sweet guy," she said. "We were able to enjoy ourselves, experiment— and we both had orgasms. We've agreed we want to keep this casual. If there's anything going on with us, it's 'friends with benefits.' We are definitely friends. Maybe if it continues, perhaps I'll want it to be something more. But that's an 'if,' because this is all new." Looking back, Holly couldn't believe how far she'd come.

Only a year ago, she was a virgin. Only a year ago, she would have said she'd need to be in a committed relationship for at least six months before she'd have intercourse. "That's clearly changed," she said. "I've pushed the line, pushed the line, pushed the line. But it's interesting where it's taken me. I don't know if it's the culture around me that tells me my behavior is okay, so therefore I'm fine with it, or if it's because I'm older and more mature and have grown as a person." She shook her head, incredulous. "It's been such a strange journey."

The girls I met often talked about "friends with benefits" as the Holy Grail of romantic arrangements: regular sex with a caring-enough partner who makes no emotional demands of you. The truth was, though, that it could be a tricky balance to strike. "'Friends with benefits' is something college students say they want," said Lisa Wade, the sociologist, "and maybe for good reason—it might be a very functional way to go. But that's theoretical. I don't see it happening." Among the students she followed, neither the "benefits" nor the friendships could be maintained. "The problem is, friendliness is off the script in hookup culture. The minute someone says, 'I like you,' it's interpreted as wanting a relationship. If you can't tell someone you like them as a person, then you can't really be friends, can you? So the only way to maintain an ongoing sexual relationship is to treat the other person badly, to be a jerk, so they know it's not a romantic thing." The less enthusiastic partner in those FWB encounters was not necessarily the boy. "I had two FWB situations in the past year," said one college freshman I met. "Each time, I told the guy I don't want a boyfriend right now. One kind of sputtered out without being discussed, but in one case he got more attached. He said, 'I kind of want something more,' and I was like"—she shrugged—"'I kinda don't.' I liked him. It was fun to spend time together, and I was attracted to him, but in the end, I didn't like him *enough*. That's what it comes down to. And now we're not friends anymore, really, which sucks."

Holly and Robert continued their . . . whatever it was, through the fall and winter of her sophomore year. But in March, when I checked in with her one last time via Skype, he had just broken it off. Holly, it turned out, had "caught feelings" for him and initiated "the Talk," to DTR (define the relationship). He wasn't interested. They hooked up one last time, on St. Patrick's Day, when she was "incredibly intoxicated." She described lying on top of him, naked from the waist down, and leaning in for a kiss; he turned his face away and said no. That had hurt. "I'll say it," she told me. "I definitely loved him, and the times he and I spent together were some of the happiest I have spent this year. To be honest, right now I feel like complete shit. But I want to make it clear: I don't regret any of this nonrelationship. Even though we were never officially boyfriend and girlfriend, we had feelings for one another, cared for one another, and enjoyed ourselves together. So, though in many respects this is the classic example of the way the hookup culture has 'damaged' relationships, I want you to know: I am not a victim of that culture, but a participant in it."

BY ELEVEN O'CLOCK, the streets around Megan's campus were crowded with girls in tiny skirts, boys hoisting beers. It was the first weekend of spring, and everyone was partying. As we cut through a quiet quad, a couple of boys called out, "Come here!" to Megan. When she didn't respond, they yelled, "Where are *you* going!" Then, still met with rejection, they sneered, "*Sluts!*"

"I hate that," Megan said, rolling her eyes.

Like Holly, Megan tended to blame herself rather than a

persistent double standard when she was treated disrespectfully. "Boys don't take me seriously," she'd told me. "I kind of ruined that. I sabotaged myself. I try to meet new people and go to parties where I can be seen differently. If they find out about me, they feel like they have more leeway to grab my ass or try to make out with me on the dance floor. No one wants to take the slutty girl on a date. It bothers me, but not enough for me to change my behavior."

Leslie Bell, the psychologist and the author of *Hard to Get*, has said that women are neither "primarily victims nor victors in hookup culture, but they are often misinformed." They need, she believes, to clearly understand what they can and will not get out of casual encounters—hookups are unlikely, for instance, to help them develop the skills necessary to have either good sex or good relationships. That's wise advice, but it doesn't change the terms of the debate. Some girls bragged to me that they could "have sex like a guy," by which they meant they could engage without emotion, they could objectify their partners as fully and reductively as boys often objectified them. That seemed a sad, low road to equality. What if, instead, they expected boys to be as sexually giving as girls? What if they were taught that all sexual partners, whether total strangers or intimates, deserved esteem and generosity, just as people do in any human interaction? What if they refused to settle for anything less?

It was time for me to return to the land of the grownups—Megan was heading to a frat party, and we both knew that I'd never get past the bouncer at the front door. Megan fussed over me, worrying about whether I could find my way across campus alone, where I'd get a cab, whether I'd be all right. We said good-bye and hugged, and I began to walk away.

"Be safe!" Megan called after me.

And I thought to myself, "You too."

CHAPTER 5

Out: Online and IRL

The snow had been falling thick and wet all morning outside my hotel room window. Two inches. Four inches. Six. By two o'clock, everything in the midwestern college town I was visiting had shut down. Classes had been called off. No cars or buses braved the slick roads. Students from the ski and snowboard club had jury-rigged a speaker system at the top of a hill that was barely steep enough for a child to sled down, and they were giddily, somewhat tipsily, freestyling to their beats. By three o'clock dusk was settling, and all my appointments for the day had been cancelled.

Except for one. Far down the street, I spotted a figure trudging in Timberland boots and a down jacket, hands jammed into pockets, shoulders hunched against the wind. I headed to the lobby, arriving just in time to catch a blast of cold air as the revolving door spun. There was the stomping of snow-covered boots, the unwrapping of a scarf from pink cheeks, the doffing of gloves. A hand extended to give mine a firm-gripped shake. "You must be Peggy." A smile, a look squarely into my eyes. "I'm Amber McNeill."

The New Street Corner

I shouldn't have been surprised that Amber braved a blizzard to meet me. The gay girls who responded to my e-mail queries were the most insistent about being heard. "I am a young, queer woman of color," one girl wrote to me. "We *have* to talk—I am your unicorn!" I received more responses than I expected from queer girls across spectrums of both ethnicity and orientation. One eighteen-year-old Korean American identified as asexual: not physically attracted to either men or women. I have to admit, that one threw me—interviewing her, I felt like I was talking to a lifelong vegan for a book on the joys of eating meat. But she wanted it on the record that hers was a legitimate sexual orientation, not arising from abuse or rejection. "I don't recall ever feeling any other way," she said. "I was just never interested in sex. I find it kind of . . . gross." What's more, she added, there is a thriving asexual community on the Internet: support groups, educational material, meetup sites.

At the beginning of every interview I conducted, I asked which pronoun—or combination of pronouns—to use when referring to a girl's sexual partners. Many identified unambiguously as straight or gay, others as bisexual or bi-curious. Several times an interview itself became a place to explore incipient feelings. Lizzy, for instance, a soft-spoken eighteen-year-old in the first month of her freshman year at a mid-Atlantic college, fidgeted and blushed through much of our discussion, staring at the floor or past my shoulder as she spoke. A miasma of low-grade depression seemed to hover around her, and she was so unresponsive that I began to wonder why she had volunteered to talk to me at all. She told me she had been the type of girl who was excluded and bullied in high school, called "bitch" and "fat" by the "athletic-pretty-smart 'whole package' girls that boys generally like." Still, she did have a boyfriend during her junior year, a fellow clarinetist in the school orchestra named Will. "I never really felt sexual desire for him, though," she said. "It was more like he was my best friend. We would hang out, watch TV, go to the movies. Sometimes we'd kiss a little bit, but not full-on making out."

I asked her what those sessions felt like. She shrugged. "Nice, I guess. It wasn't really my thing. To be honest, I don't really understand what's so great about it." After about four months, Will began to push her to go further—much further—via increasingly insistent texts: "We should totally have sex!" he wrote, and "Come on! It will be fun! It will be great!" and "Why not? I don't understand!" "I told him he was making me uncomfortable," Lizzy said. "We'd never even done anything below the neck! But he would just keep bringing it up, texting me over and over."

Although Lizzy didn't think she should have to justify a disinterest in intercourse with a boy she'd barely kissed, one who demonstrably had no respect for her limits and whose conversational skills did not extend past the keyboard, she nonetheless tried. Maybe, she said, her reluctance stemmed from shame over her body. "You see a lot of models and superstars, and they're so skinny and gorgeous," she said, looking down at her soft belly. "Even shopping for clothes—clothes are cut for people who are skinny, and I'm just not skinny." Then she shook her head. "But really, I wasn't attracted to him enough to even want to try. It was just, 'Oh, no! He wants to have sex and I don't.'" After two months of fending him off, she suggested they "take a break." Will, her supposed "best friend," never spoke to her again.

Other boys, and even adult men, had shown interest in her since, but she never reciprocated; the prospect of physical intimacy repelled her. I asked her to recall a time when she felt sexual pleasure in her body. She blushed. "I can't think of one," she said. What about arousal? The color in her cheeks deepened. "I haven't explored any of that. I just want to get through my classes and do my work. And it's hard to open up to people. It takes a lot of effort."

I could see that for her it did—our conversation proceeded in fits and starts; she was perhaps the least voluble of the girls I met. Then I asked, "We've really only discussed boys. Have you ever felt attraction to other girls?" Again, Lizzy's face grew pink, but this time it seemed to be with pleasure. "I have this really good friend," she admitted, and then, for the first time in our conversation, she laughed. "I kind of like her both ways, you know? It's like I'm balanced on the edge. There's just something . . . amazing about her." She laughed again, her smile lighting up her face. "I can't even put my finger on it. I've never met a person where I've felt . . . it's just *there*."

Lizzy had never personally known anyone who was gay, but she'd read about homosexuality on the Internet, specifically in fan fiction: original stories penned and passed around online by devotees of popular books, TV shows, plays, movies, or pop songs. The erotic novel *Fifty Shades of Grey* famously started out as fan fiction based on *Twilight*. Harry Potter has eighty thousand fanfic stories on one site alone. A fan fiction story based on *The Hunger Games* had, at this writing, over two million views. Fan fiction may "cross over" between worlds or genres, so Harry Styles, for instance, might lose his Direction and find himself in Middle Earth. It also often includes erotic, typically same-sex, canoodling (presumably) never dreamed of by the characters' creators: Mr. Spock gets with Captain Kirk; Holmes with Watson; Batman with the Joker; Hermione with Ginny. Women and girls are the largest creators and consumers of fan fiction. It's hard to say why, then, the overwhelming percentage of its sexual encounters are between men. Maybe it's because women are still underrepresented in mainstream media, and so are less compelling as characters. Or maybe writing about male bodies liberates women from the judgments about appearance, behavior, or assertiveness that typically freight their sexual exploration. Whatever the reason, fan fiction provides a form of freedom to young women: it's generally without commercial motive or viability, a corner of the media from which, with few exceptions, no one is profiting.

Like anything in the boundless olio of the Internet, that breadth can have drawbacks as well as advantages: one eighteen-year-old girl from Staten Island recalled stumbling on graphic fan fiction in middle school. "Little girls and big girls and occasionally guys write a *lot* of porn based on characters they like," she said. "I would read it all. I didn't know about BDSM until I read fan fiction; it's in a lot of the sex scenes. And for a long time, I thought the average size of a limp penis was eight inches—and that *then* they grow larger. And I thought, 'I never want one of those near me!'"

Lizzy, an avid fan of the TV show *Dr. Who*, was first exposed to lesbianism by chance, on a Tumblr blog that coupled two characters who, in the show itself, are straight. "At first it was weird," Lizzy said, "but the actual story was really good. It worked. So I kept reading. And it broadened my view of the world. I mean, I hadn't really thought about this stuff before. It was . . . not embarrassing. Just strange. Foreign. Exciting."

Adults, me included, often fret over the hazards of the Internet for kids, especially where sex is concerned. Our fears are understandable: the easy access to extreme porn, the distorted female bodies, the sexting scandals: it is enough to make anyone born before 1980 feel that Armageddon is nigh. But as with so much of contemporary culture, it is hardly that simple. As long as adults still avoid open discussion of sexuality, teens will inevitably seek information on today's electronic street corner. That presents both problem and opportunity. Yes, there are discussion board sites such as Reddit, which can quickly devolve into creepshots of women's cleavage or teen girls' butts in short shorts, bikinis, and the like. (The company's policy against posting nonconsensual porn, announced in early 2015, has so far done nothing to abate such "communities.") But there are also Scarleteen, Go Ask Alice!, and Sex, Etc., where the advice offered may be explicit but is scrupulously medically accurate.

As with their straight peers, the Internet can be double-edged for LGBTQ teens. According to the Gay, Lesbian, and Straight Education Network's 2013 report *Out Online*, they experience cyberbullying at three times the rate of heterosexuals—girls more often than boys. Yet LGBTQ kids also turn to the Web for information and support—crucial for a population whose attempted suicide rate is still five times that of other teens. Over half of LGBTQ young people who were not out in person used the Internet to connect virtually with others like them, according to the report. More than one in ten disclosed their sexual identity to someone online before telling anyone in the "real" world, and over a quarter were more out on the Internet than they were in their offline lives.

Ideally, queer teens wouldn't need to resort to trolling gay chat rooms for information or acceptance. At the same time, the Internet has provided an unprecedented pathway to normalizing and embracing sexual identity. Lizzy offered a glimmer of how that might begin, as did the young woman who'd found online support for her asexuality. But it was nineteen-year-old Amber, at a college hundreds of miles from Lizzy's, who best illustrated the potential (and a little of the weirdness) of our hyperconnected world.

After introducing ourselves in the chilly hotel lobby, we headed up to my room; Amber settled into a wingback chair under a circle of lamplight and began to tell me how, even while keeping up the appearance of the straight, popular girl her parents expected her to be, she was secretly working through something else online, something she didn't always understand, building a second identity that, in the end, proved the most real of all.

Playing the Straight Girl

The first time Amber misrepresented herself online, she was just nine years old, doing exactly the sort of thing parents fear: chatting with strangers on a gaming site. "People would try to start these sexual conversations with me," she said. "I don't even know if I really knew what sex was. I was just a naïve kid." Eventually her parents wondered why she was spending so much time on the computer and checked her history. When they discovered what she'd been doing they instantly forbade her, indefinitely, from going online. Amber didn't mind the punishment so much as her parents' horrified reaction. "I felt like I'd been doing something really, really bad," she recalled. "I was a wreck. I didn't touch a keyboard again for a year."

When she did, though, she got into *Second Life* and *The Sims*, virtual worlds in which users, represented by onscreen avatars, can once again interact with one another. Whether on the Internet or a PlayStation, Amber always chose to be male. "I didn't think anything of it," she explained. "It was just what I liked. I would make my boy avatar, then go on these websites and talk to girls, tell them they were pretty or whatever a fifth-grader would say. I never really questioned it. I honestly didn't even know what the word *gay* meant. Nobody talked about it: not my parents, not my school. Which is weird because it's not like I grew up in the middle of nowhere: we lived near a big university. I went to a high school of three thousand students. But no one said anything. So I never questioned my sexuality."

This was, of course, years before the Supreme Court ruling that made same-sex marriage legal in all fifty states. Still, it wasn't exactly the Dark Ages: celebrities such as Melissa Etheridge and Ellen DeGeneres publicly embraced their sexuality in the 1990s. Openly gay characters were increasingly common (and nuanced) on TV and in movies, too. Perhaps as a result, the average age of coming out in the United States began to plummet: from twenty-five in 1991 to between fourteen and sixteen today. "Children report awareness of sexual attraction at about age ten," Caitlin Ryan, director of the Family Acceptance Project at San Francisco State University, told me. "That's earlier than most adults, including parents, believe. But sexual orientation isn't only about sex. It's also about social and emotional relatedness, human relationships, feelings of connection." As an example, she pointed to the Broadway musical *Fun Home*, based on cartoonist Alison Bechdel's graphic memoir. Nine-year-old "Small Alison" first confronts her own difference when she sees a butch deliverywoman enter a diner. "Ring of Keys," the show-stopping song she sings, is not about eroticism but identity, recognition: a paean to the woman's "swagger" and "bearing," her "just right" cropped hair, jeans, and lace-up boots, her way of being, of presenting to the world.

Maybe Amber's avatars were her "ring of keys." At any rate, it didn't last—once again, her parents checked her computer history and discovered what she was up to. By then they had divorced, and her father had moved out of state. Amber remembers an airport handoff, sitting in her mom's car while her parents conferred on the curb. "It happened again," she heard her dad say grimly. Later, her mother asked Amber why she'd chosen male avatars, but before Amber could answer, her mother fed her the response she wanted to hear. "She said, 'You just wanted to see what it was like, right?'" Amber recalled. "And I was like, 'Yeah, yeah, that's right—I wanted to see what it was like.'" If her mother harbored any ideas about her daughter's sexuality, she didn't let Amber know.

It doesn't take long for kids to exceed their parents' competence online. By eighth grade, Amber was savvy enough to erase her browsing history, create untraceable free e-mail accounts, cover her tracks. Posing as a boy named Jake, she built a fake MySpace page, posting a profile picture she'd downloaded of a cute guy from her school and claiming to be from Los Angeles. If you'd asked her at the time, she wouldn't have been able to say why she was doing it; only in retrospect can she connect her behavior to her sexual orientation. For two years she used the page as a cover to flirt with what she described as "oodles and oodles" of girls. None of them ever caught on, even when they spoke to her on the phone. (Amber demonstrated her quite credible imitation of a teenage boy's voice.) She did make one mistake, though: she gave them her real cell phone number, attributing its midwestern area code to a recent move. That was six years ago: she still gets texts from some of those girls. "I got one the other day out of the clear blue sky that said, 'I miss you,'" she said. "It's sort of weird."

It occurred to me that perhaps the ideal imaginary boyfriend for a teenage girl might very well be another girl pretending to be a guy. Who would better know what she wanted to hear? Amber agreed. "I think they look back to when they were in high school and think, 'Oh, I remember that one guy: he was so nice, and he always really *understood*.'"

Recalling that period herself, though, brings Amber pain. She feels ashamed and guilty about deceiving other girls. "It bothered me for a long time," she said. "I'm mostly over it now, but then I get these text messages and I'm like, *What the hell?* They come out of the woodwork. You'd think after you've watched enough *Catfish* episodes, you'd realize that I probably wasn't actually a real person with the wrong area code.

"It's sort of sad," she added, "when you think about it."

If Amber was impersonating a boy online, in real life she was learning, after a fashion, to impersonate a girl—or at least a certain kind of girl. Up until puberty, Amber passed as a "tomboy." She wore loose clothes, slicked back her hair, sometimes pretended to shave with her dad. If she was occasionally mistaken for male? Well, that was fine with her. No one *forced* her to change, exactly, but as she hit middle school, the expectation was clear. Her mom had been a cheerleader in high school; her dad is an orthodontist. Appearances mattered to both of them. Maybe her parents had their suspicions about Amber's sexual orientation; maybe they were hoping to stifle it. At the very least they were eager to have her behave like a conventionally feminine girl. They encouraged her to wear skirts, and her mom taught Amber to apply makeup. "I didn't want to be the 'weird' kid," Amber recalled. "So I just had to, you know, go with the flow. I'd wear mascara and I would say, 'Oh yeah, I *love* Zac Efron!' because I wanted to fit in. But I was always tugging on the clothes, I never felt comfortable. I was just going with the flow—I was always going with the flow."

Amber tried to join in as her friends experimented with "relationships" that would last a week or so, but whenever a boy put his arm around her, she pushed it off. "I'd tell my friends he was weird or creepy or clingy," she said. "Then I'd ask them to 'break up' with him for me." At fifteen, though, Amber met a boy who, coincidentally, was named Jake. She was drawn to him immediately. "We were best friends. My mom used to say we were like the same person in different bodies. We would play video games and watch movies. I would hang out with his family; he would hang out with mine." She didn't encourage a romance, but, she said, as with the miniskirts and lip gloss, "I was going along with things, so why not go along with having a boyfriend, too?"

To Amber's relief, Jake was a devout Christian who planned to remain a virgin until marriage. So, she figured, she had "nothing to worry about." For a few months, through the fall of her sophomore year, the couple did little more than kiss. While Amber didn't enjoy it, neither was she unwilling. "I never really had any feelings when we were doing it," she recalled. "It didn't turn me on. It just . . . happened."

In January, Jake invited her to their school's winter formal. She said yes, though the idea of grinding on the dance floor in a short skirt was not appealing. She found a knee-length red dress that, as she said, "was edgy, but didn't show any boob" and wore stiletto heels ("but not strappy," she said; "and they had a closed toe"). As for the dancing? She tolerated it—which, truth be told, was the case for many of the straight girls I spoke to as well. Afterward, Jake suggested they grab a soda at a McDonald's drive-thru, and then sit and talk in the car for a while. Amber agreed. "I'm thinking, it's me and Jake, you know?" she said. "So, fine, whatever." They pulled into a church parking lot. Jake turned off the motor and leaned in for a kiss. Then, without warning, he slid his hand under Amber's skirt. She broke out in a cold sweat and her stomach clenched, but she remained silent. When he suggested they move to the backseat, Amber, yet again, "went with the flow."

She went with the flow as Jake took her hand and shoved it into his pants. She went with the flow as he slid her underwear aside. "Then," Amber said, "God, he was only a sixteen-year-old boy—his finger goes in the wrong place. It goes up my butt hole!"

Jake was mortified. "I'm so sorry! I'm so sorry!" he repeated. Amber assured him she was fine—she didn't want him to feel bad, she said—but the mood, such as it was, was shattered. He zipped his pants and slunk into the front seat. "It was actually the best thing that could've happened," Amber said now. "Because it ended things. He just drove me home, and I was like, '*Yes!* It's over!'"

Though of course it wasn't. Since she'd allowed him to touch her once, Jake assumed he could do it again. And Amber never did say no. She also never said yes, and he interpreted her passivity as consent. She would sit unmoving, hands at her side, staring into space as he groped and rubbed against her. "Once he asked why I didn't make the same noises as girls in porn videos," she said. "He watched a *lot* of porn. I told him I was quiet because I was so into it. So, he thought I liked it. He thought it was normal, and I let him think that. Because I was go-with-the-flow Amber."

Most of the gay and bisexual girls I met had gone through a period of trying to pass as straight, sometimes experimenting with lesbianism under cover of heterosexuality. A bisexual high school senior in San Francisco, for instance, would go to an all-ages club so she could make out with other girls on the dance floor. "They were doing it mostly to get attention from boys," she recalled. "Whereas I wasn't. But they didn't know that. So it was really great." Later, she went further, bringing a second girl into bed with her boyfriend; by her freshman year of college, she was dating a woman. In general, girls have become more open to same-sex attraction in recent years, more accepting of sexual fluidity. In the early 1990s, for instance, only 3 percent of women who identified as heterosexual in *The Sex Lives of College Students* reported some same-sex experience; by 2008 nearly a third did (though, again, no distinction was drawn between girl-on-girl action performed mainly to titillate guys and the real thing).

For Amber, flowing with the hetero current became increasingly difficult. She knew she did not—*could* not—feel about Jake, or any boy, the way her friends did. "They would pull out pictures of guys they met over the summer or on Facebook and be like, 'Oh, he's so hot, I just want him to fuck me,'" Amber said. "And I'd be like, 'Um, *yeah*, me, too.' That was all I could say. Or sometimes: 'He's really attractive.' I never said a guy was hot or even good-looking. I never thought any of them were."

Like Lizzy, Amber had not to her knowledge personally met a lesbian, though she had seen them on TV shows such as *The L Word*. She worried that her feelings wouldn't be seen as normal, that she would embarrass her mother, disappoint her father, alienate her friends. By the fall of her junior year of high school, the effort of keeping up the straight-girl facade was leaving her exhausted and depressed. So she turned to the only outlet she could think of: the Internet. "I needed to find someone to vent to," Amber recalled. "I thought I would release it all and that would be enough; I'd be able to suppress it again for a few more years." She searched Tumblr for gay blogs, something I tried myself and that, at least initially, returned an array of photos of men: some kissing sweetly; others naked, stroking outsize erections; ejaculating onto one another's faces; performing oral or anal sex in duos, trios, or larger groups. The results for "lesbian" were equally graphic, though adding "teen" pulled up, along with the XXX fare, a smattering of angsty quotes, pictures of dancing cats, and carefully curated selfies. On a page called "Girls Who Like Girls," Amber stumbled on Hannah, who was squarely in the nonexplicit, angsty quote camp. Hannah posted her own writing as well as pictures of places she dreamed of visiting in Paris, London, and Rome. There were no photos of her face, Amber recalled. "That made it seem like she really just wanted to talk." She also lived far away, in Ottawa, Canada. "It was perfect. I was going to vent to her about all the fucked-up things that I'd done, and then I would never talk to her again."

Amber paused, shaking her head. "So wrong," she continued. "*So* wrong.

"Hannah rocked my world."

Coming Out in the Twenty-First Century

On another winter evening, a few months after we first met, Amber introduced me to Hannah. They were nearly three thousand miles and an international border away from my California home, but thanks to Skype, we were all in the same room. Hannah jumped up every few minutes to check on a chocolate chip banana bread she was baking for Amber. ("It's her favorite," she explained.) They talked about the party they went to on New Year's Eve; about how, for Christmas, Amber took Hannah ice skating and gave her a necklace; about the last time they were together with their families. They sat close, draping their arms around each other, touching constantly in the way of young lovers. Amber wore a hoodie from Hannah's university; Hannah wore a T-shirt from Amber's college, her long dark hair covering the school's insignia.

Five minutes after Amber sent that first, fateful message, she got a reply from Hannah suggesting they Skype. They did, and ended up talking until four in the morning. "I told her everything," Amber said now, gazing at Hannah affectionately. "About the fake MySpace profile, about getting caught by my parents, everything. It was crazy. I knew in, like, a split second that I didn't want to talk to anybody else ever for the rest of my life. She was the first person to tell me my feelings were okay. And I realized: *this* is what a relationship is supposed to feel like. You're supposed to feel appreciated and accepted and comfortable and able to say anything." Hannah's eyes welled up, and Amber pulled her close. "Why are you crying?" she asked.

"Because you were so sad," Hannah replied. "You needed someone to listen to you. I remember thinking, 'This girl really needs someone to tell her it's okay.'"

Within a few weeks, Amber's relationship with Jake fizzled, and they agreed to split up. While she was now free, she was only sixteen, and the new object of her affection lived in Canada. There was no way Amber could see Hannah in person—not, at least, without coming clean to her parents.

YouTube is full of "coming out videos"—that phrase returns about twenty-one million results. There are poignant and funny videos, and some that are heartrending, as parents accept or reject their children live on-screen. There are videos of twins coming out together. There is a subgenre of "how to come out" videos, and another of songs people have written about coming out. Amber watched dozens of them, trying to get up her nerve to talk to her mother. She resolved to do it over winter break, but as Christmas turned to New Year's, she continued to put off the conversation. Finally, just before school restarted, she invited her mother out to lunch, not something she typically did. It was a strategic choice: her mom wouldn't make a scene, Amber figured, in a public place. They agreed to meet at a deli. Amber was so nervous that morning she was shaking: she still wonders how she drove there without crashing the car. Her mother was already at a table, looking stricken. "Are you pregnant?" she burst out, before Amber was even seated. Amber laughed, and said, "No, Mom," thinking to herself, "The farthest thing from it."

Amber unfolded a piece of paper, a letter she'd written a month earlier and carried with her ever since. "I love you and I don't want to disappoint you and I always want to make you happy," she read. Then came the two words: *I'm gay*. But when she got to them, she choked. "I couldn't say it, I think because I had not accepted it myself. Finally, I don't even know how, it just came out." At first her mother seemed relieved. Her daughter wasn't on drugs. She hadn't stolen anything. She wasn't pregnant and didn't have an STD. Nor did Amber want to move in with her dad. Her mother hugged Amber, told her it was fine, just fine. "I love you," she said. Then the conversation took a turn. "How do you *know* you're gay?" she asked. "Maybe it's just a phase." Maybe, she continued, it had something to do with the divorce, with having a poor masculine role model. "There was no way in hell she was going to believe I was born this way," Amber said. "She just didn't understand."

As the age of coming out has dropped, parental support has become more crucial than ever. It's one thing for your mom and dad to banish you from the home at twenty-five; it's quite another at twelve. In a survey of more than ten thousand teenagers, those who were LGBT-identified listed tolerance and their family situation as the things they would most like to change in their lives; other kids said finances and their weight or appearance. LGBT kids also cited family as their "most important problem"; other kids said grades. According to Caitlin Ryan, family acceptance is the single biggest factor in an LGBT child's well-being. Ryan's organization has linked rejection by parents to increased risk of suicide, depression, abuse of illegal drugs, and HIV/AIDS. To a degree, this would seem self-evident. Less obvious is what teens experience as "rejection." Parental silence, for instance: one girl mentioned angrily to me that while her mother's Facebook page was plastered with pictures of her brother and his girlfriend, there was not a single photo of her and *her* girlfriend. Kids also consider the kind of comments Amber's mom made ("Are you sure?" or "Maybe it's a phase") as profoundly hurtful. Letting insulting comments by extended family slide is right up there as well. That said, Ryan found that most of those negative or ambivalent responses come from a place of love. "Parents are often expressing fear and anxiety exacerbated by misinformation," she said. "They wonder: 'What's going to happen to my child in the world? How do I deal with this in my own family? How do I reconcile conflicting beliefs?' The good news is that a little change in their response can make a huge difference."

It would take months of arguments and tension for Amber's mother to come around; it certainly did not seem the right time to tell her about Hannah. So Amber put that part of the conversation off, and then put it off some more. Meanwhile, the two girls continued to Skype late into the night.

"Who are you always talking to?" Amber's little sister would ask.

Amber would shrug. "A friend," she'd respond.

That did not satisfy the younger girl's curiosity. She began to grow suspicious, hostile. There was the time she snuck up behind Amber in the family's laundry room and said, "You're a fag, Amber. You're a dyke." Other times she would hiss, "You're such a *lesbian*."

"I think my sister just didn't know a healthy way to get me to come out to her, and she really wanted to know," Amber said. When I admired her generosity of spirit, she added, "Well, it definitely hurt my feelings. And even today it puts a damper on our relationship. I mean, who does that to their sister?"

Coming out, of course, is not a one-time deal. A person has to do it over and over, not only to people she already knows, but to everyone she will ever meet. Amber tried confiding in a few trusted friends, breaking the news, perhaps unsurprisingly, over Facebook chat or text. "I could never do it in person," she said. The girls always assured her that nothing had changed, but they wouldn't mention the conversation again, and invariably the friendships drifted. "I would think, 'All right, I guess you're just busy.' But, looking back, I realize they didn't want to be friends with me anymore once they knew I was gay."

Amber never did work up the nerve to tell her mom about Hannah—not directly. One day, though, while she was in her room, her mother stormed in, pushing the door open so hard that it banged against the wall. She brandished Amber's cell phone. "Who the hell is *this*?" she yelled.

She had read all Amber's and Hannah's texts, including the ones in which the two declared their love for each other. Amber just stared. "It was the worst possible way she could have found out," she recalled. "It was so upsetting. Because if she wasn't really accepting about my being gay, she sure as hell was not going to accept a long-distance relationship with some random girl."

"What do you think you're doing?" her mother continued. "How old is this person? How do you know she's not thirty-five?"

Hannah's mother—her father had passed away—was more accepting of her daughter's sexuality and budding relationship: she offered to try to smooth things over with Amber's mom and arrange for the girls to visit. Amber's mother refused. No way was her daughter visiting some stranger in Canada. "I would *beg* her to let me see Hannah, just for a day," Amber recalled. "It didn't have to be in Canada: her mom would let her visit us. But my mom said no. It was like she thought if she kept us apart, I wouldn't be gay anymore."

By summer, Amber's mother had calmed down enough to allow Hannah to visit for three days. She could stay at their house, but the girls had to sleep two levels apart. Amber didn't care. She was going to see her girlfriend in person. Nervously, she Googled "what do two girls do together." She needn't have worried: the instant they were alone, Amber and Hannah began kissing, and the feeling was unlike anything Amber had previously experienced. "I was so into it," she recalled. "It was just a natural, normal thing, exactly how it was supposed to be. That's how it probably is for everybody else when they're in an intimate relationship, that kind of feeling I had."

Girls in relationships with other girls spoke very differently about sex from those who were involved with boys. A senior at a California public high school who identified as bisexual told me that she enjoyed the reciprocity she found—and had found *only*—in her same-sex encounters. "It's so different," she explained. "It's like my turn, her turn, my turn, her turn." Another bisexual high school senior said she tended to be more passive with male partners. "With another girl . . . well, you can't *both* be passive. Nothing would happen. With a guy it feels like he's doing something *to* you, but with a girl, you're doing it *with* each other." A college junior in the Midwest told me that sex with her girlfriend felt "off the script": since there was nothing they were *supposed* to do, they were free to create the sex life that worked for them.

Because she had never had intercourse with Jake, Amber considered herself a virgin when she and Hannah met. I asked her if she believed herself to be one now. She shook her head. "I was so confused, though, so unclear about what 'gay' meant, that I had to Google 'When is a lesbian not a virgin?'"

What was the answer? I asked her. "There wasn't one," Amber said. "For me . . ." She paused for a long moment. "I think it's just the second that you are being intimate, touching each other more than just kissing. Not your breasts, necessarily, but below the waist. The second you touch there, you're not a virgin anymore.

"But honestly, I don't really have a definition. I just knew. I guess I would define it . . . maybe once you have an orgasm with someone? Once you have an orgasm with someone, you're definitely not a virgin anymore. Yeah, that's how I would define it."

When Is a Girl Not a Girl?

Amber and Hannah's relationship deepened during their senior year of high school, and as it did, Amber grew more confident in other parts of her life. She discovered she liked public speaking and acted as emcee for a school-wide talent show; she was elected to the homecoming court; she socialized more. Although she stayed in the closet for the most part, she ditched the skirts and makeup in favor of a more pared-down, androgynous look. "I would just own it," she said. "It was fun! And nobody had a problem with it."

That first afternoon we met, she pulled up a photo on her phone of what she used to look like and passed it over to me. The girl in the photograph—her blond-streaked, carefully styled hair flowing to her shoulders, candy-pink lipstick, blue eyeliner and mascara—looked nothing like the young woman in front of me. At the same time, the current version of Amber wasn't much different from any of the straight girls I'd met, at least when they were dressed for school rather than for the party scene: she wore jeans—she said they were men's, but I wouldn't have guessed—a hoodie emblazoned with her college's name, and hiking boots. She wore no makeup, but neither, during the day, did many other girls. Her hair was pulled back with a black headband and fastened into a short ponytail. Even so, during our first conversation, the planes and shadows of her face seemed perpetually to shift: maybe it was a trick of the light, or maybe I was just tired, but sometimes she looked clearly like a girl and other times, quite suddenly, she could easily have passed for a boy.

Amber was not always certain herself which she was. It was in trying to answer that question that she found the Internet, previously so dependable, finally failing her. YouTube videos and websites she scoured suggested she might be transgender, a term she had never before heard. (It would be years before Laverne Cox and Caitlyn Jenner graced the covers of glossy magazines.) She spent the next twelve months, until just before she left for college, worrying that it was true. "It scared the living shit out of me," she said. "I was like, what am I going to do? I was going to have to go through all these surgeries and get my name changed. I thought it was the only option."

Certainly the Internet can be a trove of misinformation, distortion, dis-expertise, and bad advice. On Google, a nicked cuticle becomes a life-threatening emergency; so does working out or taking a shower (though, if you stopped exercising, you could bathe less and minimize both risks). So a young gay woman who had never heard the word *butch*, let alone *transgender*, could easily become confused, especially if, like Amber, she was raised in a community with conventional ideas about masculinity and femininity. An estimated 0.3 percent of Americans are thought to identify as transgender—that's close to seven hundred thousand individuals. (About 3.5 percent of adults identify as gay, lesbian, or bisexual, though rates are higher among those ages eighteen to twenty-nine.) The true number is hard to quantify, though, since it may or may not include those who identify as "genderqueer"—living between genders, beyond genders, or as a combination of genders. At its fullest (and some would say most threatening) manifestation, genderqueer upends notions of femaleness and maleness, masculinity and femininity, changing them from a biological inevitability into a customizable, ever-changing buffet of identities, expressions, and preferences. There was the 2013 story, for instance, of Arin Andrews, who began life in a girl's body, and Katie Hill, who began life as a boy. They fell in love in a support group for transgender teens, went through their transitions together, and continued forward as a heterosexual couple. Or the darker tale of Sasha Fleischman, born a boy in Oakland, California, who is agender—that is, not identified with either sex, preferring to be addressed by the pronoun "they." As a high school senior, Sasha suffered severe burns to the legs when another teen set Sasha's skirt on fire aboard a city bus. An outpouring of support followed—a local protest march peopled by boys wearing "skirts for Sasha"; thousands of dollars raised on the Internet to offset medical bills; local school policies changed to allow gender-nonconforming students to choose which bathrooms and locker rooms they want to use, which sports teams they want to join.

Modern college campuses are replete with gender warriors who specify whether they are cis-gender (meaning their emotional, psychological, physiological, and genetic genders match), nonconforming, or transgender. They may replace *he* and *she* with neutral pronouns such as *ze, ne, ou, hir, they,* or even *it.* The rejection of the "gender binary" can be truly radically liberating. At the same time, a rush to label a young person as "nonconforming" may risk unwittingly calcifying traditional categories. Consider the case of a male-to-female transgender first-grader whose family sued her Colorado school for forbidding her to use the girls' bathroom: her parents said their first inkling that their son, the only boy in a set of triplets, was unusual came when he was five months old and reached for a pink blanket meant for one of his sisters. Later, he rejected a car he was given for Christmas, showed no interest in sports-themed clothing, and donned a princess dress rather than a fireman's uniform in fantasy play. Five-month-olds don't know pink from blue. And choosing tulle over tools? With all due respect to the family and the child, who may indeed be transgender, that hardly seems like "proof" of anything other than adult bias. Yet nearly every press report I read not only trotted out those anecdotes but placed them in the story's lead. Even as I admired the child's parents for supporting their daughter, that inflexible definition of masculinity—which would see a boy as actually *female* before accommodating his love for sparkly gowns—concerned me.

Some of Amber's reasons for questioning her gender identity were similarly retrograde: they included being more dominant in bed, standing up for herself, planning to pursue a career in business, and hating to cook. Nor was Amber the only young lesbian I met who wondered whether her clothing and attitudes meant she was actually male. Valentina, eighteen, the girl who called herself my "unicorn," also spent her senior year of high school thinking she "must" be transgender. Growing up in a low-income, largely Mexican American neighborhood in Chicago, she shunned anything conventionally feminine: Barbies, pink, skirts, frills. Dressed in a flannel shirt and loose jeans, she told me that in middle school other girls would crawl into her lap to cuddle, calling her "Big Daddy" (she was broadly built) and ask advice about boys. By high school, she was scouring the Internet for clues as to her identity. "I wanted to know," she said, " 'Am I gay?' 'Am I transgender?' "

"Did you feel like you were in the wrong body?" I asked her.

"No."

"Did you feel like you wanted to be a man?"

"No," she said again.

"Then why did you think you might be transgender?"

"That's exactly it!" she said. "What finally made me realize I wasn't trans was reading about people who said, 'I felt like there was a guy inside of me trying to get out.' I never felt that. I never felt like I should be a guy. I like my vagina. I wouldn't want anything to happen to it. But I wasn't sure I wanted to be a girl, either."

Such confusion is understandable, according to Jack Halberstam, professor of English and director of the Center for Feminist Research at the University of Southern California, who writes about transgender issues. Even as some young people may be helped—sometimes saved—by the recent visibility of transwomen such as Cox and Jenner or by TV shows such as Amazon's *Transparent*, tensions between "butch" women and transmen have been building. "The whole concept of 'butch' is now seen as a kind of waiting room in which you stay until you change your gender physically," Halberstam said. "We don't have words for someone who has strong cross-gender identification but feels good about their bodies. *Butch* has become anachronistic, but *trans* implies transition, possibly hormones and surgery. *Genderqueer* is as good a holding term, but it's clumsy, really." I pondered the idea of "cross-gender identification." That, too, seems often culturally determined, to the detriment of girls such as Valentina and Amber. When we've defined femininity for their generation so narrowly, in such a sexualized, commercialized, heteroeroticized way, where is the space, the vision, the celebration of other ways to be a girl?

As for Amber, "I looked heavily into it," she told me during our first meeting. "I could tell you everything under the sun about being transgender. I'd go through these lists I'd find online. They would ask questions like, 'Do you cry when you think about having a vagina?' And I'd think, 'No, not really.' Maybe if somebody told me I could choose one sex or the other I would have picked the other, but I don't feel upset about it. I had all these conflicting feelings. Like, I don't really care about my boobs. That's weird, right? So then I dealt with 'Am I a biological *mistake?*' "

Ultimately, Amber realized she did not want to give up who she was, did not want to be someone completely new: "I mean, say your name is Cheryl," she explained, "and you're becoming Sean. You have to not want to be Cheryl anymore and never talk about Cheryl again.

"Well," she added, sitting forward in her chair, "I love being Amber. I could never in a million years imagine not being Amber. *I am Amber.* And I don't know if I fit being a lesbian perfectly, but I'm definitely not a transgender person. I can live my life in this body, confident and happy, and in a healthy relationship." She leaned back again, letting her hands drop to her lap. "And it took me a year, an entire year, to be able to sit here and tell you that."

DURING OUR CONVERSATION on Skype, Amber and Hannah told me they have no fear of holding hands, snuggling, or kissing on the streets of Ottawa. They're a bit more circumspect when Hannah visits Amber. Amber's mom still hasn't fully come around. ("She'll never accept us like she would if I were with a straight person," Amber said.) And while people have been mostly accepting on her college campus, the couple has occasionally been harassed by groups of young men. Still, Amber has been experimenting with being more public about who she is. She recently volunteered to serve on a panel of LGBTQ people who visit classes at her school to talk about their experiences and answer questions. She has also declared a double major in economics and public policy and is toying with going to law school and ultimately entering politics. "I'd like to try and get a House of Representatives seat," she told me, and then laughed. "I've got a little bit against me in running for office—I'm both a girl and gay. But I'll figure it out."

"Well," I said, "it just might be your time."

She nodded, smiling. "I always tell myself that," she said. "Things are opening up for women and us gay people. I guess we'll see."

CHAPTER 6

Blurred Lines, Take Two

I met Maddie Reed at the community college where she was enrolled in a special program for home-schooled or otherwise "independent" high schoolers. She shook my hand and smiled, a pale, curvy girl with a spray of freckles across her nose and reddish-brown hair that hung past her shoulders. She'd attended classes here for a semester and planned to stay another year, until graduation. That meant she wouldn't, as she once dreamed, write for her high school newspaper, or go out for the softball team, or attend the prom. "I don't think about it," she said as we strolled through campus, looking for a quiet corner where we could talk. "I don't let myself. It's still a fresh wound. And I know other girls have it way worse. At least I have a vague idea what happened to me. At least there weren't pictures of it going around. But I wasn't really aware that this was a problem before. I thought it was just something that happened in . . . I don't know, other parts of the world."

Who Stole Consent

The attention to sexual assault over the past few years has been unprecedented. From dorm rooms to press rooms to the White House, fighting rape, especially on college campuses, has become one of the most prominent, contentious civil rights issues of our time, up there with gay marriage, abortion, and police brutality. What is the definition of sexual assault? What constitutes consent? How should schools fairly handle allegations? This is not, though, the first time that acquaintance rape has sparked debate. The late 1980s and early 1990s saw a flurry of divisive, high-profile cases. The first, and perhaps most appalling, was in 1989, in Glen Ridge, New Jersey, where a group of high school boys assaulted a mentally disabled girl (a young woman they'd known since childhood) with a broomstick and a baseball bat. The case featured several elements that would resurface in the current national upheaval: the boys were star athletes in an idyllic, football-crazy town; although their actions had been initially reported as out of character for them—a "stupid mistake" by otherwise "decent" kids—they had in truth been abusing their godlike status since middle school: bullying classmates, destroying property, creating mayhem. They were disdainful of girls and female teachers (one of the boys regularly exposed himself in school and frequently masturbated during class); treated sex primarily as a form of male bonding (watching porn together, convincing younger girls to give them successive blow jobs, and secretly watching one another's escapades with unsuspecting partners). The girl they assaulted was incapacitated, though in this case mentally rather than by drugs or alcohol; bystanders declined to intervene. After the boys' arrest, many of the town's adult residents defended them, claiming that the girl was a "sexual aggressor" who had "asked for it."

Around that same time, allegations against thirty-year-old William Kennedy Smith stunned the public in a different way: he was, after all, a medical student, clean cut, wealthy, privileged—a *Kennedy*. He met his alleged victim while drinking at a Florida bar with his uncle, Senator Edward Kennedy, and his cousin Patrick, a future congressman. The woman later claimed that in the wee morning hours, Smith tackled her as they strolled on the sand near the family's Palm Beach estate; then he pinned her down and raped her. Smith insisted their sex was consensual. He was ultimately acquitted; many believed the verdict might have been different had the judge admitted testimony by three other women (a doctor, a law student, and a medical student) who, in sworn depositions, said that Smith had also assaulted them, though they didn't report those incidents to the police. Before the media had finished dissecting that case, former heavyweight champion Mike Tyson was charged and convicted in Indiana of raping an eighteen-year-old Miss Black America pageant contestant during a late-night date; he served three years of a six-year sentence. None of these assailants fit the prevailing image of the rapist as a deranged guy in a ski mask leaping out from a dark alley. The accusers knew their attackers, and had, to a point, gone with them willingly. That was, of course, used by defense lawyers as proof of consent, or at least partial collusion— the women "should have known" what was going to happen to them. Anyway, supporters argued, why would these high-status, upstanding males "need" to rape anyone? They could get all the women they wanted. It wouldn't be until 2015 that Tyson's former manager admitted that such charges were "inevitable" for the boxer, adding that the only surprise was that Tyson was not the subject of further complaints. Several of the Glen Ridge boys eventually went to prison for their crime; another, against whom

169

charges were dropped, joined the military. In 2005 he entered his estranged wife's house, shot her and a fellow soldier, wounding them both, then killed himself—all as his infant daughter lay in the next room. As for Smith? A 2004 assault charge by an employee was dismissed in civil court; in 2005 he settled another suit with a different employee, who accused him of sexual harassment.

Less than a month after Tyson's conviction, the Supreme Court granted students the right to sue colleges and universities for monetary damages under Title IX, which prohibits sex discrimination in education. That gave immediate leverage to young women across the country—at the University of Southern California; Stanford University; University of California at Berkeley; University of Wisconsin; University of Michigan; Tufts; Cornell; Yale; Columbia—who had begun speaking out about campus sexual assault. Most famously, girls at Brown University, frustrated by the administration's indifference, scrawled a list of alleged rapists on the walls of the women's bathroom in the school library. (Boys later retaliated with their own list: "Women Who Need to Be Raped.") Even after the walls were painted black as a deterrent, girls used white paint pens to keep the list going; at one point it swelled to thirty names.

Also during this period, the media began reporting on what was perceived as a sharp and shocking trend of "acquaintance rape" on campus. In December 1990 alone, the *Washington Post* revealed "The Statistic That No One Can Bear to Believe"; *People* ran a cover story on "a crime that too many colleges have ignored"; and Fox TV produced a documentary, *Campus Rape: When No Means No.* As evidence, many pointed to a 1987 study funded by the National Institute of Mental Health and conducted by Mary P. Koss, then a professor of psychology at Kent

State University. Koss surveyed six thousand students at thirty-two universities and found that 27.5 percent—more than one in four—of the girls had, since the age of fourteen, experienced a sexual encounter fitting the legal definition of rape. Eighty-four percent of those attacks were committed by someone the girl knew; 57 percent took place on dates. That led Koss to coin the term *date rape.* When she factored in other forms of unwanted sexual activity ("fondling, kissing, or petting but not intercourse"), the victimization rate shot up to nearly 54 percent. Only a quarter of the boys surveyed admitted involvement in some form of sexual aggression; one in ten said they had verbally pressured a girl into intercourse; 3.3 percent had attempted physical force; and 4.4 percent had raped someone. None of those in the latter two categories considered their acts criminal, largely because they had faced no consequences. "They would say, 'Yes, I held a woman down to have sex with her against her consent,'" Koss told NPR, "'but that was definitely not rape.'" Sexual violence was so pervasive, Koss concluded, that it was part of what the culture defined as "normal" interaction between women and men.

Then came the backlash. In her 1993 polemic, *The Morning After,* Katie Roiphe, a telegenic graduate student in English literature at Princeton, dismissed the campus "rape crisis" as overblown. "If twenty-five percent of my women friends were really being raped, wouldn't I know it?" she reasoned. Perhaps not, considering her main beef: the inclusion in Koss's rape tally of those who answered yes to the question "Have you had sexual intercourse when you didn't want to because a man gave you alcohol or drugs?" To Roiphe, "real" rape involved brute force. Silence alone did not indicate nonconsent; neither did incapacitation. It was a classic conservative argument, and one that endures to this day, but Roiphe gave it a contrarian, "feminist" spin: scolding campus activists for undermining the very agency with which the movement provided them. "A man may give [a woman] drugs," she wrote, "but she herself decides to take them. If we assume that women are not all helpless and naïve, then they should be held responsible for their choice to drink or take drugs." "Rape crisis" feminists, in other words, needed to pull up their Big Girl pants and deal with a few embarrassing nights. Roiphe rejected what she considered their attempt to expand rape's definition as being "a way of interpreting," "a way of seeing" rather than a "physical fact." As if reinterpretation—of citizenship, of suffrage, of who may hold property, even of who are, themselves, property—is not at the core of women's rights: it was just two months before Roiphe's book was published, for instance, that all fifty states finally recognized marital rape as a crime.

Roiphe's book grew out of an editorial in the *New York Times*, which also excerpted it on the cover of its Sunday *Magazine*. Other media outlets (*Newsweek*, *The Atlantic*, ABC, NBC, PBS) soon began churning out stories and programming on what was suddenly demoted to "the date rape controversy." Few mentioned that even when Koss's data were recalculated without the alcohol question, one in six women had still been legally raped. (To be fair, the statistic was often misstated by activists as the number of girls who would be raped *while on campus*, rather than *since age fourteen*, which is certainly horrifying enough.) When Roiphe lost her novelty, reporters turned to Camille Paglia, who proclaimed, "date rape is bullshit," and Christina Hoff Sommers, currently a resident scholar at the right-wing American Enterprise Institute, whose book *Who Stole Feminism* accused Koss of "[opening] the door wide to regarding as a rape victim anyone who regretted her liaison of the previous night." (Of course, by *excluding* alcohol-facilitated rape, Sommers herself would slam shut the door on "regarding as a rape victim" anyone who was penetrated while passed out drunk.)

By October 1993, campus antirape activism was so maligned that it became fodder for a notorious *Saturday Night Live* sketch, a mock game show called "Is It Date Rape?" Ostensibly set at Antioch College, it lampooned that school's pioneering requirement that partners obtain a clear, verbal "yes" before engaging in sexual activity. Chris Farley, as a frat boy, squared off against Shannen Doherty, as a dowdy "Victimization Studies" major—yes, that's funny—over categories such as "Halter Top," "She Was Drunk," "I Was Drunk," "Kegger," "Off-Campus Kegger," and "Ragin' Kegger." Other cast members, wearing "Date Rape Players" T-shirts, acted out permissible interactions involving such stilted requests as "May I elevate the level of sexual intimacy by feeling your buttocks?" and "I sure had a nice time at that ragin' kegger. May I kiss you on the mouth?" The implication was that the whole date rape thing had gone too far; a bunch of dour, unattractive feminists were trying to shut down the Animal House and ruin heterosexual sex. Days later, the *New York Times*, citing the sketch, weighed in with a staff editorial, scolding Antioch for inappropriately "legislating kisses." Although the director of the school's sexual offense prevention program responded in a letter to the editor that "We are not trying to reduce the romance, passion, or spontaneity of sex; we are trying to reduce the spontaneity of *rape*," the damage was done. "Affirmative consent" (along with Antioch College) became little more than a punch line; date rape was quickly downgraded from "epidemic" to "controversy" to "hype," and further outcry by advocates was essentially quashed. By November of that year, 17.8 million people, mostly teens, tuned in to *Beverly Hills 90210* to see an episode in which Steve, the series' resident goofball, "accidentally" raped a girl who never vocalized the word *no*. She ended up apologizing to *him* in front of a crowd at a Take Back the Night rally. The lesson learned? The "misunderstanding" was actually her own fault because, she said, "I didn't say yes, but I didn't say no, either."

Love and War

Maddie loved Kyle. She did. She'd met him at a party just before her fifteenth birthday; he was a grade ahead of her at a different high school. The two hooked up—nothing serious, just a little kissing. He told her straight out that he liked another girl, though he was willing to be her "friend with benefits." When she saw him at another party a few weeks later, after they'd both been drinking, they hooked up again. Again, they kissed a bit, but this time he informed her he couldn't continue unless she gave him a blow job; otherwise he would develop "blue balls." (Parents, take note: a number of girls I spoke with fell for that chestnut.) Maddie agreed: she had never gone down on a boy, but she already felt she was falling in love with Kyle, and she wanted to make him happy.

Nothing changed between them afterward. Instead, they fell into a pattern: when they saw each other at parties, they would make out, he might "finger" her (though not to orgasm), and she would give him a blow job. They never went out on a date. They never met each other's parents. She'd never even been to his house until they decided to have intercourse. Maddie was sixteen by then and wanted her first time to be with Kyle. They even bought condoms together beforehand, "like a real boyfriend and girlfriend." She remembers the event itself as sweet, but uncomfortable and a little boring: "It hurt really badly for about two minutes, and then I mostly looked at my nails," she told me. She was proud, though, to have had sex sober, during the day, in a bedroom, with someone she loved. Until, that is, a few weeks later, when she heard that Kyle was also having sex with someone else.

Maddie was livid. Her plot for revenge seemed ripped from a script of *Gossip Girl*: that weekend, she would go "looking all hot" to a party where she knew he'd be. And then? She would hook up with one of his friends. "I'm going to *win!*" she remembered thinking. Somehow, though, in a series of convoluted mishaps that don't make sense to anyone over seventeen, she ended up at the wrong place—a houseful of seniors from a neighboring town, mostly boys, none of whom she knew well, all of whom had been drinking. One was a football player named Josh, who had been the sort-of boyfriend of a girl Maddie knew ("like a Kyle-and-me kind of thing"), toward whom he'd been "super abusive." When she informed Josh that the girl had told her "a lot about him," he scoffed. "Don't listen to anything *she* says. She's crazy!" Maddie remained polite but distant, making it clear (at least she thought) that she was uninterested. Somehow, though, word got around the party that the two were going to hook up.

"How did he get *that* message?" Maddie said when another boy asked her about the rumor. "I'm not going to hook up with him. He's an asshole."

The boy smirked. "Well, we'll see after a couple of drinks."

"What does *that* mean?" Maddie replied. "You can't just say that stuff to girls!"

The boy laughed, holding up his hands. "I'm kidding!" he said.

Rape by the Numbers

Throughout the 1990s and early 2000s, research on campus assault quietly continued to accrue, as did skepticism about the results. Using the narrowest definition of rape—as involving physical force—most studies found an annual incidence of between 3 and 5 percent. That is not one in four or even the more recently asserted one in five. Still, given that according to the Census Bureau, there were 4.6 million female full-time undergraduates at four-year institutions in 2013, it would mean that between 138,000 and 230,000 were raped each year—not so comforting. What's more, that conservative definition is no longer employed by such notoriously radical feminist cabals as, say, the FBI, which as of 2013 defined rape as "penetration, no matter how slight, of the vagina or anus with any body part or object, or oral penetration by a sex organ of another person, without the consent of the victim." (That revised definition, incidentally, does not assume the victim is female.)

In 2015 two significant reports came out that should (but probably won't) put an end to all the squabbling. The Association of American Universities' Campus Climate Survey, comprised of over 150,000 students, found that a third of female undergraduate respondents had been victims of nonconsensual sexual contact. Meanwhile, sociologists Jessie Ford and Paula England analyzed assault rates among seniors who had participated in the Online College Social Life Survey. Unlike the AAU report, Ford and England focused solely on acts of intercourse or attempted intercourse—they did not include the incidents of unwanted touching, oral sex, or psychological coercion that critics insist unfairly pad the numbers. Ten percent of the girls said they had been physically forced to have sex since starting college;

15 percent said that someone had tried to physically force them, but that they had escaped without having intercourse (the survey didn't ask whether they had been forced into other acts instead); 11 percent reported someone had unwanted intercourse with them while they were "drunk, passed out, asleep, drugged, or otherwise incapacitated"; and 25 percent reported at least one of these things had happened to them. Including the types of assaults while intoxicated that Roiphe, Paglia, Sommers, and their supporters (if not the criminal justice system) reject, that brings us back to one in four.

Since 1990, colleges and universities have been legally obliged to report to the Department of Education all crimes occurring on or near campus. Those that don't can lose federal financial aid funding, something few schools, no matter how well endowed, can afford. The impetus for that was the rape and murder of nineteen-year-old Jeanne Clery in her Lehigh University dorm room. Clery's parents later learned that there had been multiple violent crimes at the school over the previous three years, but with no consistent tracking policy, students were left oblivious, overestimating their safety on campus. Clery's attacker, who was not a student, had passed through three doors equipped with automatic locks, all of which had been propped open with boxes by dorm residents. Despite that, sanctions for fudging crime stats remained rare, and given that high rates of rape are not a big selling point for prospective students, it's probably not surprising that by 2006, 77 percent of campuses reported their number of sexual assaults at an implausible zero.

That, however, will no longer cut it. In 2011, Russlynn Ali, Obama's new assistant secretary for civil rights, fired off a nineteen-page "Dear Colleague" letter reminding campus officials of their responsibility to uphold all aspects of Title IX, including those involving sexual harassment and violence. Along with a mandate to resolve cases quickly and ensure the physical and psychological safety of accusers (rearranging the class schedule of the accused or removing him from the alleged victim's dorm), the letter laid down a new, reduced burden of proof: "a preponderance of evidence," typically used in civil cases, rather than the more demanding "clear and convincing evidence" then being used on many campuses. More controversy ensued, with conservative activists denouncing the standard as too low given the seriousness of the crime and the potential stigmatization of the accused. The thing is, though, as legal blogger Michael Dorf has written, the lower burden of proof in civil court is not based on either a crime's brutality or its potential to defame the perpetrator, but on the nature of the *punishment*: so someone such as O.J. Simpson could be found not guilty of murder by the standards of criminal court, where life in prison was at stake, but guilty in civil court where the penalty was solely to the pocketbook. Given, then, that colleges expel or suspend rather than jail rapists, "a preponderance of evidence" standard is, in fact, reasonable.

The Department of Education's warning roiled the academic world. As with the right to sue for monetary damages in the 1990s, it also galvanized female students, who no longer needed traditional media to champion their cause: they had the Internet. In 2012, Angie Epifano, a former student at Amherst, published a signed editorial in the school newspaper about college administrators' callous response to her rape allegations. The detailed description of a skeptical sexual assault counselor, her subsequent suicidal depression, a stint in a psych ward, and her ultimate withdrawal from school went viral, generating more than 750,000 page views. "Silence has the rusty taste of shame," she declared. "I will not be quiet." Soon a national movement began to form—activists, often assault survivors themselves, at Amherst, the University of North Carolina, Tufts, Yale, Berkeley—all connecting through social media. That caught the attention of the mainstream press. This round, the *New York Times* seemed all in: running, among other stories, front-page pieces on the student activists and on the White House initiatives; an account in the Sunday Review section by a University of Virginia rape survivor about the lax punishment meted out to her assailant; and numerous opinion pieces and online debates on institutional responsibility, alcohol abuse, the underreporting of assault, and the dubious culture of fraternities and sports teams. The paper also profiled Emma Sulkowicz, a senior at Columbia University who had vowed to lug a fifty-pound dormitory mattress on her back everywhere she went during the 2014/15 school year until the boy she accused of raping her—who had been found "not responsible"—was expelled. (He filed a suit against the university, claiming the administration's failure to protect him from Sulkowicz's accusations, which he said destroyed his college experience and reputation.) Some hailed Sulkowicz as a hero; others called her unhinged. Regardless, it is clear that public witness bearing—rejecting traditional anonymity with its attendant assumption of shame—had become girls' best weapon in the fight against rape.

By the spring of 2015 more than a hundred colleges were under investigation for possible mishandling of sexual assault cases. Among them were the most prestigious in the country: Amherst, Brandeis, Dartmouth, Emerson, Emory, Hampshire, Harvard (the college and the law school), Princeton, Sarah Lawrence, Stanford, Swarthmore, the University of California–Berkeley, the University of Chicago, the University of Michigan–Ann Arbor, the University of North Carolina at Chapel Hill, the University of Southern California, the University of Virginia, and Vanderbilt. Will those inquiries make a difference? It's hard to say. The number of reported campus sexual assaults nearly doubled between 2009 and 2013, from 3,264 to 6,016. Although that wouldn't seem like good news, it is: rather than an increase in the incidence of rapes, the rise appears to reflect a new willingness of victims to step forward, a new belief that they will be heard. The key may be to keep the bright light of public attention shining. According to a study by the American Psychological Association, the reported numbers of assaults increase an average of about 44 percent when campuses are under formal scrutiny. Afterward, though, they sink back to their original levels, indicating that some schools provide a more accurate picture of sexual assault only when forced to do so.

In any case, I would argue that waiting to address rape until college is years too late. Sexual assault is even more common among secondary students; the difference is that their schools don't have the same duty to report it. Twenty-eight percent of female college freshmen in a 2015 survey of a large private university in upstate New York said they had been victims of either attempted or completed forcible or incapacitated rape *before* college—between the ages of fourteen and eighteen. As in the early 1990s, many of the recent incidents that have shocked the nation also took place among younger kids. In the fall of 2012, Steubenville, Ohio, became the Glen Ridge of its day after two football players hauled a drunk, insensible sixteen-year-old girl from party to party, taking turns sexually violating her, spitting on her, even urinating on her as classmates looked on, some cheering. Like the Glen Ridge jocks, who would, without asking their partners, Scotch tape photos to their high school's trophy case of themselves in flagrante delicto, these boys weren't content simply to assault their victim; they needed to document the "achievement." One member of the Steubenville "rape crew" tweeted such gems as "Some people deserve to be peed on" and "You don't sleep through a wang in the butthole" and "Song of the night is definitely Rape Me by Nirvana." Another boy posted a picture of the victim on Instagram, her head lolling back as the boys carried her by her wrists and ankles. In a YouTube video, a laughing young man calls her "deader than," respectively, Nicole Simpson, John F. Kennedy, Trayvon Martin, and the toddler Caylee Anthony. Was online bragging about rape part of a new, ominous trend? A year earlier, a pair of boys in Louisville, Kentucky (fine students and athletes at a prestigious Catholic school), made news when they passed around cell phone pictures of themselves assaulting a sixteen-year-old who lay drunk and semiconscious in her kitchen. Audrie Pott, a fifteen-year-old from Saratoga, California, committed suicide after photos of an assault perpetrated while she was passed out drunk were posted on the Internet. Ditto Rehtaeh Parsons, a seventeen-year-old girl from Nova Scotia, Canada, who was gang-raped while incapacitated.

Tracking those incidents, it struck me how often the words *funny* or, more commonly, *hilarious* came up among boys recounting stories of women's sexual degradation. When, during the Steubenville video an off-camera voice says rape isn't funny, Michael Nodianos, then a high school baseball player, responds, "It isn't funny. It's *hilarious!*" One of the Louisville boys told police he thought it would be "funny" to take pictures of himself assaulting his victim. A young woman I met at a California university told me how, freshman year, a male resident of her dorm invited her to watch a video he'd shot on his phone of a friend having sex with a girl who was out cold. "Come look at this," he had said. "It's *hilarious*." A boy on a midwestern campus I visited, recalling the first time he saw hard-core porn, remembered thinking that was "hilarious," too; his classmate used the word while describing how the "ugly band girls" were the most sexually active in his high school. "Hilarious" seemed to be the default position for some boys—something like "awkward" for girls—when they were unsure of how to respond, particularly to something that was both sexually explicit and dehumanizing, something that perhaps actually upset them, offended them, unnerved them, repulsed them, confused them, or defied their ethics. "Hilarious" offered distance, allowing them to look without feeling, to subvert a more compassionate response that might be read as weak, overly sensitive, and unmasculine. "Hilarious" is particularly disturbing as a safe haven for bystanders—if assault is "hilarious," they don't have to take it seriously, they don't have to respond: there is no problem.

The photos shared by the assailants in Steubenville, Louisville, Nova Scotia, and Saratoga revictimized the girls—potentially in perpetuity, as the images could be endlessly copied, downloaded, and passed along. They also provided unique evidence that crimes had indeed been committed, though that made neither conviction inevitable nor punishments necessarily more severe. One of the Steubenville rapists was given a year in juvenile detention; the other got two years, including credit for time already served. The Louisville boys were ordered to perform fifty hours of community service, which, until the local newspaper intervened, they were fulfilling by putting away equipment after lacrosse practice. Two of Audrie Pott's assailants received thirty-day sentences in juvenile detention, to be served on weekends; a third served forty-five consecutive days. Rehtaeh Parsons's attackers were placed on probation. As in Glen Ridge, there was often a groundswell of sympathy for the boys in these cases: claims that their actions were unusual, a one-time mistake; anguish over the damage convictions would do to their bright futures; denunciations of the girl involved. One of the Louisville assailants took his appeal straight to his victim, texting her to ask that she stop pursuing her case against him. "There is another way to deal with this other than jeopardizing our lives forever. . . . I'm not a bad person just a dumb one."

"You don't think you ruined my life forever?" she shot back.

Uncool

Through another series of jumbled, and by now somewhat alcohol-tinged, events, Maddie found herself in the backseat of a car with Josh, heading to the party she was supposed to have gone to in the first place. A boy named Anthony, another senior, was driving; his girlfriend, Paige, rode shotgun. Maddie ignored them all, focusing on the texts she'd begun trading with Kyle, occasionally yelling at her phone. Josh, seeming truly concerned, asked what was wrong. "There's this guy I've been in love with for a year and a half," Maddie told him, her voice teary, "and I lost my virginity to him and now he's had sex with another girl."

"Have *you* had sex with anyone else?" Anthony asked from the front seat.

"No," Maddie said, still weepy. "I only have sex with people I'm in love with."

"Well, that's your problem!" Anthony told her. "If you just have sex with someone else, you'll get over it!"

Maddie may have been upset with Kyle, but she wasn't stupid; she ignored Anthony's "advice." The group drove around for a while, but they couldn't find the party. Maybe, Anthony said, it had already been broken up by the cops. The boys suggested they head to a familiar park instead, and the girls agreed. When Anthony drove to a wooded area that Maddie didn't recognize, she didn't say anything—she didn't want to appear uncool in front of older kids—but she surreptitiously took a screenshot with her phone. The next day, the Geotag showed the boys had lied: they were nowhere near where they claimed to be. Anthony and Paige strolled off into the trees, leaving Maddie alone with Josh. He pushed her against the car door and began to kiss her. Maddie didn't want to be there, didn't want to be kissing him. She felt angry, confused, maybe a little scared. "God damn it," she thought, "what am I supposed to do?" She tried to tell herself it would be over soon: Anthony and Paige would come back and they'd go to a real party, where she could ditch Josh. When she described what she actually said to him, though, she used the tiny, helpless voice teenage girls lapse into when they're uncomfortable, when they don't want to offend. "I was like, 'Okay, we don't have to keep doing this, get off now!'" she said.

Josh grabbed her wrist and pulled her deeper into the woods. He backed her against a tree and began kissing her again. "I knew this was not good, that I needed to leave," Maddie said. But where could she go? When Josh began pushing down on her shoulders, she shrugged him off. He persisted. She moved his hands. After a few more tries, he finally said, "Oh, is that too hard for you? Do you not want to do it?"

"No, it's not 'too hard,'" Maddie replied, "I just don't want to do *anything* with you." To spare his feelings, she said it was out of respect for her friend, the one he'd called "crazy."

"She doesn't have to know," Josh said.

Maddie shook her head. "No. I just don't want to." At that, she said, Josh began to pout, acting injured and rejected. Just then, Anthony began honking his car horn.

They scrambled into the backseat and Josh brandished a bottle of rum. "I don't know where the top is," he said, "and we can't drive with an open bottle in the car." He thrust it toward Maddie, adding, "So you have to drink it."

Maddie shook her head. She did not want to drink any more.

"Oh, it's okay," Anthony explained. "Rum makes your blood alcohol go up, but you won't feel drunk."

Maybe she was just trying to get through a dicey evening, trying to avoid antagonizing two large, older boys; besides, Anthony wouldn't start the car until that bottle was empty. "Be cool," she told herself as they passed it around. "Just get yourself home, get to bed." She tried faking a few sips, but in the end, she guesses she downed about six shots. After that, her memory fragmented. She recalled crying more over Kyle's betrayal. She remembered going to a fast-food drive-thru. She remembered Josh pulling her onto his lap. And then she blacked out.

Don't Tell Girls Not to Drink; Tell Rapists Not to Rape

At the heart of the argument over consent is another argument over alcohol. How drunk is too drunk to mean yes? How drunk is too drunk to be unable to say no? Who bears responsibility for making that call? An estimated 80 percent of campus assaults involve alcohol, typically consumed voluntarily; often both victim and assailant (or assailants) have been drinking. As I wrote earlier, the party culture on college campuses (as well as in many high school communities) can act as cover for rapists, especially repeat rapists. Yet in 2013, when Emily Yoffe wrote on *Slate DoubleX* that girls should be warned that heavy drinking increases their vulnerability to having sexual violence perpetrated against them, she was pilloried for victim-blaming. *The Atlantic*, *New York Magazine*, *Jezebel*, *Salon*, *Huffington Post*, the *Daily Mail*, *Feministing*, and even colleagues at *Slate DoubleX* itself labeled her a "rape apologist." During the ensuing furor, a generation gap emerged. Older women—that is, women the same age as Yoffe (a category that includes this author)—thought her advice sounded sensible. She wasn't, after all, saying that a drunk girl *deserved* to be raped or that it was her fault if she was. Nor was she saying that sobriety guaranteed protection against sexual assault. She only seemed to be voicing what most of us would tell our daughters: alcohol reduces your ability to recognize and escape a dangerous situation. Women metabolize liquor differently from men, too, reaching a higher blood alcohol level drink for drink and becoming more impaired than a guy the same size and weight. Given the prevalence of binge drinking on campus, shouldn't they know that?

Many young women, though, countered with a stance similar to the one they held on dress codes: don't tell us not to drink, tell rapists not to rape. If you really want to reduce assault, they said, wouldn't it be equally, if not more, logical to target *boys'* alcohol abuse, especially since perpetrators are about as likely to be drinking as victims? Alcohol has proven to have a profound influence on would-be rapists' behavior. It lowers their inhibition; it allows them to disregard social cues or a partner's hesitation; it gives them the nerve they may not otherwise have to use force; and it offers a ready justification for misconduct. The more that potential rapists drink, the more aggressive they are during an assault, and the less aware of their victims' distress. By contrast, sober guys not only are less sexually coercive but will more readily step up if they believe an alcohol-related assault is in the offing.

Activists are correct in saying that the only thing that 100 percent of rapes have in common is a rapist. You can shroud women from head to toe, forbid them alcohol, imprison them in their homes—and there will still be rape. Plus, you will live in Afghanistan. To me, this seems like another of those both/and situations. I have a hard time defending *anyone's* inalienable right to get shit-faced, male or female, especially when they're underage. What's that, you say? Harmless collegiate rite of passage? Six hundred thousand students ages eighteen to twenty-four are unintentionally injured each year while under the influence; 1,825 die. Teens who drink in high school, confident in their heightened alcohol tolerance, are at particular risk of harm in college.

I happen to live in Berkeley, California, the town where my state's best and brightest come for their education—the average high school grade point average of incoming freshmen here is 4.46. Yet, in the first two months of the 2013/14 school year, paramedics transported 107 of these smarty-pants students, all perilously intoxicated, to the hospital. During "move-in weekend" alone, the volume of calls about alcohol poisoning to 911 was so high that the city had to request ambulances from neighboring towns; the local ER was overrun with drunk students, forcing diversion of those vehicles elsewhere. (Heaven help the "townie" who happened to have a stroke or a heart attack on one of those nights.) In that same two-month period, incidentally, campus police cited exactly two kids for underage drinking. And yet when binge drinking rises, so does sexual assault. As part of an investigative story by the local ABC-TV affiliate, a paramedic who responded to some UC Berkeley calls, his face blurred and voice distorted to avoid reprisals, told a reporter that he had personally stopped a group of these top-tier college boys as they dragged an unconscious girl out of a party; one admitted he didn't even know her. "Who knows what their intentions were?" the paramedic mused. Nine rapes were reported in the first three months of the 2014/15 school year; five on one night when members of a non-recognized fraternity allegedly slipped "roofies" into their female classmates' drinks, rendering them defenseless.

As a parent, I am all for harm reduction. So I will absolutely explain to my daughter the particular effects of alcohol on the female body. I will explain how predators leverage that difference by using liquor itself as a date rape drug, and how bingeing increases everyone's vulnerability to a variety of health and safety concerns. I know that getting loaded can seem an easy way to reduce social anxiety, help you feel like you fit in, quiet the nagging voice in your head of paralytic self-doubt. Still, knocking back six shots in an hour in order to have fun—or, for that matter, to prove *you* are fun—is, perhaps, overkill. Nor is it ideal to gin up courage to have sex that would otherwise feel too "awkward"—even if the results are consensual, the sex will probably suck. Two people who are lit may *both* behave in a manner they will later regret—or not fully remember, making consent difficult to determine. Should that constitute assault? Students themselves are divided. Nearly everyone in a 2015 *Washington Post*/Kaiser Family Foundation poll of current and former college students agreed that sex with someone who is incapacitated or passed out is rape (a huge and welcome cultural shift). But if *both* people are incapacitated? Only about one in five agree; roughly the same percentage say that is *not* assault, and nearly 60 percent are unsure. That's understandable, given the paradox of students' sexual lives: drunkenness is obligatory for hookups, yet liquor negates consent. There are bright lines—lots of them—and they are too often crossed. But there are also situations that are confusing and complicated for everyone. Recall Holly, who mixed Red Bull and shots (a combination that makes a person appear deceptively sober) before blacking out? Maybe she seemed coherent and eager to have sex; maybe her partner was equally drunk and oblivious; maybe he was stone-cold sober and consciously targeted her; she'll never know.

So I'll tell my daughter that it's possible to make mistakes, that not all scenarios are as clear as we would like. That said, if, for whatever reason, she does get wasted—because it's part of the culture she's in or because she wants to see what it feels like or because the drink didn't taste strong—and, God forbid, is targeted for assault, it is positively, in no way, under any circumstances, her fault. I will tell her that nothing ever, ever, *ever* justifies rape. Victims are *never* responsible for an assailant's actions and need not feel shame or be silenced. If I had a son? I would be equally clear with him: drunk girls are not "easy pickings"; their poor choices are not your free pass to sex. I would tell him that heavy drinking, in addition to potential long-term physical harm, impairs boys' ability to detect or respect nonconsent. I would say that if there is *any* doubt about a girl's capacity to say yes—if the thought even flits across his mind—he should, for his own safety as well as hers, move along. There will be other opportunities to have sex (truly, there will be). So although I get why, for both parents and policy makers, focusing on girls' drinking is tempting, it is simply not enough.

"Maddie, You Were Raped"

Later, Paige filled Maddie in on what had happened. The boys dared her to kiss Paige, which she did. Then she kissed Josh, crowing, "I'm the queen of the car because all of you like me the best!"

"If you really want to be queen of the car," Anthony told her, "you have to have sex in the car."

"Okay," Maddie replied, turning to Josh. "Let's do it!"

Maddie insisted on a condom, which made Paige believe the girl was lucid. Anthony, who had one, passed it back to Josh. Maddie remembered, sort of, telling Josh to take off her pants because, drifting in and out of consciousness, she was too drunk to do it herself. She remembered waking up at one point as the car sped through the side streets of her town; she was on top of someone but didn't know who it was or how she'd gotten there. When she realized the person was having intercourse with her, she began to cry. "But I couldn't talk and I couldn't really move," she said. "And I don't think he realized I was crying because he was so into what he was doing." There are more shards of memory, but they are much the same: confusion, tears, incapacitation. Finally, Josh finished, and Maddie rolled to the corner of the car, managing somehow to pull on her pants.

"I want to go home," she said, but the other three were looking for another party.

"No!" Maddie said. "Take me home!"

"What's your problem?" Paige asked, annoyed. "Why are you crying?"

Maddie only cried harder, repeating that she wanted to go home. At that, the other three grew nervous. "Get her out of here," someone said, and they dropped her off, alone, at a strip mall near her house.

The next morning, during an early shift at her job at a neighborhood café, Maddie would periodically start to cry, though she couldn't quite say why. "I knew something bad had happened," she told me, "but I couldn't put my finger on why I was so upset about it." When she got off work, she asked a friend to meet her, and confided what she remembered.

"Maddie," the girl said, "you were raped."

Maddie denied it, but her friend knew Anthony, the boy driving the car, and called him on the spot. "You let this girl get raped in the back of your car!" she told him. He denied it, too, asking to talk to Maddie directly. She remembered his voice as gentle, soothing. "Look," he said, "I know you had a bad night, and you're upset, but you didn't get raped. Stop telling people that."

"I'm *not* telling people that," she said and hung up. When she and her friend got to her home, her friend said she was going to tell Maddie's mom. "I'm sorry," she said, "but I don't know what to do, and someone needs to take care of this."

Maddie went to her room so she wouldn't have to see her parents' reaction. A little while later, her father knocked on the door, a notebook in hand. She told him the story in as much detail as she could muster.

"Why didn't you say no?" he asked.

"I did!" she said. "But then I just got drunker and . . . I don't know, I can't explain." Maddie didn't go back to school that Monday, or the day after that, or the day after that. She hardly got out of bed for a week. Paige, meanwhile, began spreading rumors, claiming that Maddie had cried rape because she was embarrassed to have lost her virginity in the back of a moving car. Strangers on Facebook posted that Maddie was "a lying whore." Few classmates, boys or girls, took her side. "None of them knew what actually happened," Maddie said. "*I* didn't know what actually happened. I still don't. There are still parts of the story I'm not clear on."

Not even her (now former) friends stood by her. "They'd say, 'I wasn't there, so I can't judge if it was true or not.' And I'd be like, 'Why aren't you just taking my side? I thought we were friends!' " Josh, unsurprisingly, called her a liar, too. He did contact her directly once, via text, early on. "Are you telling people I raped you?" he asked. She texted back that she was not. He never got in touch again. "Obviously no guy is going to admit to that," she said. "I don't expect him to. I don't expect him to ever apologize. Why would he? In his eyes he didn't do anything wrong. It's not like he took me to a dark alley to rape me. He just really wanted to have sex, and I said no, and it hurt his pride."

One of the only people to stick by Maddie was Josh's former girlfriend—or hookup buddy, or whatever she was: the one Maddie said he'd treated badly. "She believed me without question," Maddie said. "That stuff with him pushing on my shoulders? He did that kind of thing to her, too. And there have been two other girls who told me he's done similar stuff to them. But mine was the only time it turned into this huge mess." Maddie shook her head and sighed. "I think he'll get in trouble at some point, though."

Christmas break came, and Maddie hoped that, with it, the incident would be forgotten; it wasn't. As December turned to January and classes resumed, the gossip spiraled out of control: Maddie was pregnant! Maddie had had an abortion! She withdrew from school and stopped going online or checking texts. Eventually, she enrolled here, at the community college. At least one of her female classmates, she has discovered, was there for the same reason.

What Yes Means

One of the Big Bads that conservatives warned of in the 1990s was that if alcohol-induced assaults were included in the defini-

tion of rape, college administrators would be swamped by venge-
ful girls who regretted their previous night's encounters. As if
it's easy for a victim of sexual assault to come forward. As if girls
have been readily believed. As if it weren't social suicide. As if
they wouldn't be shunned, called sluts, blamed, harassed, and
threatened. Consider the reaction in 2014 on CollegiateACB, a
forum where students anonymously discuss campus issues, after
a Vanderbilt University student's rape accusations resulted in the
suspension of a fraternity. Forum users demanded to know the
identity of "the girl who ratted"—a name was actually posted—
and called her, among other things, "manic depressive," "a crazy
bitch," "psycho," "NASTY AS SHIT," "a no good CUNT," and,
over and over, a "snitch." "This repeated use of the word 'snitch-
ing' in the thread," wrote André Rouillard, editor of the school's
newspaper, "implies that the victim has revealed a secret that
should have been kept hidden behind closed doors—under the
rug and on floors that stick like flypaper and stink of old beer.
. . . The OP [original poster] issues a rallying cry: 'we need to
stick together and prevent shit like this from being ok.'" By "shit
like this" he didn't mean rape; he meant girls' reporting of it.

Those trying to prove that campuses are rife with psycho
young women just itching to ruin their male classmates' lives
were inadvertently handed an opportunity in the spring of 2015,
when *Rolling Stone* magazine retracted an article on a gang rape
at the University of Virginia that had fallen apart under scrutiny.
I don't know if that scandal will become the cornerstone of a
new suppression of activism—these are different times than the
1990s—but as a Columbia University Graduate School of Journalism investigation concluded, *Rolling Stone*'s editors "hoped
their investigation would sound an alarm about campus sexual
assault and would challenge Virginia and other universities to do

better. Instead, the magazine's failure may have spread the idea that many women invent rape allegations."

There are, absolutely, false charges of rape. To say otherwise would be absurd. But they are rarer than alarmists would like you to believe. Legally, a "false report" is one in which it can be *demonstrably* proven that a rape was not committed. When investigators find that assault did not occur, that is something else: an unsubstantiated or inconclusive report. Conservative pundits such as Hoff Sommers, Cathy Young, and Wendy McElroy—plus every troll ever on the Internet—assert that 40 to 50 percent of sexual assault accusations are actually *false*. (Although, oddly, as criminologist Jan Jordan has pointed out, while adamant that half of accusers lie, such critics believe women who recant are unfailingly truthful.) In her book *Rape Is Rape*, Jody Raphael explains that this statistic comes from a 1994 report for which Eugene J. Kanin, a sociologist at Purdue University, compiled one police agency's characterizations of forty-five assault claims made over nine years in a small midwestern town—assessments that were not necessarily based on evidence or investigation. Kanin himself cautioned that his findings should not be generalized, and admitted, "Rape recantations could be the result of the complainants' desire to avoid a 'second assault' at the hands of the police." More credible, Raphael wrote, are seven rigorous studies conducted in the United States and the United Kingdom over more than three decades. They place false claim rates at between 2 and 8 percent, a number, according to FBI statistics, that has been steadily dropping since 1990, when the controversy over acquaintance rape emerged. Certainly it is important to bear in mind the potential for false claims, but our fear of them seems strangely disproportionate, especially given that most victims are not believed, that 80 percent of campus rapes are never even reported, and a mere 13 to 30 percent of assailants are found responsible among the sliver that are.

Emily Yoffe, who also raises the specter of an "overcorrection" on campus rape, has objected that lumping psychologically coerced or pressured sex into statistics risks "trivializing" assault. She, too, fears it would tempt any girl who "regrets making out with a boy who has 'persuaded' her" to file a complaint that could lead to his expulsion. "We may be teaching a generation of young men that pressuring a woman into sexual activity is never a good idea," she acknowledged, "but we are also teaching a generation of young women that they are malleable, weak, 'overwhelmed,' and helpless in the face of male persuasion."

This is where she and I part ways. Most sexual interludes among high school or college students are, obviously, not violent: They are consensual and wanted, if not always reciprocal. That said, a sizable percentage is coerced; rather than "trivializing" rape, Yoffe risks "trivializing" the way such pressure is seen as a masculine right and how that shapes our understanding of consent— even of sex itself. Despite changing roles in other realms, boys continue to be seen as the proper initiators of sexual contact. (If you don't believe me, listen to the outrage of mothers of teen boys when discussing today's "aggressive" girls.) Boys' sex drive is considered natural, and their pleasure a given. They are supposed to be sexually confident, secure, and knowledgeable. Young women, as I've said, remain the gatekeepers of sex, the inertia that stops the velocity of the male libido. Those dynamics create a haven for below-the-radar offenses that make a certain level of sexual manipulation, even violence, normal and acceptable. I don't know that such acts deserve expulsion, but they are worthy of serious discussion. As Lorelei Simpson Rowe, a clinical psychologist at

Southern Methodist University who works with girls on refusal skills, explains, "The vast majority of sexual violence and coercion occurs in situations that are not obviously dangerous . . . so if nine times you go out with a boy and engage in consensual activity, and it's pleasant and you're excited to be developing a relationship, that doesn't prepare you for that one time when it switches."

While such transformations may be sudden, frequently, Simpson Rowe says, they're not. "Guys will start saying, 'Come on, let's go further' or 'Why not?' or 'I really like you. Don't you like me?' There's a lot of persuading and pleading and guilt-inducing tactics, along with a lot of complimenting and flattery. And because it's subtle, you see a lot of self-questioning among girls. They wonder, 'Am I reading this right?' 'Did he actually say that?' 'Did he actually mean that?'" Simpson Rowe and her colleagues have developed a training program that uses virtual reality simulations to help girls recognize and resist those cues. In pilot trials of high school and college students, incoming participants generally rated themselves as confident that they could rebuff unwanted advances or escape threatening situations. Yet, when role-playing a range of increasingly fraught scenarios—from a male avatar who badgers girls for their phone numbers to one who threatens violence if they don't submit to sex—they would freeze. Simpson Rowe was quick to say that only perpetrators are responsible for assault, but assertiveness and self-advocacy are crucial defensive skills. "What we found is the importance of women being able to make quick, cognitive switches between normal sexual interaction and protecting their safety," she said. "And part of that involves being able to notice when something has gone from being a normal interaction to pressure."

The girls in her program worried that a direct rejection would hurt boys' feelings; they felt guilty and uncomfortable saying no.

"Girls have all this modeling for being nice and polite and caring and compassionate about others' feelings," Simpson Rowe explained. "These are wonderful things—good characteristics. But because they're so ingrained, a lot of women think this is how they're supposed to be when faced with an unsafe situation, and they're afraid of being seen as rude. The word that comes up a lot is *bitchy*. So, it's kind of an 'aha' moment when they realize a guy who is pressuring and persuading and not stopping when you say you don't want to do something is not respecting you or your boundaries—and at that point, *you don't have to worry about hurting his feelings*. We emphasize how early the coercive process begins and help them respond to it before it ever gets to violence." Preliminary data showed that three months after completing the ninety-minute training, participants had experienced half the rate of sexual victimization than a control group. Another risk-reduction program piloted among more than four hundred fifty Canadian college freshmen had similar results: a year later, rates of rape among participants were half that of girls who had only received a brochure. "We want to send the message that no one has the right to push or pressure you into what you don't want to do," Simpson Rowe said. "You have the right to stand up for yourself as loudly and physically as you want to and can."

Listening to Simpson Rowe, I thought about Megan, who told her rapist, "Thanks, I had fun." I thought about another girl I met, a freshman in college, who told me her high school boyfriend had raped her twice—once while they were together and once after they'd broken up, when he lured her into his car at a party to talk. Both times, she was drunk. Both times she told him no. Both times he ignored her. "I probably could have pushed him off of me or rolled over or screamed loud enough so someone could hear," she said, "but something prevented me from doing it each time. I'm a very strong person. I have very strong morals. I'm not embarrassed about talking about anything. But I didn't do anything. It was kind of like being paralyzed." I recalled Simpson Rowe's words again in the summer of 2015, when I read the court testimony of a former student at St. Paul's prep school in New Hampshire. A popular senior boy had assaulted her in the spring of her freshman year, she recounted, during an end-of-year rite known as "the senior salute," in which graduating male students compete to have sexual encounters with as many younger female students as possible. Initially flattered by his attentions, she testified, she joined him in a dark maintenance room but was at a loss as to how to respond to his escalating aggression. "I said, 'No, no, no! Keep it up here,'" she told the jury, gesturing to the area above her waist. "I tried to be as polite as possible." Even as he groped, bit, and penetrated her, she said, "I wanted to not cause a conflict."

Each of those girls could have used a session in Simpson Rowe's virtual reality simulator. At the same time, I also thought about a 2014 study in which nearly a third of college men agreed they would rape a woman if they could get away with it—though that percentage dropped to 13.6 percent when the word *rape* (as opposed to "force a woman to have sexual intercourse") was actually used in the question. Teaching girls to self-advocate, to name and express their feelings in relationships, is important for all kinds of reasons, and it may indeed help some of them stop or escape an assault. Yet, just as focusing on girls' drinking disregards rapists' behavior, keeping the onus on victims to repel boys' advances leaves the prerogative to pressure in place; it also maintains sexual availability as a girl's default position even if, as feminist pundit Katha Pollitt has written, she "lies there like lox with tears running down her cheeks, too frozen or frightened or trapped by lifelong habits of demureness to utter the magic word." Even if that girl were to say no loud and clear, the boy might not hear it.

"Affirmative consent" policies—versions of the one pioneered by Antioch—have once again become the hope for change. In 2014, California was the first state to pass a "yes means yes" law directed at colleges and universities receiving state funds. Rather than requiring an accuser to prove she said no, it demands that an alleged assailant prove that there was "an affirmative, unambiguous, and conscious decision by each participant to engage in mutually agreed-upon sexual activity." In other words, that a clear, enthusiastic "you bet," either verbally or through body language, was given. Consent may also be revoked anytime, and a person incapacitated due to drugs or alcohol is not legally able to give it. That's a fundamental shift in power relations, and twelve years after the "Is It Date Rape?" *SNL* sketch, fewer people are laughing. New York passed affirmative consent legislation in 2015. New Hampshire, Maryland, and Colorado are all considering similar bills. Every Ivy League school except Harvard now has a version of "yes means yes" in place as well.

Conservatives have predictably warned that thousands of boys will soon be ejected from colleges for trying for a good-night kiss. But the policies have made liberals uneasy as well. Ezra Klein, editor in chief of Vox, wrote that he supported the law, though he believed it would "settle like a cold winter on college campuses, throwing everyday sexual practice into doubt and creating a haze of fear and confusion over what counts as consent." The anxiety on both sides reminded me of the 1993 fears about California's then-innovative law against peer-to-peer sexual harassment in schools, which allowed districts to expel offenders as young as nine years old. But you know what? Twenty-plus years later, no fourth-graders have been shipped off to San Quentin for hazarding a playground smooch. Nor have school districts been bankrupted by a deluge of frivolous lawsuits. At the same time, the legislation has not stopped sexual harassment. It has, however, provided a framework through which students can understand and discuss the issue, and the potential for recourse, on a number of levels, when it happens. Remember Camila Ortiz, the girl who called out her vice principal when he told girls to cover up and "respect yourself"? She and a friend later organized a group of girls *and* boys to fight sexual harassment at their school. In the winter of 2015, group members addressed a meeting of the school board, presenting a petition signed by more than 750 students, both female and male; among their concerns was that the high school was out of compliance with both state and federal laws. The district's policy is now being redrafted. No one was expelled; no one was sued; no one went to jail. Plus, the students got a great lesson in civic responsibility, leadership, and making social change. Increased awareness has also reduced tolerance for the winking acceptance of harassment and assault. Anheuser-Busch found that out in 2015, when the company unveiled a new tag line for Bud Light: "The perfect beer for removing 'no' from your vocabulary for the night." American sensibilities had changed since the 1990s, as had the targets of influential comedians' humor. So, rather than mocking overly sensitive women, John Oliver drew cheers from his college-age studio audience by skewering the frat-boy mentality that allowed the slogan's approval: imagining Bud executives fist-pumping and shouting, "Sick idea, brah!" "That's what I'm talkin' about, *a'ight*," "*No, no, no, no*. That's what *I'm* talkin' about, son!" and a wordless, "*Blaaaaaaaaaaaaah!*" (The beer company had been forced several days prior to issue a public apology after news of the slogan had careened around Twitter.)

Will affirmative consent laws reduce campus assault? Will cases be more readily resolved? I can't say. As Pollitt pointed out, adjudication in many instances will still be based on he said/she said, with accused assailants replacing "She didn't say no" with "Dude, she said yes!" Among the students in the *Washington Post*/Kaiser Family Foundation poll, only 20 percent said the yes means yes standard was "very realistic" in practice, though an additional 49 percent considered it "somewhat realistic." What "yes means yes" may do, though, especially if states aim solid curricular efforts at younger students, as California plans to, is create a desperately needed reframing of the public conversation away from the negative—away from viewing boys as exclusively aggressive and girls as exclusively vulnerable, away from the embattled and the acrimonious—and toward what healthy, consensual, mutual encounters between young people ought to look like. Maybe it will allow girls to consider what they want—what they *really* want—sexually, and at last give them license to communicate it; maybe it will allow boys to more readily listen.

THAT WAS THE hope of a Bay Area nonprofit that invited me to observe a focus group of high schoolers convened on a November afternoon to discuss consent.

The kids—two African American boys, two white boys, two white girls, a Latina, and an Asian girl—sprawled across couches in a borrowed living room, their conversation subtly guided by a twenty-something facilitator. Over the course of several hours, they wrestled with how alcohol-fueled hookups made "yes" feel like a moving target; with the social costs of saying a direct "no"; with the awkwardness of intervening when a drunk friend was hurtling toward regret; with how they negotiated, or didn't, consent in their long-term relationships. They talked about assault, too. Two of the girls had experienced some form of violation; another was trying to come to terms with troubling accusations by one close friend against another. One of the boys, too, had been lured into sex by an older classmate when he was too drunk to refuse. He wanted to know: was that rape?

More often, though, they talked about the complexity of establishing basic boundaries, with partners and within themselves, in a culture of contradiction, in which there has been some, but not enough, change in the expectations for, consequences of, and meaning of sex for both boys and girls. "Like, okay, 'yes means yes,'" said Michael, who had pushed his shaggy hair, Mark Sanchez style, back in a headband. "But how does that 'yes' change with every situation you're in? When you're drunk, what does that 'yes' mean? Or is it only really 'yes' when you're sober?"

"And what about people getting drunk in *order* to say yes?" Annika added, sitting forward eagerly, her elbows resting on her knees. "I know a situation where two people were interested in each other and asked a friend to have a party so that they could get drunk and hook up."

Caleb, who had a "fade" haircut and red plastic glasses, jumped in. "The whole problem is that hooking up sober is not so attractive."

Annika nodded and continued. "And yes can mean different things, *especially* if I'm drunk. Like, did I say yes because I wanted to hook up with *this* person or because I wanted to hook up with *someone*, or because my friends think it would be cool if I hooked up with that person?"

Nicole confided that when her "gut" told her to end a hookup, she would immediately start a mental tally of everything she had done up until that point—locked eyes with a boy across a room, flirted, touched his shoulder, kissed him, taken off her shirt—that would have led him to believe she would say yes to more. "And I'm already feeling guilty and worrying about what will happen in that moment of confrontation when I actually say to him, 'This is my boundary.'"

"It's so complex," said Gabriel, who wore a five-panel cap and a U.S. Marine Corps T-shirt. "As a guy, you have to do the best *you* can do to prevent a situation from happening in the future. You have to train yourself to look at someone and say, 'Are you okay with this? Are you one hundred percent sure? Is this definitely a yes?'"

Lauren, who had recently broken up with her boyfriend, quietly offered that even in a long-term relationship, consent could feel tricky. "It's like if you've had sex once, you've said yes forever," she said, and two other girls nodded. "And it's always going to end that way no matter what was voiced or what was wanted at that moment, because once you get to that point with someone, that's what always happens." "Good girlfriends" say yes, no matter what. They consent—or at least comply—freely, even if the sex is unwanted. They take one for the team to keep their relationships stable, their partners happy. What, these young people wondered, do you call that?

"You know," Michael said, "hearing all this . . . I was in a relationship for about a year and I think . . . I was probably on the other side of that equation. I think . . . I didn't mean to, but I was probably subconsciously pressuring my girlfriend." He fell silent for a moment, pondering that. "I don't know that I want to be, like, a leader in gender equality," he continued, "but whatever I end up doing, wherever I end up going, this is going to be something I incorporate. I think just by doing that with the people you meet at school or the people you work with that you can have considerable influence in changing a culture, a community. I really do."

"I Know What It Feels Like to Be Told, 'It's Not Rape.'"

"Do you think you were raped?" I asked Maddie.

She gazed down at her fingers and shrugged. I considered the decades of argument behind that question: not long ago, the answer, maybe my own answer, would have been a definitive no. So much had changed, and so much had not. "Legally?" Maddie asked. "Yes, I was. Asking for a condom doesn't imply consent. But the way everyone treated me afterward . . ." She shrugged. "People will say, 'You had to switch schools because of *that*? That's *nothing*.' And guys are like, 'Oh, that's not rape.' So, I don't know." Maddie fell silent a moment. "Lately, I've been writing blog posts and articles on changing 'rape culture.' Because I know what it feels like to be told, 'It's not rape.' And I know how horrible it was afterward. If I can prevent that, or worse, from happening to someone else, that's all I want to do."

Maddie had been careful during our conversation never to use her assailant's real name. At one point, though, she slipped, and once I was home, it was the work of a moment to find him online. He'd been on the basketball and track teams in his high school, appeared to be a solid student. He'd joined a frat this year, as a college freshman. None of that meant he'd assault someone, though both his history and interests put him at risk: fraternity brothers and athletes are disproportionately represented among repeat offenders. My eyes fell on the name of the large university he attended. I had, at that time, eight nieces who were also college students. It chilled me to realize that he was in school with one of them.

CHAPTER 7

What If We Told Them the Truth?

Charis Denison stood before seventy tenth-graders in the all-purpose room of a Northern California high school. A blond woman in her early fifties, permanently tanned from a former career as a wilderness ranger, she was barefoot, having kicked off her boho-chic wedge sandals, and was wearing her habitual tunic and jeans. A silver chain encircled one ankle, and a beaded mesh bracelet wound up her left arm. On her right hand, above a stack of jangling bangles, she sported a plush, anatomically correct vulva puppet. At the moment, her finger was fondling its clitoris as she commented, "I talk to so many girls where the first person to actually touch their clitoris is somebody else." There have been times over the past two hours when the students—both boys and girls—who were sprawled across the carpeted floor, were a little squirrelly, a bit inattentive. Now, though, they were rapt. "It's hard when you're trying to have a sexual experience with someone and you don't know what feels good to *you*," Denison said. "It's hard to let someone else have that power to decide. So if someone is choosing to become sexually active with someone else, it's really good to be sexual with oneself first. It's good to figure out what you like."

That's right. Denison just encouraged teenage girls to masturbate, and she did it in front of teenage boys. She told the whole class not only that girls have clitorises but what those organs are for—the *only* thing that they are for: to make them feel good. And that, in the annals of American sex education, is nearly unheard of. Denison doesn't call herself a sex educator, though. She sees herself as a "youth advocate," providing accurate information and a nonjudgmental forum in which kids can discuss sex and substance use along with larger ideas of ethics and social justice. She travels to high school communities across California—most, given her frank approach, are private like this one, though an increasing number are public—visiting each class several times a year, building cumulatively on what came before. Her curriculum incorporates decision making, assertiveness skills, sexual consent, personal responsibility, gender roles, and the diversity of sexual orientation and gender identity. But "my job," as she told today's tenth-graders, "my *whole* job is to help you make as many decisions as possible that end in joy and honor rather than regret, guilt, or shame."

Denison talks about risk and danger in her classes (though she doesn't necessarily use that language). She addresses anatomy and contraception, if those aren't part of students' regular health curriculum. By graduation, even if her students plan to stay abstinent until marriage ("which is *awesome!*") or will never have sex with a man, she expects them, nonetheless, to be able to put on a condom, "drunk, dizzy, and in the dark." She also talks about something usually omitted in the parental "talk" and by the football coaches who, inexplicably, teach "health": sexual activity should be a source of pleasure for teenagers. Not only is hers a more honest perspective, but she believes (and research confirms) that it is ultimately the most effective strategy for reducing risk. "To some parents in school communities, that doesn't sound right," Denison told me, "but it *is* right. [Teens] abstain with more information because they have options, because they have knowledge, because they have alternatives. It's so clear to me that in this area the less specific and the less open we are, the more and more at risk we're putting these kids—especially girls."

Denison's approach is controversial, so controversial that I had a hard time finding a school that would let me observe her in action. Her philosophy doesn't exactly jibe with the just-say-no thinking that's dominated sex ed for the last three decades, but it's one that is slowly, gradually gaining credence. In 2011 the *New York Times Magazine* profiled Al Vernacchio, a revolutionary Philadelphia educator who famously compares sex to eating a pizza: Both start with internal desire—with hunger, with appetite. In both cases, you may decide, for any number of reasons, that it's not the right time to indulge. If you do proceed, there should be some discussion, some negotiation—maybe you like pepperoni and your dining companion doesn't, so you go halfsies, or agree that one person will get his pick next time, or choose a different topping altogether—and a good-faith effort to satisfy everyone involved. There is no rounding bases in that metaphor, no striking out. The emphases are desire, mutual consent, communication, collaboration, process, and shared enjoyment.

Similarly, in 2009 the Population Council published the *It's All One Curriculum*, downloadable for free online, created in conjunction with, among others, the United Nations General Assembly, the World Health Organization, UNAIDS, and UNESCO. Integrating ideas about human rights and gender sensitivity, these guidelines aim to help educators and others "develop the capacity of young people to enjoy—and advocate for their rights to—dignity, equality and responsible satisfying and healthy sexual lives." That curriculum, like Denison's and Vernacchio's, presents sexual exploration (whether alone or with others) as a normal part of adolescence. Sure, there are hazards, but there are also joys, and our role as caring adults is to help our kids balance the two. I admit that, as a mom, the idea of my child becoming sexually active is only marginally less mortifying than the thought of my parents doing anything beyond the three reproductively necessary acts it took to conceive my brothers and me. But the consequences of parental silence, classroom moralizing, and media distortion are far worse. There has to be a better way.

Strange Bedfellows: Sex and Politics

In 1959 abortion was still criminal. Unmarried women could not legally procure contraception, and pharmacists, according to sociologist Kristin Luker, author of *When Sex Goes to School*, would refuse to sell condoms to men they thought were single. Although, even then, over half of women and three-quarters of men had intercourse before their wedding day, there was broad public agreement that sex should be reserved for marriage. That was about to change—radically and quickly. The introduction of the birth control pill in 1960 was the first salvo in the sexual revolution. That was followed three years later by the publication of *The Feminine Mystique*, which launched a new wave of feminism. A decade after that, the Supreme Court guaranteed women's right to abortion. As sex became untethered from reproduction, the notion of "waiting until marriage," or even until adulthood, grew increasingly obsolete: between 1965 and 1980 the percentage of sixteen-year-old girls who'd ever had intercourse doubled. A group of activists, led by Mary Calderone, the physician who founded the Sex Information and Education Council of the United States (SIECUS), hoped those changes would herald an age of positive, value-neutral, medically accurate sex education.

That was not to be. Instead, according to Jeffrey Moran, author of *Teaching Sex*, to ensure minors' ongoing access to contraception, congressional liberals skewed negative, popularizing the idea that teen sex, while perhaps inevitable, was inherently risky and a "crisis" requiring damage control. They argued that the "epidemic" of teen motherhood triggered by the new sexual freedom was, particularly among African Americans, responsible for spiraling poverty. (In truth, although the birth rate among black girls was three times higher than among whites, the overall teen birth rate dropped steadily through the 1960s and 1970s.) The only pragmatic response was to teach kids to protect themselves. So the Adolescent Health Services and Pregnancy Prevention and Care Act of 1978, introduced by Senator Edward Kennedy, while perpetually underfunded, championed educational programs that would focus on risk management, contraception, abortion education, counseling, and "values clarification." It also established a murky, nonspecific idea of "readiness," rather than marriage, as the expected standard for sexual behavior. That, Moran wrote, infuriated conservatives. As Diane Ravitch, an educational consultant and activist, railed (inaccurately, by the way), "Is it appropriate for the government to teach its citizenry how to masturbate? To explain how to perform cunnilingus? To reassure them that infidelity is widespread?"

With that, sex education, previously relegated to innocuous "Family Life" classes, where it was embedded in lessons on successful marriage, became a battleground: a vector for right-wing trepidation about the erosion of traditional matrimony, the rise of women's rights, the growing acceptance of homosexuality, even the potential dismantling of gender itself. In 1981, partly as a reward for the New Right's support of his presidential bid, Ronald Reagan signed what was nicknamed "the chastity law," the first legislation requiring that federally funded sex education, as its sole purpose, teach "the social, psychological and health gains to be realized by abstaining from sexual activity." Reagan, however, allocated only $4 million a year to the bill; it wasn't until the Clinton administration—oh, the irony!—that annual funding for abstinence education shot up to $60 million, a slab of pork tucked into the 1996 Welfare Reform Act. As the money grew, the message it promoted became even more restrictive: to get the cash, public schools would now have to teach that marriage was the *only* acceptable sphere for physical relations, and that sex outside of it at any age (including after divorce or widowhood) would lead to irreparable physical and emotional harm.

Under George W. Bush, the funding for abstinence-until-marriage programs continued to rise, reaching, at its peak, $176 million a year. So it was that in 1988, when the AIDS epidemic was in full swing, only 2 percent of sex ed teachers taught abstinence as the best way to prevent pregnancy or disease, yet by 1999, 40 percent of those supposedly teaching comprehensive sex ed considered it the most important message they were trying to convey. By 2003, 30 percent of public school sex education classes provided *no information whatsoever* about condoms or other contraceptives (beyond their failure rates) and by 2005 over 80 percent of federally funded abstinence-only programs were found by a congressional report to be teaching blatantly inaccurate information, including such "facts" as that the Pill is only 20 percent effective in preventing pregnancy, that latex condoms cause cancer, that HIV can be transmitted through sweat or tears, and that half of homosexual teen boys already have the virus.

All together, the federal government has spent $1.7 billion plus on abstinence-only programs since 1982; that money might just as well have been set on fire. As I mentioned earlier, while virginity pledgers delayed intercourse for a few months longer than their nonpledging peers, when they did become sexually active, they were less likely to protect themselves or their partners against pregnancy or disease. The same holds true for participants in abstinence-only classes. Studies stretching back over a decade have found that, at best, when compared to a control group, participants neither abstain entirely from sex nor delay intercourse; they also do not have fewer sexual partners. They are, however, a lot more likely to become unintentionally pregnant: as much as 60 percent more likely. That could lead one to suspect that abstinence-only advocates are more concerned with ideology than with public health or even sexual restraint— otherwise they would have given it up long ago for something that has been repeatedly proven to reduce teens' sexual activity, increase their use of contraception and disease protection, and improve their relationships: comprehensive sex education.

Under President Barack Obama, comprehensive sex ed finally got its first federal love, although the focus remained squarely on reducing negative consequences: $185 million earmarked for research and programs that have been shown, through rigorous evaluation, to reduce teen pregnancy. That money, of course, could easily disappear under another, less progressive commander in chief, and probably will: for instance, a clause buried in the Student Success Act, a Republican rewrite of No Child Left Behind that passed the House in the summer of 2015, zeros out any funding for programs that "normalize teen sexual activity as an expected behavior, implicitly or explicitly, whether homosexual or heterosexual." Meanwhile, $75 million in abstinence-only funds continued to be doled out each year through the Affordable Care Act. While substantially less than under President Bush, that's still an awful lot to blow on the sex ed equivalent of a tinfoil hat.

What this means for parents is that you never know what your child's "sex education" class may entail. Only fourteen states require that sex ed be medically accurate. Yet even that is no guarantee. Mine is supposed to be one of them. Yet it wasn't until the spring of 2015 that a judge ruled for the first time against a public school system that was actively teaching misinformation: students in the city of Clovis, California, had for years been made to watch videos that compared an unmarried woman who had intercourse to a "dirty shoe" and were encouraged to chant the antigay motto "One man, one woman, one life." Around that same time, Alice Dreger, a professor of medical humanities and bioethics at Northwestern University's Feinberg School of Medicine, live-tweeted her son's abstinence-based sex education class from a public high school in politically progressive East Lansing, Michigan. Instructors there warned about the potential failure rates of contraceptives, citing, as an example, a box of condoms in which *every single one had a hole*! They also advised the boys to seek out "good girls" who say no to sex. At one point, Dreger tweeted, the students were told, " 'We are going to roll this dice 8 times. Every time your number comes up, pretend your condom failed and you get a paper baby.' " She followed that up shortly with "Paper babies are being handed out to EVERYONE. They have ALL HAD CONDOM FAILURE AND THE WHOLE CLASS IS PREGNANT." When it was over, Dreger tweeted, "I just want to grab all those kids after school and say HERE IS

THE TRUTH. SEX FEELS GOOD. THAT'S WHY YOU SEEK IT. TAKE CARE & HAVE FUN."

Life Is Like an English Essay

Nearly twenty-five years ago, while teaching English and leading outdoor programs at an all-girls' private school, Charis Denison had an epiphany. So many of the critical lessons of middle and high school took place outside the classroom. Her students wanted (needed) to talk about their experience, but didn't know how, and anyway, there was nowhere they could try. "I started feeling that we were failing these kids," she told me. What would happen if she carved out a formal space for those conversations? What would happen if she encouraged students to apply the rigorous critical skills they used in the classroom to life beyond it? "You wouldn't walk into an essay exam wondering which book the test was on, right?" she said. "But people will go to a party without any thought at all, not even of what they *don't* want to happen." Rather than blaming themselves when things go awry, students needed to remember, Denison began urging them, the "reflect-revise-redraft" strategy they used when editing a paper. "Instead of just thinking, 'Oh my God, that night was awful, that was horrible!' I want them to back it up and think, '*Why* did that suck? And what part did I play in it, and what part was out of my control?' Just like you would with a bad grade, or with anything else that goes wrong. Avoiding the blame game—just backing up, figuring it out, reflecting on it, revising your plan, forgiving yourself, and moving forward."

Denison consciously avoids labels like "good" and "bad," "responsible" and "irresponsible," even "healthy" and "unhealthy," in her classes. "Those are a matter of personal belief," she explained. "The idea of 'regret' works regardless." That's important, she said, because she teaches in communities that encompass a broad range of backgrounds and values. During time devoted to anonymous questions, one student might want to know, "Is it okay that I have casual hookups on a pretty regular basis?" Another, in the same class, might ask, "Is it okay if I wait until I get married to have sex?" "In that context, the idea of 'good' choices doesn't make sense," she explained. "What's key is to be able to talk about sex in a way that makes it equally comfortable for both of those students. So, if Monday morning, after you hooked up with a couple of guys, you feel joy, then that's the right choice. And from there we can back up and ask: Is that serving your partners, too? Is it clear that you're on the same page? And if you're not, does that really serve you? Then, for that girl who perceives sex as something she's holding on to and wants to keep as a part of her to give to a partner that she made a commitment to be with for the rest of her life: How does that feel? If you don't feel guilt, if you don't feel shame, if you're feeling joy and honor, then *bingo*. And if you are feeling guilt and shame, then let's talk about that. Where is it coming from? So developing this idea of 'How are the choices affecting me *and* the people around me? How are they serving me, and how are they serving my partner?'"

Much of Denison's curriculum, perhaps most of it, is not specifically about sex. It's about decision making and communication, skills that are useful in any realm. On another afternoon, I watched her with a group of ninth-graders she was meeting for the first time. She was explaining what she calls "fallbacks," unconscious, reflexive behaviors we resort to when we're uncomfortable. "A lot of fallbacks come from gender roles," she said. "A lot of them come from ways we cope in our families. Like, what if you want to do one thing after school and your friends want to do something else? Or you're in a situation and all of a sudden you're super uncomfortable and you don't know what to do?"

Book smarts won't necessarily help in those fight-or-flight moments, especially, perhaps, for girls. "I talk to a hundred girls a month who are superassertive, feminist, who can correct their teachers about the symbolism of a novel in class," she said. "Then they're at a party and some dude's hand is on their leg—or between their legs—and they feel like duct tape is over their mouths. They literally can't say, 'Can you move your hand?' Superassertive, but not in that situation, because they're using a different part of themselves. And then there's regret and shame. And that's just because we need to practice." Once again, the room has fallen silent, the kind of hush that occurs when a teacher has truly touched a nerve.

Denison asked for a volunteer, and Jackson, a lanky boy in a Chicago Bulls T-shirt, stood up. "People talk about 'assertive' all the time," Denison said. "And 'aggressive' and 'passive-aggressive.' Those are ways to think about how we react in the real world, especially when we are uncomfortable." She pulled out her cell phone. "So, let's say I borrowed Jackson's phone and said I'd have it back in a day. But it's been three days. Also, I've cracked the screen. Now I'm going to return it to him, and he's going to show us what a passive response would be."

She sauntered over and dumped the device in his hand. "Thanks for the phone, Jackson. It's awesome." She casually gestured to the imaginary crack, adding, "There's just, like, that little thing here."

"No problem," Jackson said.

"Really?" Denison took a step toward him. "Can I borrow it again, then?"

"No, um . . ."

She took another step. "Oh. Well, do you have a car?"

"Yeah, it's over there."

"Can I have the keys?" Jackson pretended to toss them to her, and the scene was over.

Denison turned to the class. "So his fallback was 'I'm uncomfortable, this is unpleasant, I want it to end, and agreeing with her is the fastest way.' But did you see how when I stepped forward and he backed away I was like, 'Yeah, I've got this. I do not have to be accountable in any way. I can take advantage.' So the bummer of that response is 'Am I going to come back?' Oh, *hell* yeah. He's got a Post-it on his forehead with a bull's-eye now. But if he could get to a place of thinking, 'How do I feel right now? What do I think? And what do I want to have happen?' Maybe it would be worth thirty seconds of doing something different so that this obnoxious girl will not come back."

A thin boy in a red-and-white striped shirt raised his hand. "So what exactly is an aggressive fallback?"

"Pushing back against someone before they can go after you," another boy said. "Or saying someone's an asshole."

"Or, like, yelling back if your parents start yelling at you," said one of the girls.

Denison had invited a handful of seniors, students the underclassmen respected, to join her today as de facto teaching assistants. One of them, a girl wearing a fedora and a vintage Violent Femmes T-shirt, raised her hand. "My fallback was, when someone asked, like, 'What do you want to eat?' I'd say, 'Whatever you want.' And I would never, ever, *ever* say what I wanted to do. I've been trying to change that, at least with people I'm comfortable around."

"So it must not have been working for you . . ." Dennison prompted.

The girl nodded. "I still do it often. But I didn't like never having the power within myself to say what I wanted. I was always so worried about people not liking me if I said what I might want to do."

"Bringing that back to the situations we're talking about," Denison said, "especially in the hookup scene, especially in the city, where there's so much more access to underage dance clubs—if that's your fallback, it's like a potential minefield of regret. Because there's a lot of ninth-graders who go to those clubs and they say they're not going to drink, they're just going to dance, but they don't think through situations that might make them uncomfortable, or come up with a plan.

"There's a lot of oral sex happening in these clubs, in the back hallways," she continued. "Sometimes it's because people know they don't want to have intercourse, but they haven't practiced saying, 'No, I'm not going to go down on you.' That just seems impossible to them. And then there's a lot of regrettable sexual behavior. And drinking, too. Because you get tired of saying no or getting your mom to text you that you have to come home. So, trying to come up with some real, workable tools, and especially working with your seniors here, people who've been there, is really helpful. And trying to get you guys at the beginning to identify two or three of your fallbacks, even by the end of this semester. Then let's talk about it over the next few years. Let's really work that muscle. To avoid regret and practice that assertiveness is so important. And what's cool is the more you practice the easier it gets."

They acted out a few more passive, aggressive, and assertive scenarios, with Denison urging volunteers to state firmly "How you feel right now, what you think, what you want to have happen." In the few minutes of class time that remained, she fielded several anonymous questions that students had submitted on index cards, then gave out the number for a cell phone she keeps specifically for their calls and texts. Some of her colleagues over the years have questioned Denison's willingness to let kids intrude on her life at any hour of the day or night. "They say it's a boundary issue," she told me later, "but I disagree. I come here and encourage students to question themselves, to name a situation when it's not going well, to acknowledge that it's not going well, and reflect on it. I promise I will advocate for them. If after that I disappeared, if I bailed, I wouldn't be doing my job." Most of the messages she receives are queries about basic facts involving sex and drugs; sometimes they are about relationship dilemmas or the choice between dueling visions of "regret"; sometimes they are just notes of gratitude. Typically they are anonymous, sometimes from friends of friends of students she's taught, kids she'll never meet. Among the texts she had recently received:

"My boyfriend won't touch me after he comes. Is that valid?"

"My girlfriend and I had a mishap with a condom and were wondering if we should get Plan B, but she is on a hormonal birth control pill. Would it be a bad idea to mix medication?"

"I am talking to this guy and he told me (through text), 'You act like you're never gonna suck a dick. That's, like, a girl's job. . . .' We've been 'a thing' for about two months, and I don't know what to do because I want to make a decision on handling this that I won't regret."

"I just took four busses and a train to follow a boy who called me a bitch a month ago and I need to know why I'm here."

"Charis: I so appreciate everything you do. You were such an incredible resource while I was in high school and have motivated me to start a sex ed radio show/podcast at my college!"

Scrolling through the texts, Denison shakes her head in

wonder. "If adults thought about their world and their choices as deeply as the teens who reach out to me do . . ." she said. "They're so thoughtful. Thoughtful before they do something. Thoughtful after they do something. Thoughtful while they do something. It's inspiring."

Going Dutch

Here's a solution for concerned parents: move to the Netherlands. Okay, maybe that's not the most practical advice. Perhaps, though, we can move a little of the Netherlands here. Because the Dutch seem to have it all figured out. While we in the United States have the highest teen pregnancy rate in the industrialized world, they have among the lowest. Our teen birth rate? Eight times higher than theirs, and our teen abortion rate is 1.7 times higher. Yes, there are some significant demographic differences that affect those numbers: we are a more diverse nation than Holland, with higher rates of childhood poverty, fewer social welfare guarantees, and more social conservatives. Yet even when controlling for all that, the difference holds. Consider a study comparing the early sexual experiences of four hundred randomly chosen American and Dutch women at two similar colleges—nearly all white, all middle class, with similar religious backgrounds. So, apples to apples. The American girls had become sexually active at a younger age than the Dutch, had had more encounters with more partners, and were less likely to use birth control. They were more likely to say they'd had first intercourse because of "opportunity" or pressure from friends or partners. In subsequent interviews with some of the participants, the Americans, much like the ones I met, described interactions that were "driven by hormones," in which boys determined re-lationships, male pleasure was prioritized, and reciprocity was rare. As for the Dutch girls? Their early sexual activity took place in loving, respectful relationships in which they communicated openly with their partners (whom they said they knew "very well") about what felt good and what didn't, about how "far" they wanted to go, and about what kind of protection they would need along the way. They reported more comfort with their bod-ies and their desires than the Americans and were more in touch with their own pleasure.

It's enough to make you rush out to buy a pair of wooden shoes.

What's their secret? The Dutch girls said that teachers and doctors had talked candidly to them about sex, pleasure, and the importance of a loving relationship. More than that, though, there was a stark difference in how their parents approached those topics. The American moms had focused on the potential risks and dangers of sex, while their dads, if they said anything at all, stuck to lame jokes. Dutch parents, by contrast, had talked to their daughters from an early age about both the joys and re-sponsibilities of intimacy. As a result, one Dutch girl said she told her mother immediately after her first intercourse, "because we talk very open[ly] about this. My friend's mother also asked me how it was, if I had an orgasm and if he had one."

The attitudes of the two nations weren't always so far apart. According to Amy Schalet, an associate professor of sociology at the University of Massachusetts and author of *Not Under My Roof*, in the late 1960s the Dutch, like Americans, roundly dis-approved of premarital sex. The sexual revolution transformed attitudes in both countries, but whereas American parents and policy makers responded by treating teen sex as a health crisis, the Dutch went another way: they consciously embraced it as natural, though requiring proper guidance. Their government made pelvic exams, birth control, and abortion free to anyone under twenty-two, with no requirements for parental consent. By the 1990s, when Americans were shoveling millions into the maw of useless abstinence-only education, Dutch teachers (and parents) were busy discussing the positive aspects of sex and relationships, as well as anatomy, reproduction, disease prevention, contraception, and abortion. They emphasized respect for self and others in intimate encounters, and openly addressed masturbation, oral sex, homosexuality, and orgasm. When a Dutch national poll found that most teenagers still believed that boys should be the more active partner during sex, the government added "interaction" skills to its sex ed curricula, such as how to let "the other person know exactly what feels good" and how to set boundaries. By 2005, four out of five Dutch youth said that their first sexual experiences were well timed, within their control, and fun. Eighty-six percent of girls and 93 percent of boys agreed that "We both were equally eager to have it." Compare that to the United States, where two-thirds of sexually experienced teenagers say they wish they had waited longer to have intercourse for the first time.

It's not just about sex, though—according to Schalet, there's a fundamental difference in the two countries' conceptions of how teenagers become adults. American parents consider adolescents to be innately rebellious, in thrall to their "raging hormones." We respond by cracking down on them, setting stringent limits, forbidding or restricting any behavior that might lead to sex or substance use. We end up with a self-fulfilling prophecy: teens assert independence by breaking rules, rupturing their relationships with parents, separating from the family. Sex, which typically involves sneaking around or straight-up lying, becomes a vehicle through which to do that. Charis Denison, for instance, told me that roughly half the questions she fields from students about parents involve how to get contraception or STD testing without Mom and Dad finding out; the other half are on how to bring up sensitive issues so they will actually listen. Both speak to a rift between teenagers and those who love them most—one we parents more or less create. Girls, Schalet said, particularly suffer, wrestling with the incompatibility of remaining a "good daughter" while becoming sexual. They end up either lying to their parents or copping to their behavior but keeping it invisible, outside the home. Either way, closeness can be compromised. Think back to Sam, who said her politically progressive parents behaved "more like a conservative household" where sex was concerned; Megan, who laughingly told me her dad "thinks I'm a virgin"; Holly, whose mother told her "you shouldn't be having sex" when she asked, at age nineteen, to go on the Pill. Each girl was forced to pretend with her parents, to act the innocent. That didn't change her behavior; it just left her unsupported and vulnerable.

Dutch teens, on the other hand, remain closely connected to parents, growing up in an atmosphere of *gezelligheid,* a word most Americans can't even pronounce, but which Schalet translates loosely as "cozy togetherness." Parents and teens are expected to discuss the children's psychological and emotional development, including their burgeoning sexual drives. As part of that, Dutch parents permit—wait for it—sleepovers, which are rare in the United States, except in the most progressive circles. A full two thirds of Dutch teens ages fifteen to seventeen with a steady boy or girlfriend report that the person was welcome to spend the night in their bedrooms. That's not to say it's a free-for-all over there. Quite the opposite: the Dutch actively discourage promiscuity in their children, teaching that sex should emerge from a loving relationship. Negotiating the ground rules for sleepovers, while not always easy (parents admit to a period of "adjustment" and some embarrassment), provides yet another opportunity to exert influence, reinforce ethics, and emphasize the need for protection. Schalet calls it a kind of "soft control." And you can't really argue with the results.

Holland is not perfect. Girls are still more likely than boys to report having been forced to do something sexually. They are more likely to experience pain during sex or have difficulty reaching orgasm. Although they express equal interest to boys in pursuing both lust and love, and can freely admit to sexual desire, Dutch girls who have multiple casual partners or one-night stands do risk being labeled "sluts." Schalet found, though, that the word didn't carry the same sting or stigma that it does in America. The Dutch boys she interviewed, meanwhile, expected to combine sex and love. They said that their fathers had expressly taught them that their partners must be equally up for any sexual activity, that the girls could (and should) enjoy themselves as much as boys, and that, as one boy said, "of course you should not be so stupid to [have sex] with a drunken head." Although she found American boys often yearned for love, too, they tended to consider this a personal quirk, a trait their peers, who were always DTF ("down to fuck"), did not share.

Getting Down and Dirty—and Ethical

"I'm comfortable talking to my parents about sex."

Charis Denison watched as the ninth-graders began to move. Those who agreed with the statement she had just made headed to the north end of the room; those who disagreed went to the south. Denison had made clear that staying in the middle was not an option: the point of this exercise was to force students to take a stand, to defend or maybe even change deeply held beliefs. In this case, however, nearly everyone chose "disagree."

"My parents are weird," one girl explained, seeming to speak for the entire group.

Some of the statements Denison tossed out during this lesson seemed like ringers. When asked, "If a teen does have sex, he or she should use a condom every single time," everyone obviously agreed. Then Denison said, "Oral sex isn't real sex." A few kids tried to stick in the center of the room, but Denison wouldn't let them. "Sometimes in life," she told them, "you have to make a hard choice. You don't get to stay in the middle. Sometimes you just have to bust a move." In the end, the class was divided. "Well," said a girl who had reluctantly disagreed, "it's not *really* sex. But it's not really not-sex, either. It's kind of . . ." She shrugged helplessly. "I don't know."

A boy standing next to her added, "I think you have to be able to get pregnant to be having actual sex."

Denison raised an eyebrow. "So, my thirty-five-year-old friend who is a lesbian and has never been with a guy is a virgin?" she said. At that, the boy looked confused. "No," he said, slowly, "but . . ."

A girl on the "agree" side interrupted. "I think sex is having an intimate moment with someone," she said. "It doesn't have to mean putting something inside of someone." She received several "snaps" of approval for that reply.

Denison's statements became more provocative later, when she repeated this exercise with eleventh-graders. Chaos broke out over whether "a guy going down on a girl is basically the same as a girl going down on a guy." Several students asked Denison,

"It *should* be or it *is*?" but she stayed mum. A handful refused to move from the noncommittal center of the room. Eventually, though, nearly everyone landed in the "agree" camp.

"That's a big group," Denison said, looking them over. "Do you see it playing out that way in reality? Raise your hand if you think that girls are getting as much oral sex as guys." Not a single hand went up. "So I guess we need to talk about what's going on," Denison said.

Next up: "I know someone who has had unwanted sex." Again, nearly everyone landed on the "agree" side of the room.

A boy in a Matchbox Twenty T-shirt raised his hand. "What is 'unwanted'?" he asked. "Is it when you're drunk and you have sex and then the next day you say, 'Ugh, I didn't want that'?"

"Would you call that unwanted sex?" Denison replied.

"Yeah," he said.

A girl in a striped maxi-dress cut in. "But, I think it's kind of unfair to say the guy's a bastard for doing that to you," she said. "If you were like"—she puts on a ditsy, drunken voice—"'Oh that sounds cool!' And then later you go, 'Not cool, dude.' That's not on his plate."

"Does it have to be on someone's plate to feel unwanted?" Denison asked.

The girl shrugged. "No, I guess not."

Denison gestured to the agree side. "People over here: raise your hand if you know more than one person who's had unwanted sex." Most did. "Keep your hand up if you know more than two people who've had unwanted sex." Most hands stayed up. "More than three." Still a lot of hands. "Four." She paused for a long moment. "I'm in love with the teenage population," she finally said. "I think they're the smartest, most creative, most brave population on the planet, but there's a lot of regret going on around this, a lot of confusion and a lot of messiness. What do we need to lessen that? What are we not doing or what do we need to do?"

A boy in a stocking cap raised his hand. "I think that mind-altering substances are called that for a reason. You make decisions under the influence that you wouldn't make sober."

Denison nodded. "Every choice we make we either surrender or gain power, right?" she said. "With alcohol and drugs, you're surrendering power. Which is why people do it sometimes, because they want that. But let's not be ignorant. Let's realize that with each sip, you lose some power to discern what's going on around you; you lose the power to take care of yourself, to judge your emotions."

A girl in a gray sweatshirt chomping on a big wad of bubble gum raised her hand. "I think that you have to make the definition of consent very clear," she said. "If someone doesn't literally say, 'Yes I want to,' then stop. Even if they didn't say no. Even if they're intoxicated. Even if they said they wanted to and then changed their mind. That's not consensual."

"She's saying *make consent clear*," Denison said. "You're making a lot of sense. Someone is hooking up with someone, they're totally into it. The other person is like, 'Is this okay?' And they say, 'Yeah, bring it on!' But then, all of a sudden, it starts *not* being okay. What needs to happen then?"

"The person needs to say, 'I'm not okay with this now,'" the girl said. "'We can either stop or turn it back and do what we were doing.'"

"That's awesome. But what if the person isn't saying it. What could the other person do?"

"Ask if it's okay," the girl replied.

"Excellent," Denison said. "It is super sexy to get consent. The idea of just saying"—she dropped her voice an octave, jutted out her chin like a teenage boy—" 'Hey, is this all right? You okay?' " She paused for a second to let that sink in. "That's *nice*. It's not, 'I would like to take out my legal documentation right now and get my attorney.' " The kids laughed. "And part of it is recognizing that there are a lot of ways to be sexual. It doesn't have to be this linear thing of going from point A to point B. We have all this language, all these metaphors that say you have to go from here to there." She brought up the baseball metaphor, with its familiar images of "rounding the bases," "home runs," and "scoring." "There's never this idea that someone might go up to bat, hit the ball, round second, and say, 'You know what? I kind of like it here. I'm just going to stay here. I'm not going to go all the way home.' You'd lose the game, right? But if someone says yes, that doesn't mean yes all the way through. There's this useful thing around consent: Any good lover is a good listener. And a bad listener is at best a bad lover and at worst a rapist."

The kids gasped. "*Whoa!*" someone said.

"It's about communication," Denison continued. "That doesn't mean you sing 'Kumbaya' in the middle of intercourse, but it does mean you are sharing with your partner. You are being *intimate*. You get to decide what that intimacy looks like and feels like, and you get to define what 'intimate' is. But there are *two* people involved—that 'you' is plural. Another way you can think about it is: 'What will be a positive sexual experience for everyone involved?' "

A boy in a football jersey, both of whose earlobes were pierced, raised his hand. "I never thought of it before, but in that baseball metaphor? You're trying to score *against* them."

"Exactly," Denison agreed. "There's a winner and a loser in baseball. It's a competition."

"So who is supposed to be the loser?" a girl asked. "The other person?"

Denison just smiled.

Watching the kids' interchange reminded me of a conversation I'd had with one of Denison's former students, Olivia, now a freshman in college. Olivia had told me she'd hooked up a lot during ninth and tenth grades. She couldn't say why—she certainly wasn't enjoying herself, and it made her feel, as she put it, "gross." "There wasn't a moment that things changed for me," she said one afternoon as we chatted in a café near her former high school. "I just started to understand that I wasn't behaving how I wanted to behave and I wasn't the person I wanted to be. Charis's class was a huge part of it, though. I learned to consciously make decisions instead of just letting things happen. And I began to really think about my values and my morals." She tugged thoughtfully at a lock of dark hair. "I think the biggest difference is that now I try to live consciously, with intent. Like, I used to think, 'Oh, okay, I guess we're hooking up now,' instead of thinking about whether I really wanted to be doing it. It's not that I stopped hooking up entirely, but by my junior year, I was less impulsive. And I felt very much like I was participating in it, not just going along with it."

Two tenth-graders held up a poster-size piece of butcher paper with the words "HOOKING UP IS . . ." printed in purple block letters across the top. A few minutes earlier, Denison had handed out markers and had students write responses to phrases she'd penned on a row of similar papers, such as "ABSTINENCE IS . . . ," "SEX IS . . . ," "SEX AND ALCOHOL . . . ," "BEING A VIRGIN IS . . . ," "SLUT SHAMING IS . . . ," "PRUDE

SHAMING IS . . ." They'd broken up into small groups to analyze the results and were now reporting to the class. "We observed that hooking up could be a bunch of different things to a bunch of different people," said a girl whose wavy dark hair fell to her waist. "But it's usually thought of as 'no strings attached' and less complicated. Like something you do at a party." She laughed. "But sometimes it actually turns out to be *more* complicated."

"That's really common for teenagers," Denison said. "You go into a hookup to make things easy, and then sometimes it back-fires. Is that what you're saying? What does that look like?"

"In some cases one person becomes more attached than the other," the girl said, "and believes there's something between them."

"If I were to say the word *hookup*," Denison asked, "how many people, as a gut reaction, see it as a negative thing?" No hands went up. "A positive thing?" Only boys raised their hands. "How many people imagine it just being a thing—not positive or nega-tive but just another choice?" More hands went up, this time split equally between boys and girls.

As they continued the lesson, a number of familiar themes emerged. Although all the responses to "Sex is . . ." were enthusiastic—"In a word," said the tall blond boy who presented for his group, "people think it's 'great!'"—everyone raised a hand when Denison asked who among them knew someone who'd had a negative sexual experience. "Yet there wasn't a sin-gle negative thing on that paper," she mused. "Why do you think that is?" Again, too, they discussed whether oral sex was, indeed, "sex"; only two people agreed that it was, until Denison men-tioned her lesbian friend. "Honestly?" the blond boy said. "Sex should be whatever you want it to be." More snaps.

Over the next hour or so, they discussed their feelings about virginity ("In our group, we didn't like the connotation of 'clean' and 'pure,'" said one of the girls) and abstinence (comments on that had included "sad," "a choice," and "anal"). A boy wearing a basketball jersey sparked a cacophony of responses to the question, "But what *is* abstinence anyway? Is it doing anything but intercourse or is it no contact at all, or what?" The group presenting on sex and alcohol initially suggested, sanctimoniously, that mixing the two was a bad idea. But when Denison asked who knew someone who had hooked up sober, not a single hand went up. Not one. "I'm hearing more and more that nobody gets sexual with someone unless they're in an altered state," she said. "And that can really feed into that regret factor."

"I think in some ways it's easier, though," a girl said. "You can be like, 'Oh, I wasn't thinking. I was drinking.'"

"That's what I call a setup," Denison responded. "Especially for girls: if you're a prude for setting limits and you're a slut if you decide to have sex, then you're screwed no matter what. At least if you get drunk, you can say, 'Well, yeah, I didn't know what I was doing.' So it's a way to not be accountable. And you have to have some empathy around that. It's pretty seductive to be able to have an out of some kind if you're going to be shamed or feel regret either way. So what are you supposed to do? We have to look at that more closely. We'll be talking more about that next time."

In the final moments, as she did every session, Denison answered anonymous questions. Here is a smattering from the classes I observed:

What if I pee during intercourse?

How do you get STDs from oral sex?

Is it true that when girls come, they can squirt fluid halfway across the room?

How big is a normal penis?

How many calories are in sperm?

Does your hymen always break when you lose your virginity?

Do you need lube to give a hand job?

How can I make anal sex feel better to my partner?

Denison answered them matter-of-factly, dispensing facts and correcting myths—including that "everyone" is "doing it." "There's such a perception that everyone is having sex and hooking up," she said, responding to a ninth-grader's concerns, "and that is just not the case. There is such pressure and it's just not that common, especially in ninth grade. There's plenty of people who don't even have their first kiss until at least sophomore year, much less go beyond that. So this notion that someone needs to hook up because it's 'time'?" She shook her head. "We have to really work on that. We have to get back to this idea of 'What am I actually feeling, what do I think about it, what do I want to have happen, and how can I look back without regret?' "

At the same time, she offered this to an eleventh-grader whose friend was having sex with many different people. "Your response doesn't have to be 'That's gross' or 'That's good' or 'That's bad.' You can ask, 'How did that feel to you? What does it bring you? How does it serve you?' Approached in the right way, that can be a great conversation. Then, if you really care about that person, your job is to be their human shield from shame."

There were times, listening to Denison answer those anonymous questions, that I felt a little uncertain. Like when someone in an eleventh-grade class asked how to have intercourse in a way that wouldn't hurt his partner. She talked about easing the penis in and out of the vagina gradually, rather than doing the porn-inspired jack hammer thrust, allowing a girl's body time to acclimate. She suggested a boy could shift his weight so he wasn't always bashing into the same spot, and could "empower" a female partner to grab his hips to control the depth of the penetration. There was no denying it: she was explaining how to have sex. It was the worst nightmare of conservative policy makers realized. Yet this is exactly the kind of discussion that, if Holland is any indication, is needed to combat the pop porn culture, reduce regret, and improve teens' satisfaction when they do choose to have sex (whenever that may be). So what about it makes me cringe? Surely, I'd rather have a daughter in bed with a boy who had a question like this asked and answered than one whose only point of reference was what he'd seen on the Internet. "I am not telling them what to do," Denison would explain to me later. "I am responding to a direct question—one that I get ninety-nine percent of the time, by the way—that rises from a student's respect and sense of accountability to both himself and his partner. If I didn't answer specifically, I'd be a fake, just another adult testing their trust." To the class, she concluded with "It's all about *communication*." And of course she was right.

At the end of each session, Denison pulled several handfuls of condoms from a silver tackle box she carried everywhere with her, sort of like Mary Poppins's carpet bag: it also held the vulva puppet, a model of a penis (nicknamed Richard) for demonstrating proper condom use, individual capsules of personal lubricant, and other tools of her trade. "Keep talking, keep asking questions," she would say. "Knowledge is power." True, I saw a group of boys make a show of scooping up the condoms and tossing them in the air. "Children, be free!" one of them said, laughing. But more often students, both boys and girls, approached respectfully. Some took the condoms casually; others sidled up, pretended to pick up an errant index card or pen, and then subtly slipped one or two condoms into their pockets.

A few kids always hung around as the room emptied, hoping for a private moment with Denison. One girl wanted clarification on the definition of statutory rape. Another wanted to know about Denison's career path so she could emulate it. One afternoon, the last student to approach her was a boy with dark curly hair and wide brown eyes. He ground the toe of his sneaker into the floor as he confided that his girlfriend was pushing to have intercourse, but he wasn't ready. "You'd be surprised at how often boys tell me that," Denison told him. "It must be hard and feel lonely." The boy nodded, his eyes welling up. Denison talked to him for a while, in a voice too low for me to hear. Then she gave him her phone number and e-mail address and told him to feel free to contact her. He nodded and walked away, a little less alone.

THIS BOOK IS about girls, about the ongoing obstacles to their full, healthy sexual expression and the costs of that to their well-being. But I want to leave Denison there, with a boy, because making change has to include them as well. It's no longer enough simply to caution young men against "getting a girl pregnant," or, more likely in the current climate, to warn about the shifting definition of rape. Parents need to discuss the spectrum of pressure, coercion, and consent with their sons, the forces urging them to see girls' limits as a challenge to overcome. Boys need to understand how they, too, are harmed by sexualized media and porn. They need to see models of masculine sexuality that are not grounded in aggression against women, in denigration or conquest. They need to know about shared pleasure, mutuality, reciprocity—to transform from baseball players to pizza eaters. That may not be as hard to do as one might think.

Charis Denison taught mostly high school, so one afternoon I sat in on a week-long coeducational puberty class for fourth- and fifth-graders taught by a pink-haired woman aptly named Jennifer Devine, who was a Unitarian minister as well as a certified sex educator. She spent the first session talking about how, with a few notable differences, puberty was basically the same for what she referred to as "people with vulvas and people with penises": everyone gets taller, everyone gets zits, everyone grows hair in new places, everyone's genitals mature, everyone gets "tingly feelings," everyone becomes capable of making a baby. She also spent a session each on the intricacies of male and female anatomy. After those lessons, she asked students to label drawings of men's and women's reproductive systems, both internal and external, which were rendered with clinical precision. That meant both boys and girls had to name the vulva, the outer and inner labia, the vaginal and urethral openings, the anus. I sat behind two boys, Terrell and Gabe, who were doing fine until suddenly Terrell drew a blank. "Hey, Gabe," he said, pointing to his booklet. "What's this again?" Gabe glanced over. "Oh, that's the clitoris," he replied. "That's for making good feelings."

It's a start.

Parents could learn a thing or two from Gabe. I recently suggested to a friend of mine, a woman who, like me, is a feminist, politically progressive mom of a preteen girl, that it was not enough to teach our daughters about the mechanics of reproduction, not enough to encourage resistance to unwanted sexual pressure, or to tell them that rape is not their fault. It was not even enough to equip them with birth control pills and condoms when the time came. We needed to talk to them about *good* sex, starting with how their own bodies worked, with masturbation and orgasm. She balked. "They don't want to hear about that kind of thing from *us*," she said. No? From where will they hear

234

it, then? They deserve something better than the distorted, false voices that blare at them from TVs, computers, iPhones, tablets, and movie screens. They deserve our guidance rather than our fear and denial in their sexual development. They deserve our help in understanding the dangers that lurk, but also in embracing their desire with respect and responsibility, in understanding the complexities and nuances of sexuality.

After studying the Dutch, Amy Schalet whipped up a four-part "ABCD" model for raising sexually healthy kids. First off, we want them to be autonomous (that's A), to understand desire and pleasure, to be able to assert sexual wishes and set limits, and to prepare responsibly for sexual encounters. Moving slowly, with awareness of desire and comfort, is the best way to gain those skills. Who, after all, is truly more sexually "experienced," a person who has intercourse while drunk to divest herself of virginity or the one who spends three hours kissing a partner, learning about erotic tension, mutual pleasure, intentionality? Frankly, if American parents didn't get any further than A, we'd be ahead of the game.

Nonetheless, there are three more letters. B, for building egalitarian, supportive relationships that value shared interest, respect, care, and trust; C for maintaining and nurturing connection with your child; and D for recognizing the diversity and range of sexual orientation, cultural beliefs, and development among their peers. As for that sleepover? I don't know whether I could get there myself, but I'm not saying never—the argument is awfully compelling. Regardless of how we navigate the details, though, we still can, and must, be more open with our daughters and our sons—and encourage them to be more open with us. My friend is actually wrong: Kids *do* want to hear that from their parents. They really do. In a 2012 survey of over four thousand young people, most said they wish they'd had more information, especially from Mom or Dad, before their first sexual experiences. They particularly wanted to know more from us about relationships and the emotional side of sex. So, think about it: Would you like your teenager to explore and understand her own body thoroughly before plunging ahead with partnered sex? Would you like her notion of what constitutes intimacy to extend beyond intercourse? Would you like her to have fewer partners, and consistently protect herself against disease and pregnancy? How about enjoying her sexual encounters? Transcending gender stereotypes? Would you hope she'll find caring, reciprocal, egalitarian relationships in which she can express her needs and limits? If she does pursue sexual pleasure outside relationships, do you want those experiences, too, to be safe, mutual, and respectful? I know I would. All the more reason to take a deep breath and forge ahead with discussions (that's *multiple* discussions) that include ideas about healthy relationships, communication, satisfaction, joy, mutuality, ethics, and, yes, toe-curling bliss.

After talking to so many girls, I now know what to hope for—for my own daughter and for them. I want sexuality to be a source of self-knowledge and creativity and communication despite its potential risks. I want them to revel in their bodies' sensuality without being reduced to it. I want them to be able to ask for what they want in bed, and to get it. I want them to be safe from disease, unwanted pregnancy, cruelty, dehumanization, and violence. If they are assaulted, I want them to have recourse from their school administrators, employers, the courts. It's a lot to ask for, but it's not too much. We've raised a generation of girls to have a voice, to expect egalitarian treatment in the home, in the classroom, in the workplace. Now it's time to demand that "intimate justice" in their personal lives as well.

Acknowledgments

Usually at this point I write about how while authorship is a solitary pursuit, there were many who supported me in it, blah, blah, blah. But that's such a civilized, sanitized way of putting it. What I really mean is this: I am difficult to live with, difficult to be around, difficult to know or interact with in any way while I am engrossed in book writing. The work consumes me. It makes me anxious, obsessive, flaky, and self-absorbed. It makes me grouchy. It makes me emotionally and often physically distant. Sometimes I don't know how those who love me—my friends, my family—can stand it. And yet they do, and that is, for me, the definition of grace.

So let me put it out there for real. For living through this with me yet again, for chewing over the issues, for challenging me, cajoling me, housing me, and enduring me, I would like to thank: Barbara Swaiman, Peggy Kalb, Ruth Halpern, Eva Eilenberg, Ayelet Waldman, Michael Chabon, Sylvia Brownrigg, Natalie Compagni Portis, Ann Packer, Rachel Silvers, Youseef Elias, Stevie Kaplan, Joan Semling Bostian, Mitch Bostian, Judith Belzer, Michael Pollan, Simone Marean, Rachel Simmons, Julia Sweeney Blum, Michael Blum, Danny Sager, Brian McCarthy, Diane Espaldon, Dan Wilson, Teresa Tauchi, Courtney Martin, Moira Kenney, Neal Karlen, ReCheng Tsang Jaffe, Sara Corbett, and Ilena Silverman.

For their assistance with research, I would like to thank Kaela Elias, Sara Birnel-Henderson, Pearl Xu, Evelyn Wang, Henry Bergman, and Sarah Caduto. For acting as sounding boards (and sometimes contending with some very personal questions), thanks to my nieces and nephews, especially Julie Ann Orenstein, Lucy Orenstein, Arielle Orenstein, Harry Orenstein, Matthew Orenstein, and Shirley Kawafuchi. For their guidance, I thank my agent, Suzanne Gluck, my ever-patient editor, Jennifer Barth, as well as Debby Herbenick, Leslie Bell, Patti Wolter, Lucia O'Sullivan, Lisa Wade, Jack Halberstam, Jackie Krasas, Paul Wright, and Bryant Paul. For the luxury of space and time to write uninterrupted, I am profoundly grateful to Peter Barnes and the Mesa Refuge, as well as to the Cindy-licious Ucross Foundation.

Greg Knowles deserves a special place in heaven for rescuing my manuscript when it disappeared into the technological ether. And while looks aren't everything, I sure appreciate what Michael Todd did with mine. Thanks, too, to the staff of *The California Sunday Magazine* and especially Doug McGray for your support and understanding. Special thanks to Charis Denison for all that my reporting put her through.

Most of all, thank you to the generous young women who participated in my interviews and the adults who helped me find them. To protect their privacy, I can't name them here, but you know who you are. It was a pleasure to get to know each and every one of you, and there is no way I could have written this book without you.

Finally, thank you to my family, both extended and immediate. To my husband, Steven Okazaki, so much more love than I could ever express; and to my beloved daughter, Daisy, I hope I haven't embarrassed you too much. I love you boundlessly and wish you the gift of ever and always being fully yourself.

Notes

Introduction: Everything You Never Wanted to Know About Girls and Sex (but Really Need to Ask)

3   The average American has first intercourse: Finer and Philbin, "Sexual Initiation, Contraceptive Use, and Pregnancy Among Young Adolescents."

5   Teen intimacy, it said, ought to be: Haffner, ed., *Facing Facts: Sexual Health for America's Adolescents* .

5   Sara McClelland, a professor of psychology: McClelland, "Intimate Justice."

Chapter 1: Matilda Oh Is Not an Object—Except When She Wants to Be

12   "If they aren't," Moran wrote, "chances are": Moran, *How to Be a Woman*, p. 283.

12   Preschoolers worship Disney princesses: Glenn Boozan, "11 Disney Princesses Whose Eyes Are Literally Bigger Than Their Stomachs," Above Average, June 22, 2015.

12   Self-objectification: American Psychological Association, *Report of the APA Task Force on the Sexualization of Girls*. The groundbreaking report defines sexualization as comprising any one or any combination of the following: "a person's value comes only from his or her sexual appeal or behavior, to the exclusion of other characteristics; a person is held to a standard

that equates physical attractiveness (narrowly defined) with being sexy; a person is sexually objectified—that is, made into a thing for others' sexual use, rather than seen as a person with the capacity for independent action and decision making; and/ or sexuality is inappropriately imposed upon a person." See also Madeline Fisher, "Sweeping Analysis of Research Reinforces Media Influence on Women's Body Image," *University of Wisconsin–Madison News*, May 8, 2008.

12   In one study of eighth-graders: Tolman and Impett, "Looking Good, Sounding Good." See also Impett, Schooler, and Tolman, "To Be Seen and Not Heard."

12   Another study linked girls' focus on appearance: Slater and Tiggeman, "A Test of Objectification Theory in Adolescent Girls."

13   A study of twelfth-graders connected self-objectification: Hirschman et al., "Dis/Embodied Voices."

13   Self-objectification has also been correlated: Caroline Heldman, "The Beast of Beauty Culture: An Analysis of the Political Effects of Self-Objectification," paper presented at the annual meeting of the Western Political Science Association, Las Vegas, NV, March 8, 2007. See also Calogero, "Objects Don't Object"; *Miss Representation*, dir. Jennifer Siebel Newsom and Kimberlee Acquaro, San Francisco: Representation Project, 2011.

13   Or, as one alumna put it: Steering Committee on Undergraduate Women's Leadership at Princeton University, *Report of the Steering Committee on Undergraduate Women's Leadership*, 2011; Evan Thomas, "Princeton's Woman Problem," *Daily Beast*, March 21, 2011.

13   "the pressure to look or dress": Liz Dennerlein, "Study: Females Lose Self-Confidence Throughout College," *USA Today*, September 26, 2013.

13   "effortless perfection": Sara Rimer, "Social Expectations Pressuring Women at Duke, Study Finds," *New York Times*, September 24, 2003.

13   It is a commercialized, one-dimensional, infinitely replicated: Levy, *Female Chauvinist Pigs*.

16   rejecting the torture device commonly known as: Haley

Phelan,"Young Women Say No to Thongs," *New York Times*, May 27, 2015.

17 "I will lose weight, get new lenses": Brumberg, *The Body Project*.

18 Comments on girls' pages, too: Steyer, *Talking Back to Facebook*; Fardouly, Diedrichs, Vartanian, et al., "Social Comparisons on Social Media." See also Shari Roan, "Women Who Post Lots of Photos of Themselves on Facebook Value Appearance, Need Attention, Study Finds," *Los Angeles Times*, March 10, 2011; Lizette Borrel, "Facebook Use Linked to Negative Body Image in Teen Girls: How Publicly Sharing Photos Can Lead to Eating Disorders," *Medical Daily*, December 3, 2013; Jess Weiner, "The Impact of Social Media and Body Image: Does Social Networking Actually Trigger Body Obsession in Today's Teenage Girls?" *Dove Self Esteem Project* (blog), June 26, 2013.

19 Their "friends" become an audience: Author's interview with Adriana Manago, Department of Psychology and Children's Digital Media Center, UCLA, May 7, 2010. See also Manago, Graham, Greenfield, et al., "Self-Presentation and Gender on MySpace."

19 Also, especially on photo-sharing sites such as Instagram: Lenhart, "Teens, Social Media and Technology Overview 2015."

19 This despite the fact that 1,499 of the profiles: Bailey, Steeves, Burkell, et al., "Negotiating with Gender Stereotypes on Social Networking Sites."

20 *selfie* was named the "international word of the year": The first recorded use of the word *selfie* was in 2002, in an online chat room by a drunken Australian. It became the word of the year after Oxford's researchers established that its use had spiked 17 percent since the same time in 2012. Ben Brumfield, "Selfie Named Word of the Year in 2013," CNN.com, November 20, 2013.

20 Anyone with a Facebook or Instagram account: Mehrdad Yazdani, "Gender, Age, and Ambiguity of Selfies on Instagram," *Software Studies Initiative* (blog), February 28, 2014.

20 "If you write off the endless stream": Rachel Simmons, "Selfies Are Good for Girls," *Slate DoubleX*, December 1, 2013.

21 But about half also said: Melissa Dahl, "Selfie-Esteem: Teens Say Selfies Give a Confidence Boost," Today.com, February 26, 2014.

21   Body dissatisfaction seems less driven by: Meier and Gray, "Facebook Photo Activity Associated with Body Image Disturbance in Adolescent Girls."

21   the more they look at others' pictures: Fadouly and Vartanian, "Negative Comparisons About One's Appearance Mediate the Relationship Between Facebook Usage and Body Image Concerns." See also Kendyl M. Klein, "Why Don't I Look Like Her? The Impact of Social Media on Female Body Image," CMC Senior Theses, Paper 720, 2013.

21   In 2011 there was a 71 percent increase: Sara Gates, "Teen Chin Implants: More Teenagers Are Seeking Plastic Surgery Before Prom," *Huffington Post*, April 30, 2013.

21   One of every three members: American Academy of Facial Plastic and Reconstructive Surgery, "Selfie Trend Increases Demand for Facial Plastic Surgery," Press release, March 11, 2014. Alexandria, VA: American Academy of Facial Plastic and Reconstructive Surgery.

22   In truth, it's hard to know: Ringrose, Gill, Livingstone, et al., *A Qualitative Study of Children, Young People, and "Sexting."* See also Lounsbury, Mitchell, Finkelhor, et al., "The True Prevalence of 'Sexting.'"

22   one large-scale survey: Englander, "Low Risk Associated with Most Teen Sexting."

22   That's particularly disturbing: Caitlin Dewey, "The Sexting Scandal No One Sees," *Washington Post*, April 28, 2015. This survey of 480 undergraduates found that, for both women and men, being coerced into sexting was more traumatic than being coerced into physical sex.

23   Management consultants use: Roger Schwarz, "Moving from Either/Or to Both/And Thinking," Schwarzassociates.com. If you find you can't make this trick work, try doing it backward, starting with your finger at your waist tracing a counterclockwise circle and moving it up.

23   Deborah Tolman has suggested: Personal conversation, September 20, 2011.

25   Between 2012 and 2013 the number of "Brazilian butt lifts":

American Society of Plastic Surgeons, *2013 Plastic Surgery Statistics Report*, Arlington Heights, IL: American Society of Plastic Surgeons, 2014.

25   "Milk, Milk, Lemonade": "Watch 'Inside Amy Schumer' Tease New Season with Booty Video Parody," *Rolling Stone*, April 12, 2015.

27   As with those pop culture memes: Kat Stoeffel, "bell hooks Was Bored by 'Anaconda,'" *The Cut, New York Magazine* blog, October 9, 2014.

31   "Sexy, but not sexual": Levy, *Female Chauvinist Pigs*.

32   When she was fifteen: Katherine Thomson, "Miley Cyrus on God, Remaking 'Sex and the City,' and Her Purity Ring," *Huffington Post,* July 15, 2008. Other lapsed promise ring Disney Kids include Selena Gomez, Demi Lovato, and the Jonas Brothers. Britney Spears also claimed she was saving intercourse until her wedding night. It turned out she was "not that innocent": she had sex for the first time in high school, years before her famed relationship with Justin Timberlake.

33   Mirroring (and raising further questions about): Foubert, Brosi, Bannon, et al., "Pornography Viewing Among Fraternity Men." See also Bridges, Wosnitzer, Scharrer, et al., "Aggression and Sexual Behavior in Best-Selling Pornography Videos."

34   41 percent of videos also included: Bridges, Wosnitzer, Scharrer, et al., "Aggression and Sexual Behavior in Best-Selling Pornography Videos."

34   Watching natural-looking people: Chris Morris, "Porn Industry Feeling Upbeat About 2014," NBCnews.com, January 14, 2014.

34   nearly 90 percent of 304 random scenes: Bridges, Wosnitzer, Scharrer, et al., "Aggression and Sexual Behavior in Best-Selling Pornography." An earlier study found that whether the director was male or female made little difference in the level of aggression or degradation of women in the films. Chyng, Bridges, Wosnitzer, et al., "A Comparison of Male and Female Directors in Popular Pornography." See also Monk-Turner and Purcell, "Sexual Violence in Pornography," which analyzed a random sample of adult videos and found that most had "sexually violent or dehumanizing/degrading themes." For

example, 17 percent of scenes showed aggression against women, 39 percent of scenes featured female subordination, and 85 percent of scenes showed men ejaculating on women. Barron and Kimmel, "Sexual Violence in Three Pornographic Media," found a progressive increase in sexual violence in pornographic materials from magazines to videos to the Internet.

34 as one eighteen-year-old pursuing: *Hot Girls Wanted*, directed by Jill Bauer and Ronna Gradus, Netflix, 2015.

35 "So when you see consistent depictions of women": Personal interview, Bryant Paul, Indiana University–Bloomington, December 4, 2013.

35 Over 40 percent of children ages ten to seventeen have been exposed: Wolak, Mitchell, and Finkelhor, "Unwanted and Wanted Exposure to Online Pornography in a National Sample of Youth Internet Users." Rates of unwanted or accidental exposure to porn rose from 26 percent in 1999 to 34 percent in 2005, Wolak and her colleagues found.

35 By college, according to a survey of more than eight hundred students: Carroll et al., "Generation XXX."

36 There is some indication that porn has: Regnerus, "Porn Use and Support of Same-Sex Marriage."

36 On the other hand, they're also less likely: Wright and Funk, "Pornography Consumption and Opposition to Affirmative Action for Women." This was true for both men and women, even when controlling for prior attitudes on affirmative action.

36 Among teenage boys, regular porn use: Peter and Valkenburg, "Adolescents' Exposure to Sexually Explicit Online Material and Recreational Attitudes Toward Sex"; Peter and Valkenburg, "The Use of Sexually Explicit Internet Material and Its Antecedents." See also Wright and Tokunaga, "Activating the Centerfold Syndrome"; and Wright, "Show Me the Data!"

36 Porn users are also more likely: Wright and Tokunaga, "Activating the Centerfold Syndrome"; Wright, "Show me the Data!"

36 Male *and* female college students who report recent porn use: Wright and Funk, "Pornography Consumption and Opposition

to Affirmative Action for Women"; Brosi, Foubert, Bannon, et al., "Effects of Women's Pornography Use on Bystander Intervention in a Sexual Assault Situation and Rape Myth Acceptance"; Foubert, Brosi, Bannon, et al., "Pornography Viewing Among Fraternity Men." For a study involving high school students, see Peter and Valkenburg, "Adolescents' Exposure to a Sexualized Media Environment and Notions of Women as Sex Objects."

36   female porn users are less likely than others to: Brosi, Foubert, Bannon, et al., "Effects of Women's Pornography Use on Bystander Intervention in a Sexual Assault Situation and Rape Myth Acceptance." One of the arguments *for* pornography is that rates of sexual assault drop in countries where bans against it have been lifted. But as Paul Wright, a professor of telecommunications at Indiana University–Bloomington, told me, if both male and female porn users are more likely buy into rape myths, if women users are less likely to notice when they are at risk, and if women who are objectified are more likely to be blamed when assaulted, then it may not be that there are fewer rapes in such countries so much as that they go unrecognized or unreported. Author interview, Paul Wright, December 6, 2013.

36   Only 3 percent of females do: Carroll et al., "Generation XXX."

37   They believed that the unnatural thinness: Paul, *Pornified*.

38   "What I'm saying is whether it's rated X": "Joseph Gordon-Levitt, on Life and the Lenses We Look Through," Interview on *Weekend Edition*. National Public Radio, September 29, 2013.

39   And the impact of that garden-variety, "pornified" media: Author interview, Paul Wright, December 6, 2013. See also Fisher, "Sweeping Analysis of Research Reinforces Media Influence on Women's Body Image."

39   The average teenager is exposed to: Fisher et. al., "Televised Sexual Content and Parental Mediation."

39   70 percent of prime-time TV: That's up from 56 percent in 1998, the first year tracked. Ninety-one percent of comedies and 87 percent of dramas contained sexual content, ranging from

innuendo to implied intercourse. Ward and Friedman, "Using TV as a Guide"; Shiver Jr, "Television Awash in Sex, Study Says," *Los Angeles Times*, November 20, 2005.

39 College men who play violent, sexualized video games: Stermer and Burkley, "SeX-Box."

39 College women who, in experiments: Fox, Ralston, Cooper, et al., "Sexualized Avatars Lead to Women's Self-Objectification and Acceptance of Rape Myths"; Calogero, "Objects Don't Object."

39 Meanwhile, in a study of middle and high school girls, those who were: Aligo, "Media Coverage of Female Athletes and Its Effect on the Self-Esteem of Young Women"; Daniels, "Sex Objects, Athletes, and Sexy Athletes."

39 Young women who consume more objectifying media: Calogero, "Objects Don't Object."

39 In other words, as Rachel Calogero: Ibid.

39 The sex in TV and movies: Thirty-five percent of sex on TV occurs between two people who either have never met or are not in a relationship: Kunkel, Eyal, Finnerty, et al., *Sex on TV 4*.

42 Kim's true contribution has been an ingenious "patriarchal bargain": Lisa Wade, "Why Is Kim Kardashian Famous?" *Sociological Images* (blog), December 21, 2010.

43 "Our hopes have gotten so cheesy": Tina Brown, "Why Kim Kardashian Isn't 'Aspirational,'" *Daily Beast*, April 1, 2014.

Chapter 2: Are We Having Fun Yet?

48 "'Do you spit or do you swallow?'": Tamar Lewin, "Teen-Agers Alter Sexual Practices, Thinking Risks Will Be Avoided," *New York Times*, April 5, 1997.

48 The reporter linked that incident: Laura Sessions Stepp, "Unsettling New Fad Alarms Parents: Middle School Oral Sex," *Washington Post*, July 8, 1991.

48 Girls' bodies have always been vectors: Brumberg, *The Body Project*.

49 In 1994, just a few years before: Laumann, Michael, Kolata, et al., *Sex in America*.

49 By 2014, oral sex was so common: Author interview, Debby Herbenick, Indiana University, December 5, 2013.

50   Oral sex practices of minors: Remez, "Oral Sex Among Adolescents."

50   By 2000 the Clinton presidency was winding down: Anne Jarrell, "The Face of Teenage Sex Grows Younger," *New York Times*, April 2, 2000.

50   That was not true: Kann, Kinchen, Shanklin, et al., "Youth Risk Behavior Surveillance—United States, 2013."

50   An article in the now-defunct *Talk* magazine: Linda Franks, "The Sex Lives of Your Children," *Talk*, February 2000; See also Liza Mundy, "Young Teens and Sex: Sex and Sensibility," *Washington Post Magazine*, July 16, 2000.

51   The girl whose color hit farthest down: "Is Your Child Leading a Double Life?" *The Oprah Winfrey Show*. Broadcast October 2003/ April 2004.

51   A 2004 NBC News/*People* survey taken: Tamar Lewin, "Are These Parties for Real?" *New York Times*, June 30, 2005.

52   By the end of ninth grade: Halpern-Felsher, Cornell, Kropp, and Tschann, "Oral Versus Vaginal Sex Among Adolescents," found that one in five ninth-graders reported having experience with oral sex; 37 percent of boys and 32 percent of girls ages fifteen to seventeen reported oral sex experience; by ages eighteen to nineteen, those numbers had roughly doubled, to 66 percent and 64 percent, respectively. Child Trends DataBank, "Oral Sex Behaviors Among Teens." See also Herbenick et al., "Sexual Behavior in the United States"; Fortenberry, "Puberty and Adolescent Sexuality"; Copen, Chandra, and Martinez, "Prevalence and Timing of Oral Sex with Opposite-Sex Partners Among Females and Males Aged 15–24 Years." Over half of fifteen- to nineteen-year-old girls had oral sex before having first intercourse. See Chandra, Mosher, Copen, et al., "Sexual Behavior, Sexual Attraction, and Sexual Identity in the United States"; Chambers, "Oral Sex"; Henry J. Kaiser Family Foundation, "Teen Sexual Activity," *Fact Sheet*; Hoff, Green, and Davis, "National Survey of Adolescents and Young Adults."

52   Right-wing influence on sex education: Dotson-Blake, Knox, and Zusman, "Exploring Social Sexual Scripts Related to Oral Sex."

52   over a third of teenagers included it: Dillard, "Adolescent Sexual Behavior: Demographics."

52   70 percent agreed that someone: Child Trends DataBank, "Oral Sex Behaviors Among Teens."

53   a widespread belief among teens that it is risk free: Halpern-Felsher, Cornell, Kropp, and Tschann, "Oral Versus Vaginal Sex Among Adolescents." Only 9 percent of teens engaging in oral sex report using a condom. See Child Trends DataBank, "Oral Sex Behaviors Among Teens." See also Copen, Chandra, and Martinez, "Prevalence and Timing of Oral Sex with Opposite-Sex Partners Among Females and Males Aged 15–24 Years."

53   rates of sexually transmitted diseases: Advocates for Youth, "Adolescents and Sexually Transmitted Infections"; See also "A Costly and Dangerous Global Phenomenon." *Fact Sheet.* Advocates for Youth, Washington, DC, 2010; "Comprehensive Sex Education: Research and Result"; Braxton, Carey, Davis, et al., *Sexually Transmitted Disease Surveillance 2013.*

53   The new popularity of oral sex: Steven Reinberg, "U.S. Teens More Vulnerable to Genital Herpes," WebMD, October 17, 2013. See also Jerome Groopman, "Sex and the Superbug," *New Yorker,* October 1, 2012; Katie Baker, "Rethinking the Blow Job: Condoms or Gonorrhea? Take Your Pick," *Jezebel* (blog), September 27, 2012.

53   The number one reason they do it: avoiding STDs ranked fifth for girls in a list of motivations for engaging in oral sex, after improving relationships, popularity, pleasure, and curiosity. It ranked third for boys. Cornell and Halpern-Felsher, "Adolescent Health Brief."

53   For years, psychologists have warned: Gilligan et al., *Making Connections*; Brown and Gilligan, *Meeting at the Crossroads*; Pipher, *Reviving Ophelia.* See also: Simmons, *Odd Girl Out*; Simmons, *The Curse of the Good Girl*; Orenstein, *Schoolgirls.*

54   Boys, incidentally, far and away, said: They were also twice as likely as girls to report feeling good about themselves after oral sex; girls were three times more likely to say they felt used. Brady and Halpern-Felsher, "Adolescents' Reported Consequences of Having

Oral Sex Versus Vaginal Sex." This study specifically looked at consequences of oral sex among ninth- and tenth-graders.

54 For both sexes, but particularly for girls: Cornell and Halpern-Felsher, "Adolescent Health Brief."

54 Intercourse could bring stigma, turn you into a "slut": Initiating fellatio earlier than their peers, however, was associated with low self-esteem for girls. Fava and Bay-Cheng, "Young Women's Adolescent Experiences of Oral Sex." Although they said oral sex was a strategy to gain popularity, ninth- and tenth-grade girls were only half as likely as boys to feel that strategy was successful. Brady and Halpern-Felsher, "Adolescents' Reported Consequences of Having Oral Sex Versus Vaginal Sex"; Cornell and Halpern-Felsher, "Adolescent Health Brief."

54 the calculus and compromises they made to curry favor: One in three girls in a national survey of teens reported engaging in oral sex specifically to avoid intercourse. Hoff, Green, and Davis, "National Survey of Adolescents and Young Adults."

55 They were both dispassionate and nonpassionate about: Burns, Futch, and Tolman, " 'It's Like Doing Homework.' "

60 As Anna said, reciprocity in casual encounters: In their research on college students, Laura A. Backstrom and her colleagues similarly found that cunnilingus was an assumed part of relationships but not of hookups. Women who wanted oral sex in hookups had to be assertive to get it; those who did not want it were found to be relieved. In relationships, women who did not want oral sex were uncomfortable, whereas it was considered a source of pleasure for those who enjoyed it. Backstrom et al., "Women's Negotiation of Cunnilingus in College Hookups and Relationships."

62 Around a third masturbated regularly: According to the National Survey of Sexual Health and Behavior (NSSHB), more than three quarters of boys ages fourteen to seventeen say they have ever masturbated; less than half of girls have; about a third of girls in every age group masturbate regularly, while the percentage of boys rises steadily with time. Fortenberry, Schick, Herbenick, et al., "Sexual Behaviors and Condom Use at Last

Vaginal Intercourse"; Robbins, Schick, Reese, et al., "Prevalence, Frequency, and Associations of Masturbation with Other Sexual Behaviors Among Adolescents Living in the United States of America"; Alan Mozes, "Study Tracks Masturbation Trends Among U.S. Teens," *U.S. News and World Report*, August 1, 2011. According to Caron, *The Sex Lives of College Students*, 65 percent of male students masturbate once a week compared to 19 percent of female students.

63 "Like once you've done *that*, you really must be": Most of the college students Backstrom et al. studied likewise viewed cunnilingus as intimate and emotional, and so more desirable within a relationship. Backstrom et al., "Women's Negotiation of Cunnilingus in College Hookups and Relationships." See also Bay-Cheng, Robinson, and Zucker, "Behavioral and Relational Contexts of Adolescent Desire, Wanting, and Pleasure."

64 They are dirty, the male writer continues: Wayne Nutnot, "I'm a Feminist but I Don't Eat Pussy," Thought Catalog, June 7, 2013.

65 Those early experiences can have a lasting: Schick, Calabrese, Rima, et al., "Genital Appearance Dissatisfaction."

66 Women's feelings about their genitals: Author interview, Debby Herbenick, Indiana University, December 5, 2013; Schick, Calabrese, Rima, et al., "Genital Appearance Dissatisfaction." See also Widerman, "Women's Body Image Self-Consciousness During Physical Intimacy with a Partner."

66 College women in one study who were uncomfortable: Schick, Calabrese, Rima, et al., "Genital Appearance Dissatisfaction." See also Widerman, "Women's Body Image Self-Consciousness During Physical Intimacy with a Partner."

66 Another study, of more than four hundred undergraduates: Bay-Cheng and Fava, "Young Women's Experiences and Perceptions of Cunnilingus During Adolescence."

66 Young women who feel confident: Armstrong, England, and Fogarty, "Accounting for Women's Orgasm and Sexual Enjoyment in College Hookups and Relationships."

69 Largely as a result of the Brazilian trend: American Society for

Aesthetic Plastic Surgery, "Labiaplasty and Buttock Augmentation Show Marked Increase in Popularity," Press release, February 5, 2014; American Society for Aesthetic Plastic Surgery, "Rising Demand for Female Cosmetic Genital Surgery Begets New Beautification Techniques," Press release, April 15, 2013.

69　The most sought-after look: Alanna Nuñez, "Would You Get Labiaplasty to Look Like Barbie?" *Shape*, May 24, 2013. See also Mireya Navarro, "The Most Private of Makeovers," *New York Times*, November 28, 2004.

70　"Thirty percent of female college students say": Herbenick et al., "Sexual Behavior in the United States." The National Survey of Sexual Health and Behavior is the largest survey ever conducted on the sexual practices of men and women ages fourteen to ninety-four.

70　The rates of pain among women: Ibid.

70　In 1992 only 16 percent of women: Herbenick et al., "Sexual Behaviors in the United States." See also: Susan Donaldson James, "Study Reports Anal Sex on Rise Among Teens," ABC. com, December 10, 2008.

70　Girls were expected to endure the act: Bahar Gholipour, "Teen Anal Sex Study: 6 Unexpected Findings," Livescience.com, August 13, 2014.

71　Consider that at every age: Laumann et al., *Sex in America*.

71　Or that girls are four times more: Twelve percent of young women said they tolerate unwanted sexual activity versus 3 percent of young men. Kaestle, "Sexual Insistence and Disliked Sexual Activities in Young Adulthood."

71　According to Sara McClelland, who coined the term: McClelland, "Intimate Justice"; author interview, Sara McClelland, January 27, 2014.

72　For men, it was the opposite: McClelland, "Intimate Justice"; McClelland, "What Do You Mean When You Say That You Are Sexually Satisfied?"; McClelland, "Who Is the 'Self' in Self-Reports of Sexual Satisfaction?"

72　Women's commitment to their partner's satisfaction: In sexual encounters between women, both partners have orgasms 83 percent of the time. Author interview, Lisa Wade, March 19, 2014. See also Douglass and Douglass, *Are We Having Fun Yet?*; Thompson, *Going All the Way.*

Chapter 3: Like a Virgin, Whatever That Is

76 Just last week, Christina told me: In 2012, filmmaker Lina Esco launched a movement called "Free the Nipple," focused on ending the double standard that sexualizes women's upper bodies but not men's. In August 2015, "Go Topless Day" protesters demonstrated in sixty cities across the globe for gender equality in public breast-baring. *Free the Nipple*, dir. Linda Esco New York: IFC Films; Kristie McCrum, "Go Topless Day Protesters Take Over New York and 60 Other Cities for 'Free the Nipple' Campaign,'" *Mirror*, August 24, 2015.

77 Nearly two thirds of teenagers: Sixty-four percent of twelfth-graders have had intercourse at least once. Kann, Kinchen, Shanklin, et al., "Youth Risk Behavior Surveillance—United States, 2013."

77 a sizable number of girls: Seventy percent of sexually experienced girls report their first intercourse was with a steady partner; 16 percent say it was with someone they'd just met or with a friend. Martinez, Copen, and Abma, "Teenagers in the United States: Sexual Activity, Contraceptive Use, and Childbearing, 2006–2010 National Survey of Family Growth."

77 Over half, both in national: Leigh and Morrison, "Alcohol Consumption and Sexual Risk-Taking in Adolescents."

77 Most say they regret their experience: Martino, Collins, Elliott, et al., "It's Better on TV"; Carpenter, *Virginity Lost.* While research doesn't answer the question "Waited for *what?*," Martino and colleagues write that "youth who say they wish they had waited longer to have sex for the first time apparently come to regret their decision to have sex, whether because they felt unprepared for the experience, wish they had shared it with someone else or been at a different point in their relationship, found the sex itself to be unsatisfying, or found that the consequences were not what they hoped or expected they would be."

78   in her book *The Purity Myth*: Valenti, *The Purity Myth*.

81   One in four eighteen-year-olds: Jayson, "More College 'Hookups'
      but More Virgins, Too."

81   unless they're religious, most don't advertise: Carpenter, *Virginity
      Lost*.

82   each, more or less, reflected in: Ibid.

83   first intercourse was just a natural: This could be why researcher
      Sharon Thompson found that young women who recognize and
      make sexual decisions based on their own desire are more likely
      than those who ignore or deny it to find pleasure in virginity
      loss. Thompson, *Going All the Way*.

85   By 2004 more than 2.5 million: Bearman and Brückner,
      "Promising the Future."

85   I made a note to myself to check: Rector, Jonson, Noyes, et al.,
      *Sexually Active Teenagers Are More Likely to Be Depressed and to Attempt
      Suicide.*

86   Girls, for instance, are also more likely than boys to be bullied:
      Dunn, Gjelsvik, Pearlman, et al., "Association Between Sexual
      Behaviors, Bullying Victimization, and Suicidal Ideation in a
      National Sample of High School Students."

88   perhaps due to a lack of education, or perhaps: Regnerus,
      Forbidden Fruit. Regnerus found that only half of sexually
      active teenagers who report seeking guidance from God or
      the Scriptures when making a tough decision say they use
      protection every time they have intercourse. Among sexually
      active youth who say they look to parents or another trusted
      adult for advice, 69 percent do. Regnerus's findings were drawn
      from the National Longitudinal Study of Adolescent Health
      (hereafter Add Health) as well as a national survey he and his
      colleagues conducted of about 3,400 children ages thirteen to
      seventeen.

88   Pledging has to feel special: Bearman and Brückner, "Promising
      the Future." Bearman and Brückner's data were drawn from
      Add Health.

89   Male pledgers are four times more: Bearman and Brückner,
      "After the Promise."

89   by their twenties, over 80 percent: Rosenbaum, "Patient Teenagers?"

89   The only lesson that sticks: Ibid.

90   Once wed, they found that talking to friends: Molly McElroy, "Virginity Pledges for Men Can Lead to Sexual Confusion— Even After the Wedding Day," *UW Today*, August 16, 2014.

90   A young woman who had taken: Samantha Pugsley, "It Happened to Me: I Waited Until My Wedding Night to Lose My Virginity and I Wish I Hadn't," *XOJane*, August 1, 2014." See also Jessica Ciencin Henriquez, "My Virginity Mistake: I Took an Abstinence Pledge Hoping It Would Ensure a Strong Marriage. Instead, It Led to a Quick Divorce," *Salon*, May 5, 2013.

90   Meanwhile, a 2011 survey: Darrel Ray and Amanda Brown, *Sex and Secularism*, Bonner Springs, KS: IPC Press, 2011.

92   Again, his concern seemed less: Relationships in middle adolescence have been linked with positive, healthy commitment in later relationships; but they can also sometimes be a symptom of pathology. Like so many of these issues, it depends on the context and the couple. Simpson, Collins, and Salvatore, "The Impact of Early Interpersonal Experience on Adult Romantic Relationship Functioning."

92   What's more, if Dave really: U.S. Census Bureau, "Divorce Rates Highest in the South, Lowest in the Northeast, Census Bureau Reports," News brief, Washington, DC: U.S. Census Bureau, August 25, 2011. See also Vincent Trivett and Vivian Giang, "The Highest and Lowest Divorce Rates in America," *Business Insider*, July 23, 2011.

92   Statistically, the strongest factor: Jennifer Glass, "Red States, Blue States, and Divorce: Understanding the Impact of Conservative Protestantism on Regional Variation in Divorce Rates," Press release, January 16, 2014. Council on Contemporary American Families.

95   even those who believe they've talked: According to a joint poll of readers conducted by *O Magazine* and *Seventeen* that involved a thousand fifteen- to twenty-two-year-olds and a thousand mothers of girls those ages, 22 percent of mothers

believed their daughters were uncomfortable talking to them about sex; 61 percent of girls said they were. The percentage of girls having oral sex (30 percent) was double what mothers knew or suspected. Forty-six percent of girls who'd had intercourse did not tell their mothers. Among the girls who'd had an abortion, many also never told their mothers. Liz Brody, "The *O/Seventeen* Sex Survey: Mothers and Daughters Talk About Sex," *O* Magazine, May 2009. A 2012 Planned Parenthood survey found that while about half of parents said they were comfortable talking about sex with their teenagers, only 19 percent of teens said they were comfortable talking to their parents; and while 42 percent of parents said they'd talked "repeatedly" to their children about sex, only 27 percent of teens agreed. Thirty-four percent said their parents have either talked to them only once or never. Parents in the survey believed they were giving their kids nuanced guidance; the kids were only hearing simple directives, such as "don't." Planned Parenthood. "Parents and Teens Talk About Sexuality: A National Poll," *Let's Talk*, October 2012. See also Planned Parenthood, "New Poll: Parents Are Talking with Their Kids About Sex but Often Not Tackling Harder Issues," Plannedparenthood.org, October 3, 2011.

101 What if, as Jessica Valenti suggests: Valenti, *The Purity Myth*.

Chapter 4: Hookups and Hang-Ups

104 The seismic tectonic shift in premarital sexual behavior really took place: Armstrong, Hamilton, and England, "Is Hooking Up Bad for Young Women?"

104 That's what is meant by the term: Wade and Heldman, "Hooking Up and Opting Out."

105 According to the Online College Social Life Survey: Armstrong, Hamilton, and England, "Is Hooking Up Bad for Young Women?"

105 The behavior is most typical among affluent: Ibid. African American women and Asian men have historically been most marginalized in the sexual marketplace. Gay students, too, have

lower hookup rates, perhaps because, on many campuses, their numbers are small and concerns about safety remain high. See Garcia, Reiber, Massey, et al., "Sexual Hook-Up Culture." According to sociologist Lisa Wade, black students are also more conscious of appearing "respectable" and avoiding stereotypes of the "Mandingo" or "Jezebel." The hookup culture centers around fraternity parties, too, and black frats tend not to have their own houses. Poor and working-class students, often the first in their families to attend college, also avoid the party/hookup scene. Lisa Wade, "The Hookup Elites," *Slate DoubleX*, July 19, 2013.

105 Only a third of these hookups included intercourse: Armstrong, Hamilton, and England, "Is Hooking Up Bad for Young Women?"

105 Kids themselves tend to overestimate: Alissa Skelton, "Study: Students Not 'Hooking Up' As Much As You Might Think," *USA Today*, October 5, 2011; Erin Brodwin, "Students Today 'Hook Up' No More Than Their Parents Did in College," *Scientific American*, August 16, 2013.

105 from the 92 percent of songs on the *Billboard* charts: Dino Grandoni, "92% of Top Ten Billboard Songs Are About Sex," The Wire: News from *The Atlantic*, September 30, 2011.

105 Mindy Kaling, creator and star of: "Not My Job: Mindy Kaling Gets Quizzed on Do-It-Yourself Projects," *Wait, Wait . . . Don't Tell Me!*, National Public Radio, June 20, 2015.

106 The truth is, nearly three quarters: Debby Herbenick, unpublished survey, February 2014.

106 In hookups involving intercourse: Armstrong, England, and Fogarty, "Accounting for Women's Orgasm and Sexual Enjoyment in College Hookups and Relationships."

106 Orgasm may not be the only measure of sexual satisfaction: Ibid.

106 As one boy put it to Armstrong: Ibid.

107 That may partly explain why 82 percent of men said: Garcia, Reiber, Massey, et al., "Sexual Hook-Up Culture." A 2010 study of 832 college students found only 26 percent of women and 50 percent of men reported feeling positive after a hookup. Other studies have found that roughly three quarters of students

regretted at least one previous instance of sexual activity. Owen et al., " 'Hooking up' Among College Students."

107 As the age of first marriage rose: Armstrong, Hamilton, and England, "Is Hooking Up Bad for Young Women?"; Hamilton and Armstrong, "Gendered Sexuality in Young Adulthood."

111 Her schoolwork was suffering, too: The breakup of a relationship is among the most distressing, traumatic events teens report, and evidence is growing that it is a major cause of suicide among youth. Joyner and Udry, "You Don't Bring Me Anything but Down"; Monroe, Rhode, Seeley, et al., "Life Events and Depression in Adolescence."

111 More than half of physical and sexual abuse: According to the CDC, more than one in seven high school girls were physically abused by a romantic partner in the past year, and one in seven was sexually assaulted. Latina and white girls were victims of dating abuse more than black girls. Kann, Kinchen, Shanklin, et al., "Youth Risk Behavior Surveillance—United States, 2013."

111 those experiences prime girls to be victimized again: Exner-Cortens, Eckenrode, and Rothman, "Longitudinal Associations Between Teen Dating Violence Victimization and Adverse Health Outcomes."

114 On most of the campuses I visited: There has recently been some effort to change this as a strategy to reduce sexual assault. Amanda Hess, "Sorority Girls Fight for Their Right to Party," *Slate XXFactor.* January 20, 2015

117 in order to create what Lisa Wade, an associate: Author's interview with Lisa Wade, June 9, 2015.

117 As with intercourse, the proportion of young people: Reductions in rates of binge drinking have been driven by college men, not women. National Center for Chronic Disease Prevention and Health Promotion, "Binge-Drinking: A Serious, Unrecognized Problem Among Women and Girls." See also Rachel Pomerance Berl, "Making Sense of the Stats on Binge Drinking," *U.S. News and World Report*, January 17, 2013.

117 one out of four college women and one out of five: National Center for Chronic Disease Prevention and Health Promotion,

"Binge-Drinking: A Serious, Unrecognized Problem Among Women and Girls." See also Berl, "Making Sense of the Stats on Binge Drinking."

117 Other surveys have found that nearly: "College Drinking," *Fact Sheet*. Kelly-Weeder, "Binge Drinking and Disordered Eating in College Students"; Dave Moore and Bill Manville, "Drunkorexia: Disordered Eating Goes Hand-in-Glass with Drinking Binges," *New York Daily News*, February 1, 2013; Ashley Jennings, "Drunkorexia: Alcohol Mixes with Eating Disorders," ABC News, October 21, 2010.

118 They're most likely to be the most drunk: In one study of men and women who engaged in an uncommitted sexual encounter that included penetrative sex, 71 percent were drunk at the time. Fisher, Worth, Garcia, et al., "Feelings of Regret Following Uncommitted Sexual Encounters in Canadian University Students."

118 a process that involved asceticism: Caitlan Flanagan, "The Dark Power of Fraternities," *Atlantic*, March 2014.

125 the number who fake: Caron, *The Sex Lives of College Students*.

129 Mixing energy drinks with alcohol leaves a person: Centers for Disease Control, "Caffeine and Alcohol," *Fact Sheet*; Linda Carroll, "Mixing Energy Drinks and Alcohol Can 'Prime' You for a Binge," Today.com, *News* (blog), July 17, 2014; Allison Aubrey, "Caffeine and Alcohol Just Make a Wide-Awake Drunk," *Shots: Health News from NPR* (blog), February 11, 2013.

131 But as Armstrong and her colleagues have pointed out: Armstrong, Hamilton, and Sweeney, "Sexual Assault on Campus."

131 Since victims have a hard time: Ibid.

133 A report by the Justice Department released: Thirty-two percent of victims the same age who are *not* in college report their assaults. Laura Sullivan, "Study: Just 20 Percent of Female Campus Sexual Assault Victims Go to Police," *The Two Way*, National Public Radio, December 11, 2014.

137 When they do, boys tend to feel remorse about: Oswalt, Cameron, and Koob, "Sexual Regret in College Students."

Chapter 5: Out: Online and IRL

145 Or maybe writing about male bodies liberates women: For more
on fan fiction, see Alexandra Alter, "The Weird World of Fan
Fiction," *Wall Street Journal,* June 14, 2012; and Jarrah Hodge,
"Fanfiction and Feminism." For a fascinating discussion of
why so many "slash" stories are male on male, including those
written by lesbians, see Melissa Pittman, "The Joy of Slash: Why
Do Women Want It?" *The High Hat,* Spring 2005. In the spring
of 2014, Chinese officials arrested twenty authors for the crime
of writing male/male slash fiction—most were young women in
their twenties. Ala Romano, "Chinese Authorities Are Arresting
Writers of Slash Fanfiction," *Daily Dot,* April 18, 2014.

146 The company's policy against posting: It's impossible to know
who posts the photos on Reddit, since users are anonymous.
Ben Branstetter, "Why Reddit Had to Compromise on Revenge
Porn," *Daily Dot,* February 27, 2015.

146 As with their straight peers, the Internet can be: "Girls" includes
both cisgender LGB girls, whose self-identified gender conforms
to their biological sex, and male-to-female transgender girls.
Ditto "boys." See GLSEN, *Out Online.*

146 Yet, LGBTQ kids also turn to the Web for information: LGBT
teens are five times as likely as their non-LGBT peers to search
for information on sexuality and sexual attraction. They are
substantially more likely to have a close online friend. Ibid.

146 More than one in ten disclosed: Ibid. According to a 2012 report
by the Human Rights Campaign, *Growing Up LGBT in America,* 73
percent of gay teens are "more honest" about themselves online
than in the real world, as opposed to 43 percent of teens who
identify as heterosexual—though that, too, seems concerning.

148 the average age of coming out: "Age of 'Coming Out' Is Now
Dramatically Younger: Gay, Lesbian and Bisexual Teens Find
Wider Family Support, Says Researcher," *Science News,* October
11, 2011.

153 In the early 1990s: Caron, *The Sex Lives of College Students.*
According to the Centers for Disease Control, 12 percent
of women ages 25–44 report having had a same-sex sexual

encounter in their lifetimes; 6 percent of men do. Chandra, Mosher, Copen, et al., "Sexual Behavior, Sexual Attraction, and Sexual Identity in the United States."

156 In a survey of more than ten thousand: Human Rights Campaign, *Growing Up LGBT in America.*

157 Ryan's organization has linked rejection: Zack Ford, "Family Acceptance Is the Biggest Factor for Positive LGBT Youth Outcomes, Study Finds," ThinkProgress.org, June 24, 2015; Ryan, "Generating a Revolution in Prevention, Wellness, and Care for LGBT Children and Youth."

162 An estimated 0.3 percent of Americans are thought to identify: Gary J. Gates, "How Many People Are Lesbian, Gay, Bisexual, and Transgender?" April 2011, Williams Institute on Sexual Orientation Law and Public Policy, UCLA School of Law, Los Angeles.

162 About 3.5 percent of adults identify as gay: Gates, "How Many People Are Lesbian, Gay, Bisexual, and Transgender?" See also Gary J. Gates and Frank Newport, "Special Report: 3.4% of U.S. Adults Identify as LGBT," poll, Gallup.com, October 8, 2012. 4.6 percent of men and 8.3 percent of women ages eighteen to twenty-nine identify as LGBT, the highest rate of any age group. The American public, when polled, believed that 23 percent of adults were gay: Frank Newport, "Americans Greatly Overestimate Percent Gay, Lesbian in U.S," poll, Gallup.com, May 21, 2015.

162 The true number is hard to quantify: There is some dispute over whether "genderqueer" individuals are transgender, or vice versa. Gates, "How Many People Are Lesbian, Gay, Bisexual, and Transgender?"

162 They fell in love in a support group for transgender teens: They have since broken up, and each plans to publish a memoir. Janine Radford Rubenstein, "Arin Andrews and Katie Hill, Transgender Former Couple, to Release Memoirs," *People*, March 11, 2014.

163 They may replace *he* and *she* with: For a rundown of gender-neutral pronouns and their meanings, see "The Need for a Gender Neutral Pronoun," *Gender Neutral Pronoun Blog*, January 24, 2010.

See also Margot Adler, "Young People Push Back Against Gender Categories."

163 her parents said their first inkling: Solomon P. Banda and Nicholas Riccardi, "Coy Mathis Case: Colorado Civil Rights Division Rules in Favor of Transgender 6-Year-Old in Bathroom Dispute," Associated Press, June 24, 2013; Sabrina Rubin Erdely, "About a Girl: Coy Mathis' Fight to Change Gender," *Rolling Stone*, October 28, 2013.

Chapter 6: Blurred Lines, Take Two

168 They were disdainful of girls and female teachers: For an outstanding account of the Glen Ridge rape and its impact, see Lefkowitz, *Our Guys*.

169 It wouldn't be until 2015 that Tyson's former manager: Nicholas Godden, "'Mike Tyson Rape Case Was Inevitable, I'm Surprised More Girls Didn't Make Claims Against Him,'" *Mail Online*, February 9, 2015.

171 "They would say, 'Yes, I held'": Kamenetz, "The History of Campus Sexual Assault."

172 Other media outlets: *The Date Rape Backlash Media and the Denial of Rape*, Jhally, prod.

172 When Roiphe lost her novelty: Zoe Heller, "Shooting from the Hip," *Independent*, January 17, 1993.

172 whose book *Who Stole Feminism*: Hoff Sommers, *Who Stole Feminism*.

176 Using the narrowest definition of rape: Raphael, *Rape Is Rape*.

176 Still, given that according to the Census Bureau: There was a total of more than 5.7 million female undergraduates at four-year institutions and more than 3.8 million at two-year institutions. U.S. Census Bureau, *School Enrollment in the United States 2013*, Washington, DC: U.S. Census Bureau, September 24, 2014.

176 The Association of American Universities': Cantor, Fisher, Chibnall, et al., *Report on the AAU Campus Climate Survey on Sexual Assault and Sexual Misconduct*.

177 and 25 percent reported at least one: Ford and England, "What Percent of College Women Are Sexually Assaulted in College?"

A third survey, released in 2015 by United Educators, which provides liability insurance to schools, found that 30 percent of rapes reported at its 104 client schools between 2011 and 2013 were committed through force or threat of force and 33 percent were committed while the victim was incapacitated. In another 13 percent of cases, the perpetrator didn't use force, but continued engaging in sexual contact after the victim hesitated or verbally refused. Eighteen percent of cases were labeled "failed consent": the perpetrator used no force, threat of force, or coercion but "ignored or misinterpreted cues or inferred consent from silence or lack of resistance." The remaining 7 percent of rapes involved the use of a knockout drug. Ninety-nine percent of perpetrators were male. Claire Gordon, "Study: College Athletes Are More Likely to Gang Rape," *Al Jazeera America*, February 26, 2015.

177 that brings us back to one in four: Another 2015 study, of 483 students at an unnamed private university in upstate New York, found that 18.6 percent of freshman women were victims of rape or attempted rape. Carey, Durney, Shepardson, et al., "Incapacitated and Forcible Rape of College Women."

177 it's probably not surprising that by 2006: Kristen Lombardi, "Campus Sexual Assault Statistics Don't Add Up," Center for Public Integrity, December 2009. Between 2009 and 2014, over 40 percent of schools in a national sample had not conducted a single assault investigation. United States Senate, U.S. Senate Subcommittee on Financial and Contracting Oversight, *Sexual Violence on Campus.*

178 lower burden of proof: Michael Dorf, " 'Yes Means Yes' and Preponderance of the Evidence," *Dorf on Law* (blog), October 29, 2014.

179 Among them were the most prestigious in the country: Edwin Rios, "The Feds Are Investigating 106 Colleges for Mishandling Sexual Assault. Is Yours One of Them?" *Mother Jones*, April 8, 2015.

180 appears to reflect a new willingness: "New Education Department Data Shows Increase in Title IX Sexual Violence

Complaints on College Campuses," Press release, May 5, 2015, Office of Barbara Boxer, U.S. Senator, California.

180 Afterward, though, they sink back: Yung, "Concealing Campus Sexual Assault."

180 Twenty-eight percent of female college freshmen in a 2015: Unlike some other surveys, this one limited itself to the legal definition of rape; it did not include forced fondling or forced kissing. Carey et al., "Incapacitated and Forcible Rape of Women." The U.S. Justice Department has found that nearly one in five girls ages fourteen to seventeen had been the victims of attempted or completed assault. Finkelhor, Turner, and Ormrod, "Children's Exposure to Violence."

183 "You don't think you ruined my life forever?": Jason Riley and Andrew Wolfson, "Louisville Boys Sexually Assaulted Savannah Dietrich 'Cause We Thought It Would Be Funny,'" *Courier Journal*, August 30, 2012.

185 often both victim and assailant: Krebs, Lindquist, and Warner, *The Campus Sexual Assault (CSA) Study Final Report.*

185 Yet in 2013, when Emily Yoffe wrote on *Slate DoubleX*: Emily Yoffe, "College Women: Stop Getting Drunk," *Slate DoubleX*, October 15, 2013.

186 Women metabolize liquor differently from men, too: Centers for Disease Control, "Binge Drinking: A Serious Under-Recognized Problem Among Women and Girls."

186 If you really want to reduce assault, they said, wouldn't it be equally: Gordon, "Study: College Athletes Are More Likely to Gang Rape"; Abbey, "Alcohol's Role in Sexual Violence Perpetration"; Davis, "The Influence of Alcohol Expectancies and Intoxication on Men's Aggressive Unprotected Sexual Intentions"; Foubert, Newberry, and Tatum, "Behavior Differences Seven Months Later"; Carr and VanDeusen, "Risk Factors for Male Sexual Aggression on College Campuses"; Abbey, Clinton-Sherrod, McAuslan, et al., "The Relationship Between the Quantity of Alcohol Consumed and Severity of Sexual Assaults Committed by College Men"; Norris, Davis, George, et al., "Alcohol's Direct and Indirect Effects on

Men's Self-Reported Sexual Aggression Likelihood"; Abbey et al., "Alcohol and Sexual Assault"; Norris et al., "Alcohol and Hypermasculinity as Determinants of Men's Empathic Responses to Violent Pornography."

186 It lowers their inhibition; it allows them to disregard: Abbey, "Alcohol's Role in Sexual Violence Perpetration"; Davis, "The Influence of Alcohol Expectancies and Intoxication on Men's Aggressive Unprotected Sexual Intentions"; Abbey et al., "Alcohol and Sexual Assault."

186 By contrast, sober guys not only are less sexually coercive: Abbey, "Alcohol's Role in Sexual Violence Perpetration"; Orchowski, Berkowitz, Boggis, et al., "Bystander Intervention Among College Men."

187 Six hundred thousand students ages eighteen to twenty-four: Nicole Kosanake and Jeffrey Foote, "Binge Thinking: How to Stop College Kids from Majoring in Intoxication," *Observer*, January 21, 2015.

187 In that same two-month period: Dan Noyes, "Binge Drinking at UC Berkeley Strains EMS System," *Eyewitness News*, ABC, November 7, 2013; Emilie Raguso, "Student Drinking at Cal Taxes Berkeley Paramedics," Berkeleyside.com, November 12, 2013; Nico Correia, "UCPD Responds to 8 Cases of Alcohol-Related Illness Monday Morning," *Daily Californian*, August 26, 2013. In 2012, twelve students were transported to the hospital during the first two weeks of school at UC Berkeley; in 2011 there were eleven incidents in the month of August alone. In 2014, however, the number of incidents during the first weekend of school dropped by half. *Daily Californian*, "Drinking Is a Responsibility," August 26, 2014.

187 And yet when binge drinking rises, so does sexual assault: Mohler-Kuo, Dowdall, Koss, et al., "Correlates of Rape While Intoxicated in a National Sample of College Women." This is not, again, to say alcohol causes rape, but that rapists use alcohol in a variety of ways to abet their crimes.

188 "Who knows what their intentions were?": Noyes, "Binge Drinking at UC Berkeley Strains EMS System."

188 nearly 60 percent are unsure: "Poll: One in 5 Women Say They Have Been Sexually Assaulted in College," *Washington Post*, June 12, 2015.

193 "'we need to stick together and prevent shit like this'": André Rouillard, "The Girl Who Ratted," *Vanderbilt Hustler*, April 16, 2014.

194 Although, oddly, as criminologist Jan Jordan has pointed out: Raphael, *Rape Is Rape.*

194 "Rape recantations could be the result of the complainants'": Additionally, victims were urged to take a polygraph test, a practice that has since been abandoned as adversely affecting their willingness to come forward. Rape victims asked to take a polygraph test believe they are being doubted from the get-go. Kanin, "False Rape Allegations."

194 They place false claim rates at between 2 and 8 percent: Raphael, *Rape Is Rape*; Lisak, Gardinier, Nicksa, et al., "False Allegations of Sexual Assault: An Analysis of Ten Years of Reported Cases."

194 Certainly it is important to bear in mind the potential for false claims: Sinozich and Langton, *Special Report: Rape and Sexual Assault Victimization Among College-Age Females, 1995–2013*; Tyler Kingkade, "Fewer Than One-Third of Campus Sexual Assault Cases Result in Expulsion," *Huffington Post*, September 29, 2014; Nick Anderson, "Colleges Often Reluctant to Expel for Sexual Violence," *Washington Post*, December 15, 2014.

195 Emily Yoffe, who also raises the specter. Emily Yoffe, "The College Rape Overcorrection," *Slate DoubleX*, December 7, 2014.

195 "we are also teaching a generation of young women": Emily Yoffe, "How *The Hunting Ground* Blurs the Truth," *Slate DoubleX*, February 27, 2015.

195 Young women, as I've said, remain: See Tolman, Davis, and Bowman, "That's Just How It Is."

197 Another risk-reduction program: Senn, Eliasziw, Barata, et al., "Efficacy of a Sexual Assault Resistance Program for University Women." This is particularly important because rapists target freshman women. The resistance program involved four three-hour units in which skills were taught and practiced.

The goal was for young women to be able to assess risk from acquaintances, overcome emotional barriers in acknowledging danger, and engage in effective verbal and physical self-defense.

198 "I wanted to not cause a conflict": Bidgood, "In Girl's Account, Rite at St. Paul's Boarding School Turned into Rape."

198 though that percentage dropped to 13.6 percent: Edwards et al., "Denying Rape but Endorsing Forceful Intercourse."

198 it also maintains sexual availability as: Katha Pollitt, "Why Is 'Yes Means Yes' So Misunderstood?" *Nation*, October 8, 2014.

203 "Good girlfriends" say yes: Laina Y. Bay-Cheng and Rebecca Eliseo-Arras, "The Making of Unwanted Sex: Gendered and Neoliberal Norms in College Women's Unwanted Sexual Experiences," *Journal of Sex Research* 45, no. 4 (2008): 386–97.

203 What, these young people wondered: For some college women, complying with unwanted sex may be a reaction to having refused in the past and then been coerced by their partner. In a study of undergraduates, a woman was seven times more likely to have engaged in sexual compliance if her partner had previously coerced or assaulted her. Katz and Tirone, "Going Along with It."

204 fraternity brothers and athletes are disproportionately: In 2015, United Educators, which offers liability insurance to schools, released an analysis of 305 sexual assault reports from 104 client colleges made between 2011 and 2013. Although 10 percent of accused perpetrators were fraternity brothers (proportionate to their presence on campus), they made up 24 percent of repeat offenders; 15 percent of accused assailants were athletes, also proportionate to their presence on campus, yet they made up 20 percent of repeat offenders. Athletes were also three times more likely than other students to be involved in gang assaults, committing 40 percent of multiple perpetrator attacks reported to schools. Gordon, "Study: College Athletes Are More Likely to Gang Rape."

Chapter 7: What If We Told Them the Truth?

207 and a good-faith effort to satisfy everyone involved: Abraham, "Teaching Good Sex."

208 Unmarried women could not legally procure contraception: Luker, *When Sex Goes to School.*

208 Although, even then, over half of women: Schalet, *Not Under My Roof.* As late as 1969, two thirds of Americans thought it was wrong to have sexual relations before marriage. Lydia Saad, "Majority Considers Sex Before Marriage Morally Okay," Gallup News Service, May 24, 2001.

208 As sex became untethered: By the early 1970s the disapproval rate for premarital sex had dropped to 47 percent. By 1985, more than half of Americans agreed that premarital sex was "morally okay." Saad, "Majority Considers Sex Before Marriage Morally Okay." In 2014, 66 percent of Americans felt sex between an unmarried man and woman was "largely acceptable." Rebecca Riffkin, "New Record Highs in Moral Acceptability," poll, Gallup.com, May 2014.

209 They argued that the "epidemic" of teen motherhood: Moran, *Teaching Sex.*

209 "To reassure them that infidelity is widespread?": Moran, *Teaching Sex.*

210 "the social, psychological and health gains": Ibid.

210 by 1999, 40 percent of those supposedly teaching comprehensive sex ed: Ibid.

210 By 2003, 30 percent of public school sex: U.S. House of Representatives, *The Content of Federally Funded Abstinence-Only Education Programs.*

211 that money might just as well have been set on fire: Nicole Cushman and Debra Hauser, "We've Been Here Before: Congress Quietly Increases Funding for Abstinence-Only Programs," *RH Reality Check*, April 23, 2015.

211 Studies stretching back over a decade have found: U.S. House of Representatives, *The Content of Federally Funded Abstinence-Only Education Programs*; Hauser, "Five Years of Abstinence-Only-Until-Marriage Education: Assessing the Impact," 2004, Advocates for Youth, Washington, DC; Kirby, "Sex and HIV Programs"; Trenholm, Devaney, Fortson, et al., "Impacts of Four Title V, Section 510 Abstinence Education Programs."

211 They are, however, a lot more likely to become: Kohler,

Manhart, and Lafferty, "Abstinence-Only and Comprehensive Sex Education and the Initiation of Sexual Activity and Teen Pregnancy."

211 otherwise they would have given it up long ago for: Amanda Peterson Beadle, "Teen Pregnancies Highest in States with Abstinence-Only Policies," ThinkProgress, April 10, 2012; Rebecca Wind, "Sex Education Linked to Delay in First Sex," Media Center, Guttmacher Institute, March 8, 2012; Advocates for Youth, "Comprehensive Sex Education"; and "What Research Says About Comprehensive Sex Education."

211 $185 million earmarked for research and programs that: This discretionary funding stream includes $110 million for the president's Teen Pregnancy Prevention Initiative (TPPI), which is under the jurisdiction of the Office of Adolescent Health, and $75 million for the Personal Responsibility Education Program (PREP), which was part of the Affordable Care Act. See "A Brief History of Federal Funding for Sex Education and Related Programs."

212 Meanwhile, $75 million in abstinence-only funds: "Senate Passes Compromise Bill Increasing Federal Funding for Abstinence-Only Sex Education," *Feminist Majority Foundation: Feminist Newswire* (blog), April 17, 2015.

212 What this means for parents is that you never know: For information on individual state requirements as of 2015, see Guttmacher Institute, "Sex and HIV Education."

212 a judge ruled for the first time against: Bob Egeiko, "Abstinence-Only Curriculum Not Sex Education, Judge Rules," *San Francisco Chronicle*, May 14, 2015. A 2011 study conducted by UC San Francisco found uneven compliance with California state laws on sex education. In a sampling of California school districts, more than 40 percent failed to teach about condoms and other contraceptive methods in middle school; and in high school, 16 percent of students were taught that condoms were ineffective, and 70 percent of districts failed to comply with provisions of the law that require age-appropriate materials about sexual orientation.

Sarah Combellick and Claire Brindis, *Uneven Progress: Sex Education in California Public Schools*, November 2011, San Francisco: University of California–San Francisco Bixby Center for Global Reproductive Health.

213 "TAKE CARE & HAVE FUN": Alice Dreger, "I Sat In on My Son's Sex-Ed Class, and I Was Shocked by What I Heard," *The Stranger*, April 15, 2015; Sarah Kaplan, "What Happened When a Medical Professor Live-Tweeted Her Son's Sex-Ed Class on Abstinence," *Washington Post*, April 17, 2015.

219 Consider a study comparing the early sexual experiences: Brugman, Caron, and Rademakers, "Emerging Adolescent Sexuality."

220 "My friend's mother also asked me how it was": Ibid.

220 they consciously embraced it as natural: Schalet, *Not Under My Roof*. See also Saad, "Majority Considers Sex Before Marriage Morally Okay." Gallup did not measure Americans' attitudes toward teen sex in particular until 2013, when it found a significant age discrepancy in beliefs. Only 22 percent of adults over fifty-five agreed that sex between teenagers was "morally acceptable," whereas 30 percent of adults thirty-five to fifty-four and 48 percent of those eighteen to thirty-four agreed it was. Joy Wilke and Lydia Saad, "Older Americans' Moral Attitudes Changing," poll, Gallup.com, May 2013.

221 When a Dutch national poll found that most teenagers still: Schalet, *Not Under My Roof*.

221 Compare that to the United States, where two thirds: Martino, Collins, Elliott, et al., "It's Better on TV."

222 Either way, closeness can be compromised: Schalet, *Not Under My Roof*.

223 Girls are still more likely than boys to report: Vanwesenbeeck, "Sexual Health Behaviour Among Young People in the Netherlands."

223 Dutch girls who have multiple casual partners: Schalet, *Not Under My Roof*.

235 After studying the Dutch: Schalet, "The New ABCD's of Talking About Sex with Teenagers."

236 They particularly wanted to know more from us about: Alexandra Ossola, "Kids Really Do Want to Have 'The Talk' with Parents," *Popular Science*, March 5, 2015.

236 All the more reason to take a deep breath: Schear, *Factors That Contribute to, and Constrain, Conversations Between Adolescent Females and Their M––others About Sexual Matters*. William Fisher, a professor of psychology as well as obstetrics and gynecology, found that teens who felt positively about sex were more likely to use contraception and disease protection. They were also more likely to communicate with their partner. Fisher, "All Together Now."

Selected Bibliography

Abbey, Antonia. "Alcohol's Role in Sexual Violence Perpetration: Theoretical Explanations, Existing Evidence, and Future Directions." *Drug and Alcohol Review* 30, no. 5 (2011): 481–89.

Abbey, Antonia, A. Monique Clinton-Sherrod, Pam McAuslan, et al. "The Relationship Between the Quantity of Alcohol Consumed and Severity of Sexual Assaults Committed by College Men." *Journal of Interpersonal Violence* 18, no. 7 (2003): 813–33.

Abbey, Antonia, Tina Zawacki, Philip O. Buck, and A. Monique Clinton. "Alcohol and Sexual Assault." *Alcohol Research and Health* 25, no. 1 (2001): 43–51.

Abraham, Laurie. "Teaching Good Sex." *New York Times Magazine*, November 16, 2011.

Advocates for Youth. "Comprehensive Sex Education: Research and Results." *Fact Sheet*. Washington, DC, 2009.

Aligo, Scott. "Media Coverage of Female Athletes and Its Effect on the Self-Esteem of Young Women." *Research Brief: Youth Development Initiative* 29, September 15, 2014, Texas A&M University, College Station, TX.

Allison, Rachel, and Barbara J. Risman. "A Double Standard for 'Hooking Up': How Far Have We Come Toward Gender Equality?" *Social Science Research* 42, no. 5 (2013): 1191–206.

———. "'It Goes Hand in Hand with the Parties': Race, Class, and Residence in College Student Negotiations of Hooking Up." *Sociological Perspectives* 57, no. 1 (2014): 102–23.

American Psychological Association. *Report of the APA Task Force on the Sexualization of Girls.* Washington, DC: American Psychological Association, 2007.

American Sociological Association. "Virginity Pledges for Men Can Lead to Sexual Confusion—Even After the Wedding Day." *Science Daily,* August 17, 2014.

Anonymous. "The Pretty Game: Objectification, Humiliation and the Liberal Arts." *Bowdoin Orient,* February 13, 2014.

Armstrong, Elizabeth A., Paula England, and Alison C. K. Fogarty. "Accounting for Women's Orgasm and Sexual Enjoyment in College Hookups and Relationships." *American Sociological Review* 77 (2012): 435–62.

Armstrong, Elizabeth A., Laura Hamilton, and Paula England. "Is Hooking Up Bad for Young Women?" *Contexts* 9, no. 3 (2010): 22–27.

Armstrong, Elizabeth, and Brian Sweeney. "Sexual Assault on Campus: A Multilevel, Integrative Approach to Party Rape." *Social Problems* 53, no. 4 (2006): 483–99.

Backstrom, Laura, et al. "Women's Negotiation of Cunnilingus in College Hookups and Relationships." *Journal of Sex Research* 49, no. 1 (2012): 1–12.

Bailey, Jane, Valerie Steeves, Jacquelyn Burkell, et al. "Negotiating with Gender Stereotypes on Social Networking Sites: From 'Bicycle Face' to Facebook." *Journal of Communication Inquiry* 37, no. 2 (2013): 91–112.

Barron, Martin, and Michael Kimmel. "Sexual Violence in Three Pornographic Media: Toward a Sociological Explanation." *Journal of Sex Research* 37, no. 2 (2000): 161–68.

Bay-Cheng, Laina Y., and Nicole M. Fava. "Young Women's Experiences and Perceptions of Cunnilingus During Adolescence." *Journal of Sex Research* 48, no. 6 (2010): 531–42.

Bay-Cheng, Laina Y., Adjoa D. Robinson, and Alyssa N. Zucker. "Behavioral and Relational Contexts of Adolescent Desire, Wanting, and Pleasure: Undergraduate Women's Retrospective Accounts." *Journal of Sex Research* 46 (2009): 511–24.

Bearman, Peter S., and Hanna Brückner. "Promising the Future: Virginity Pledges and First Intercourse." *American Journal of Sociology* 106, no. 4 (2001): 859–912.

Bersamin, Melina, Deborah A. Fisher, Samantha Walker, Douglas L. Hill, et al. "Defining Virginity and Abstinence: Adolescents' Interpretations of Sexual Behaviors." *Journal of Adolescent Health* 41, no. 2 (2007): 182–88.

Bersamin, Melina, Samantha Walker, Elizabeth. D. Walters, et al. "Promising to Wait: Virginity Pledges and Adolescent Sexual Behavior." *Journal of Adolescent Health* 36, no. 5 (2005): 428–36.

Bisson, Melissa A., and Timothy R. Levine. "Negotiating a Friends with Benefits Relationship." *Archives of Sexual Behavior* 38 (2009): 66–73.

Black, M. C., K. C. Basile, M. J. Breiding, et al. *The National Intimate Partner and Sexual Violence Survey (NISVS): 2010 Summary Report*. Atlanta: National Center for Injury Prevention and Control, Centers for Disease Control and Prevention, 2011.

Bonino, S. et al. "Use of Pornography and Self-Reported Engagement in Sexual Violence Among Adolescents." *European Journal of Developmental Psychology* 3 (2006): 265–88.

Brady, Sonya S., and Bonnie L. Halpern-Felsher. "Adolescents' Reported Consequences of Having Oral Sex Versus Vaginal Sex." *Pediatrics* 119, no. 2 (2007): 229–36.

Bridges, Ana J., Robert Wosnitzer, Erica Scharrer, et al. "Aggression and Sexual Behavior in Best-Selling Pornography Videos: A Content Analysis Update." *Violence Against Women* 16, no. 10 (2010): 1065–85.

Brixton, James, Delicia Carey, Darlene Davis, et al. *Sexually Transmitted Disease Surveillance, 2013*. Atlanta: Centers for Disease Control and Prevention, 2014.

Brosi, Matthew, John D. Foubert, R. Sean Bannon, et al. "Effects of Women's Pornography Use on Bystander Intervention in a Sexual Assault Situation and Rape Myth Acceptance." *Oracle: The Research Journal of the Association of Fraternity/Sorority Advisors* 6, no. 2 (2011): 26–35.

Brown, Lyn Mikel, and Carol Gilligan. *Meeting at the Crossroads: Women's Psychology and Girls' Development*. New York: Ballantine Books, 1993.

Brown, Jane D. "Mass Media Influences on Sexuality." *Journal of Sex Research* 39, no. 1 (2002): 42–45.

Brown, Jane D., and Kelly L. L'Engle. "X-Rated: Sexual Attitudes and Behaviors Associated with U.S. Early Adolescents' Exposure to Sexually Explicit Media." *Communication Research* 36, no. 1 (2009): 129–51.

Brückner, Hannah, and Peter Bearman. "After the Promise: The STD Consequences of Adolescent Virginity Pledges." *Journal of Adolescent Health* 36 (2005): 271–78.

Brugman, Margaret, Sandra L. Caron, and Jany Rademakers. "Emerging Adolescent Sexuality: A Comparison of American and Dutch College Women's Experiences." *International Journal of Sexual Health* 22, no. 1 (2010): 32–46.

Brumberg, Joan Jacobs. *The Body Project: An Intimate History of American Girls.* New York: Random House, 1997.

Burns, April, Valerie A. Futch, and Deborah L. Tolman. "It's Like Doing Homework." *Sexuality Research and Social Policy* 7, no. 1 (2011).

Calogero, Rachel M. "Objects Don't Object: Evidence That Self-Objectification Disrupts Women's Social Activism." *Psychological Science* 24, no. 3 (2013): 312–18.

Cantor, David, Bonnie Fisher, Susan Chibnall, et al. *Report on the AAU Campus Climate Survey on Sexual Assault and Sexual Misconduct.* Washington, DC: Association of American Universities, 2015.

Carey, Kate, Sarah Durney, Robyn Shepardson, et al. "Incapacitated and Forcible Rape of College Women: Prevalence Across the First Year." *Journal of Adolescent Health* 56 (2015): 678–80.

Caron, Sandra L. *The Sex Lives of College Students: Two Decades of Attitudes and Behaviors.* Orono: Maine College Press, 2013.

Carpenter, Laura M. *Virginity Lost: An Intimate Portrait of First Sexual Experiences.* New York: New York University Press, 2005.

Carr, Joetta L., and Karen M. VanDeusen. "Risk Factors for Male Sexual Aggression on College Campuses." *Journal of Family Violence* 19, no. 5 (2004): 279–89.

Carroll, Jason S., et al. "Generation XXX: Pornography Acceptance and Use Among Emerging Adults." *Journal of Adolescent Research* 23 (2008): 6–30.

Centers for Disease Control and Prevention. "Binge Drinking: A
    Serious, Under-Recognized Problem Among Women and Girls."
    CDC Vital Signs (blog), January 2013. Atlanta: Centers for Disease
    Control and Prevention.

———. "Caffeine and Alcohol." *Fact Sheet*, November 19, 2014.
    Atlanta: Centers for Disease Control and Prevention.

———. "Reproductive Health: Teen Pregnancy, About Teen
    Pregnancy," 2014. Atlanta: Centers for Disease Control and
    Prevention.

———. "Youth Risk Behavior Surveillance." *Morbidity and Mortality
    Weekly Report*, June 13, 2014. Atlanta: Centers for Disease Control
    and Prevention.

Chambers, Wendy C. "Oral Sex: Varied Behaviors and Perceptions in a
    College Population." *Journal of Sex Research* 44, no. 1 (2007): 28–42.

Chandra, Anjani, William D. Mosher, Casey E. Copen, et al.
    "Sexual Behavior, Sexual Attraction, and Sexual Identity in the
    United States: Data from the 2006–2008 National Survey of
    Family Growth." *National Health Statistics Reports* 36, March 3,
    2011. Washington, DC: U.S. Department of Health and Human
    Services.

Child Trends DataBank. "Oral Sex Behaviors Among Teens."
    Bethesda, MD: Child Trends DataBank, 2013.

Chyng, Sun, Ana Bridges, Robert Wosnitzer, et al. "A Comparison
    of Male and Female Directors in Popular Pornography: What
    Happens When Women Are at the Helm?" *Psychology of Women
    Quarterly* 32, no. 3 (2008): 312–25.

Collins, W. Andrew, Deborah P. Welsh, and Wyndol Furman.
    "Adolescent Romantic Relationships." *Annual Review of Psychology*
    60 (2009): 631–52.

"Consent: Not Actually That Complicated,"
    Rockstardinosaurpirateprincess.com, March 2, 2015.

Copen, Casey E., Anjani Chandra, and Gladys Martinez. "Prevalence
    and Timing of Oral Sex with Opposite-Sex Partners Among
    Females and Males Aged 15–24 Years: United States 2007–2010,"
    National Health Statistics Reports 56 (August 16, 2012).

Corinna, Heather. *S.E.X.: The All-You-Need-to-Know Progressive Sexuality*

Guide to Get You Through High School and College. Boston: Da Capo Press, 2007.

Cornell, Jodi L., and Bonnie L. Halpern-Felsher. "Adolescent Health Brief: Adolescents Tell Us Why Teens Have Oral Sex." *Journal of Adolescent Health* 38 (2006): 299–301.

Daniels, Elizabeth A. "Sex Objects, Athletes, and Sexy Athletes: How Media Representations of Women Athletes Can Impact Adolescent Girls and Young Women." *Journal of Adolescent Research* 24 (2009): 399–422.

The Date Rape Backlash: Media and the Denial of Rape. Transcript. Documentary produced by Sut Jhally, 1994.

Davis, Kelly Cue. "The Influence of Alcohol Expectancies and Intoxication on Men's Aggressive Unprotected Sexual Intentions." *Experimental and Clinical Psychopharmacology* 18, no. 5 (2010): 418–28.

Diamond, Lisa. "Introduction: In Search of Good Sexual-Developmental Pathways for Adolescent Girls." In *Rethinking Positive Adolescent Female Sexual Development.* Edited by Lisa Diamond. San Francisco: Jossey-Bass, 2006, pp. 1–7.

Diamond, Lisa, and Ritch Savin-Williams. "Adolescent Sexuality." In *Handbook of Adolescent Psychology.* Edited by Richard M. Lerner and Laurence Steinberg. 3rd ed. New York: Wiley, 2009, pp. 479–523.

Dillard, Katie. "Adolescent Sexual Behavior: Demographics." 2002. Advocates for Youth, Washington, DC.

Dotson-Blake, Kylie P., David Knox, and Marty E. Zusman. "Exploring Social Sexual Scripts Related to Oral Sex: A Profile of College Student Perceptions." *Professional Counselor* 2 (2012): 1–11.

Douglass, Marcia, and Lisa Douglass. *Are We Having Fun Yet? The Intelligent Woman's Guide to Sex.* New York: Hyperion, 1997.

Dunn, Hailee, A. Gjelsvik, D. N. Pearlman, et al. "Association Between Sexual Behaviors, Bullying Victimization and Suicidal Ideation in a National Sample of High School Students: Implications of a Sexual Double Standard." *Women's Health Issues* 24, no. 5 (2014): 567–74.

Edwards, Sarah R., Kathryn A. Bradshaw, and Verlin B. Hinsz. "Denying Rape but Endorsing Forceful Intercourse: Exploring

Differences Among Responders." *Violence and Gender* 1, no. 4 (2014): 188–93.

England, Paula, et al. "Hooking Up and Forming Romantic Relationships on Today's College Campuses." In *Gendered Society Reader*. Edited by Michael S. Kimmel and Amy Aronson. 3rd ed. New York: Oxford University Press, 2008.

Englander, Elizabeth. "Low Risk Associated with Most Teenage Sexting: A Study of 617 18-Year-Olds." *MARC Research Reports*, Paper 6, 2012. Bridgewater, MA: Virtual Commons–Bridgewater State University.

Exner-Cortens, Deinera, John Eckenrode, and Emily Rothman. "Longitudinal Associations Between Teen Dating Violence Victimization and Adverse Health Outcomes." *Pediatrics* 131, no. 1 (2013): 71–78.

Fardouly, Jasmine, Phillipa C. Diedrichs, Lenny R. Vartanian, et al. "Social Comparisons on Social Media: The Impact of Facebook on Young Women's Body Image Concerns and Mood." *Body Image* 13 (2015): 38–45.

Fava, Nicole M., and Laina Y. Bay-Cheng. "Young Women's Adolescent Experiences of Oral Sex: Relation of Age of Initiation to Sexual Motivation, Sexual Coercion, and Psychological Functioning." *Journal of Adolescence* 30 (2012): 1–11.

Fay, Joe. "Teaching Teens About Sexual Pleasure." *SIEUS Report* 30, no. 4 (2002): 1–7.

Fine, Michelle. "Sexuality, Schooling, and Adolescent Females: The Missing Discourse of Desire." *Harvard Educational Review* 58 (1988): 29–53.

Fine, Michelle, and Sara McClelland. "Sexuality Education and Desire: Still Missing After All These Years." *Harvard Educational Review* 76 (2006): 297–338.

Finer, Lawrence B., and Jesse M. Philbin. "Sexual Initiation, Contraceptive Use, and Pregnancy Among Young Adolescents." *Pediatrics* 131, no. 5 (2013): 886–91.

Finkelhor, David, Heather Turner, and Richard Ormrod. "Children's Exposure to Violence: A Comprehensive National Survey." *Juvenile Justice Bulletin*, October 2009.

Fisher, Deborah A., Douglas L. Hill, Joel W. Grube, et al. "Televised Sexual Content and Parental Mediation: Influences on Adolescent Sexuality." *Media Psychology* 12, no. 2 (2009): 121–47.

Fisher, Maryanne, Kerry Worth, Justin Garcia, et al. "Feelings of Regret Following Uncommitted Sexual Encounters in Canadian University Students." *Culture, Health and Sexuality* 14, no. 1 (2012): 45–57.

Fisher, William A. "All Together Now: An Integrated Approach to Preventing Adolescent Pregnancy and STD/HIV Infection." *SIECUS Report* 18, no. 4 (1990): 1–14.

Fortenberry, Dennis J. "Puberty and Adolescent Sexuality." *Hormones and Behavior* 64, no. 2 (2013): 280–87.

Fortenberry, Dennis J., Vanessa Schick, Debby Herbenick, et al. "Sexual Behaviors and Condom Use at Last Vaginal Intercourse: A National Sample of Adolescents Ages 14 to 17 Years." *Journal of Sexual Medicine* 7, suppl. 5 (2010): 305–14.

Foubert, John D., Matthew W. Brossi, and R. Sean Bannon. "Pornography Viewing Among Fraternity Men: Effects on Bystander Intervention, Rape Myth Acceptance, and Behavioral Intent to Commit Sexual Assault." *Sexual Addiction and Compulsivity: The Journal of Treatment and Prevention* 18, no. 4 (2011): 212–31.

Foubert, John D., Jonathan T. Newberry, and Jerry L. Tatum. "Behavior Differences Seven Months Later: Effects of a Rape Prevention Program on First-Year Men Who Join Fraternities." *NASPA Journal* 44 (2007): 728–49.

Ford, Jessie, and Paula England. "What Percent of College Women Are Sexually Assaulted in College?" Contexts.com, January 12, 2015.

Fox, Jesse, Rachel A. Ralston, Cody K. Cooper, et al. "Sexualized Avatars Lead to Women's Self-Objectification and Acceptance of Rape Myths." *Psychology of Women Quarterly*, October 2014.

Fredrickson, Barbara, et al. "That Swimsuit Becomes You: Sex Differences in Self-Objectification, Restrained Eating, and Math Performance." *Journal of Personality and Social Psychology* 75 (1998): 269–84.

Fredrickson, Barbara, and Tomi-Ann Roberts. "Objectification

Theory: Toward Understanding Women's Lived Experience and Mental Health Risks." *Psychology of Women Quarterly* 21 (1997): 173–206.

Friedman, Jaclyn, and Jessica Valenti. *Yes Means Yes!: Visions of Female Sexual Power and a World Without Rape.* New York: Seal Press, 2008.

Garcia, Justin R., Chris Reiber, Sean G. Massey, et al. "Sexual Hook-Up Culture: A Review." *Review of General Psychology* 16, no. 2 (2012): 161–76.

Gerressu, Makeda, et al. "Prevalence of Masturbation and Associated Factors in a British National Probability Survey." *Archives of Sexual Behavior* 37 (2008): 266–78.

Gilligan, Carol, Nona Lyons, and Trudy Hanmer, eds. *Making Connections: The Relational Worlds of Adolescent Girls at Emma Willard School.* Cambridge, MA: Harvard University Press, 1990.

GLSEN. *Out Online: The Experiences of Lesbian, Gay, Bisexual and Transgender Youth on the Internet.* New York: GLSEN, July 10, 2013.

Gomillion Sarah C., and Traci A. Giuliano. "The Influence of Media Role Models on Gay, Lesbian, and Bisexual Identity." *Journal of Homosexuality* 58 (2011): 330–54.

Grello, Catherine M., et al. "No Strings Attached: The Nature of Casual Sex in College Students." *Journal of Sex Research* 43 (2006): 255–67.

Grunbaum, J. A., et al. "Youth Risk Behavior Surveillance— United States, 2001." *Morbidity and Mortality Weekly Report. CDC Surveillance Summaries* 51 (2002): 1–64.

Guttmacher Institute. "American Teens' Sexual and Reproductive Health." *Fact Sheet,* May 2014. New York: Guttmacher Institute.

———. "Sex and HIV Education." *State Policies in Brief,* June 1, 2015. New York: Guttmacher Institute.

Haffner, Debra W., ed. *Facing Facts: Sexual Health for America's Adolescents: The Report of the National Commission on Adolescent Sexual Health.* Washington, DC: Sexuality Information and Education Council of the United States, 1995.

Halliwell, Emma, et al. "Are Contemporary Media Images Which Seem to Display Women as Sexually Empowered Actually

Harmful to Women?" *Psychology of Women Quarterly* 35, no. 1 (2011): 38–45.

Halpern-Felsher, Bonnie L., Jodi L. Cornell, Rhonda Y. Kropp, and Jeanne M. Tschann. "Oral Versus Vaginal Sex Among Adolescents: Perceptions, Attitudes, and Behavior." *Pediatrics* 4 (2005): 845–51.

Hamilton, Laura, and Elizabeth A. Armstrong. "Gendered Sexuality in Young Adulthood: Double Binds and Flawed Options." *Gender and Society* 23 (2009): 589–616.

Harris, Michelle. "Shaved Paradise: A Sociological Study of Pubic Hair Removal Among Lehigh University Undergraduates." Senior thesis, 2009, Lehigh University, Bethlehem, PA.

Henry J. Kaiser Family Foundation. "Teen Sexual Activity." *Fact Sheet*, December 2002. Menlo Park, CA: Henry J. Kaiser Family Foundation.

Henry J. Kaiser Family Foundation/YM Magazine. *National Survey of Teens: Teens Talk About Dating, Intimacy, and Their Sexual Experiences.* Menlo Park, CA: Henry J. Kaiser Family Foundation, March 27, 1998.

Herbenick, Debby, et al. "Sexual Behavior in the United States: Results from a National Probability Sample of Men and Women Ages 14–94." *Journal of Sexual Medicine* 7, suppl. 5 (2010): 255–65.

Hirschman, Celeste, Emily A. Impett, and Deborah Schooler. "Dis/Embodied Voices: What Late-Adolescent Girls Can Teach Us About Objectification and Sexuality." *Sexuality Research and Social Policy* 3, no. 4 (2006): 8–20.

Hoff, Tina, Liberty Green, and Julia Davis. "National Survey of Adolescents and Young Adults: Sexual Health Knowledge, Attitudes and Experiences," 2004. Henry J. Kaiser Family Foundation, Menlo Park, CA, p. 14.

Horan, Patricia F., Jennifer Phillips, and Nancy E. Hagan. "The Meaning of Abstinence for College Students." *Journal of HIV/AIDS Prevention and Education for Adolescents and Children* 2, no. 2 (1998): 51–66.

Human Rights Campaign. *Growing Up LGBT in America.* Human Rights Campaign, Washington, DC, 2012.

Impett, Emily, Deborah Schooler, and Deborah Tolman. "To Be Seen and Not Heard: Femininity Ideology and Adolescent Girls' Sexual Health." *Archives of Sexual Behavior* 35 (2006): 129–42.

Impett, Emily, and Deborah Tolman. "Late Adolescent Girls' Sexual Experiences and Sexual Satisfaction." *Journal of Adolescent Research* 6 (2006): 628–46.

Joyner, Kara, and J. Richard Udry. "You Don't Bring Me Anything but Down: Adolescent Romance and Depression." *Journal of Health and Social Behavior* 41, no. 4 (2000): 369–91.

Kaestle, Christine Elizabeth. "Sexual Insistence and Disliked Sexual Activities in Young Adulthood: Differences by Gender and Relationship Characteristics." *Perspectives on Sexual and Reproductive Health* 41, no. 1 (2009): 33–39.

Kanin, Eugene J. "False Rape Allegations." *Archives of Sexual Behavior* 23, no. 1 (1994): 81–92.

Kann, Laura, Steven Kinchen, Shari L. Shanklin, et al. "Youth Risk Behavior Surveillance: United States, 2013." *Morbidity and Mortality Weekly Report.* Atlanta: Centers for Disease Control and Prevention, 2014.

Katz, Jennifer, and Vanessa Tirone. "Going Along with It: Sexually Coercive Partner Behavior Predicts Dating Women's Compliance with Unwanted Sex." *Violence Against Women* 16, no. 7 (2010): 730–42.

Kelly-Weeder, Susan. "Binge Drinking and Disordered Eating in College Students." *Journal of the American Academy of Nurse Practitioners* 23, no. 1 (2011): 33–41.

Kipnis, Laura. *The Female Thing: Dirt, Sex, Envy, Vulnerability.* New York: Pantheon Books, 2006.

Kirby, Douglas. *Emerging Answers 2007: Research Findings on Programs to Reduce Teen Pregnancy and Sexually Transmitted Diseases.* Washington, DC: National Campaign to Prevent Teen and Unplanned Pregnancy, 2007.

———. "Sex and HIV Programs: Their Impact on Sexual Behaviors of Young People Throughout the World." *Journal of Adolescent Health* 40 (2007): 206–17.

Kohler, Pamela K., Lisa E. Manhart, and William E. Lafferty.

"Abstinence-Only and Comprehensive Sex Education and the Initiation of Sexual Activity and Teen Pregnancy." *Journal of Adolescent Health* 42 (2008): 334–51.

Krebs, Christopher P., Christine H. Lindquist, and Tara D. Warner. *The Campus Sexual Assault (CSA) Study Final Report.* Washington, DC: National Institute of Justice, 2007.

Kunkel, D., Keren Eyal, Keli Finnerty, et al. *Sex on TV 4.* Menlo Park, CA: Henry J. Kaiser Family Foundation, 2005.

Lamb, Sharon. "Feminist Ideals for a Healthy Female Adolescent Sexuality: A Critique." *Sex Roles* 62 (2010): 294–306.

Laumann, Edward O., Robert T. Michael, Gina Kolata, et al. *Sex in America: A Definitive Survey.* New York: Grand Central Publishing, 1995.

Lefkowitz, Bernard. *Our Guys: The Glen Ridge Rape and the Secret Life of the Perfect Suburb.* Berkeley: University of California Press, 1997.

Leigh, Barbara, and D. M. Morrison. "Alcohol Consumption and Sexual Risk-Taking in Adolescents." *Alcohol Health and Research World* 15 (1991): 58–63.

Lenhart, Amanda. "Teens and Sexting." Internet, Science, and Tech. Pew Research Center, December 15, 2009.

Lescano, Celia, et al. "Correlates of Heterosexual Anal Intercourse Among At-Risk Adolescents and Young Adults." *American Journal of Public Health* 99 (2009): 1131–36.

Levine, Judith. *Harmful to Minors: The Perils of Protecting Children from Sex.* Cambridge, MA: Da Capo Press, 2003.

Levy, Ariel. *Female Chauvinist Pigs: Women and the Rise of Raunch Culture.* New York: Free Press, 2006.

Lindberg, Laura Duberstein, Rachel Jones, and John S. Santelli. "Noncoital Sexual Activities Among Adolescents." *Journal of Adolescent Health* 43, no. 3 (2008): 231–38.

Lindberg, Laura Duberstein, John S. Santelli, and Susheela Singh. "Changes in Formal Sex Education: 1995–2002." *Perspectives on Sexual and Reproductive Health* 38 (2006): 182–89.

Lisak, David, Lori Gardinier, Sarah C. Nicksa, et al. "False Allegations of Sexual Assault: An Analysis of Ten Years of Reported Cases." *Violence Against Women* 16, no. 12 (2010): 1318–34.

Lisak, David, and Paul M. Miller Brown. "Repeat Rape and Multiple Offending Among Undetected Rapists." *Violence and Victims* 17, no. 1 (2002): 73–84.

Livingston, Jennifer, Laina Y. Bay-Cheng, et al. "Mixed Drinks and Mixed Messages: Adolescent Girls' Perspectives on Alcohol and Sexuality." *Psychology of Women Quarterly* 37, no. 1 (2013): 38–50.

Lounsbury, Kaitlin, Kimberly J. Mitchell, and David Finkelhor. "The True Prevalence of 'Sexting.'" *Fact Sheet*, April 2011. Crimes Against Children Research Center, Durham, NH.

Luker, Kristin. *When Sex Goes to School: Warring Views on Sex—and Sex Education—Since the Sixties*. New York: W. W. Norton, 2006.

Manago, Adriana, Michael B. Graham, Patricia M. Greenfield, et al. "Self-Presentation and Gender on MySpace." *Journal of Applied Developmental Psychology* 29, no. 6 (2008): 446–58.

Martinez, Gladys, Casey E. Copen, and Joyce C. Abma. "Teenagers in the United States: Sexual Activity, Contraceptive Use, and Childbearing, 2006–2010 National Survey of Family Growth." *Vital Health Statistics* 31 (2011): 1–35.

Martino, Steven C., Rebecca L. Collins, Marc N. Elliott, et al. "It's Better on TV: Does Television Set Teenagers Up for Regret Following Sexual Initiation?" *Perspectives on Sexual and Reproductive Health* 41, no. 2 (2009): 92–100.

McAnulty, Richard D., and Arnie Cann. "College Student Dating in Perspective: 'Hanging Out,' 'Hooking Up,' and Friendly Benefits." In *Sex in College*. Edited by Richard D. McAnulty. Santa Barbara, CA: Praeger, 2012, pp. 1–18.

McClelland, Sara I. "Intimate Justice: A Critical Analysis of Sexual Satisfaction." *Social and Personality Psychology Compass* 4, no. 9 (2010): 663–80.

———. "What Do You Mean When You Say That You Are Sexually Satisfied? A Mixed Methods Study." *Feminism and Psychology* 24, no. 1 (2014): 74–96.

———. "Who Is the 'Self' in Self-Reports of Sexual Satisfaction? Research and Policy Implications." *Sexuality Research and Social Policy* 8, no. 4 (2011): 304–20.

Meier, Evelyn P., and James Gray. "Facebook Photo Activity Associated with Body Image Disturbance in Adolescent Girls." *Cyberpsychology, Behavior, and Social Networking* 10, no. 10 (2013).

Mohler-Kuo, Meichun, George W. Dowdall, Mary P. Koss, et al. "Correlates of Rape While Intoxicated in a National Sample of College Women." *Journal of Studies on Alcohol* 65, no. 1 (2004).

Monk-Turner, Elizabeth, and H. Christine Purcell. "Sexual Violence in Pornography: How Prevalent Is It?" *Gender Issues* 2 (1999): 58–67.

Monroe, Scott M., Paul Rhode, John R. Seeley, et al. "Life Events and Depression in Adolescence: Relationship Loss as a Prospective Risk Factor for First Onset of Major Depressive Disorder." *Journal of Abnormal Psychology* 180, no. 4 (1999): 606–14.

Moore, Mignon R., and Jeanne Brooks-Gunn. "Healthy Sexual Development: Notes on Programs That Reduce Risk of Early Sexual Initiation and Adolescent Pregnancy." In *Reducing Adolescent Risk: Toward an Integrated Approach.* Edited by Daniel Romer. Thousand Oaks, CA: Sage Publications, 2003.

Moran, Caitlin. *How to Be a Woman.* New York: HarperPerennial, 2012.

Moran, Jeffrey. *Teaching Sex: The Shaping of Adolescence in the Twentieth Century.* Cambridge, MA: Harvard University Press, 2002.

National Center for Chronic Disease Prevention and Health Promotion. "Binge-Drinking: A Serious, Unrecognized Problem Among Women and Girls." *CDC Vital Signs* (blog), 2013. National Center for Chronic Disease Prevention and Health Promotion. Atlanta: Centers for Disease Control and Prevention, 2013.

National Institute on Alcohol Abuse and Alcoholism. "College Drinking." *Fact Sheet*, April 5, 2015. Washington, DC: National Institute on Alcohol Abuse and Alcoholism.

Norris, Jeanette, Kelly Cue Davis, William H. George, et al. "Alcohol's Direct and Indirect Effects on Men's Self-Reported Sexual Aggression Likelihood." *Journal of Studies on Alcohol* 63 (2002): 688–69.

Norris, Jeanette, William H. George, Kelly Cue Davis, Joel Martell, and R. Jacob Leonesio. "Alcohol and Hypermasculinity as Determinants of Men's Empathic Responses to Violent Pornography." *Journal of Interpersonal Violence* 14 (1999): 683–700.

Orchowski, Lindsay M., Alan Berkowitz, Jesse Boggis, et al. "Bystander Intervention Among College Men: The Role of Alcohol and Correlates of Sexual Aggression." *Journal of Interpersonal Violence* (2015): 1–23.

Orenstein, Peggy. *Cinderella Ate My Daughter: Dispatches from the Front Lines of the New Girlie-Girl Culture.* New York: HarperPaperbacks, 2012.

———. *Flux: Women on Sex, Work, Love, Kids, and Life in a Half-Changed World.* New York: Anchor, 2001.

———. *Schoolgirls: Young Women, Self-Esteem, and the Confidence Gap.* New York: Anchor, 1995.

O'Sullivan, Lucia, et al. "I Wanna Hold Your Hand: The Progression of Social, Romantic and Sexual Events in Adolescent Relationships." *Perspectives in Sexual and Reproductive Health* 39, no. 2 (2007): 100–107.

Oswalt, Sara B., Kenzie A. Cameron, and Jeffrey Koob. "Sexual Regret in College Students." *Archives of Sexual Behavior* 34 (2005): 663–69.

Owen, Janice, G. K. Rhoades, S. M. Stanley, et al. " 'Hooking up' Among College Students: Demographic and Psychosocial Correlates." *Archives of Sexual Behavior* 39 (2010): 653–63.

Paul, Elizabeth L., et al., " 'Hookups': Characteristics and Correlates of College Students' Spontaneous and Anonymous Sexual Experiences." *Journal of Sexual Research* 37 (2000): 76–88.

Paul, Pamela. *Pornified: How Pornography Is Transforming Our Lives, Our Relationships, and Our Families.* New York: Times Books, 2005.

Peter, Jochen, and Patti Valkenburg. "Adolescents' Exposure to a Sexualized Media Environment and Notions of Women as Sex Objects." *Sex Roles* 56 (2007): 381–95.

———. "Adolescents' Exposure to Sexually Explicit Online Material and Recreational Attitudes Toward Sex." *Journal of Communication* 56, no. 4 (2006): 639–60.

———. "The Use of Sexually Explicit Internet Material and Its Antecedents: A Longitudinal Comparison of Adolescents and

Adults." *Archives of Sexual Behavior* 40, no. 5 (October 2011): 1015–25.

Peterson, Zoe D., and Charlene L. Muehlenhard. "What Is Sex and Why Does It Matter? A Motivational Approach to Exploring Individuals' Definitions of Sex." *Journal of Sex Research* 44, no. 3 (2007): 256–68.

Phillips, Lynn M. *Flirting with Danger: Young Women's Reflections on Sexuality and Domination.* New York: New York University Press, 2000.

Pittman, Melissa. "The Joy of Slash: Why Do Women Want It?" *The High Hat*, Spring 2005.

Ponton, Lynn. *The Sex Lives of Teenagers: Revealing the Secret World of Adolescent Boys and Girls.* New York: Dutton, 2000.

Raphael, Jody. *Rape Is Rape: How Denial, Distortion, and Victim Blaming Are Fueling a Hidden Acquaintance Rape Crisis.* Chicago: Chicago Review Press, 2013.

Rector, Robert E., Kirk A. Jonson, and Laura R. Noyes. *Sexually Active Teenagers Are More Likely to Be Depressed and to Attempt Suicide: A Report of the Heritage Center for Data Analysis.* Washington, DC: Heritage Foundation, Center for Data Analysis, 2003.

Regnerus, Mark. *Forbidden Fruit: Sex and Religion in the Lives of American Teenagers.* New York: Oxford University Press, 2007.

———. "Porn Use and Support of Same-Sex Marriage." *Public Discourse*, December 20, 2012.

Remez, Lisa. "Oral Sex Among Adolescents: Is It Sex or Is It Abstinence?" *Family Planning Perspectives* 32 (2000): 298–304.

Ringrose, Jessica, Rosalind Gill, Sonia Livingstone, et al. *A Qualitative Study of Children, Young People, and 'Sexting': A Report Prepared for the NSPCC.* London: National Society for the Prevention of Cruelty to Children, 2012.

Robbins, Cynthia, Vanessa Schick, Michael Reece, et al. "Prevalence, Frequency, and Associations of Masturbation with Other Sexual Behaviors Among Adolescents Living in the United States of America." *Archives of Pediatric and Adolescent Medicine* 165, no. 12 (2011): 1087–93.

Rosenbaum, Janet Elise. "Patient Teenagers? A Comparison

of the Sexual Behavior of Virginity Pledgers and Matched Nonpledgers." *Pediatrics* 123 (2009): 110–20.

Ryan, Caitlin. "Generating a Revolution in Prevention, Wellness, and Care for LGBT Children and Youth." *Temple Political and Civil Rights Law Review* 23, no. 2 (2014): 331–44.

Sanders, Stephanie, Brandon J. Hill, William L. Yarber, et al. "Misclassification Bias: Diversity in Conceptualisations About Having 'Had Sex.'" *Sexual Health* 7, no. 1 (2010): 31–34.

Schalet, Amy T. "The New ABCD's of Talking About Sex with Teenagers." *Huffington Post*, November 2, 2011.

———. *Not Under My Roof: Parents, Teens, and the Culture of Sex.* Chicago: University of Chicago Press, 2011.

Schear, Kimberlee S. *Factors That Contribute to, and Constrain, Conversations Between Adolescent Females and Their Mothers About Sexual Matters.* Urbana, IL: Forum on Public Policy, 2006.

Schick, Vanessa R., Sarah K. Calabrese, Brandi N. Rima, et al. "Genital Appearance Dissatisfaction: Implications for Women's Genital Image Self-Consciousness, Sexual Esteem, Sexual Satisfaction, and Sexual Risk." *Psychology of Women Quarterly* 34 (2010): 394–404.

Sedgh, Gilda, Lawrence B. Finer, Akinrinola Bankole, et al. "Adolescent Pregnancy, Birth, and Abortion Rates Across Countries: Levels and Recent Trends." *Journal of Adolescent Health* 58, no. 2 (2012): 223–30.

Senn, Charlene Y., Misha Eliasziw, Paula C. Barata, et al. "Efficacy of a Sexual Assault Resistance Program for University Women." *New England Journal of Medicine* 372 (2015): 2326–35.

"Sexual Health of Adolescents and Young Adults in the United States." *Fact Sheet*, August 20, 2104. Menlo Park, CA: Henry J. Kaiser Family Foundation.

Sharpley-Whiting, Tracy D. *Pimps Up, Ho's Down: Hip Hop's Hold on Young Black Women.* New York: New York University Press, 2008.

SIECUS. "A Brief History of Federal Funding for Sex Education and Related Programs." *Fact Sheet*. Washington, DC: SIECUS, n.d.

———. "Questions and Answers: Adolescent Sexuality." Washington, DC: SIECUS, November 12, 2012.

————. "What Research Says . . . Comprehensive Sex Education." *Fact Sheet*. Washington, DC: SIECUS, October 2009.

Simmons, Rachel. *The Curse of the Good Girl: Raising Authentic Girls with Courage and Confidence*. Reprint. New York: Penguin, 2010.

————. *Odd Girl Out, Revised and Updated: The Hidden Culture of Aggression in Girls*. New York: Mariner Books, 2011.

Simpson, Jeffry A., W. Andrew Collins, and Jessica E. Salvatore. "The Impact of Early Interpersonal Experience on Adult Romantic Relationship Functioning: Recent Findings from the Minnesota Longitudinal Study of Risk and Adaptation." *Current Directions in Psychological Science* 20, no. 6 (2011): 355–59.

Sinozich, Sofi, and Lynn Langton. *Special Report: Rape and Sexual Assault Victimization Among College-Age Females, 1995–2013*. Washington, DC: Office of Justice Programs, Bureau of Justice Statistics, U.S. Department of Justice, 2014.

Slater, Amy, and Marika Tiggeman. "A Test of Objectification Theory in Adolescent Girls." *Sex Roles* 46, no. 9/10 (May 2002): 343–49.

Sommers, Christina Hoff. *Who Stole Feminism? How Women Have Betrayed Women*. New York: Simon & Schuster, 1994.

Steering Committee on Undergraduate Women's Leadership at Princeton University. *Report of the Steering Committee on Undergraduate Women's Leadership*. Princeton, NJ: Princeton University, 2011.

Stermer, S. Paul, and Melissa Burkley. "SeX-Box: Exposure to Sexist Video Games Predicts Benevolent Sexism." *Psychology of Popular Media Culture* 4, no. 1 (2015): 47–55.

Steyer, James. *Talking Back to Facebook: The Common Sense Guide to Raising Kids in the Digital Age*. New York: Scribner, 2012, pp. 22–23.

Strasburger, Victor. "Policy Statement from the American Academy of Pediatrics: Sexuality, Contraception, and the Media." *Pediatrics* 126, no. 3 (September 1, 2010): 576–82.

Tanenbaum, Leora. *Slut: Growing Up Female with a Bad Reputation*. New York: HarperPerennial, 2002.

Thomas, J. "Virginity Pledgers Are Just as Likely as Matched Nonpledgers to Report Premarital Intercourse." *Perspectives on Sexual and Reproductive Health* 41, no. 63 (March 2009).

Thompson, Sharon. *Going All the Way: Teenage Girls' Tales of Sex, Romance, and Pregnancy.* New York: Hill and Wang, 1995.

Tolman, Deborah. *Dilemmas of Desire: Teenage Girls Talk About Sexuality.* Cambridge, MA: Harvard University Press, 2002.

Tolman, Deborah, Brian R. Davis, and Christin P. Bowman. "That's Just How It Is": A Gendered Analysis of Masculinity and Femininity Ideologies in Adolescent Girls' and Boys' Heterosexual Relationships." *Journal of Adolescent Research* (June 2015).

Tolman, Deborah, Emily Impett, et al. "Looking Good, Sounding Good: Femininity Ideology and Adolescent Girls' Mental Health." *Psychology of Women Quarterly* 30 (2006): 85–95.

Trenholm, Christopher, Barbara Devaney, Ken Fortson, et al. "Impacts of Four Title V, Section 510 Abstinence Education Programs." Office of the Assistant Secretary for Planning and Evaluation, U.S. Department of Health and Human Services. Princeton, NJ: Mathematics Policy Research, 2007.

U.S. House of Representatives, Committee on Government Reform Minority Staff, Special Investigations Division. *The Content of Federally Funded Abstinence-Only Education Programs.* Prepared for Rep. Henry A. Waxman. Washington, DC: U.S. Government Printing Office, 2004.

U.S. Senate Subcommittee on Financial and Contracting Oversight. *Sexual Violence on Campus.* By Claire McCaskill. 113th Congress. Senate Report, July 9, 2014.

Valenti, Jessica. *The Purity Myth: How America's Obsession with Virginity Is Hurting Young Women.* Berkeley, CA: Seal Press, 2009.

Vanwesenbeeck, Ine. "Sexual Health Behaviour Among Young People in the Netherlands." Presentation at the Sexual Health Forum, Brussels, March 13, 2009.

Vernacchio, Al. *For Goodness Sex: Changing the Way We Talk to Teens About Sexuality, Values, and Health.* New York: HarperWave, 2014.

Wade, Lisa, and Caroline Heldman. "Hooking Up and Opting Out." In *Sex for Life: From Virginity to Viagra, How Sexuality Changes Throughout Our Lives.* Edited by Laura Carpenter and John DeLamater. New York: New York University Press, 2012, pp. 128–45.

Ward, L. Monique. "Understanding the Role of the Entertainment Media in the Sexual Socialization of American Youth: A Review of Empirical Research." *Developmental Review* 23 (2003): 347–88.

Ward, L. Monique, Edwina Hansbrough, and Eboni Walker. "Contributions of Music Video Exposure to Black Adolescents' Gender and Sexual Schemas." *Journal of Adolescent Research* 20 (2005): 143–66.

Ward, L. Monique, and Kimberly Friedman. "Using TV as a Guide: Associations Between Television Viewing and Adolescents' Sexual Attitudes and Behavior." *Journal of Research on Adolescence* 16 (2006): 133–56.

Widerman, Michael M. "Women's Body Image Self-Consciousness During Physical Intimacy with a Partner." *Journal of Sex Research* 37, no. 1 (2000): 60–68.

Widman, Laura, et al. "Sexual Communication and Contraceptive Use in Adolescent Dating Couples." *Journal of Adolescent Health* 39 (2006): 893–99.

Wolak, Janis, Kimberly Mitchell, and David Finkelhor. "Unwanted and Wanted Exposure to Online Pornography in a National Sample of Youth Internet Users." *Pediatrics* 119, no. 2 (2007): 247–57.

Wright, Paul J. "Show Me the Data! Empirical Support for the 'Centerfold Syndrome.'" *Psychology of Men and Masculinity* 13, no. 2 (2011): 180–98.

———. "A Three-Wave Longitudinal Analysis of Preexisting Beliefs, Exposure to Pornography, and Attitude Change." *Communication Reports* 26, no. 1 (2013): 13–25.

Wright, Paul J., and Michelle Funk. "Pornography Consumption and Opposition to Affirmative Action for Women: A Prospective Study." *Psychology of Women Quarterly* 38, no. 2 (2013): 208–21.

Wright, Paul J., and Robert S. Tokunaga. "Activating the Centerfold Syndrome: Recency of Exposure, Sexual Explicitness, Past Exposure to Objectifying Media." *Communications Research* 20, no. 10 (2013): 1–34.

Yung, Corey Rayburn. "Concealing Campus Sexual Assault: An Empirical Examination." *Psychology, Public Policy, and Law* 21, no. 1 (2015): 1–9.

Index

About the Author

Peggy Orenstein is the *New York Times* bestselling author of *Cinderella Ate My Daughter*, *Waiting for Daisy*, *Flux*, and *Schoolgirls*. A contributing writer for the *New York Times Magazine*, she has been published in *USA Today*, *Parenting*, *Salon*, the *New Yorker*, and other publications, and has contributed commentary to NPR's *All Things Considered*. She lives in Northern California with her husband and daughter.

DRAGONFIRE

DRAGONFIRE

TED BELL

BERKLEY
NEW YORK

BERKLEY
An imprint of Penguin Random House LLC
penguinrandomhouse.com

Copyright © 2020 by Theodore A. Bell
Penguin Random House supports copyright. Copyright fuels creativity, encourages diverse voices,
promotes free speech, and creates a vibrant culture. Thank you for buying an authorized edition of
this book and for complying with copyright laws by not reproducing, scanning, or distributing
any part of it in any form without permission. You are supporting writers and allowing
Penguin Random House to continue to publish books for every reader.

BERKLEY and the BERKLEY & B colophon are registered trademarks of Penguin Random House LLC.

Library of Congress Cataloging-in-Publication Data

Names: Bell, Ted, author.
Title: Dragonfire / Ted Bell.
Description: First edition. | New York: Berkley, 2020. |
Series: An Alex Hawke novel
Identifiers: LCCN 2020015891 (print) | LCCN 2020015892 (ebook) |
ISBN 9780593101209 (hardcover) | ISBN 9780593101223 (ebook)
Subjects: GSAFD: Adventure fiction. | Suspense fiction.
Classification: LCC PS3602.E6455 D73 2020 (print) | LCC PS3602.E6455 (ebook) |
DDC 813/.6—dc23
LC record available at https://lccn.loc.gov/2020015891
LC ebook record available at https://lccn.loc.gov/2020015892

Printed in the United States of America
10   9   8   7   6   5   4   3   2   1

Cover art: *Person on motorcycle* by Westersoe / GettyImages
Cover design by Steve Meditz
Book design by Laura K. Corless

This battered old heart of mine has finally learned
that even if you have to wait a lifetime,
you can find the one true love of your life.
This book is dedicated, with abiding love, laughter,
and admiration to my one and only Lady of Spain,
the beautiful, gracious, and kind Victoria de la Maza.
One in a million.

War is never about what is in front of you.
It is always about what's behind you.
And war is never about who is right, but who is left.

—Alexander Hawke's "The Warrior's Code,"
written during the Battle of Kamdesh
October 2009

GREYBEARD HOUSE

Greybeard Island
The Channel Islands, UK
June 1939

My dear grandson,

In light of your recent decision, which I wholeheartedly support, and of which I'm quite sure your late father would applaud, to join the Secret Service when your Royal Navy commission expires next spring, I would like to share some thoughts that I think will serve you in good stead. I'm an old man now, Blackie, but once I was you, straining at the traces and wishing to do important work in serving your King and Country. . . .

Be true to yourself. Honesty and integrity are absolutes, but you will need more. You will need the determination and the courage to see matters through, even when fainter hearts have already taken counsel of their fears. You will need to take hardship, danger, fatigue, and—perhaps above all—uncertainty in your stride. . . .

You will need the strength of will and confidence to take the right road when it is not an easy one.

Your loving grandfather,
(Signed)

(Letter from Admiral Lord Hawke to his grandson, Commander Horatio Black Hawke, RN Flying Service)

PROLOGUE

Bermuda
Present Day

A nd, pray tell, what fresh Hell is this? Mother of God!"
Lord Alexander Hawke flung his few anguished words into the warring windstorms in the heavens high above. He was shouting down the elements, calling them out, berating the brute natural forces that had conspired to turn on him in this, his darkest hour. "Traitors, what treason is this?" His words were whipped away, lost in the blow, vanished in the operatic rumble of thunder resounding in the dark and purplish clouds on the far horizon.

Then, of course, the rains came, solid curtains of water, a deluge upon this small spit of land, this lonely midocean isle breasting the oncoming tumult of the deep and heaving Atlantic Ocean.

Grumbling to himself, Hawke throttled way back on the vintage motorcycle, making every effort to squint the flood of stinging rainwater from his eyes. Damn the torpedoes, he thought. Full speed ahead! Hawke wound up the revs and surged forward at a breathtaking, if not suicidal, pace.

A dire situation was, at this very moment, evolving at his Bermuda hideaway, Teakettle Cottage.

His beloved Pelham's life was in danger. There was not a precious second to be lost. Calling upon his reserves of resolve, he leaned hard over into a hairpin turn, his right knee grazing the macadam. Now upright once more, he was accelerating furiously into a tight descending turn. Danger lurked around every bend along the old Coast Road. Flying home on a wing and prayer, as the RAF Spitfire lads at No. 76 Squadron would have back in the Battle of Britain.

His iron steed was an unforgiving mistress on even the driest of the dry summer days. On a night like this? A twisting, curvy coastal road practically marinated in decades of Castrol motor oil? God help you, boy. It was, Hawke thought, like racing a school bus across a frozen lake in a whiteout snowstorm.

As it happened, a suicidal vortex of two torrential maelstroms had come crashing ashore at the same time. Yet he somehow remained in the saddle. Cannon to the left of him, cannon to the right, volleyed and thundered. One storm, boiling up from the southernmost reaches of the Caribbean, battered him from the right. The other, a veritable freight train, roaring southward from the turbulent North Atlantic, whipped at him from the left.

Hawke had no illusions about himself now; he knew he was little more than a bit player, a sole actor occupying center stage at this epic meterological drama, The Tempest. God's Perfect Storm. But was he up to tonight's performance? The stomach for it? Or the *huevos*, as his Spanish friends call them?

Alexander Hawke, age thirty-five, had always kept himself in impeccable shape. His profession, senior counterterrorism officer at MI6, demanded it. Rising daily at dawn and beginning with free weights, squats, push-ups, and lunges, et cetera, the much-decorated fighter pilot performed the Royal Navy airman's standard exercise routine with a vengeance. Afterward, a six-mile swim in the open ocean. Three miles down to Bloody Bay on Bermuda's north shore and three miles back.

With his lean, muscular build, his sharply etched features, his prominent chin, and aquiline Roman nose, his fine head of unruly black hair and startling glacial blue eyes—which not a few London gossip columnists had said resembled "liquid pools of frozen Arctic rain"—he was no pretty boy. He was, in the end, simply a creature of radiant violence, a warrior to his molten core.

Also, a gentleman spy and a bit of a dandy for all that. A well-regarded citizen of London town of whom it was oft said, "Men loved to stand him a drink, whilst women much preferred him horizontal." Some wag once opined that this was the reason his mug had appeared so frequently on the cover of *Tatler* magazine's annual "Bachelor of the Year" edition.

The overpowered Norton was now racing flat out on twisting rain-slick roads. The bike was not cut out for this kind of a double-triple-whammy confluence of typhoon crap. Most definitely not. The old girl was a dry-track bike built for flats and racing against other vintage bikes, full stop. Not this bleeding nightmare. Bloody hell . . .

Suddenly, the bike went airborne. He'd completely miscalculated the sudden drop off of the steep hill that made a sharp descent down to Blackbeard's Bay. Undaunted by his error, the decorated ex–Royal Navy fighter pilot summoned an old air-combat trick. In the dogfight of your life, when all the chips are down and the fit has most certainly hit the bloody shan, with both your engines flamed out and a big fat bogie right up your arse and lighting off air-to-airs into the bargain, what do the Magnificent Men in Their Flying Machines do then, flyboy?

First, you mentally slow everything down, relax your grip on the stick a bit and force yourself to summon up every ounce of luck, every bit of skill you've got and even ones you've not, and you bloody well laser-focus on perfecting a soft landing. . . . Ah, here it comes!

"Hold fast," he said to himself, repeating the old credo of Nelson's Navy. Those two words, Admiral Lord Nelson's lifelong credo, tattooed on the underside of Hawke's left wrist were his permanent reminder of a temporary feeling: "Hold fast!" In red ink and acquired one very late red-light night when he and his sidekick, Stokely Jones Jr., had been barn-storming about Bangkok's infamous Soi Cowboy district in hot pursuit of the rumlike Mekhong Thai whiskey and other pleasures of the flesh . . .

———————

The wind and rain lashed the rider. Yet Hawke managed to zone in tight, but stay loose. Not fight the bike, but "fly with your eyes," as he called his technique. He'd done a bit of road racing in his twenties. Just pick the exact spot where you want the vehicle to go next and maintain a quiet mind, a light touch on the throttle ... yes ... and a bit of rear brake here, easy ... steer with your eyes ... and ...

Touchdown! Still upright. Bloody hell! One day, one more of these mistakes might bloody well kill me.

Hawke's most urgent thoughts now were of his beloved lifelong friend and gentleman's gentleman, Pelham Grenville.

"Hold fast, Pelham," he whispered. "Hold fast, old son!"

And now it was Pelham's life that hung in the balance. The old dear had somehow, through no fault of his own, fallen into the hands of a truly evil animal, a nightmarish creature only thinly disguised as a human being.

The monstrous American assassin, now in the service of one Vladimir Putin, was known politely as "Mr. Smith." Mr. Smith's given name went unsaid in polite company. It was actually an acronym derived from the days when the British trade clippers carried massive shipments of manure from the West Indies back to England. In the beginning they stowed the cargo low in the bowels of the ships to minimize the stink above deck. But the fleets were plagued with horrific fires and explosions for many years. Finally, they realized that the gases generated down low in the hold were the cause. And going forward, all the bales of animal waste carried the stenciled words "Stow High in Transit."

Shit. That was Mr. Smith's given name and it suited him to a T.

And now this fiend in human form had managed to gain entry to Teakettle Cottage, Hawke's quaint bungalow overlooking the sea. And the man was holding Pelham as ransom to ensure Hawke returned home. This West Texas cowboy chap, this former rodeo star and CIA contract killer, went by the highly unlikely name of "Shit Smith."

Smith was a murderous psychopath who enforced Putin's every will and whim with the blade of his razor-edged Bowie knife. His two-foot-long blade was always holstered to his right thigh. He was a man who belied the old verity "Never take a knife to a gunfight." Shit Smith would never take anything but a knife to a gunfight. He could pull the Bowie from its holster and hurl it with deadly accuracy as fast as any gunman could pull a trigger.

Smith was just one of countless Russian, Chinese, North Korean, and other contract killers around the globe who, for a brief time, had been out for Hawke's head, and all the fortune and fame that came with it. Putin had been offering a vast sum with a single condition: In order to reap the Kremlin's rewards, the killer must arrive at the Kremlin in Moscow in person. He must deliver Alex Hawke's head to Vladimir Putin on a sterling silver platter. The reward—ten million pounds British sterling. Cash, of course.

Hawke, who knew the Russian leader on a personal level, had ensured that Vlad got to keep his ten million pounds sterling in one of his Swiss bank accounts. He had dispatched all the would-be assassins to hell.

Twenty minutes earlier, Hawke had been interrupted at a black-tie dinner party at Shadowlands, a sprawling twenty-two-acre estate that had once belonged to the American businessman Vincent Astor. Now it was home to Hawke's closest friends, Chief Inspector Ambrose Congreve and his wife, the lovely Lady Diana Mars. After being seated at the table, and just as the roast of veal was being served, a servant had hastily bent down and whispered into Hawke's ear.

"Sorry to disturb," he had whispered. "There is a phone call from Teakettle Cottage." Pelham, Lady Mars's butler said, was now on the line asking for him. "Most urgent, Your Lordship," the man in the crisp white jacket with silver buttons had said.

Hawke went straightaway to the library, pulled a chair up to the fire, and took the call and a sip of his claret.

"Pelham," Hawke said, "it's me. Tell me what's wrong."

"M'lord, you must return home at once," he said. "N-now."

And indeed it was most urgent. According to Pelham, a strange man clothed entirely in black, nearly invisible in the downpour of rain, had appeared outside the cottage door. The stranger had been asking after his lordship's whereabouts and demanding entry to the cottage to wait for him. Finally, he had succeeded in forcing himself inside despite Pelham Grenville's most extreme objections.

Alex heard the palpable terror and tremor in his old friend's voice. When asked if he was all right, Pelham had whispered, "He c-cut my hand, Your—Your Lordship, the . . . Sorry . . . the right one . . . I'm afraid, sir. . . ."

"How deep is it, Pelham?" Hawke said. "Tell the truth for God's sake!"

There was a brief pause and then Pelham said: "Ah, the blood flows like wine, m'lord."

This degree of detached coolness under fire could have come only from a blythe spirit like Pelham Grenville. He of the heart of purest gold and the spine of Sheffield steel. Hawke could now overhear the shouted threats and epithets of the intruder before he violently ripped the phone from the old fellow's hand. Clicked and disconnected. Hawke silently uttered a profanity, the one word, he'd vowed never to say aloud.

Less than thirty seconds after that call, the British spy sprinted out across Shadowland's expansive lawns and gardens onto the broad hewn-stone drive outside the row of garages. He climbed aboard his beloved bike and the race-modified engine instantly roared into throbbing life.

Someone, lost in the mists of time, had once said that Alex Hawke was a man who was "naturally good at war." At his squalling birth on a stormy night up in Hawkesmoor's third-floor nursery, his father, the late Admiral Lord Hawke, had proclaimed to the midwife and to his darling wife: "He is a boy born with a heart for any fate, Mother."

CHAPTER 1

A very good morning to you, gentlemen!" President Franklin Delano Roosevelt said, appearing in the White House cabinet room all hale and hearty.

The president then lit a cigarette and fixed it into a tortoiseshell holder and placed it in his mouth at the jaunty angle that the press liked so much. The act served as a signal for everyone to light up as well. Missy LeHand, the president's secretary and the woman closest to him on the White House staff, handed round the coffee.

Then Roosevelt got right down to cases. Winston Churchill wanted a face-to-face meeting with him as soon as humanly possible. Harry Hopkins had passed on the message and urged FDR to agree to such a meeting.

The president sensed a ripple of unease among the cabinet members, including a deep frown on the face of Secretary of State, Cordell Hull. Old Hopkins had gotten his way again, jamming up the cabinet members' diplomatic channels with his own private agenda.

FDR was well aware that his cabinet resented Hopkins, but then so did all the other politicians in town. He also knew that every man in front of him, on this cold and sunny Saturday morning, was engaged in some sort of feud or other with their own deputies or rivals. He could step in at any time and replace any one of them. And they damn well knew it! So they could listen to what Harry was reporting back and advise their president on what he should do.

He cleared his throat loudly and said, "Well, gentlemen, what do you think?"

One by one, they spoke in turn. Cordell Hull's cautious view was reinforced by an even more negative reaction from Ickes. He said, "What would America gain from such a public meeting, one which would be feted by the British press and interpreted as just one more step down the road to war? Lindbergh and all the other isolationists would absolutely crucify this administration. I'll tell you that much, Mr. President!"

Even Knox, who was the most pro-British, was against the idea. He said, "The merest suggestion that the president was going to such a meeting would only strengthen the isolationist case and swing public opinion further behind them."

When wrapping up a discussion, Roosevelt always made sure that everyone had had their say. He listened carefully to the balance of the men in the room. "Well, does anyone have anything else to add?"

"I certainly do, Mr. President," Cordell Hull said. "I wonder, is that really all that Harry Hopkins had to say?"

"Yes, he said a good deal. Now, anyone got anything else?"

There was silence.

"Good," said the president. "That's decided, then."

Hull fired back, "What's been decided?"

"I've decided that I'm going to think about it," said Roosevelt, looking down his nose at the man.

———————

At 9:30 P.M., on that December 6, a certain Lieutenant Lester Schulz, paunchy and slightly out of breath, arrived at the White House with a locked pouch containing a top secret document. The leather pouch contained thirteen parts of the fourteen-part Japanese reply to the hard-line U.S. proposal presented to Japan in November. The messages had been sent from Tokyo to the Japanese Embassy in Washington, but they had been intercepted by American intelligence. The United States had cracked the Japanese diplomatic code, code-named "Purple" in August 1940.

American officials had been reading top secret Japanese messages before her diplomats received them, meaning that President Roosevelt had the advantage of knowing what the Japanese government was doing and saying for the sixteen months prior to the sneak attack on Pearl Harbor. They had not, however, thus far cracked the military code. So, while the U.S. government was aware of Japan's diplomatic maneuvering, it remained cloaked in darkness about the specific movements of Tokyo's Imperial Navy.

Harry Hopkins, former secretary of commerce and one of Roosevelt's speechwriters and his closest confidant, delivered the documents to the president in his study. The president, in a pensive mood, his Scottie Fala perched on his lap, said, "What have we got here, Harry?"

"You'll see," Hopkins said. "It ain't good. I'll tell you that much."

As Hopkins paced back and forth, the president read the fifteen type-written pages carefully for about ten minutes. Most of it outlined Japan's peaceful intentions in the region and laid the blame for the rising tensions on the United States. The final section of the document announced there was no chance of reaching a diplomatic settlement with the United States "because of American attitudes."

Roosevelt looked up, stared at Hopkins, and said, "This amounts to a declaration of war, Harry. Sooner rather than later. Most likely precipitated by a Japanese attack on British, or possibly Dutch, possessions somewhere in the region. Maybe the Philippines."

Hopkins pulled up a chair and sat. He was doing what he was best at, which was why he was held in the highest esteem by the president and his closest thing to a real friend in Washington.

"Yes, by God. And I think we damn well ought to consider pushing the Pentagon for a preemptive strike against those bastards. Rather than sit back and wait for war to come at the convenience of the Japanese. Strike the first blow at their homeland and prevent any sort of unpleasant surprises. I urge you to immediately get the Navy and Army Air Corps brass over here and—give these bastards a righteous punch."

But Roosevelt was a student of history. And like Lincoln on the eve of the Civil War, he understood the political appeal of having the enemy fire the opening shot.

"No, Harry. No, we can't do that. We are a democracy and a peaceful people." And then, raising his voice, he said somewhat cryptically, "But by God, we have a damn good record when it comes to waging war! And by God and all that's holy, I will take it to them!"

FDR was still in his bed with the newsapers on that frosty Sunday morning when he received notice that his military aide, Admiral Alex Beardall, would be bringing the locked pouch containing the missing fourteenth, and final, part of Japan's diplomatic response. The man delivered it to the president at 10:00 A.M. and waited patiently at his bedside while the president read it. Then read it again.

This document, Roosevelt clearly saw, instructed the Japanese ambassador to destroy the code machines at their Washington embassy and to deliver the message to the secretary of state at 1:00 P.M. And said that the "chances of achieving peace in the Pacific were gone, because cooperation with the American government has been lost."

The president turned to the admiral and said, "It looks as though they are breaking off negotiations. They're planning to strike, Alex. But when? And where?"

Roosevelt's first scheduled appointment on Sunday, December 7, was with the outgoing Chinese ambassador, Dr. Hu Shih, at 12:30 P.M. The elderly ambassador had taken the midnight train down from New York for the meeting. They met in the Oval Study. FDR was anxious to let the ambassador know that he had sent a private appeal directly to the Japanese emperor.

He told Dr. Hu: "I want to assure you, sir, that if the Japanese emperor does not intervene and restrain his military, war between the United States and Japan is utterly inevitable. We will be in this fight together, your country and mine. To the bitter end. May I have your unbridled assurances that your replacement here in Washington will be up to the Herculean task before us? He has some mighty big shoes to fill, I will say."

"Indeed," the ambassador replied, still holding his hat in his lap. "Too kind. But more than up to it, Mr. President."

"He's coming to see me tomorrow. I've read every last scrap they've given me. What I would appreciate is not our appraisal, but your personal appraisal. He's very young, isn't he? A bit untested in the intricacies of world affairs? Current events in Europe as well as the Pacific, especially in this most tenuous of times? You know him, of course. You were part of the team that selected him."

"Of course. Since boyhood. I'm an old friend of his father's. A man who, outside of Chiang Kai-shek, is probably the most powerful man in China not in the government. The Tang clan is one of the oldest and most powerful families in the country, dating back four or five hundred years. They have amassed vast holdings around the world, vast wealth.

"The son has been groomed by his father since the age of two to take over leadership of the family. But also to assume a position of power on the world stage. He has been to the finest schools. Eton, then Le Rosey, in Switzerland of course, in the early years. Later, he completed his undergraduate studies at Christ's College, Cambridge. He read history, of course, literature, and political studies. Took a first in all three."

"Impressive," FDR agreed.

"Then on to Oxford for his postgraduate PhD candidate work. Again, political studies and history. He took a first in both, I can tell you. The boy looks like some Hollywood action hero. But I will say that he is brilliantly educated—that, no one can deny."

"A love of history. I like that. Did he concentrate on any particular period?"

Hu smiled. "So glad you asked, Mr. President. Yes, he did. He has made his lifetime of study attaining a first-rate understanding of one country and its internal workings. The political life of the United States of America."

"I'm beginning to like this young fellow."

"You'll like him even more when you meet. He has a natural charm, a warmth from within, that belies his fierce intelligence. He's almost pre-ternaturally attractive to the ladies, I'm afraid. His father and I have dis-cussed this potential weakness, and I've already assigned someone in the embassy to watch him like a hawk. My old secretary, actually. I believe you've met her."

"Miss Li?"

"Ah, yes, Miss Li. God, I'll miss her, Mr. President."

"I must say, you've made my day, old sport. I've been worried about seeing you go for months now. But I think I'm going to like the cut of this fellow's jib. I really do. Yes. Very much looking forward to our meeting."

The two old comrades gossiped a bit more and then said their final good-byes.

Both of them almost blissfully unaware that all hell was about to rain down on them in a matter of hours.

CHAPTER 2

Washington, D.C.
December 8, 1941

I t was ice-cold in Washington, D.C., that memorable morning in the first week of December. It was also the day after the Day of Infamy, when unending waves of Japanese "Zeros" and carrier bombers had dropped their ordnance and left burning what had once been home to the most powerful Navy in the Pacific.

As it happened, it was also the day that the new Chinese ambassador disembarked from his train at Union Station.

Whether or not he intuited this, this new posting was going to take him for what would prove to be an extremely wild ride. He would remember those days years later and wonder how on earth he'd survived.

"Oh, no, no, no. That cannot be accurate," Tai Shing Tang, age thirty-one, said as he leaned forward across the polished mahogany dresser top, rubbing his raw red eyes. He blinked a few times, then peered more closely at his reflection in the cloudy glass of the gilded dresser mirror.

He could not believe his eyes.

Who is that dreadful-looking old fellow staring me down? Cannot possibly be me . . . some kind of flaw in the old mirror glass? An apparition? Surely, a ghost of Christmas past?

What he faced was not a pretty sight. By the looks of him, last night had obviously been a very late night. Most of it had taken place downstairs in the chaotic Chinese Embassy, in the gilded Grand Ballroom. A room from another time, another place. Some wag reporter had given it a nickname that had stuck. In a *Washington Post* article on the new Chinese ambassador, the room had been labeled "the Chinese Versailles."

To say the least, the ambassador could not remember any of the many moments at the boisterous welcome reception the embassy staff had pitched in his honor.

The early part of the evening was all pretty much a wash now. A fleeting parade of blurry faces, a fading rosy blush on a passing young girl's cheek, a succession of snapshots of evanescent flirtations, some serious eye contact, foolish sideways glances, firm diplomatic handshakes, snippets of broken conversations, and lipstick phone numbers scrawled on cocktail napkins or scribbled inside restaurant matchbooks and stuffed willy-nilly into one's jacket pockets.

And now this morning, his jaw ached from the fixed smile he'd worn all the night long.

Ah, well, after all, he was the new Chinese ambassador to the United States. If all this hoopla and folderol were to be his new life in Washington, then so be it. And he'd damn well better get used to it. He undid his pajamas and dropped them in a puddle on the hardwood floor, then donned his dark red velvet bathrobe and headed for the steaming bath his valet had drawn ready.

In the aftermath of the all the hullabaloo surrounding his arrival, he'd sought escape beyond the walls of the embassy. Luckily, as the last guests began drifting off, there were those anxious to help him leave the dregs of the evening to others. Tiger had looked round for Yang Yang-Tsing, his new minder. "Minder" was not a word he was familiar with, but minder he was.

His new aide-de-camp was the ever-smiling, deferential personage who was now his constant shadow. Yang-Tsing, of the angelic countenance framed by silky black hair, the potbellied, small-footed physique, and the semitransparent yet sometimes caustic wit. And yet... and yet...

And yet... there was just something about the man that didn't ring true. He seemed to have little to no idea what the position of ADC to a major political figure entailed. And he had a disturbing habit of staring at the ambassador that was both discomfiting and annoying. Like the ambassador was mere bacteria on a glass slide under a microscope. And sometimes when Yang-Tsing stared, it felt like he was surreptitiously trying to hypnotize Tang! Gave him terrible headaches . . .

And then one day it hit him. He'd seen this fellow once, long ago, in China. He picked up the telephone and asked his secretary to summon Yang-Tsing to his office immediately.

"Come in!" Tiger said, and the man almost seemed to slide into the room.

"No! Don't sit down. This won't take long."

"Yes, sir!" Yang-Tsing said, eyes darting nervously about.

"We've met before, haven't we?"

"Yes, sir."

"And where might that have been?"

"In Guangzhou, sir."

"Where in Guangzhou?"

"Your father's automobile factory, sir. Brilliance China Auto."

"You worked there?"

"Yes, sir. I was your father's driver at that time."

"And how is it that you appear in Washington?"

"Your father, he helped me get my job."

"He did? Why?"

"He says he worries about you all the time. Wants me to keep an eye on you. Make sure you're okay, he said."

"So you talk to him about me?"

"Once a week, yes, sir."

"All right. Go back to work. I don't want to be disturbed. Show yourself out. No! Stop. Turn around."

"Yes?"

"I will give you this warning but once. Disobey me and you will not be around long enough for regrets. This conversation never took place. I will be listening in on your weekly calls with my father. And I will tell you exactly what you can and cannot say! Do you understand that?"

"Yes, Mr. Ambassador!"

"Get out of my sight."

There was, that same evening, also in attendance, a devilishly handsome young Brit, a Royal Navy commander on loan from Navy Command Headquarters based at Whale Island, Portsmouth. Horatio Black Hawke was his name, former Spitfire pilot shot down by the *Luftwaffe* over the English Channel. Assigned as liaison to the military attaché here at the Chinese Embassy. A hail-fellow-well-met type, but with charm to burn, a flyboy with acres of military decorations upon his breast.

Hawke, then. His smart uniform a dark navy blue tailcoat with a standing collar, white with gold edging, and worn with gold shoulder boards, plus a ceremonial saber with full-dress sword belt with three gold stripes.

Tang had asked around about this hale English fellow with whom he would soon be working. Lord Hawke, for starters. Aristocrat. But apparently the man never used his title, which the ambassador found amusing but becoming. Sixth richest man in England, indeed! Direct descendant of Alex Black Hawke, or Blackhawke, an infamous pirate who'd carved a name for himself with his bloodstained cutlass, looting more than half the gold and treasure in Port Royal and on the Spanish Main. Apparently, his portrait had long hung above the hearth in the White Dog Inn in Port Royal, Jamaica. Beneath it, some wag had carved the words:

Black be his name, and black be the colour of his heart.

This current "Blackhawke," born in Oxfordshire in the same year Tiger had been born, 1910, was a cat of a madly different stripe. One of the most popular boys on the society pages, clearly a piratical swordsman in his inevitable ascendancy. "Debutante catnip," one society columnist had called him.

These two handlers had emerged from the crowd and steered the young diplomat out the embassy's front entrance and into an idling black Cadillac limousine with great plumes issuing from the exhaust pipe.

And then it was round and round Washington town, with stops at 1789 in Georgetown and Martin's Tavern and Old Ebbitt's Grill and, last, a mandatory nightcap at the bar known as Off the Record. It was centrally located, downstairs at the Hay-Adams Hotel situated directly across the street opposite the White House.

"Do you play squash, Doc?" Hawke asked before crossing the slushy street.

"Actually, my title is 'Ambassador.' What's this 'Doc' business?"

"You nabbed a doctorate at Oxford, I read somewhere. In American political thought of all things . . ."

"What of it?"

"It was a joke for Crissakes, Doc," Hawke said. "So, do you play squash, or don't you? Yes-or-no question."

"Some might claim I do. Not well, but I do play, Commander. Let's have a go sometime."

"Splendid. I'll book a court at my club," Hawke replied, "the Fauquier Club over in Virginia."

They eyed each other, mentally circling like boxers, looking for an opening, each warily deciding if they could be friends with the other. Time would tell. But judging by first impressions on both sides, there was a high probability they would get along. Two tall, good-looking, and athletic chaps like these had a habit of getting extremely competitive at the drop of a hat. Whether it was women or skeet shooting, poker or polo.

The recently minted Chinese ambassador to America paused briefly before crossing the slushy avenue. He wanted to look back at the lovely facade of the White House with a mantel of snow. A huge colorfully lit Christmas tree stood before the South Portico, with Christmas candles flickering in every window, the white palace all but shimmering in the powdery swirling snowfall. Ever since his boyhood, he'd admired depictions of the White House's neoclassical architecture. It did not disappoint tonight.

At the pretty little church across the street, a choir standing outside in the snow started singing "O Holy Night." With the lovely song floating on the night air, all looked so peaceful, stately, and serene . . . but tonight at the White House, it was all just beautiful facade. Inside, the president, his staff, and the occupants of 1600 were very much on edge. They suddenly had a world war to win.

And it didn't look good for the home team.

In fact, Tiger mused, it could not possibly have looked worse. He gazed at his gold wristwatch. Almost three in the A.M. Oh, well. One and done, as they used to say in college. Yeah, right, mate. The phrase inevitably ending up as a joke.

As they entered the Hay-Adams lobby, Commander Hawke squeezed his right shoulder and said, "Mr. Ambassador, brace yourself. You are now about to enter Washington's 'best spot to be seen and not heard.' Noisy as hell. No worries about discretion down there. No one can hear a word you say, so go have fun!"

"I'm all for that, Alex Black!" the ambassador said, giving Hawke a nickname that would not stick. The two men, now united in an unspoken common purpose, quickly descended the stairs.

Hawke added, "If you can't get lucky down there, you might as well jump off the Brooklyn Bridge and get it over with. Put yourself out of your misery, old man!"

No understatement there. It was indeed a mad scene down in the bar: a raucous crowd, high on high-test fuel provided by the drunker-than-lords bartenders, red-faced chaps who'd long ago in the evening given up on measuring out drinks and accepting payments. Not to mention the gorilla in the room: America's endless nightmare of waves of zealously suicidal Japanese Zero pilots who had, earlier that very day, killed three thousand and reduced America's Pacific Navy to a sinking, stinking, smoking rubble at Pearl.

Hawke looked around, somewhat dizzily, at the mob of patrons gathered six deep round the bar. Small wonder. Atop the bar, an alluring young woman in a low-cut red satin gown was giving the word "shimmy" a brand-new meaning. Perhaps she'd indulged in a glass too many. Make that definitely too many. But who was counting? On that particular December night in 1941, on that unholiest of nights, many of the celebrants had the very strong feeling that this might well be America's last hurrah. . . . Another round, please?

"What do you think, Mr. Ambassador?" the smiling Englishman said. "Have I overstated the case?"

"Sheer bedlam. I want in, m'lord!" Tiger Tang replied with a wide smile. "I feel like I'm swimming in secretaries! Come on, cover my six. I'm diving in!" And then he did, indeed, wade in. Commander Hawke followed in his wake, along with the potbellied little Yang-Tsing, Tiger's relentless minder. In a matter of mere seconds, the holy trio was separated, giving themselves over to the mad frenzy of the amorphous crowd, and soon subsumed deep into the writhing mass.

Commander Hawke managed to find a spot at the horseshoe bar and ordered a Guinness. Immediately, two boisterous redheads to his right tried to chat him up. "Not me." He smiled. "I'm getting married in the morning. But that handsome gentleman over there in the corner is desperately lonely." He smiled as the two damsels appeared to glide over to the table of his new friend Tiger.

Two carrot-topped moths to the flame.

CHAPTER 3

Bermuda
Present Day

He saw the cottage now, yellow lights blazing in the windows, standing out to sea on a rocky promontory. He'd made it, by God. Now, nearing his quaint pale pink bungalow, Hawke would need to silence his approach and quickly, or he'd telegraph his position to precisely the wrong ears.

He throttled all the way back on the black Norton and let gravity and momentum coast him in silence, save the hissing tires, all the long way down to the bottom of Royal Guardsmen's Hill. At last, arriving at his hidden drive, he braked hard, shut the bike down, and jumped off. A thicket of banana trees concealed the sandy road from all but the most prying of eyes, and he hid the black Norton deep among the thick mangroves and elephant ears.

Wiping the rainwater from his eyes, he then whipped his mobile from the pocket of the old Barbour shooting jacket Ambrose had lent him. He speed-dialed Edward VII Hospital's emergency number, said he needed an ambulance immediately, gave his name and address, and said, "Please, hurry! It's life or death!" before ringing off.

And then he ran like hell up the twisting sandy lane that was his drive, wet leaves slapping at his face, looping vines threatening to catch a foot and bring him down . . . very dark out here in the garden . . . but he knew every inch of it.

There was a great deal of rattling thunder and hissing lightning now, as the tropical storm moved farther ashore. A loud and sizzling strike nearby suddenly lit up a strange three-wheeled electric vehicle he didn't recognize as his own. Parked under a palm tree near the entrance, it looked like a little silver spaceship. A Twyzy, they called them, the latest tourist toy to grace the island's ways and byways. Our Mr. Smith had certainly arrived in style.

Hawke moved swiftly to his left, avoiding the front lawns of the house entirely, staying just inside the green jungle cover of the banana trees until he could surveil the enemy target, locate his position inside, and come up with a plan that would somehow enable him to— What? He'd learned from Chang Hu, his ancient kung fu master, long ago that no fight has to last more than five seconds, and in that short span of time, the man who lands the first two sharp blows inevitably wins, if he's not bound to conventions of sportsmanship, or to the effete nonsense of any given technique.

He paused beneath a banyan tree. Closing his eyes, he touched his palms together, the thumbs beneath his chin, the forefingers pressed against his lips. He exhaled completely and breathed very shallowly, using only the bottom of his lungs, sharply reducing his intake of oxygen. Holding the image of the still pool that was now his mind, he brought his face ever closer to the pool's surface until he was almost under and—

A scream in the night from within the house.

A long, plaintive howl that sounded like a grievously wounded animal . . . Pelham. Hawke sprinted seaward to the rain-swept waterfront side of the house and leapt over the wall that enclosed the broad terrace. He was running for the rear door, ready to crash through the glass if that was necessary, get in there, and kill the crazy bastard who had hurt his Pelham.

That's when the house went dark, every room, at the same instant. Another cry of pain . . .

"Pelham! Pelham!" Hawke stood stock-still and cried out. His gun now in his hand, the trusty old American .45—five cartridges in and the hammer down on the empty. The bulky blue steel revolver felt heavy and cold in his hand as he quickly snapped out the cylinder and checked the load. The slugs were scooped out and a deep cross had been cut into the head of each. No range. No accuracy to speak of. The bullet would begin to tumble five yards from the barrel. But when it hit, it would splat as wide and thin as a piece of tinfoil. A nick in the forearm would slam the victim down as though he'd been struck by a freight train. Good professional job of dumdumming. Reassuring.

He ran with the gun out in front of him now, barreling straight ahead, and smashed right through the wide locked cedar door, splintering wood and glass and hurtling inward as he powered into the darkness within. He stopped, got his bearings, peering into the inky darkness and listening. . . .

"Pelham?" he whispered. He heard a stir from behind the bar.

"Alex . . . over . . . here . . . ," he heard Pelham choke out.

"Where?"

"I'm just behind the bar, m'lord . . . ," the gravely wounded old gentleman croaked.

Hawke leapt up onto the wide rattan bar, his eyes moving everywhere, his .45 revolver still clutched firmly in his right hand. With his left, he flicked the flint on his old Zippo and had a look. Two startlingly blue eyes gleamed back up at him from the blackness. Pelham was lying on his back, and he—Good Lord—he was lying on the floor atop a bed of broken glasses and bottles, holding up his bloody right hand with his left, his shirtfront blood soaked.

Hawke got to his knees, reached down, and managed to get a grasp on both of the poor fellow's wrists. He paused and said, "Ready?" and his old friend managed a thin smile. The injury to his right hand was severe, and the pain of being lifted from all that jagged glass was no doubt rather hellish.

As Hawke began to lift him higher, the trembling Pelham winced and cried out in pain. Hawke carefully hauled him up and over the edge of the wide bamboo bar, stretching him out horizontally on the bar top as carefully and as painlessly as he could.

"Talk to me, Pelham. Where is he?" he whispered.

Pelham gathered up amazing strength, considering the blood he must have lost, and pulled Hawke's face down toward him, clearly wanting to whisper something in Alex's ear.

"What is it, old fellow? Hurry now," he said. He could sense a nearing presence but saw nothing in the all-enveloping blackness.

"He's here. . . . He's hiding, sir . . . front of the house . . . just inside the ladies' loo by the front door . . . waiting. . . . He will have heard you come in. . . ."

Despite the dire situation, Hawke had to smile. Heard the resounding crash of glass and splintered wood, had he? Despite the awful condition of the old fellow, despite all he'd just gone through, all the pain and all the blood he'd already lost . . . he managed to draw on those great depths of English understatement with "He will have heard you come in. . . ."

It was at that very instant that he felt hot breath on the back of his neck and heard a whiskery voice a few inches behind his right ear say, "Howdy, dead man. It's your old compadre, Shit. Come to pay my last respects. . . ."

Hawke's gut instinct was to whip his head straight back without warning. Use his skull to deal a sharp blow to the tip of Shit's nose. One that would have disabled him, possibly killed him if a bone splinter was driven into his brain. Failing that, he'd at least have had Shit Smith by the larynx, the life of the murderous bastard between his thumb and forefinger, a hostage. . . .

"Ah, my old friend Mr. Smith," Hawke said, feigning a coolness he did not feel. "Forgot the first name. Sorry, old chap, something to do with excrement, no? Potty talk, what? Pee-pee? Wait! I remember! Shit, that's it! Hello, Shit. Welcome to Bermuda, old fellow. . . . And, please say hello to my old friend Persifor Fraser, III. He's always looking for new members here at the Royal Bermuda Yacht Club, don't you know."

He expected some kind of reflexive trash talk in return.

Instead, there came cruel paroxysms of razor-sharp steel on Hawke's vulnerable flesh, Shit's big Bowie knife, slicing through his belly and girdle of muscle with the swift ease of a hot wire through cheese. The pain was pyrotechnic as everything within him began to give way and burst.

Now Alex Hawke himself screamed, more in excruciating pain than in fear for his life.

He fell forward, his very guts threatening to spill out or already spilling, the upper part of his torso crushing Pelham to the bar top, smothering him. He summoned the strength to slide his right hand beneath his belly and somehow seize up the wound. Dear God, this was it. Hold on. Just hold the heavy green-grey folds of . . . of . . . Damn it to hell, his own bloody intestines . . . inside his yawning belly long enough for him to get Pelham's bleeding under—

Smith had bent down and grabbed a handful of Hawke's unruly black hair, yanking his head back so the two of them were nose to nose.

"How you doin', Lordship? Ouch. I bet that hurts. Everything copacetic? You okeydokey?"

"I will be," Hawke spat out.

"Ya think so, podnuh?"

"If it's the last thing I do. And then I will hunt you down, and I will bloody erase you, you miserable piece of shit. . . ."

Shit put the blade of the Bowie under Hawke's chin and started sawing the blade back and forth slowly, with a light touch, smiling at him while he did it, producing another warm spill of blood over his hand.

"I—I'll come for you. . . ."

"Well, hell, boss. Good luck with that," Shit said in a lighthearted way as he pricked Hawke's nose with the tip of the Bowie knife. "I reckon I best be runnin' along now. But you notice I ain't taking your pretty head along with me, right? Hell, no, I ain't! Even though the Big Boss offered me double for it if I delivered it to him on a platter. But, y'know, I just couldn't see it. I said—I told him right up front—I said, 'Hell, Vladimir, save yer money! I just don't want to deal with getting it back to Moscow! Lug that bloody noggin of his around with me in a bowling ball bag for a week or so? I can't check it with my luggage, and I don't believe I could get past them TSA machines. Naw, fuck that shit, man. Airport security, railway stations? No way, José.' He tole me to think on it. How much fresh pussy I could get with ten or twenty mil in the bank."

He dropped Hawke's head and stood straight up, wiping the Englishman's blood and guts from his knife on his shirttail before holstering the bloody Bowie.

"So, I guess I'll bid you two happy campers a fond adieu. Skedaddle on back to where I come from . . . Git while the gittin' is good, as the man said. One step ahead of the sheriff, as per usual."

"Safe travels," Hawke said with all the strength he had left in him. "Just make sure you keep your eyes open. I'll be coming for you, you bloody arsehole."

Shit laughed out loud at that one.

"Oh, hell yeah! Yes, indeedy, I certainly will do that. Don't you worry none. Now, say good night and go away . . . yer done."

And the cowboy faded to black, leaving his two victims to their fate. Tonight was almost certain to be, Hawke considered, a fatal rendezvous with his longtime sidekick, sometimes known as the Pale Rider. Hawke's pain was vast. But, at least, he reflected sadly, it was finite. This couldn't go on much longer. Sharp-edged waves of agony climaxed in intensity until his body convulsed and his mind was awash. And then, just before the madness took over, the crests broke and surmounted the limits of his consciousness, and promised an escape, if only briefly, into oblivion.

Hawke had no idea how long they lay there like that, the two of them, two mortally wounded men, inseparable in life and now together in death's embrace. Half an hour? Six hours? Half his life? His existence seemed equally divided into two parts, one containing thirty or so active, colorful years; the other, the second half, some unknown span of pain. And now it was the second half that really mattered.

A spasm in his bowels awakened him. He felt warm fluid running down his leg. It wasn't blood. . . . It was . . . oh, God . . . dear God . . . release me . . . the stench emanating from his exposed bowels was intolerable.

Slowly, the numbing of his overloaded nerves came into balance with each new level of agony and neutralized it. He knew that more exquisite levels of pain might still come. But pain was no longer an animate enemy he might get by the throat and crush and crush! His pain and his life had finally welded into one.

The two would always be together now. These few remaining moments would be his epitaph, his final memories. . . . . He called an old and happy image to his mind. He and his beloved son, Alexei, standing on a wind-swept mountain in the Highlands of Scotland. They'd been stalking a great stag all morning when they chanced upon him off a ledge twenty feet below, and now his son was filled with wonder at the sight of such a magnificent animal . . . and the beauty of the heather in full bloom.

When there was no longer pain, after all, there would no longer be life.

Alex Hawke, he of the purported lionlike courage and strong heart for any fate, suddenly felt very cold and alone.

And very sad.

CHAPTER 4

Washington, D.C.
December 8, 1941

For his part, Tiger Tang, trying to conserve his resources, found a deserted corner table and retired there and summoned a waiter, determined to fly solo and nurse a small pitcher of white wine until Yang-Tsing intervened and said otherwise.

"Belay that order," Yang-Tsing told the waiter. "He'll have soda water. . . ."

But then . . .

But then, of course, events intervened.

And here they were, magically appearing at Tiger's refuge table. Yes, yes, those gymnastic Topsy Twins, as well put together a pair of statuesque redheads as one could imagine. Both working up on Capitol Hill, rowdy secretaries simply dripping in Mr. Woolworth's jewelry and faux-fox-fur wraps, known, apparently, as Agnes and Flora. Two lovelies whom he found himself charming over nightcaps.

"What will you two lovely ladies be having?" Tang asked, caving in completely and ordering a magnum of Pol Roger Brut. And then they were all three off to the races. "Keep it coming," Ambassador Tang heard himself telling the champagne-bearing waiter. And so it went, and so it goes. . . .

A short time later, in a moment of wanton indiscretion, fueled by numberless swills of chilled Pol Roger, the ambassador had bedded the voraciously hungry, exceptionally pneumatic, and athletic twins simultaneously in a king-sized bed in the hastily arranged Presidential Suite upstairs.

"I'm Agnes," one of them had said, clinging to him in the elevator going up, fumes of some exotic perfume welling up between them. "I'm the quiet one. That's my sister, Flora. Known in some circles around town as 'the Human Trampoline.' She's the rich one, from Bryn Mawr, the Main Line, Philadelphia. Right, honey?"

"Please, try not to embarrass me, Agnes. Seriously. No one cares about things like that. Where one went to college. You're awfully silly tonight."

These two ebullient ladies, plainly intoxicated, were staffers in the Office of the Speaker of the House. And very loose-lipped about their famous boss, Sam Rayburn, rumored to have dallied with both. The young ambassador smiled inwardly at the thought: Pay attention. Listen carefully. These two might well prove very helpful to you someday. What fun! An underground pipeline out of the House of Representatives! And he hadn't even been there twenty-four hours!

Dear God, it was a miracle he'd gotten out of that madhouse on the twenty-fifth floor alive. He was aware of two black eyes staring at him across the lobby. And there, of course, he spied the omnipresent Yang-Tsing, seated in a wing chair beside a roaring fire, having a coffee and pretending to be reading the morning *Post* while he surveilled the ambassador. "Ah, there you are, Ambassador," he said, rising to greet him. "Your car is outside waiting. . . ."

"Good heavens, man. Have you been here all night?"

"Yes, sir. My job, you see."

"Let's be off, then."

At least he'd had the fortitude and presence of mind to haul himself out of bed in time to find Yang-Tsing and make it back to the Chinese Embassy before dawn, leaving the two sleeping beauties to their dreams. Crept up three flights of stairs and slid into his bed without waking a soul or raising a ruckus.

He leaned once more into the looking glass above the bathroom sink and inspected himself more carefully.

Hmm. Ah, yes, the familiar bloodshot eyes. The sallow complexion. And, God, the dry mouth, a condition that none but some godforsaken Gila monster lizard, spending all day splayed out on a flat rock under the broiling desert sun of Arizona, might comprehend.

Yes, the old Tiger, as he'd been nicknamed at university, was a bit grey around the gills, a bit haggard around the edges this morning. A haze of black stubble on his chin and jaw. Ah, well, a perhaps a wee touch of the Irish flu? Yes, that would explain it. What time was it, anyway?

He sighed and looked at his father's gold wristwatch. Patek Philippe, of course. A parting gift from the old man as they'd stood side by side on the pier at Xiamen, waiting for him to board the steamer that would ferry him to San Francisco and thence to the city of San Francisco, the Union Pacific train to Union Station, Washington. It was nearly nine o'clock.

Christ! There was an extremely important meeting today at noon. And because of the earthshaking events of yesterday, it was a big one. Meaning he had just a few short hours to pull himself together before walking into the lion's den.

He was, he had to keep reminding himself, the newly minted Chinese ambassador to the United States. First impressions would indeed be critical in this town for at least the next few months or so. And then there'd been a spot of bad luck. The timing of his arrival simply could not have been worse. He had, after all, arrived at Union Station only yesterday.

One day after that fateful day, December 7, 1941.

And today? It was shortly after the day that the American president had loudly proclaimed would "live in infamy." He sighed and took a step back from the mirror, straightening his tie. A watery light filled the high-ceilinged cream-colored bedroom. The peaceful snowy view of the Capitol outside the soaring windows of the room was deceptive. Tensions in Washington could not be ratcheted one notch higher. The sleeping town lay under a fresh blanket of pure white snow, but it was anything but peaceful out there. Citizens would awaken to a shockingly new and vastly more dangerous world.

The entire Western world was suddenly dangling by a thread. With the voracious Nazi wolves at the door everywhere in Europe, and now

Imperial Japan eager to devour the Pacific theater in one sitting . . . Tiger could only wonder at Roosevelt's state of mind at this moment. One of the twins had told him that, during a dinner on the eve of December 7, a White House butler had overheard FDR speculating about the possibility of a Japanese invasion on the West Coast that could spread as far as the Midwest.

There was indeed widespread shock and panic in most quarters of the government, and gut-wrenching fear in most if not all of the Capitol itself. America's Pacific Fleet had been decimated, neutralized in a single devastating surprise attack. In the blink of an eye, Japan's mighty Imperial Navy had seized control of the Pacific. Already, Japan's Navy and Imperial Japanese Army Air Service were leapfrogging north toward the pole, rapidly building naval bases and airstrips ever closer to the American-held Aleutian Islands. From there, they would be just a short hop, skip, and jump away from America's Western coastline. And then who the hell knew? Japanese troops marching into downtown Chicago? It certainly seemed possible. . . .

Tiger grabbed the stack of newspapers and decoded Chinese news and military démarches and dispatches waiting on his bureau. He then went over to the deep leather armchair beneath the window, speed-reading all the relevant articles that caught his eye. He was no stranger to this kind of stuff. He had taken his PhD, a "double first" in history and political science at Oxford, with a focus on American history in both.

And he had been deep in study of the American geopolitical landscape for months now, perhaps a year, all leading up to his imminent appointment as ambassador. One thing was clear from his survey of the news from the political and war fronts. In a heartbeat, the entire global political landscape had changed. And not for the better. And he didn't have a whole lot of time to get up to speed.

Precisely at twelve noon, Ambassador Tang was scheduled to present himself and his credentials to the vice president at a welcoming ceremony for him at the White House. In the East Room, to be exact. The president would not be able to attend, as he would be up on the Hill at that hour, giving what would become his famous speech on the dastardly

Japanese sneak attack. "A day that will live in infamy!" Afterward, there was to be a long-scheduled one-hour private meeting with the beleaguered Franklin Delano Roosevelt himself and his right-hand man, the ghostlike, wraith-thin, and mysterious Harry Hopkins.

Tiger Tang had been amazed that, given the epic events of yesterday, the long-planned meeting was still taking place. He was sure he'd soon be notified that the White House had called to reschedule upon his arrival at his embassy. It didn't happen. Still on, apparently.

His adjutant had explained his situation at drinks and over dinner. "You must understand your own unique position in this town, Excellency," the fellow said. "America is now fighting on two fronts: Europe and Asia. You, and you alone, are now Roosevelt's only hope for victory in Asia. The war in Europe must take precedence because America's allies are already struggling for their very survival. Under Churchill, Britain is a formidable foe for Hitler. But it's a losing battle as of now. U-boats are cutting off most of the food being transported by freighters to the island fortress of England, now in danger of starvation. In all of Asia, only China can provide the military might, manpower, and sea power that America now so desperately needs to bring Japan to its knees."

The ambassador looked at his adjutant and smiled. "I am ready on all counts," Tiger said. "I've been getting ready for this all of my life."

And that was the unvarnished truth.

If you happened to look at it from a certain angle.

CHAPTER 5

Washington, D.C.
December, 1941

Soaking in his steaming bath, a pungent Cuban stogie clenched in his strong white teeth, Ambassador Tai Shing Tang knew that, in the wake of the attack on Pearl Harbor, today's meeting at the White House was clearly going to be the most important meeting of his young diplomatic life. A handsome young man, he was possessed of a finely boned face and gleaming jet-black hair sweeping back from a prominent forehead. A man some said was too beautiful for his own good, he was also a chap with some charm and a demonstrably formidable intellect.

The Chinese diplomat abruptly stood up, toweled dry, and went to the window. He knew he needed to gather his wits and quickly. He must compose himself. He must be ready with intelligent responses to each and every query, all this before strolling into the Oval Office. Roosevelt would have home-field advantage; that much was sure. The old lion would be ready for him, this young Chinese upstart, fresh from the playing fields of Eton, Le Rosey, Cambridge, and Oxford. His academic pedigree was a match for any in this town. But he also knew that the aristocratic American president always placed character high above pedigree.

He smiled in spite of himself. The brilliantly educated new ambassador was a man of many diverse talents. But he was also a man of secrets. Secrets he must guard with his very life, which he must protect at all costs. Generational secrets as well as his own. His was the first ray of light to shine on a family that had operated in the shadows for five centuries. The Tangs literally knew where all the bodies were buried because it was the Tang Triad that had put them all there in the first place.

On a more personal level, one of Tiger's best-kept secrets was that although he was privately ridiculed by his enemies as something of a dandy, a fop, he was in fact a kung fu master, one of the Highest Order. His ancestors, monks of the Triad Society, had all practiced this highly specialized form of physical self-defense. This to counter the torture and mass murder they had long suffered at the hands of the sadistic Manchu emperors.

They had perfected the art for themselves in great secrecy; they called it kung fu. The Dark Arts, some called it. Tiger himself owed his high position in the society known as the Triad as a "red pole" or "enforcer"—all was due to his almost inhuman prowess in the art of kung fu. He could, in fact, kill you blindfolded with one hand tied behind his back and only his ears and nose to guide him.

Although Tiger could never reveal this fact, he actually had a gourmand's taste for hot blood. He liked a good fight any old time. And there had been times when the dictates of his circumstances had caused him to take desperate measures. Permanent measures. Otherwise, he was the consummate, perfectly well-mannered gentleman dressed in the finest bespoke haberdashery that Savile Row could offer.

Of all the many Chinese secret societies, none had wielded greater power for longer than his family, the Triad. Mentioned in nearly every history book of the Chinese peoples, their members were bound together by an intricate system of secret oaths, rituals, passwords, ceremonial intermingling of their blood. And, of course, the ancient and mystical Chinese arts of mind control, serving to weld the disparate members of the clan together with unbreakable bonds.

During the long and arduous years of preparation he'd endured under his father at the ancestral home in Foochow, in Fukein Province, he had learned many things. But the one that had been hammered into his thick skull was that he would have to hide the fierce Tiger burning inside him.

Let no man catch a glimpse of the smoldering coal of power that was the engine at the very core of his very being, his soul.

It was the fire of ancient warriors running in his blood.

Just as the Mafia was founded by Giuseppe Mazzini in Palermo, Sicily, in 1860 as a guerrilla force to drive out a foreign ruler and unite with mainland Italy in the name of patriotism and liberty, so, too, had the earliest of the Triad Societies come into existence in Fukein Province in the latter part of the seventeenth century.

His direct monk ancestors had been valiant resistance fighters against the alien oppression of the Manchus, the "barbarian" tribesmen. Godless creatures who had swept across the Great Wall of China and in 1644 defeated the ruling native Ming Dynasty of Emperors to set up their own Ch'ing Dynasty. Legend dates the founding of the first Triad Society to a militant group of one hundred twenty-eight Buddhist monks at a monastery near Foochow in Fukein Province in 1674.

Such was the largely unheralded birth of Tiger's extended family nearly five hundred years earlier.

Before they started writing their history in blood and making a fearful name for themselves.

Now, as he began to fulfill his American mission, his destiny, driving himself ever deeper and deeper into the freshly bleeding heart of his new ally, this country newly under siege, he would take pains to insinuate himself into the bleeding heart of America. Wounded, yes, but possessed of a force still so mighty and powerful as to be the world's only hope to defy and deny the Axis Powers now conquering Europe. And then there was China. The only country in the world at that moment that perhaps hated the Japanese even more than the Americans.

Yes, China. He would fulfill his mandate. He would make China and, indeed, himself indispensable to President Roosevelt. He would make a great and trusted friend of the staunch and valiant American president. Shoulder to shoulder they would stand. It would be—yes, he knew it—it would be a Grand Alliance, with the Triad Society providing the steel hand of vengeance, wielded against those who would try to humble America.

He straightened up to his full height of six feet three inches and brushed his pomaded black hair straight back from the high forehead with two silver military brushes. The suit was good, he saw, a bespoke chalk-striped grey flannel from his Savile Row tailors in London, Huntsman & Co. He straightened his tie. The tie was good, too, a well-worn number from Sydney Sussex, his college at Cambridge. But something was off. What was it? Ah. The bulge under his left arm was going to be a problem. His Nambu 8mm automatic pistol was at issue.

Would the White House Secret Service guys dare to frisk him, to pat him down?

He smiled. Of course they would.

He pulled the automatic from his leather shoulder holster and fondled it, as if it were some iconic piece of art from the Ming Dynasty.

For the last ten years, the little black Nambu had provided him with a small measure of security. Tiger Tang, as he was known in the provinces and at home, had his enemies' blood on his hands. Enough to float a bloody sampan on! He was, without ever drawing attention to the fact, an enforcer.

At home, he never traveled anywhere without his Nambu and several well-armed bodyguards as well. His family had many enemies in Beijing, after all, both within the government and without. He sat atop a powerful family, one with deep and secret tentacles reaching inside the Chinese government and even to Generalissimo Chiang Kai-shek himself. The man whose power and influence had swiftly elevated himself to such a position of immense power despite all the protests that he was far too young and too inexperienced in statecraft, much less world affairs.

His enemies in the press, the *Asahi Shibumi* newspaper, and the Party and elsewhere had screamed that his sudden elevation by Chiang Kai-shek was an outrage. Those enemies had been silenced by soldiers of his family, of course, permanently. In a manner befitting the chairman of the Chinese Nationalist Party, the Kuomintang. Not to mention the Tang Triad Society, his family's own secret police.

They had been laid to rest, yes. But not necessarily in peace.

Still, the Tiger considered that, here in Washington, in America, the Chinese ambassador would have formidable security around him at all times. Here at the official residence and at the embassy and wherever he traveled . . . including the White House.

He removed his jacket.

The Nambu would have to go. Carrying a concealed weapon into the Oval Office for a meeting with Roosevelt was decidedly a bad idea. China and the Americans were going to war. Together, he would tell Roosevelt, the new allies would roll up the Japanese and push them into the sea. . . .

Somewhat wistfully, he unfastened the shoulder holster, removed it, and placed it in the top drawer of his dresser. He had a new life now. This was a new day. He was no longer Tiger Tang, a dangerous man-about-town in Beijing. He was now Ambassador Tang, cultured diplomat. His Excellency. America's most formidable ally in the war against their common enemy. History was in the making. Before he'd left Mainland China, he had vowed to represent his emperor and his country to the very best of his considerable abilities.

The ambassador grabbed his worn leather briefcase and made his way to the vast kitchens, a sudden desire for hot black coffee having arisen. He was hungry, too, and he then wanted to get outside in the frosty air, pull it deep into his lungs.

He wanted to go for a long brisk walk, somewhere where he could think for an hour or so in private, alone with his swirling sea of thoughts. He would never admit it, of course, but there were times, like this morning, when the enormity of what was happening threatened to overwhelm him. Tiger Tang willfully slowed his breathing down to meditation rate and recited the comforting verses of the William Blake poem that he had come to revere while at Cambridge. . . .

Tyger Tyger, burning bright,
In the forests of the night;
What immortal hand or eye,
Could frame thy fearful symmetry?

In what distant deeps or skies,
Burnt the fire of thine eyes?
On what wings dare he aspire?
What the hand, dare seize the fire?

He stepped outside into a snow-white wonderland. The little town of Washington, completely covered under a mantle of pure white snow lit by early-morning light, was captivating. The trees on the grounds of the Chinese Embassy shifted and swayed in breezes that sent soft flutterings of snow falling to the ground below. It was, Tiger thought, enchanting. For the first time, he realized that his new home was to be this exquisitely beautiful metropolis. Home to magnificent monuments, wide boulevards, neoclassical architecture (by far his favorite period), great stone mansions with sweeping lawns rising up to greet them . . . it was, well, what it was, was perfect.

CHAPTER 6

Bermuda
Present Day

Sigrid Kissl pressed forward, her chin stretched over the steering wheel, putting her nose against the cold windshield of the old Bentley as she raced to the side of her lover. The wipers could scarcely keep up with the curtains of rain that thrashed Bermuda's Coast Road. It was a dark night, anyway, neither moon nor stars, only the weak Lucas beams of her lover's ancient grey saloon piercing the veils of tears beyond.

"Bugger all!" she shouted, banging her right fist on the leather-covered dash. "Seriously!"

She turned up the windscreen defroster, hoping to reduce the fog that kept threatening to cloud her view of the rain-slick road snaking along the coast. She'd waited at the table as long as she could, not wanting to be rude, only jumping to her feet halfway through dessert, startling the other guests and saying to her hostess, Lady Mars: "Sorry, darling! I have to go. Something's terribly wrong. I could see it in his eyes. I can feel it! Please excuse me and—"

"Go, my sweet," Lady Mars said to her. "Go to him. He's all that counts, anyway. . . ."

And here she was, a woman on a mission. She had never felt comfortable in this role. She always felt she was either letting her beautiful lover down or right on the verge of doing so. Not that he demanded so much, no. At least not intellectually. He was a patient soul when it came to her, in the kitchen and on the golf course. Everywhere, that is, except in bed. Oh, yes, he was an ardent companion in that arena, a man who gave much, but demanded much in return.

"Christ!" she heard herself scream.

She hit the brakes and turned the wheel over hard in an attempt to avoid the big coconut palm that had just come down less than a hundred feet in front of her. She was nearing the crux of the bend and threatening to go off the road and down onto the rocks and into the crashing sea.

Somehow, she got the old grey Bentley under control and back onto the macadam. She was close now; she could see the black humpback of Teakettle Cottage standing out to sea, braving the roar of waves rolling ashore and the lashings of wind and rain.

As she crested the hill, she saw flashing red and blue lights at the bottom, pulled up just outside the hidden drive up to the cottage. Two or three Bermuda Police Service cruisers were blocking the coast road in both directions. . . . There was yellow crime scene tape festooning the banana plants, stretched across the entrance to the sandy lane that wound its way up the hill through the thick jungle of vegetation.

She rolled down the hill and pulled off on the verge. A young officer turned to look at her, shining his powerful flashlight on her face.

He tapped on the window, and she wound it down halfway.

"Sorry, madam. Police action. Crime scene. This road is closed. You'll have to turn around and head back the other way."

Crime scene? she thought. Crime scene?

"Sorry, Officer, but this is m-my home. I think my . . . my, uh . . . my companion might be in grave danger. I have to go to him."

"Let me see some identification, please. Proof of residency."

"Yes, yes. Of course. It's right here in my purse. . . . Here you go. . . ."

He shone the light on her Bermuda driver's license, noting the address on the South Shore Road. "All right, Miss Kissl. You may proceed on foot up the drive. The police are probably wrapping this scene up by now, and you can—"

Wrapping it up? She'd come as quickly as she possibly could, hadn't she? Hadn't she?

She leapt from the Bentley, whipped off her high-heeled shoes, and brushed her way past the young officer, racing barefoot up the sandy lane to save her man.

There were two ambulances and two or three more police vehicles, lights still flashing red and blue, parked in the drive nearest the front entrance-way. Yellow crime scene tape up here, too, draped across the front door, and, God, someone draped in blood-soaked sheets was about to be loaded into the rear of the ambulance. Alex? She dashed up the final stretch of wet sand. There was so much blood. . . .

"Alex! Alex! Oh, my darling! What did . . . ? What happened . . . ? What's going on?"

One of the two EMS medics turned and said, "This is Mr. Grenville, ma'am. . . . We need to get him to the ER right now! Please step back. . . ."

"Oh, dear God, Pelham. My poor, poor Pelham. . . ."

She took his hand.

"You're going to be all right, darling Pelham. Do you hear me? Everything is going to be . . ."

It was clear that Pelham was unconscious. Or was it? Was he . . . Could he be?

Sigrid grabbed the medic by his sleeve.

"Where is Lord Hawke? En route to hospital? Inside? Where?"

"Lord Hawke is receiving emergency medical treatment inside the house, Miss Kissl. We need to stabilize him before we can—"

She ran for the opened front door, ignoring the policeman standing guard outside and tearing at the yellow crime scene tape, moaning and sobbing, near hysteria.

The policeman took her by the upper right arm and guided her off the front walk and out onto the grass and the gardens beyond.

"All right, please calm down. They're coming out with him now."

Seconds later, two EMS medics emerged from the cottage, a man on a blood-soaked stretcher between them.

"We've got a code red," the man shouted. "Everyone out of the way. Code red!"

She turned to the policeman, wiping the tears from her eyes. "Is he still alive?"

"Ma'am, we found him in very bad shape. I'm sure these guys are doing everything humanly possible to save him and—"

"Alex!" she cried, seeing the stretcher surrounded by medics racing him frantically toward the waiting ambulance. "Alex, my darling man! I love you!"

"Please try to calm down, miss."

"Did you catch the man who did this, Officer?"

"I'm afraid not. We searched the house in its entirety as well as the gardens and down on the beach. Nothing."

"Oh, my God . . . Can I go with him in the ambulance?"

"No room with all those EMS techs working on him. Sorry."

"That's all right. I'll drive my own car. I can't spend the next twenty-four or so hours in this evening gown. . . . I'll just go inside and change and get a few things he might need during his stay. Are there still police inside?"

"No. We're done here until tomorrow first light. We'll be back with forensics and crime scene boys. . . . Hold on, miss. Here they come with the stretcher! Get back!"

And in wink of an eye, her lover was loaded inside, and the ambulance, lights flashing and sirens wailing, fishtailed around in the sandy drive and disappeared down into the green jungle below.

———————

Only one cop remained, pulling the front door shut. Sigrid put on her most alluring posture and addressed him.

"I am Alex Hawke's personal assistant. May I please go inside? I need to change and get some of Lord Hawke's prescription medications before I go to the hospital. I won't be ten minutes."

"No worries, ma'am. Forensics is all done here. I'm headed back to the station. Are you sure you're all right?"

"Yes. And . . . thank you for everything."

"All right, then. Just one question. Does the victim have any enemies here on Bermuda? Anyone wishing to do him harm?"

"Well, obviously he does, doesn't he, for God's sake? Look at him!"

"Anyone you know, is what I meant, ma'am."

"No. No one I know. He has enemies in every corner of the world."

"Well. I'd hurry up then, if you want to get to the hospital . . . in time."

Sigrid raced to the front door, pulled it open, and stepped inside. The house was cold and as dark as a tomb. She made her way through the front room, feeling her way along the pieces of furniture. Their bedroom faced the sea, at the end of a hallway leading away from the circular bar that opened onto the beach below.

She suddenly felt a cold, wet wind blowing in from the sea. Had she left the door open? She didn't think so. Maybe one of the seaward French doors? She thought not because Alex was always so careful to—

A searing white light suddenly stopped her in her tracks, left her staggering and blinded.

"What?" she cried. "What the hell is that?"

"So you're Sigrid," a bizarre voice, barely a whisper but audible. "Your Instagram pictures don't lie, baby. I see what his lordship sees in you, honey. Come over here and let ole Shit get a closer look at you. . . . I wanna smell you, baby. I wanna lick you."

"Leave me alone! There are police out there! Get out now, or I'll scream. . . ."

"I love to hear a woman scream," he said. "You jes' go ahead and let 'er rip, baby. . . . Give it yer best shot."

"I'm warning you. . . ."

"Go ahead and scream, woman, afore you make me mad. Do something to you I'll regret . . ."

Sigrid gathered her strength and screamed as loudly as she ever had in her entire life. "Help! Help meeeee. . . ."

She knew the cops had all gone. But he didn't, and maybe it would be enough to—

A rough hand had her by the throat, coming from behind, squeezing her larynx. . . .

"All righty, all righty," he said. "That was a good one. You going to behave, little lady? I don't want to hurt you none. . . ."

She squirmed and hiked her tight black skirt up. Then she kicked her right heel upward and behind her as hard as she could, hoping to catch his knee or, better yet, his groin . . . but she didn't catch either.

"Ah, honey. You don't want to hurt ole Shit, now, do you? He's going to take care of you tonight. Maybe give you a hot bath, tuck you in bed, right? Give you a nice back rub maybe. I will warn you though, baby face. You let the Big Dog out? Hell, that monster will hunt! I sincerely shit you not. . . ."

She felt the sting of the blade at her throat. . . .

"Just do what you're told. You don't . . . this ain't going to end well for you, little lady."

"Please! Please don't hurt me!"

"Aw, baby, spare me the agony. You just remember that everybody has a breaking point. Learned that in my CIA days. Tonight, you and me? We're going to find out what yours is. I'm gonna make you feel things no woman has ever felt. You're gonna be down on your knees, begging for the end by the time I'm done. . . ."

It was then that she saw the Taser in his hand.

"Time I introduced you to my zaptastic friend." He smiled at her as he zapped the back of her fleshy thigh with fifty thousand watts for at least fifteen seconds, until her bones became a conduction system, her nerve endings afire, her entire body shaking uncontrollably.

He zapped her again, slightly below the curve of her ass, this time for much longer.

The scream that then issued from her throat was at a pitch and of such rampant power and blistering intensity as to cause the countless multicolored tropical birds, hidden in the plantation of thick green banana trees outside the cottage windows, to rise up as one and flee, winging away en masse out over the breaking waves and the dark Atlantic Ocean beyond.

Inside the little cottage by the sea, all was still. All was quiet.

The Reaper had come and gone.

And it had been grim.

CHAPTER 7

Washington, D.C.
December 1941

Ambassador Tang stood waiting patiently under the porte cochere. The bulbous black 1939 Cadillac limousine that had ferried him all round Georgetown last night was paused at the security gate, white smoke billowing from its exhaust. The cavernous grey felt interior of the American car, after all the diminutive Chinese government vehicles, would be a welcome change for his six-foot-plus frame.

And the U.S. Army driver who'd been assigned to him was a pleasant surprise. He was an easygoing chap, a Southern fellow from—where was it?—Georgia. Bobby Ray, his name was. Tiger had been calling him "Mr. Ray" for most of the evening until he'd finally been informed that "Ray" was not his chauffeur's last name, but in fact was his middle name. His last name, he said, was Beavers. And then added, somewhat mysteriously, "Bobby Ray Beavers of the Beavers of Claxton, Georgia, fruitcake capital of the world, and welcome to it."

He had a way of talking, Mr. Beavers did. Fruitcake? What in God's name was that?

The limo wound its way up the long, serpentine drive, gliding through the snow-covered ornamental trees. Tiger followed the Cadillac's path, his nostrils flaring at the bite of the frosty air. A chill went up his spine that straightened him up, and he realized his recovery from the previous night's debauchery was well on its way. Now he just needed a good long walk somewhere, get his heart rate up and his thoughts to settle and coalesce. . . .

The black car pulled under the covered entry, out of the snow, and Bobby Ray Beavers swung his door open and climbed out, smiling at Tang across the snowy rooftop of the Cadillac. And then came that long, slow drawl, must have crawled all the way up from Georgia.

"Well, good morning, suh! Sorry I'm a touch late. Damn traffic's backed up from the Key Bridge all the way into Arlington. . . ."

The driver made his way through the freshly fallen knee-deep snow to open the rear door for his new passenger and swung it wide.

"We've got plenty of time," Tang said, climbing inside the darkness of the rear and stretching his long legs out before him, luxuriating in the grey felt upholstery. The Americans seemed to have an appreciation for luxury that had not yet reached the shores of his homeland. He was a sensual creature, after all, and that fact boded well for his tenure here in this garden of earthly delights. He said:

"I'd like to stop and take a walk somewhere on the way to the White House. Get some air. Get my blood flowing to my brain. Where do you suggest, Bobby Ray?"

The chauffeur shut the door securely and went back around to his opened door. He climbed in and turned around, his arm along the top of the seat, and smiled.

"Well, lessee. Let me think on it a spell. Place I like? Is to walk in Potomac Park, down by the Lincoln Memorial. Hardly ever anybody down there, and it's real pretty, you know . . . exspecially in all this snow!"

"Sounds extra special to me. Let's go, Bobby Ray. We've got about an hour to kill before we're expected. Let's make good use of it."

"Yessir, Mr. Ambassador. Don't you worry neither. I won't spare the horses. . . ."

———————

Within minutes of this swift and pleasant ride through uncharted urban territory, the new Chinese ambassador decided that Washington was indeed one of the loveliest capital cities he'd ever visited in his life. He loved all the gleaming white monuments, the parks at every turn, each filled with elegant statuary depicting great heroes of the young country's glorious past. He was deeply proud of his homeland's ancient culture and modern achievements. That was China. But he felt something more akin to love for the story that was America.

He'd studied American history while an undergraduate at Cambridge, his focus the profound effects on society and political history in the aftermath of the American Revolution. In fact, he'd written his undergraduate thesis on General George Washington. In the process of his studies, he'd met all the great man's friends and colleagues, including, Jefferson, Hamilton, Adams, Franklin, Madison, and finally, his personal favorite, the gloriously swashbuckling Marquis de Lafayette, who had saved the day at Yorktown.

And, later, as a postdoctoral candidate at Oxford, he'd shifted his focus to the man from Illinois, Abraham Lincoln. And here, he'd at last found his one true hero.

The ambassador leaned forward, putting a hand on the back of the front seat and peering ahead through the snow-blown windows of the big black car.

"That's it, isn't it? The Lincoln Memorial?"

"Yessiree, Mr. Ambassador. There she is all right."

"She? Who?"

"Well, you know, figger of speech. Down South, land o' cotton, is what I mean."

Tiger knew enough now to stop trying to decode the things Bobby Ray Beavers said. So he just said:

"Pull over, Bobby Ray. I want to go have a look."

He was immediately taken aback by the majestic, templelike appearance of the edifice, one that reminded him of the Parthenon. He found his thoughts were not of classical architecture or war, but of the magnificent mind of the man picked out in marble, seated so resolutely inside the central chamber. It was, he thought, staring up at Lincoln with a shudder of emotion, with the possible exception of Michelangelo's *David* in Florence, the most powerful inanimate object he'd ever encountered in his life.

Looking up, he saw that the names of the thirty-six reunited states appeared in the frieze above the columns. A testament to Honest Abe's steadfast hand on the tiller in the fight to save the Union. He began climbing the steps, hastening his pace, as he wanted to have as much time alone with the great man as he could. He found a marble bench and sat down, staring up at the power of that heroic head as clearly held in his mind now as those of his own country's heroes.

He sat there for nearly half an hour, quiet, centering himself, imagining his first glimpse of the Oval Office and the imposing American president, considering and discarding multiple greetings before he settled on one imperfect one that might have to do. And then, rising, he quickly looked into the two chambers flanking the great man himself. For this is where his words were to be found. . . .

In the first of the two, he paused and read this, quietly whispering the words aloud as he read . . .

With malice toward none; with charity for all; with firmness in the right, as God gives us to see the right, let us strive on to finish the work we are in; to bind up the nation's wounds; to care for him who shall have borne the battle, and for his widow, and his orphan—to do all which may achieve and cherish a just and lasting peace, among ourselves, and with all nations.

And in the quiet sanctity of the second chamber . . .

The world will little note, nor long remember what we say here, but it can never forget what they did here. It is for us the living, rather, to be dedicated here to the unfinished work which they who fought here have thus far so nobly advanced. It is rather for us to be here dedicated to the great task remaining before us—that from these honored dead we take increased devotion to that cause for which they gave the last full measure of devotion—that we here highly resolve that these dead shall not have died in vain—that this nation, under God, shall have a new birth of freedom—and that government of the people, by the people, for the people, shall not perish from the earth.

Tiger rose, hot tears stinging his eyes at the roiling emotions Lincoln's words had stirred within him, rubbing his gloved hands together for warmth, and he gazed up one final time at the profile frozen in stone looming above. As always, he'd been humbled by the great man's words, even more powerful carved in stone than printed on paper. He felt a twinge of guilt as he tried as ever to reconcile his love and admiration for some of America's heroes . . . and his erstwhile dedication to his father, his family, to Chiang Kai-shek and his country. He was, after all, sailing under a false flag. He had two masters now.

And he would do well to remember that.

He would do all within his power to help Roosevelt and the Americans crush the evil Japanese, those murderous bastards behind the horrific Rape of Nanking, China, beneath their boots. But his true mission, the real reason he'd been chosen by Kai-shek, was to funnel top secret information from within the seats of power of the American government. He was to be both ally and spy to the Americans.

For better or for worse, he was now, and always would be, the Divided Spy.

CHAPTER 8

R ain rattled against the windows of the snug little study with its damp wood fire releasing bluish flames that lapped lambently at the wrought iron grate. "Come here, Fala, good dog! Come, Fala!" the president said, motioning for his beloved Scottie to spring up into his waiting arms. In a single bound, Fala landed on the president's lap.

"Ah," FDR said, "my good soldier, home from the front, battered and bowed, but unbroken. . . ." He stroked Fala's long black ears as was his habit. Had Fala been a cat, he would have surely purred like a feline demon.

The president had gotten the black-and-white Scottie last year. An early Christmas 1940 gift from his first cousin and closest companion, Margaret "Daisy" Suckley. The president, instantly smitten with the dog, had immediately named the little fellow "Murray the Outlaw of Falahill" after his famous Scottish ancestor. And Fala it was, evermore.

"Harry, listen up," the president said to his friend, closest confidant, and lone companion in his private office, upstairs at the White House residence.

For some reason or other, the old gent was bent forward with his head down, shaking his shaggy locks in front of the heat radiator. Fala had leapt to the carpet and was now at his feet. "Yes?" Harry murmured, still shaking.

FDR said, "I want you to make me a promise. If anything should happen to me, if I somehow don't have the physical and mental wherewithal to survive the monolithic challenge I now find myself confronted with— no, no, hear me out. I want you personally to take Fala by train down to Georgia, to the Little White House at Warm Springs. Privately and discreetly, of course. No publicity, no press corps. Are you listening to me?"

"Yes, Mr. President, of course," Harry Hopkins replied. "Just give a me a moment here," he said, shivering and pulling his old grey woolen sweater over his head.

The rainwater had finally stopped dripping from Hopkins's silver hair down his collar. He'd returned just moments ago to the president's study. As was his custom, rain or shine, he'd been taking Fala for a lovely morning walk in the rain across the North Lawn. Both of them soaked to the skin by the watery adventure. The room was becoming close and steamy with the drying of his hair, clothes, and Fala's luxuriant coat.

After Harry's cancer ordeal, the president chided him about catching a chill during his rainy walkabouts, but he would not be dissuaded. Cold rain on his cheeks was about the only thing that made him feel alive anymore.

Over the years the two men had formed a near invincible bond. Hopkins understood his boss's moods. He knew the appropriate moment to talk business and when the president needed to relax. If Roosevelt was the "thinker," Hopkins was the "doer." His real talent was turning FDR's sometimes inchoate ideas into concrete programs that would serve the country well. He'd made it his job—his religion, really—to elicit just what it was that Roosevelt really wanted and then see to it that neither hell nor high water, not even possible vacillations by the man himself, blocked its achievement.

Roosevelt, staring into the flickering firelight, cleared his throat and said, "My butler, Horace Spain, as you well know, is already aware of this plan. He will be expecting you and Fala to arrive by train at Warm Springs shortly after all the funeral hoopla up at Hyde Park has been concluded. Horace is a lifelong bachelor, never married, no children. The great love of his life is Fala. In my will, I'm bequeathing the gardener's cottage to Horace for the duration of his life. It is my fervent hope that he and his boon companion, Fala, will live out their years happily ever after there, long after I'm gone. All right, Harry, we're clear on that?"

"Yes, sir."

"Good, good. Well. Who's up at bat next, then?"

"That would be the brand-new ambassador from China, sir. I've scheduled the meeting to take place upstairs here in your study. More private. Shall I remain? I've got plenty on my plate today, Lord knows. . . ."

"Please stick around for this, Harry. I want your take on this young fellow. I hear marvelous things about him from his predecessor. Almost too good to be true, to be quite honest. Anyway, there's nothing for it. Other than my admirals and generals across the river at the Pentagon, this one man will be absolutely vital to our cause in Asia for the foreseeable future. I daresay, we simply cannot defeat the Japanese Imperial Army without him."

"Yes, quite right," Hopkins said, obviously ruminating on the president's remarks. "I agree. Like many Americans, I cling to a romantic image of the Chinese. An image reinforced by my ancestors' ties to the China trade, I suppose."

"I, too, have always had the deepest sympathy for the Chinese," the president sighed. "How could I not embrace them now, when we are united by a mutual adversary?"

At the very last moment, FDR changed his mind about the venue for meeting with the new Chinese ambassador. The study was overly warm, damp, and close.

"It stinks in here, Harry," the president said, raising his prominent Roman nose into the air. "It's that ancient tweed jacket of yours, old sport. Starts to smell like hell when you wear it in the rain."

"Hardly the jacket. I do believe it's Fala, sir."

"Fala? Don't be absurd. Fala doesn't stink! Do you, Fala? Of course not."

"Nevertheless, Mr. President, it is a bit ripe in here. I'll grant you that. I'll move us down to the Oval, sir."

"Good, good. Ambassador Tang is presenting his credentials to the vice president and the secretary of state in the East Room right now. Should be finishing up in a few minutes. Let's shove off, shall we?"

Fifteen minutes later, the president's pretty secretary, Marguerite "Missy" LeHand, peeked inside and announced that Ambassador Tang had arrived.

"Thank you, Missy. Please show him in," the president said.

Roosevelt liked the cut of the ambassador's jib from the very second he laid eyes on the young man who walked through his door.

Tang strode into the Oval Office like a movie star onto a set. Tall, handsome, brimming with confidence, good health, a twinkle of humor in his eyes, and a toothy white smile. He approached the Resolute Desk and offered the president his outstretched hand. Roosevelt shook it first, then Hopkins, who stood by his side.

"A very great honor, Mr. President," Tang said. "You have both figured very prominently in my thoughts these last days. I extend my deepest sympathies for the losses America has suffered, both in human terms and the Pacific Fleet itself."

Roosevelt smiled wanly. "Please take a seat, Mr. Ambassador. Over there by the fire. Secretary Hopkins has agreed to join us. He is my confidant, my closest friend, and my good right hand. You will quickly come to know that Harry deserves your confidence every bit as much as he does my own. Thank God they appear to have overlooked all the oil tank storage."

"I've not the shadow of a doubt, sir," Tang said.

Hopkins showed Tang to the nearest green leather armchair and took the one opposite him. As always in the Oval, Roosevelt remained ensconced in the wheelchair hidden behind his desk. Hopkins smiled at the young man and said, "You see, he considers us as one, Mr. Ambassador. But I, for one, know that he has no equal."

"Well said, sir!" Tang beamed. "We will win this war, Mr. President, Mr. Hopkins. We will rout those bloody Jap bastards, and we shall never look back!"

Inside, the ambassador felt the stirring of things beginning to loosen up a bit. Tang had intuited almost instantly that he was going to get on with these two men. They already shared a good deal in common, beyond just brains and political acuity, most notably, a common enemy. Japan would loom large for their foreseeable future, to be sure. But he, Tang, would endeavor to build many bridges among the trio. And many walls around them. Most important, he would win their confidence as well as their friendship, a wartime triad of cavaliers bound by cause and embowered in bonhomie.

That was his plan, at any rate, Tang thought, as he bid the president farewell.

Everyone knew full well, of course, what could happen to the most carefully laid plans, exorbitant dreams, and stealthy schemes. And at that precise moment, another one of the president's many political schemes popped into his brain, fully baked and ready to be served up.

Churchill was about to drive him up the walls.

Constantly calling, asking to be reassured of the American president's affection and sense of duty regarding the plight of Britain, now taking a horrific thrashing by the Nazis.

"Harry, I've a thought. I would very much like for you to move up your scheduled travel to Britain in order to parley with Winston Churchill. As I've already made clear, he is desperate for ever-increasing amounts of aid, both in cash and war matériel. I'd like for you to spend a goodly amount of time with him. Listening to him, observing him, his habits good and bad, his strengths, and, of course, his weaknesses. A fondness for female companionship, alcohol, gambling on the ponies, whatever you find. Your primary mission? Listen. And learn.

"When you return home from Jolly Old England, I would like to meet with you and hear how you think I should deal with him, because, sooner rather than later, I'll be doing just that."

"I'll go all right. But as I said before, I won't put up with any high-hatting behavior. The Brits and their oh-so-obvious condescending behavior toward Americans get under my skin, as you well know. I'm damn serious, Mr. President. I mean, just who the hell do these people think they are? Rule Britannia, my ass! Go have another look at the battlefield at Yorktown. Their fancy-pants General Cornwallis didn't even have the stones to come out of his tent and concede defeat once Washington's Continental Army had whipped the living daylights out of those redcoats!"

"Well, then, Harry, might I suggest you hold your nose in his company. All the while considering the inescapable fact that it is only the fate of Western civilization that hangs in the balance."

Hopkins smiled at the not-too-subtle dig. "Well played, Mr. President. Right up to snuff lately, I must admit."

Well, that's it, then, Hopkins thought to himself, he's thrown me to the lions this time!

CHAPTER 9

Bermuda
Present Day

Dr. Nathaniel Wetherell, chief of surgery at Edward VII Hospital, was quietly reading in his office that morning when the telephone on his desk jangled.

"Dr. Wetherell?"

"Yes, yes, what is it?"

"Your patient in three fifteen, sir," the head nurse said. "He seems to be coming out of the vegetative state and—"

"Alex Hawke?"

"Yes, sir. Lord Hawke."

"Good Lord! Has he entered MCS?" Wetherell said, referring to the most welcome next phase of a coma, the minimally conscious state.

"I've been with him for half an hour. Appears to be drifting in and out, breathing, sleeping, and waking regularly."

"I'll be right there. Stay where you are. Keep talking to him. Patients in a coma can hear you, you know. Hearing is always the last of the senses to go."

"Yes, Doctor, of course. Oh, one other thing you should know— He, uh, well . . . I don't know how to say it other than to tell you that Lord Hawke has been mumbling in word perfect Chinese. Mandarin, I think. My mother spoke Mandarin."

"Bilingual aphasia! Good Lord, I'm on my way!"

Wetherell bolted from his office, ran down two flights of stairs, and rushed down the hall to Hawke's room. At the bedside, the chief of surgery took Hawke's hand and massaged it vigorously, saying, "Alex! Alex, can you hear me?"

No response.

But then—a slight tightening of the patient's fist around his own. Weak at first, but gathering strength. Wetherell emitted a huge sigh of relief. When the patient had arrived at hospital that night, he was as near to death's door as one could get without stepping through. No one had had believed that he would survive the night. Nor did anyone on duty that night think that the other, much older, victim of the killer's heinous knife attack stood the ghost of a chance.

"He's on his way up," Dr. Wetherell said, gazing up at Nurse Vicky with a broad smile. "On his way up, indeed!"

"Thank God," she said. "We've all been praying for him, you know. His lordship is very popular with our Women's League ladies at the annual benefit picnic. . . ." She trailed off, looking dreamily down at the sleeping patient she'd been caring for lo these many long weeks of healing and resting.

"So, when he first spoke, it was Chinese?" Wetherell said.

"Yes, sir. At first I thought it was just gobbeldygook, but then it was definitely Chinese. Never seen this before, Doctor. How does it manifest?"

"Very rare. But bilingual aphasia manifests when an area of the brain that learns a language is damaged while another remains untouched. Apparently, at some point in his life, he learned Mandarin . . . as did I, myself, whilst working for Her Majesty's government in Shanghai. . . ."

"I think I should remain here with him, Doctor. And keep you informed of all significant progress."

"Just about to suggest that, Nurse. And don't stop praying, dear. He's not out of the woods yet. His abdominal wounds were the worst I've seen in thirty years of practice."

"Where is Pelham?" were the first three words in English issuing from the mouth of Alex Hawke. The old gent, Pelham Grenville, whom

Hawke sometimes referred to as "My Octogenarian," was truly a "gentle" man, a white-haired wraith of a chap from Cornwall who never "entered" a room, but rather one who shimmered in. Nor did the fellow, Hawke said, ever simply appear.

No, no, not him. Pelham materialized.

Along with Chief Inspector Ambrose Congreve of Scotland Yard, Pelham had helped the young Hawke's grandfather raise the boy up from boyhood. Hawke's early days were spent at the home of his grandfather on Greybeard Island. It was an ancestral home—more of a castle really—perched on the small island near France in the Channel Islands, and how he'd adored scampering about its walled gardens and beaches with his beloved dog, Jip.

His grampy, a Royal Navy man, taught the boy all he could impart: celestial navigation, how to overcome fear, how to treat the fairer sex with respect, how to sharpen a knife and swing an axe or a golf club, how to hold a fork, the art of fair play, and how to clean a shotgun, how to reef, bend, and steer a sailing boat, how to train a field dog, how to comport oneself as a gentleman, what to look for in a woman, how to repair the triple downdraft SU carburetors on a Triumph TR3 roadster. And how to respect the flag, history, and traditions of one's country.

And more, so much more. A lovely chap, really.

But it was chiefly dear old Pelham who, subsequent to the murder of Alex's parents by drug pirates in the Caribbean, took over as Hawke's guardian.

It was little more than a week after Hawke had begun the process of entering the final phase of disordered consciousness. Now he was sitting upright in his hospital bed, chatting merrily with Nurse Vicky, who was lovingly and vigorously massaging his right hand.

"Why, Pelham's at home, sir," she said, smiling. "Resting comfortably."

"Resting? At home? Good Lord, you don't mean to say he—"

"Survived? Recovered from his wounds? Yes, indeed he did, although no one who attended to him that first night would have believed it possible. There's a toughness to him belied by his genteel exterior. He was discharged this past Tuesday and is now resting quietly at Teakettle Cottage with round-the-clock nurses tending to his every need. Doing very well, eating normally, gaining strength day by day. . . ."

"I cannot believe it," Hawke said. "I was pretty sure he'd died there on the bar. I remember feeling terribly sad about that just before I lost consciousness. How on earth did you save the old boy?"

"Wasn't me, dearie. Was our beloved Dr. Wetherell that did it. For all the blood loss, most of his wounds were superficial. The wound to the hand was severe, but the doctor managed to repair all the damage to the tendons. He won't be using it for a while, but eventually, with therapy, he might recover full use."

"God love his soul! You see before you a happy man, a man who, for all intents and purposes, thought he'd lost the one soul closest to him and—" He looked up. "Why, it's Pelham! It's old Pelham come to call! Can it be? Pelham? Is that really you? I cannot believe—just a delusion. . . ."

A sob escaped from deep inside. Confusion and pain were in a tug-of-war within him. As the pain diminished, the confusion began to reign supreme.

The nurse reached over and placed her warm, dry hand on Hawke's forearm.

"My lord," she said. "I don't think you realize that—"

"That what?"

"That you are crying."

"What?" Hawke put his hand to his cheek. It was wet with tears. My God, how long had he been crying? "I'm sorry. It's just . . . that night, the night we were dying . . . I was just so sure I'd never see him again . . . see that beautiful old soul again. I'm so sorry. . . . I do love him dearly."

"Top of the morning, m'lord," Pelham said, executing a slight bow before he fully deatomized in the doorway, trying not to notice the flood of tears continuing to flow from his lordship's eyes. "I do hope I'm not interrupting what appears to be an inconvenient moment. . . ."

Nurse Vicky said, "No, no. It's not you, dear Mr. Grenville. He's just emerging from his coma. It's often difficult to come to grips with the new reality of one's life. Besides, these fresh tears are tears of purest joy."

The nurse hurriedly dropped Hawke's hand from the death grip she'd been holding it in. "Don't be silly, Mr. Grenville. Massage is just standard therapy for a recovering coma patient."

Hawke sat straight up in bed, gazing goggle-eyed at this walking miracle. Pelham's ancient blue eyes were shining bright, and his cheeks were flushed a rosy pink with the chilly November air outside.

"Welcome, good sir," Hawke said, smiling. "You're either a convincing ghost, or you're my dear old Pelham in the flesh! Is it true what they say? You've bloody well been raised from the dead! The man is a god, I tell you! Positively immortal!"

"It would appear so, yes, m'lord," Pelham said, floating on winged feet into the small room. "I did hear the angels singing, m'lord. For both of us. How do you feel, sir? You've been away for some time now."

"Bloody marvelous, considering, that's how. At least, I've apparently stopped speaking all that bloody Mandarin. Learned it while a guest of the Chinese government, you'll recall. But not nearly as good as you look, old son."

"Might I sit down, sir?"

"Of course you can. I say, Nurse, would you be so kind as to pull that chair up to my bedside?"

Vicky jumped up and got Pelham situated.

The old fellow coughed discreetly into his closed fist before he spoke. "M'lord, I hate to spoil what is indeed a most salubrious recovery and reunion. But I have grave news. Before he and Lady Mars left for London a few days ago, Chief Inspector Congreve charged me with delivering some very sad tidings, indeed, sir. Assuming you would come out of the coma at some point . . ."

"Yes, of course, assuming . . . ," Hawke said, a grey cloud suddenly descending on the happy moment.

"It's Miss Kissl, sir. Sigrid Kissl."

"What about her? Is she ill?"

"No, sir, I'm afraid not. She's dead."

Hawke looked stricken. "Dead, you say? My God!" He looked at the nurse and said, "She's bloody dead? Why didn't you say something? Nurse? You've not mentioned this?"

"We were instructed not to, sir. By Dr. Wetherell. He was afraid it might be too much of a blow for you at this early stage of your recovery. I'm very sorry, sir. I'm sure it comes as a tremendous shock."

Hawke closed his eyes and took a few deep breaths to compose himself. He looked at Pelham, suddenly thinking about his last night together with Sigrid. A hard rain had descended with the evening, enveloping his little seaside cottage in the white noise of frying bacon. She'd been terribly unhappy all day long. Her back was to the window, and wet, diffused light illuminated her face with unkind surgical accuracy. The short platinum blond hair looked lifeless, and the lines etched in her thin face constituted a hieroglyphic biography of wit and bitterness, laughter and intelligence—a life of accomplishment without fulfillment.

It was the first time he'd seen her so ineffably sad. . . . She had stood up and wiped the haze off a pane of the window, and for a while, she had stared out past the gardens and the rain to the banana trees undulating hypnotically in the wind. Then she had turned and faced him. "Alex. I know I've often described my life as a pile of shit," she said, then smiled wanly. "But it's the only pile of shit I've got."

They'd dressed in silence before leaving for the dinner party with Ambrose Congreve and Lady Mars.

"Pelham? Help me understand this. . . . How did it happen?"

"Yes, m'lord. So sorry to be the bearer of such very sad news, m'lord. But I felt you should know now. . . ."

"She's dead? How on earth? Last time I saw her, she was at Shadowlands chatting with Ambrose over a good claret at a dinner party. She was drinking heavily. I was worried about her. I told the chief inspector and Lady Mars not to let her out of their sight until I sounded the all clear at the cottage."

"Yes, sir, but, as we know now, that all clear was never sounded. I'm sorry to tell you that Miss Kissl was murdered there at the cottage later that night. Attacked and killed in cold blood."

"But, good Lord, Pelham, who killed her?"

"The crime was without an eyewitness, m'lord."

"Who found her?"

"Your gardener found her early next morning. Still alive, but barely. Sigrid had crawled from your bedroom, where the attack took place, all the way out to the rear terrace overlooking the sea. The gardener then left her there and ran inside to call for an ambulance. When he returned, she was lying there on the flagstones, unmoving. But she had. . . ."

"She had what?" Hawke said. "What did she do?"

"Before she died, she had used her own blood to scrawl two letters on the pale flagstone. . . ."

"Yes?"

"The letters were: *S S.*"

"Shit Smith," Hawke said, anger dripping from the spoken name. "When are the funeral services?"

"There are none scheduled, m'lord. Miss Kissl is no longer on the island."

"Really? Then where on earth is she?"

"Chief Inspector Congreve took it upon himself to try to track down her family in Switzerland. He finally located the grandfather, a sheep-herder in Tiefenthaler, a small mountain town near St. Moritz. Ambrose took it upon himself to make arrangements for the body to be returned to the family, sir."

Hawke sat up straight in bed.

"Putin is carrying out his threat to me when last we saw each other. He said that my immediate family members and I were no longer under his protection. We were first on his list for punishment. Alexei is next."

"A reasonable surmise, Your Lordship."

"Pelham. Listen carefully. As you well know, my son is at sea. He's on a Cunard Line circumnavigation. Under the care of my dear Spanish friend, Carlos Martinez de Irujo, the Duque of Alba. And two Royal Protection Officers from the Yard. I want confirmation that those two officers are now guarding him night and day. One within six feet of him at all times. Also, I want a call put through to Carlos aboard the liner. I want to warn him that Mr. Smith is out and about, killed my colleague Sigrid, and nearly killed you and me here in Bermuda. I want Alexei's two Scotland Yard Royal Protection Officers to be on the highest alert.

Understand? In each and every port of call. For the balance of the voyage, I want daily reports as to his safety."

"Of course, m'lord. I'll ring him as soon as I get home."

"Be sure that you do."

"I've always perceived your wishes as commands, sir. Fear not."

"All right, Pelham, good on you. Now. It's high time we went on offense against this crazy bastard. Not to mention that maniac in the Kremlin who put a multimillion-dollar price tag on my head. I want to assemble every fighter worth his salt that we've got. First two calls go to Chief Inspector Congreve and Stokely Jones Jr. Next, those two crazy mercenaries known as Thunder and Lightning. As soon as I can get out of this bloody sickbed and recover some strength, I'm going to call my pilot to get us the hell out of here. Do we think that Mr. Smith, now that he believes he's delivered his triple death blows, has left Bermuda? I wouldn't guarantee it."

"What is the basis for your fears, sir?" Pelham said, leaning forward in his chair.

"I'll tell you. Putin knows I survived the attack. The morning of the dinner party at Shadowlands, I got a call from my friend who's a CIA officer in Miami. According to Harry Brock, the CIA recently intercepted a heavily encrypted message from the very highest levels at the Kremlin. It was short and sweet and sent to every Russian contract killer out there. 'Bring me the head of Alex Hawke. On a silver platter. Reward. Signed, Vladimir Putin.'"

Pelham looked at Dr. Wetherell and said, "Doctor, I think you need to alert the Bermuda constabulary immediately. We will need at least two armed guards, one in this room, the other in the hallway. Yes? As soon as they can get here."

"Yes, of course, of course!"

"I need to get out of here as soon as humanly possible, Dr. Wetherell. Now would be good."

Pelham said, "He's a freak of nature, Doctor. Near supernatural powers of recovery."

"I'm starting him on physical therapy this very afternoon. I think I should be able to spring him, say, in a week's time? Ten days? Say, Monday after next? Certainly by that Tuesday."

"Alex?" Pelham said.

"Yes, yes. Yes to the guards and the gym training, all of it. Pelham, you need to return to Teakettle and pack two of my handguns. The forty-five revolver and the Walther PPK if the police didn't take it as evidence. Two boxes of ammunition each. . . . Also, Doctor, I think you should issue a discreet message to all the nurses on the floor. Should they see anyone suspicious, or anything at all out of the ordinary, come to me immediately."

"Good idea, Alex. You really think the killer stuck around the island after he'd done the deed?"

"I've no idea. I hope so. I'd like to see him again. Under different circumstances, of course."

"What is your plan, if I may be so bold as to ask?"

"Dr. Wetherell, you saved my life. You can ask me anything you wish. I'm going, with a little help, to heal myself as quickly as is humanly possible. Then I'm going to scour the ends of the earth and sail the seven seas in search of Mr. Smith. When I find him, I will kill him."

"From the extent and style of your injuries, I would be very careful as to how you approach this monster. Frankly, you need time to heal."

"Oh, I'm not going it alone, Doctor. It will not surprise you to learn that, in addition to Chief Inspector Congreve, I have a few unsavory yet very formidable friends around the globe. Men of a certain stripe who help me—how to say it?—with unpleasant circumstances and individuals. Mercenaries, soldiers of fortune, adventurers, chaps of that sort."

"Of course, sir. One only assumes these things based on rumors that swirl around this island when you are off on another adventure."

"Ah, yes, I see," Hawke said. "If you would be so kind, I would be grateful if you could get the chief inspector on the line? He's now at his home in Oxfordshire, England. Here is his mobile number. If his wife picks up, ask her to put you through straightaway. Tell her it's urgent and that I wish to speak with him as quickly as possible."

CHAPTER 10

Sunningdale Golf Club, London, England
Present Day

Sir David Trulove, chief of MI6, England's famed Secret Service, was standing impatiently outside the men's locker room at Sunningdale, his golf club outside of London. As always, the former Royal Navy admiral, an eminent hero of the Falklands War with Argentina, was looking rather magisterial. A tough feat to pull off while a chappie was wearing golf attire, but he managed it. It was a splendid day, clear and sunny, yet worry clouded his pale blue eyes and well-lined face. The Queen had awakened him shortly after dawn, a call from Buck House. Her Majesty the Queen was fit to be tied.

It seemed her beloved grandson, secretly her favorite of the lot, Prince Henry, having just attained the threshold of twenty-five, had been invited down to some fancy resort in the Bahamas. Very exclusive. Invitation only. Apparently, someone at the club had seen the photo spread of him in *Vanity Fair.* The resort was called Dragonfire Club, and owned by a major Chinese industrial family by the name of Tang, Her Majesty had said. Sailing, gambling, golf, women, the usual. That had been ten days ago. Her Majesty had subsequently received two of Henry's e-mails, quite glib and jolly, and a lively phone call from him last Friday evening. Then an odd call around midnight. She'd picked up on the first ring. There was no one there.

Despite her own subsequent calls to the young prince's suite, which went unanswered, there had been no communication since.

Sir David was convinced that the rambunctious Royal—who was "Jane crazy" as the doughboys used to call an infantryman overly fond of women, and who was also the godson of Alex Hawke—had met some louche heiress or other and swum off to another happy, sun-kissed tropic isle, just another boy looking for the heart of Saturday night, as they used to say.

Trulove had asked Scotland Yard to send two of their topmost investigators down to Dragonfire Club, posing as wealthy British businessmen, and have a look round. Dig in and see if they could get on the wayward prince's trail.

Apparently, the young man had simply vanished. No one knew anything more. Scotland Yard had offered to put a missing-person alert on the missing prince and hope for the best. The Queen was not amused.

After a week in the Bahamas, the detectives had filed a report saying that the young prince had simply vanished. Along with all of his belongings. The Yard detectives had found a scrawled phone number on a pad on the desk in his room. Turned out to be the reservations line for Raffles Hotel in Hong Kong. The two men were en route now in an effort to locate the young prince somewhere in China. Since then, complete radio silence from the Yard. After a week or so of digging, the detectives had come to naught and were recalled to London.

And now, in the wee small hours, the Queen was back on Sir David's case.

"I am not at all happy. I want you to do something, Sir David. And I want it done now. That's why I'm calling so early. I'm told you're playing golf with Chief Inspector Congreve at Sunningdale today. Is that correct?"

"Yes, ma'am."

"Good. Because I want you to inform the chief inspector that the Yard's assistance is no longer required in the search for my grandson. Tell him he's been made redundant. Because you, personally, will be heading up the case from this moment forward. Is that quite clear, Sir David?"

"Abundantly, Your Royal Majesty. Crystal clear."

"Good. There's only one man in England who can find my grandson and bring him home safely. Yes, and we both know very well who he is.

Therefore, I want Lord Hawke on this case. And I want him now. Do we understand each other? Should anything happen to that child, I shall hold you personally accountable. Is that clearly understood, Sir David?"

"Crystal. I understand with perfect clarity, Your Majesty," Trulove asserted, having no earthly idea how he was going to deliver the goods to Buckingham Palace in a timely fashion. At last report, Hawke had been hovering at death's door in a hospital on Bermuda.

"Good. The only member of your staff at Six who is capable of bringing this situation to its proper conclusion is that dear boy, Alex Hawke. No one else will suit. I want his immediate attention on this nightmare, and I want him now! Do we understand each other, Sir David? I want Hawke to go wherever the trail may lead; find the prince and return with him to England posthaste. Alex Hawke has never let me down. Not once, including the time he almost single-handedly saved me and my entire family from assassination by al Qaeda fiends that Christmas at Balmoral Castle! Please give that dear boy the Queen's best regards, will you? Tell him I hope he's recovering nicely from that horrid attack."

"My pleasure, Your Majesty."

The Queen had rung off without waiting for Trulove's reply. SOP, as far as such matters went with Her Majesty. When on the phone with the Queen, a final farewell was always just a click away.

———

A man of a certain age, a fringe of silver hair and a bit rotund round about the middle and wearing heavy tweed plus fours in an unnerving shade of yellow, paused in the arched doorway of the clubhouse. He withdrew a leather tobacco pouch, lit his meerschaum pipe, then emerged from the looming shadows of the old clubhouse and onto the sun-splashed golf terrace.

"Aha! There you are, Congreve! Good God, man. What were you doing in the loo for so long? I must say, no one of my acquaintance spends longer in the loo than you! Of course, with the sole exception of my late wife, Claire. What the devil were you up to for so long?"

Congreve regarded Trulove carefully, took a quick pull on the meer-schaum, and blew a big smoke ring and then a little one straight through it.

"I cannot tell you how that rankles," a plainly rattled Trulove barked at the world-famous detective. As Stokely Jones Jr., Alex Hawke's boon companion, had once said to him under similar circumstances, "Queen ain't happy, ain't nobody happy."

"Really? Do tell us why? A simple enough trick, really."

"Because I can't bloody well master it, can I? No matter how I try. You do it merely to taunt me when I'm in a state."

"High dudgeon, if I take your meaning?"

"What of it? You mock me, sir."

"Not at all, Sir David. I do the feat in honor of my great hero and mentor, Sherlock Holmes. Similarly, when Holmes demonstrated the smoky trick to Dr. Watson, the man was, likewise, never quite able to master it."

"So, what were you doing in the bloody locker room? Your hair? I was afraid we'd miss our tee time."

"On the blower, Sir David. Alex Hawke rang me from hospital in Bermuda."

"He's out of the coma? Thank you, dear God! In His heaven this morning after all and taking care of all God's children!"

"Well out of his coma, so it would seem. He's being released from hospital in a week or ten days to continue his rehab therapy with a phys-ical trainer at the cottage."

"Oh, saints above. That's the best news I've heard all day! Tell me more, my good fellow. *Hors de combat* no longer then, is he?"

"Save the death of Miss Kissl, it would appear that there is much to be thankful for."

"Sigrid Kissl is dead? How awful. Accident? Illness?"

"Murder. Perpetrator used a knife with a razor-sharp serrated blade. Victim was chopped practically to pieces."

"Terrible. Any idea who?"

"An idea, but no proof as of yet."

"She was a lovely girl, and I know you and Lady Mars were terribly fond of her. I always thought she had the makings of a fine detective, and I know she was well respected at Scotland Yard."

"Yes, she was. Over the years, whilst she was living in our gardener's cottage, we became rather close. So it was that I arranged with her grandfather to have her body returned to the family in the Swiss Alps. The funeral is next Monday on the family farm at the mountain town of Tiefenthaler. My wife, Diana, and I are attending."

"Poor dear. So. Tell me about Hawke. The timing of his reawakening is most fortuitous, believe you me. Beyond fortuitous, as I was in a bit of a pickle!"

Congreve said, "Bloody lucky to be alive, he is, and he knows it. As you'll recall, when they found him, he had a gaping abdominal wound eighteen inches across. For Alex, there's been no sign of infection as yet, and the wound is on the mend. Not sure how long that process will take. He says he can't wait to get back to his daily open-ocean swims."

"All right, I'll speak with his physician this afternoon for an update. I got a dawn wake-up call from Buckingham Palace. The Queen. Terribly agitated about your lack of progress in this case, this business of locating her missing grandson, Prince Henry. You, my dear fellow, have become redundant. You, meaning Scotland Yard, she believes, have failed her miserably. Her words, not mine. She's firing you and hiring me. To be more specific, your chum Hawke. There is an urgent need for his services at the moment. She wants him out to the Bahamas posthaste. And I intend to see that he abides by her wishes."

"Oh, good Lord. You really do ask the impossible. The man was cruelly mutilated, for all love! Horrific injuries. Have you no sympathy?"

"While I'm sure you're aware of the fact, I will remind you that Prince Henry is also Hawke's godson? The child of his closest friend throughout his career as a Royal Navy combat pilot?"

"Lord Peter Windsor, who, in Afghanistan, when he died in Hawke's arms before they could be rescued, begged Hawke to protect and support his only child."

"Indeed. Hawke's godson and the Queen's grandson are one and the same. I want you to inform his decision in this grave matter by providing him with that information."

"Sir David, with all due respect, I will, of course, inform the Yard that Six will be taking over the case. However, I must beg you to find someone else to join the fray. If Hawke asks my opinion in the matter, I will insist that he remain at his Bermuda cottage, swim and work out, rest and read until he is fully healed and recovered."

"Really? You will insist, will you? And why on the good green earth would you wish to endanger, nay, to destroy my at long last relatively good relationship with the sovereign? Have you gone completely mad?"

"Three reasons. One, Putin has a price on Hawke's head. Ten million pounds sterling. He's a marked man wherever he goes. Two, he's recently suffered grievous bodily wounds, as you well know. He needs time to recover! And three, he's in mourning. Sigrid was a lovely woman but very complicated."

"Whatever do you mean by that, old boy? All women are complicated."

"Well, I learned only recently that she suffered from depression. Alcoholism. That she lied on her application to the training program at Scotland Yard. She was a convicted felon at age twenty-two. Incarcerated. There was also an ex-husband from Zurich who was blackmailing her. He died in a rather bizarre motor accident somewhere in Morocco. Sigrid was in the car with him just before it ran off a cliff. Hawke confided to me that he thought perhaps she had murdered the man. . . . Apparently, he was threatening to kidnap Lord Hawke's son, Alexei."

"My Lord. I had no idea."

"No one did. Hawke was in semi-love-hate with her. He protected her. His son adored her."

Sir David turned away and surveyed the scene on the distant first tee. One foursome was teeing off, and a twosome was waiting on one of the benches.

"All right, then, Constable," he said. "Our tee time is fast approaching. Let's get a buggy and head out to the course."

"You wait here. I'll go fetch the buggy," Congreve said, and strode off in the direction of the caddy master's shack.

In a shake of a lamb's tail, Congreve came barreling around the side of the buggy barn and squealed to a halt right in front of Trulove.

"Jump in!" he said, and Trulove did just that.

Trulove, hanging on for dear life as Congreve raced up the twisting cart path leading up the hill, said, "Damnably rotten luck, you know, the Queen insisting on Hawke traveling to the Bahamas just now. . . ."

"Bad luck? There's understatement for you. The man's in hospital after a near-death experience of the first order! But it's your bad luck?"

"I didn't mean to infer that—"

"Sir David, grow a pair. Don't let the Crown push you around like this. Why don't you bloody well man up, as our American cousins would have it? Tell Lizzie you can't produce your glamour boy until he's fully recovered from this little episode of hors de combat. His doctor told me he was amazed that, due to the severity of his gut wounds, Alex had not died in the ambulance en route to the hospital."

"Her Royal Majesty wants him now," Sir David said, somewhat irked, "and the young man, Prince Henry, a young man whose life Hawke has sworn to protect, may well be in grave danger. Hawke alone will serve, so says the Queen. And that, as they say, is that."

"All ashore that's going ashore," Ambrose said as they pulled up near the steps to the elevated tee box. He hefted his girth out of the golf buggy, grabbed his bag, and started huffing and puffing up the wooden staircase.

"I say, is that a new driver?" Trulove asked, reaching the top as Ambrose withdrew the magnificent weapon from his bag. "American, isn't it? That clubhead looks rather like a giant white egg."

"An egg, you say? Hardly," the chief inspector said with evident pride of ownership, taking a few inelegant practice swings. "Behold the new M-Three by TaylorMade. The very club Tiger Woods used throughout his comeback year. If eggs are good enough for Tiger, they're bloody well good enough for me."

"Good enough for what?"

"My comeback, of course."

"Comeback? Comeback, did you say?"

"Age before beauty," Congreve said, motioning Trulove to take his tee shot.

Trulove bent to tee up his ball for the short par four, then straightened and said, "Are you actually planning to stage some kind of a comeback? What on earth are you going on about?"

"Indeed, I am, sir. And it starts here and it starts now. Not tomorrow, but right now."

"Don't be ridiculous, Constable," Trulove said, using the affectionate nickname Alex Hawke had given to the brainy detective. "You can't possibly stage a comeback."

"And pray tell why not?"

"Because one has to go somewhere else before one can stage a comeback. Your great hero Woods went into hiding for years before his comeback."

"I beg your pardon? In my case, it was my game that went away from me, not me from it," Congreve said, mildly miffed. He backed away from his ball and began his practice-swing routine.

But Trulove was not to be denied. He said:

"Look here, Ambrose. We've played golf together for going on two decades now. The game you have now is exactly the same game you had twenty years ago when you first came striding out of the men's locker room, wearing those tatty bright yellow plus fours of yours and causing a few raised eyebrows among the membership. Since I was the one who had proposed you for membership, it was my duty to inform you that some among us—and I include myself in their number—found your livery . . . a bit vivid for dear old Sunningdale, shall we say? Yes, we did. And then there was . . ."

"And then there was what?"

"Then there was . . . well, your golf game."

"What about my golf game?" Congreve huffed, a grey cloud suddenly shading his sunny mood.

"What about it? You appeared on the first tee that very first day, acting like the very reincarnation of Tommy Jones and then—"

"Bobby. Bobby Jones."

"Fine. Bobby Jones you were not. You teed up your ball, took what may be politely called an exorbitant backswing, and whiffed it. Then you took two illegal mulligans before you finally hit a ball a few feet beyond the confines of the tee box."

"Thank you for reminding me of that, Sir David. I agree. It was not my finest hour. But may I remind you that I was leading in the men's four ball that year when the match was canceled due to the heavy rain? Leading the bloody match! Surely you remember that!"

"Yes, you were leading. We were on the second hole. On the first, through some bizarre miracle on the part of the golf gods, you appear to have gotten an ace. The cherished hole in one."

"Correct. My finest hour."

"And your last hole in one. Look here. You have no long game. You have no short game. You're hopeless hitting out of the sand hazards, and you cannot read a putt for love nor money. In short, Ambrose, you have no game. You had no game then, and you have no game now. I don't mean to appear so harsh, but you simply cannot make a comeback to a game you never had in the first place!"

"May I take my shot now?" Congreve said, plainly irritated.

"Have at it, Constable. By all means, have bloody at it."

Congreve took a mighty swing and snap-hooked the ball into the water hazard.

"Practice swing," Ambrose said. "Didn't mean to hit it. Mulligan?"

"Bad luck," Sir David said. "If you wish to take an illegal mulligan, do so by all means. I shan't breathe a word to the rules committee. I'm afraid I was a bit harsh on you. I suppose I'm a bit upset by my pressing dilemma with the Crown. Do forgive me."

"Can you please stop chatting away during my practice swings? May I hit?"

"Now. Surely while we're young, Constable. Fire at will. With the understanding, of course, that mulligans are not permitted."

"Oh, for heaven's sake," Congreve said, and whiffed it.

CHAPTER 11

Washington, D.C.
December 1941

The Chinese ambassador was keenly aware, within the first couple of weeks or so, that, due to his hectic new life in D.C., he would need some kind of an escape hatch from the Chinese Embassy. From dawn to dusk, his life was not his own. He belonged to everyone but himself. FDR had him constantly running in circles. Persistent demands that China could and should do far more than they were currently doing for the Americans. Asking him to intervene for the White House in every messy matter dealing with Chang Kai-shek's government in Beijing, now that the communist Mao was nipping at everyone's heels.

In the evenings, Tang made the rounds of various high-society black-tie dinner parties in Georgetown and at the beautiful old grande dame Chevy Chase Club beneath the spreading oaks in Maryland. An avalanche of invitations to meet the daughters of the social biddies came flowing his way, all courtesy of his burgeoning friendship with the extraordinarily popular Commander Hawke. They made a good team. They would kid each mercilessly and make all the pretty girls giggle in an admittedly attractive fashion.

One society girl had caught his eye at a Hunt Club dinner in Maryland. A tall and statuesque young blonde, a student at Georgetown Law School. He'd gone out onto the terrace for a quick cigarette to escape all the hubbub, and she'd magically appeared right on his heels.

"So, who are you and what do you want?" he said, turning to her, his white grin freighted with charm.

"What did you say?"

"What's your name?"

"Winfield Woolworth."

"Winfield. Lovely."

"A few of my friends all call me Winnie, actually. My enemies, whose numbers are legion, call me Five 'n' Dime."

"Winnie suits. Not sure about the other one, actually."

"Woolworth? My greatgrampy F. W. Woolworth? Frank Winfield Woolworth? Five-and-dime stores?"

"Of course! That Woolworth. The name did stir a memory, but I was so preoccupied with the face that I—"

"Oh, piffle. Just call me Winnie, please. So. However did you end up at this damn thing?" she asked him, joining him at the stone balustrade overlooking the paddocks and the rolling snow-covered hills in the distance beyond the river. She extracted a cigarette from her clutch and waited for him to fish out his lighter. "Yummy!" she exclaimed. "So, Mystery Man, what brings you to this dismal affair?"

"Just lucky, I guess. I've a friend of a friend who pulled massive amounts of strings to get me on the invitation list."

"Lucky you. I abhor this crap. You believe this band? Have they never heard of swing? Dorsey and Sinatra? Am I the only girl here because her mother made her come? Hardly. So. Who's your friend?"

"He prefers to remain anonymous."

"Ah. One of those. I wonder. Do you have any notion at all of kissing me?"

"Oh, I have many notions at all of kissing you."

"Well, Mr. Whosis, or whatever your name is, the lady is ready, willing, and able."

And so he kissed her. It lasted a long time. She pressed her considerable bosom against his chest, and he felt like clinging to her as a drowning man might cling to a buoy in a storm. The kiss seemed forever. American women apparently could extend a kiss like nobody's business.

"Here. Take this," she said, pushing something into his left hand as she pushed away from him.

"What is it?"

"Besides a ransom note? My name and telephone number, you idiot."

"Ah."

"'Ah,' the man says. This mysterious Oriental gentleman who, with his faithful companion, Lord Hawke, has taken Washington society by storm. See you around the campus at the next soiree, big boy. If you get lucky. If not? See you in the funny papers."

And, with that, like Scarlett, Winnie was gone with the wind.

Upon returning to the ballroom, he saw her dancing with Commander Hawke. Close. Closer than she'd been to him. Much closer. And she was nipping at his ear between sweet nothings whispered into it.

Tiger tore his eyes away from them and opened up the stiff squib of paper she'd given him. The clouds of gin parted.

Winnie Woolworth. 421-6843.

"Damn it to hell," he said to himself. Remembering Hawke's last words to him that very afternoon.

"Come on," he'd said on the phone. "Don't be such a damn wallflower. It'll be fun. Besides, you'll get to meet old Woolworth. She's my girl, brother, and what a girl she is. You'll see!"

Tang folded the paper she'd given him carefully, placed it in his waistcoat pocket, and headed for the bar. All being fair in love and war and all that. And besides, he could use a drink.

On the weekends, Ambassador Tang would frequently find himself up at Hyde Park, the president's spectacular country estate, two hundred eleven acres on the banks of the Hudson River. His practice, weather permitting, was to take long strolls along the riverbank, Tiger and his pungent Cuban companion, happy as a lark, as they said these days.

In these early days, the president was keen to extract every scintilla of inside information on the innermost workings of the very highest level of the Chinese government in Beijing. When they weren't talking by the fire, the two allies were sitting in the president's private study up on the second floor. The tall windows overlooked the broad Hudson and the Catskill Mountains beyond. The river was dotted with sparse maritime traffic due to winter weather and freezing conditions.

The president would sit beside these windows with the winter sun streaming down and work tirelessly on his precious stamp collection. Tang was content to relax in a deep, well-worn leather club chair pulled close to the hearth. There, he would read random books from the president's library quietly for hours, his peace periodically interrupted by Roosevelt suddenly holding up a specimen to the sunlight and exclaiming, "Say, will you look at that! A Ben Franklin one-center! I'll be darned!" Or some such thing. Tiger was many things, but a philatelist he was not.

Should Tiger stumble upon some literary gem while reading, he would pause and share it, reciting the passage aloud to the great man. For instance, just this morning, he'd said:

"Here's one, Mr. President. Some American writer chap named Hemingway, recalling the saddest short story ever written . . . only six words long."

"Yes?"

"'For sale,'" Tiger read aloud. "'Baby shoes, never worn.'"

"Good Lord," FDR said, and the ambassador saw his eyes shining with tears. "I think it's high time we poured ourselves an evening restorative. Don't you agree? A rejuvenating libation? Maybe squeeze in a second before the dinner bell. . . ."

"Superb idea, Mr. President," Tiger said, getting up and going to the drinks table, where he poured two generous beakers of Cutty Sark.

"You've met Dr. Ross McIntire, I believe. No? My personal physician up here at Hyde Park. Has the nerve to say I'm drinking too much! Asked me for a daily cocktail accounting. Know what I told him?"

"I do not."

"I said, 'Doc, at Hyde Park, dinner is served promptly at seven. So, between five thirty and seven, I drink as much as I possibly can!'"

"Ha!" the ambassador exclaimed. "Good one, sir! That's showing him who's boss!"

He looked at the beaming president returning to his stamps, fully at ease here in his splendid manor house high above the river. Ah, the life of the country squire in America was a fine thing to behold. And then it came to him, a flash out of the blue.

He bloody well needed a country place of his own!

Somewhere outside of the frantically whirling orbit that was the Washington universe. And so, in his free time, he would go for long drives in his convertible, searching out his refuge. Wheeling his brand-spanking-new lemon-colored Rolls-Royce Phantom III up into Maryland, through the rolling cornfields and all the way out to the charming little seaport of Annapolis on Chesapeake Bay.

His new sidekick, or wingman, as he now called himself, Commander Hawke, had arranged for him to join him for luncheon at the Annapolis Yacht Club. They walked the docks afterward, puffing cigars while admiring the gorgeous yachts, especially the yawls, always his favorite rig. Someday, he said to himself, a smile suddenly appearing. "What do you think of the big white yawl at the end of the pier, Your Lordship?" Tiger said.

"She's mine," Hawke said with a wry smile. "Glad you like her. We'll take her out on the Chesapeake some weekend if you'd like. Woolworth has me teaching her how to sail."

And sometimes he headed south, across the Key Bridge and bound for parts unknown down in Virginia horse country.

The more he saw of the rolling Virginia countryside, the more he came to love it. Yes. Virginia. That was the place for him. Perhaps he'd find a little hideaway, a cabin where he could go for solace, to escape the mad state the war-torn town was in at the moment. A place where he could escape, far from the madding crowd.

A weekend getaway. Somewhere to relax in privacy such as Roosevelt enjoyed on the Hudson. Where he could entertain his friends. Or his women, away from the prying eyes of the nosy gossip columnists and radio political pundits who hounded the handsome young bachelor and man-about-town relentlessly.

A place where the old Tiger could just be himself. Stride around naked and growl out loud if he felt like it. Scratch his private parts to his heart's content while admiring his leather album filled to bursting with bawdy French postcards purchased from Paris newsstands down by the Seine. Listening to Crosby and Sinatra and Tommy Dorsey on the wireless all the while. Hell, you know. Smoke his bloody opium pipe in peace, for once!

A week later, he found himself driving around in the Virginia horse country outside the little village of Warrenton. This was the land of the long driveways, he'd noticed. Great manicured estates and Old South plantations waited at the other end of those winding drives, great white Georgian mansions standing amid the magnolias and azaleas and camellias! And famous stud farms . . . It was all so very beautiful. He was charmed by the serenity of it, the palpable peace that pervaded, the pristine beauty unmarred by foreign wars.

And then, one fine day, there was the house he'd been searching for.

Sevenoaks, it was called.

He had found his dream cottage, all right; it just happened to be a sprawling plantation. Sight unseen, he sensed it, just from the beauty and gravitas of the great black wrought iron gates swung wide at the entrance. There was a discreet Realtor's sign, faded. Appleton Farm Realty. He made a mental note of the telephone number, passed through those exquisite gates, and started up the steep and gracefully winding drive. When he breasted the last hill, he paused to catch his breath. But what was revealed took his breath away all over again.

A slightly larger version of Tara, the name of the plantation where Miss Scarlett had wooed Captain Butler in that fabulous movie he'd seen at the London premier back in 1939, *Gone With the Wind*. Sevenoaks was all white marble columns splayed across the front with acres of slate roof, massive ivy-strewn brick chimneys popping up here and there. The rambling covered porches all overlooked the gardens and the beautiful horse

country of Virginia. There were winding paths everywhere. Paths leading down to the barn and stables, to the tennis courts, to the Olympic-
sized pool. . . .

Sevenoaks was nestled in a wooded area of some fifty acres. It presided
atop a hilltop beside a large blue lake. That lake, he would later learn, was
called Botts Lake, after the family who built the estate in the 1920s. And
that the locals all called it "Bottomless Lake," as it had resisted the at-
tempts of decades' worth of divers trying to plumb its depths.

All green, he could see spring in his mind's eye even now, rolling
emerald grass crisscrossed by infinite miles of whitewashed fences winding their ways hither and thither across the majestic countryside as if
some giant had just flung out handfuls of them to bind up the earth.

In a fever, he rushed back across the Potomac. Speeding as usual because no one had ever enjoyed diplomatic immunity quite as much as
Tiger Tang when behind the wheel of his yellow Rolls-Royce. He'd call
Appleton Farm Realty and make an offer on Sevenoaks. He wanted to be
fully installed, staffed up, and comfortably ensconced by springtime. He
would buy a great big mahogany four-poster in which he could lie in
state of a morning and listen to birdsong rising up from his gardens on
warmer days when every new day brought colorful floral explosions into
view.

CHAPTER 12

Sevenoaks Plantation, Virginia
January 1942

Not very long after he'd bought Sevenoaks lock, stock, and barrel, Ambassador Tang got a call in his office—one that caught him a tad off guard. His secretary, Kimberly Li, strode in with his coffee and the morning mail and said, "An old friend of yours rang up earlier, Mr. Ambassador. Left his private number and asked you to please call him at the Chinese Trade Mission."

"I don't have any friends at the Chinese Trade Mission. What's his name?"

"Tony Chow, sir."

"Tony Chow?" he said, rising from his desk and turning to stare out the window, gathering himself for the coming storm of emotions that would surely be heading his way.

"Yes, sir."

"Do you mind leaving me alone for a little while, Kimberly? Please do not put any more calls through."

"Of course, sir," she said, pulling the heavy door closed behind her.

He stared down at the flow of traffic slowly moving up Pennsylvania Avenue. Slow because of all the snow they'd had the night before.

Tony Chow. It was a name he'd not heard in years. It was a name he'd heard a lot about from his father. This was about a time during the bad years. The time of the great war between the Tangs and the Chows. Going to the mattresses, the Mafia called it in America. In China, the mob called it going to ground, but it was the same thing. Moving out of your homes and taking up residence somewhere else with little or no furniture. All done in preparation for war.

Soon, all-out war between two powerful crime families raged throughout the country, mainly in Shanghai, but also engulfing Beijing, and extending even to Quangzhou and Hong Kong and Singapore. Archrivals in narcotics, prostitution, extortion, kidnapping, et cetera, each side had everything to gain and everything to lose.

Still, the war dragged on for far too long, with neither side willing to retreat from the field of battle. It wasn't until Tiger's father ordered the murder of the scion of the Chow family that the killing on both sides escalated exponentially. There was much suffering to be endured. Especially the murder that finally ended the conflict, at least for a time.

And then a Tang soldier who had ignored the call to go to ground was murdered in his bed at his palatial estate outside Shanghai. Decapitated. His head was placed on a lamppost in the street below. His wife was sleeping in a different wing of the house. His child as well. No one was ever sure who it was who severed the head of the most powerful young Tang in the family's long and storied history, dating back four hundred years. But Tiger's father, Deng Tang, always believed he knew who'd done it. To avoid rekindling the epic battles, it was a name that could never leave the confines of the dinner table.

The victim of the assassination was Deng's son, Jackie Tang.

Jackie's younger brother, little Tiger, had been born on the very night of his brother's murder. Tiger never got to meet his much-revered older sibling, though the stories of his valor were legend throughout the land.

The killer, his blessed father had always believed, was a young thug, a nasty piece of business named Tony Chow.

"Mr. Chow's office," the woman on the other end of the line said. "How may I direct your call?"

"This is Ambassador Tang. I'm returning his call."

"He's expecting you. I'll put you right through."

"Hello," said a voice.

"Hello?" said Tiger.

"Tiger! It's really you? Good to hear your voice. Where the hell did you disappear to? I heard you left Foochow for good and went off to be educated in England. And here you are, our new ambassador. Moving up in the world, I'd say."

"Time does fly," Tiger said, not signing up for this happy-horseshit mob patter these damn Chow boys were known for. "What can I do for you, Tony? I'm a little busy around here. . . ."

"A lot. It's about time I had friends in high places. You and I can work miracles. I help you. You help me."

"Help you what?"

"You know. Grease the skids a little. Press the flesh. My bagman days are over, buddy. Big shot now. Quit the rackets. But this American bureaucracy moves at the speed of fucking lava. You make a phone call here and drop a note there. . . . You know how it works."

"Not really. I've not been here all that long."

"Long enough to call your old friend, let him buy you a drink, right. I'm calling to invite you to join me for a welcome dinner Saturday night at the George Town Club. I'm a member, if you can believe that. It would be good for you. Meet some of the inner-circle boys, shake a few hands— you get the picture."

"Yeah, well, I dunno. . . ."

"You still got a beef with me? Is that it? Still not good enough company for you?"

"No, no, not at all. Sounds swell, Tony, but look here. I've bought a little weekend place out in the country. I go out Friday nights and come back to town Sunday nights . . . but listen. I've got an idea. You give me a rain check on the George Town Club, and instead, you come out here for the weekend. Come out Saturday morning, spend Saturday night. We'll grab a couple of horses down at the stables and go for a nice long ride in the countryside. I'll have Cook do a roast leg of lamb tarragon. Oh, and by the way, we dress for dinner at Sevenoaks, Tony."

"What? You mean you don't eat naked?"

"That expression means black tie and dinner jacket."

"Yeah, yeah, I know. Just kidding around. Not a total idiot."

"Well, uh . . . listen. If you've somehow managed to remain single, I can provide a little female companionship. American friend of mine. Her name is Flora the Human Trampoline."

"Human Trampoline, huh?"

"That's an understatement, Tony. I have firsthand experience. For a high-society dame from the Main Line, she's got—how shall I say it?—appetites."

"You got yourself a deal, old friend," Tony Chow said, the eagerness in his voice palpable.

———————

So it was that Tiger and his old pal Tony found themselves riding horse-back and hell-bent for leather on that drizzly Saturday afternoon, making bets and having match races from pillar to post, hither and thither across the muddy meadows, snowy hills and valleys of some of the finest horse country in the world. Tiger's new purebred stallion, the cleverly named Teabiscuit, was more than a match for the gimpy mare he'd ordered up for his guest. The funny thing was that Tony, who'd clearly not spent a whole lot of time in the saddle, didn't even know he'd been had.

"How much do I owe you?" Tony said as the horses were led away by the grooms.

"Let's see, Tony. Fifty dollars a race? Four races? Two hundred dollars will do nicely, old chap."

"It wasn't a fair race. After all, you know the territory like the back of your hand and—"

"Fork it over."

If Tiger had worried about spending too much time with Chow that weekend, he needn't have. The big bald man, whom everyone at home had long considered little more than a thug, was making a supreme effort to look and sound very much like a proper gentleman. Telling off-color jokes, mixing the martinis, playing gin rummy, all with a lot of hail-fellow backslapping and general levity.

It was decided that the two of them would reconvene in the library for cocktails at six. When Tiger gave him the hour, Tony said brightly, given a chance to show off his newly acquired status, "Oh, yeah. You mean like when the sun is over the yardstick, right?"

"Wrong. It's an old Royal Navy expression, Tony. Eighteenth century. 'When the sun is over the *yardarm*.' The yardarm is a horizontal spar mounted up on the masts of the old square riggers from which the square sails were hung."

"Oh. That's fascinating, Mr. College Boy. See you at six. What's the trampoline's name again?"

"Flora. She'll be here. Don't worry. I lied and told her you were the greatest swordsman this side of Chinatown."

"That's no lie."

"Well, then, I'll leave you to it. Time for my beauty rest."

Tiger retreated to his quarters, stripped off his muddy clothes and riding boots, and tossed them into a hamper. After an invigorating piping-hot shower, he climbed up onto the big mahogany four-poster. Spying the splayed novel on the bedside table, he reached for it.

His new friend Commander Hawke had given him the book as a house present when he came for a weekend. He had been anxious to return to it all day. *For Whom the Bell Tolls*, by this American writer named Ernest Hemingway who was new to Tang, told the tale of an American chap fighting in the Spanish Civil War, and Tiger found the unadorned, stripped-down prose so very modern and a wonder to read.

He dove in, reaching for a Lucky Strike cigarette from the silver box embossed in gold with his intertwined initials, TT. Hearing tires crunching on gravel in the courtyard below, he lit up, rose, and went to the window. A yellow D.C. taxi was just pulling up at the front entrance. Since he'd dispatched all the servants save the cook, he hurried downstairs to meet his new guest.

She was climbing out of the rear when he opened the front door. He went to the driver's window and said, in his best imitation of an American gangster, "What do I owe ya, bub?"

He paid the driver and turned to see a woman he hardly recognized. She was dressed beautifully in a navy crepe de chine skirt, falling just below the knee, with a red bolero jacket over a frothy white blouse. Her ginger-red hair was up in the Gibson girl fashion, and her makeup was sheer perfection.

"Flora," he said, making the statement sound like a question.

She looked at him, smiled, then returned her gaze to the imposing facade of Sevenoaks. "Hey, Tiger, swell place you've got here."

He smiled. "Small, but it works for a single gentleman living alone." He took her hat, black lambswool overcoat, and small red overnight suitcase. "Let's get out of this cold. Follow me," he said, and led the way up the stone pathway to the front entrance. Two massive double oaken doors were flanked by a formidable array of Doric pillars.

"Oh, Flora?" Tiger said.

She paused in the double-height foyer filled with massive gilt-framed English sporting paintings amid the odd suit of armor. She took it all in and whistled like a sailor. "Yes?" she said.

"I do hope you remembered our agreement. That you would not breathe a word of this invitation or me or my whereabouts to another living soul?"

"Of course. You have to be good at keeping secrets if you want to work for Speaker Sam Rayburn. Secrets are our currency, our stock-in-trade My pretty red lips are forever sealed."

"Of course. It's just that this is my only sanctuary. My escape hatch. My privacy here must remain inviolate."

She kissed his check and said, "Relax, boy. I'm the living soul of discretion."

"Good girl. Now, what do you think of my little country house?"

"I applaud the catholicity of your art collection, Mr. Ambassador!"

"Why, thank you. Catholicity, huh? Spoken like a true Bryn Mawr graduate. Been a collector ever since I first went to England. I love horses and—dogs. As you can see. Like that fine four-legged gentleman running down the staircase . . . Captain! Come meet this fancy woman!" The gorgeous black-and-white purebred spaniel raced over to her with his usual grace and stood at her feet, looking up at Flora, clearly longing for love or, at least, affection. Captain, for all his exceptional field skills, was, at heart, a Romeo.

"Sit!" she said with authority. And he did. "He's very handsome. What breed is he?"

"An English springer spaniel. A national champion actually. I found him at a breeder up in Sharon, Connecticut. Let's have a look around, shall we?"

He gave his guest a quick tour, a summary survey of the ground floor, visiting the notable parts of the house: the main dining room, breakfast room, billiard room, solarium, living room, all culminating in the library.

"Drinks here at six, Flora. What kind of wine do you like?"

"Expensive will do nicely."

"I'll check the cellar. I think we've got a few bottles of that vintage."

"Tiger?"

"Yes."

"Thanks for inviting me out. It's lovely here. I thought I'd never hear from you again. And anyway, Agnes told me you were a cad who'd break my heart."

"Never, my sweet. Never. See you at six."

"I believe there might be a nice hot bath somewhere up that very grand staircase. And if not, I shall draw one. I hope we're still dressing for dinner. I brought a lovely Dior evening dress that I'm positively dying to show off. . . . Tell me the name of my beau for the evening again?"

"Tony Chow. Our two families were quasifriendly back home in Foochow. When I went to Eton, he went to St. Paul's in America, and then to Dartmouth whilst I went to Cambridge. We lost track after that, until he invited me to the George Town Club the other day. Apparently, he's a member there."

"Very posh. Is Tony a fancy boy?"

"I'll let you be the judge of that, Flora. So, see you back here by the fire at six on the dot."

She smiled, then turned and tiptoed quickly up the broad marble staircase. Light as a feather, that one. And hotter than a Guadalajara jalapeño on a withering July afternoon. He regretted now not calling her after she'd given him her phone number. He'd figured her for a hot potato, just another D.C. secretary who'd pulled herself up by her bra straps.

He watched her all the way up the staircase, bewitched, bothered, and bewildered by the fetching sight of Flora's fetching derrière and seamed black silk stockings as viewed from the rear.

CHAPTER 13

Sevenoaks Plantation, Virginia
December 1941

When Tony Chow strode into the pine-paneled, book-stuffed room at twenty past six that evening, Tiger and Flora were sipping champagne, seated in the two facing leather chairs in front of the blazing hearth. Tiger was resplendent in his starched white shirt with wing collar and black tie, a Savile Row green velvet smoking jacket, striped trousers, and black velvet evening pumps on his feet. Flora was dazzling in a floor-length Alice blue gown gleaming with sequins. The fire was crackling; the air smelled of woodsmoke, probably maple. Beyond the floor-to-ceiling windows, snow was swirling about in the wintry sky.

It was all quite pleasant aside from the fact that Flora, nervous about meeting her date for the evening, had already knocked back four glasses of champers.

"Ah, here's our hero right on time, Tony!" Tiger said as the man made his way over to them.

"Hello, old sport!" Tony said to Tiger, staring at Flora with a rather lascivious grin. Tiger winced at the sound of his voice. He sounded like someone trying to pry open a manhole cover with a crowbar.

Tiger looked up at the man standing beside him, and a shadow clouded his face. He didn't show it, but he was shocked by the man's appearance and not quite sure what to say. He essayed, "Tony, come have a drink, won't you? Say hello to Flora here."

Tony had not dressed for dinner as instructed. He was still unwashed and filthy in his mud-caked riding clothes and boots. He gave the pretty girl a wink and said, "Know what you call a female detective?"

Tiger winced. The old joke had been floating around the capital for weeks now, and it was plainly shopworn and no longer funny.

"No, what?" She giggled.

"A Dickless Tracy, that's what, sweetheart."

"Oh, my!" she said, trying not to laugh at his dirty joke. In Washington, such quips were common currency, and it wasn't like she'd not heard this one before. Countless times.

Tiger managed a thin smile and said to Tony, "Listen up, old sport. I believe I told you we dress for dinner here at Sevenoaks."

"I'm dressed. What's the problem?"

Tony ignored Tiger and went straight for Flora, grabbing her pale white hand from her lap and giving it a sloppy kiss. Tiger observed that while he'd been napping, Tony had been nipping and not at the cooking sherry. He reeked of Gordon's Gin. Tiger's father had long warned him of the dangers of too much "loudmouth soup" as he'd called the stuff. The British antimalarial had brought sorrows to many of his friends and professors at Cambridge. Tiger had once considered writing a short story about those years entitled "The Sorrows of Gin."

"How about a glass of champagne, Tony?" Tiger said, getting up from his seat and going over to the drinks table. There was a bottle of vintage Pol Roger Brut nesting in crushed ice in a silver bucket. He poured himself a glass and stood listening to Tony already trying to sweet-talk his way into Flora's knickers. She was giggling a little too much, betraying her nervousness at the sheer size of the unkempt man.

The former enforcer had put on a lot of weight in the intervening years, muscle gone to fat. Lost most of his hair, too. The gleaming bald pate atop the thick neck and shoulders, the squinty black eyes, all gave the dim-witted gangster the alarming presence of a giant gnome, which was, of course, an oxymoron of the first rank.

Tiger drained his crystal flute and poured himself another, thinking that this thing could turn ugly before the night was over.

He faced his two guests and with a slight bow said, quoting Bette Davis, "Fasten your seat belts, ladies and gents, it's going to be a bumpy night."

So saying, he withdrew from the room and went out to the kitchen to check on the roast leg of lamb and have a word with Cook. He wanted dinner moved up an hour to seven instead of eight, which was his wont. Early side, seven, but at least his two guests might still be capable of rational table talk. He also ordered that dinner be served at the small table by the bay window at the far end of the dining room. The main table sat eighteen and would have been pretentious, and rather silly, for three people.

In any event, dinner was served. The lamb pink, the mint sauce divine.

Wine was poured, a good claret, and glasses were raised.

Tony Chow, still muddy and clearly soused to the gills, had his chin on his chest, snoring loudly.

Tiger, looking only at Flora, said, "Here's to us, our noble selves. None finer, and many a damn sight worse! Like our friend Tony over there."

And so it came to pass that Tiger and Flora had devoured the tasty roasted lamb and mint sauce, pommes soufflé fromage, and petits pois with pearl onions, polished off two bottles of Château Mouton Rothschild, and were deep into a large bottle of 1921 Château d'Yquem when Tony Chow suddenly lifted his chin off his sternum and blurted out, "What? Oh, hey. Sorry. I must have dozed off."

"Yes," Tiger said, feeling the wine a bit now. "Your dinner has gone cold. If you like, I can have it reheated."

"No, no, forget about the food. I'll have a glass of whatever you're having."

Tiger poured Tony a glass, and Flora, her cheeks burning bright red, said, slurring her words, "Is there any more of that red wine? I could drink that all night long."

Tiger looked at her closely.

"Are you quite sure you're all right? Perhaps you should just go to bed, darling," the ambassador told her. "Yes. That might be best."

"No, no! I want to see the horsies!"

Tiger kissed the Trampoline on the cheek and bade her good night. The woman had her own set of troubles; of that, he was sure.

Tony gave her shoulder a good squeeze and said, "Yeah, good idea, kid. We'll go down to the barn and see the horsies."

Tiger rose from the table and went over to the mahogany sideboard, plucked a fresh bottle from the tray, and opened it. He was suddenly feeling extraordinarily tired. Especially tired of this Tony Chow and his unbelievable rudeness. He put a glass and the opened wine bottle in front of Flora and said, "Well, I'm off to bed. You two help yourselves to dessert or anything else your little heart's desire. Good night, sleep tight, and I'll see you at breakfast at eight. Tony, I'll only say this once. If you come down in the morning in those filthy clothes, I'll show you the door. I bid you both good night."

CHAPTER 14

Sevenoaks Plantation, Virginia
January 1942

Having previously given the entire staff, save the cook, the day off, the host went through the butler's pantry and out into the kitchen and said to the cook, "Delicious dinner, Armand. The lamb was superb. *C'est très délicieux!* Don't you worry about clearing the table tonight. Just go home and get some rest. Breakfast at eight tomorrow?"

"*Mais oui, monsieur!*"

Armand took off his toque blanche and bolted straight for the back door. He was always in a great hurry, every night, to get home to that plump little *poulet* he'd married in Paris, Gigi, who was the very love of his life. She'd served at the table a few nights, and Tiger had clearly seen what his chef saw in the woman. She had an aura about her. She was a garden of earthly delights in human form.

Tiger, ever so glad of his escape from the nightmare dinner party, took the servants' back stairs up to the third floor and leapt into his four-poster bed. The sheets were crisply ironed and cool to the touch. He liked to leave a few windows open, even on a cold night like this, and snuggled down under the duvet covers with Mr. Hemingway's wonderful latest novel *For Whom the Bell Tolls*.

And soon, he had drifted off to dreamland. In his dreams, Spanish women, stripped to the waist, protected a wounded man from the Fascist soldiers. . . .

Sometime later, his dreams were disturbed by the faint sound of screams drifting in through the open windows on the frigid night air.

What the hell?

He rolled out of bed, grabbed his woolen robe from an armchair, and went over to the half-opened windows on the southern side of the house.

There was screaming all right; he hadn't been dreaming.

He dressed quickly in cords and a sweater and put on his heavy Royal Navy peacoat, another gift from Hawke and one that he treasured. Leaving his room, he ran down the main staircase, over to the double doors at the entrance, and out into the frigid white night. The screams were louder out here in the cold night air. He could tell where they were coming from. . . .

The stables. Of course.

Tony had likely dragged Flora down the hill to the barn. And not to say good night to the horses. Tiger ran all the way to the bottom.

The screaming was indeed coming from inside the hay barn. It was Flora, of course. Furious with himself for being so stupid as to leave her in the company of that disgusting animal, Tony, he sprinted across the paddocks and raced to the barn's double doors. Locked. What the hell? He ran around to the back and tried that door. Locked as well, but he had an idea. Above the entrance to the barn was the hayloft. From it hung a pulley on a rope for the lifting the bales that drooped down almost to the ground. He grabbed hold of the bitter end and started climbing, hoisting himself up hand over hand. In less than a minute, he was scrambling inside.

The screaming was much louder up here. Tiger walked softly, trying not to make a sound on the squeaky floor boards.

There was a hole in the floor where the ladder emerged.

He got down on his belly and slid forward so he could get a good look below. . . . There they were! Tony and Flora in the light of the flickering gas lantern.

Jesus Christ.

He had her down on the hay-strewn wooden floor beneath him. Most of her dress had been torn away. Her lacy underwear and silk stockings had been ripped off as well and cast aside. Her face was red as if he'd been slapping her repeatedly and very hard. He was still beating her, first one cheek, then the other, yelling at her to shut up, to stop her crying, or he was going to hurt her badly. . . .

Tiger was in luck.

Tony was facing away from the ladder. Flora could see him descending, yes, but he thought she was too far gone to call out his name and reveal him to her attacker.

He started down swiftly, one rung at a time, spun around, and dropped lightly to the wooden floor.

Made it! And without being seen by either of them. He crept across the floor toward them, the hay making his footsteps almost silent. . . .

"Get off her, Tony," he said to the man's back when he was ten feet and closing. "Leave the poor girl alone!"

"Wha ?" Tony seemed disoriented.

"Leave her alone, I said. Get on your feet, you bastard. Now. You heard me. Now turn around."

Tony turned and stared at him, his face a mask of purple rage. Once again, a Tang kid was ruining his party.

Tiger treated him to the gently clouded, almost beatific smile that other men had recalled only in retrospect when the battle had been lost. During the period of warming up for any fight, there were the angry words before a barroom brawl, the bowing and shuffling of kung fu. Although the kung fu master didn't need any weapons besides himself, Tiger always looked around for whatever was handy.

He could remember an incident in Taipei in which his assailant had ended up with a Ticonderoga No. 3 lead pencil driven in four inches between his ribs. He'd been taught the rule of thumb by the ancients: that no fight needed to last more than five seconds and that the man who landed the first two blows always emerged victorious.

He saw Tony's grin of derision, believing he was watching his opponent search in vain for some kind of weapon. Tiger, in return, grinned sheepishly at Chow's sneering smile, all the while lulling him deeper into a false sense of security.

Tiger, who had the true warrior's keen perception of an enemy's base emotions at a time like this, could see the combination of hatred and jealous rage in the eyes of his brother's killer and his frustration that he had been interrupted in the midst of consummating his savage attack. After all, Tony was probably thinking the girl was a tramp, a trampoline, but still a little slut and she deserved to be treated like one, didn't she?

Tony straightened, reached inside his jacket, and pulled out a nasty little automatic, holding it in front of himself a bit unsteadily. He was having a boozy go of it staying on his pins. He muttered to Tiger, barely audibly, "You got fifteen seconds to get the hell out of here and leave us alone. Now go—"

"You're not going to shoot me, Tony. You don't have the guts."

"Oh, yeah? You don't think I've ever killed anybody?"

"On the contrary. I'm quite sure you have. My father told me about you, Tony."

"You know what gets me? Here I am, an old friend of your father and your brother, Jackie, and here you treat me like dirt, like garbage. You've always looked down on me. I never could figure it out, but now I have. You're a snob, Tiger. You think you're better than everyone. Well, news flash: You're not, pal. Nothing worse than a nobody who thinks he's a somebody because he went to some fancy university. News flash number two: You're a nobody in this town. Me, I've got more pull and more contacts than you'll ever have and—"

"Oh, shut up," Tiger said, slowly edging a little bit closer, his incremental movements nearly invisible, his eyes on the gun pointed at his belly.

"You were never a friend of Jackie's," Tiger said. "Maybe you thought so, but he never did. Father always said Jackie never had one good word to say about you. Never."

"Bull crap. He looked up to me. Jackie, that kid, he loved me. And I loved him."

"You loved him? My brother? Is that what you said?"

"It's the truth, goddamn it. I could give a good hot damn what you think."

"If you loved him so much, then why the hell did you murder him? In cold blood? Cut his head off and stuck it on a lamppost for his family to see when they came home that night? His mother had to see that? That's how much you loved him? I ought to kill you. Right now. . . ."

"Are you paying attention? Guess who's got the gun. You?"

"Guns don't scare me, Tony. Never have. Give it up."

"You know what? I could care what you think, Mr. Head-up-his-ass Ambassador. Whether or not I killed Jackie, who cares at this point? We were at war. But one thing's for sure. I'm going to kill you tonight, you arrogant son of a bitch . . . just as sure as we're standing here. . . ."

Tiger saw the shaky gun start an upward arc as he, too, moved, but with blinding speed. Tony never knew what hit him.

The young ambassador leapt forward onto his left foot, composed himself, and spun his body clockwise like a lethal ballet dancer, with his right leg extended upward about waist high. His right foot, with a slashing, twisting motion, caught Tony's gun hand with a wallop, hard as hell, and sent the little silver automatic skittering across the barn floor.

With an imperceptible pause, Tiger reversed his direction and spun counterclockwise, his left leg now extended head high this time. His left bootheel caught Tony in the right temple, with enough brute force to fracture his skull. He spun again, right foot to left temple. Whiplash times three. Then he drove three rock-solid fingers deep into the man's throat, cutting off all his oxygen. He started to slump. He was out of gas.

Then the simultaneous flat-handed cymbal slaps on Tony's ears punctured his eardrums with air implosions. After the powerful jab of his right fist into Tony's stomach that brought his hands down and left his nose undefended, Tiger went for the kill. He brought his right knee up with such blinding speed as to catch his adversary right on the tip of his nose with enough sheer force and might as to drive splinters of bone deep up into Tony's brain and snap his head backward . . . and break his neck.

Tony Chow was a dead man before the fat dumbass hit the floor.

CHAPTER 15

Sevenoaks Plantation, Virginia
January 1942

Tiger looked over at Flora. She was still down on the floor, half naked, her head down on her forearm, sobbing hard enough to make her shoulders rise and fall violently. He walked toward her, pausing to pick up Tony's .38 as he did so. He knelt beside her, putting his hand on her head with a comforting pat. He bent down and cradled her in his arms, whispering softly to her as he plucked hay straw from her tangled red hair.

"It's all right, Flora. It's all right. It's all over. He can't hurt you anymore. He's gone now. He'll never hurt anyone again."

A moaning cry from her filled the barn with her pain and anguish.

Tiger said, "I'm so sorry that I ever involved you in this. I'll never forgive myself. God. The night we met, I thought you were just another fun gal looking for a good time. Now I know that you're a woman of great substance and intelligence. . . . I'm so sorry that you . . . had the misfortune to meet me."

"You're why I came here, Tiger," she sobbed, "the only reason I came. Didn't you know that? Did you really think I came for that . . . that thing over there?"

"I don't know, Flora. I don't know what to think now. . . ."

"Please don't hate me, Tiger. I'm not a bad person. I never, ever meant to cause you all this terrible trouble, I promise you. I'm just a simple girl who fell in love with you . . . that's all."

He stroked her tangled hair, wiped tears from her eyes, not wanting to see those blue eyes weeping, not wanting her to see his own face, the deep pain in his own eyes. The self-loathing and all the remorse, his guilt . . . What kind of man was he, after all? He liked to think he was a good man. An honorable man. A kind man even . . . And yet he knew without the slightest equivocation that he had to be rid of her somehow.

This woman, who worked at the pinnacle of the political pyramid, spending her days within earshot of one the most powerful men in Washington. Speaker of the House Samuel Taliaferro Rayburn. And all of the attendant D.C. powerhouses who daily sought his blessing for their machinations and critical roles inside the U.S. government. He could almost hear Flora having cocktails with her coworkers, talking about this man she'd fallen head over heels for, who just happened to be the new Chinese ambassador to the United States.

No. This could not stand. She'd just seen him kill a man. A man politically powerful enough that his disappearance would be noted and thoroughly investigated by the FBI. This woman could destroy him in the blink of an eye and a slip of the tongue, not out of anger or vengeance, but out of vanity. Her "romantic" friendship with the rich and powerful. An ambassador! The man who had the ear of President Roosevelt . . .

"Tiger," he heard her whisper and looked down at her bruised face and her blue eyes and her face so wet with tears.

"Yes?" he said as gently as he could. The poor, innocent girl was in terrible distress, physically and emotionally.

"Would you mind kissing me? Just once, please. It would mean the world to me, I promise you. I would never forget it. . . ."

He felt like he was about to burst into tears himself, but he smiled down at her, then bent his head and kissed her softly on her lips. . . .

She spoke, her gleaming eyes staring up at him. "I love only you, Tiger. I loved you from the moment I saw you that very first night. I knew you were the picture-perfect man I had always dreamed of since I was a little girl. You were him, Tiger. The only man I've ever really loved. And if this is the end of us? Tonight, I mean? Well, I will always be able to say, 'Yes, I was in love once upon a time. With the kind of man who only comes along once in a lifetime. . . .'"

"Oh, my dear Flora" was all he could get out.

"Do you think you could ever find it in your heart to love a simple girl like me?"

He choked back his own his own hot tears and said, "I love you, sweet Flora. And I always will."

"Oh, Tiger. I've so wanted to hear that. . . ."

And then he pressed the muzzle of the silver Browning Hi-Power pistol gently against the back of her skull, squeezed the trigger, and fired a bullet into her brain.

He sat there for a long while afterward, crying. Feeling sorry for both of them, star-crossed lovers in the worst possible way. . . .

Still stroking her bare shoulder with tears running down both cheeks and splashing on her deathly still white bosom. His thoughts came tumbling:

God forgive me, what else could I do? She was a witness. She could have destroyed me. Derailed my mission for my beloved China. Deprived America of any chance of victory against Japan. My father, who has invested so much in me, would have been shattered. My entire family disgraced at home by the scandal in America. All of this, all of it, hung in the balance. So, whatever was I to do? God help me, what?

He sat there, thinking. And smoking his cigarettes over the body of the poor, sad dead girl from the Philadelphia Main Line.

What to do with the two of them? That was the question now. Think like a murderer, he told himself. Not like you haven't done it before. Don't kid yourself, Tiger. Dispose of the bodies somewhere where they can never, ever be found. . . .

He looked around the barn. In the corner was a huge stack of burlap sacks. Big enough to hold a human body . . . And there was a pile of heavy stones behind the barn. . . .

When he'd gathered up the ripped clothing and the torn undergarments and used them to wipe away every trace of the blood Tony had spilled, he stuffed them, along with the little silver Browning pistol, in sacks. When the two bodies were all sealed inside bags filled with heavy rocks, he tied a thick rope to each bag. The other ends of the ropes he tied to the rear of the old John Deere tractor the groom kept in the barn. He turned the key in the ignition and fired up the aging farm machine, loving the sound of it sputtering to life, clouds of exhaust billowing up from the stacks.

Ten minutes later, he was driving the ancient green tractor, chugging through heavy snowdrifts in the deep woods, rolling down the twisting path to the lake. He was going slowly. He was in no rush, and he was dragging the two bodies behind him through the snow. The moon suddenly appeared above the treetops, gleaming down through a break in the clouds, and the world around him turned a surreal shade of moonlight blue. The sight of it cheered him a little. He pulled out a pack of Luckys and lit one up, inhaling deep with the shuddering pleasure of satisfaction.

It was two o'clock in the bloody morning.

Everyone was fast asleep.

The lake was bottomless.

No one would ever find the bodies.

No one would ever know.

He came over a rise and saw the dock below, stretching out about forty feet over the silvery ebony of Bottomless Lake.

He stopped at the shoreline and climbed down from the Deere. Slogged back behind the big wheels to the rear and untied the lines to the bags. He thought that if he did them one at a time, he could drag the two bodies out to the end of the dock despite the weight of all those damn rocks.

For some reason he chose to do Flora first. Remove her from this mortal realm, out of sight and out of his life and far away from his deeply troubled conscience. At some point, he had to let it go. Sometimes a man simply had to do what a man had to do. . . .

After he spoke a few words of blessing over her, Flora went into the lake, slipping silently beneath the waves. Tony Chow got deep-sixed as well. Tiger didn't waste any words on that piece of human refuse.

He was now just a bad memory, a lump of rotting flesh at the bottom of a bottomless lake. Fish fodder. And somewhere up in heaven, his brother, Jackie, was smiling down. His father and his dead brother had finally been granted their revenge. After putting the tractor back in the barn, after hosing all the remaining bloody straw off the floor and out into the paddocks, where he buried it, he made his way up the snowy path through the woods to Sevenoaks. The windows on the front were still glowing warmly, smoke still rising from a few chimneys. . . . It was enchanting, and he paused to light another Lucky and just take it all in.

Climbing into bed with his brandy and opening his book, he felt a palpable lifting of his spirits. He read the opening lines of the Hemingway masterpiece.

He lay on the brown, pine-needled floor of the forest, his chin on his folded arms, and high overhead the wind blew in the tops of the pine trees.

He smiled at the simple words. He was actually beginning to feel a bit less guilty about the death of the poor Philadelphia girl. Sacrificed on the altar of history, actually. A casualty of the great war that now needed to be won. Not really his fault. God only knew what role she had played in the grand story that would be this war. But her death had been, he told himself, in the service of righteousness and the preservation of democracy and peace. He was trying to do the right thing by history itself.

He had learned a valuable lesson this night. To wit:

A man who was not who he appeared to be needed to be ever mindful of who he really was. And thus, to keep the truth of that man forever and ever out of sight and to do so at all costs.

He could live with that.

Yes, by God, he could do that.

CHAPTER 16

The elevator door pressure pad repeatedly opens and closes on the obdurate obstruction of the dead Iranian gunman's head. The man returns to life and slides upward on the wall. The bloody hole in his palm disappears, and he tugs the bullet out of his back. He runs backward through a gaggle of English schoolchildren, one of whom floats up off the floor as a red stain on her pretty pink pinafore is sucked back into her stomach. When he reaches the light-blurred main entrance, the Iranian assassin ducks as fragments of broken glass rush together to form a windowpane. The second gunman jumps up from the floor and catches a flying automatic weapon, and the two of them run backward, until a swish pan leaves them and discovers a Japanese boy on the tiled floor. A vacuum snaps the top of his skull back into place; the bloody stream of gore recoils back into his hip. He leaps up and runs backward, snatching up his rucksack as he passes it. The camera waves around, then finds a third Iranian killer just in time to see his cheek pop back on. He rises from his knees, and blood implodes into his chest as the khaki shirt instantly mends itself. The three Iranians, clad in mufti, walk backward side by side. One turns and smiles. They saunter back through a group of Israelis pushing and standing on tiptoe, there to greet some relatives disembarking the El Al flight from London Heathrow. The trio backs down the lane to the immigration counters, and the Israeli official uses his rubber stamp to suck the entrance permissions off their passports. A redheaded girl shakes her head, then smiles thanks. . . .

Hawke, who'd entered the darkened MI6 fifth-floor screening room just as the video began to unfold in reverse to an audience of one, said, "Morning, Sir David! Yeoman First-Class Hawke, reporting for duty as ordered. What the hell was that all about? *Looney Tunes?* All ahead reverse?"

· "Come down here, and I'll tell you, Alex."

"As ordered, sir." Hawke strode down the center aisle to the first row, where Trulove was seated on the left side. The man got to his feet and shook his hand.

"You look like hell, son," he said, stepping back to appraise his senior counterintelligence officer. The one man in all of Six who had easy access to Her Royal Majesty, and a man for whom she had only the highest esteem. Trulove would never verbalize an instinct he had, but he believed that, on some level, the two of them might actually have feelings akin to love for each other. He'd seen it. He'd felt it. At some moments, such as when the Queen presented Alex with the Victoria Cross for almost single-handedly saving the lives of all the Royal Family at the hands of al Qaeda terrorists. All in the space of one awful Christmas up at Balmoral Castle in Scotland.

Hawke was staring at him for some reason.

"I beg your pardon?" Alex said. "I'm know I'm still a bit shaky, but . . . hard to bounce back from a disembowelment."

"Oh, that. You know I can't help a barb when I'm so bloody delighted to see you risen from the dead. I cannot possibly express my gratitude, Alex. I don't know how you managed to collapse your prescribed recovery therapy down to a matter of weeks. But I will assure you that before you stands a profoundly grateful man."

"Queen and Country, as they say, Sir David. Besides, I've never been one for sitting on the shelf *hors de combat* for any length of time. I'm forbidden by my doctors everything save deep knee bends and applesauce. And as you well know, I cannot stomach even the sight of applesauce."

Trulove rarely allowed himself to laugh aloud, but in this case, the reflex caught him by surprise. "That's the spirit! Back to your old self, I see. You have no idea how pleased the Queen will be to learn that you've resurfaced. She's in quite a state over her missing grandson. And of course, your godson."

"Yes, indeed. We're to meet with the Queen, I suppose."

"Indeed. We've a meeting with the sovereign tomorrow morning at ten. At Buck House."

"I look forward to being of assistance. I made a solemn promise to Prince Henry's father, my copilot and dearest friend, on his deathbed in a field hospital outside Kabul, that I would protect and guard his only child to the end of my days. I haven't done a very good job of either, it seems. I want to correct that grievous absence right now."

"Duly noted. I'm glad you grasp the situation. Have a seat, won't you?"

Hawke took the seat across the aisle from his superior. "What are we watching?"

"The Iranian terror attack last weekend. Tel Aviv. Ben Gurion Airport. They claim it's retribution for the Israelis moving troops into Gaza."

"A nightmare. And you are watching the CC tapes backward because?"

"I go back and forth. Try it sometime. You pick up new things both ways. Until you don't."

"El Al out of London, correct?"

"Hmm. We lost six British citizens, three of them schoolchildren."

"Where are we with this? What does Mossad say?"

"Nowhere. All of us still at ground zero. I'll run the thing again, forward direction. Pay particular attention to the chap facedown in the elevator using his head as a door stopper. Ready?"

"Roll tape."

Trulove dimmed the lights and pushed PLAY on the remote. Hawke leaned forward in his seat, his focus and concentration unwavering during the film's run time.

A few minutes in, he said, "Pause it right there, please, sir."

The screen froze. The still image showed the dead terrorist facedown in the elevator, seconds before the pressure pads on the doors were impacting his skull and then reopening the doors. You couldn't see the entire face, but the eyes and nose were visible.

"I know that chap," Hawke said.

"I know you do. That's why I asked you to join me here. How do you know him, Alex?"

"I used to work with him, sir. Here at Six. Shortly after I joined the firm."

"Two thousand eleven, was it not upon your return from Afghanistan."

"Indeed it was."

"Name?"

"Stern, I think. Yes, that's it. Moishe Stern. More passion for causes than realpolitik as I recall. A bad actor in the making."

"Good. Thanks for your confirmation. Most helpful to the investigation. Let's go up to my office, shall we, and continue this conversation over tea?"

The chief of MI6 had recently had his suite of offices redone. Gone were the walnut paneling, the serious collection of eighteenth-century British marine art, the heavy mahogany furnishings, the Persian rugs, the bust of Admiral Lord Nelson.

Hawke followed Trulove into the white work space on the sixteenth floor, the walls and carpets all in matte white. In the center was a discussion area consisting of six lightly padded white leather chairs arrayed around a table with an etched glass top that served as a screen upon which appeared television, satellite imagery, and all the myriad media images generated by the mainframe computer banks in the basement.

Of the six chairs, only one would swivel: Sir David's. The others were set rigidly into the floor and were designed to provide minimal comfort. This area was for work, for quick, alert discussion—not for small talk and social fencing office gossip, that sort of tommy rot.

Sir David's own desk was conspicuously modest, with its white glass surface only fifty centimeters by sixty-five. It had no drawers or shelves, nowhere to lose or overlook material, no way to delay one matter by pushing it aside on the excuse of attending to something else.

He'd devised a priority system ordered by a complicated set of strict criteria that brought each problem to his desk only when there was sufficient research available for decisions, which were made quickly, and matters were disposed of. It went without saying, Hawke knew, that Sir David despised both physical and emotional clutter.

He crossed to his desk chair, designed and constructed by an orthopedic specialist to reduce fatigue without providing narcotizing comfort. "Have a seat," he said, waving at one of the chairs facing him.

Alex Hawke smiled and sat down.

He'd donned his old cloak and dagger once more.

He was back in the game.

And, as Dr. Watson would have it, the game was most definitely afoot!

CHAPTER 17

Dragonfire Club, the Bahamas
Present Day

Alex Hawke's dark blue Gulfstream G650 jet touched down at Lynden Pindling International, the Nassau airport, just after dawn. The flight had been uneventful, and he'd gotten a good eight hours of sleep in his owner's cabin located at the aft end of the plane. Anjelica, one of the two flight stewards, had served him huevos rancheros for breakfast. He ate with gusto while watching the BBC international news on the plane's visual system. A special treat. His rapid recovery from the abdominal surgery continued to astound him as well as his MI6 physician and physical trainer in London.

Alex had, in fact, rarely felt better or stronger. It was a good thing, too. He had much to do, and his Queen was counting on him to get it done in a hurry. Her Majesty's grandson, his own dear godson, Prince Henry, could well be in danger. Given the threats to Alex's own life by Putin's paid assassins around the globe, there was a chance, as he'd pointed out to both Congreve and Sir David, that the prince was merely a pawn here, meant to lure Hawke to his certain death.

He'd shrugged that off, of course. It was hardly the first time such a plot had unfolded. And it would most certainly not be the last.

Alex's pilots grabbed his suite of brown leather Goyard luggage from the aft stowage compartment and arrayed them on the tarmac. With the midnight-blue Gulfstream G650 in the background, the scene could have been mistaken for a luggage ad in one of the glossies. He looked up to see a gleaming black Bentley Flying Spur, the new four-door sedan, racing across the tarmac in his direction. Sent by the hotel? If indeed one must work for one's living, it helped to do so under pleasant circumstances.

The big car braked to a halt just forward of the portside wing of his airplane. Hawke went back aboard and had a final word with his captain and copilot. He'd booked two rooms for them at one of the Dragonfire Club's private seaside cottages. He said they should just take it easy, have a little fun, and get some sun, but be ready to take off at any moment. He wanted the plane's fuel tanks topped off, and his aircraft ready to fly at the drop of a hat.

"Are you by any chance Lord Alexander Hawke?" a woman's silky voice behind him said.

He turned and smiled, saying, "Just Alex will do. Never use the title. Who are you?"

She was stunning, was who she was.

Dressed entirely in chauffeur's livery, pale blue with dark blue piping and black riding boots, polished within an inch of their lives, to the knees. He'd been in love with a Chinese woman once, long ago. The daughter of a rogue Chinese general of the Army whom he'd ultimately had to kill. Her name was China Moon, and for a long time she'd been a wonder at keeping him happy . . . Ah, well, she had worked her magic for a time . . .

"I'm Zhang Tang, m'lord. Beautiful airplane, sir, stunning. My bosses, the Tang brothers, will be extremely jealous. It is my pleasure to meet you and to welcome you to Dragonfire Club. The Bentley and I will be at your disposal for a few days or weeks, at least until the owners return from Beijing."

"How kind. But please, call me Alex. I don't use my title unless I'm dining with the Queen, who insists on using it. Just curious. Who are the owners, by the way? I'm not at all sure I've ever met them," Hawke said innocently, having been extensively briefed by both Trulove and Chief Inspector Congreve and knowing full well who they were, having memorized both of their bios backward and forward.

"Tommy Tang and Jackie Tang," she said, "Twins, actually. Identical, in fact."

"No relation?"

"On the contrary. They are my big brothers. They've made me a sort of unofficial hostess here at the resort. When we have a guest of your magnitude, someone of such international importance as yourself, I get assigned to ensure that everything that is required for an enjoyable stay is provided. I will provide you with a mobile dedicated to me. I'm on call every day from five A.M. to midnight."

"You're assigned to me?"

She smiled and the sun came out. "I am at your command, Your Lordship. In a manner of speaking, of course. I don't mean that literally."

"Of course."

She smiled again, and so did Hawke.

Game on, he thought. A stroke of luck. A beautiful girl to show him around. And one who could grant him unfettered access to the infamous Tang brothers. He'd watched a recent documentary about their extraordinary lives of crime on the plane from Bermuda. It was called *High Crimes and Misdemeanors*, and it was chilling to say the least. Drugs, human trafficking, gambling, extortion, torture . . . with a recurring tendency toward murder most foul.

The Tang Empire, derived from the centuries-old Tang Dynasty, had extended its reach around the world. On the surface, it was a vast and amazingly successful holding company with dozens of legitimate corporate entities. Casinos, high-end resorts such as the Jewel in the Crown, the famous Dragonfire Club, and many others throughout the world. They were in legit businesses, too, oil and gas production and feature Hollywood films, and they owned many national power companies, controlling the power grids of entire nations throughout Latin America, East Asia, and Eastern Europe.

Once she had her passenger well situated in the rear of the cavernous Bentley, Zhang climbed behind the wheel, and off they went. She'd suggested a tour of the resort, and Hawke had eagerly agreed. He needed to get his bearings.

They sped past a building with a fire-spewing black dragon emblazoned on the doors.

"That's just the shore station, where I have one of my two offices," she said. "From there, I facilitate club departures and arrivals by air and sea. There's another one over on Paradise Island, where both Atlantis and the Ocean Club are located. Are you familiar with the Ocean Club over on Paradise Island, Mr. Hawke? Sorry. I mean, Alex?"

"Indeed, I am. One of my very favorite spots in the Caribbean."

She thought about that one for a second and said, "So, you know about our ferry service from there out to Black Dragon Island?"

"Never took the ferry. Only way to get out there, right? Other than if you dock your yacht at your marina. Sadly, I seem to have forgotten mine."

"Helicopter service as well. That traffic light up ahead is for the bridge over to Paradise Island. We'll park at the Ocean Club and catch the next chopper flying out to the Dragofire Club."

"Marvelous."

"As you'll soon see, the resort consists of seven man-made islands surrounding one very large natural island at the center. Hilly for the Bahamas and parts of it are still dense tropic jungle. An infamous pirate of the Caribbean dubbed it "Fire of the Dragon Isle" back in the early seventeenth century. Sixteen thirteen, I think, or thereabouts. There were rumors of a large fire-breathing dragon prowling about the island in those days, and even sketches of such a creature done by sailors and natural philosophers on shipboard along with various whalebone scrimshaw carvings depicting such a fiery dragon."

"Fascinating," Hawke said, going along with the tale. "Giving rise to the name 'Dragonfire Club,' no doubt."

"Indeed. Did you happen to notice my gold charm bracelet?"

"Sorry, no. Should I have?"

"Yes. See the scrimshaw dragon? Very old. My brothers gave it to me when I came from China to join them here. I love it."

As predicted, Zhang entered the grounds of the Ocean Club and drove straight through the jungle green to the main entrance. A doorman or bellman rushed out to open the rear door for Hawke. He emerged and shook the man's hand. "What's your name?" He smiled at the fellow as the man began to arrange Hawke's luggage on a trolley.

"Benoit, sir. Jenson Benoit."

"Lovely to see you again, Jenson. Remember you well. I played you in the *Casino Royale* picture . . . yes? Borrowed that very jacket of yours to do the shot. . . ."

"Hawke? Why, yes, it is you! The man everybody in the Paradise Island cast thought was Errol Flynn himself! How do you do, sir? Been a while, sir. Sorry. Right this way if you'll follow me."

Zhang key-fob-beeped the locks on the Flying Spur and joined Hawke and Jensen, who said:

"Hello, Miss Tang. Nice to see you again."

"And you, Jenson. Thanks for your help. You've met Lord Hawke, of course."

Hawke put his hand on Jenson's shoulder and said, "I'm headed out to Dragonfire Club. Have you been?"

"Many times, sir. We have guests who stay here at the Ocean Club who sometimes venture out there to the islands for lunch or dinner, the casino, or a Vegas show. Or even stay out there for a night or two. It's quite something, don't you know? I'm sure you'll enjoy it. Down here for business or pleasure this time, sir?"

"Strictly pleasure, believe me. I've been in hospital on Bermuda for a while. I'm here to marinate in sea and salty air for as long as it takes to get my strength back. May try my hand at chemin de fer if the mood strikes."

"Sorry to hear you were ill."

"Nothing serious. Bit of a tummy ache, that's all. Had my bowels in an uproar for quite a while, however. Comes and goes. You know how it is. One gives fate the evil eye and moves on."

CHAPTER 18

Tiger cracked an eye, regarding the silver-plated phone by his bed with some annoyance. It had jangled shortly after seven that morning. With a slight grimace, Ambassador Tang reached over and picked up the receiver. He said, "Who are you, and what do you want?" not mincing any words in his husky, whiskied, late-night-last-night voice. Whereupon Kimberly Li, his private secretary, informed him that the White House social secretary had just called to leave a message for the ambassador. An invitation, to be clear. It seemed that President Roosevelt wanted to invite him to go fishing. A cruise up the New England coast was mentioned aboard the presidential yacht, *Potomac*.

"Fishing?" Tiger said, plumping the pillow beneath his head. "I'll say this once: I don't fish."

"Shall I ring them back and tell them no, Mr. Ambassador?"

"Of course not. You shall ring them back and say I'm honored. I'd be delighted. When is this grand adventure to commence?"

"Next Saturday morning, departing at ten. You'll be joining the presidential party aboard the *Potomac*."

"Pray tell, how long shall I be lost at sea? You'll have to clear my calendar."

"Five days, the White House social secretary said. Give or take."

"Mother of God. A lifetime."

"Yes, sir. You'll need to be at the Gangplank Marina in Southwest Washington at nine sharp so that your luggage can be brought aboard and stowed on the *Potomac*. Shall I arrange for your driver here at the embassy at, say, eight-thirty?"

"Please do. Any idea at all what one wears whilst fishing? Those heavy rubber trousers one sees on men all over the north of Scotland, one suspects."

"Waders."

"Precisely. Waders."

"You'll be fishing from aboard the presidential yacht, so I rather doubt waders will be called for unless the *Potomac* strikes an iceberg and starts to go down. However, I'll find out and get back to you with proper wardrobe suggestions."

"Thank you. One more thing. Who are my fellow travelers?"

"I have the passenger manifest right here, sir. In addition to his two sons, Franklin Jr. and Elliott, the president has invited a small group of his most senior military commanders. Their number includes Generals George Marshall and Henry 'Hap' Arnold and Admirals Ernest King and Harold Stark. You're the sole nongovernment invitee."

"Lucky me."

"Indeed."

"Hmm. Something bothers me, Kimberly."

"What, precisely, sir?"

"I don't know. But something smells fishy."

"Fishy, did you say?" She giggled and said, "Oh, and one more thing. Your new friend, Commander Hawke, rang about fifteen minutes ago. He's headed right back to England tonight and would like you to join him for a farewell luncheon today at twelve thirty. The Cosmos Club. He said you knew the location. Is that a yes or a no, Mr. Ambassador?"

"Definite yes. I haven't seen that scoundrel Hawke in weeks. He's been in London, as you know, out at Bletchley Park with Churchill. And up to some kind of nefarious business or other, chasing the Nazis all over the map, I'm sure. Good-bye. . . ." Click.

She'd hung up.

Miss Li sighed, sad to lose the brief connection to him on the line.

She sat back in her leather chair, held up her compact, and pursed her Estée Lauder red lips. She loved her job. Oh, hell, let's at least be honest with yourself, Kimberly.

She loved her boss. But then again, what girl did not?

After a brisk walk over to Massachusetts Avenue, Ambassador Tang was a good ten minutes early to the Cosmos Club, a rambling Victorian affair in Georgetown. Instead of taking a chair in the small but cozy visitors' lounge on the main floor, he bounded up the large, curving mahogany staircase to the men's grille. The bar in the grille was the best in Washington in terms of the things he cherished when it came to bars.

His taste in bars had been honed to a razor's edge in the various gentlemen's clubs of London. White's. Boodle's. The Carlton Club. Here, huge atmosphere dominated: low lighting, comfortable dark red leather banquettes, and deep, worn club chairs scattered hither and thither across the wine red carpeting.

In such rarefied air, there, too, could be found the deliciously intermingled scents of ancient Persian rugs marinating in decades of spilled whiskey, centuries-old leather books, English Leather shaving lotion, and, of course, Cuban cigars. The haze of pipe and cigar smoke found shape in the great shafts of sunlight slanting downward from the imperious leaded windows and skylights.

At the far end of the long, curving mahogany bar, beyond the rowdy American officers gathered nearby, were the British Foreign Service chaps, celebrating something or other. All resplendent in terms of attire and demeanor. Suits by Huntsman. Shirts by Turnbull & Asser. Shoes by Lobb and hats by Lock. In an homage to Churchill, many of the UK lads sported the familiar navy blue polka-dot bow tie. College ties from Cambridge and Oxford were there, too.

Tiger ordered a Rob Roy and relaxed, absorbing the many moods of this sanctum sanctorum for these powerful men at war while he sipped at his cocktail, his keen black eyes roving and appraising all he saw.

"I knew you'd beat me here, you competitive bastard," he heard a hearty voice say behind him. It could have only belonged to Blackie Hawke. "Didn't I tell you, Winnie? This guy kicks life into an entirely new gear."

Tiger spun round at the mere mention of the name Winnie and regarded his friend. "Hullo, Commander." He smiled.

Hawke grinned and said, "Hullo, yourself! You remember old Winnie, of course, Tiger? Winnie Woolworth? Now that I've delivered the goods, you'll both have to excuse me. I need to duck into the head," he said, and disappeared into the pulsing throng of young manhood. Pausing, he looked back over his shoulder and said, "Don't you two do anything I wouldn't do!"

"As if," an unsmiling Winnie said, rather cool and distant, looking into her gold pocket mirror as if nonchalantly powdering her pretty nose.

"Hello, Winnie," Tiger said, getting to his feet.

"Tiger!" she said. "What an unexpected pleasure!"

He extended his well-manicured hand to the goddess. She smiled sweetly with an extremely discreet wink only he could see. Her honey blond hair was done up in a splendid chignon pinned with a dark blue velvet ribbon. She was wearing a red Mainbocher sweater with pearl buttons and a tight navy skirt of silk. A massive alligator handbag hung from her shoulder.

"Yes, of course I remember!" the ambassador said. "We met at that dance out in the country. Your club. Forgot the name. How have you been, Winnie? Aside from spending time in the company of that reprobate Commander Hawke, I mean?"

She laughed politely. "You never called me, you naughty boy. I might as well have slipped my private number to one of those cute parking attendants."

"You needn't have bothered, my dear girl. I'd already slipped it to one of them. Chap who brought round my lovely lemon yellow Rolls-Royce when I left the club, to be honest. The head valet parker at the club. Rather attractive chap named Chuckie as I remember . . . I'm sure you'll be hearing from him any day now. . . ."

"If I do hear from this Chuckie character or whatever he is, Tiger, you will live to regret it. . . ."

CHAPTER 19

Cosmos Club, Washington, D.C.
January 1942

P lease tell me you're joking about the parking attendant," she said.

"Don't be absurd. Of course I'm joking."

"So, just out of idle curiosity, why didn't you call me?"

"I was actually trying to be the well-behaved gentleman. His lordship has become quite a good personal friend. And I tend to honor my friendships. Dreadfully old-fashioned notions of loyalty around here, I'm sure."

"I see. You're probably unaware of that old expression about love and war...."

"All's fair in love and war, et cetera?"

"Hmm. Apparently not in your case. But all *is* fair in love and war! It is. Get down on your knees and praise the Lord!"

A smile crinkled his eyes as he replied, "Is Alex aware of this? Perhaps I'll tell him you said so."

"Don't even try to be funny. You won't say a word."

"True. I won't."

"Whatever have you been up to, Mr. Ambassador? Aside from your well-chronicled romantic adventures in the social pages of the *Post?* Rumor has it you and President Roosevelt spend your every waking moment together. Weekends at Hyde Park, private dinners at the White House ... joined at the hip, so they say."

"Hardly, my dear Miss Woolworth. As a matter of fact, I've acquired a little country place of my own for the weekends."

"So I hear."

He tried to blink back his shock. "So you hear? Is that what you said?"

"Yes."

"And may I ask, from whom did you hear this idle gossip?"

"Why so upset, silly? Is it such a deep, dark secret?"

"Of course not! A bit curious, that's all. I'm a private person, as you may or may not know."

"Quite innocent, all of it, I assure you. Mummy and Daddy have been looking for a country place in Virginia. Last weekend, a Realtor showed us a place they loved. A house called Southlands. We were walking the grounds when I noticed a rather massive affair on the hillside, looming above us. I pointed it out and the Realtor said, 'Oh, yes, a lovely old plantation called Sevenoaks. Dates to the early nineteenth century. Rumor has it the new Chinese ambassador is the buyer.' So anyhoo, that's how I know. Don't worry. I won't spill your precious beans to any reporters, Mr. International Man of Mystery."

Before he could reply, a waiter appeared at her side. He was bearing a silver tray upon which lay a crisp white envelope with the Cosmos Club seal embossed in gold. Winnie whispered, "Thank you" and ripped open the sealed flap.

"Oh, gosh," she said.

"Bad news?"

"Rather."

"Do tell."

"My parents."

"What about them? Lost at sea? Killed ascending Everest? Kidnapped by pirates? Mauled by tigers in the Bengal? Down with the grippe?"

"I wish. No. Nothing so dramatic. They're downstairs having lunch in the grille. They saw me come in, apparently. I've been ordered by Daddy to put in an appearance at their table posthaste. It's their anniversary, apparently. No one bothered to tell me."

"Do you think your mother's going to like me?"

"Oh, don't be ridiculous, Tiger. You are not invited."

"So. The country. Did your parents buy the house?"

"Of course. Daddy collects houses the way the president collects stamps."

"Hmm. So. Do you plan to spend any time out there?"

"Are you kidding? Oodles! I love the country. I'm whip of the Virginia Hunt, you see."

"I beg your pardon?"

"Foxhunting, silly. I've a lovely pair of Arabian jumpers, you see, a gift from the shah of Persia, don't you know? Lovely mares for hunting. You must come out. Do you ride?"

"A bit."

"Hunting, Mr. Ambassador? Is that a Chinese sport?"

"No, nothing much to speak of. I've ridden, of course, in England. Dressage mostly. A bit of polo and show jumping while I was still at Oxford. My team was called Dr. Odd. Prince of Wales formed us up at Balliol."

"I see," she said, taking his hand and batting her lashes. "You must bring the prince out for a day with me sometime. He's divine. All the girls say so."

"I'd like nothing better, Winnie, but I can't promise I can deliver the Prince of Wales."

"My God, I'm kidding! Better be careful, Tiger. Don't stand me up this time. I might just show up at your door some dark and stormy night and borrow a cup of sugar. . . . Well . . . gotta run. Daddy beckons."

"Say, here comes your handsome beau now. . . ."

She smiled at Tiger, winked, and giggled. "To be continued, buster . . . so, keep your strength up!" she said to Tiger.

She stopped Hawke midstream, pecked him on the cheek, whispered that she'd be right back, and vanished into the mob at the bar on her way out the door. Hawke took her place at the bar and said:

"Sorry. Had to take another private call from Number Ten Downing. My new nanny, Winston. It appears I'm headed right back there, for God's sake. I just got here! Winnie will bloody kill me when she gets wind of this development. . . . I'm dead nuts on that gal, you know."

"Yeah. I know."

Tiger, deciding it best to remain mum on the subject of Miss Woolworth's decidedly flirtatious behavior toward him, said, "There's a war on, flyboy. Your country is calling. Or hadn't you heard?"

"Yes, yes. You know what strikes me, Tiger? Winston treats me precisely the way Franklin treats you. Like his bloody puppy dog, Fala. Come, Tiger! Sit! Fetch! Good boy!"

"Tell me about it, brother," Tang said. "What's up back in Blighty? Anything you can talk about without compromise?"

"Hmm. Maybe. Got a lot on my mind. Things could get pretty spicy for me in the next few weeks. I'd like your input. Let's go get a quiet table in the corner."

They sat down, ordered a pair of matching Rob Roys and club sandwiches, and got right down to business. Hawke collected his thoughts before he spoke. It was completely unlike him to talk about the kind of hush-hush things he did for the Department of Naval Intelligence. On the other hand, after all, this wasn't some admiral of the Swiss Navy he was buying a drink for. This was the bloody Chinese ambassador to the United States! He was one of his closest friends. And certainly one of Britain's and America's most powerful allies in the two-front wars against raging tyranny.

"Ready?" Hawke asked.

"Fire away," Tiger said, enjoying all the new American wartime slang he was picking up around town.

"Here's the skinny, Mr. Ambassador. Whitehall Naval Intelligence has put me in charge of a secret squad of six highly battle-hardened commandos. Blinker Godfrey, our supreme leader, calls us Hawke's Headbangers. My remit, our remit, is to come up with new and even more ingenious ways to torture Herr Hitler and his bullyboys behind the lines, where it hurts most. It seems my latest scheme, long on the shelf, has suddenly won the endorsement of my boss, Rear Admiral Blinker Godfrey. Winston has just blessed it as well, so I guess it's game on."

"Can you give me some broad strokes without your loose lips sinking any ships?"

"You're closer to the truth than you know. You do know, of course, about Germany's Enigma code machine?"

"Of course."

"Well. Here's the thing. The beautiful minds out at Bletchley Park cracked the code on that one. But no one has been able to lay a hand on the other one, the three-rotor encoding machine that all the *Kriegsmarine* (War Navy) ships and subs at sea use in lieu of the Enigma. Until I figured out how we might actually acquire one of these damn things. As well as the companion codebooks. We'd be sitting pretty then, in terms of intelligence . . . for the balance of the war, actually. It would give us a huge leg up on the German Navy. Save thousands of our boys' lives . . . that sort of thing."

"Brilliant. Go on. . . ."

"Well, at Naval Intelligence, if you come up with a juicy idea within your own section, you project-manage it yourself, and your reputation sinks or swims accordingly. So. Here goes nothing, right?"

"And your idea for staying afloat long enough to fight another day?"

Hawke lowered his voice and said, "Okay, I suggested we might get our hands on the loot by the following means. One, we obtain from the air ministry an airworthy German bomber. Preferably a Heinkel."

"Really? Easier said than done, one would imagine. And then what?"

"We crash-dive our bomber into the English Channel."

"Brilliant. There will be survivors, one would hope?"

"Hmm."

"I'm serious, Blackie. That's the plan? Good God."

"It's as much as I'm comfortable with revealing, Mr. Ambassador. Safe to say, there's a lot more to my scheme than ditching a German bomber in the drink."

"Dangerous as heck, but to hell with it. Do what you've got to do."

"Why is it dangerous?" Hawke asked. It was a notion he'd not considered.

"Oh, I don't know. What if you sink? How long does a long-range German bomber typically stay afloat?"

Hawke, irritated, said, "All airplanes will sink eventually, Tiger. But there are air pockets throughout the fuselage. The area between the outside skin of the fuselage and the interior is a space that is insulated and has air that needs to be displaced by the sea. Also, the petrol tanks in the wings help. Since water is heavier than fuel, the fuel inside the wings helps offset some of the weight of the plane . . . not a lot, but some."

"Well, you've clearly thought this through."

"Yeah, it's what I do for a living. The prime minister of my country likes it that way."

"There is that, I suppose."

"All right, then. Are you going to wish me Godspeed? Wish me luck at least?"

"No, Commander Hawke. I'm going to wish you a long and happy life full of cheap wine, expensive women, to a soaring overture of songs fit for angels."

"More's the better. I'm off. I've not even packed a valise. One last thing. I want you to keep an eye on little Miss Five 'n' Dime whilst I'm away. Will you?"

"Why? She needs watching, does she?"

"She's . . . complicated. As you know, headstrong and impulsive. Sometimes she doesn't think straight. Living in a world of her own half the time. I'm just asking you to see that she doesn't get herself into any trouble while I'm gone. Will you do it?"

"Of course I'll do it, old chap. I'd do anything in my power for you. You know that. We're comrades-in-arms, right? You know that."

"Can you keep a secret, old fellow? Should a handsome swain step in, say?"

"Certainly."

"Last weekend, Winnie and I drove out to Annapolis and got secretly engaged. No one knows. I gave her my mother's engagement ring, but she's never worn it in public. . . ."

"I see. Well, congratulations, old man! That's marvelous news!"

"Yes, I suppose so. I do fear she's going to prove a handful. But what can I do? I'm crazy about that girl! Cheerio, old fellow. See you soon, I hope."

"Not if I see you first." Hawke grinned at him.

And he was gone.

Tiger took a swig of his cocktail and watched his friend disappear into the crowd.

So, they were secretly engaged now, were they? This would require a steady hand on the tiller. And his ability to keep Winnie at arm's length no matter what webs the little vixen purported to use to seduce him.

CHAPTER 20

The Bahamas
Present Day

To say that Lord Alexander Hawke was somewhat shocked at the aerial view of the sprawling Dragonfire Club complex from the circling chopper would have been the epitome of British understatement. First, it was far larger and vastly more grandiose than anything he could have imagined. He leaned over and peered through the Plexiglas beneath his feet at the wonders arrayed below. It would only have been a slight exaggeration to say that what he beheld was "another world" altogether.

One central island, called Black Dragon Isle, was very large, possibly a few thousand acres or more. In a swath of cleared jungle, situated high atop the highest hilltop, was an imposing residence of soaring, cutting-edge architecture worthy of note. Think Bill Gates meets Elon Musk meets I. M. Pei. A sleek and gleaming silver elevated monorail connected the sprawling Tang family homestead with other locations scattered about the main island. One expansive complex by the sea boasted a hotel of at least fifty stories, and with a lavish rooftop pool, tennis courts, and a nine-hole golf course, it was obviously the resort's primary hotel.

The Hotel di Qing, it was called. The Star God of War, in Chinese mythology. Odd choice for a hotel name, Hawke thought.

Situated on the opposite side of the island, where it was largely undeveloped, all thick tropical jungle, was a strange monolithic white structure, large, and of poured concrete. The monstrosity was a city-block-sized rect-angular building, one that was built into the hillside but stretched far out over the water. No windows and no visible entry points, at least from above. Some kind of marine research facility, Hawke imagined. Bio-agriculture maybe. He'd heard they had irons in every fire, these Tangs. Chinese bio-warfare maybe. He'd seen a top secret M16 dossier that said the Chinese were experimenting with militarizing a virus.

But his spy brain kicked in almost immediately. Something familiar or other about the dull architecture. The location . . . size . . . It would come to him. He'd have a midnight recon one of these nights; that much was a given.

He counted seven other satellite islands of varying sizes and features, all connected by the gleaming silver monorail, plus a system of hyper-postmodern pedestrian and single-lane auto bridges. There was, too, a traditional British Colonial–style yacht club, bustling and colorful and overlooking the vast marina. The slips were jam-packed with the world's most expensive megayachts and futuristic Wally speedboats.

And all of this magnificence and architectural grandeur was hidden away in some Bahamian backwater, not unlike the endless miles of man-grove swamps and no-name keys south of Key West.

A thought about Prince Henry, his young godson, struck him like an exploding lightbulb in a pitch-black room. A young Royal—an adventur-ous bachelor of considerable wealth, charm, and exceeding beauty—might well think this place was a highly desirable vacation destination. And with his high profile on social media, and the wall-to-wall coverage in the celebrity press, it was scant wonder that the missing Prince Henry had petitioned, as Ambrose had discovered, the coveted invitation from Tommy and Jackie, also known internationally as the Tang Twins.

In other words, he had not been lured here. He had wanted to come. It was his idea. Here he had met his fate, whatever it would prove to be, and done so at his own hands. This was, at the very least, Hawke thought, a starting place . . . a wormhole into the mystery, and, hopefully, out of it.

The beauteous Miss Zhang Tang, seated across the narrow aisle, sud-denly placed a delicate warm hand on Hawke's deepwater-tanned forearm. On her naked brown arms, she wore lovely gold Van Cleef cuff bracelets, which clinked softly as she moved her hands. Around her neck, a gold choker studded with diamonds set off her magnificent bosom, rather frankly on display in her low-cut blouse.

"You like it?" She smiled, catching his reaction to the affectionate overture. "Our little island, I mean."

"My God," he said. "I had no idea."

"No one ever does. It's one of the reasons I love my job. Seeing the expressions of my clients when they first set eyes on Black Dragon from the skies above. Now, before we land, is there anything else you might require during your stay, beyond the typical amenities? A car perhaps? A small boat?"

Hawke thought about it, gazing out at the earth below, or at least pretended to do so. "Let's see. A mint under my pillow?"

She laughed and said, "Be serious, please. I'm here to help. It's my job. Name your poison."

"Yes, now that you mention it: not a car, but a motorcycle, if that's possible. My favorite mode of transportation. I want to have a good look round. I assume each island has its own style of restaurants and cuisine and nightclubs, casinos?"

"Good assumption. Whatever your heart desires. Michelin chefs at each restaurant. Monte Carlo dealers and stewards at every casino table. You enjoy chemin de fer, no doubt, Lord Hawke."

"I do. But, please, call me Alex, won't you? I don't use my title. I'm descended from pirate stock, you see, not fat little pink lords who wear silk stockings to Parliament and raise fat little pigs in the country."

"Of course, Alex. I'll call you anything you like, except late for dinner."

He laughed at the old joke. "Good Lord, your brothers don't tred lightly, do they?"

"Just you wait. Alone, a force of nature. Left to their own devices, together, an existential geostorm."

"When do they return? I look forward to meeting them."

"I would guess ten days, maybe two or three weeks. Depends entirely on how much they get accomplished. They have to be back by the first because we're having our annual corporate retreat that week. They always host that themselves."

"Good. That's about how long I planned to stay before returning to England. So, yes, I'd love the use of a motorcycle whilst here. And if possible, a small speedboat, preferably fast, of course. I've friends over in Nassau with homes on the water. It would make dinner parties or visiting with them ever so much simpler. And a great way for me to explore the club from the water."

"Just so. I'll make it happen. You know what? My brother Tommy has a lovely little Wally boat he uses as a tender for the yacht sometimes. I'm sure he wouldn't mind if you borrowed it in his absence."

"Hmm. Maybe. What's his yacht called, by the way?"

"*Chop-Chop*. You've heard of her?"

Hawke laughed. The pidgin English word for "quickly" was one of his favorite yacht names. Until now, he'd never been able to determine who her owner was.

"Are you quite sure he wouldn't mind? I'm quite keen on the Wally tenders. I have a pair aboard my own boat, *Blackhawke*. . . ."

"Done and done," she said, squeezing his hand and turning on those emerald-colored high beams. "Anything else?"

"Oh, I'm sure I'll think of something," Hawke managed to say with a semistraight face, all the while letting his eyes wander down below her chin to her Promethean bosom, a physical marvel that could well be described as the "curvature of the earth" without fear of overstatement!

He was suddenly reminded of something an American chum of his, who'd been a Visiting Scholar at Cambridge while he as there, had said about his girlfriend's considerable assets:

"My God, Hawke! I'd crawl over a mile of broken glass just to drink her bathwater!"

CHAPTER 21

Hotel di Qing, the Bahamas
Present Day

Hawke's two-bedroom penthouse suite was located just one floor down from the pinnacle of the rather epic Hotel di Qing. In the suite's foyer, Hawke discovered a private elevator up to the pool and sports club on the rooftop. The elevator, all glass including the floor, was mounted on the outside of the building. So the view, especially the one between your shoes, was exciting enough.

He pushed UP.

Up there, Hawke knew he'd have a good three sixty of the entire Dragonfire complex, encompassing all eight islands. A view that might well come in handy, should things get a little spicy at some point during this little vacay of his. He smiled at the notion of offering himself up as a sacrifice to the Sun Gods. Pictured himself gladly marinating in the tropical salt and sun, saving his explorations and investigations for the midnight hours.

When he emerged from the elevator, he was surprised to see that the free-form aquamarine pool boasted a high diving board. You never saw those back home in England anymore—insurance premiums had been the death of them—but as a youth, he'd loved doing full gainers off the high dives no end. He welcomed the opportunity to hone his skills once more. He did a circumnavigation of the rooftop, including the sports club and the

Dragonfire Bay Restaurant (which reminded him of his old haunt, Trader Vic's). At the bar, he ordered his old favorite cocktail, the infamous Suffering Bastard. Delicious rum concoction at the Plaza Hotel, New York.

When a lissome mermaid, topless and with flowing golden locks, swam behind the bartender, he thought perhaps he'd better stop at just one rum. The wall behind the bar was thick glass, and one could peer into the deep end of the pool above from his barstool. He saw a second and then a third topless mermaid swim right up to the glass, point at him, and then swim up to kiss the glass in front of him. It was entertaining, but, still, he felt a bit Peeping Tom–ish looking at all the bathing beauties. . . . He paid his tab and beat a hasty retreat to his elevator.

Back in his suite, he smiled at his prudishness after all these years. He sighed, forgiving himself, and went to the little mahogany bar in the living room. He wasn't surprised to see a silver bucket filled with ice and an unopened bottle of Mr. Gosling's famous 151 Black Seal Rum. These people did their homework.

He poured a short glass, neat, and carried it out to the terrace off his bedroom.

The lambent sun was loitering about the horizon, turning the whole wide world pink and gold. It was lovely. Mr. Gosling's potion was working its magic, and Hawke was beginning to relax. He even considered ringing the beauteous Miss Zhang and inviting her to join him for a quiet dinner at the rooftop club restaurant . . . and quickly reconsidered. Best to remain a bit distant and a tad aloof. Let her do the chasing.

His grandfather Admiral Hawke, a man famous for his daring sabotage exploits against the Nazis in World War Two, who had adopted him after the murder of his parents when he was seven years old, had once imparted the following wisdom: "Alex, never, ever chase a girl who doesn't want to get caught!"

Hawke stood at the railing, savoring the fire of deep dark rum in his belly and waiting patiently for the full tropic moon to bounce up and get everyone's attention. He took a deep breath of the cooling northern breezes. He'd been an extraordinarily lucky fellow. He'd almost died at the hands of a psychopathic madman. So had his dear old Pelham. But,

but, but . . . hadn't they'd beaten the devil? Hadn't they both lived to fight another day?

Here he was about to take on his first Chinese adversaries since General Moon had come to a fitting end in yet another messy affair that was nearly the end of him . . . a stormy love affair with the general's daughter. The unforgettable and exquisite China Moon. Long ago and far away now . . .

He saw a rather large and powerful-looking craft hove into view, steaming around the coast from the other side of the island. She was doing about ten knots, maybe half a mile from shore. . . . Hmm. He ducked back into his room and grabbed the small Leica binos from his leather briefcase.

Patrol boat?

Back at the rail, his suspicions were confirmed. He recognized her immediately. Big deck guns fore, aft, and amidships. A chopper pad on the stern, complete with a missile-attack chopper. No doubt. She was nothing if not a Type 056 Jiangdao Class Corvette. A guided-missile light frigate. Also known by the Chinese Navy as the guided-missile frigate "Bengbu."

What the hell was a Chinese Navy vessel doing on this side of the planet? Half a world away? News flash, note to self: nothing good.

His thoughts were interrupted by the soft ring of his encrypted mobile phone resting in its cradle on the bedside table in his bedroom. He stepped inside.

"Hullo?" he said, expecting a call from the front desk asking him if all and sundry were satisfactory.

"Alex?" It was Ambrose Congreve.

"Ambrose?"

"The one and only. Have I reached you at an inconvenient moment? Sir David gave me your whereabouts. How's your health?"

"Depends. Who wants to know?"

"Her Royal Majesty the Queen of England, basically."

"Ah. Well. Pain is pretty much gone. Doctors on Bermuda are still a bit worried about abdominal infection. But, apparently, there's a first-rate hospital right here on this island. I'll pop round in the morning and have them take a look at things . . . blood work. You know the drill."

"Good, good. Do that. Now, listen. I've some new information for you. I asked the two Yard detectives who went out to the Bahamas to Black Dragon Island—Operation Dragonbreath they called it—to come out to our country house for a daylong debrief and—"

"Well, good on you, old sod. Hard to believe Sir David didn't do that himself before he sent me packing."

"I'll not speak ill of your boss behind his back. Maybe he assumed I'd already done it. But needless to say, I wholeheartedly agree. At any rate, I did it. Pumped them dry or at least until I thought they'd strangle me. I came away with some bits and bobs I thought might help you."

"God bless you. Fire away."

"All right, then. Number one: Before they left the resort, Sergeant Detectives William and Morris furtively interviewed club staff on property. Waiters, bartenders, gardeners, caddies at the golf course, et cetera, anyone who may have had chance encounters with our missing Royal, yes?"

"Yes."

"It seems our young prince somehow managed to get on the nerves of the Tang brothers whilst out there. He was indifferent to all the rules and regs of the place. Seduced half the female population of the waitstaff and most of the housekeepers. Paid caddies hundreds of pounds to look the other way while he surreptitiously kicked his golf ball out of hazards in the middle of a money match with other members who thereupon, of course, complained to the caddy master, who complained to a Miss Tang, who apparently is a very big cheese down there. That sort of thing. Poor chap had to be carried out of the casinos at dawn. You know how he is."

"That's my boy, all right."

"Yes. I know. But he finally did something that really raised the ire of the twins."

"I'm all ears."

"One of the young boys working on the petrol dock at the marina told my men that the prince had rented a small runabout for a—as he rather grandly called it—'complete circumnavigation of the island.' Apparently, during this epic voyage, he stuck his nose into some dark places where it didn't belong. Saw things he wasn't supposed to see. . . . You know how that goes, too. . . ."

"And?"

"And the next day, he and all his belongings vanished into the thinnest of air."

"Interesting. I'll take that all into consideration. By the way, what are you up to these days? Pruning peonies? Waltzing Matilda? Counting your blessings? Listening to Benny Goodman swing music on Auntie Beeb in the evenings?"

"I must say, Alex, despite your recent duel with death, you've lost none of your irritating gift for sarcasm. As a matter of fact, I'm writing a book, if you must know. A novel, to be perfectly honest."

"A book? About what, pray tell."

"Sherlock Holmes. The untold story. A mystery novel, of course, in which the ghost of Professor Moriarty returns to haunt Sherlock and Dr. Watson whilst on a golfing holiday in Barbados. Diana has read the opening chapters. It's called *The Banshee of Barbados*. My wife's already comparing me to Le Carré and Ian Fleming, for all love! To say that the word 'masterpiece' left her lips on numerous occasions would not be stretching the truth."

"How marvelous. And as we all know, Diana is nothing if not a stickler for top-notch literary endeavors."

"Don't you dare patronize me, boy!"

"I'm not! You've been a lifelong Sherlockian, Ambrose. Not to mention the fact that the whole world knows you as the brainiest chap ever to grace Scotland Yard, as celebrated a criminalist mastermind as ever there was in England. If ever anyone could be the one to pen such an epic tome, it would be you. Love the title, by the by."

"Well, thanks for that. Now, what's your take on the scene out there so far?"

"The twins are not here for a week or so. I can roam about a bit without raising any alarms. Unlike my dear godson, Henry, I'm going to be the perfect guest by day, a stealthy spy by night. And to make things interesting, there is already a woman. There's always a woman, isn't there, Ambrose?"

"Always, dear boy. Always."

CHAPTER 22

RAF Archbury, Oxfordshire, England
January 1942

The shimmering blood orange sun was barely peeking over the horizon when Hawke rolled the snarling Norton motorcycle to a stop outside the HQ at RAF Archbury, 18th Bomber Group, Oxfordshire. He dismounted and went round to the entrance to the rusting World War One Quonset hut building. The small gardens to either side of the walkway looked to have been there since the long, silent roar of Sopwith Camels taking off in World War One.

The name of the small village nearby was spelled out with rather quaint arrangements of white stones on the twin green oblongs of lawn inside the beds of roses and peonies: ARCHBURY.

Hawke lit a cigarette and reflected on the path that had led to this place in time. Cigarettes were the latest addition to his doctor's all-clear list, now allowing both alcohol and tobacco. He saw an immediate boost in his moods. When asked by his Harley Street physician, "And how's the drinking these days, Blackie?" He had promptly replied, "Fabulous, thank you. Never better, to be honest."

He looked up into the warring storm clouds high above and took a deep breath. No time like the present, he said to himself. Yes. It was finally time to execute Operation Skyhook.

After a long liquid supper at Number 10 Downing last evening, he'd laid the entire scheme, Operation Skyhook, out for Winston in very succinct, simple terms. Primary objective: obtain the *Kriegsmarine*'s 3-rotor code machine, and the germane codebooks, by the following means:

1. Obtain from the Air Ministry an airworthy German bomber. Preferably a Heinkel 111, warhorse of the *Luftwaffe*.

2. Recruit a tough crew of six that includes myself as pilot. Also including a W/T (wireless/telegraph) operator and a word-perfect German speaker. Dress them all in well-worn German *Luftwaffe* uniforms; add blood and bandages to suit.

3. Crash the bomber in the English Channel off France after making SOS call to Rescue Service in P/L (plain language) and within visual range of a German *Minensuchboot* (a large minesweeper) on patrol in mid-Channel.

4. Once crew is safely aboard the German rescue boat, seize control, neutralize the German crew, and sail the vessel and the encoder forthwith to Portsmouth Harbour on the southern tip of England.

The HQ doors suddenly swung wide and Colonel Peter Mainwaring came strolling down the brick paved walk with a broad smile. They were old friends, having gone to the Naval College at Dartmouth together. Peter was wearing his leather combat flight jacket, as was Hawke.

"Commander Hawke, you old bounder, welcome to RAF Archbury. How's life in the colonies treating you? Word has it you're the toast of all Washington, celebrated by high-society debutantes and their grande dame mothers, all with an eye toward a titled military officer for little Susie. We've been expecting you to come over for an inspection, ever since the request for the German bomber came through from on high," Colonel Mainwaring said as Hawke climbed off his motorcycle.

Hawke had made short work of the run out from London, having left his small flat in Chelsea at dark thirty that morning. He looked at his ancient Rolex steel dive watch. Well, how about that? Seems, despite the rain showers, he'd arrived right on time.

"Glad to be here, Peter. Why do you look tan and healthy whilst I'm a mere shadow of my former self? Stealing afternoons out on the local links, old fellow?"

Mainwaring smiled. "Honeymoon, old chap. Two sunny weeks in Barbados with my bride. Sandy Lane Hotel. Lovely spot. I think you're the one who originally reco'd it to me at our engagement binge at Claridge's, no?"

"I love it out there, yes. I used to go whenever I got the chance. A lot of romance in the air, in the islands."

"Yes, I quite agree. Do you remember a chappie named Bajun by any chance? A waiter at Sandy Lane. He remembers you."

"Yes, I do remember him quite well. He's still around?"

"Indeed. Only now he's the club's general manager."

"So, apparently, there's a groundswell of RAF enthusiasm for my mission? The one the boys at DNI Whitehall have taken to calling 'Hawke and His Suicide Six.'"

"To be sure. Everyone's convinced a successful Operation Skyhook mission could well change the whole course of the war in Britain's favor. Those Nazi wolf packs lurking about out in the Channel will get a well-seasoned taste of their own bloody medicine, I'll warrant. Your crew, the new Skyhook lads here at Archbury, are all quite keen about the previous exploits of you and your commandos this past year. The men are thrilled to be under your command for such an important go. Especially this new *Kriegsmarine* scheme of yours. It's only brilliant!"

"They're all here this morning?" Hawke said. "Been looking forward to saying hello."

"Affirmative. Been here for a month, training in the actual bomber seven days a week. Just a heads-up if you don't mind. They've organized a bit of a surprise for you . . . by way of a welcome to RAF ARCHBURY this morning."

"Much appreciated. Good on you, mate. I'd no idea you lads were this far along. I've been buried in Washington red tape these last few weeks, dealing with Winston's demands and President Roosevelt's keenly anticipated lend-lease program. But I'm glad the lads are all so enthusiastic.

We're going to need that, I imagine. Once the gravity of what we're doing starts to sink in . . ."

"Well, the sheer simplicity of your idea is stunning, Blackie. I think it was Flight Lieutenant Alastair Stauffenberg, your new number two and copilot, who said, just the other day, 'It's so bloody obvious, sir, this idea. It's a wonder no one's had the notion before!' Everyone in your crew wants to throw in their two cents on how to properly ditch that bomber in the Channel. Tricky bit of business, they say, a risky bit of flying to be sure."

"Understatement. Problem is, I can't follow any of the bloody water-landing protocols. I've got to make the damn thing look totally realistic when I deep-six her in plain sight of a German minesweeper. A horrific crash dive into the Channel. And then I've got to get the crew out in one piece. A matter of minutes and seconds. Since I can't put her down on the water properly, we'll have a very short time afloat, I'm afraid. I will have an audience, you know. Aboard that Nazi minesweeper, every sailor who sees the smoke streaming from my portside engines will come to the rail to watch us go down."

"Duly noted. It won't be any picnic for sure. But listen, old boy, if anyone in this man's outfit can do it, it's you. And that's not flattery. It's the bloody truth."

"Don't be so modest. You could do it, too, Peter."

"Thanks for that. By the by, procuring this Nazi flying machine was a breeze for us. I think you had a little help at the Air Ministry from on high. From Number Ten Downing Street. Apparently, despite a lot of pushback from the backbenchers that Operation SKYHOOK is plainly a foolhardy scheme that will no doubt lead to disaster. But the prime minister is very optimistic that you can pull this thing off, if anyone can. I'm inclined to go along with Winston's assessment, sir. You can do it. And it will be such an enormous step forward in the war effort. Those wolf packs in the Channel will get a jolly good taste of their own medicine. That much is certain!"

"Thanks, Peter. And thanks ever so much for finding that damn *Luftwaffe* bomber for me. I wasn't quite sure how this was all going to come together, to be honest. Still not, actually."

"Well, as I said, I had a great deal of help procuring the necessary equipment. I looked through mountains of captured enemy equipment at Cardington and acquired suitable German uniforms and weapons. You'll look the part. I can guarantee that.

"At any rate, the lads of the eighteenth are glad they might get a chance to say hullo whilst you're here at Archbury. Wish you luck, that sort of thing. Everybody's rooting for you and your Deep Six crew, sir."

"Appreciate that, Peter. Now, tell me about the crew."

"You'll meet them this morning. All five of them handpicked by the air vice marshal at Whitehall. They're all here for a familiarization tour of the airplane with yours truly."

"You're happy with the lot of them?"

"Beyond happy. These lads are all first-rate. Every one of them as good as they come. And straining at the traces to get under way."

"Remind me to ring up the old man, give him my personal thanks."

"Of course. Happy to oblige, Alex. I can't tell you how much I've been looking forward to this very moment. A lot of us believe this idea of yours has been long overdue, too long on the shelf."

"Well, we'll see, won't we? I just hope the Nazi bomber you got me is airworthy."

"Oh, I think you're going to be more than pleased. What we've found for you is a sterling example of its kind, to tell you the truth. Never shot down. Not a bullet hole anywhere. Virgin."

"How the hell did you come by such a find?"

"Simple. The Krauts on her inaugural mission across the Channel ran out of fuel after an extended bombing run at Canterbury. Had to ditch her just off the cliffs of Dover. Pristine condition. Royal Navy boys plucked the crew out of the water, some of them still alive. Then they towed the old girl back to Portsmouth Harbour, where she was first mothballed. The Air Ministry was reluctant to let her go, to be honest."

"Where is she now?"

Hawke stood back as a mud-spattered RAF four-door sedan, with big RAF roulons on the back doors, rolled to a stop on the tarmac. The driver, a sergeant who looked hardly old enough to be in long pants, saluted the two officers smartly. Mainwaring pulled open the rear passenger door for his friend.

"Hop in the back, and we'll go have a look at your new bird. She's on the other side of the field, just outside the officers' club, where everyone can get a good look at her."

"Delighted, let's go," Hawke said as Mainwaring climbed into the backseat next to him. The driver engaged first gear, and they roared off down the runway where the gallant Spitfires would shortly be lined up for takeoff, headed up into the skies for the day's sorties against the Nazi flyboys.

"Tell me more about my new joyride, Colonel," Hawke said above the unmuffled roar of the engine. He found himself strangely excited about the prospect of actually, finally, seeing his grand scheme come together. "A Heinkel, I would imagine?"

"Most certainly. The Heinkel HE One Eleven is the most numerous of the German bombers we see daily over England. Actually, it's been the primary *Luftwaffe* bomber at this stage of the war as Göring brings the new Junkers on line. How much detail can you stand, Commander Hawke?"

"All you got, Colonel."

"All right, then. Don't say I didn't warn you. I eat, dream, and sleep these bloody things, so stop me if I bore you to tears. . . ."

"Hardly likely. I'm all ears."

"The HE One Eleven is a fast medium German bomber designed by Siegfried and Walter Günter in the early nineteen thirties. She was built in secret and in direct violation of the Treaty of Versailles. The Germans insisted it was merely a transport aircraft, causing it to be dubbed a 'sheep in wolf's clothing.'"

"Are they any good? The Heinkel One Elevens, I mean. By our standards?"

"I'd say so, yes. Up to a point. It's been a moderately successful war fighter, but its weaknesses became all too apparent when our fighters started engaging them with a will as soon as they crossed the Channel. That's when the One Elevens' weak defensive armament, relatively low speed, and poor maneuverability left them exposed to aerial attacks. Continue?"

"Please."

"Nevertheless, the twin-engined HE One Eleven, despite all of its shortcomings, is the workhorse of the *Luftwaffe*. With their distinctive 'greenhouse' noses, the One Elevens have been used in a variety of roles not only in the air war here in England, but on every front in the European theater. Göring used them as strategic bombers during the Battle of Britain, but as a torpedo bomber during the Battle of the Atlantic, and a medium bomber and a transport aircraft on the Western, Eastern, Mediterranean, Middle Eastern, and North African fronts. . . ."

"Is that it?" Hawke said, leaning forward to peer more closely through the dirty windscreen. "All I need to know?"

"Indeed it is. I ordered her parked over here so the lads at the officers' club could have a good look-see."

The sedan slowed coming around the side of the officers' club and braked to a halt at the port wingtip of the *Luftwaffe* bomber. Hawke had to blink rapidly to make sure he was seeing what he thought he was seeing.

The men looked like hell. Five rugged young men, bloodied, battered, and bandaged, stood beneath the broad portside wing. They all snapped to attention and saluted as the two young officers emerged from the rear doors of the sedan and approached them.

Each man was dressed in the authentic uniform of a Nazi *Luftwaffe* airman. They all looked like they'd been through hell, having barely survived a horrific crash dive into the English Channel. They looked so authentic, Hawke felt like pulling his sidearm.

"At ease, gentlemen," he said. "Which one of you dashing young characters is Flight Lieutenant Alastair Stauffenberg?"

"I am, sir," a lanky young pilot with curly blond hair said, stepping forward.

Hawke stuck out his right hand, and Stauffenberg shook it vigorously. *"Wie geht's, mein Herr,"* Hawke said, smiling at the fellow.

"Sehr gut, danke shön, mein Herr! Und sie?"

Hawke said, *"Alles gut. Bitte, haben-sie eine rot Kugleschriber?"*

"Habe nicht, Commander Hawke. No red ballpoint pen at all, I'm afraid, sir."

Hawke laughed. "You knew that was a test," he said. "I thought if this boy wonder knows the English word for *Kugleschriber*, he'll be good enough for me!"

The young flyboy had passed his first test. When the nut-cutting moment came at last, when they were all yanked from the sea and hauled aboard the German minesweeper, the young lieutenant would be known as Kapitän Fritz von Richter. He would represent the crew until they had gained the confidence of the German officers aboard.

"Let me ask you a question, Lieutenant," Hawke said, "seeing as how you're going to be sitting in the right-hand seat next week. . . ."

"Yes, sir?"

"How many flying hours do you have in this old bird?"

"Just over a few hundred, sir."

"Do you think that, in your wildest dreams, you could crash-dive this bird into the drink at a realistic and believable angle and still get the entire crew out of the aircraft before it sinks like a bloody stone?"

"Absolutely, sir! I'm convinced of it. I've been thinking of little else during the last month of training. Got it all figured out, sir!"

"Good answer," Hawke said. "I'm glad at least one of us bloody has."

The crew erupted into spontaneous laughter at Hawke's self-deprecation.

He added: "When we have a spare moment I'd like you to share the basis of all that youthful optimism with me, would you? I'll tell you one thing, Lieutenant Stauffenberg. This thing's going to be dicey. A real bitch. It's been keeping me up at night for weeks! I've convinced myself no sane man save myself could ever have come up with such a hare-brained scheme."

"Yes, sir." Stauffenberg saluted. "Shall we take the old girl up in the wild blue yonder for a dry run over the Channel, sir?"

Hawke said, "I'd say that's a cracking good scheme, son! Colonel Mainwaring, you're welcome to come along for the ride."

"I'd like nothing better, Commander. Let's get aboard this ugly Nazi bitch, and she what kind of tricks she can do, shall we?"

CHAPTER 23

Dragonfire Club, the Bahamas
Present Day

A morning shot through with azure skies, the surrounding seas below a resolute blue, and great clouds of swirling white seagulls riding the wind, hovering just beyond his reach at the rail of his rooftop terrace. All the swooping white birds were crying what sounded very much like "mine-mine-mine-mine-mine!" and greedily eyeing the lavish repast laid out on the table. No bubble and squeak for this boy, nosiree.

Out on his spacious terrace, Hawke's splendid breakfast of French toast, smoked Canadian bacon, and his beloved Blue Mountain coffee from Jamaica was just what the doctor hadn't ordered. He ate *con* both *brio* and *mucho gusto*, all of his senses awakened, his heart pumping away like a finely tuned engine, good health returning every day now, it seemed.

And with it, a vast improvement in his moods.

Enjoying the fresh sea breeze, laced with a whiff of iodine, he was leafing through yesterday's *Times* and all that jolly old rag entailed: the current dustup with Iran, a surprise state visit to North Korea by the American president, Britain's Brexit mess, the Chelsea Flower Show, et cetera, et cetera, as the King of Siam would have put it.

His attention span fluttered like a darting hummingbird through the newspaper pages, skipping from page to page out of sheer habit, bored by the news of the day, which was already old news by the time the *Times* arrived here in the Bahamas from London.

Then his symphonic mobile rang, an all-too-brief snatch of ringtone, one of Puccini's ravishingly beautiful arias from *Madama Butterfly*. He answered, somehow already knowing while reaching for the device who might be calling. He wasn't disappointed. It was Miss Tang, of course.

"Hullo?" the voice said. "Lord Hawke?" A female. Had to be her. Had he not told her he never used his bloody title? He decided to have a little fun at the dragon lady's expense. He said: "Oh, so sorry. His lordship is not available. He's not here. This is his alter ego. My name is Big Al."

There was a pregnant pause. Hawke thought he sounded a bit posh for a chap named Big Al, but he was having fun with her and decided to roll with it. Besides, he'd told her very specifically not to use his title and she'd deliberately disregarded his instructions, naughty girl.

There was a pause, and she said, "I'm sorry. Did you say, Big Al?"

"I did, lady," Hawke said, in his punch-drunk boxer from Manchester voice. "It's my name. You got a problem with that?"

"Fine, uh . . . Big Al. But could I please leave him a message? This is Miss Tang calling. He knows who I am."

"Oh, yes, Miss Tang. Matter of fact, he mentioned you to me! Yes, he did! Had some very nice things to say about you, actually. Said you were quite attractive. I believe the word 'babe' crossed his lips. Oh! And some other things I'd best keep to myself, really—don't you see? We have to keep our secrets, don't we? Anyhoo. You have a message for him, sweetie? Fire away."

"Yes. Please tell his lordship that I have a lovely surprise for him. If he's not busy this morning, I could swing by and pick him up around eleven. His surprise is over at the marina, but please don't mention that. All right?"

"Of course not. So I should tell him to expect you around eleven?"

"Better make it eleven, sharp."

"Don't you worry your pretty little head about a thing. I'll be sure to let him know. Ta-ta for now!" he trilled gaily.

And hung up.

That wasn't very nice, Alex, he thought to himself. Pulling that girl's leg like that.

He had to smile, though. Happy to be back in a sunny mood in a sunny place in life where he didn't take every damn thing to heart. The recent loss of someone in his life he had cared for, for instance, or like living for one more day with the pain of his injuries.

He got up from the table and grabbed his encrypted mobile as he left the room.

He speed-dialed one of his most well-loved friends and comrade in arms.

"Stokely Jones," he heard that basso profundo voice in Miami say.

"Stoke, it's me."

"Alex?"

"Yes. Of course, Alex."

"If you say so. How are the Bahamas this time of year?"

"Swell. Wish you were here."

"Ditto. I'm all alone here at Casa Encantada. Fancha got herself a big fat two-week singing gig at the Palms Casino Resort in Vegas. Calling her show, 'Moon over Fancha's Miami.' Must be some joint, boss. You know how much the top suite out there goes for? A night?"

"No idea."

"Hope you're sitting down for this. One. Hundred. And. Forty. Large. Per. Night!"

"Hold those horses, Stoke. Are you serious?"

"Yessir."

"Stoke. Reason I called is I could use a little help down here. Dragon-fire Club is a very big place, a lot of ground for one man to cover. Crawling with heavily armed security forces, a couple of Chinese missile frigates patrolling night and day. Sounds like you're all by yourself for a while . . . so I thought maybe you could—"

"I'm on my way."

"How soon can you get packed?"

"I'm prepacked. I'm always prepacked for this kinda thing. You know that. You want me to bring along some firepower?"

"Right, I do. I anticipate trouble when the Tang brothers return here. I want you to call the boys in Costa Rica, Thunder and Lightning. Tell them I want them on standby effective immediately. Also, Harry Brock.

I've ordered my captain aboard *Blackhawke* to steam to Nassau Harbor immediately and put the crew on a war footing. My new pilot, Colin Falconer, just landed at Pindling Airport so my plane's already over in Nassau. I could ask Colin to gun it to Miami and probably touch down at Miami Jetstream Aviation around noon. That work?"

"You got it, boss. See you when I see you."

Hawke smiled and rang off. He was glad Stoke was coming. He was going to need help. Maybe the Costa Rica boys, too. But, maybe not. He'd have to see how things played out.

To get out of the fierce sun, Hawke was standing among the many potted hibiscus bushes beneath the porte cochere at the Hotel di Qing entrance. He heard a melodious toot and looked up to see the sleek black Bentley Spur piloted by the lovely Miss Tang pull up under the porte co-chere and roll to a stop. She got out, resplendent in her powder blue chauffeur's livery and mirror-polished riding boots, and pulled open the rear passenger door.

"Good morning," she said with a bright smile. "So glad you were free this morning!"

"Well, I could hardly say no when I heard you had some brilliant surprise for me. I'm quite keen on surprises, you see, always have been. Fair warning. I hate—no, I loathe—surprise parties. Throw one of those for me, and you'll live to regret it."

"Duly noted, sir. Hop in. We're headed over to the marina."

"Marina, eh? I do like the sound of that."

"You're going to like it even better when you see what I've left for you there."

"Don't tell me. You found me a motorcycle."

"Yes! You guessed it! It's an old one, I'm afraid. But the man at the garage told me it was quite a good one. It's a called a Vincent. I believe he said a Vincent Black Shadow."

"You're kidding me."

"I never kid."

And, as it turned out, she wasn't kidding at all.

CHAPTER 24

Dragonfire Club, the Bahamas
Present Day

Zhang climbed behind the wheel inside the deeply aromatic Bentley interior, turned her head round to smile at him, and said, "Well, we try, we try. How are you enjoying Dragonfire Club so far, Alex?"

"So far, it's very refreshing. Bermuda owns my heart, but she lacks for all this chic glamour and . . . What do the Americans say . . . ? Uh . . . they call it . . . pa—something or other . . . like pizza!"

"Pizzazz."

"Precisely so. Pizzazz, it is! Good for you."

"We get many Americans. Politicians and movie stars looking for a certain kind of . . . stimulus, shall we say? A taste for the exotic they cannot find at home."

"Fascinating," Hawke said, his mind somewhere else entirely.

"Perhaps I can arrange a complimentary evening for you? Over at the Castle?"

"Castle? I haven't seen any castles."

"You won't, not unless you know where to look. It's well hidden in the jungles high in the hills. This castle, the exact one that Charlemagne had built in 802 AD, was located in Italy on the border of Tuscany and Umbria. Completely disassembled on the site, stone by stone, and shipped here to Dragonfire. Completely rebuilt with modern plumbing and electrics. And including a ninth-century dungeon."

Hawke smiled. "Any self-respecting castle has to have a dungeon."

"There's an unmarked sandy lane that leads up to the Castle's moat. Only a privileged few ever get invited inside: an American president or two, a South American dictator, an international movie star or two. . . . You get the idea."

"Oh, yes. Indeed, I do. What kind of entertainments does this castle provide?"

"I'll leave that to your imagination. But all the islands are replete with rare amusements and gorgeous hostesses catering to every whim, every taste. One of the favorites is our dungeon, of course."

"'Of course'? Why of course?"

"The human mind has many dark passages, Lord Hawke, and many of them lead straight to the dungeon. All right, here we are at the marina. We just need to walk out to the end of this pier. Are you excited?"

"By your dungeon? Good Lord, no!"

"No, no! By your surprise? The one your partner, Big Al, told you about. I hope he gave you my message."

"My partner? Is that what you said? Really?"

"Oh, gosh, I don't know. I assumed as much."

"You assumed as much? You assumed I was gay? That's a first. What-ever makes you think that, pray tell?"

"Well, for starters, a man like you? Filthy rich, war hero, impossibly attractive, with that veddy, veddy posh title and British accent of yours? And not yet married? You're far too pretty to be taken seriously as straight, darling. Trust me on that one."

"This Big Al you spoke to. What did he sound like?"

"Oh, hell, I don't know. Your sister, maybe?"

Hawke laughed. "Tell me about my surprise. How about that? Yes, I'm terribly excited. If it floats, flies, or . . . well, whatever, I'm keen! But I thought the Black Shadow was my surprise."

"No, that was just a little gift. You're real surprise is moored right out there at the end of the pier. Have a look!"

Hawke raced ahead, really rather anxious to see what kind of marine equipment he'd have at his disposal, should the two brothers prove to be inhospitable at some point. He foresaw a time when he just might need to leave Dragonfire Bay in rather a dire hurry. He needn't have worried.

The surprise (which really wasn't one) was moored at the very end of the dock. It was a Wallytender 48, built in Forlì, Italy, forty-eight feet in length, just like the two aboard his own *Blackhawke*, but done up from stem to stern in an aggressive matte black finish, very stealthy, indeed, and perfect for his needs.

At her stern, two powerful Volvo Penta IPS 650HP engines, totaling thirteen hundred horsepower. She was capable of speeds nearing sixty miles per hour and could get him into, and out of, trouble without much bother.

"May I take her out for a little shakedown cruise?" he asked Miss Tang, whom he now thought of as perfect in the role of the despotic Mistress of Darkness down in her Dungeon of Despair.

"By all means, Alex," she said. "Go anywhere you wish, of course. The petrol tanks are all topped off. There's beer and frozen vodka and tomato juice in the galley as well as finger sandwiches for your midmorning snack."

"Jolly good!" Hawke said, picturing a big fat Bloody Mary as soon as he'd moored somewhere to get his bearings and catch a few golden rays to cover up what he called his fish-belly white "hospital tan."

"A brief cautionary note, sir," the woman said, bending down to tend to the fore and aft dock lines as well as to be better heard, not to mention giving him visual access to her voluminous womanly charms and somehow managing to simultaneously look like a very incautious woman indeed.

She said, "There are some areas throughout the islands clearly marked 'restricted.' Take them seriously, please. Those waters you may not enter, of course. Otherwise, you're free to fly. Have fun! Perhaps I'll see you later? I'm having a few friends over at my house for cocktails and supper this evening. Over on Snow Egret Bay. Locals. Perhaps you'd like to come?"

"I should be honored, madam. Delighted to come."

"It's a date. Cocktails at seven, dinner at eight." She turned to leave.

"Madam Zhang?" Hawke said "One question, dear girl. The name on the door to my suite in Chinese. *Jin*. What does it mean, that symbol?"

"Gold. He who owns the gold owns the world, Lord Hawke. That's my brother's motto."

"Couldn't agree more," Hawke said, and stepped nimbly aboard, planted himself at the helm, checked the fuel and batteries, turned the key, fired the matching outsized outboards, and waved good-bye to Miss Tang. Then he grinned boyishly and sped away from the docks and out into open water at full throttle. He put the wheel over, banked hard astarboard, and headed toward the other, and far more sinister, more interesting side of the central island, Black Dragon Bay.

He looked at his dive watch and felt a twinge. It had been a gift from Sigrid on their first Christmas together in Switzerland. A Rolex, a Sea-Dweller, of course, but one hell of a Rolex. He'd done the research. It had been created for saturation divers working at great depths, reliable and robust, but mainly to withstand incredible levels of water pressure. Earlier models, when used at extreme depths, had had shortcomings. After a number of deep dives at extreme depths for prolonged periods of time, the crystal of the Submariner was prone to pop out in the decompression chamber.

To remedy this, the Sea-Dweller had had a helium escape valve developed on the side of the case. Hawke's Double Red Sea-Dweller had been made for COMEX (*Compagnie Maritime D'Expertises*), a professional diving company based in Marseilles.

It was going on eleven thirty. Stokely was arriving at the airstrip at two. So the MI6 officer had just enough time to begin his initial foray into what he'd now come to suspect just might well be an enemy Chinese military installation right in America's backyard.

Hawke was racing flat out about two miles offshore, the throttles firewalled, bow angled up sharply, the Wally boat on plane, throwing off huge bow waves to either side. He saw passengers aboard oncoming sailing yachts gather at the rail to watch his approach. While Wally boats were quite the thing in the Med, they'd not yet reached significant numbers here in the Bahamas. He now had the hillside jungle with the bizarre white concrete structure in sight. He slowed way down and was altering course to intercept it when he noticed one of the big missile frigate patrol boats following in his wake and closing fast. No sirens or flashing blue and white lights, not yet anyway.

When they got within a thousand yards, sirens commenced to wail, horns started blaring, and flashing blue-and-white lights atop the bridge deck roof started flashing.

So sorry, chaps. Was I speeding?

He put the hammer down and soon the Chinese patrol boat was just a distant memory way back there at the end of his frothing, hissing wake. He wasn't ready to go public or cause any trouble at this juncture, not quite. He needed a helluva lot more information before doing that. He made a course correction that was a beeline to the mouth of the main harbor over at Nassau Town.

The big frigate would be tracking him on radar all the way over the horizon, figuring him for some rich tourist day-tripper over from Nassau, having a good look round Dragon Bay. Since he was headed to Paradise Island, anyway, he thought, why not tie up at Atlantis and have a little fun at the roulette tables or try his hand a bit of vignt-et-un, his favorite form of gambling?

At around one, he'd take his winnings or his lumps, jump back into the Wally, and race over to Pindling Airport to pick up pilot, copilot, and his old pal Stokely Jones Jr. Harry Brock was supposed to be aboard as well but events in Miami had delayed his departure. Hawke was not disappointed. He had always found the man exasperating and once had asked Stokely why that was.

Stoke had looked at him and said, "Ain't that difficult to understand, boss," he'd said. "Fact is, you just can't trust a man who was brought up inside a gated community in Orange County, California." Hawke, having no idea what he was talking about, had opted to take the sagacity of the advice at face value.

"Just think about it, boss. Give the man a little rope, is all I'm sayin,'" Stoke had said.

"Enough to hang himself with? Sound thinking." Hawke had smiled.

"You got to see the true inner cat before you go making up your mind. All that cocky attitude? Shit. Based on good old-fashioned insecurity. That's always been Milk's problem."

"'Milk's problem'? You've lost me now, Stoke."

"Milk's his nickname. Had it since he was in grade school. . . ."

"Dare I ask how he came by it?"

"He was in the third grade at the Newport Beach Middle School, got a score of two percent on his math exam. One of the kids started calling him 'Milk.' You know, like two percent milk. It stuck with him. All the way through college."

"That's actually funny. Milk. I like it. Mr. Two Percent. When do you suppose he'll show up?"

"Week or so, I suppose."

Hawke had booked rooms for all the men at the hotel. Good chance for some crew R & R and for his team to get down to the business at hand. He'd not seen Stoke in an age. Not since Switzerland, where they'd rescued the kidnapped Alexei from the clutches of that rapidly deteriorating ex friend of his, one Vladimir Putin by name.

Stoke lived the life of a Miami Beach pasha on his wife, Fancha's, island estate, Casa Que Canta, over on Key Biscayne. Since the tragic death of Stoke's sole employee—the little, one-armed Cuban sportfishing guide, the man so nice they named him twice, Sharkey Rodrigues-Rodrigues, to a shark attack down in the Florida Keys—Stoke had been hanging out in the company of Hawke's old nemesis, an American CIA field officer at the Miami station named Harry Brock. Hawke was interested to see whether or not any of Brock's inestimable number of bad habits had worn off on Stokely. His four-letter vocabulary, his fondness for marijuana, his skirt-chasing, his cocky attitude. . . .

Hawke shifted the chrome throttles back to idle speed, let the vessel settle into the seas, and stood at the helm to throw a coiled bowline to the eager young dockmaster at the Atlantis docks, then raced aft and shut down the twin Volvo Pentas while drifting in toward the dock with the current. Looking up at that amazing pink Atlantis architecture, he was beginning to get that old tingling sensation deep in his belly.

The one he got when he knew Lady Luck would be standing shoulder to shoulder beside him when he rolled those bones out across the green baize of the tables at the much overwrought and over-gilded Atlantis Casino!

Luck be a lady tonight!

CHAPTER 25

The English Channel
January 1942

D ay dawned with streaks red and gold racing one another out of the east trooping in formation across the wave tops of the English Channel. Burnished rays of the rising sun washed over the white cliffs of Dover and the emerald green downs in the south of England.

Commander Hawke, on this day of days, had risen hours earlier than the sun. He was a man determined to leave no nit unpicked, no dangling detail regarding today's mission left unreconsidered for perhaps the twentieth time. Exhausted by his efforts well into the wee small hours, he'd finally collapsed, fully clothed, atop his narrow iron bed.

The unit would be wheels up shortly and would tuck in behind the wake of a German air-raid heavy bomber squadron, en route home from attacks over the industrial north of England. For the German crews who'd survived the vicious battles in the skies to fight another day, it was all bombs away and homeward bound across the Channel to Berlin.

Once out over the Channel, Commander Hawke, when he'd at last located a Nazi minesweeper of sufficient size to have the coveted 3-rotor decoder, would peel away from the rear of the homeward bound German bomber formation. Then, once he'd fully committed to the minesweeper in question, he'd waggle his wings to ensure he had the German skipper's attention, cut his engines, and ditch the aircraft into the water in full view of every man aboard the big Nazi warship. And thus it was his most fervent hope to fake a convincing and believable emergency crash dive into the drink.

This would be his critical moment. The absolute time when perfection in every aspect of a decade of flying warplanes would be the difference between life and death for the pilot and his crew. There would be no retakes, no second chances. He'd stick the crash landing at the perfect angle of attack . . . or he would not.

In the dark of the predawn hours, Hawke, who'd be flying the German bomber on this mission, had calculated and recalculated the airship's precise angle of attack at the moment of impact with the surface of the water. This would be no gentle splashdown. It had to be at a very steep angle and look utterly realistic. He'd also gone over the figures for the precise amount of fuel to be left remaining in the wing tanks at the appointed moment of splashdown. The air-filled wing tanks would directly affect the floatation duration once his ship was down.

Lieutenant Stauffenberg, copilot and navigator, who'd be manning the cockpit's right-hand seat this morning, was at his side in the staff room in those predawn hours as the skipper and his five-man crew pored over every phase of the flight plans, studied printouts of mid-Channel weather systems, high-level aerial photos of all German naval activity in the area of engagement in the last five days, and pages upon pages of other critical details as the clock wound down to zero hour.

Stauffenberg, the young lieutenant born in Bavaria to an English mother and a German captain in the *Luftwaffe*, was a critical component of Hawke's crew. German was the boy's first language, and he was word-perfect in that language. He would be the team's leader once they'd been safely plucked from the wreckage and delivered on board the mine-sweeper.

Stauffenberg checked and double-checked everything the skipper asked him to look at and wasn't surprised to find that Commander Hawke was every bit as thorough about the details as he himself was. Hawke took charge of everyone and everything. He commanded a loyal team of battle-hardened commandos.

Even in the smallest moment, to see Hawke in control was inspiring.

He was the living epitome of the commanding officer you would willingly die for; he conveyed the kind of courage that convinced you that he would unhesitatingly give his life for you, too. He was one of the few men you would put your trust in absolutely.

And that is why his crew of volunteers was so upbeat and positive that morning, some of them whistling and jostling one another as the hour drew nigh. Even when it had been made painfully clear to them that the odds of surviving the initial crash that day were not even slightly in their favor.

But the crash was critical to the mission success of Hawke and the entire team. And on that fateful day, their unalloyed allegiance was to the man who would lead them into battle and, they believed, to the ultimate victory. He'd make admiral one day soon, the lieutenant was sure of it.

Today was just two short weeks to the day after Hawke had arrived at RAF Archbury and taken that very first flight out over the Channel in the purloined *Luftwaffe* bomber. Now Hawke and his elite crew would take to the skies once more. And this time, it was no practice run. He'd sent an encrypted telex to Winston at Bletchley Park. Operation Skyhook has officially commenced, the missive read. The stakes could not have been higher certainly. But Hawke was pleased to see that the morale of his crew, and their determination to succeed, was far higher by a factor of ten. Hawke had seen to maintaining that level every waking moment since his arrival here at RAF HQ.

"Time to go flying, Skipper," Ballantine, the tail gunner, said, getting to his feet and slipping into his leather flight jacket.

The air was clear but bitterly cold. "Weather?" Hawke asked him.

"Iffy here, sir. Limited visibility and ground fog out on the field. But it looks good out over the target area, sir. A bit of high cirrus scattered here and there at around fifteen thousand but no visibility problems at all. RAF camera footage from yesterday shows two German minelayers and one very large minesweeper patrolling mission target perimeters until late afternoon. The lads say we can expect those vessels back on station later on this morning."

"Good, good, Lieutenant," Hawke said, taking Stauffenberg aside and speaking in low tones. "Now, listen. I assume that you've spoken to the lads about me being last out the door once we hit the water? No matter what?"

"Yes, sir. They're not very happy about it, sir."

"Too bloody bad. This is going to be a very close thing today, no matter how much sugar and sunshine you and the crew manage to pour on it. And believe me when I tell you that I am not abandoning that bloody ship until every last one of our lads is safely outside the damn plane. Look here, if you don't think you can convince them to—"

Stauffenberg was immutable. He said, "Sir, I beg you to reconsider. The lads and I just don't think we can afford to lose our team leader when we get hauled aboard that Nazi minesweeper and—"

He was decisively interrupted by Hawke. "Listen carefully, Lieutenant. I'm safe in saying that I am the only one here at RAF HQ who is a charter member of Churchill's 'Ministry of Ungentlemanly Warfare'! Not you and your poor sods who had the nasty luck to get yourselves caught up in this little web of intrigue created by Uncle Winston and me. This is my own bloody idea and I'll damn well sink or swim with it. All by myself! Do I make myself perfectly clear, Lieutenant Stauffenberg?"

He snapped to, saluted, and said, "Crystal clear, sir, aye-aye!"

Commander Hawke smiled and said, "Well, then, by God, man, let's get the lads upstairs and find ourselves a big fat Nazi minesweeper!"

CHAPTER 26

The English Channel
January 1942

Nothing untoward happened on the flight out over the crystalline blue Channel to the target zone, save the appearance of the *Aleksandr Kolchak* at about twenty miles off Calais. Stauffenberg was flying the plane, and Hawke told him to descend and maintain three thousand so he could get a closer look at her. An intelligence officer had told him about a rogue Soviet Navy vessel cruising around off the coast of France. A PR stunt, the man said, the Russkies just showing the flag in the Channel.

She was a Soviet Kirov-class cruiser, all right, a six hundred footer with double-shaft-geared steam turbines and the usual array of guns and rows of antisub depth charges at her stern. She had nine six-inch B-38 guns mounted in Mark 5 triple turrets. And as Hawke watched, they were already slowly swinging around.

Hawke, riveted, watched as the barrels of the big guns were being elevated and converged on his bomber. Would the Soviets be crazy enough to shoot down a German bomber in the middle of a public relations ploy? Not bloody likely.

Hawke used the little Leica he'd bought in Zurich to snap photos of the Russian vessel, just in case anybody at Whitehall was curious as to what the hell she was doing twenty miles from the French coastline. Steady on they flew for another half hour, engines droning, climbing steadily back up to twenty thousand feet and a course bearing south-southwest.

They'd spotted the two German *Kriegsmarine* minelayers first, both busily depositing their deadly wares in the waters where channel markers outlined the approach to the busy harbor at German-occupied Le Havre. Ignoring them, the camo-colored *Luftwaffe* attack bomber lumbered, its four engines emitting a rather low and muted growl, for another twenty minutes.

That was when Hawke, growing tired and frustrated at gazing down at empty seas, first saw a sight he'd seen in his dreams a hundred times or more. A big fat German minesweeper cruising along at about fifteen knots on a northerly course that would most likely take her around Lizard Point, the southernmost tip of England, and then probably north to Norway.

"Skipper, I have radar contact. It's the large minesweeper, all right. Right on schedule.... I have visual contact at two miles' separation. Target heading three-twenty degrees, speed over water twelve knots...."

"Okay, Lieutenant, I'll take it from here," Hawke said, shedding altitude as he put the bomber's nose down sharply, easily reaching and exceeding crash-dive speeds.... He watched his airspeed indicator increasing rapidly and fought the natural inclination to pull her nose up and bleed speed.

"Could you put the revs up, please? Need to get her nose up just a bit...."

"Aye-aye, sir. At eleven thousand, descending through ten thousand, Skipper."

"I want visible smoke pouring from the portside engines descending through cloud cover at five thousand...."

"Portside smoke at five thousand ... aye."

"Steady, steady," the skipper said, a grim look of complete and utter determination on his face as they dropped into clean air. "Give me smoke at the outboard starboard engines. All you've got, Lieutenant!"

"Aye, Skipper!"

"Time to make the SOS call to Rescue Service."

Lieutnant Stauffenberg grabbed his mike and switched the wireless to an open mike, uncoded, then spoke in his word-perfect German. He said: "Mayday, Mayday, Mayday! We're on fire and going down! Attention, all ships in mid-Channel. We are a *Luftwaffe* Heinkel bomber in a crash dive at thirty-two-point-zero-one west latitude and ninety-eight-point-thirty-three north longitude. . . . Again, this is an SOS, repeat, SOS, and we require immediate assistance! *Kommen-sie, bitte, kommen-sie!*"

Hawke then pushed forward on the yoke, pushing the big airplane into a near vertical dive. All the while trailing thick black smoke from the engines. He dove down at an ever-steeper angle of attack. They were two nautical miles from the approaching German vessel, now increasing her speed to twenty knots. The water was coming up to meet them in a big hurry now. . . . Hawke throttled back, bleeding off a little speed. He wanted to land in the direct path of the German vessel, and he wanted to crash-dive his bomber at a surface point exactly two miles from the boat's current position.

"Good show, sir! You're right on the money, Skipper, on target flight path. . . . Crew's out on her decks now. . . . Lots of German eyes on us down there . . . All crew and officers gathering on her starboard rail for the big show, sir."

"Give me more smoke . . . all you've got. . . . Gentlemen, drop your cocks and grab your socks, boys. We're going in!" Hawke was determined to keep his eyes open until the exact moment of impact. But in those last few seconds, his instincts prevailed, and he squeezed his eyes shut.

It was like hitting a solid-brick wall in an automobile going two hundred miles an hour. The tip of the port wing caught a wave first, and the entire wing was ripped off, but they were still afloat. The nose was still intact as well as the battered fuselage. All the Perspex in the cockpit windows was immediately blown out. A flying dagger of synthetic glass caught his copilot in the forehead and a solid sheet of blood already covered his face.

He appeared to be unconscious, but when Hawke unbuckled his harness and pulled him to his feet, the man opened his eyes and smiled, wiping the blood from his eyes.

"Still alive, am I?" he said.

"It appears that way," Hawke said. Hawke got his arm around him and kicked open the cockpit door, and they started aft to help the crew. Assuming they were still alive.

"Hurry up, Lieutenant," Hawke added, feeling the nose of the plane slowly dipping about five degrees. Five more and seawater would flood the cockpit.

The bloody Nazi bomber had already begun to sink.

And suddenly, she was going down faster, picking up momentum. . . . If he was to get five men out of the doomed airplane alive, he was fast running out of time.

CHAPTER 27

Paradise Island, Nassau, the Bahamas
Present Day

She was sitting at the roulette table. Enwreathed in a haze of cigarette smoke and black silk, Dior, casually betting red and black, odds or evens. A beginner's game, a waste of time. Why play a game over which you had literally zero control? He knew her well enough to know that she had not an ounce of gambler's blood in her. She was only here for the scene. Or perhaps she was here on duty, just like he was. When they'd met, she had been one of the highest-ranking officers in the Chinese Secret Police. He had no reason to think she wasn't still.

He had to blink a few times to make sure he wasn't just seeing things. He caught a sidewise glimpse of those smoldering black eyes.

He was not seeing things. It was her, all right. Of all the women in the world. It was China Moon.

Hawke could not take his eyes off her. She was poised. A long white ivory cigarette holder in her right hand caught the eye. She had one elbow on the table with her arm and hand shaped like a swan's neck. As if she were modeling for a cigarette advertisement. Her hair was gleaming jet-black and hung luxuriously, framing a face that was, at the moment, all business.

Hawke could sense she possessed a steely determination to never lose. Yet here she was dressed in Dior, a black shantung dress with a tightly fitting bodice. It was the bodice that had him stifling old memories of the way they were back then. Her bosom was lush, and the bodice exaggerated her bust. It was classic China and classic haute couture. A dress that could easily have been made for her and, Alex Hawke reflected, most likely had been. A gold-and-diamond collier cravate with matching earrings put the final touches on the female masterpiece that had stolen his heart so long ago.

Hawke had first met China years earlier in the Côte d'Azur, in the south of France. In Cannes, in the wee small hours of the morning at the Petite Bar at the famous—some said infamous—Carlton Hotel one night so long ago. Her beauty and magnetism drew him to her like a moth to a flame. He'd eagerly embraced that flickering flame, and he had embraced her as well. Not to mention his soul and his body.

China, then the beloved daughter of one the most powerful military officers in Beijing. And China herself had been a very high-ranking officer and political assassin in the Chinese Secret Police. Little did Alex know that she'd been lying in wait at that bar for three hours, sure that he'd pass right by the Petite Bar on his way to the elevators. It was only much later that Hawke finally stumbled on the truth. China had been there in France on an important mission: to assassinate Lord Alexander Hawke, a master British spy who had gotten his name high on the death roster of the Secret Service's list of foreign espionage agents. He had meddled once too often in Chinese internal affairs of state. After a good deal of scintillating Pol Roger, and Hawke's arctic blue eyes looking deep into hers, she slowly adjusted her game plan. Course correction.

She didn't want to kill this beautiful man, at least not until after she'd bedded him.

Later, each enjoying a cigarette in his vast bed, in his suite overlooking the bustle of busy traffic along the wide and fashionable boulevard known as the Croisette and the blue sea beyond, she confessed her duplicity. She was still a foreign agent, and she'd been sent to kill him, she said. She leaned over and kissed him hard on the lips, her darting tongue probing, pleading. And then her grasping hand found him, and China Moon had announced that she'd changed her mind and damn the consequences in Beijing.

Alive and in the flesh, here she was again, always the one he'd loved and lost. Ten long years ago. The woman who'd seduced him that first night at the famous Carlton Hotel. He'd learned a hard lesson from her. If you really love a woman, it's a very bad idea to assassinate her father, no matter how much he may deserve it. They can't seem to get over it. But if ever one man had it coming, it was her infamous father, General Sun Yung Moon.

Sun Moon, the billionaire, was amassing a private army of paid legionnaires in China. His goal: a military insurrection in Beijing that would put him in power. He would then devote 80 percent of China's wealth to the military and declare war in Asia, first invading Japan after threatening to bomb all of Tokyo into oblivion. Hawke was the only man who could have stopped him. And, a world war.

Now his heartbreakingly beautiful daughter was sitting in a relaxed fashion, her two elbows on the banquette, alone, no other players. She smoked a fresh cigarette, glowing orange at the tip of a long holder in her right hand. He'd always loved the way she looked when in her casino mode.

Her bare arms, sculpted by incessant hours in strength training. The graceful curve of her neck, the glittering gold choker studded with diamonds, the largest of which was nestling in the cavern of her throat. Black silk seemed to flow around her hips. As always, she was wearing classic black satin stiletto heels decorated with rhinestones. She was concentrating on the careless little ball bouncing around on the roulette wheel.

He walked up behind her, pausing when he was in whispering distance and softly saying: "Diamonds on the soles of her shoes. . . ."

She turned in her chair and gazed up at him. "Alex Hawke," she said with the barest trace of a smile of surprise on her lips. "Of all the men in the world."

"China Moon," Hawke said, smiling at her. "I thought I'd never see you again."

"You almost didn't," she replied. "If I'd seen you first, I would have disappeared."

"China, please don't go down this road. I tried a thousand times to see you or talk with you on the phone. To explain what happened with your father and me. I knew my explanation might not lead to forgiveness, but at least I'd have the comfort of you knowing it was anything but cold-blooded murder. I took the only action I could take to prevent a holocaust in Asia and, after that, worldwide nuclear war."

She looked at him for a very long time before she spoke again. "You killed my father, you bastard. I lost my twin sister because of what you did to her in Hong Kong. Go away. I vowed to my father and my sister never to set eyes on you again."

"I had no choices that terrible day. China, please give me a chance to explain myself. I was doing my duty. I have sworn an oath to protect my country and its allies. That's what I do. I am honor bound to act on behalf of my country's best interests, just as you were when you were Chinese Secret Police."

"I still am."

"I should have guessed as much."

She looked at him, felt her heart cave an inch, sighed, and said, "Buy me a drink, will you?"

"Where are you staying? Here at Atlantis?"

"Good God, no. Tourist trap. Look at all these sun-toasted Americans. I'm staying at Dragonfire Club, of course. Vastly more elegant. But the casinos out there are all rigged so that the house wins. I come over to Nassau whenever the gambling bug bites me."

Hawke sat down in the chair next to her and took her hand. "Listen, China, I've an idea. I have to be over at Pindling Airport in half an hour. You may remember my good friend Stokely Jones Jr.? Rather a large chap, approximately the size of your average armoire."

"To say he is unforgettable is the very height of understatement. Funny, too. The man is a living monument to masculinity."

"Indeed, he is. I'm picking him up and ferrying him and my crew over to Black Dragon Bay. So, listen. I have a lovely little speedboat tied up here at the Atlantis dock. Why don't you join me aboard? We'll gather up the human armoire, that man mountain, and his luggage and speed you back to the Dragonfire Club. We can have our drink there, the three of us, up on the roof for the setting sun. Sound good to you?"

"Let's get out of here," she said, grinding her cigarette to ashes in the silver tray and getting gracefully to her feet.

China looked very Jackie O in her big black sunglasses and red and gold Hermès scarf. She was enjoying the ride, the wind, and the sudden sea spray coming over the bow. She was continually urging Hawke to ever-greater speeds. The forty-eight-foot Wally was an effortless speed demon, capable of thirty-eight knots or more. She said: "You always had exquisite taste in boats, automobiles, and airplanes, Alex. But this thing is amazing. What the hell is it?"

"Oh, it's a Wally boat. Most beautiful boats out there in my view."

"How long have you had her?"

"About two hours, actually."

"You just bought it?"

"No, actually, I just borrowed it. Someone named Tommy Tang is the actual owner."

China suddenly went deadly serious. She stared at Hawke for many long seconds before she said, "Hold on. Are you telling me that you're friends with Tommy Tang?"

"No. Never met the man. It was his sister who told me he wouldn't mind if I borrowed her for a few days."

"Zhang Tang? If you borrowed her?"

"Mmm. No, not Zhang. The boat, dear. I'll grant you, she may well be available for rent, but I've been given no indication of that so far."

"Beware that one, my friend. She's the big black spider in the deep dark web. A real-life Mata Hari. That bitch will be the death of you yet, Lord Hawke. Mark my words."

"I don't think that's exactly what she has in mind. . . ."

"Of course you don't. You're just a man. You don't think when it comes to women like that. You just yank at your zipper and have at it. So, tell me, lover boy, are you're actually staying at Dragonfire Club?"

"If that's all right with you, then, yes, that's where I'm staying."

"Did they give you one of the new seaside villas? Over on Foochow Island?"

"No. I've got the penthouse at the hotel."

"On that island, a penthouse is the outhouse, Alex. And by the way, has the Mistress of Dragonfire Club gotten her claws into you? Gotten you into her bed yet? Or better yet, down into her deep, dark dungeon of desire?"

"Neither. I've taken a vow of chastity since last we met."

"Very funny, Alex. How much do you know about these Tangs?"

"Not enough, apparently. I'm down here on business, you see. Government work for Her Majesty the Queen."

"The infamous missing prince, I assume? Prince Henry, Duke of Bedford, I believe his name is."

He looked at her, his blue eyes gone stone cold. "Listen to me. I know who you are. I've seen your files. I know all about some of the people who have been your victims."

"Hmm. I prefer to call them clients."

"I'm sure you do. But look here, China. This may all be a game to you. But a godson of mine, whose life I've sworn to protect, is missing and may well be dead. And that's no game, believe me."

"I'm sorry, Alex. Really I am."

"I've been sent down here to find Henry or find his kidnappers, perhaps his murderers. Right now I'd say you were one of the most likely suspects."

"Me?" China laughed. "Don't be absurd. Believe it or not, my business here has nothing at all to do with you, hard as it may be on your precious ego to accept."

Hawke smiled at the barb and throttled back, letting the big boat ghost toward the dock at a burbling idle speed. The wind was out of the west now, right on his starboard bow, in his favor. The light wind would push the Wally right up against the dock with no effort on his part.

"If you could possibly go forward and throw that coiled bowline to the dockmaster? And then the aft? That would be lovely."

China Moon was up on the bow with the coiled bowline to hand in a matter of seconds. As Hawke slowed the Wally and let the wind and tide gradually push her portside up against the wooden pilings of the dock, China tossed the line to the dockmaster perfectly. He caught it in midair and quickly secured the tender to the dock.

Hawke scanned the skies above, hoping to see his aircraft nearby. He wasn't disappointed. A large dark blue aircraft suddenly dropped through the thin cloud layer and banked sharply to starboard, lining up on final approach to the airport at Nassau.

"That's my new airplane on final. Rather good-looking, don't you think? The latest Gulfstream."

"Oh, please, spare me. Men and their toys. Don't be a bore, Alex. I don't get impressed anymore. So, that's what brings you to the Bahamas. The mysterious disappearance of Prince Henry. I actually had dinner a few times with the prince before he disappeared. Charming boy. We had fun."

Now she had Hawke's complete attention. "How much fun, exactly, China?"

"Mind your manners, Mr. Hawke. My private life is none of your affair."

"Everything regarding Prince Henry is my affair. Now, how much do you know about the prince's vanishing without a trace?"

"Nothing at all. Here's what I can tell you. One minute he was everywhere. The next minute he was nowhere."

"Oh, he's somewhere, China. And I'm going to find him and take him home, wherever he is. Bet on it."

Later, waiting out on the tarmac for Stoke to disembark from the dark blue Gulfstream, he remembered her words regarding the missing prince: One minute he was everywhere. The next minute he was nowhere.

As good a place the start as any, Hawke supposed. And here came his pal Stokely, with a big white smile on his face as wide as a mile. They embraced, pounding each other on the back and laughing happily at the idea of being in the game again, with the one person they could each rely on to bring the fight to the enemy and then some.

CHAPTER 28

The big bomber was an ungainly thing now, wallowing about in the sloppy seas like a wounded duck missing one wing. Hawke pushed his copilot through the opening ahead of him, into the darkened fuselage. It was dank and reeked of spilled petrol and oil. The sea was relentless, now beginning to flood the cockpit. The first thing Hawke saw upon emerging from the flight deck was three of his crewmen, all perhaps injured to one extent or another, down on the deck amidships, attending to the apparently seriously injured wireless operator. A jocular, freckled young lad from Cornwall, Airman Campbell.

The midships exit over the remaining wing was swung wide open to the air and water. It had already started to flow inside the fuselage. They were standing in about six inches of water even now. Swiftly, and without saying a word, Hawke placed his big hands on his copilot's broad shoulders and shoved him out into the sea. Stauffenberg hit the water with a splash, whirled around, and gave his skipper a big thumbs-up. He was okay. And he had understood that Commander Hawke had no time for argument right now. . . .

"What is it, lads?" Hawke said, rushing to the boys gathered around the injured crew member.

"It's Campbell, sir. The aft bulwark folded on impact and came down on his right leg just above the ankle. We can't pull him free, sir! Can't budge him an inch."

"Just go. Get out of here," the trapped boy croaked through his feverish pain. "Leave me to it, please, I beg you."

Another crewman spoke up. "We're not leaving him like this, sir. We can't!"

"Get out of the way, and let me see him for God's sake!" Hawke shouted. They parted and Hawke leaned in. He got a good look at the boy's perilous situation.

Hawke acted instinctively.

There was a medical cupboard here amidships full of emergency surgical supplies, including morphine, thank God, and equipment in the event of a crash. There was an item in there that might save the young aviator. Hawke pulled open the cabinet door and dragged the bulky leather bag off the shelf. Then he dropped to his knees next to the badly injured boy. He looked the three crewmen in the eye before he spoke, giving them a look that said he would brook no disagreement with his orders. They all saw the hacksaw in his hand and knew what was coming next.

Airman Campbell was about to lose his left foot to a surgeon who'd never performed surgery in his life.

"Gentlemen, I'm assuming you're all wearing your Sten guns and your sidearms attached to a webbed bandolier under your tunics. Is that correct?"

"Aye!" they said, checking. Each man had the standard issue for Royal Navy pilots. The Sten gun, a British submachine gun chambered in 9X19mm. And a snub-nosed Smith &Wesson .38 Spec. revolver.

"Ensure that all weapons are securely attached to your torso and free of any encumbrance when the time comes to first show our weapons in a hurry."

"We're good, sir!" one of the young crewmen assured him.

"I order you to abandon ship, gentlemen," Hawke shouted. "Now!"

"Aye-aye, sir!" they shouted. "Good luck, Campbell!" And one and all raced to the midships open port. Stauffenberg, the copilot, was bobbing about twenty feet from the doomed bomber, waiting for them and urging them to hurry before she went down.

Hawke, now on his knees beside the fallen airman, rolled up a fresh white surgical towel. "Open your mouth," he told the boy before placing the towel between his teeth.

"Please help me, sir! I don't want to die. . . ."

"You're not going to, sonny boy. But there's going to be some pain involved. I want you to bite down on that towel as hard as you possibly can when I tell you to. Understood?"

"Aye, sir." Campbell shivered, already in horrible pain. The sloshing water inside was now almost ten inches deep and rising fast. Hawke did what he had to do.

"Bite down, son! Now!"

Hawke steadied the boy's leg with his left hand and began to saw relentlessly at his shinbone with his right hand. The tibia, Hawke knew from training, was the strongest bone in the leg. And the hardest to sever.

Suddenly, the bomber's nose dropped precipitously. She was going down, and so were the two remaining crewmen.

"Oh, God! Oh, God!" the boy screamed as the jagged teeth of the saw edge began to cut away at his leg, going through both flesh and bone.

Hawke, trying to pretend he wasn't affected by the smells and sounds of his saw grinding through bone, said, "You're going to be all right, Campbell. Just hold that thought! Bear with me. It'll be over in a few seconds."

The young man was having none of it, pain blinding him to everything else. "Somebody, help me! Please! I can't take it! I can't take it!"

Hawke, sawing with as much strength and speed as he could muster, went at the task now with a vengeance. The boy passed out, which helped. Even though it was an eternity, two minutes later, the deed was done. The foot was finally separated from the tibia, or shank bone. Hawke took the towel from the boy's mouth and bound it tightly around the stump of the grievously wounded leg. He knew it wouldn't help much, but it was all he had, and it was better than nothing.

As he got to his feet, something—he was not sure what—made him pick up the bloody severed foot and, with reverence, place it inside his flight jacket. It seemed an obscenity for this German ship to go down with even a part of this brave young English warrior still aboard.

Water had now risen so that the boy's head was completely submerged. He was unconsciously swallowing gulps of seawater. Seconds counted now. They had to get out or go down . . . get out or go down . . . get out or go down.

He bent down and grabbed Campbell's wrists and pulled and yanked at his torso for all he was worth. A minute later, the boy was finally freed from the crushed bulkhead. He got an arm underneath him and got him upright. He headed toward the opening in the fuselage, sloshing through water now up to his knees. The water was icy cold, and he knew, if he'd miscalculated, and help was not soon on its way, they'd all be dead of hypothermia in less than half an hour. They'd live just long enough to die.

Moments later, they were all in the bitterly cold water, life jackets inflated. About two hundred yards away, his bomber (amazing that he thought of the German airship that way) was in her death throes. All the air in her remaining wing and fuselage was gone, replaced by the unrelenting surge of seawater.

As the crew all watched, the tail of the Heinkel, emblazoned with a large red swastika, suddenly rose up from the sea and into the sky, just like the bow of *Titanic* had done, and she silently slipped beneath the waves, headed for her final resting place on the bottom. Operation Skyhook was now in full swing. No deaths and only one casualty.

And now for the hard part, Hawke thought to himself.

CHAPTER 29

Sevenoaks Plantation, Virginia
January 1942

The Chinese ambassador downed the balance of the amber whiskey in his crystal tumbler and then, suddenly and inexplicably rising to his feet, heaved it as hard as he could into the fireplace in frustration. Flints of gleaming crystal sprayed everywhere, but the fire screen helped him avoid getting sliced to ribbons.

It was cold as hell in this goddamn house.

He'd had a fire going in practically every room downstairs all day long, and still the house was cold as a crypt. He sighed and padded over to the wide-open hearth. Choosing the largest pine log he could find, he heaved it onto the conflagration. Then another for good measure.

"Damn it to hell," he shouted into the empty library. It had been pissing rain or sleeting or snowing all bloody weekend. He had been like a caged Tiger, padding about his gargantuan lair like a wounded animal who'd just lost his mate. And in a way, that was exactly what had happened.

If he was not quite in love, he was certainly in lust, and he had it bad. If that weren't bad enough, it was a love tainted with another, much-less-desirable emotion.

Guilt.

His girl had called early that morning from the comfort of her warm bed at her parents' house not a mile away from Sevenoaks. She was hungry, she said, hungry for his touch, for the smell of him, for the taste of him. She would go insane if she couldn't share his bed on this, what promised to be the coldest night in years. Her parents were driving her mad, all of them cooped up in the big farmhouse on the lake because of the fucking weather. How long could she pretend interest in the jigsaw puzzle, pieces of which were scattered all over the kitchen table? A picture of the goddamn Champs-Élysées? I mean, really, who bloody cared? Someone at Farmington had told her a good one, though. "Question: Why did the French plant trees all along both sides of the Champs-Élysées? Answer: So the conquering Nazis could walk in the shade."

It was just a street, for God's sake. Seen it once, you've seen it a million times. Anyway, back to her miserable parents. It was her mother, really, who was driving her up the walls. Daddy was much more sanguine about her behavior. Mummy kept telling her nothing good could come of her well-publicized affair with the Chinese ambassador. Insisting that she must break it off. Stay away from him. "He's a climber, darling. What Daddy and I used to refer to as a 'social alpinist.' He's just using you as a girl on the side for as long as he can until his best friend and—may I remind you, your bloody fiancé—returns home from England."

"Oh, get off your high horse, Mummy dearest. We both know why you really want me to save myself for Hawke."

"We do? I don't. Pray tell, darling."

"Because, and I dare you to deny this, because he's got that fancy bloody title, that's why. Because his name is Lord Blackie Hawke! Yes! And because nothing, oh, nothing on this big green planet would elevate you into that rarefied air that you so fervently seek to breathe more than having an oh-so-grand daughter named Lady Winfield Hawke!"

"How dare you! How dare you accuse me of such base behavior? I ought to slap your face, young woman."

"Go ahead. No? Well, let me tell you something else, Mumsie, old girl. You also lie awake nights dreaming about a grandson or a granddaughter with a fucking English title! Look at you! You're blushing because you know it's all true! Every word! Christ in a barrel, I'm sure you've already got Queen Elizabeth and the Duke of Edinburgh on the guest list for the wedding at the Chevy Chase Club!"

"How you despise me! Go! Get out of my sight, damn you!"

"With pleasure. I'm going out tonight. Don't wait up." So saying, she dashed out of the kitchen and bounded up the staircase to her room on the third floor. She couldn't last another second without hearing his voice. Or with hearing another word out of her mother.

The ambassador wandered over to the drinks table, looking for some-thing, anything, to ease his troubled mind. It wasn't just this girl driving him mad with desire. Hell, he knew that. Oh, no. That wasn't the real problem. It was the guilt. What had Hawke said to him that last day standing at the bar at the Cosmos Club?

"Look after her while I'm gone, will you, buddy? She can get a little crazy sometimes, as you know. I don't want her getting into any trouble while I'm gone. . . . Besides, we secretly got engaged last weekend up in Kennebunkport."

Or maybe it was Hyannis Port. Something Republican like that.

Hawke hadn't been gone long when she'd first shown up unannounced at his doorstep at midnight one snowy night. A Friday or a Saturday when he was home alone out in the country.

At the deep tolling of the door chimes down in the front hall, he raced down the stairs and yanked open his front door. He narrowly avoided fainting. She was wearing a full-length mink, a rich dark brown affair with a cowl collar pulled up and framing her face and her honeyed curls. Her plump cheeks had been tinted pink by the frigid air, the perfect face amid a swirl of whirling snowflakes, her bright eyes beaming up at him, daring him to refuse her entry on this frigid night.

"I was in the neighborhood, kind sir," she said in her best Scarlett O'Hara drawl as she brushed by him and into the center of the black-and-white-checkered entrance hall.

"Your timing is perfect, darling. I was just about to commit suicide."

"Don't be silly! Aren't you going to take a girl's coat, Mr. Ambassador? I do declare I believe you've forgotten your manners, Captain Butler."

He laughed and moved toward her.

"Let me help you," she said. She stepped out of her shoes and, shrugging her shoulders and kicking at her L.L.Beans, let the long mink coat fall to puddle around her pretty little white feet.

He took a breath and paused in midstride, staring at her.

She was carrying an open bottle of Pol Roger in her right hand and wearing nothing but a smile. She looked down at her magnificent bosom and said, "Is it chilly in here, or is it just you, Mr. Ambassador? My goodness, everybody's all puckered up!"

And so it had begun.

And so it continued.

And so one day it would end.

The following week, on the Friday, they'd had their first row. It wasn't his fault really.

"I need you, baby. I need you real bad," she said that afternoon on the phone, her voice a smoky blend of passion, cigarettes, and strong spirits. She was drinking again, and there didn't seem to be a damn thing he could do about it.

"Six o'clock tonight," he told her, his own voice suddenly husky and freighted with lust. His love was sodden with the want of her. He was besotted by the touch of her hand, the hot press of her lips. He went directly upstairs and took a steaming-hot shower, dressed in his best silk pajamas and his maroon paisley robe from Charvet in Paris.

They'd mutually agreed it would be ill-advised for them to be seen together in Washington society. They would limit their weekly trysts to his house in the country, where they could come and go under the radar. It was his new habit to entertain her in his pj's. It made him more relaxed and added to the style he wished to employ at his new country home. He thought of it as "relaxed elegance yet still elegant."

Around five that evening, keen with anticipation of her imminent arrival, he'd gone down to the kitchen to check on dinner with the cook and make sure there was fresh ice in the silver bucket on the drinks table in the library. He fixed himself a Rob Roy and collapsed into his favorite wine red leather club chair beside the roaring fire.

He was sipping his delicious concoction when, five minutes later, Hamish, his English butler, floated in on a cloud of unflappable serenity. Hamish, of the stiff upper lip and the crisp white collars and the formidable brain power.

Now Hamish was telling him that there was a call for him in his study.

"Who is it, Hamish? Miss Woolworth?"

"Indeed not, sir. It is, in fact, your father who's asking for you."

"Don't be ridiculous. My father is half a world away in China. It's the middle of the night there. Or . . . day, or something!"

"I beg to disagree, Mr. Ambassador. He is calling from town. He's down at the railroad station."

"Good Lord. How extraordinary. All right, please tell him I'll be right there. . . ."

"As you wish, sir." Hamish withdrew.

"Hullo?" Tiger said, half expecting it to be Winnie pulling some kind of a prank or just calling about something or other.

It wasn't.

It really was his father calling from the local train station.

"Hello, son. Surprise, surprise!"

"Pop? Is that really you? Where are you?"

"Just pulled into the station. My plan was to take a taxi to your house and surprise you. But due to the snowstorm, nothing's moving on the roads out here. Can you come pick me up?"

"Wow, Pop, this is a surprise. Yes. Yes, of course, I can come fetch you. It's just that—"

"Just that what?" his father said, irritation already coloring his voice. He was not a man who took being dismissed lightly.

"Nothing, Dad. Nothing. I'll tell you when I see you. Be there in two shakes of a lamb's tail, as they say."

"Good boy. I'll be standing under that lantern by the station house door. I'm freezing my nuts off out here, for God's sake!"

Tiger downed the balance of his cocktail and picked up the receiver and dialed Winnie's number. This was not going to be fun. She picked up on the first ring.

"Hullo?"

"Darling, it's me. I'm so awfully sorry, but I'm afraid we're going to have to reschedule. Something's come up."

"Something like what?" she asked, her voice already ringing with indignation and suspicion.

"An unexpected guest has shown up. There's really nothing I can do and—"

"Who is it? Some cheap, tawdry little trick you keep on the side?"

"That's grossly unfair. And offensive, I might add."

"Oh, *you're* the one who's offended. I get it. Not me."

"It's my father, for Crissakes, baby. Come all the way from China, apparently. Had no earthly idea he was coming. What more can I tell you?"

Silence.

"All right, then. Call me when you get a free moment."

Click.

"Fuck!" he muttered under his breath. What the hell could the old man want, anyway?

What the old boy wanted was a lot, as it turned out. It was a nightmare, actually.

A bad dream with a tragic ending as it turned out.

CHAPTER 30

The English Channel
January 1942

Commander Hawke and his crew had already been bobbing about in the icy water for a good ten minutes. Hawke's current favorite worry for his crew was hypothermia. Next to him in the frigid water, Stauffenberg held young Campbell, still unconscious, between them, keeping his chin up out of the water. The crew was huddled around the two officers in order to better stay in communication with one another. Hawke also had a whistle in case of unanticipated foggy conditions at splashdown, or to use as a call to action once aboard their objective.

The chill had already begun to seep inside them, reaching for their bones. The worn flannel German uniforms were no match for these temperatures. Hawke had just begun to fear that, somehow, he'd miscalculated the time between ditching, the onset of hypothermia, and the big Nazi *Kriegsmarine* minesweeper coming to their rescue.

But then he was much heartened to hear Lieutanant Stauffenberg shout with joy: "Look, sir. There's a launch from the minesweeper headed this way at very high speed, sir!"

"Where away, Lieutenant?" Hawke said, using an antiquated Royal Navy expression, meaning "What compass point are you referring to?"

"Just there, sir," Stauffenberg said, pointing in the fast-moving launch's direction, out of the south.

Hawke raised a hand to his forehead to shade his eyes from the brilliant play of sunlight dancing on the surface of the water. The big gray launch was up on plane, throwing off a huge bow wave to both sides of the hull. Hawke took joy in the fact that she was headed straight to the position where the Heinkel had gone down.

"By God, you're right. Here they come, all right. Are you men ready?"

"Aye, sir!" the other three crewmen said in unison.

"I've got just time enough for a final recap of key points of our actions once in German hands. Remember this: Your answer to any direct question from a German officer or crew member is strictly limited to the use of the following five German words. *Bitte* or please. *Nicht verstehen* or I don't understand. Also, *danke* or thank you. *Nein* or no. *Ja* or yes. Understood? Also, memorize this one catchphrase. Use it whenever you're confronted by a crew member with a direct question. You say, *Alles gut, alles gut!* It's not a perfect answer, but it beats the hell out of a stupid blank stare."

"Aye-aye!"

"That's it, then, men. Once we're safely aboard that minesweeper, you will take all your behavioral cues from me or Lieutenant Stauffenberg. Do what we do, not what we say. If we head aft, you head aft. If we stand on our heads, you stand on your heads. We two will do *all* of the verbal interactions with the Germans."

"Aye-aye, Skipper."

"Final reminder: When we've been aboard the minesweeper for exactly one hour, long enough for them to get comfortable with us and not on their guard, we split up, casually, so as not to draw attention to our movement. I'll take Colin Hood with me to the bow. Lieutenant Stauffenberg will station himself at the stern rail. Wallace and Graebner will join up with him there.

"Good. Now, at precisely ten minutes after the hour, one way or another, I plan to be on the bridge. I will take out Donitz and whoever else is up there with him. I will sound some kind of an alarm or other throughout the ship. Anything to give us the cover of chaos. When you hear it, you immediately remove your weapons and begin approaching the Germans from behind, preferably using your blade to drop them silently. Yes? 'Stealth' is the operative word here. Take as many down silently as you possibly can. When they start shooting at us, grab your Sten gun from under your tunic and return fire at any and all remaining enemy. They will scatter. You will follow. We will have earned the advantage of surprise, and very few of them will be armed. You keep up the automatic fire until the last of the crew is dead or neutralized.

"At that point, young Hood and I will start moving aft from the bow, taking out Germans as silently and as quickly as we can, then make our way up to the bridge. Stauffenberg and you two men will likewise move forward from the stern, killing as many as you can, and thus creating a pincer movement amidships.

"When it's clear that the very last combatant is nullified, we'll hold a service for the brave sailors. I'll say a few words and then we will commit them to the deep. I will assume command of the vessel and steer a direct course for Plymouth harbor, full speed ahead. All of our land, sea, and air forces have been alerted to expect us, granting safe passage to a heavy German minesweeper approaching Plymouth harbor from out of the south, flying a Union Jack from her main staff."

He pulled the folded flag from inside his flight jacket and showed it to the men.

Hawke smiled at that and earned himself a cheer from his crew.

"I want to see lots of those smiles when the launch arrives here. These are your comrades, remember, and they've come to save you from a watery grave. Any questions? No. That's good. You've got your orders. All of England will recognize and remember what we do here this day. Let's not let them down, shall we? My uncle, Winston Churchill, would be terribly annoyed with me."

"On to victory then, sir!" one of the men said, and the others joined with the victory cry.

"Good on you. Lieutenant, first order of business, as soon as we're aboard the primary target, is to inform the German officers that your crewman is badly wounded, has lost his foot, and needs a tourniquet and the attention of the ship's surgeon in sick bay immediately. Understood?"

"Of course, sir."

"All right, lads," Hawke said, "here they come. Keep your heads down, and don't give away a thing. If you've got any prayers, right now might be a particularly good time to use them."

One by one, the British boys, wolves in wolves' clothing, were pulled up from the freezing sea and up over the gunwales of the German *Schnellboot*, a fast launch of about fifty tons and equipped with a twenty-millimeter gun forward and two torpedoes.

Hawke, who'd identified himself as the pilot of the downed bomber, Kapitän Ludwig von Reuter, was first aboard the launch. He stood at the rail and assisted the German crewmen who were grabbing his near frozen men by the wrists and hauling them aboard.

Next up was Stauffenberg, called Fritz by *das Kapitän*, who had already charmed his captors and was laughing over something the German sailor helping him had said about the sad state of his uniform. So far, so good, Hawke thought to himself. Just keep doing what you're doing, Fritzy, old boy.

Ten minutes later, they were aboard the minesweeper, and they had all been taken belowdecks for coffee and bowls of steaming potato and leek soup doled out by the ship's cook. Hawke ate his rapidly and went back for seconds. He hadn't even realized he was hungry, but the soup was seasoned with fresh chives and by far the most delicious soup he'd ever tasted. He watched his boys, shivering with frostbite and keeping their heads down, saying nothing, happy to be alive, wrapped in woolen blankets and being treated like heroes.

Which, unbeknownst to their German hosts, they actually were, with the distinction that they were playing for the opposing team! Or, at any rate, soon would be, in England, anyway.

"Mein Kapitän?" he heard a young German officer with a shock of blond hair and a ready smile say as he approached the table where Hawke and Stauffenberg were quietly gathering their strength for the coming battle. Just in case anyone was listening, they confined their German conversation to a discussion of their great good fortune in going down within sight of the good ship *Tannenberg* and its Michelin-star cook.

"Bitte schoen, mein Herr," a young sailor said to Hawke.

"Jawohl? Yes?" Hawke said to the boy in word-perfect German. *"Was bekommen Sie? Haben Sie eine Wunsch?* What will you have? Do you have a wish?"

"Only that Captain Donitz would like a word with you, sir. I'm to bring you up to the bridge, if you'd be so kind, sir."

"Of course!" Hawke said, getting to his feet. "Lead on. I'm right behind you." Thinking this was a great opportunity to suss out the situation up on the bridge, he gave Stauffenberg a concealed look that said, "Nothing to worry about, mate. I'm fine here."

Hawke could feel the vibrations of the *Tannenberg's* massive engines below, coming up through the soles of his boot as he climbed the steep steel steps up to the bridge. He smiled at his sudden good fortune. Besides Donitz, there were only two other duty officers. They would be getting the ship under way again shortly, he realized, all their attention taken by tricky channel navigation. Also, keeping a weather eye out for British Spitfires, a squadron having been notified the big German minesweeper was conducting operations in mid-Channel.

"Willkommen an bord. Welcome aboard, Captain!" the fabled seaman said in German. "I am Donitz, forever after heralded as your savior."

Hawke snapped to attention, saluted, then smiled, and replied in his best boarding-school German accent.

"Ich bin immer in Enrer Schuld, mein Herr! I am forever in your debt, sir!" he said.

The captain said, "I've just heard from my ship's surgeon. The amputee is stabilized, his wound has been dealt with, and he has been given morphine for the pain and a mild sedative. He is resting comfortably."

"Deeply appreciated, sir!"

"Do you want for anything, Captain? Or your crew?"

"No, sir. We've been watered and fed the most delicious potato soup outside the Reich, sir. *Danke, danke.*"

"Well," Donitz said, "I won't keep you. I just wanted to introduce myself and say hello. I've got a ship to run now. Perhaps you'll dine at my table this evening?"

"Sehr gut!" Very well.

The bridge was just what Hawke had expected of a tightly run ship such as Donitz had a reputation for, and out of the corner of his eye he immediately saw what he was looking for.

In the unfrosted windows of the small comms room, he saw an empty chair that meant the radio operator was not on duty.

He also saw, to his great delight, what he instantly recognized as the much-vaunted cypher machine, the 3-rotor *Kriegsmarine* encoder. Carefully arranged on a bulkhead shelf above the radio and wireless equipment was a neatly ordered set of codebooks bound in red leather.

The lever he sought, also painted bright red, was on the portside of the bridge, within easy access of any man on the bridge. In order to exit the bridge deck, he had to walk right past it. . . .

"Bis diese abend! See you this evening, then, Captain!" he said cheerily, but the captain did not turn around. He was bent over a chart table, poring over a map of the channel with his navigator. Oblivious to all else.

"Auf Wiedersehen." Hawke smiled at the handsome young officer as he passed. He kept right on going, praying that Stauffenberg and his crew would recognize his actions for what they were—a perfect way to wreak havoc and cause confusion on board.

He paused at the top of the steps, pulled his sidearm from its holster under his tunic, turned to face the Germans with their backs to him, using binoculars to search for more targets. He raised the snub-nosed revolver and took dead aim. He then dropped them quickly, one by one, to the deck with nice clean head shots.

He reached for the bright red handle and yanked it down hard. Immediately, sirens and horns everywhere started their shrill wail. A prerecorded voiced screamed on the ship's PA system:

ACHTUNG! ACHTUNG! *BATTLE STATIONS!*
MAN YOUR BATTLE STATIONS!

The battle *für das Boot, für das Tannenberg* had just begun in earnest.

CHAPTER 31

Sevenoaks Plantation, Virginia
January 1942

The evening meteorologist on the NBC forecast over the wireless had predicted blizzard conditions in the District of Columbia and the northeastern parts of Virginia. For once, they'd gotten it right. American meteorologists, Tiger had noted, only got it right about 30 percent of the time. But apparently that was good enough for Americans, for he'd never heard a single complaint about the latest botched forecast.

The twisty two-lane country road leading down the side of the mountain to the tiny village of Warrenton, Virginia, was something akin to a roller coaster. You didn't have to steer; you just had to hold on to your hat. In the time that Tiger had been here, two parallel tire tracks had been etched deep into the hard-packed snow. There they were, day after day, waiting to guide you safely down. So all the driver had to do was get his wheels aligned in the proper track, put the vehicle in neutral, take his foot off the brakes, and let 'er roll on down. Rather like bobsledding, he'd thought when first he'd tried it.

It was snowing like hell when the ambassador made the trek from the kitchen door down the hill to the garages. His father was not notorious for his patience, and the son had witnessed his wrath on a personal basis far more times than he cared to admit. He tried to take his father's surprise visit in stride, but to be honest, he was having a hard go of it.

He'd finally managed to escape the old boy's orbit when he happily relocated to Washington. But he could remember times at Cambridge, and later at Oxford, hell, even back during his heady Etonian days, when the crusty old son of a bitch had shown up at the most inopportune times. Not that, for Tiger, any particular time was opportune. He had read in some psychiatric journal somewhere that powerful fathers did not relish sons who proceeded to achieve even greater measures of success at earlier ages than their sires had.

They let you know this, through your formative years, by continuing to damn you with faint praise. Or by no praise at all, no matter how much it might have been warranted. And Tiger could not recall a single time when, at some celebration or other, his father had said he was proud of Tiger's latest achievement. Nor had he ever heard his father utter those three little words that carry such weight: "I," "love," and "you."

Some of these fathers, suddenly finding themselves eclipsed by the shining glory of their offspring, would resort to malevolence or, in extremis, violence.

Tiger had been sent to Washington by the government of Chiang Kai-shek. But Chiang's was a weak government, riven by dissension and riddled with corruption. The strongest force in Tiger's life was, by far, his responsibility to his ancestors and his family, especially his father.

The Tang crime family had been involved with illicit and criminal activities for centuries. Tiger was the celebrated black sheep of the family specifically because he was the only good egg they'd laid in centuries.

It was, to be sure, a love-hate relationship he had with his father. True, his father had never beaten him, per se, but he had done worse. His father's method, when angered sufficiently, was to slap his son's face hard enough to whip his head around. Slapping, as any man will tell you, is the greatest insult that one man can bestow upon another—to wit, the object of your disaffection. The grossest of insults in a man's world, to be sure.

Just recalling that one thought made Tiger curse when he clambered behind the wheel of the big yellow Rolls-Royce, turned the ignition switch, and depressed the starter button down by his left foot. The engine failed to turn over out in this cold. Once, twice, three times. If that bastard tried to replay old behavior, Tiger was prepared to give him a little refresher course in the dark arts of kung fu before he sent him packing.

Tiger sat back, took a deep breath, and tried to get this anger under control. Obviously, he didn't want to hurt the old boy, but he'd need to watch himself. It was near zero out tonight in the garages, and he reached to turn the key again with little expectation that the old girl would fire.

A pause, then a muffled explosion as the massive sixteen-cylinder engine roared to life. Thank God. He engaged first gear and made his way carefully down the long winding drive to the road. It was minimum visibility now, and he was glad when he pulled out onto the state road and slotted the big Rolls into the tracks.

All that was required of him, all the way to the bottom, was a little judicious braking every now and then. The bright white eye of the moon was hanging high in the sky and gave a lustrous feel to the whole valley. The experience of gliding silently down through the trees, over the many small bridges, and past waterfalls silvered by moonlight was exquisitely pleasant. He found his mood much improved by the time he pulled up in front of the stationmaster's door and hopped out to help his father with his luggage.

"This is quite a car you've got yourself, son," the old bald-headed gentleman with the gold-rimmed glasses said as soon as he was comfortably seated with a woolen lap robe for warmth. "A Rolls-Royce, is it not?"

"It is, Pop! I get lots of compliments on it. She's a mint-condition Rolls-Royce Phantom Three."

His father favored him with narrowed eyes that expressed his holier-than-thou disapproval. His father said, "Upon what meat doth this our Caesar feed that he is grown so great?"

Tiger's eyes shone with righteous indignation at this Sheakespearean insult.

"This is the United States, old man. We prefer to eat a roast joint of lamb, or filet mignon, or roast prime rib of beef. We also enjoy Beluga caviar with a nice glass of Pol Roger."

He waited for a reply but got none, nor an expression of his approval. Typical.

He couldn't help himself. He looked over at the old man and said, "All this leather around you? It is not English, Pop. I assure you. It's rich Cordoban leather, from the the Andalusia region of Spain."

He waited once more in vain.

"Say something, for Crissakes!"

No reply.

"Sorry you had to come all the way to town in this weather, Tiger. I meant to take a taxi up to the house and surprise you."

"Dad, it's nothing. I'm so glad to see you. You look well. What brings you to Washington?"

"If you mean by that, did I come all this way just to see you? Certainly not. The generalissimo has entrusted me with a very private message he wishes delivered in person to Roosevelt."

"Exciting. I've grown rather close to the president over the last month. Spend weekends out at his country place on the Hudson River. That sort of thing. He's invited me to go on a fishing trip off the coast of New England aboard the presidential yacht. *Potomac*, by name."

"Has he, now?" The words dripped with acid as if Tiger's deepening relationship with Roosevelt was beneath the patriarch's comment.

Tiger bit his tongue and tried to remain above the fray. He said, "Oh, never mind. You don't give a damn, I know. How long are you planning to stay, anyway? An hour? Two?"

"Oh, I'm not staying the night. I'm just having dinner and catching a late train back to Union Station. If that's all right with you, of course."

"Of course," Tiger muttered. Much more than all right.

They rode in silence the rest of the way up the mountain, each man alone with his thoughts.

Tiger, his anger simmering on a low boil, felt like stopping the car and shoving the old man out into the bloody snow. Let him freeze to death. No one would miss him. In America, he was a nobody. He was just another petitioner diplomat, looking for a handout from Roosevelt.

Tiger vowed not to say one more word to him unless he was asked a question. The old bastard could hitchhike back to the station if he wanted to leave, by God.

Tiger was finally done with this conceited, obnoxious, trumped-up old fool. There was no more room for him in Tiger's life, not from this day forward. Never had been really.

He was just so much dust in the wind.

Always had been.

Had he had his Nambo handy, he might as well have shot the son of a bitch on the spot!

CHAPTER 32

Sevenoaks Plantation, Virginia
January 1942

The long yellow Rolls-Royce glided up under the snow-covered porte cochere. The white stuff was still coming down, snowing harder than ever if that were possible. Hamish was standing at the ready, practically at attention. He came down the steps, pulled open the passenger door, and helped Tiger's aging father climb out of the car. Hamish, ever the consummate professional, said: "Mind these steps, sir. They are glazed with thick black ice."

Hamish took the old fellow's elbow and guided him safely to the top without saying a word. At the door he took Tiger's father's overcoat, offering a comment to the gent regarding the quality of the navy cashmere.

Tiger then drove down the hill to the garages, a huge sense of relief from just getting some room between the two of them for a few moments. Climbing on foot back up the snowy hill, he took his time. He was in no rush to be honored by his father's presence any further than the minimum. He'd get through the dinner somehow, with a little help from a couple of whiskies and a very nice 1933 vintage Château Margaux.

"Lovely chap, your father," Hamish said, smiling when he saw the master of the house coming up the snowy walkway.

"You're kidding, right, Hamish? I mean, really."

"Tough old bird, I meant to say, sir. Wouldn't want to rattle his cage if I were you, sir."

"Better. He flits from one encounter to another, collecting poison the way bees collect honey. Tell Cook to speed this dinner along, will you? I want my father fed and out the door as soon as humanly possible. Oh, and would you be so kind as to run him back down to the station after supper? I've a bit of a headache and may wish to retire early."

"Certainly, sir."

"That's good. And a good bit of good riddance to him."

When Tiger entered the large candlelit dining room, his father was already in his seat at the far end of the long mahogany table, barely within shouting distance, halfway through a fresh shrimp cocktail. Manners dictate that the guests are never seated until the host or hostess. But not for Papa, not for him the polished manners of refined people everywhere, oh, no. A man unto himself and might he ever remain one.

Tiger had poured himself a healthy splash of Scotch, and he brought the drink to the table. He'd arranged it so that the two of them would be sitting at opposite ends of the rectangular table he'd had shipped over from Mallett's in London.

It would not be too much of a stretch to say that dinner that evening was a strained affair. Cook had outdone himself. There was a rack of lamb, perfectly pink, with freshly made mint sauce, which was a specialty of the house. As well as gaufrette potatoes, a New Orleans delicacy, and creamed spinach such as Tiger had never tasted before. A dish to make the angels cry with pleasure.

His father ate with gusto. Tiger could see how much he was enjoying the food. But were any compliments to the chef forthcoming? Not on your life, brother. Compliments were not something in the old buzzard's repertoire. Cruel criticism was his stock-in-trade.

One year, Tiger had sent him a needlepoint pillow he'd picked up while Christmas shopping in Portobello Road. Green velvet with "If you can't say something nice about anyone, please come sit by me" embroidered on one side.

Tiger could not recall receiving a thank-you note that Christmas.

Tiger managed to get through the meal without the outbreak of a food fight but the long silences were unbearable. All he could hear from his father's end of the table was the sound of him masticating loudly, eating, as was his habit, with his mouth wide open. Unspeakable. Unbearable.

When Tiger couldn't take it a second longer, he said, "What news of Beijing, Pop? Rather an exciting place to be now that there's a war on, I'd imagine. Any sensational rumors floating around town? Any forbidden activities in the Forbidden City?"

"One that my friend Chiang has got terminal cancer. He doesn't. Another that your father is going to be feted at a magnificent state dinner at the Summer Palace, hosted by the generalissimo himself. . . ."

"Wow, Pop. Is that one true?"

"Of course it's true. Don't be ridiculous. It's my second one, actually. There was one back in thirty-nine, now that you mention it. It was quite a splendid affair. The great man had me seated next to . . ." *Blah-blah-blah.*

God save me.

Tiger said nothing, just tucked into the delicious lamb, pink and smelling of rosemary, just the way he liked it. The Margaux made for good company with the rest of the meal. For the most part, they ate in solitary silence, which was fine with him. And just when he'd given up all hope on any conversation at all, his father spoke up.

"You asked me something about rumors floating around Beijing."

"Did I, really? I don't recall that."

"Well, you certainly did. At any rate, there was one some weeks back surrounding one of your childhood friends. You remember Tony Chow, of course?"

An alarm bell sounded at the name Chow somewhere deep within Ambassador Tang's cerebellum. But he collected himself enough to say with some nonchalance: "I do. The one you always claimed murdered Jackie."

"That's him."

"Well, what about him?"

"There was a rumor floating around town in Beijing that he'd gone missing."

"Missing?" Tiger said, the alarm bells sounding inside his brain, and put his wineglass down on the white linen. "Really, now? How extraordinary. Anyone have any idea what happened to him?"

"Police have no idea. FBI is looking into it, apparently. J. Edgar Hoover has decided to investigate the case himself. Kidnapping, possibly. But there's never been any ransom note. . . . I hear the case is still open."

"Hmm," Tiger said, wheels within wheels spinning furiously inside his mind.

His father looked at him with a strangely malevolent cast to his eyes, like a cat toying with a frightened mouse or small bird. He finally said, "It is a bit odd, though. Someone who worked with Tony at the Chinese Trade Bureau told a colleague of mine in Beijing that on the Friday before he disappeared, Tony Chow was making plans to spend the weekend with you here in the country."

"What? Absurd on the face of it. I'd sooner have a nest of poisonous vipers in this house than that fat thug."

"You never heard from him?"

"Oh, yes. Of course I heard from him. He called me one day. Wanted to tell me what a big shot he was in Washington. Wanted to introduce me round to all his friends at the club. I said there was a war on and that I was terribly busy at the White House and would have to pass on the invitation. That was the end of it. I have to say that, wherever the hell he's got himself to, I hope to God he's sleeping undergound these days. Or"— and here he allowed himself a sly smile—"with the fishes."

"I'd no idea you disliked him so intensely. And then—"

"He murdered my fucking brother, for God's sake, Dad."

"I can't say I'm sad Tony's gone. But . . . you and your brother would never have been suited to each other. He was very much the outdoor type. A true sportsman. Cricket, shooting, skiing, deep-sea fishing. Falconry, even. As compared to you, always a rather pale child, hidden as you were behind your fortress towers of books."

"All right, that's just fucking enough!" Tiger half shouted, half coming out of his chair with his fists clenched. At that moment, he knew he was capable of anything. Including killing his own father.

His father threw down his linen napkin and rose, red-faced, to his feet. "Well, it's the damn truth, isn't it, boy? You were never half the man your brother was!"

With that, Tiger got to his feet, rang the dinner bell, and summoned Hamish to have the table cleared.

"Dinner is officially over," Tiger said, moving toward the door.

His father leaned back in his chair and smiled, very serpentine, and hissed, "Really? No dessert?"

"Not tonight, Josephine. And just so you know, I usually take coffee in the library after dinner. I'm going there now. Join me if you like. Or not. You know your way out. Hamish will show you the door."

CHAPTER 33

Sevenoaks Plantation, Virginia
January 1942

Tiger escaped down the hall to the library, his favorite room. There, he poured a fresh Scotch and lit a lovely Romeo y Julieta Cuban cigar. He was seated calmly by the crackling fire when the old monster slithered in with all the reptilian charm of an anaconda. There had always been this horrid aspect to the man. If ever there was a human being you could visualize shedding his skin before wriggling back under the bushes, it would have been his father.

The old boy had a rather large box in his hands; it was wrapped up in silver foil paper and red satin ribbons like some kind of a Christmas present. Now what?

"I wanted to give you this before I left. It's a gift from Beijing. In honor of your high-and-mighty status these days."

"Thanks, Pop. Put it on the sideboard. I'll open it later."

"I'd prefer you open it now. I have my reasons."

"Oh, Christ, fine. I'll open the damn thing. Just so you know, Hamish has brought my car around to the front entrance with the engine running, keeping the interior warm. To take you to the station. He's ready to go whenever you feel like leaving."

Without looking at the gift giver, he strode over to the sideboard and picked up the silver box. It was surprisingly heavy. He tore the paper off, rather furiously because he was very, very angry now. His evening had been ruined by the one person in his family who, for all of his life, had managed to ruin everything.

There was a heavy crystal chandelier full of burning tapers hanging above. And in the flicker of soft light was revealed an exquisite black lacquered box, inlaid with swirls of magnificent ivory. Tiger had to admit it was beautiful. What was the old boy up to now?

"Open it," his father said. "The present is what's inside the box, not the box."

Tiger lifted the lid.

It was a gun.

His heart lifted. He'd always loved guns, especially beautiful ones, which this one certainly was. He lifted it out and examined it in the light. Stunningly beautiful, this one. It was a short-barreled Colt .45, a gun of the Old West, but this one had ivory handles and incredibly intricate inlay work. How his father had picked this one, he'd never know, but, still he was now holding this work of art in his right hand, and it felt as if it belonged there.

"It's beautiful, Pop, truly beautiful."

"I hoped you'd like it. I know how fond you are of all things American."

"Yes, I am. I'm out of the spy trade, Dad, now that I'm an ambassador. Don't really have much use for guns to be honest. But I'll treasure this one."

"Since you're up, do you mind going over and pulling those doors closed?"

"Not at all," he said. "What's up, Pop?"

Something was definitely up; that was for damn sure.

"Come back and sit next to me. We're going to have a very important and very confidential conversation."

Starting to feel a bit uneasy, Tiger sat in the chair opposite his father and put his new treasure on the side table, where he could study it.

"Chiang Kai-shek is the one who picked that gun for you, not me. I've no love of guns, as you know. But he does, and he assured me that from all he'd heard about you, you would treasure this one and put it to good use."

"Ambassadors don't really carry guns, Pop. Or even use them very much. We have bodyguards."

"I'm sure you do. However, you remember I told you the reason for my visit to Washington? That Chiang wanted me to deliver a highly personal message to President Roosevelt?"

"I do. You're going to the White House tomorrow, I'd guess."

"No, I'm not. The one who's going to deliver the generalissimo's message to Roosevelt . . . is you, Tiger. You yourself."

"What on earth are you talking about?"

"There's a letter inside the box for you. Handwritten by our great leader at the Gate of Divine Might, the northern gate of the Forbidden City. Read the letter at your leisure, but read it you must."

"Slow down. What's going on here? I'm starting not to enjoy this conversation. . . ."

"The generalissimo has anointed you to carry out a divine mission. You should be honored beyond comprehension. And may I say, for the first time, I can honestly say that I am prepared to be proud of you, Tiger. If you somehow manage to grow some backbone even at this late stage."

"Yeah, right, fine, sure you are. Tell me about this divine mission of mine."

"Very straightforward. You have been ordered to carry out the will of Chiang and all of his people. . . ."

"And how do I do that again?"

"Simple enough. You put a bullet in President Roosevelt's head."

Tiger let that remark register while taking a large gulp of the Cutty Sark. He stared at his father, thinking about how the old man was dealing with turning eighty. Not well, was the answer.

"What? Say that again. . . ."

"Hear me now, and remember my words: You are going to use that gun to assassinate the president of the United States."

"Are you insane? What? Kill FDR? Lunacy! He's our great ally. Doesn't Chiang know that?"

"Be quiet and listen for a change. The leader is of the strong opinion that Roosevelt has betrayed him. Betrayed our beloved fatherland. That his focus and all of his singular energy and resources are going to Churchill and England. Because of the so-called 'special relationship.' We in Beijing do not relish the idea of playing second fiddle to anyone. And yet every time we make a request for critical aid, it winds up in Britain's coffers. We want a true partner in the White House. And that will never be Roosevelt. . . ."

"Sorry. Where did you hatch this bizarre scheme? Some squalid whorehouse or backstreet opium den, no doubt. Wrong number, old boy. I simply won't do it."

"You have to do it. Chiang Kai-shek makes that perfectly clear. He fears his government is coming unglued. That Mao Tse-tung and the communists will soon force him out of office. If that should happen . . . Well, I should say no more at this point. Friends are mysteriously disappearing. Some have died."

"Let me guess. You've spent a lifetime cultivating your personal relationship with Chiang. You needed his help to keep the Tang pot on the stove from boiling over. Now you're losing your power base. And you need to shore it up. You're in a blind panic. It's all over your face. You are the one who wants to take some radical action to remind the world that the Chinese government is still a force to be reckoned with. And that force is you."

"What drivel. I spent a fortune educating you in the best universities. What a waste. Now, when your father really needs you, you bow out. You have to do this for me. For our great family."

"And if I refuse?"

"You will die. And I will pass the beautiful little gun on to your successor. Someone with vision and guts and strength of will. And—dare I say it?—loyalty to Chiang and our nation. I think you still foolishly believe that you can safely ignore the force of my will. But I am telling you what you are to do, and by God, you are going to do it!"

"This ancient Chinese mind-control crap of yours worked when I was five or six. You made me feel alone and stupid and like some kind of a sissy boy. It was all bullshit, Pop. I've erected walls against you, old man. Six feet thick. That crap doesn't work anymore. Not in this house."

The old fiend actually cackled. "You think not? We shall see. I've planted the seed. It's already sprouting roots inside that brain of yours. You just don't know it yet."

"Show yourself out, Pop. I want to be alone now. I'll probably never see you again. So, this is good-bye."

"But damn it to hell, you still need to—you have to—*do as I say!*"

"I said, 'Good-bye.' That means leave. Get the hell out of my bloody house before I pick up that gun and use it on you! I'm glad you came. It made me realize just how insane you really are. And how much I hate your rotten guts and always have. Now, you get out. Or I'll have the servants throw you out on your fat ass."

"Not without telling you one more thing, you puffed-up little princeling pretty boy. Your cowardice besmirches the proud and ancient name of Tang. As far as I'm concerned, you are no longer part of this family."

"Fuck you, old man. I never was part of it. Now, get the hell out of my sight. Good-bye and good riddance!"

A minute or two later, Tiger heard the yellow Rolls rumble out of the porte cochere and looked out the window to see his father in the rear seat, his black top hat clearly visible in the oval rear window. He was gone. Thank God. Tiger went over to the drinks table and poured some more Scotch whiskey.

Sitting down close to the warmth of the fire, he picked up the phone and dialed a number he knew by heart.

"Hullo?" the sleepy voice said.

"Are you asleep, beautiful?"

"Not anymore, darling. What's going on? You sound horrible."

"My father just left. Miserable bastard."

"Thank God. He's not staying the night?"

"No. I threw him out in the cold."

"Good for you. What? Why in heaven's name would you do that?"

"He's crazy. It was a nightmare. I'll tell you all about it. Can you come now?"

"What time is it?"

"Almost midnight. I could come down the hill to collect you?"

"No, no. I've got my brother's car. He's down from Princeton for the weekend."

"Good. Would you like a nice hot bath before I tuck you in? I could scrub your back . . . your front . . . your pretty little feet?"

"That sounds divine. I'll see you soon, darling. . . ."

"Hurry, for God's sake! Hurry!"

CHAPTER 34

The English Channel
January 1942

Commander Hawke left the dead Germans to their own devices up on the bridge and stepped outside onto the bridge wing. The air was frigid and his threadbare German tunic provided a bare minimum of protection. The steel structure of the wing projected out from the bridge deck, one on each side of the bridge, high above the deck. This was where the ship's captain or first mate did their celestial navigation, took sightings on the North Star to locate their position on the charts. And supervised all close-in docking maneuvers with an unsurpassed view of his entire ship from this height.

Hawke could see and hear the fierce firefight that had just broken out on the stern afterdeck. He picked up the Zeiss binoculars hanging from the rail and scanned the ship from amidships aft. He counted six enemy down on the deck, all either wounded badly or dead.

Apparently, the stern had been cleared because he saw his three crewmen, visibly unhurt, beginning to work their way forward toward the bow, moving slowly, Sten guns at the ready.

The ship's company of three officers and twelve seamen was rapidly being depleted. Probably gone into hiding at this point . . . but not for long.

The wind out of the south was freshening now, a vast parade of orderly white caps marching across the sea to starboard. Purple cloud banks tinged with gold and crackling with lightning were stacking up on the far horizon. None of this had been in the forecast. They'd have to make for Plymouth in a blow, but it was nothing the big minesweeper couldn't take in her stride.

He heard a muffled shout from somewhere near the bow. He turned to look and saw to his great dismay that Stauffenberg was in a jam. He was cornered and clearly wounded, the right shoulder of his tunic saturated with blood, forcing him to fire with his left hand.

Three enemy combatants had him trapped. One was advancing toward his position at a crouch; the other two fanned out, providing the lead with covering fire. The lieutenant had his back against the bow rail with no place to go but the sea below; he was taking cover behind two mammoth anchors, one to port and one to starboard. . . . Another thirty seconds and his assailant would have him dead to rights.

Hawke cupped his hands round his mouth and shouted loudly in the direction of the advancing German. *"Achtung! Achtung!"* he cried out. *"Nicht schießen. Er ist harmlos!"* ("Don't shoot! That man is harmless!")

The stupefied seaman paused just long enough to look back over his shoulder, and up to the bridge, to see what officer was shouting at them and why. Likewise, he caught the attention of the two Germans who were providing covering fire. It was just long enough. The man lost a step and the focus of his attention. The other two were still staring up into the glare of the sun behind the bridge, wondering at the order not to shoot. Hawke was swift to take advantage of the distraction he'd created at the bow.

He quickly raised the Sten and sighted along the barrel, leading his moving target just a hair. His finger tightened around the trigger, and he squeezed off a quick burst. The lead man instantly crumpled to the deck, having taken three or four rounds in the back. Hawke then unleashed a hail of lead on the bow, suppressing the two remaining combatants.

He saw Stauffenberg rise up and give him the V-for-victory sign before opening up on the two remaining German crewmen. They were caught in a cross fire, Hawke pounding them from above and behind, and the cornered Englishman letting them have holy hell from the front. Just then a round ricocheted off the steel bulkhead behind Hawke with a re-sounding twang! Hawke spun around and looked below where the shot had obviously come from.

Two more Germans were coming up the steel staircase en route to the bridge to check up on the captain no doubt. At the last minute, back at RAF ARCHBURY, Hawke had decided to clip two frag grenades to his utility belt. He reached up under his tunic and plucked one out. His thought was just to pull the pin and then bounce the grenade down the steps, timing it so it would detonate somewhere within lethal vicinity of the advancing enemy.

He could literally see one of the German's eyes widen at the sight of the lethal pineapple bouncing merrily down the steps toward him. The Nazi sailor raised his Luger 9mm but never quite got the chance to get a shot off. The grenade exploded at knee level, knocking him off his feet and backward into his comrade, the two of them falling to their deaths some thirty feet to the steel deck below.

Two more down, only one remaining.

Hawke started down the staircase, keeping his Sten at hand as long as there was any remaining resistance to him and his pirates capturing the enemy vessel.

He had wounded, of course. He needed to get Stauffenberg down to the sick bay pronto, where he could find a medical kit to patch up the lads and to stanch the blood flow. Also, he had to locate the badly wounded Campbell and see how he was doing.

The commander and his lieutenant found the last remaining German alive down in sick bay. A tall blond boy who couldn't have been a day over twenty was seated beside Campbell's blood-soaked bed linens, holding the boy's limp white hand. He turned to them, and they saw the tears running down both the German boy's cheeks.

"Don't move," Hawke shouted in German, covering him with his automatic pistol.

"*Nein! Nein! Alles gut!*" the boy said, turning again to look at the two Englishmen standing in the doorway. Men who'd completely outwitted Captain Donitz.

"Is he dead, sailor?"

"*Jawohl, mein Herr,*" the boy said, swiping the back of his hand across his eyes, ashamed of his copious tears.

"Christ. What happened here, boy?"

"He bled out, sir. There was just no way of stopping all that blood. I'm a medical orderly, and I know how to do it. But nothing I tried would stop all that arterial blood, sir. I'm—I'm very sorry, sir. He was a fine soldier and very kind to me. . . . He was crying. . . . I held his head and tried to comfort him . . . but it was no good. I lost him. . . . I just wasn't good enough. . . . I'm sorry, sir."

"Lieutenant, arrest that man and take him into custody. We'll hand him over to the Navy at Plymouth. He can sit the rest of this one out, lucky lad."

The young orderly looked at Hawke quizzically and said, "You are all English? Not German?"

"I'm English. He's German. We're friends."

"Oh. I see."

He plainly did not see, but Hawke just let it go. He was in far too good a mood to trifle with such matters.

It was blowing like stink all the way north to England. Stauffenberg sat in the comms room on the bridge just behind Hawke, who manned the helm with Hood at his side. It was the young lieutenant's pleasant duty to inform Royal Navy Command and the DNI at Whitehall about the success of the mission. Donitz and the two other officers were gone. Like all the dead today, they'd been given burials at sea. Hawke was not so crass as to simply have their corpses heaved overboard. He'd said a few words over each one as the fallen men slipped beneath the waves.

It was done with the utmost respect, which he hoped the Germans would accord to English combatants caught in a similar situation.

Lieutenant Stauffenberg had fared a lot better than young Campbell. His was only a flesh wound, the round hadn't hit any bone or nicked his lungs. He'd been on the radio for most of the voyage back across the

Channel. He'd finally been able to summon the prime minister to the radio so Hawke could personally be the first to deliver the good news.

"I've the prime minister on the line for you, sir," he said to Hawke, poking his head out the door.

Hawke lit up, relinquished the helm, and rushed inside the small comms room.

"Who the bloody hell is this?" he heard his famous relative say.

"Hawke, your nephew, Uncle."

"You! By God! You boys survived the crash dive, did you?"

"Indeed we did, sir. And I'm happy to say a great deal more."

"Don't tell me you've got hold of the bloody prize!"

"Indeed, we have, sir. We've got a very nice present for you, Uncle Winston," Hawke told his delighted relative.

"Tell me! I've been on pins and needles since daybreak, worrying about you and the lads!" Winston shouted, unable to contain his excitement.

"Bit of piracy on the open seas, I'm afraid, sir. We lost our portside wing on surface impact, but still managed to get out before she sank. The lads and I got fished out of the briny by a big *Kriegsmarine* minesweeper in mid-Channel. The *Tannenberg.* That phony-uniform idea of yours did the trick, and we got aboard without a hitch. As soon as they got lazy, we gave 'em hell with the Stens."

"Atta boy! Hitler will be spitting bullets when he hears about this one!"

"Indeed, he will. There was only one German survivor, a medical orderly who helped me try to save one of my crew—a lad named Campbell, who sadly lost his right foot in the crash dive and didn't make it. Other than that, and a flesh wound suffered by my copilot, we're returning in good health, sir."

"And the three-rotor cypher machine? Intact? They didn't have time to take an axe to it? And burn the codebooks?"

"Negative. Both well in hand, sir. We're en route to Plymouth Harbor. Do you want to arrange for someone to come fetch the presents up to you at Bletchley Park?"

"Indeed, I do. I'll arrange for a nondescript army van with a military escort to be there when you pull into port."

"Perfect."

"May the saints preserve us! You bloody well pulled it off, didn't you? Good work! Someday this amazing story will be declassified, and you will be hailed as a great hero of this war, my boy. But in the meantime, I want you to bring your entire crew here to Number Ten for a little reception tomorrow, in your team's honor. I'll even invite the Queen Mother. Nothing she likes better than the gin and Dubonnet fizz my barman here at Ten makes for her."

Hawke laughed. "Sounds delightful, Uncle! What time should we be expected?"

"What time is the sun setting over the yardarm, sir?"

"One o'clock somewhere in the British Empire, I should guess. Does that suit?"

"Eminently. I'm very proud of my young nephew on this glad day for England. You've done an enormous service to the nation. It could even be a tipping point in this war. And please tell the lads that I am very, very proud of all of you."

"I will, sir."

Hawke was beaming from ear to ear as he emerged from the comms station. What remained of his crew on the lost bomber had now gathered round the helm, eager to hear what the skipper had to say.

Hawke stood before them, hands clasped behind his back, looking each and every man dead in the eye before he spoke a word.

"I'm sure some of you armchair historians have, like me, knowledge of Admiral Lord Nelson's dying words as he lay on the blood-soaked decks of his flagship *Victory* at Cape Trafalgar . . . the battle surely won. But the loss of England's greatest naval hero would be felt for years to come.

"Nelson said, to his adoring captain, 'Kiss me, Hardy.' And then, his pale blue woebegone eyes cast to the heavens, he said, 'Thank God, I have done my duty!' And then he died, thankfully conscious of his magnificent victory that day. Of Britain's victory! I want each and every one of you to remember Nelson's dying words when your hour finally comes. Remember this day and thank your God that, before you died, you were able to do your duty! And, remember this, my brave and hardy lads. You, here today, have earned every right to say those words before you leave this earthly coil. Well-done, chaps! Well-done!"

And then, at that instant, from the poop deck to the foredeck, from the mizzen to the mainmast, from bow to stern and from the very heights of the rigging, the *Tannenberg* erupted with a roar, shouts, and cries from his crew.

"Huzzah! Huzzah! Huzzah!"

CHAPTER 35

Dragonfire Lagoon, the Bahamas
Present Day

D usk. The sun seemed in no hurry to slip away. The upended bowl of sky above was on fire in the west. Hawke, his attention locked on the rim of the far horizon, saw what could very well have been flames from Dante's inferno, rippling across the vast perimeter where sea meets sky, and rays of gold were streaking seaward toward Black Dragon Lagoon. From this height, atop his fifty-story hotel, the views were literally breathtaking.

He'd made a last-minute decision for himself, Stoke, and Mr. Brock to go directly up to the rooftop club for drinks and dinner alfresco.

"What do you guys think, Stoke?" he asked his old friend and comrade in arms, still staring at Mother Nature's fiery display out on the far edge of the world.

"About what? Her?" Stoke said, smiling at his new friend, China Moon.

China looked, Hawke thought, incredibly beautiful tonight. She was wearing Dior, a strapless pink gown with a wasp waist decorated with intricate beading and pearlescent sequins. She wore an exquisitely simple diamond necklace around her throat matched by two teardrop earrings. A metallic silver clutch bag was tucked under her bare arm.

"Yes," China said overtly flirtatiously. "What do you think about her, big boy?"

China certainly appeared to have fallen hard for that man mountain, Stokely Jones Jr., and she was lost in a deep conversation with him. Hawke smiled, just happy as he could be to have one of his old flames and one of his oldest and dearest friends within speaking distance. When you hadn't seen Stoke in a while, it was almost easy to forget just how essentially large a human being he actually was.

Hawke had once said, by way of introduction, "So, this is my good friend, Detective Sergeant Jones. He's only slightly larger than your average refrigerator." Six months later, Stoke found himself living in London, having left the force, and working as a bodyguard and man Friday for none other than Lord Alexander Hawke himself.

Hawke had met Stoke a decade ago. He'd been kidnapped for ransom by the Tucci family mob and left to die in a burning warehouse in Flatbush. Detective Sergeant Stokely Jones Jr., NYPD, had been working Hawke's case for nearly a month when he finally caught up with a mob capo with a rap sheet a mile long. He'd offered him a deal he couldn't refuse. "Just gimme a location, Tuna, and I'll forget about all that smuggling crap you're really going down for."

Half an hour later, he was driving his unmarked Crown Victoria at speeds of one hundred plus mph, through the streets, deserted at 3:00 A.M. He saw orange flames climbing into the black sky from two blocks away and really put the pedal down. It had to be the warehouse. The final resting place where Hawke had been left to die.

Any building burning that hot had to be bad news for the man he was trying to save. Stoke, following three combat tours as a U.S. Navy SEAL, had been drafted by the New York Jets. Fullback. He was badly injured scoring a touchdown against the Cleveland Browns, out for the game, out for the season, probably out forever. Then he'd applied for the NYPD police gig, starting out as a young patrolman on the beat down in Soho and ending up a detective.

Without a thought, Stoke careened into the warehouse's deserted car park, then raced through the flames licking at the entrance and into the dilapidated ruin. With nary a thought for his own skin, he charged up five flights of burning wooden staircases. He finally found Hawke, bound hand and foot and left to die in small closet full of cleaning solvents. Hawke had inhaled a lot of bad shit, including smoke, asbestos, and other poisonous chemicals, but he was still breathing.

"Can you hear me?" Stoke said, pulling the unconscious man to his feet. "We gotta get outta here, like, now!"

No response.

Shrugging off the weight of the six-foot-three Englishman, Stoke hoisted him upon his shoulders and raced to the bottom, but not before a burning ember embedded itself in his hair, scorching his scalp. He got to the ground floor, glad he could remember where the exit was because the entire room was now almost completely engulfed in flames. He'd never run this fast on a football field in his life, and it was only sheer speed that kept them from being trapped and burned alive.

"How'd you happen to meet my boss?" Stoke asked China.

"Oh, I dunno. We had a thing, I guess. Long time ago. Now we're just old friends. Despite the fact that he killed my father."

"He what?" Stoke said.

Hawke said, "General Sun Yung Moon, Stoke. Remember, I told you about him after we got the hell out of China. That was her father."

"Aw, man. I'm sorry to hear that, China. But you got to cut the man some slack. I was actually there that day. It was one of those kill-or-be-killed kinda situations. It was flat-out war. It was a kill-or-be-killed kinda war. Your father did not leave Alex any choice but to defend himself. We were in a firefight. A lot of people died that day, a lot them probably people just in the wrong place at the wrong time. Including one of my oldest and bestest friends. Little Frenchman, ex–French Foreign Legion and one the toughest cats on the planet. His name was Froggy."

"Froggy," Hawke said. "Braver than any ten men I've ever met, may God rest his soul."

"Got that right," Stoke said. "Well. The black hats had us on the run, closing in fast. Froggy got shot bad, a round took half his leg off. Boss here picked him up and hiked him up on his shoulders. Slowed us down while were trying to make it down to the beach, see? Get out of a free-fire zone. We weren't going to make it. Froggy kept screaming. Wanted the boss to set him down. Said he'd have our backs. Slow them down and cover our retreat. We never saw Froggy after that. . . ."

Stoke wiped his eyes with the back of his hand. He had gotten emotional, remembering that terrible day.

China just sipped at her mojito, eyes downcast, saying nothing for a long time.

Hawke cupped her chin in his hand and lifted her face up where he could look her in the eyes. He said, "Like the man says, it was war, for God's sake, China. You of all people know how that works. You've been there, I know."

China stood up, dabbed at her lips with the white linen napkin, and said, "You'll excuse me, gentlemen. I need to use the loo."

After she'd left the table, Stoke leaned in closer to Hawke and said, "Man, I'm sorry about that. Getting all weepy and shit. My bad."

"Hell, no. This isn't about you or me. That's just her. She's touchy about that subject. I might be, too, were I her, confronting the man who killed her father. But don't blame yourself."

"Who is she, anyway?"

"Chinese Secret Police. Way up the totem pole. She's here on assignment, to look into the business affairs of the owners here, twin brothers. Part of the Tang Family. Another ancient Chinese crime family that still practices its ancient traditions. Gambling, prostitution, vast plantations of poppy fields to supply global heroin markets, human slave trade, et cetera. China now admits she actually had dinner with Prince Henry a few times before his disappearance. She doesn't want to talk about it, but I'm going to get whatever I can out of her. I think she knows a hell of a lot more than she's saying about the prince."

"Are you getting anywhere on that?"

"Just scratching the surface. But I'll tell you one thing. The Tang twins are rotten apples. There are two Chinese PLA Navy missile frigates patrolling what I think may well be a secret Chinese military installation, right here on this little island in the Bahamas, not even a two-hour flight from Key West, from the east coast of Florida. I saw a huge structure on the other side of the island. Massive, built out over the water on four gigantic white pillars, two ashore on the mountainside and two way out in deep water. Thing looks like an angry dog ready to pounce. If it's what I think it is, we could well be heading into the Cuban Missile Crisis to the tenth power. I believe it could well be military, specifically naval."

"You thinking submarines? In America's backyard? God help us."

"Yeah. I'm thinking subs.

"You and I are doing a recon there tonight in the wee smalls. Have a look around. Did you bring all the scuba equipment and arms I asked for?"

"Damn straight. And some more goodies you didn't ask for. Since I was flying Air Hawke and not Delta, I figured why the hell not?"

"For example, what?"

"An M-60 machine gun and a grenade launcher. NVG goggles. A couple of M4A1 assault rifles. A couple of SIG Sauer P226s. A sniper rifle. A pair of KA-BAR fighting knives. A few other goodies. Flashbangs and smokers, that kind of struff."

"Well, I know you had your choice of air travel and I'm very glad you flew with me as opposed to Delta."

Stoke laughed.

"Yeah, boss. So, tell me. Who've we got in this business? Just you and me and Mr. B over there?"

"For now. I've asked Ambrose Congreve to come down here and snoop around, but he's tied up handling some scandal involving the Royal Family. Very hush-hush, apparently. We're just doing the exploratory. Get the lay of the land. Should the situation escalate and demand more fighters, we're going to call our pals down in Costa Rica to jump into the fray."

"Thunder and Lightning, you're talking about? Froggy's old outfit?"

"Nobody does it better."

"You got that right, boss! Who we going up against end of the day?"

"The whole bloody Tang Empire maybe. Even here they have vast security forces scattered about on all six islands of the Dragonfire Club complex. Plus, Chinese military forces and heavily armed naval patrol vessels that make no secret of their presence here."

"Now, that's some serious shit right there, boss."

"Hmm," Hawke replied, thinking about something else.

Alex then felt a hand landing on his right shoulder, and then a disembodied voice said, "Well, well, well. Look who's here. My new friend Hawke. And this gentleman must be—just a guess—Big Al?"

Hawke and Stoke both stood up at the presence of a lady at the table.

"Zhang Tang, say hello to my business partner, Mr. Stokely Jones Jr. and his bodyguard, Mr. Brock."

"Hello, Mr. Brock. Hello, Mr. Stokely Jones Jr. Nice to have you with us tonight. Are you boys staying on the island?"

"Just checked in."

"Welcome, then. Is anyone sitting in that seat?"

"Yes," Hawke said. "She's just gone to the loo. It's China Moon, actually. I believe you two know each other?"

Zhang took the empty seat as if she hadn't heard about China being in the loo.

"Oh, everybody knows China. That crazy chick is always poking her pretty little nose into places she shouldn't. I'm amazed my brothers, Tommy and Jackie, didn't sent her packing long ago. She's a high-ranking Chinese Secret Police officer—did you know, Alex?"

"No! Is she? I had no idea."

"Well, you just keep your nose clean around her."

"So sorry!" China said, suddenly reappearing at the table. "There was a wait list to get into the ladies' loo."

"Yes?" Zhang said, looking up, startled, as if puzzled by China's sudden arrival.

"That chair belongs to me," China said, the color rising in her cheeks. "Please vacate it, Zhang. Now."

"Actually, it belongs to me, as, obviously, do all the rest of the chairs out here. How do you know lover boy, over there?"

"Actually, that's none of your fucking business, Zhang."

Zhang said, "Down, girl! It's not nice to insult the owner. Especially if you don't want to get locked out of the spa, and your hairdresser, darling."

China smiled ever so sweetly and said, "Well! Zhang, my dear, here I was, all prepared for a battle of wits, but you appear to be unarmed. . . ."

Hawke tried not to laugh but it bubbled out of him anyway.

"Oh, do fuck off, won't you, China?" Zhang said.

"China, stop it," Hawke said, seeing the possibility that this vitriolic verbal sparring might well lead to a physical battle. He added, "This is getting ridiculous, ladies. Please take a deep breath and calm down."

China looked at Hawke and smiled. "Thanks for the drink, lover boy. I'm going to skip dinner tonight. I've suddenly got a terrible taste in my mouth. The cheap liquor they serve here at this dump, I suppose. Anyway, I'm off. Call me if you want to chat some more about you know what." With that, she turned and made her way through all the tables to the elevator bank.

Zhang said, "Touchy, touchy, that girl. It seems I've ruined your little party, Alex. I'm sorry. Are you two an item? You and China Moon?"

"We were, a decade or so ago. Just having a drink for old times' sake."

"Good. She's gone. I'm starving! What is everyone having?"

"May I suggest the crow?" Hawke said to her with a smile to take the sting out of it.

"Crow, did you say? How rude!" she said, throwing her napkin down on the table and getting up to her feet.

"If you're going to pick sides in a battle royale, Alex, you're always better off going with the winning side. Call me when you're ready to apologize. Good-bye, Stokely. Mr. Brock. It was lovely meeting you." She turned and walked away, disappearing into the Zinc Bar.

"Lover boy, huh?" Stoke said. "Looks like you've been pretty busy down here, boss man. Man, you got 'em coming and going all over the place!"

"Right. Just what I needed. To get caught in the middle between those two vixens."

"'Vixen,' huh?" Stoke said. "I've heard that word before. What's it mean, anyway? Witch or something along those lines?"

Hawke smiled and said, "Let me see. I do know. I believe it means a sexually attractive woman who also just happens to be a mean, shrewish, and ill-tempered bitch on wheels."

Stoke laughed. "You got that right, man, I'm tellin' you. Those two gals? Shit."

"Stoke, China was coming on to you. Despite that big fat gold wedding ring on your hand."

"Yeah, I picked up on that. I feel like whatever happens in Dragonfire Bay stays in Dragonfire Bay. Still, something bothers me about that chick China Moon. I think she's dangerous. I think she's the spider in this web. Girl is flat-out poisonous. Beautiful, I'll grant you that, but otherwise . . ."

"Hmm," Hawke said. "What's your read on the other chick?"

"'Bout the same. I don't much trust either one of them. The Tang girl? Mata Hari personified. You know, that belly dancer who spied for both the Germans and the French in World War One. Got her ass executed by a French firing squad. This one you've got? She's after your ass, man. Maybe for a good reason, maybe not. But she's got you smack-dab in the middle of her crosshairs. Hell, both of 'em do! I think that's the problem. Which one of them is gonna pull the trigger first?"

"That's a comforting thought," Hawke said. "Any more where that came from?"

"Just give me time, my brotha. Give me a little time. I'm a damn hotbed of good ideas lately."

CHAPTER 36

Black Dragon Lagoon, the Bahamas
Present Day

Hawke and Stokely, both clad in Six Wolf grey night combat uniforms and wearing light body armor underneath, arrived at the Dragonfire Club Marina at 2:45 A.M. They had not passed a single soul or vehicle since leaving the hotel on Hawke's motorcycle. Hawke had been carefully noting the comings and goings of security at the gate for the last three nights. There was a shift change at 2:30 A.M., and the 3:00 A.M. guy never rolled in until after 3:30 A.M., whereupon he promptly fell asleep in the little guardhouse after about half an hour of swigging from a rum bottle and watching porn on his computer terminal.

It was dead quiet, save the softly tinkling sound of sailboat halyards whipped around by a fresh breeze, slapping the hollow aluminum masts of yachts of varying size, all the way up to three hundred feet in length overall. Hawke and Stoke dismounted and walked quickly out onto the main pier, but not so quickly as to arouse the interest of some insomniac skipper up on deck for a smoke. Hawke could see the Wally moored all the way at the end of the narrow pier where he'd left it late that afternoon. He'd sent Brock ahead to the marina to organize the weapons and ammo on the boat prior to their arrival. He was also expected to top off the tanks with petrol, and, most importantly, to mount the fifty-cal machine gun on its mini-mount up on the bow.

"Man, oh, man, where'd you come up with this sweet little piece of naval beauty?"

"A loaner. I call her Wally. Belongs to Zhang's brother, Tommy. Let's do try not to sink it tonight, shall we? Might spoil the party."

"What the hell is it, boss? And what does that name mean? Chop-chop?"

"It means 'Hurry-Hurry.' The boat's a Wallytender. Piece of bloody work, isn't she?"

"What's her power situation?"

"The new Volvo Penta 650s outboard propulsion."

"Whoa, Mama. That's some serious shit right there."

"Tell me about it. I've been having fun with it."

"You want me to drive?"

Hawke said, "Absolutely. Hop aboard. I'll free the lines."

Stoke stepped aboard and lowered his six-five, three-hundred-pound frame down into the helm seat. "You got the keys, I hope. . . ."

"Oh, yeah," Hawke said, and Harry Brock tossed them down to him.

Stoke twisted the key in the ignition, and the big outboards at the stern roared to life. "Sweet Jesus! Listen to that! I want one of these babies for Christmas!"

"Be a good boy, and I'll get Santa on it," Hawke said, jumping down into the cockpit and freeing the spring line. Then he loaded all the scuba gear and assault weaponry Stoke had brought to the party, stowing it in the aft storage locker below the deck.

Stoke said, "We outta here now?"

"Lines are free. Equipment stowed. Let's go. Take it nice and easy till we're well clear of the harbor entrance and out in open water . . . as in dead slow."

"You got that right," Stoke said, easing back on the throttles until they were running at idle speed, a soft burble gurgling at the stern.

Once they were out in open water, Hawke turned on the GPS and said, "Okay, all good. You see this piece of protected coast here, on the other side of the island? That's our destination. We'll approach dead slow from the south. Beach the boat, run her up into the mangroves to keep her out of sight, and swim the rest of the way to the target."

"And that's where we're headed?"

"No," Hawke said, pointing his finger at the coastline on the GPS screen. "The house is here, up on the mountaintop. The target is massive. Looks like heavy steel-reinforced concrete. No windows, no doors."

"Huh. I smell military, boss."

"Yeah. Place reeks of it. Light up our radar, Stoke. See who we've got for company. I told you about those two big Chinese missile frigates. They are now on the other side of the island, heading toward each other and coming back around every two hours, so we've got to get a move on. We don't want to get anywhere near those bad boys. Put Wally on a course for this spit of land here. We'll run in at full throttle until we get around that isthmus. We'll nip inside that peninsula into the bay and get off the bloody radar."

"How do we get inside that place, boss?"

"Swim in, I guess, submerged, from the sea. That is, if there's a way in, I suppose."

"I love to swim. Just a natural-born SEAL baby, I'm tellin' ya."

"I guess so, baby," Hawke said, playfully punching Stoke in his right shoulder. He might as well have punched a two-foot-thick wall of concrete.

Twenty minutes later, Hawke shoved the twin throttles forward, firewalling them. They sped across the small inland bay, where Hawke had first spotted the strange structure, and ran the bow up onto the soft white sand. After off-loading all the scuba equipment, weapons, and gear, they tied a line to the bow. Then, thanks to the powerful Mr. Jones, they managed to pull the tender up inside the heavy thicket of mangroves growing down from the mountainside and spreading out along the beach to the sea.

The merest suggestion of a crescent moon, hiding behind the high cloud cover, along with a careless scattering of pinpoint stars crowding out the black velvet skies vaulting above painted a soft bluish light on the bunches of palms and the white sandy beach. They were not been able to get the Wally completely hidden inside the mangroves. Still, only a small portion of the aft hull remained visible, and Hawke thought she was safe enough in Brock's care until the break of dawn. He hoped they'd get in and out of the facility much sooner than that.

The two warriors stood on the beach, donning their gear and checking their ammo and weapons. Each man took an M4A1 assault rifle. Hawke had made the decision that the heavy M-60 machine gun was not really portable enough for a lengthy underwater swim, and Stoke stowed it in the Wally. They each took a SIG Sauer P226 sidearm and a KA-BAR assault knife. As had been agreed earlier, Brock would remain with the boat in case they had any unexpected guests on the beach.

"All right," Hawke said, putting a round into the chamber of his P226, "the target is that way. Let's go up the side of the mountain a bit and keep to the jungle until we get within five hundred yards of the target. Then we get wet, swim out until we're facing the seaward side of that monstrosity. Stay submerged all the way in, surface inside. Good?"

"Good for me."

"Break a leg, gentlemen," Brock said, chambering a round in his weapon as they walked away.

"See that big leafy plant over there? Stay well away from it, Stoke. They've got it growing all over the place, especially in places where they don't want us going."

"What the heck is it?"

"Bahamians call it gympie-gympie. Also known as the moonlighter and the mulberry-leaved stinger. It's a nettle. But it's the most painful stinging nettle in the entire world. If those tiny silica hairs on the leaves come in contact with your skin, it's only a matter of seconds before you experience a level of pain you wouldn't believe possible."

"That bad, huh?"

"Yeah, only worse. You get the sort of pain that stabs at every inch of your body with a series of electric jolts that can drive your body into anaphylactic shock in a heartbeat. I heard from a training instructor at a jungle-warfare seminar the story of a serviceman who had unwittingly used a handful of gympie-gympie leaves as toilet paper during a training exercise. Thirty minutes later? Unable to bear any more, he shot himself dead."

"That's some bad shit, man. Glad you pointed that out."

"Yeah. So, God only knows what we'll find inside that thing. But I can tell you one thing: They definitely don't want anyone nosing around the premises or, God forbid, getting inside. My assumption is that Prince Henry ran afoul of the Tang twins, not because of his Randy Andy sexual behavior with the resort staff, although I'm sure that was part of it."

"Bad move on his part."

"I think he was just as curious about this installation as I am. And that he got caught nosing around out here."

"You think they took him out to keep him quiet?"

"Maybe, yeah. But what I really think is that the prince represented an extremely valuable piece of property to the Tangs. Either as political leverage in a pinch or asking a queen's ransom for his safe return at some point in time. Or worst case, he's sleeping with the fishes."

"Makes sense. You think, if he's still alive, he's maybe still on this island?"

"I don't know. But it's a good place to start looking, once we find out what this place is really all about. Okay, let's climb up through that little break in the mangroves until we're in sight of that big bunker or whatever the hell it is. . . . There are two watchtowers, one at each corner of the structure on the landward side. Searchlights, guards with machine guns, you know the drill. So, stay low and stay alive. . . .

"There it is," Hawke said, though you really couldn't miss the damn thing, massive as it was.

Fifteen minutes later, they had emerged into a small clearing on a promontory elevated about fifty feet above the white beach. Stoke followed Hawke out to the edge to have a look at the monstrosity. They were well above the structure and even the two twenty-foot watchtowers, so they could take their own sweet time figuring out the best route down through the jungle to the sandy white crescent beach.

"Lordy, I see what you mean. I don't know what the hell it is, but I can tell you one damn thing: Some serious shit going on down there, whatever it is. And they clearly want nobody but nobody finding out what."

Hawke looked at his steel dive watch.

"Let's go find out, then, Stokely," Hawke said, and started down the angled cliff face to the sand and sea.

Stoke was a step or two behind him. When they got to the water's edge, they both kept walking, and moments later, they disappeared from sight. Nor was there a trail of bubbles from the two divers below the surface. Stoke had chosen the new Russian rebreather equipment. The latest thing for swimmers conducting combat operations in a heavily guarded war zone situation.

No bubbles, no troubles, was what the man had said.

In the end, it would not quite work out that way.

CHAPTER 37

Devil's Island, the Bahamas
Present Day

The two men, both exceptionally strong swimmers, had been in the water for nearly half an hour. They were swimming at a depth of roughly ten meters when they became aware of a faint greenish glow in the water beneath them. It seemed to emanate directly from the mysterious white structure. Hawke had judged its size to be approximately three hundred meters in width, by maybe four hundred meters in length. By his calculations, they must have been getting very close to the target.

Out of the corner of his eye, he saw Stokely gesticulating with very apparent excitement and pointing below them at the bottom of the sea. Hawke looked down and saw what all the excitement was about.

Three rows of small green lights dotted the sandy bottom! All fanned out in three separate lines from the seaward portion of the complex. In the middle, one straight line protruding out across the seabed at least five hundred yards, and two other identical lines of green lights, one to the left, the other to the right of center. To Hawke, they resembled nothing so much as the runway lights you'd see coming from an aerial view of an airfield at night.

What the hell?

Some kind of guidance system perhaps, he thought, swimming hard to catch up with Stokely, who had been increasing his speed the closer they got to finally solving this mystery. Within a couple of minutes, both swimmers saw a massive white structure looming up ahead. It was maybe fifty meters from top to bottom and about twenty meters above the bottom of the bay. The green "runway lights" all disappeared inside the massive opening, spanning the whole width of the structure, right in the middle.

They both paused, treading water about fifty feet away from what they could only believe had to be the entrance to the damn thing. That is, if it even had an entrance! Behind his dive mask, Stoke was all smiles. He shrugged his big muscular shoulders as if to say, "What the hell, partner? Let's go see what gives here. See exactly what kind of mischief these boys are up to."

The green glow was far stronger here, coming from somewhere deep inside, it seemed.

What the hell, indeed? Hawke thought, and the two of them swam side by side and disappeared into the glow inside.

It was eerie, all right, as if they had suddenly found themselves swimming underwater in some massive swimming pool of the gods lit up by unseen underwater illumination. Hawke motioned for Stoke to stay at this depth, while he went up to the surface to recon the place for the strong possibility of armed guards up there. Or one of the missile frigates cruising offshore.

Hawke kicked his swim fins hard three times and shot to the surface.

He broached with only his mask visible above the surface. Using his hands and his fins, and rotating his body through 360 degrees, and seeing no sign of guards or personnel, he rose higher out of the water and was greeted with a sight that told him his instincts upon sighting this thing had been right all along.

His instincts had not lied. It was a bloody nuclear submarine pen, one hundred eighty miles from America's shores! A Chinese sub pen, no less!

Hawke dove back down and motioned to Stoke to come up and see what he'd seen.

"Holy shit," Stoke said as he and Hawke each pushed their masks back to the tops of their heads and swiveled 360 degrees, getting their bearings. "I mean, seriously? Are you kidding me? Are those what I think they are?"

"If you think those are advanced Chinese Navy Shine-class nuclear submarines, you'd be correct, Stoke," Hawke said. "Five hundred seventy-five feet on the waterline, seventy-six-foot beam, and she draws about forty feet and is equipped with nuclear-powered torpedoes. Shine-class subs are powered by two fifty-thousand-horsepower steam turbines and four thirty-two-hundred-kilowatt turbogenerators. Speed is highly classified, but at MI-Six we book her in about twenty-two-point-twenty-two knots on the surface, and twenty-seven knots submerged."

Stoke said, "One of those babies could slip out of this pen on a moonless night, dive deep, and be patrolling deep down beneath Biscayne Bay in Miami in less than five hours. Shit, man. This is crazy-pants time!"

"It is indeed, crazy pants, Stoke. No idea how they've managed to maintain the secrecy of this operation. But mystery of the underwater runway lights solved. Some kind of guidance coming and going for the big subs on patrol arriving or departing during typhoon, or even combat, conditions here in this little corner of the Bahamas. Now I know why they have those watchtowers. And the two missile frigates patrolling out here day and night. I need to communicate this with my friend Brick Kelly at CIA and fast."

Hawke lifted a Nikon WP-1, a waterproof camera that was hung on a strap round his neck, and began rapidly snapping pictures of everything in sight, capturing the vast interior spaces of the sub pen, the one empty pen, and the two Shine-class subs that were currently moored there. He dove down to grab a few shots of the lower hull and the propulsion system.

Surfacing, he got what he could of the pen's vast interior. Above, there were various steel gantries and thick tubing snaking around, which indicated a sophisticated fresh-air-circulation system. At the very rear of the structure, he could barely make out a soft reddish glow that appeared from what looked to be the thick glass of the control room operation.

Hawke and Stoke clearly hadn't been spotted yet. If they had been, the whole place would have instantly lit up like the Vegas Strip.

Hawke checked his dive watch. They would have to get a move on. By his calculation, the two missile frigates were crisscrossing each other right now on the opposite side of the island. Two ships passing in the night and en route to the sub pen.

Views of a secret Chinese naval base the chief of staff at the Pentagon had never laid eyes on were now priority one. The Shine class of nuke subs was, Hawke knew, the most advanced of China's fleet of six nuclear subs, with more under construction, plus another fifty assorted diesel-electrics, now deployed in the Indian Ocean, off Australia and Cambodia, and other hot spots around the globe. It would take China a while to have a sub fleet as extensive as the Americans', but they were building these subs as fast as they could . . . a total of sixty now, but they were on track to vastly exceed the U.S. fleet by 2029. . . .

The fact that the Chinese Navy had been able to operate out of sight in these waters for so long was both surprising and disturbing. Somebody, somewhere, had dropped a very large ball. Heads would no doubt roll. The American president, the secretary of state, the Pentagon, and the CIA were all going to pitch a fit when Hawke brought this to their mutual attention. And the Tang brothers were going to have to account for their complicity at some point.

And the Dragonfire Club? It was a powder keg primed to explode.

Suddenly, Hawke knew that the secret of the prince's disappearance, while deeply troubling to both Hawke and the Queen, was only the tip of the iceberg here at Dragonfire Club. The fact that China Moon was here, too, sniffing around on behalf of the Chinese Secret Police was becoming more understandable. The Chinese military, not to mention the notorious Tangs, had a great deal at stake down here. A whole lot to hide. And a whole lot to lose.

"Seen enough, boss?" Stoke said.

"More than enough. Let's get the hell out of here before those two missile frigates arrive back on the scene up top."

They managed to return to the hotel without incident. Hawke wondered how long their luck would hold. He and Stoke were no doubt pushing their luck; that much was for sure.

Hawke took the elevator up and used the key card to gain admittance to his penthouse suite a little after 4 A.M. The night had turned cold and rainy when he and Stokely had left the marina and ridden back to the hotel after shedding their combat gear and uniforms, stowing them in the forward anchor locker. His ivory white silk shirt and linen trousers were soaked through by the time he shut down the big bike.

As soon as he stepped inside the darkened penthouse foyer, he knew that something was amiss. He could smell it. There was a faint scent of French perfume and spilled champagne and Gauloises cigarettes in the air. The scent of a woman. And from his bedroom, empty when he'd left it, the sound of someone softly snoring. It was a woman.

He went to the bar to get a bottle of sparkling water from the fridge. Snapping on the light, he saw that there was an empty bottle of Krug Champagne upside down in an ice bucket and two glasses with lipstick smudges around the rim. What the devil? And then there was the crystal ashtray, once empty, now filled with stubbed-out cigarettes, also bearing the traces of two shades of lipstick.

Correction. There were *two* women in his bed?

He entered the darkened room and turned on a table lamp beside the door. Somewhat to his relief, or chagrin, as the case might have been, there was only one woman in his bed. She was sleeping on her back, her lustrous black hair arrayed back on the pillows. She was naked. Her large breasts rose and fell. Her lips parted, to a soft, almost inaudible whistle, and she stirred, pulling up the bedcovers.

As always, something resembling heat inside him stirred as well. China Moon had always had that effect on him. Not trusting his ability to resist her charms, he decided not to climb into bed beside her. Instead, he padded out into the living room, lit the gas fire, stripped naked, and wrapped himself in the pale blue cashmere throw that was on the sofa. Then he plopped himself down in the overstuffed club chair, lit a cigarette, and stared into the make-believe fire.

A lot to think about tonight. A lot on the line. And the sooner he downloaded the chip in the Nikon WP-1 and forwarded all those encrypted images to Brick Kelly at the CIA, Langley, Virginia, the better.

Behind him, a voice said, "We waited up a long time for you, darling."

He didn't turn around. Just took a drag on his Morland cigarette and expelled a long blue plume.

It was China all right.

"Whatever do you mean, *we* waited up?"

"I mean, me and Zhang. You won't believe what happened after we left you. We ran into each other again at the Disco Inferno and ended up burying the hatchet over drinks at the Zodiac Club. A few too many drinks, as it happens. She had the idea to surprise you here in your penthouse when you got back from whatever mysterious secret mission you and Mr. Jones were on."

"How did you get in here?" Hawke asked. "And please tell me you didn't go through my sock drawer."

"Zhang used her master key card to get us in. She found the bottle of Krug in the refrigerator, and we decided, what the hell? Drank it and fell into your bed and went to sleep. She gave up on you around two and went home. I, rather obviously, did not."

"It occurs to me, my darling, that you are drunk."

"It's four o'clock in the morning! Everybody's drunk!"

Hawke sighed and, against his better judgment, felt himself succumbing yet again to her considerable charms. "Come over here. Right now. Stand in front of me, hands behind your back."

"Yes, sir, m'lord. Anything you say, sir."

She complied with his demands. She was one of those supremely strong and confident women who sometimes liked being told exactly what to do. Let someone else be boss, be in control for a while, giving the orders. That was something, Hawke had long ago discovered, that powerful women needed in order not to burn themselves out; everyone needed a brief hiatus now and then. Just like alpha males needed to let strong women take control of them sometimes.

China had put his maroon paisley silk Charvet robe on, but left it untied, allowing the nipple of her right breast to play peekaboo with the English spy.

Hawke said, "Still all about games, aren't you, China? Well, guess what. We're in one now. I can see it in your eyes. You want someone to boss you around? Okay, I'm your boss. And this time, the boss wants every scrap of information about events leading up to Prince Henry's disappearance. Not much scares me. But I saw something on this island tonight that made me afraid. Very afraid. I know you're hiding something, and I want it now."

China's cheeks suddenly flushed red. "Those are almost exactly the words you said that other night when we met at the Casino in Monte Carlo. Where's the devil-may-care boy I knew in Cannes a decade ago? You've become a bore in your old age. Spare me the agony, please."

"Yes, I did say those words or something to that effect. But this time is going to be different. Because tonight you, my dear, are bloody well going to tell me what I want to know."

"Oh, really, Alex? You think you can force me? And how, exactly, do you propose to get it out of me? Are you going to bend me over a chair and take me from behind, you big brute? Make me whimper and beg?"

An open invitation now hung in the air between them. She had told him what she wanted. It was all he needed. He had already decided to take what he wanted, and devil take the hindmost. He took a step toward her, grabbed hold of her arms, and pulled her close, pressing his mouth onto hers, forcing his tongue between her lips. Her breasts were large and warm against his naked chest, and he swept his arms around her, drawing her still closer. He examined the deep dark eyes, the red lips, the gleam of firelight on all that voluminous jet-black hair.

The last thing he expected was for her to resist. But he was somewhat shocked to suddenly find both of his wrists clamped in the iron grip of her two hands! Puzzled, he stared at her. Had he simply misread her signals? Maybe. But then, with a mischievous smile, she lowered herself down onto her knees. She was on the faux-fur rug before the fire, pulling him down onto the rug with her. Still, she held his wrists tightly captive, not allowing him to come close to her.

Hawke now felt the heat rising within him, but he got the message. If this game was going to continue, it would be on China's terms alone.

He knew that he wanted her, but he also knew that he had to wait for her to give her assent, and a part of him cursed the fact that, even now, in this most intimate of moments, she insisted on playing her bloody games.

He pulled her toward him, the flickering flames painting the silhouettes on the ceiling. He kissed the pale sheen of moisture on her cheeks. . . .

When they had finished and were both lying on their stomachs on the rug, smoking cigarettes and staring into the fire, she smiled at him and said: "Well, Alex, my dear man, if that's your new interrogation technique, I must confess that I like it. A lot. Any more questions for me, sir?"

Hawke smiled, but had no reply to that one.

CHAPTER 38

Sevenoaks Plantation, Virginia
February 1942

Tiger Tang sat straight up in bed. He'd heard the unmistakable sound of rubber automobile tires crunching on gravel in the drive below his bedroom windows. Now, blinking his sleep-encrusted eyes, he looked over at the illuminated alarm clock on his bedside table. His brain was still half asleep. What day of the week was this? It wasn't yet seven o'clock in the morning, for Crissakes! Okay, Sunday morning, that was it. What in hell was Hamish doing, calling his bedroom on a Sunday and at this unholy hour? Had the man lost all of his marbles? Was he entirely off the rails?

Tiger stared at the squat black Bakelite telephone and dared it to keep ringing, burying his sleepy head beneath his pillows. The lighted button on the phone was blinking BUTLER'S PANTRY. Muffled a scosh, but he could still hear the damn instrument, damn it to hell!

After an eternity, it stopped ringing.

Five minutes later, someone, most likely Hamish, was back at it.

Tiger picked up this time.

"This had better be good, by God," Tiger said, not bothering to hide the noxious fumes of his simmering anger.

Hamish sighed and said, "Frightfully sorry to disturb you, sir. But I thought it only prudent to make you aware that a yellow taxicab is waiting outside under the porte cochere. No one has made any move to exit the vehicle. It's just sitting out there with the motor running. Perhaps someone gave the driver the wrong address? The windows are all steamed up, and I cannot even tell you how many of them are inside the taxi and just sitting out there, sir. All a bit on the bizarre side, if you ask me, sir."

"Oh, Christ," Tiger said. Incredibly, this was a repeat of what had happened at midnight, just last night!

Miss Woolworth had shown up at his door sometime in the wee hours last night. He had been in bed, fast asleep, for more than an hour. But Hamish, with his usual fervor, had rung him up to announce her arrival, and he'd hauled himself out of bed and padded down the wide sweeping staircase to pull open the front door to the frigid night air. The evening snowfall had turned to sleet and freezing rain.

"You look like a drowned rat, my darling," he had said, eyeing her mop of drenched wet hair and the rain droplets running down from her chin.

She'd been to a big soiree her parents were hosting down at the Sagamore Hill Golf Club, and apparently, she was well into her cups. She had an open bottle of Dom Pérignon and two crystal champagne coupes. She stood up on her tiptoes and gave him a sloppy wet kiss.

"Take me to bed, Daddy," she whispered. "Your baby girl has been a bad girl, but she still needs it bad. And I'm freezing to death out here."

And so inside and so to bed.

And now someone else—God only knew whom—had decided it was a very bright idea to show up at his very private country home at this time of the morning! Bloody well uninvited and bloody well unannounced, waiting outside his front door! With a sigh of deepest regret at not getting a few more hours of much-needed sleep, Tiger rolled out of the cozy, high-thread-count Egyptian sheets and the huge four-poster bed piled high with goose-down pillows, and slipped his feet into the leather slippers waiting by his bedside.

He tried not to make a sound, lest he wake the sleeping beauty who now so frequently shared his bed, keeping him busy into the wee small hours. There were four large windows in his boudoir overlooking the rolling lawns and gardens in the front of the house and the sweeping drive mounting the hill and opening into the gravel car park and the porte cochere.

He made his way over to the nearest window and looked down at the car park and the drive. The automobile he'd heard on the gravel was idling under the porte cochere, its rooftop still weighted down by last night's snow squalls. He squinted at the legend painted on the passenger door at the rear. GEORGETOWN YELLOW TAXI, he saw, was emblazoned in dark green on the cab's flanks.

Still, who the hell had come to call at this ungodly hour?

The rear door swung open, and gazing down, the ambassador saw a tall, well-built fellow who was attired in a tailored Royal Navy officer's uniform and who now removed his white cap, the one with all the scrambled eggs on the black brim, uncovering a full head of unruly black hair. The still sleepy ambassador had an instant flash of recognition. Hawke! If it wasn't bloody Lord Hawke knocking on his door! Back from England already? He hadn't heard a peep out of him since the day he'd left for England, right after asking Tiger, at the Cosmo Club bar, to promise to keep an eye on his fiancée while he was gone because she had a tendency to find trouble wherever she went looking for it. . . .

And he'd pledged that he would. And then the pretty little troublemaker had wound up spending a whole lot of time in his bed. And his treachery ate away at him. His own. And, *hers*!

He stood for a moment at her bedside, looking down at the sleeping Winfield Woolworth, aka little Miss Five 'n' Dime. He was aware, as usual, of his mixed emotions surrounding his new paramour. His duplicity in this affair gnawed at him day and night. Secrets and lies. Many times, he'd felt he should end it right now. But somehow she always worked her magic.

Keep her stashed upstairs until Lord Hawke was gone. At which point he would tell her it was over between them. And now that Blackie was back in Washington, their relationship must always remain a secret. Hawke would do that very thing.

And suddenly he knew he couldn't do it.

The doorbell now sounded its deep tolling chime down in the front hall and reverberated up the elegant curving and freestanding staircase that soared to the second and third floors, just as Winnie's big blues popped wide open.

"Darling," she said, "where on God's green earth are you going at this hour? Do come back to bed, won't you, please, with sugar on top? You won't be sorryyyy. . . ."

"I don't understand a thing about you, Win. What is it with you? You go behind your fiancé's back the second he leaves town? I know your mother is very excited about you marrying a fancy British title. But still . . . why get engaged to a man if you don't even love him? What's that all about? I need to know something. What is it you really want? That's a question. Answer me."

"What do I want?"

"You heard me."

"I want the world, damn you. And everything in it. That's what I want, Mr. Ambassador. Now, get back in this bed and make Mama happy, mister."

"I'll do no such thing. You see, your precious fiancé has just arrived back from England and is now standing down at my front door, very persistently ringing my bell. So, I'm going down to see what he wants. And I want you to go back to sleep and stay out of sight upstairs for as long as he's here. Not a word out of you. You hear me? Not a bloody peep."

"You need to calm down, Tiger. Don't worry about it! I can handle him."

"'Handle him'? He may well shoot you if he sees you here with me at seven o'clock in the morning! Hell, he might shoot both of us! Listen to me, young lady. I don't imagine either of us would savor what is sure to be, if not an awkward moment, most certainly one that will cause great pain to the offended party, the only innocent party here, the man who entrusted the care of you to me, once, and formally, his best friend. My friendship with Blackie is important to me. We're rather like brothers at this point. I won't let you ruin that for him or me. Promise me you'll stay right here."

She sighed, pulled the covers over her head, and uttered the muffled words, "I promise, Daddy."

"And, for heaven's sake, stop calling me Daddy. I am not your father. Thank God! I'd be married to that harridan mother of yours!"

Rattled by his conflicting emotions, and descending the elegant curving suspended staircase, he reflected on the fact that in two days he'd be leaving Washington on the presidential yacht, headed for points north as a member of FDR's much ballyhooed fishing expedition. And following that trip, he'd been invited down to Warm Springs, Georgia, to spend the long holiday weekend with the president.

It was only then that Tiger recalled the very painful and very dangerous situation that, thanks to his godforsaken father, he now found himself in. Chiang Kai-shek had ordered him to assassinate the very man he served. A man he had come to not only revere, but someone for whom he now felt something distinctly akin to the love a son might feel for his father.

Not that he'd know a damn thing about that.

CHAPTER 39

Sevenoaks Plantation, Virgina
February 1942

His upcoming presidential travel invitations, Tiger considered, were two particularly convenient ways for him to stay well off the social radar for a few weeks. Take this romantic pot of his off the boil, he thought, and see what happened between the happy couple. Now, in his current situation, he was actually glad he'd accepted the fishing trip invitation, as well as a long, relaxing train ride down to Warm Springs, Georgia, deep in the heart of the southland.

Padding down the marble staircase, Tiger was feeling, more than ever, suffocated by this bewitching woman of his. He needed air and a whole lot of space. His nerves were frayed to the breaking point, and it was not a good feeling, not even close. Sometimes, when he felt he couldn't stand another minute of her company, he'd realized he couldn't stand the idea of breaking it off between them. He had never in his life met a woman this wanton, this libidinous. How to deal with her would require what they called at Oxford, Occam's razor. Usually in Latin, of course. *"Numquam ponenda est pluralitas sine necessitate,"* or something like that. His Latin, never a strong suit, but still able to dredge up a translation. "Plurality must never be posited without necessity." KISS, or Keep it simple stupid, as the Americans would have it.

There was a simple solution to the Woolworth dilemma: Bid her a fond farewell.

He stood before the closed front door for a few seconds and tried to compose himself. He mentally pictured himself as a man overjoyed to see Commander Hawke standing there in the cold. His lordship was a dear friend whom he'd worried he'd never see alive again. And a man whom he'd repeatedly betrayed with his fiancée. Stop the madness! he shouted to himself. Take control, damn you!

He took a deep breath and reached for the door handle. "Ready? Set? Go!" he said to himself, and grabbed the door handle with a will and pulled open the fifteen-foot-high oaken door, swinging it wide.

Hawke stood there on the icy steps, puffing a cigarette while staring at a brilliant red cardinal perched atop the snowy bough of an old Japanese maple tree, and looked around to see his friend standing in the open doorway, still in his pj's and quilted burgundy velvet smoking jacket with matching monogrammed slippers.

"Hawke! As I live and breathe!"

"Tiger," Hawke said with a warm smile, letting the word hang there between them.

"If it isn't his lordship in the flesh, safely home from the war! I shall henceforth consider all my prayers answered!"

Hawke returned the smile and said, "Hello, old boy! Sorry to come knocking at such a beastly hour on a Sunday. . . . Please, forgive me, Tiger. May I come in? Bit chilly out here, to be honest."

Tiger, slightly embarrassed by his lack of courtesy, stepped back into the entry hall and bowed, welcoming him inside with both arms extended.

Tiger said, "You're looking none the worse for wear, old bean. Clearly, secret commando raids on the Hun agree with you. . . . Come on back to the library. Hamish already has a wood fire going and a pot of coffee brewing. Unless my nose deceives me, I can smell them both."

"'Lay on, Macduff'!" Hawke said. "'And damn'd be him who first cries, 'Hold, enough'!"

Tiger laughed and said, "*Macbeth*, act five, scene eight!"

Hawke stopped dead in his tracks. He asked, "You actually know that? No one knows that. No one I know, anyway."

"The two of us do! Isn't that enough? A couple of old veterans of

Cambridge, Oxford, and the English public school system?" Tiger asked, reasonably enough.

Proceeding with his guest into the book-lined library, Tiger took the nearest of the two faded leather club chairs to either side of the hearth. He let himself simply breathe for a moment. The air in this room was perpetually redolent of ancient leather-bound volumes: Samuel Pepys, Pliny the Elder, Aristotle, and of course, Edward Gibbon and his dogeared copy of *The History of the Decline and Fall of the Roman Empire*. Yes, all this and the complete red leather collections of Dickens, Conan Doyle, and a good deal more.

Also, there was always the vague olfactory history of Balenciaga and other popular women's *parfums parisiennes* of the late-nineteenth and early-twentieth centuries, not to mention woodsmoke, and hundred-year-old velvet draperies so full of old dust and dirt that an archaeologist would have had a field day studying the things. And the even older leather furniture, gallons of dog pee and of spilled whiskey, and of course, *fromage*, the dominant aroma being that of an overripe Stilton from long ago and paired with a delicious dollop of Taylor's Reserve Port, put down in 1935.

Heaven on earth, in other words.

Hawke followed Tiger into the room and sat himself down in the matching opposite chair. He said, "I now know why you so love this room, Tiger. You're very lucky to have this sancturary to escape to when you need it. I envy you a bit, old boy."

Tiger replied, "Couldn't agree more. I've dreamed of a room just so for all of my adult life. So, tell me, dear Blackie, when did you arrive back upon these verdant shores?"

"Arrived on the liner from Southampton night before last. Took the train down from Penn Station in New York yesterday morning. Arrived here at Union Station in time for a homecoming lunch held for me at the Cosmos Club. You were invited. I was sorry to see you couldn't make it."

Tiger leaned forward and gave his friend his most earnest and appealing look. "As was I, as was I!" he said, "I had planned on attending, to be honest. But yesterday morning, I was summoned down to the stables as one of my favorite horses, Pale Rider, was taken during the night by some strange illness. Annie Fleming, our local vet, arrived at lunchtime to have a look. Said she'd never seen anything like it. Pulmonary, she thought. That the stallion should be carefully monitored for any signs of worsening. . . ."

Hawke said, "I'm so sorry. I know how you love that old horse. How is he doing?"

"Much improved when I went down to the stables last evening. What-ever the doctor has given him, it seems to be working. Thank God. So, what brings you out to the sticks on a cold and wet Sunday morning?"

"It's Winnie. I've looked high and low. I've been calling her George-town flat number and the one here in the country and getting no answer. I wanted to let her know I was back in Washington and wanted very much to see her. Celebrate my safe return or something like that. . . . Finally, in a bit of desperation, I called her mother and asked where she was.

"I was told she'd met some friends the night before at the Sagamore Hill Winter Dance and was going to the house of one of them for the night. Saying she'd be home for breakfast. But she never showed up. 'I honestly have no idea where she might be,' her mother said. 'She does this from time to time even though she knows it enrages her father.' At any rate, have you heard from her lately? Do you have any idea where she might have got to?"

"I'm so sorry," Tiger said.

"I very much wanted to surprise her. You can understand that?"

Tiger said, "Of course I can! What man would not? Oh, well, she'll turn up soon enough. I'm sure it's all very innocent, old boy. And, no, I myself haven't heard from her in days. I'm sure she's all right. She can take care of herself. Besides, she still doesn't even know you are home, does she?"

Meanwhile, Winnie, who'd had her ear pressed to the door for the last fifteen minutes, having overheard Tiger's story of this stallion needing attention, turned away and raced upstairs. She was shivering, still wear-ing nothing but her flimsy pink nightgown and a silk bed jacket, and she wanted to change back into the pair of old dungarees and an old flannel shirt and boots she kept in Tiger's closet. She then flew down the back stairs that led to the kitchen and out the kitchen door. She raced down the snowy hill to the barn, where Pale Rider was being cared for, and went straight to the sick stallion's stall.

The big horse appeared to be sleeping comfortably.

She dove into a corner of the hay-strewn floor, rolling around in the mounds of loose hay and straw, getting covered with the stuff, even scads of it in her long golden blond hair.

Then she jumped up and ran just as fast as her long legs would carry her, all the way back up the hill to Tiger's manse, going in through the kitchen door before making her way to the front of the house and the library.

She yanked the door open, peeked inside, and said, "Tiger, you'd better come quickly! I think your prize stallion has taken a grave turn for the worse."

"Winnie!" Tiger exclaimed, getting to his feet. "What in the world are you doing here?"

It was only then that she spied Blackie Hawke coming up out of his chair with a wide smile on his handsome face. Her heart fluttered at the sight of him. Never did one man do so much for a Royal Navy officer's uniform as his lordship Blackie Hawke.

"Oh! Oh! It's Blackie!" Winnie cried. "You're home! And safe! Oh, God, I've missed you, darling!" She fell into his arms and hugged him as tight as she possibly could.

Tiger chimed in, saying, "Winnie, when did you get here? I had no idea you were even on the property!"

"Oh, Tiger, but I've been here all night. Ever since the vet, Annie, told me that Pale Rider had suddenly taken ill, I've been worrying that no one was keeping an eye on him. I left my parents' party at the club, went home, and changed. I spent all night here, down in the stables with that beautiful animal. And the vet, my dear friend Annie, just got off the phone with me. She's coming up straightaway to have a look at her patient."

Hawke, listening to all this, had gone sneaking around behind his excited fiancée. He wrapped both arms around her tiny waist and lifted her a foot or two off the ground, high into the air, and shook her like a rag doll. Lowering her to the floor, he spun her around and kissed her full on the lips.

"My darling, you look so beautiful with all that hay in your hair. I have missed you so very much. Do you still love your old boy, still remember him after he's been away from you for so long?"

"Oh, my God, Blackie. Are you kidding? Just ask Tiger. He gets tired of hearing me talk about you. But, secretly, he missed you, too. I'd say the whole town hasn't been the same in your absence. We all love you, Commander Hawke!"

Tiger got to his feet. "All right, all right, enough of this mush talk. I'm out of this lovefest," Tiger said, moving toward the door. "What's everyone want for breakfast?"

"Bacon, fried eggs, and hash brown potatoes, fried to a crisp with oodles of Heinz ketchup!" said Winnie.

"Black coffee for me, old boy," Hawke said, "and two poached eggs on toasted muffins. God, it's good to see everyone so happy and safe!"

Winnie went to the ambassador and hugged him. She said, "Thank you, Tiger, so much for inviting us to stay for breakfast. I'm starving! Isn't it grand, having our boy back in town?"

"Grand," Tiger said, forcing a smile and pulling the heavy library door shut behind him.

"Christ in a wheelbarrow," Tiger muttered quietly to himself, making his way along the hall to the kitchen, "that bloody girl will be the death of me yet!"

CHAPTER 40

Washington, D.C.
February 1942

Exactly one week from that early morning when Hawke had first presented himself at the front door of Tiger's Sevenoaks Plantation, Commander Hawke suddenly found himself and Winnie invited to dine with Tiger, along with a bubbly blind date, a former college roommate of Winnie's. It was to be at the legendary and oh-so-fashionable George Town Club. Longtime home to distinguished and long-gone members of Congress, the rich and the powerful all had, at one time or another, sequestered themselves at this place to see and be seen, on Wisconsin Avenue in Washington.

Tiger mentioned to Hawke that he had just been made a full member of the very exclusive club, and he wanted to celebrate joining the venerable Home of the Old Guard, an establishment with a grand history. The intimate second-floor dining room where their table was situated was actually the very same room where George Washington would dine with the Frenchman, L'Enfant.

Hawke and his fiancée, Winnie, who had both resumed their somewhat attenuated feelings of deep affection for each other after his return from England, had both instantly felt at home in the place upon entering. Dark and warm walnut paneling in every room, all of it having been imported from a very grand château in Paris. Red-and-white checked tablecloths in every room. Quaint and cozy. The theme of all the art was primarily equestrian, with sporting portraits of great foxhounds of yore, and valuable old English foxhunting prints hung alongside portraits of famous winners of the Grand National and the Derby and Ascot, all adorning walls everywhere. On the ebony black baby grand piano, an embossed Tiffany silver frame, with a black-and-white autographed photo of a twelve-year-old Elizabeth Taylor on the set as Velvet Brown, starring along with Mickey Rooney in the much-beloved classic *National Velvet*.

A few centuries' worth of old sterling silver racing trophies were on all the mantels above the crackling hearth, and in the bookcases were the complete works of Shakespeare bound in red leather and many other grand titles of Sir Arthur Conan Doyle's Sherlock Holmes and Dame Agatha Christie's memorable detectives.

Guttering candles in bronze and black iron sconces provided a warm glow everywhere, as well as the fireplaces in almost every room to keep the cold winter night outside at bay. All very cozy. Hawke checked in with the maître d' and gave his name. A lovely hostess in her twenties, wearing a Colonial-period blouse, white stockings, and a floor length gathered calico skirt with slippers peeking out from beneath, appeared magically to escort the two of them to the ambassador's table.

Tiger was a noticeable figure, and Hawke and Winnie spied him instantly upon entering the room. Seated beside the ambassador was an incredibly beautiful girl with long, curly black hair that fell to her bare white shoulders. Apparently visiting from Spain and an old school chum of Winnie's.

"Welcome, all!" Hawke said, bowing slightly from the waist.

The ever-gracious ambassador, clothed in a splendid dark green velvet blazer, probably from Turnbull & Asser, beckoned the two new arrivals to join them. Tiger was enjoying all this immensely. Had you told Tiger, on that memorable morning in the country just one week ago today, that all would have been well once more, all the planets back in their customary rotation, all the tawdry secrets of his best friend's fiancée cloaked in a cape of silence, and that he would be having a cheery dinner with Blackie and his fiancée here at the George Town Club, he would have laughed out loud.

Ever since the reunification of Winnie and her affianced lover, Hawke, Tiger had been relishing the slowly evaporating clouds of despair and guilt that had plagued him during all those languid weeks of his highly charged illicit dalliance with the beautiful neighbor who lived down the hill.

He knew he was well out of that mess, and that now his life once more had that sense of order, duty, and clarity that had stood him in such good stead all the days of his life.

Winnie, alongside the handsome Englishman in his dress Royal Navy uniform, made her way through the jumble of tables and diners and wait-staff and appeared at the table in the corner that the ambassador had requested.

As was always the case, Winnie saw that the eyes of many women dining in the room were fixed on the tall and handsome Englishman in his perfectly cut uniform. She could feel the palpable waves of jealousy emanating from their tables like an ill wind out of the east.

"So sorry I'm a bit late, Tiger," Hawke said. "I was rather trapped on a lengthy call from you know who. May we sit down?"

"Let me guess. Your favorite uncle? Indeed, do sit down."

Hawke pulled out a chair and said, "Will this be all right?"

"Of course, if you two would rather stand . . . ," Tiger said, teasing him as always about his very formal English manners. "Be my guest!"

Hawke forced a grin and pulled out a second ladder-back chair for Winnie, helped her to get situated, and sat down right next to her.

Winnie leaned over and kissed the cheek of the beautiful Spanish girl sitting on her right, then turned and smiled and said, "Blackie, please say hello to my dear friend the Countess Victoria de la Maza, who's visiting me from Spain—Madrid and Seville, to be precise."

"Well, hello there, Victoria," Hawke said to the raven-haired beauty sitting between Tiger and Winnie. "I'm Horatio Hawke, but please call me Blackie. This, as you well know more than I, is my lovely fiancée, Winnie Woolworth. How do you two know each other, by the way, Victoria? You were at school together here in America?"

Victoria smiled and said with a lovely accent that sounded like a mix of British and Spanish that indicated the señorita had been schooled at some point in England. "Hello, Commander Hawke. That's it. We were at Miss Porter's boarding school together, at Farmington, which is up near Hartford in Connecticut. And we became very close. I stayed with her the summer after graduation, and then we both decided on the same college and were roomies.

"I understand you've just returned from London, Commander. Business or pleasure?"

"A little of both, actually. The usual endless meetings at my office in Whitehall. But thank God I managed to get in a bit of sailing out on the Channel with some of my late German friends...."

"Seriously? But you're at war with Germany!"

"Wartime makes for curious bedmates sometimes, my dear girl," Hawke said, hoping that answer satisfied her curiosity. It certainly was not far from the truth.

It did not satisfy her. She said, "But you say your 'late' friends. What on earth happened to them?"

"Terribly sad story, I'm afraid. It seems that, after putting me ashore at Dover, they ran afoul of a bad squall off Calais. Their splendid yacht, *Froya*, sank with all hands."

"How perfectly awful," Victoria said "And so sad for you, too.... My condolences."

Hawke gave her a sad, lingering look that he could only hope spoke volumes.

They all chatted on. Tiger took their drink orders and a mustachioed waiter magically appeared at the table. Soon enough, the two old school chums were holding hands and giggling, telling funny stories about their legions of boyfriends during the old school days, in that bygone halcyon time before the clouds of war began to gather to the east and to the west.

The two women had their heads close together, whispering secrets to each other now, casting sly glances at their two escorts, and Tiger took the opportunity to talk privately with Blackie about a matter that had come up only this morning.

"Everything fine between you two, Blackie?" he asked, keeping his voice low.

"Never better, to be honest. I don't know. She seems calmer and more collected, less like a Thoroughbred filly at the start of the Kentucky Derby at Churchill Downs, bucking and snorting in the gate and raring to go. . . ."

Tiger swiveled his head around, looking at all the diners nearby. Luckily, no tables were within good listening distance from the quiet one in the corner. Even so, when he spoke, it was with a strong sense of the warning in that poster hanging in the hall outside Hawke's office at the British Embassy: LOOSE LIPS SINK SHIPS!

"That's good, that's good," Tiger said. "That means she's putting you first now. And being your blushing bride-to-be. Well, I could not be happier for you both. Now, listen up, Your Lordship. You come bearing news, I gather. You say you were tied up on a call with you know who. No doubt your dear relation at Number Ten Downing?"

"The Lion of England? The British Bulldog? Hell, yes."

"And? What's he have to say for himself these days?"

"That's a conversation to be had in a secure bank vault at the U.S. Mint. So tell me, old sport, What's up with you two lovebirds now, Tiger? Let me guess. The president now wants you to move into the White House as a permanent resident. He's planning to install you in the Lincoln Bedroom, which, as I'm sure you know, is directly across the hall from the president's own quarters. So, you two can now have your midnight meetings and stogies and whiskey in your bloody jammies."

"Not funny," Tiger said.

"Funny," Hawke insisted. "Everyone in Washington thinks so. So, let me ask you again, Mr. Ambassador. What, precisely, is up?"

"You. You are what's up with Papa Roosevelt this morning. It seems that last night the president received a call from Churchill. The prime minister wanted to know if Roosevelt had ever met a young naval officer on loan to Washington from the Royal Navy Air Service. And that this particular British officer was widely known to be a friend of the new Chinese ambassador . . . and . . ."

"And?"

Tiger lowered his voice and continued. "And the president said he knew of you and was aware of the fact that you and I had become rather palsy-walsy, or, as FDR called it, 'chummy' as of late. Also, FDR told me that you were Churchill's nephew—a salient fact you never mentioned to me by the way but good to know—and that you had performed brilliantly in a very dangerous commando raid aboard an enemy German vessel recently. 'Brilliant tactics, heroic execution' were the words Winston used to describe it. He said you would soon receive a major honor from the Queen at Buckingham Palace at a strictly private ceremony in the spring. The story of the German bomber crash-diving into the Channel and the subsequent filching of the Nazi encrypting machine would never be made public. Or spread any further than Bletchley Park. But that wasn't the real reason he called.

"He told me all about his planned hush-hush fishing voyage off the coast of New England. And that he had invited all the members of his cabinet plus some high-ranking military and advisers from the White House. And finally, I was included. And then he—"

"Hold your horses, Tiger. Where do I fit in to this scenario?"

"Apparently Churchill might be on board, and Winston has asked FDR to invite you, of all people, on the upcoming trip. He wants you aboard when the two of them host their high-level war-planning discussions, including any number of critically important covert operations scheduled behind German lines. He said there was one new mission that he wanted very much to discuss further with you, Blackie, privately. A new scheme of yours, apparently. Very dangerous, Churchill said. It involves you and your squad parachuting behind enemy lines and making your way undercover to Berlin. . . . That's as far as he would go."

"Good Lord, Tiger, I just got back here. He told me it would be at least a month before he could get it approved by Admiral Godfrey and the powers that be at Naval Intelligence. . . ."

"Well. That's what you get for becoming a famous war hero, buddy. Anyway, I'm asking you at the president's request. Will you join me for this great adventure at sea?"

"Christ! I'm up to my ass catching up on all the war work that somehow got forgotten about whilst I was barging around Britain. . . . I don't know if I can manage to—"

"Oh, good God, man, stop it. It's Churchill, for God's sake! It's about you taking it to the Nazis once more, once more unto the breach! I'm sure your Navy superiors here in town will fully realize that you cannot even think about saying no to the prime minister. That's your first calling, Blackie. Not going to a bunch of endless meetings all over town, talking about the bloody lend-lease schedule and other endless logistical minutiae . . . right?"

"Of course you're right. There's only one man in England who knows how to win this bloody Nazi war and stave off what is sure to be the coming German invasion of our shores. It all falls to Winston, I guarantee you. He's the only man in England who has what it takes for the British Empire to emerge, stronger, more powerful, and ultimately victorious."

"Now you're talking, sailor! So, yes or no? Tell me, are you going to sign on for this epic presidential sea voyage or not? The president needs to know."

"I'm in, Tiger," Hawke said with a strange reddish gleam in his startling blue eyes. "As long as Winston doesn't give me an ultimatum to appear in London, I'm all in!"

Tiger realized for the first time that his friend was a warrior, fire and thunder to the core. And when called upon to serve his country, he'd be first in line to put his own life on the line in this epic battle against Hitler's Third Reich. Roosevelt and Churchill needed men like Blackie Hawke to come to the fore and confront evil, as powerful an enemy as ever to wage war against these two allies, Britain and America.

"Now, listen to me, Tiger. Winnie tells me you received a most unwelcome visit from your father while I was away. What was that all about?"

"Nothing, really. He was in Washington for meetings as a representative of Chiang Kai-shek, pleading for more and faster American aid. Seems the two of them have concocted some insane scheme or other.

Wanted me to lend a hand. I politely declined. The old boy's not playing with a full deck, I fear. He's got only three cards left to play, and they're all jokers."

"Sounds awful," Hawke said.

"Oh, it was a good deal worse than that," Tiger replied.

It was only then that Tiger recalled the well-oiled pistol now locked in his desk drawer in the library at Sevenoaks. A wave of despair washed over him. While Hawke was going off to fight, what was that old bastard, his father, doing?

Plotting the assassination of the heroic Roosevelt with Chiang, that's what. Biting his tongue nearly hard enough to make it bleed, Tiger simply said: "The old man's recently gone way round the bend, Blackie. Capable of literally anything."

"I'm so sorry you have to deal with that, buddy," Hawke said. "If there's anything I can do to help, just say the word, and listen, I've got to tell you something. I might not make the fishing trip. Winston wants me back in London, pronto."

"What's up? He tell you?"

Hawke lowered his voice. "Another mission. An idea I've been playing around with finally caught his attention after the salubrious ending of the last one. He and Admiral Godfrey and his number two, Commander Ian Fleming, want to ramp up immediately and—"

"Hey, excuse me, Blackie. I've got to make a trip to the loo. Be right back."

He needed air.

The Chinese ambassador arose and walked quickly past the restrooms down the hall, and then down the wine red carpeted stairs, through the smoky, crowded, and somewhat rowdy tavern room, past the packed horseshoe bar, past the maître d's station, and straight out the door into the snowy street.

He needed a cigarette and a few moments to be alone with his turbulent emotions, and the sick feeling at the pit of his stomach whenever he thought about that fucking gun from his old man, locked away in the library drawer where he wouldn't have to look at it. That awful dinner. Painfully, he was reminded of the nightmarish position he'd been put in because of his father and the generalissimo.

If ever he really did have to fire that gun, he hoped it would be to put a bullet into his father's head.

And certainly not the head of the heroic American president, for whom he'd come to feel not only abiding respect, but, even, yes, something akin to love, as a son to a father. He could never bring himself to admit it, but he'd lately come very close to thinking of FDR as his father figure. Certainly a far more fathomable choice than the wily old fiend he'd been conceived by.

President Franklin Delano Roosevelt was a man he could emulate. Someone whose leadership and wisdom he could revere who could provide a moral compass and a cherished confidante with whom he could share his innermost thoughts. . . . Oh, well.

"This is what you get by being born the devil's spawn," Tony Chow had said to him one day back in his childhood. Tiger had never forgotten or forgiven the sting of those cruel words.

And now the late Tony Chow, alone with his memories at the bottom of a bottomless lake, knew he should have been far more careful in picking his enemies.

"Oh, fuck it," Tiger said aloud, tired of all this crap.

He flicked the cigarette butt to the sidewalk and ground it out with the toe of one of his mirror-polished brogues.

Then he pasted a perpetually wry smile on his face and walked back into the warm glow of the George Town Club to be with his friends, old and new.

He was, after all, a man of the moment. An important cog among the many interwoven gears of the Washington war machine. He was, after all, now in the very thick of things, at the very nexus of Roosevelt and Churchill's vast war machinations. He found himself at the center of a British-American sabotage operation, which would give the Nazis pure unbridled hell right on their doorstep. He was suddenly far more than a mere bureaucrat. He was a functioning warrior, doing his part to help

America. He personified America's great ally, China, in the supreme struggle of the age, to win the world war for the Allies and safekeep civilization.

Tiger suddenly realized he was also somewhat jealous of his new friend Hawke. He knew he himself would be behind a desk for the remainder of the war. While Hawke would be dangling beneath a parachute canopy on a starry night, looking down at the muted lights of Berlin. Leaping into danger behind enemy lines, wreaking holy hell and havoc against his enemies.

Hell with it. He would just have to find some way or other to become more relevant to the cause, starting with getting word to his friend Mike Lotus, U.S. Secret Service. He'd tell him of rumors emanating from Beijing, that Chinese agents might attempt an assassination of Franklin Delano Roosevelt. In response, he was sure that the Secret Service would redouble their layers of protect.

One thing was certain.

He would sleep a whole lot easier.

CHAPTER 41

Number 10 Downing, London
February 1942

One week after the George Town Club dinner, as it happened, Winston Churchill did indeed give Hawke a top priority ultimatum. A wire delivered to his office appeared that afternoon informing him that a Royal Air Corps transport plane was on the ground at a secret U.S. Army Air Corps landing strip in the Maryland countryside, ready to ferry him back across the Atlantic. Tonight. An unmarked government car would be at a secret RAF airstrip to deliver him unto Churchill at Number 10.

The prime minister was expecting him tomorrow promptly at 10 A.M.

And despite his misgivings about jumping into another critical mission so soon after Skyhook, and despite that the new mission had been his idea all along, he packed his rucksack and took a taxi out to the field in Maryland. No sooner was he aboard, seated all alone behind the cockpit in the cold in a canvas sling chair, than they were airborne. It was hellishly chilly in the cavernous fuselage of the empty transport plane, the air reeking of oil and petrol. Huddled under his paper-thin Army blanket, he smoked and slept when he was able and awoke when the big plane touched down on English soil. And then to Number 10 he went.

"Enter, nephew!" a voice boomed from the cloud of steam rising from the big white porcelain bathtub. The cool white tiled walls were bathed in the sheen of condensation. "There's champagne over on the table, Blackie."

Hawke, startled and trying to imagine the sober, dignified Roosevelt entertaining company in his bathtub with an offer of chilled champagne, found the glass of champagne releasing a bubbly stream to the surface. A bottle of Pol Roger stood in a silver ice bucket beside the glass. He took a seat on the white wooden stool and, thankfully, swallowed the icy bubbly in one draft. Another? Perhaps not.

Hawke saw only the merest suggestion of a pair of chubby pink hands waving about inside the clouds of rising steam, and then he saw Churchill emerge from the mist, leaning forward in his tub, a genuine smile on his round, cherubic pink face, and examining his young nephew, just arrived from Washington.

The prime minister raised his empty wineglass and Hawke leaned forward with the icy champers and filled his glass. Hawke, desperate for a cigarette, found himself wondering if a prime minister who received visitors in his bath and offered them champagne would also allow them to smoke as well.

Probably not.

"Good ho!" Churchill said, and collapsed back into the steamy veils, sloshing a goodly bit of soapy water over the rim of the big white tub. "I do hope you're being properly looked after, Commander! Suitable lodgings on the top floor, I trust?"

"Doing well, thank you, doing well," Hawke said, grateful for the first warm glow of champagne hitting the system.

At that moment, Churchill, in all his roly-poly naked pink glory, arose from the tub, stuck out his hand, and deadpanned, "Towel, if you please, nephew!"

Seeing the look of shock on the young officer's face, the old fellow said, "Let it never be said that the prime minister of Britain has anything to hide from his nephew nor anyone else for that matter!"

Hawke averted his eyes and handed him the fluffy terry towel.

Toweling off in the steamy bathroom, Churchill said, "Listen, Horatio

Hawke, there's to be a reception in your honor at the noon hour. Down in the main reception room. Commander Fleming has organized a drinks party for DNI staff, Wild Bill Donovan, OSS, the usual suspects. At my suggestion, Admiral Godfrey wants you and Fleming to meet. Thinks you and Fleming might be a rather lethal combination going forward. This mission you call, so mysteriously, 'Phantom Locomotive.' I want the four of us to discuss it in some detail as the day wears on. Admiral Godfrey has some ideas for you. I think you will find him terribly helpful."

"Of course, Uncle. I need all the help I can get."

"Good, good! I think you and Fleming should get along splendidly. Two peas in a pod, as the saying goes . . . birds of a feather and all that, both intellectually challenged but devastatingly attractive and catnip for the ladies!" Winston stared at his nephew, waiting for a reaction.

Hawke realized his leg had been pulled, smiled at this uncle, and said, "Good one, Uncle! You had me there for a moment."

"My pleasure. You've met young Fleming, I understand."

"Ian was in my class at Eton, and again at Dartmouth Naval College, although we were never close. A rather moody boy. Bit of a loner is my memory. Haven't seen him since, actually."

"Well, he's performed brilliantly over at DNI. Godfrey's second-in-command and head of his own commando sabotage unit, 30AU. Assault Unit Thirty or, as Ian calls it, 'Indecent Assault Unit Thirty.' Now, I've ordered breakfast for you up in my private dining room. They're waiting for you now. I'll see you at Fleming's party promptly at noon."

CHAPTER 42

Fleming, tasked by Churchill himself with hosting the Naval Intelligence event honoring Hawke, was glad to finally escape from all the guffaws, backslapping, hale and hearties, and happily made his way to a quiet corner of the large, high-ceilinged room. There, waited a comfy leather sofa and two armchairs flanking a crackling fire. He loathed small talk and did not suffer well the endless stream of Winston's off-color jokes that everyone in HM government seemed to find so amusing. He was quite content to be known as a chap with no sense of humor and to sit and observe the invitees, see who was talking, or sleeping, with whom and who was not. That sort of intel was usually helpful in the hothouse environment that was Whitehall at war.

And here at last, Fleming saw, entered the man of the hour, following through the wide doorway on the coattails of Admiral Godfrey. Ian watched him closely as he smiled and shook hands and played every bit the handsome war hero in a charming fashion such as Olivier himself could not have outshone on the silver screen.

Commander Ian Fleming, who was number two to Admiral Blinker Godfrey, the head of DNI, at Whitehall, was sitting back in his chair, watching with some amusement as the man of the hour, this dashing young hero, Commander Hawke, greeted Churchill and his wife, Clementine, and other assorted brass hats, all eager to shake hands with the man who'd delivered the ultimate prize, the Nazi *Kriegsmarine*'s 3-rotor decoder along with all the relevant codebooks. It was, by all accounts, one of the more spectacular individual feats of the war.

From across the crowded room, Admiral Godfrey caught Fleming's eye, nodded, and began wading through the mob with Hawke still on his heels toward Fleming's ringside seat by the fire.

Fleming was actually of two minds about this fellow he was about to see for the first time since Eton and college. Hawke's reputation was now burnished gold. But still, Fleming himself had done a lot of similar wet work behind enemy lines. He was also the creator and inspiration for 30 Assault Team (known as 30AU), also known as "Ian's Red Indians," a crack team of commandos who'd penetrated enemy territory many times to perpetrate saboatage and gather vital intelligence and feed it back to Whitehall.

Neither he himself, nor his team, had received, nor should they have received, half the internal recognition as had Hawke's Operation Sky-hook. It was not chagrin Fleming was feeling. Just the mildest traces of envy, perhaps.

Hawke's operation had been, from the get-go, a spectacularly con-ceived and brilliantly executed blow against the Nazis' naval forces. Still top secret and surely to remain so forever, enough had leaked out around the edges for one to imagine its brilliance.

Fleming, educated at Eton and Dartmouth, came from a very old, rich, and successful Scottish banking family, and he was not, by nature, one prone to the pangs of jealousy. But this young man, Lord Hawke, filthy rich, titled, popular with the other sex, good-looking enough to find him-self frequently on the cover of the society gossip rags, rather had a ten-dency to get under one's skin at times.

Fleming stuck another cigarette into his tortoiseshell cigarette holder, clenched it between his teeth at a rather jaunty angle, and sat back to enjoy the show. Hawke was the golden boy now, the hero behind the en-coder purloined at great risk of life and limb from the Nazis. He noticed Hawke catching his eye as he began working his way over toward him.

Hawke arrived and extended his hand and Ian stood, then shook it rather firmly, just for good measure.

Godfrey said, "Well, here you are, Fleming. Did you not invite your-self to your own fling, or are you just in a grouchy mood? Say hello to Commander Hawke, won't you? He tells me you two were at school to-gether. Not, he says, that you'd remember him at all. . . ."

"Commander Hawke," Fleming said warmly, "I am honored to finally meet you officially, sir. I've followed your DNI career since the beginning and congratulate you on your countless and enormous contributions to the fight. Blinker tells me you've got some excellent new bunker-busting ideas for us with which to beleaguer the Nazis anew."

"Well, for you to judge, of course, but, I must say, Winston is fright-fully keen about the idea."

"As am I, as am I," Godfrey said. "Time is getting short, and I thought we three might have a bit of a quiet chat about the scheme. Winston was supposed to join us, but he seems otherwise engaged with the First Sea Lord. This corner is private enough if we keep our voices down. Fleming, would you mind terribly ordering whiskey for us? You recall where the bar is, I'm fairly certain."

Ian stood and excused himself, heading once more into the fray.

This Hawke fellow seemed a genuine enough chap, Ian perceived, some-one whose thoughts and deeds were not guided by guile or conceit. There was a fleeting innocence in his compelling blue eyes that spoke well of his character. A good, honest fellow, that was Fleming's first im-pression. A born warrior with a spine of steel. A man's man to be sure, the kind of fellow whose company Fleming himself most enjoyed. The kind of man, Ian was fond of saying, "Whom men would wish to stand him a drink, whilst women much preferred him horizontal."

While Fleming fulfilled his obligations, Godfrey got his pipe going, looked up at Hawke, and said, "Brilliant chap, Fleming. Nerves of steel and a frightfully colorful imagination. Should anything untoward befall me, he is the next man up. Just so you know."

"He was quite the sportsman at school. Cricket, rugby, tennis, golf. Amazing athlete. He's obviously taken good care of himself," Hawke said. "I understand he's just bought a home in Jamaica. Calls it Goldeneye. He says that after the war is over, he's going there to write the great British spy novel. Says he's got enough stories from his 30AU actions behind German lines to write fifty bloody novels if he wants to."

"Yes, so he told me. His brother, Peter, is a very successful author, and Fleming is very competitive with him. He also showed me the Jamaica pictures. Lovely water views. But back to business. We three all the share the twin burdens of fate and victory here, don't we? I'm looking forward to hearing Fleming's take on your new scheme. He can bring a lot to the party, as you know. Ah, here he is now, bearing gifts . . . a brimming bottle of Haig Pinch and three crystal glasses fit for kings."

CHAPTER 43

Number 10 Downing, London
February 1942

Once Ian had returned and poured the drinks all round, the three men sat back and savored the odd sip or two until Fleming, expelling a plume of blue smoke, said, "So, tell me about the new scheme you two have cooked up, won't you, Hawke? Apparently your latest brainstorm has got old Winston walking into meetings singing, 'Over there, over there!' at the top his lungs. I'm exceedingly curious, to be honest."

"Well," Hawke said, "it's rather a curious thing, to be honest. Came to me in a dream, as these things have a way of doing. Where would you like to start?"

"What's your primary objective, for starters?"

Hawke looked at him, smiled, and said, "Well. What we intend, Commander Fleming, is nothing less than to dismantle Germany's entire primary railway system in a single devastating blow."

Fleming tried to hide his reaction to this staggering statement. "Good grief," Fleming said, "is that all? Can we not sink the German Navy at the same blow? Ground the *Luftwaffe*? Corner the sauerkraut market? Kidnap the semi-beautiful Fraulein Eva Braun and hold her for a king's ransom?"

Hawke laughed, slapping his knee in the bargain.

"It is a rather tall order, I admit, Commander Fleming. It's sabotage, plain and simple, as no one knows better than you. But not so plain and not so simple, as I'll explain."

"Good Lord," Fleming said, gathering his wits, "you do think big, Commander Hawke! I'll give you that. The code name you've given the operation certainly piqued my curiosity, Blackie. Do you mind if I call you Blackie? I'm happy to be known as Ian. . . . So, tell me, Operation Phantom Locomotive? Sounds very dramatic, I must say. Please elaborate . . . a ghost-in-the-machine type of thing, what?"

Hawke saw Blinker Godfrey give him an approving nod and said to Fleming: "Yes. Yes, there will most definitely be a ghost at the throttles of the locomotives when they roar inside Berlin *Hauptbahnhof* at full bore. Let me paint a quick picture for you in very broad strokes. Admiral Godfrey and I have all the necessary support documents, maps, et cetera, in a file in my private office. I'll share it with you first thing tomorrow morning. Then we can discuss Operation Phantom Locomotive in great detail."

Godfrey interrupted, saying, "Well, Ian, let me interject here. I don't think you'll find what we now have in mind is nearly so complicated nor even as inherently risky as Commander Hawke's Operation Skyhook. But if successful, Phantom will yield enormous dividends at a moment critical to national morale, to turning the tide in our war effort and in the hearts and minds on the home front. And as an added enticement, it's sure to drive the jackboot boys in Berlin straight up the Reichstag walls!"

"You have my full attention, Admiral," Fleming said, leaning forward so as not to miss one word, he was so keen on it. "I must say I do rather like that code name. Operation Phantom Locomotive does have a nice ring to it."

"I agree. Now let me tell you about the plan. Broad strokes, as I say, but Hawke and his squad of fifteen intend to do a night drop deep into Germany, the countryside, perhaps within a radius of fifty miles outside of Berlin.

"Once safely on the ground, the team will split up. Each saboteur will have been assigned a specific primary German railway station at the end of the Berlin trunk line, and that is his sole target. Each of the fifteen individual stations targeted is located on one of those primary trunk rail lines into and out of Berlin. That will be important.

"Each man will be equipped with the necessary weapons and ammo, as well as tools, satchels of high explosive devices, and sufficient food and water for the amount of time he will require. I believe a maximum window of twelve hours, operating only at night, will suffice to accomplish what's necessary. As soon as a man's work is complete, and the driverless locomotives are speeding toward Berlin, he will immediately begin to make his way back to the barn at the drop location and wait with the others until exfiltration by means not yet determined. Understood?"

"Question," Fleming said. "How do the assault team members get to and from their targets, especially traveling such distances at night in unknown enemy countryside?"

"Good question, Fleming!" Blinker said. "I was going to ask you about that. I had rather a good idea. Do you still have your full network of British sympathizers and Nazi Resistance operating under cover inside Germany?"

"The Edelweiss Pirates? Couldn't live without them, sir. Literally."

"Good to hear it. As I recall, you've kitted them all out as motorcycle couriers, the Deutschesbund Courier and Post Patrol, I believe they're called. Sten guns and frag grenades in their saddlebags."

"Or," Fleming said, "monster explosive devices in the saddlebags! Yes, we're intact. All word-perfect German-born citizens with flawless papers and an encyclopedic knowledge of German history, culture, and terrain."

"Perfect!" Godfrey said. "Look here, Ian, here's what Commander Hawke and I intend. Looking at aerial photos of possible landing zones, we've seen one LZ with a huge barn in a vast field, abandoned, near primary roads. I'd like you to have your lads, en masse, sneak their motorcycles inside that barn under cover of darkness and await our arrival at the drop site. Phantom team members, given maps of their targets and wearing appropriate Postal Courier uniforms, will then use their bikes to get to their targets with the explosive devices quickly and undercover. Upon completion of the mission, they make their way back to the waiting aircraft, while Fleming's C and P Patrol riders return home before dawn. What say you, Fleming?"

"It's perfect, sir."

"Brilliant, sir!" Hawke added, not to be outshone by his new rival.

"Once in situ at his assigned station, each operative will scout his particular rail yard under cover of darkness and locate a suitable locomotive waiting on a siding. That is, one that is scheduled to depart that night for Berlin but has not yet been coupled with a train. He will then board the detached locomotive and place his explosives wherever Fleming expects they will do the most collateral damage."

"And then?" Fleming said, his curiosity getting the better of him. "What happens?"

"Ian, calm down. You'll hear all the Phantom details in good time. But I asked you and Hawke here for a very specific reason. Commander Hawke, a question I've been nursing. That is, who on your team will be responsible for designing and implementing the explosive devices to be used in the attacks? Have you designated someone for that purpose?"

"Yes, sir. Lieutenant Stauffenberg, who was my number two on Sky-hook. He's had a bit of sabotage experience, I understand. Apparently managed to blow up a bakery truck in front of the Berlin opera house on an opening night when Herr Hitler himself was in attendance."

"A bit of sabotage experience, you say, Blackie? Small-scale hit-and-run operations? Ian, this is where you come into the picture. We're going to send at least fifteen massive steam locomotives packed to the gunwales with high explosives, all hurtling along in excess of eighty to ninety miles per hour, right into the beating heart of Berlin with no one at the controls! Thoughts?"

Fleming thought a second. "Hmm. No timers. Impact detonators, obviously. I'll need to get a look at similarly designed locomotives before I can speculate on the design components and ideal placement of the explosive devices inside the locomotives. . . ."

"Thanks, Ian. Blackie, by way of background, let me tell you a little bit about Commander Fleming's 30AU, his assault unit."

"I call it my 'Indecent Assault Unit,'" Fleming said with a smile. "We're a very rowdy and destructive bunch of lads. . . ."

Blinker looked at Hawke. "Ian, behind his back, is called 'the Detonator.' There is not a more experienced man in the art of high explosives, nor a more seasoned saboteur in all of Britain. Remember the massive Rhine Valley bridge that stood in the heart of Germany for centuries? It's now a pile of rubble. The hydroelectric plants and dams at Remagen? Gone, thanks to Fleming here. . . .

"Is that right?" Hawke said. He suddenly saw exactly where this was going. "Ian, could I implore you to hop aboard the Phantom train? I'm sorry I didn't think of asking you myself. I was overwhelmed with sheer logistics. And I just was not aware of all your vast experience in modern demolition stratagems. . . . I really had no idea you were so active out in the field."

"Bringing young Ian into the picture? Yes, by all means. That would be my job, Hawke," Godfrey said. "Yours is to think these insane schemes of yours up out of thin air. Mine is to bring you back in touch with reality to ensure that they are executed perfectly. *Et voilà, Monsieur Fleming?*"

"I'm in," Fleming said. "When and where do we start training for this epic adventure?"

"Immediately. I've been scouting rail yards in the north of Scotland. Found the perfect one near the town of Dundee. There's a huge warehouse out in the rail yard built right over the tracks, open at both ends, where, out of sight, we can do all the demolition design and fabrication in complete secrecy. There's an old abandoned railway hotel, the Highlander, across the street from the yard. Holes in the floors, dust everywhere, and inundated with mice, but it will serve. That's where everyone will be housed for the duration of the training."

"Sounds ideal, sir," Hawke said. "Always rather fond of mice myself."

"It is ideal," Godfrey said. "Oh, Ian, just for fun, tell Hawke about your chocolate bombs."

"Admiral, with respect, I don't think he could care less."

"Ian, with respect, I think I could not care more," Hawke said. "Chocolate bombs? Surely, you're joking."

"Just an idea I had. Two wafer-thin pieces of steel with a film of nitro in between. Coated with best Swiss chocolate. Break off a corner and the cotton fuse ignites the explosive. A thought I had about smuggling these things into the Reichstag or the Eagle's Nest to assassinate Herr Hitler or Goebbels or any of them. No success yet, but we keep trying."

Hawke laughed out loud. "My God, that is insanely brilliant, my dear Ian."

Fleming reached out his hand to Hawke, and Blackie shook it warmly, saying, "Well, Fleming, it looks like we're going to be partners in crime for this show. The Fleming and Hawke Show. I'm sure I can learn a lot from you."

Ian smiled and said, "As can I from you, Blackie, as can I!"

"I'll drink to that," Godfrey said, all smiles that his secret plot to bring Fleming aboard the Operation Phantom Locomotive seemed to have succeeded. He raised his glass and said, "A toast, gentlemen. To our wives and girlfriends! May they never meet!"

It got a laugh as it always did.

And so it began, what would prove to be one of the most fortuitous meetings and collaborations in the storied history of British espionage and sabotage during World War Two.

Fleming. And Hawke. Known in the Navy as code names "Falcon" and "Raptor." Birds of prey, in other words!

Together at last.

And primed to kill half the Nazi hierarchy in the Reichstag Building in the heart of Berlin. Or, at the very least, blow Herr Hitler the hell out of his bloody bed in the midnight hour!

CHAPTER 44

Dragonfire Club, the Bahamas
Present Day

Alex Hawke and Stokely Jones spent the rest of that week exploring, just your basic recon. They were doing a complete reconnaissance of the entirety of the Dragonfire complex. Every island, every nook and cranny of every island. Stokely took the Wally's helm early each morning, and Hawke, using a Leica camera left over from the fifties that his late grandfather had bequeathed to him, a Minox B Subminiature camera, shot literally hundreds of pictures.

The tiny espionage camera, shaped like a small but elongated cigarette lighter, could be easily concealed in the palm of an agent's hand; it had first been conceived in Latvia in 1922. And it was finally invented and produced in 1936 by a Baltic German named Walter Zapp. It was the camera of choice on both sides of the Iron Curtain during the whole of the Cold War.

On these sun-filled Bahamian days, Hawke, wearing only his ivory white silk shirt and a navy blue Vilebrequin bathing suit, would pretend to be sunning himself on the bow of the Wally boat, while surreptitiously snapping away at anything that caught his interest. The morning after their submerged visit to the Chinese sub pen, Hawke had called his old comrade and friend, Patrick Brickhouse Kelly, director of the CIA, known to his friends as Brick.

Upon hearing Hawke's report of Chinese naval operations being conducted in secrecy just a hop, skip, and jump from the east coast of Florida, Brick suddenly went utterly and completely silent.

"Brick? Are you still with me?"

"Yeah, barely. Jesus, Mary, and Joseph, Alex! I mean, seriously? The fucking Chinese are actually operating Shine-class subs out of the fucking Bahamas? Utterly beyond the pale. The president's going to pitch a total shit fit."

"But they are. Three of them, in fact. Two of them were berthed inside when we swam inside. One, I assume, was off on patrol of our Eastern Seaboard."

"And you've got something to prove all this? You actually got inside the damn sub pen?"

"I did. Stoke and I. As soon as we ring off, I'm going to e-mail you photographic proof via my encrypted iPad."

"Christ," Brick said. "Have you any idea how serious this is? Their new subs carry the new JL-Three nuclear missiles. Range of nearly six thousand miles. And because they're new subs, unlike land-based ICBMs, Chinese subs can sail close enough to the American mainland to put all U.S. cities well within their range."

"So, it's even worse than I thought. . . ."

"It most certainly is. Doesn't get any worse, my friend. And you two are the only ones down there who have any inkling about this? You and Stokely? Say yes, Alex."

"Yes."

"What in hell are you doing down there, anyway?"

"I'm here investigating the disappearance of my godson, Henry. Prince Henry, actually, the Queen's favorite grandson. There's massive security all over the place. Including a pair of Chinese Navy missile frigates patrolling the coastline. They're painted in a generic grey camo to disguise them, but that's what they are, all right. Now I understand why they're operating in these pacific waters. 'Pacific' as in calm, of course. Not the ocean."

"Of course." Brick sighed, knowing Hawke would never tire of trying his patience with what he thought were humorous asides. "You know what you're sitting on, right, Alex?"

"Yes. A keg of dynamite. Laced with C-4 and nitroglycerin. The next Cuban Missile Crisis multiplied to the tenth power."

"Exactly. As soon as I receive your transmission, I'm going directly to the president and the Joint Chiefs. Do you two require any backup down there?"

"Not now, Brick. But maybe later. You remember the Tang brothers that I told you about? The twins who rule the vast criminal underworld? The duo behind that black ops massacre that went south in Hong Kong two years ago, remember?"

"Breathes there a soul who does not?"

"The Tangs built this place. The Dragonfire Club. They run it as an ultraexclusive resort. Six wholly individual Bahamian islands connected by a monorail and a launch service. Hotel is by invitation only. Gambling, girls, whatever. But what it really is, I believe, is a cover story. What it really is, is the worldwide HQ of their international criminal network, which is one of the reasons, in addition to their jobs as landlords for the Chinese Navy, that they have fortified this island to within an inch of its life. The security here is like nothing I've ever encountered before, trust me."

Brick said, "I'm looking at it on Google Earth right now. Impressive."

"Very," Hawke said, matter-of-factly. "A billionaire's playground on an epic scale."

"Okay. Talk to me. What's your cover down there?"

"Chairman and CEO of Hawke Industries, LLC, based in London, with offices in New York, Miami, L.A., Paris, Tokyo, and Madrid. A worldwide consortium of very important companies and up to their ears in very important people. Including the boss."

Only his old pal Hawke could get a laugh out of Brickhouse Kelly at a moment like this. But laugh he did.

"They buy that? They don't make you for a spook? Hell, Alex, they're looking for a new Bond now that Daniel Craig has abandoned ship. You could have that role if you wanted a new career. I'm only half kidding.

Listen to me. I don't want you getting sideways with these people. Especially since you and Mr. Jones are down there all by your lonesomes. If you need a few heavily armed babysitters, say the word, and they'll be down on the next thing smoking out of Joint Base Andrews."

"So far, so good right now. But you never know, Brick. If I feel like I'm about to get in over my head down here, you'll be the first to know about it. Meanwhile, I need a favor."

"Name it and claim it, buddy."

"I need you to run a name through the international criminal database at Langley. Ready?"

"Aim, fire."

"It's a woman. Her name is Zhang Tang. In her thirties, born in Shanghai. She's the younger sister of the twins. She's fancies herself the head honcho down here at Dragonfire Bay. Queen-bee sort of thing. Runs the joint in their absence. I'd love to know whose side she's on."

Brick said, "Has to be her family, right? There's no way she could not know what the boys are up to."

"Yeah. I think so, too. I'd still like whatever dossier your guys can put together on her. I think she could prove useful when we blow the lid on this. Tell me, is the secretary of state still in Beijing negotiating the trade agreement, or trade disagreement as some people in Parliament have come to call it?"

"No, he's back in town."

"He's going to have his work cut out for him when this fit hits the shan."

"Have you met him, the new guy at State? Name is Jon Adler. Fulbright scholar, Nobel Peace Prize laureate, Harvard, Kennedy fellow, the whole nine yards."

"Know his name, that's all. What the hell do you think the president is going to do with this hot potato, Brick?"

"The subs? Same thing as Kennedy did with the Soviets back in October of nineteen sixty-two. Call them out on it. Go public and go big. Give a slide presentation at the UN Security Council. Show your photos. Get the Navy to set up a naval blockade in the South China Sea. No maritime travel in or out of the Chinese mainland. Then I'm going to bring our Atlantic Fleet to bear in the Bahamas. Encircle the entire complex of islands. Give the Chinese forty-eight hours to withdraw all three subs from this hemisphere. Noncompliance with the deadline results in saturation bombing of the islands once all the civilians have evacuated. That's what I'd do, anyway."

"Sounds about right, Brick."

"Right. Too bad they had to pull this stunt. We were finally getting somewhere with all that shuttle diplomacy. Put an end to their decades of horrific trade abuses."

"Yeah, well. As I've said to you many times, any problem you can solve with money is not really a problem."

"Yeah. I guess."

"Stay safe, Hawke."

"That's me. Mr. Safe and Sound. You, too, Brick."

CHAPTER 45

Dragonfire Club, the Bahamas
Present Day

Stoke and Hawke were up early and went for a five-mile run on the beach. Two-and-a-half miles out, same thing back. On soft sand, mind you. It was the first time since the night at Teakettle Cottage when he and Pelham had been mutilated by Shit Smith that he'd really felt worth a good goddamn. He had energy again, maxed out his nitric oxide, energy to spare, and he wanted to continue on the arc of healing and restoring his body to its prior fitness.

The run was not entirely about sweat and fitness. Hawke had been looking at pictures of the Tang residence perched atop the highest hill on the island. It was certainly big enough, built on about six different levels, meandering around and down the hillside to where the jungle encroached. The postmodern structure looked to have been built on a clearing at the very top of the hill. It was totally surrounded by dense jungle and warnings like PRIVATE. NO TRESPASSING! And orders to KEEP OUT! GUARD DOGS!

His curiousity piqued, Hawke said, "Let's go take a look at this damn thing, Stoke. It's two and a half miles away, at the southern tip of the island. The beach runs along directly below it. It's jungle all the way, but we've got your machete."

"You gonna carry, boss? Just in case," Stoke said.

"Yeah. I'll stick the Walther in the waistband of my swimsuit. You?"

"Around this place? Always. Listen, before I forget, I saw something on my way down here from Miami I meant to tell you about soon as I got off the G-plane."

"Now's as good a time as any, man."

"Well, it was at the end of the flight. We were coming out of five thousand feet, descending and on final approach. I happened to be looking out the window, expecting to see blue water. But what I saw was green. It was a giant mangrove swamp, stretching out as far as I could see. And suddenly we're over water again. Right in the center of the swamp was a large bay, totally surrounded on all sides by the dense mangroves."

"Tell me this is going to be good, Stoke," Hawke said, wondering where this was going.

"Gonna be good enough, I'm tellin' ya. So, anyway, right smack-dab in the middle of this big bay? A goddamn island! Pretty big island. Completely overgrown with jungle and mangroves, just a narrow band of sand all the way around the perimeter. No sign of life whatsoever. But—and here's the thing—we were descending rapidly now, and I was amazed to see these big signs posted everywhere, on stilts out in the water, all around the whole damn island."

"Could you read them?"

"Yeah. And I did, just before we cleared the swamp about ten minutes before we touched down at Nassau. They all said the same thing: 'Private property! Intruders will be shot!' and 'Warning! Armed guards!'"

"What the hell?" Hawke said.

"My thought exactly. What the hell? Remember that time in the Amazon? That entire city that Papa Top had created under the jungle canopy where no satellites could ever see it? Houses built up in the trees and connected by wooden bridges. . . ."

"Yes, I certainly do remember. We barely got out of there. So, you're saying you think there might be something on that island? Some kind of compound hidden deep beneath the trees and the mangroves?"

"Exactly. Just what I was thinking. You think we should go take a look this afternoon, assuming we don't get eaten alive by no damn guard dogs?"

"Absolutely. Lots of secrets down here. I want to get to the bottom of every one of them. And I want to find my godson, Henry, damn it."

"We'll find him, boss. Don't you worry yourself about that! You think he's still here in the Bahamas, somewhere or other?"

"Yes. The Queen of England's grandson is a very big fish for them to have landed. I think the brothers would want to keep him close. Somewhere they could keep an eye on him, twenty-four seven. So someone like us doesn't come along and snatch him."

"Think you're right about that, brother," Stoke said, mopping the sweat from his face with the back of his hand.

"I suppose we'll see about that," Hawke said.

And, indeed, he would.

It just didn't turn out exactly as he had anticipated.

CHAPTER 46

Devil's Island, the Bahamas
Present Day

A cold front had crept ashore on cat's-paws during the night. Day had dawned on a thick, heavy layer of fog, a real pea-souper, as Hawke called it back home in dear old Blighty. He pulled the glass slider open, and he and Stokely walked out onto the broad terrace. You could hardly even see your hand in front of your face.

"Okay, Stoke. Let's do this."

"In this crap? Do what? We can't even see. Hell, I couldn't even button up my fly or tie my damn shoes."

"I know the route to the marina in my sleep. We'll be fine. Man up, Stoke!"

"Whatever."

"And don't say 'whatever.' Makes you sound like a pompous dick-head."

"Hey, hold up. Did somebody get up on the wrong side of the bed this morning? I think so. . . ."

Hawke just stared at him for a few seconds and stepped back inside the living room.

So, he and Stoke took the elevator down to the underground garage and climbed back aboard his trusty motorcycle, the amazing Vincent Black Shadow that Zhang, God bless her crazy little heart, had found for him at some old garage over in Nassau.

Even though Hawke knew the route in his sleep, he drove very slowly through the thick stuff. He wanted to fire up the Wally, shove off, and be out of the harbor before the fog lifted. He and Stoke were clearly en route to someplace they definitely should not have been going to, and the fewer people who had eyes on him leaving the harbor this morning, the better.

They were headed to, for want of a better name, No-Name Island, the place where, according to strategically located signs posted every-where, they could well expect to find themselves torn limb from limb by vicious man-eating guard dogs. No picnic on the beach was this very mysterious destination. And apparently, the island was home to some secret or other nasty business that the Tang brothers and, quite possibly, the Chinese Secret Police would very much have liked to keep all to themselves.

It had occurred to Hawke more than once that the terrible twins might even have been Chinese government intelligence agents, working all over the world in the shadows for Beijing. He'd have to ask his CIA pal Brickhouse Kelly, about that question sometime. If they were involved at the highest levels in Beijing, it would explain a lot of the very odd things that Hawke had witnessed around here since his arrival more than a week earlier.

Hawke's grandfather, Blackie, who had retired as Admiral Lord Hawke, had been a great unsung hero of the war with Hitler, someone who had spent a great deal of time in Washington during the war, posted as a naval attaché. He'd apparently struck up a great friendship with the newly arrived Chinese ambassador to America in the war years, an ever-deepening friendship that had lasted until the ends of both their lives. This very handsome and charming Chinese gentleman had once visited at his grandfather's home—a castle, really—in the Channel Islands, and Hawke could still remember him as a tall, kindly man, one who had shared a deep friendship with his grandfather, something that felt akin to love itself.

Hawke had never forgotten the man's name.

It was Tang. Tiger Tang. Same name.

Hawke had found a place where he could stow the Vincent Black

Shadow bike whenever he took the boat out, someplace where no one would really think to look. Behind a deserted building that appeared to have once been a prosperous bait-and-tackle shop, there was a dense thicket of cabbage palms. Once he'd left the bike in the thick of it, about thirty or forty feet inside, it was all but invisible to the naked eye.

Despite the fog, they made it to the marina without incident. Once he'd stowed the bike, they were out on the water and slowly making their way beyond the harbor mouth at dead-slow speed. This was to keep the engine sound down to a minimum. The fog, if anything, was even thicker out here in open water. It was a cold, wet fog, and Stoke had gone below and fetched their bright orange Henri Lloyd foul weather jackets. He'd also brewed a pot of hot black coffee, which Hawke gulped down to stave off the chill.

Hawke was at the helm, with Stoke standing beside him. Stoke had studied the marine charts of New Providence, Nassau, and the surrounding islands. Back-timing from Air Hawke's landing at Nassau, he was able to approximate the location of No-Name Island and marked it with an X on the chart and put the coordinates info into the GPS mounted above the helm station. Hawke had also fired up the radar, and given the early hour and the lack of marine traffic, he thought it was safe to open up the throttles out here and get there in somewhat of a hurry.

Half an hour later, the fog had finally dissipated. He was now able to firewall the throttles of the big Volvo Penta 650 HP outboards on the transom, coming out of the hole in the blink of an eye and getting the boat instantly up on plane, trimmed for speed.

Still, it took nearly an hour before they entered the vast reaches of the mangrove swamp. It was exactly like the ones down in the Keys, where they had once run down a murderer. Also, Stoke had done his Navy SEALs training there. So, they both knew pretty well how to get a boat in and out of these things.

At first, Hawke had to throttle back and slow the boat to idle speed to make it through the swamp to the bay that Stoke had described. It was, he'd said, almost in the very center of the sprawling mangroves, hundreds, perhaps thousands of acres in size. Off the beaten path, but plainly visible from the air. Mangroves are a very tough species of marine plant indeed, replicating themselves faster than weeds.

But the way forward, the way they managed their progress once inside the stranglehold of the mangroves, was simple and straightforward, just the way Stoke had been trained to do as a SEAL.

Stoke stood, legs wide apart, on the wide, flat bow with his trusty machete in one hand and his assault knife in the other. He would either push aside the vegetation to allow their passage or, worst case, hack his way through with his machete, creating not only a way in, but, more important, a way out. As he told Hawke, he had reason to suspect they might well need to make a very hurried exit from the isle of secrets. Hawke told him that he, too, had come to that conclusion.

If he and Stoke had to run for it, it would be because they were running for all the marbles—indeed, for their very lives.

CHAPTER 47

Devil's Island, the Bahamas
Present Day

The previous evening, Stoke had stowed all their ammo and the heavy artillery in the storage lockers located in the transom at the rear of the Wally's spacious cockpit. He'd included an M32 grenade launcher, because it would be his one chance of chasing away, or sinking, any threatening vessel that got too close for comfort. Put a grenade down the throat of a pesky patrol boat with a .50 cal mounted on the bow and watch 'em scatter—that had been his combat experience with the M32 both in training and in country.

After they'd been inside the suffocating green jungle for a good twenty minutes, Hawke shouted at Stoke on the bow, "Hey, give me a rough estimate of how far we are from the bay, Jonesie!" It was his new nickname for his partner, and Hawke knew just how crazy it drove him.

Jonesie? Gimme a damn break, man. Hawkie. How you like that? he thought but didn't say.

"Yeah, boss, I'm starting to see little pieces of daylight up ahead. I'd say another ten minutes. Maybe less. Just keep doin' what you're doin', boss man! We're making some damn progress now . . . almost out. . . . Here we go!"

The Wally tender, gliding forward now at idle speed, emerged into another world. Gone was the infernal tangle of mangrove bushes that had made Stoke so claustrophobic. In their place, a spacious, tranquil world of blue skies, clear blue water and bright sunshine. A placid bay hidden away from the rest of the world.

And, of course, dead ahead, the No-Name Island.

As on the day Stoke had first seen it from Hawke's Gulfstream, there were no signs of human life anywhere, with the possible exception of all the warning signs everywhere. Then the strangest thing. There did seem to be hundreds, if not thousands, of flocks of snow-white birds nesting on the island. Everywhere you looked, nesting in the trees all along the shoreline of the island. To Stoke's eye, it literally made this tropical coast look like there'd been a heavy snowfall the night before. "Look at this place, boss. Like a damn Bahamian Christmas card or something," he said to Hawke.

Countless more of the birds came and went, swooped in and out, whole flocks of them, by the hundreds, suddenly rising up en masse into the blue sky from somewhere in the interior of the island. They made no noise at all, no squawking like flying rats, which was what Stokely called the infernal seagulls down in the Florida Keys.

Stoke turned around and called back to Hawke, "Where we going to beach this thing, boss?"

"Does it matter?" Hawke said reasonably enough. There was not, as far as he could see, a dime's worth of difference where they beached the Wally.

"I guess not. All the same shit around here, far as I can see."

"I'm going in dead ahead. Unless you see some reason why I shouldn't. . . ."

"You mean, like, uh, like a mine? Something like that? Nothing would surprise me around here. They probably booby-trapped the beaches and shit."

"Yeah," Hawke said, throttling back and gliding into shore and powering the bow up onto the soft white sand. "Probably got Komodo dragons running loose all over the place. Although I haven't seen any yet, it's how this place got its name."

"Dragonfire?" Stoke said.

"Bingo. The original indigenous tribes in these islands passed down lurid tales of giant fire-breathing dragons that only came out of hiding in their caves at night. . . ."

"Hell is a Komodo dragon, anyway? They ain't fire-breathers, are they?"

"Much worse. Like something out of your worst nightmare. You don't want to know."

"Yeah, I do. Specially if I'm 'bout to come face-to-face with one of these bad mamajamas."

"I had to deal with Komodos once. A private island in Indonesia. The man I'd gone there to kill had two of them chained by his front door. And a lot more around the estate. Huge, ugly animals. Imagine a two-hundred-pound lizard that was over ten feet long. Incredibly fast animals, enormous powerful jaws. Capable of covering ground about as fast as a bloody cheetah. Venomous bite that secretes an anticoagulant, so one bite and you're done for. I had one chase me up to the top of a tree. It was about to take my leg off when I put a round between its eyes."

"Damn!"

"This Indonesian guy? He kept about seven or eight of these brutes penned up on his property. He caught any trespassers? Like me, for instance? Got themselves thrown in the Komodo pen at feeding time. Bad way to go."

"You trying to scare me, you are succeeding. You don't really believe they've got those damn things running around loose down here, do you?"

Hawke laughed. "C'mon, Stoke. Lighten up. I was just kidding you a little. Okay. Sorry, not sorry. I'm running this thing up onto the sand. You tie off a line to the bow cleat and run it up to the tree line and secure us to one of the big palms."

"You got it," Stoke said, and did it. "Let's move out, boss."

And then they were in dense jungle once more. Stoke couldn't believe how fast the jungle swallowed them up. Not mangroves, thank God. Just good old-fashioned palm trees and looping vines and huge banana plants and wildly colored tropical vegetation. Each man was carrying a machine gun, a sidearm, and an assault knife. They'd worn heavy khaki trousers and long-sleeve shirts to protect themselves against insect bites, mosquitoes, whatever might come their way.

Hawke held a finger to his lips, and they continued forward in silence, taking care not to step on fallen and desiccated palm fronds or anything that made a sound. A moment later, he pointed to the trunk of a tree, and Stoke saw a thick cable running up into the tree, ending at a fan-shaped microphone. The entire jungle had been wired for sound!

Hawke knew that whoever these people were, and whatever the hell they were up to around here, it was nothing good. This godforsaken hump of sand was not home to the Royal Society for the Prevention of Cruelty to Animals, the British Red Cross, or the Little Sisters of the Poor. Oh, no!

It was the devil's work they did here; he was pretty damn sure of that.

Hawke smiled. He'd finally thought of a perfectly appropriate moniker for this bloody tropical paradise.

Devil's Island.

And he knew he'd come to the right address.

CHAPTER 48

Dundee Rail Junction, Scotland
February 1942

Shortly after all the lads had arrived on station in the little village of Dundee in the north of Scotland, and established a garrison in the decidely dilapidated Hotel Royal Highlander across the road from the Dundee Railway Station, Ian Fleming, always rightly concerned about troop morale, took it upon himself to fashion something of a pub in the drafty ground-floor lobby. He'd called it the Red Indian Pub, in honor of the hardened warfighters who made up Fleming's 30AU, his assault unit.

To say that it was almost instantly a popular destination every evening would not have done it justice. Dundee was not a vast metropolis with a myriad of entertainments for young soldiers. No stompin' at the Savoy here. No cancan dancers flashing their knickers onstage at the Moulin Rouge. No, the tiny village of Dundee was famous for only two things: the River Dee, one of the world's most famous salmon fishing rivers, and for Dundee Orange Marmalade.

In something less than two weeks, Fleming's Red Indians and Hawke's Headbangers had been forged by their two extraordinarily charismatic leaders into a single twenty-man fighting unit. And deploying into Germany soon at full strength. They spent their waking hours fanned out all over the Dundee rail yard, familiarizing themselves with the equipment, primarily the locomotives, the logistics of how a rail yard operation functioned, the basic mechanics of the steam engines, and the use of the controls, especially brakes, throttles, and engine-starting procedures.

Every night during that first month, Ian Fleming and Blackie Hawke served as barmen, using the hotel's front desk as their make-do bar. One of the commados, who fancied himself as something of an artist, had painted a huge red tomahawk on the pine wall behind the bar. It reminded Fleming of the bloodred hammer and sickle painted on the wall of the bar at King's College, Cambridge.

All the lads were enjoying themselves at day's end, and the two commanders had noticed that there were more than a few local lovelies who'd begun to frequent the joint in ever-increasing numbers. Rule of nature, Fleming said to Hawke. Girls go where the boys are.

No argument there.

After a pub supper, compliments of the retired chef at the pub on the corner, the Old Silent, the two new comrades in arms would leave the lads to their own devices and adjourn back to the warehouse and discuss progress so far and what remained to be done. They worked into the wee hours every night.

Fleming, a man with a mighty work ethic who'd never spared the midnight oil, was nearing completion of the design and construction of the explosive devices. Individual commandos would be placing them inside the cabs of the locomotives.

The total package consisted of two plain matte black metal boxes, slightly larger than a man's shoebox but small enough to fit one inside each of the detachable leather saddlebags that the Deutschesbund Post & Courier Patrol motorcycles were now being fitted with. All the bikes were identical, with large red numerals on the dark green fuel tanks of the Norton 16H and the standard sidecars removed and replaced with the requisite saddlebags.

Hawke found Fleming bent over his workbench, a cigarette clenched between his teeth, puffing furiously, and sat down to have a smoke and watch the mad genius, the one they called "the Detonator" at his work.

"Hullo, Fleming," he said. "Having fun?"

"Actually, I am," Fleming said. "Discovered at an early age that there was nothing I enjoyed quite so much as blowing things up. I started with mailboxes, actually. Worked my way up to Nazi Panzer tank factories."

"Using TNT as the primary explosive, I assume?" Hawke had no basis for his assumption, but he had no wish to appear wholly ignorant of the matters at hand.

Ian looked up, shook his head, and replied, "Hardly. What you're looking at here is Torpex. Torpex is a secondary explosive fifty percent more powerful than TNT by mass. Torpex comprises forty-two percent RDX, a nitrogen explosive, forty percent TNT, trinitrotoluene, a chemical explosive, and eighteen percent powdered aluminum. Got all that?"

"Maybe. Run it by me one more time. Did you say that Torpex comprises forty-two percent RDX? Did I get that right?"

"Smart-ass. Hand me that box up there on the shelf marked 'detonators.' Think you can handle that?"

"I can try. Is this the one?"

"Quite right. Notice the word 'detonators' stenciled in red on the box lid?"

"Hmm, didn't see that. . . ."

"You know, Hawke, I think if I had a little less help from you right now, I might be finished with this part by morning. If you want to help, round up some of the lads and start unpacking all those boxes in the hotel dining room."

"Wondered about those. What are they?"

"Deutschesbund Courier and Post Patrol uniforms for the commandos. Should be about twenty-five of them. Leather helmets and goggles and riding boots. Picture-perfect Deutsch Reisebüro travel ID cards and cash in German marks. The bigger boxes are Webley and Scott sidearms, ammo, et cetera. We're just about wrapping up this process here. Spoke to Admiral Godfrey early this morning and told him that we are very near completion of this phase of the training."

"The lads are ready when you are, Ian. I can vouch for them. They've done double duty during this intensive training period. We're good to go!"

"A week from today. On the Saturday. That's what I'm going to tell Blinker. I think we should inform the lads, don't you?"

"Absolutely. I'll do it."

"Can you afford to take a few days off, Blackie? I need you to nail something down for me."

"Say the word. I'm yours to command."

"We've chosen the drop site now. Not surprisingly the one with the abandoned barn in the middle of an empty field."

"Good choice. That's where all the courier bikes will assemble?"

"Correct. They're going to start assembling there every night over the weekend. I've given your contact information to my lead chap in country. Code name Valkyrie. Your code name will be Braveheart. You will liaise with Valkyrie and keep me informed as to progress on that front. Agreeable?"

"Absolutely."

"I'd very much appreciate it if you could get on the suitcase radio set in my room tonight. Inform Valkyrie about everything he needs to know. Tell him you want to hear from him at least once every day until we arrive on the drop site."

Hawke nodded in the affirmative. "You're doing yeoman's duty here, Ian, and I feel that I'm of little help. . . ."

"Blackie, don't be silly, old boy. This is my part, not yours. Your part comes when the shooting starts. This is just chemistry. Any public school science professor could do this. By the way, so you know, the two explosive devices are connected electrically. The A device is triggered by an impact detonator. And that explosion automatically triggers a ripple effect explosion of the B device. Massive explosive power. Cataclysmic, I daresay."

"And all twenty devices explode simultaneously?" Hawke said. "That will shake Berlin to its core!" Hawke had come to despise Germany. He could stomach the sickness that had seized the entire country and put it on a path to total destruction by the Allies.

"Hmm," Fleming said, "I think that was your original intention, was it not? To set the explosions just across the Reichsstrasse from the Nazi headquarters, the Reichstag building?"

Hawke just laughed. All this verbal fencing with a man of Fleming's keen wit and superb intellect was taking a toll on his nerves.

Jousting with seriously quick minds, like Ian Fleming endured growing up with his brother, Peter, always made him feel as if he were just a step off the beat. But someday, Fleming knew in his very gut that he would show them all how it was done.

All of them.

CHAPTER 49

Devil's Island, the Bahamas
Present Day

Hawke and Stokely, dressed in khakis, were both awash in sweat. The hot and humid tropical air seemed very close. Hawke felt hemmed in by so much dense foliage and the nearness of so many massive trees towering overhead. Oppressive. It was also rather dark beneath the thick green canopy high above, which did not admit much sunlight at all. Nothing else moved. Even the birds and the butterflies seemed to have been warned off.

One species that did not get the memo? Mosquitoes.

Like the terrorist camp he'd uncovered in the Amazon jungles, the green canopy here provided the enemy with total invulnerability when it came to spy planes or spy satellites overhead. You could find them only by spending weeks or months searching in a massive jungle.

After moving through the jungle at a good clip for another twenty minutes, Hawke, looking through a gap in the dense foliage ahead, saw a metal fence with the sun glinting off the wire. It looked to be about twelve feet high, topped with coils of gleaming barbed wire.

He looked at Stoke and said, "You got this, brother?"

"Oh, yeah," his old friend said, "got this one in spades!"

Stoke reached inside his battle jacket and withdrew a pair of wire cutters. Dropping to his knees beside the hurricane fence, he quickly and expertly cut a three-sided flap at ground level, about three feet square, which, when lifted, would allow them to wiggle through on their bellies. Once they were safely inside, Stoke lowered the flap to its original position. Unless you were really looking hard, there was no sign of the flap at all.

A no-man's-land of about fifteen feet separated the first fence from an inner one. This second barrier was an almost exact match for the outer one with a significant exception—it was emitting a loud gunning sound.

It was definitely electrified. To the tune of ten thousand volts, if you believed what all the yellow warning signs said.

"Bet you ten bucks they got guard dogs running around and around inside there. . . ."

"Yeah," Hawke said. "Well, they're not here now. So, you in the mood to disable the electric one? I'd find that helpful. . . . Cut us another flap in this one, Stoke."

"Yeah, yeah, be cool. First we got to locate one of the positive terminals on the second fence, see if it's powered by an AC outlet or a large battery bank, either one. You'll know it when you see it. I suggest you go thataway and I'll go thisaway. First one to find it gives a signal, yeah?"

"Yeah. Let's get started," Hawke said, and started moving left between the two fence lines leading through the jungle.

Ten minutes later, he'd located what was obviously an electrical junction box hidden inside a large growth of weeds inside no-man's-land. It was five feet long and about three feet high, a third of the way up the secondary fence.

He stood up and whistled three times, summoning Stoke to his position. Stoke appeared three minutes later, on the run.

"Whatcha got, boss?"

"Looks like some kind of junction box to me. Hard to see in all those thick weeds. But definitely electric, I should think."

"Where is it?" Stoke asked, looking around.

"Inside, in the middle of this patch of weeds. They hid it obviously."

Stoke, dropping to his knees in the dirt, said, "Tell me this ain't that gizmo plant that guy used as toilet paper and then shot himself dead," Stoke said.

Hawke said, "Sure, Stoke. This ain't that gizmo plant that guy used as toilet paper and then shot himself dead."

"Thank you," Stokely said, and used both hands to pry the weeds apart. They'd overgrown whatever was hiding in there, and he'd have to cut them away to get at it. "Oh, yeah. That's what I'm talkin' about, right there. How the hell did you find it?"

"With my right foot. I was walking through these weeds, just in case somebody decided to hide something in there. What is it?"

Stoke was still slashing away at the weeds with his assault knife, finally revealing a large rectangular matte black metal box, about three feet wide and roughly four feet high.

"Either ion batteries or an alternating current connection, pumping out some serious voltage. Help me lift off this cover. . . ."

Hawke did and Stoke said, "Okay, we cool. It's AC. All we got to do now is unwrap the red wire from around that positive terminal right there. . . ."

"What's this 'we' business. You're the expert of this sort of thing. You do it."

"'Course I'll do it. You might find the process shocking."

"Not funny. Disconnect this thing, and let's get moving.

Stoke had a pair of rubber-covered pliers made of high-carbon steel. He got hold of the bitter end of the red wire wrapped tightly around the terminal. Slowly, and with extreme caution, he began to unwind the wire until it was free from any contact with the power source.

"Okay, we're good here. Lemme go make us a flap in that formerly electrified fence."

"You're sure it's been disabled?"

Stoke looked up at Hawke and smiled. "How much you know about electricity?"

Hawke replied, "Just the basic fundamentals. You push the switch up, it goes on. You push it down, it goes off. Pretty straightforward stuff, to be honest. Any schoolboy knows it."

"Yeah, 'bout what I figured. Yes, I'm sure you're not going to get electrified, boss man. Jeez, I got to lead you around by the hand sometimes. Let's get the hell out of here!"

CHAPTER 50

Devil's Island, the Bahamas
Present Day

The ground beneath their feet had begun a gradual rise upward, and Hawke realized there was going to be an elevated position waiting for them at the top. Ten minutes later, they were still beneath the green canopy, but standing atop a sizable hill. He and Stoke were able to remain hidden but still get a view below. From up here, by parting the big banana leaves a bit, they had a reasonably good glimpse of the hidden world of Devil's Island below them.

They found themselves looking down upon a sight that mystified both of them.

"Holy shit and Shinola!" Stoke said under his breath.

"That about sums it up," Hawke said, having a very hard time believing his eyes.

In the middle of a jungle, in a happy, sunny part of the world overrun with tourists just out to have a good time, in a location just a few hours from Miami, he had stumbled upon what looked like nothing else so much as a World War Two POW camp. It was massive. Surrounded by both barbed wire and electric fences. At each of the four corners stood identical watchtowers with guards armed with machine guns and giant searchlights silhouetted against a thin slice of sky.

There was some kind of parade ground or exercise yard in the foreground and then rows upon rows of identical barracks stretching away into the distance. They were built of dark wood on a brick base with slanting roofs formed from sheets of corrugated iron.

The long rectangular buildings had windows designed deliberately to provide no view either in or out. The buildings were set in straight lines, each marked with a large single letter painted white, exactly like the ones you'd find at a POW camp.

"What do you think it is, boss?" Stoke asked.

"Quite possibly a reeducation camp for political enemies, dissidents, whoever they don't like. These things are all over Western China. A network of 'centers' dedicated to 'transformation through education' or 'counterextremism education.'"

"Okay, I know about those. But why would they put one here?"

"An excellent question that deserves a good answer. Unfortunately, I've not got one at the moment," Hawke said. "But tens of thousands are locked up in new ones like this, thought-control camps with barbed wire, bombproof surfaces, reinforced doors, guard rooms."

"You don't think they threw the prince in there, do you?"

"It crossed my mind, yes."

"Be tough to get him out of there."

"Yeah. That's why we have friends like Thunder and Lightning down in Belize."

"Got that right."

Directly below their position was the main entrance, with a series of concrete barriers and a large security block, probably staffed with round-the-clock guards and a security force. Hawke could see a lane emerging from the jungle, eventually leading to the entrance. Just inside was a wide concrete area. Parked in multiple rows were jeeps upon jeeps. The jeeps were dark green Willys MBs with Bren guns and ammo boxes mounted in the back.

Hawke fished the Minox subminiature camera from one of the pockets in his vest and snapped off a dozen or so shots of the compound to send to Brick Kelly when he got back to the hotel. He nodded at Stokely. There was little to be gained by staying.

The two of them turned to leave and made a troublesome discovery. They were no longer alone.

Three men, all dressed in khaki, stood facing them, machine guns in hand. They had emerged soundlessly from the jungle thicket and crept up on them while they were watching the compound below. Hawke wondered if they had heard their footsteps on the jungle floor, or if by disconnecting the power source of the electric fence, they had inadvertently triggered alarms down in the security block.

Hawke knew that to allow themselves to be taken down to the mind-control camp operation might well be the end for both of them. The guards would never let them get out alive.

Hawke looked at the distance separating him from the guards. They were clearly professional, keeping the correct distance. But he and Stoke had long held a prearranged plan for uncomfortable moments like this one. The code word "lost" was a signal to Stoke that, damn the torpedoes, they were charging the enemy.

"Hands in the air!" the fat one in the center shouted.

Stoke and Hawke slowly complied, waiting for the signal.

"What are you doing here?" the one on the left demanded.

Hawke smiled at him. Then, talking out of the side of his mouth, he said to Stoke, "Get ready. . . ."

"Keep your hands in the air," Fatboy said. "You will come with us."

The leader—a squat, flat-faced fellow whose cheeks bore the horrific scars of bouts with acne—had a radio transmitter. He lifted it to his mouth and was met with a hiss of static.

Stoke said, through clenched teeth, "Boss, we let these dudes take us inside that compound down there? It's all over. . . ."

Hawke nodded. He knew he had to take these three thugs out before they called for backup. There were three machine guns pointed point-blank at the two of them. The odds were hopelessly stacked against them.

The muzzle of the leader's machine gun rose; then there were three black eyes pointing at Hawke's head, daring him to make a move, any kind of move. It was now or never.

They weren't buying what Hawke was selling.

"We got lost, damn you!" Hawke shouted at Fatboy with a sidewise glance at Stokely. "That's the bloody truth! We're *lost!*"

The two warriors bolted simultaneously, Hawke going left and Stoke right. Three fast strides into the mouth of the raised weapons, and then they both dove forward, going in low, their shoulders catching the enemies hard at their kneecaps and shoving them violently backward. Two of them were down, howling in pain with severely disjointed knees.

Hawke's and Stoke's tremendous forward momentum had carried them well beyond the bugger in the middle. Indeed, it had carried them into the heavy green vegetation and tumbling down a small hill into the undergrowth.

Suddenly, there was movement in the dense foliage above them. And staccato rounds of incoming machine-gun fire kicked up little clods of damp soil all around them as the gunner found his range. It was clear there were two guns right now; one of the injured guys was back in the fray.

"Boss!" Stoke cried, yanking Hawke's arm hard enough to dislocate his shoulder. "Get inside those trees!"

"One second," Hawke said, his sidearm suddenly in his hand. "I've got this guy!"

He pulled the trigger three times, and one of machine guns went silent. Rounds from the other were still whistling round his head as he followed Stoke's mad dash into the thick cover of the trees.

"Gimme some cover fire, boss man. I'm going upstairs."

Instantly, the big man was racing upward, grabbing branches of the nearest tree as fast as he could climb.

A moment later, a single shot rang out from the top of the tree. A scream from the thick green stuff above pierced the jungle, and then it stopped.

Stoke, hanging from the lowest branch, said, "Boss, we got to exfil and pronto. Sure they heard this little fracas down below at the camp. We got to get to the beach before they send the cavalry up here!"

Stoke and Hawke dashed back into the dense jungle on the run, headed back to the crescent of sandy white beach where they'd hidden the speedboat.

They were breathing hard by the time they got to the Wally.

Hawke reached inside the cockpit and lifted the lid of the storage locker in the transom, feeling around for something.

Stoke said, "What are you lookin' for?"

"I need that canvas tarp you wrapped the weapons in."

"Just a sec," Stoke said, and climbed into the cockpit. He bent over and looked in the locker. "This it?" he said.

Hawke said, "Yeah, thanks. I need you to drape the tarp over the transom and use the aft cleat to secure it to the boat somehow so that the wind won't blow it off."

"Okay, but why?"

"Because, Stoke, if we get one of those Chinese patrol boats on our tail, I don't want them getting a look at the name on the transom. *Chop-Chop* is the name of Jackie Tang's three-hundred-foot yacht, you know, and this tender carries its name, *TT/Chop-Chop*, back here on the transom. After what just happened? Anybody sees us leaving this island and heading back to Dragonfire Club?"

"Got it. We're F-ing toast. Let's get the F outta here, brother man! Shall we? As you would put it, boss."

"Indeed, we shall, young Jones! Tallyho!"

"Like the man said," Stokely opined.

He'd never understood what the word "Tallyho" meant, and he wasn't about to figure it out now!

CHAPTER 51

Devil's Island, the Bahamas
Present Day

The day after the "this close" call with death they'd had on Devil's Island, Hawke and Stoke decided to take a day off. After a long, lazy breakfast by the rooftop pool, they retired to a pair of chaises next to the high-dive board to catch rays. Hawke, who had been something of a diver back in the day, had not seen a board in at least a decade and he decided to put on a little show of his skills for Stoke. He wanted to see how much he still remembered.

Not much, as it turned out. The first attempted dive, a reverse dive from the tuck position, was not thrilling by any standard. The second, front tuck, got a faint clatter of applause from Stoke and nearby sunbathers. The third, and mercifully the last, was an attempt at a twisting dive from the reverse with one-and-a-half somersaults. He hit the water feetfirst and climbed out, then toweled his hair dry all the way back to his chaise.

"What did you do that for?" Stoke said.

"Because I can, that's why," Hawke said, irritated with himself for being such an obvious show-off.

"No, you can't."

"Leave it alone, Stoke," Hawke said, and picked up his book. He was reading a favorite, Alistair MacLean's *Where Eagles Dare*, and he buried his head in the soggy paperback.

On the other hand, he and Stoke were certainly enjoying the poolside scenery.

Thanks to a hot tip from Zhang he'd heard playing back his phone messages earlier that morning, Hawke learned that every Saturday the hotel pool relaxed its very strict policy of not allowing topless bathing. But only for one hour, from eleven o'clock to high noon.

And that a goodly number of female guests, as well as the "hostesses," who plied their trade in the Zodiac nightclub up at the Castle, took the opportunity to work on their tans. A few that he and Stoke had happened to meet stopped by to say hello and maybe flirt a little. Not with Hawke, but with the incredibly ripped man giant, Mr. Stokely Jones Jr.

Shortly after the twelve o'clock hour, the hostesses magically disappeared and, with them, the majority of the male guests poolside. It was hot as hell up here, Hawke thought, but now at least he could tell Stoke about his early-morning call from his friend Brick Kelly in Washington.

Hawke leaned over to whisper in Stoke's ear. "Keep your voice way down, okay. I've got news for you, and I shouldn't be shocked to learn that there are hidden mikes all over up here. Got it?"

"Oh, yeah. I think you could bet on it, boss."

Hawke lay back in his chaise, slipped his Ray-Ban Aviators on, closed his eyes against the bright overhead sun, and said: "I got a nice call from my old pal in Washington this morning."

"Really?" Stoke said. "The Brickman. How's that old coot doing?"

"Well, let's just say he wants us to ease up on the sightseeing and log more time at the pool or in the fitness center."

"How come?"

"Said he already had received enough e-mail postcards from us highlighting all the sights down here. He got all the ones from Devil's Island yesterday. He's all over that with the prez and the SecDef, but he's been watching the weather, and he worries it's going to get too hot for us very soon, us being out in the sun all the time. And that this tropical heat wave from the Far East could come at any time now."

"We're sitting on a powder keg with a short fuse. I can dig that."

"Yeah. He wants to know how we plan to get out of here if it really heats up in a hurry. Says it would be very bad for him and all his friends if we suddenly got stuck down here and couldn't get out. He said that his pal Rawhide over at Casa Blanca thinks we could easily become some kind of international celebrities. In a bad way. And he does not—I repeat, does not—want to see us on the cover of *People* magazine or the *Washington Post*."

"We might cause some kinda international incident, is what you're saying," Stoke said.

"Exactly."

"I could see that happening. You remember that time they had that damn incident over in Cuba a few years ago. Folks still talkin' 'bout that little CIA dustup. Or CIA goatfuck, as Harry Brock calls it."

"He mentioned that event, oddly enough. Said take that Cuban incident to the tenth power. Or higher. Depending on how our friends in Chinatown decide to play it when we blow the lid off this thing."

"Right about that, boss. Some serious shit would go down."

"What comes after World War Two?"

"Three?"

"Good guess. He also asked me how my English friend—'that prince of a fellow,' as he calls him—is doing. I had to be honest, so I told him I hadn't even gotten around to contacting him since we got down here."

"What did he say to that? Pissed?"

"He said I was terribly rude and that I should give him a ring sometime in the next few days or forget about it, get the hell out of here, and come home. He also said he'd told a friend of his down in Miami all about Dragonfire Bay. His friend said he could use a few days in the sun and was coming down soon to join us."

"Who is it? Do I know him?" Stoke said.

"I'm pretty damn sure you do, partner."

"Aw, man. Don't tell me. Just what you need, right?"

"Uh-huh."

"Boss, I can tell by the look on your face you ain't happy 'bout this."

"Oh, I'm not, believe me. It's Harry Brock, isn't it?"

"Yep, he's on a flight from Miami to Nassau right now. Gets in at two."

"Staying here?"

"Yes. Somebody pulled somebody else's strings apparently and got him invited."

"I sent him home, remember? After that outrageous stunt he pulled over at the Ocean Club. He got us all thrown out of there! Now, he's back? What the hell, Stoke? You tell him to come back?"

"Wouldn't never do that, boss. You know that."

"Then, who did?"

"Friend of yours. Worried about your ass."

"Both my parents are dead. No one left to be worried about me."

"It was Brick Kelly did it. Thinks we're understaffed down here. Thinks Harry's a helluva an asset in a firefight."

"So, he's coming," Hawke said.

"Yes. Somebody pulled somebody else's strings apparently and got him invited."

"Well, Harry's coming. Lucky, lucky, me," Hawke said with a sigh and an air of resignation.

CHAPTER 52

In the skies over Germany
February 1942

On the Saturday, Blackie Hawke and Ian Fleming found themselves seated upon jump seats in the cockpit, Fleming directly behind the pilot and Hawke behind the copilot. The big bomber lumbering along high above the English Channel was an Avro Lancaster four-engine heavy bomber. It could deliver payloads (bombs) of fourteen thousand pounds. It was also the only bomber capable of holding the RAF's Grand Slam bombs, weighing in at twenty-two tons. At eighteen thousand feet, the altitude allowed the bomb to attain a near supersonic concrete-penetrating terminal velocity. This old bird was known as *The Night Raider*, and Godfrey had insisted it was the only aircraft he would accept for a successful Operation Phantom Locomotive.

Tonight, however, no aerial bombardment. Fleming and the pilot had worked out a flight plan that would take them north out over the North Sea and then south over the German coastline, flying at extremely high altitude over the large industrial city of Hamburg. In addition to the twenty-man commando team, now officially called the Phantom Bombers, there were the two pilots, a navigator, a flight engineer, a bomb aimer, and a midgunner in the turret on top of the fuselage and a rear gunner in the tail turret.

"Dry feet," the pilot said when they left the North Sea and crossed over the shoreline at Nordstrand, Germany, and proceeded toward Berlin.

Ian was busy studying his maps, calculating the country roads that would get his men to their appointed targets in the least amount of time. Hawke, who knew he would get little to no sleep in the next twenty-four hours, was trying to grab a little bit of shut-eye before they hit the silk over the small village of Bad Honnef, Germany.

Captain George Frederic Beurling, nicknamed Buzz and Screwball, was Canadian, but he had been denied entry to the Royal Canadian Air Force, and he hadn't been allowed by his parents to join the Finnish Air Force, and finally, after three trips to England to plead his case, he had been accepted into the Royal Air Force at the age of eighteen in 1940. He would retire as one of the top ten fighter aces of World War Two. He had Fleming up front because they were old chums, and he'd flown the man behind enemy lines many times. He found it was helpful to have Fleming with his charts, coordinating courses and corrections with the bomber's navigator.

Suddenly, Buzz's voice was in Hawke's headphones. "Commander Hawke, I anticipate, assuming that no German *Messerschmitts* are foolish enough to rise up to engage us over Hamburg, that we will arrive over the drop zone at approximately twenty-one hundred hours. You lads should go suit up and do your final equipment checks. Please inform the squad in the back of the bus that they have one half hour before the jumpmaster is going to throw their sorry asses out of this aircraft into the middle of the back of bloody beyond."

Forty-five minutes later, every single man was safely on the ground and accounted for. The wind had carried them even closer to the big red barn than they'd anticipated. One parachutist narrowly avoided landing on the roof. The parachute bearing what they'd come to call "the package" floated down to earth beneath three chutes a few minutes later. Fleming had calculated the maximum speed at which the package could hit the ground without triggering the impact detonators. Not an *i* undotted, not a *t* uncrossed, as Ian liked to say.

Commander Fleming and Hawke were on the brink of becoming fast friends. And their partnership, engineered by Churchill and Admiral

Godfrey, was already yielding huge dividends in the death struggle with the Third Reich.

The first thing Hawke noticed upon entering the decrepit structure of the barn was the delightful smell of hot coffee and damp hay blended with high-octane petrol provided by the arriving Norton Courier motorcycles. He'd counted ten already inside with ten more arriving every few minutes. These men were carefully transporting the explosive devices inside and placing them inside the Norton's black leather saddlebags.

There was, too, a long table with food for the Phantom Bombers and the newly arriving Germans in their Deutschesbund Courier uniforms.

These were Fleming's German Resistance fighters, men who risked their lives every second of every day. And that death, if and when it finally came, would have been the most agonizing exit the Nazis could have devised. Garroted with wire and filmed for the entertainment of *der Führer* at Eagle's Nest, near Berchtesgaden. One by one, these brave men went to Ian's side and either shook his hand or, with great emotion, embraced their esteemed British leader. Hawke looked at his beat-up Rolex diver's watch. It was half past 10 P.M.

At the same time, the Phantom Bombers were studying their maps, checking their sidearms, and switching out their RAF flight suits for the German courier uniforms Fleming had ordered up. Donning the leather helmets and goggles, Hawke, donning his own uniform, saw that these men could now easily pass muster for the real thing. Very reassuring, he thought.

Across the room, Fleming pulled his goggles down over his eyes, climbed aboard the nearest Norton, fired it up, and looked at Hawke. He smiled and gave him a thumbs-up.

Time to go.

Fleming and Hawke had assigned themselves the idyllic little riverside town of Meissen, located just twenty-five kilometers north of Dresden on the banks of the River Elbe. They had chosen it because it was easily the farthest target away from the LZ, meaning the risk there was the highest.

A thick, cold fog had rolled in from the sea. Its long grey tendrils gave the night a chilling aspect, and it would certainly impact the timing of travel to and from Meissen.

On narrow roads, snaking through the countryside, the hazard factor rose considerably. You could misjudge a corner, turn into it too fast, and lose the bike. But, Fleming thought, he'd faced far worse obstacles operating behind German lines!

The roads on the twisting backcountry lanes were devoid of any signs of life, save the glow of lighted windows that shone through the fog in the cottages lining the many small villages. They were fastidious about maintaining the local speed limits and not doing anything that would draw the attention of the rural *polizei*.

Fleming had estimated that it would take them the better part of an hour to reach Meissen. In actual fact, the trip required an hour and a half. Still, they arrived at the rail station with more than enough time to do what had to be done.

The station house, enwreathed in swirling mists of fog, was dark, as was the rail yard, where they were prepared to encounter railway detectives with or without dogs. But all was quiet. Clearly, the threat of any kind of foul play, vandalism, or criminal activity was not a priority concern for the town fathers in this romantic little haven that, for more than a thousand years, had been far more famous for its beautiful porcelain than for anything else.

Hawke reckoned that the high explosives in their saddlebags were probably sufficient to level the pretty little town, which so far had been spared by British and American bombers.

Fleming slowed his bike down and stopped as they left the darkened and deserted station house car park and entered the rail yard proper. For a town the size of Meissen, the yard was extensive. Freight trains and passenger cars abounded everywhere he looked.

Fleming and Hawke both dismounted, and Hawke retrieved a sheaf of aerial photographs of the yard from his saddlebag.

He took out his penlight and showed Ian the narrow service road that separated the yard. They quickly agreed that, to save precious time, they would bifurcate the yard for the search, with Fleming taking the northern half of the yard and Hawke the southern. Their criteria were very straight-forward. They were looking for an isolated locomotive in a remote section of the yard waiting on a siding to be hooked up for the morning run to Berlin. Whoever first found the locomotive that best served their purposes would come find the other.

They remounted their bikes and roared away in different directions.

Hawke's nerves, on the search, were thrumming with excitement. This was one of those amazing moments when a man at war saw the flicker of an idea that was his coming into fruition and realizing that, no matter what might come, he was doing his duty and his very best for King and Country. He was reminded how he had felt when he'd arrived at RAF Archbury and come around a corner of the officers' club and seen that lovely German bomber that was all his.

And then he saw it.

A big black brute just sitting there on a siding, left in position before heading for Berlin, in a remote part of the yard where his actions would not be noticed. He shut down the Norton and climbed off. As he was mounting the steps up to the engine's cab, a brilliant white light swept over the locomotive, and a rough voice rang out in the stillness.

"Achtung! Was ist los?" ("Attention! What are you doing?")

A man was now running rapidly toward him. He had a snarling Do-berman on a leash, and Hawke knew that if the yard detective released the dog, he'd be dead in a minute or two. His sidearm was in a leather holster just beneath his armpit. Without showing a trace of alarm or anx-iety, he slipped his right hand inside his leather bomber jacket and with-drew the pistol, at the same time leaping up inside the cab. He now had the high ground, and he put it to good use.

There was nothing for it, he thought, turning around with his gun hand extended. At the last second, he realized he had to shoot the dog first. If he shot the guard first, the dog would come bounding and salivat-ing for his throat as soon as the leash was freed.

The guard saw the gun too late. *"Gehen-sie, Fritzy! Mach schnell, mach schnell!"*

He released the dog, and it came in leaps and bounds toward Hawke.

It went airborne at the bottom of the steps up to the cab. Hawke knew he was going to get only one chance at this. The dog was in midair, and in a second, the animal was inside the cab with him, teeth flashing and flinging great loops of saliva that reached Hawke's face just as he pulled the trigger.

The guard screamed in anger when the dog howled in pain, blown outside once more, and fell dead at the man's feet. Hawke had shot the dog in the heart. Lead rounds were now ricocheting around inside the cab like angry wasps. There was no way Hawke could rise up and draw a bead on the man, but if not, one of the angry wasps would soon find him—he heard the roar of a motorcycle and saw Fleming coming at full throttle around the rear of the locomotive. He had his left hand on the handgrip and his gun in his right, blazing away.

Ian continued firing on the German and emptied his gun into him as he crumpled to the ground beside his dog.

"Come down from there, Commander. It's safe now. I can't leave you alone for ten minutes, can I? Mount up. I found the perfect engine for us on the other side of the yard."

"I owe you one, Fleming," Hawke said.

"No, you don't," Fleming said. "This is just what we do, old man. Have each other's backs. Goes with the territory."

CHAPTER 53

Dragonfire Club, the Bahamas
Present Day

Stoke came back from the pool's tiki bar with a pair of cocktails in his hands. Piña colada for him, Gosling's Dark 'n' Stormy for Hawke. He handed the drink to Hawke and sat back down on the chaise. He said:

"You know what? I just got an idea. Let's you and me go have us some fun before we skedaddle. Let's mosey on over to that Castle place Zhang's always talkin' about. Got a great steak restaurant, she said. Called Island Prime. Yessir. Aged beef, just like me. And then go take a peek at that nightclub show at the Zodiac Club. Good idea?"

"You and Zhang getting pretty tight these days? Or, rather, nights?"

"Ah, boss. You know me better than that. Besides, my wife, Fancha? Hell, brother, she catch me sneaking around with some strange somebody like Zhang Tang? Hell, she'd Bobbittize me, and I ain't kiddin'!"

"She'd what?" Hawke said.

"Bobbittize my ass, that's what."

Hawke said, "What the bloody hell is that supposed to mean, Bobbit-tize? Some kind of American hipster slang?"

"Don't tell me you never heard of Lorena Bobbitt!"

"I've never heard of Lorena Bobbitt."

"Man, that's amazing. Back in the early nineties, that woman was front-page news all over the world. But I keep forgetting you're from

England. She was a woman who'd caught her old man cheating on her. Cut his damn pecker right off and threw it out the window! That's what you call gettin' Bobbittized back where I come from."

"Oh, come on, Stoke. Your wife would never do that to you. That sweet Fancha? No way."

"Way. Hell, boss, she's already told me she'd do it! Shit. Multiple times!"

"Well, listen up. I've got dinner plans. But I think you and Harry should go check out the Castle. Just don't let Zhang take you two down to the dungeon."

"What dungeon?"

"Told me she's got a dungeon—that's all I know."

"What do they do down there?"

"No idea. Your guess is as good as mine."

"Sounds like some of that whips-and-chains shit to me, boss."

"Knowing Zhang's sexual predilections, I would not be even slightly surprised. . . . What time is it?"

"One o'clock," Stoke said.

"Your friend Harry lands at two. JetBlue from Miami. If you take the Wally, you can be over there at the airport in half an hour to pick him up. Scoot."

"Don't you scoot my ass, boss. I'm on it. So who are you dining with tonight?"

"China. She invited me over to her house for a home-cooked meal."

"Wait. She's got a home here?"

"Apparently."

"Okay. I'm gone. You feel like it, after dinner you and China want to stop by the Zodiac for a nightcap, you'll find me and Harry at the bar."

"I'll remember that."

Five minutes after the elevator had swallowed Stoke whole, who should appear to Hawke's wandering eyes but the beauteous Miss Zhang Tang, who must have not realized what time it was because she'd forgotten she was wearing only the bottom half of her swimsuit.

"Hello there, handsome," she said, smiling at him. "Mind if I sit down?"

"Not even slightly." Hawke smiled back, forcing himself with some difficulty to keep his wandering eyes above her neck.

She sat down on Stoke's chaise and said, "Haven't seen you around much lately. Where have you and your boyfriend been keeping yourselves?"

"Well, let me see. . . . Oh, yes . . . yesterday, we took the boat over to Paradise Island to play golf with a Bahamian friend of mine. And the day before that, we hired a captain with a Hatteras GT Seventy sportfisher to take us out to marlin country. Boat isn't happy at any speed under forty knots. I'm going over to the dealer in Nassau to order one."

"So, you're having fun, are you?"

"How could I possibly have more? This is paradise."

"Oh, I'm sure I could think of a few ways, Your Lordship."

"I'm sure you could. . . ."

"Give a girl half a chance, why don't you?"

"Depends. What have you got in mind?"

"I was thinking I'd like to show you around the Castle tonight. I think you'd find the dungeon interesting. . . ."

"And why would that be?"

"It's for men with exotic appetites."

"I'm afraid my appetites, such as they are, are hopelessly vanilla, darling. I find rum raisin frightfully exotic."

"So, you see? You need to spice things up, don't you? Will you be my guest? I could pick you up at seven, and we could dine at the steak house before your tour? Sound appetizing?"

"I have to admit I'm intrigued. But I'll need a rain check."

"Oh, no. You naughty boy! Are you busy? Dare I ask with whom?"

"I'm quite sure you know. She's a friend of yours."

"China? She led me to believe it was all over between you two, the lying little bitch."

"Don't let the claws come out quite yet. Perhaps it is over, and she just hasn't gotten around to letting me in on her secret. Maybe that's why she's invited me to dine with her this evening? To tell me the news. Who knows?"

"I shouldn't be so hard on her. It must be fun, actually."

"What must be fun?"

"Having two beautiful women fighting over you. Come on, admit it. My sources tell me you're a very popular man-about-town back in London. A little too popular, some women say."

"It beats taking out the trash bin."

"Ha-ha, very funny. I've got an idea. Have you been over to my sports center yet? At the southern tip of the island?"

"I must have missed that one. Why?"

"We have a boxing gym there. And professional instructors. As a matter of fact, I've been taking boxing lessons for over a year. Gotten quite good, I have to say." She pumped her fists. "Punch! Jab! Left, right, left! Knockout!"

"And?"

"I was just thinking. What if I challenged that little minx to climb into the ring with me? Say, three rounds only. Winner take all, of course."

"All of what?"

"All of you, silly man, all of you. Would you come watch if I can talk her into it?"

"I'd certainly consider it. I'm sure she's told you, but she is a kung fu master."

"Good for her. So am I! It will be great fun!"

"If she'll do it."

"Oh, she'll do it, all right. I can be most persuasive when I really, really want something. Where are you two love doves having dinner? Let me guess, the Castle."

"At her home, apparently."

"Surely you jest!"

"Honey, I don't kid about things like that."

"I've known China for a long time. She's a man-eater. But I don't think she's ever invited a man into her private lair before. Wonder what that's all about . . . said the spider to your fly."

Hawke shrugged his muscled shoulders. He said, "We shall see, I suppose."

"Well, the little whore has but two fetishes. She'll either fuck you. Or kill you."

CHAPTER 54

Meissen Rail Yard, Germany
February 1942

Commanders Hawke and Fleming rolled their rumbling motorbikes to a stop on the far side of the yard and got their bearings. Fleming said, "It's this way, I think. On the other side of that large building. Follow me, old sport!" Ian roared off and Hawke followed in hot pursuit. The swirling fog over here to the north was even thicker than they'd dealt with on the south side. And thanks to the blackout regulations of 1939, the top half of their headlights were masked in black paint. Hawke would never admit this, but he loved fog. He thought it lent an air of mystery and suspense to any situation. Walking through Berkeley Square on a foggy night with a beautiful woman swathed in mink on your arm was far more dramatic and romantic than on a clear night when the nightingales were in full song.

"What do you think, old boy?" Ian asked Hawke as they came around a large stone equipment building. Hawke got his first look at the brutish black powerhouse of locomotion that Fleming had found for them. Towering above them, it was at least half again as large as the one Hawke had nearly died in earlier.

"I think you hit the jackpot, Ian. We've now got four of the explosive devices to dedicate to this monster. Plus, the engine in this thing has to be far more powerful, and thus much faster, than the first."

"It should be. Twenty thousand horsepower it says on this engine cowling."

"I put my money on this brute to be first to arrive at the Berlin Hauptbahnhof," Hawke said.

"Right you are!" Ian said, opening his saddlebags. First, spreading on the ground four or five worn padded blankets such as furniture-removal men used to protect the goods. And then, ever so carefully, lifting out first one of the black boxes, then the other and placing them gingerly on the pile of blankets.

He hadn't told Hawke this, but some of the ingredients the wily old bomb maker had used were notoriously unstable.

"Try not to kick one of those, would you, Commander Hawke? Or, worse yet, drop one. If it's not too much to ask . . . and for God's mighty sake, please do mind where you're going."

"Aye-aye, Admiral!" Blackie said, and extracting the two devices and carefully placing them on Ian's blankets beside the other two.

"How do you want to handle this next bit, Ian?" Hawke said. "Stowing these things aboard, I mean."

"With the finesse of a bloody brain surgeon. Very carefully. The problem with detonator devices is that they can blow you to hell and gone when you least expect it. I've seen it happen more than once, and it's quite grim, I assure you. So, here's how we do this. You climb up into the cab. Sit facing me on the top step. I will hand the four devices up to you one by one, not releasing my grip until you say you've got it securely in hand. Good?"

"Makes eminent sense," Hawke agreed.

"Well, I don't know about eminent, necessarily, but prudent to be sure. So, up you go, then. Sit facing me. Now, take a deep breath. Tell me when you're absolutely comfortable and calm, all right?"

Hawke said, "I'm absolutely comfortable and calm, yea, a veritable isle of utter tranquillity in the tempests raging all round me."

"Are you ever serious, Blackie? I mean, really, you do try my patience at times."

"Sorry."

"Here comes number one. This is A, the impact detonator device. I'll not hand it up until you say you're ready."

"I'm ready."

Fleming stood at the bottom of the steps, legs wide apart, feet planted like trees, and ever so gently raised the heavy device, swathed in one of the thick blankets, upward and within Hawke's reach.

"Have you got it?" Ian asked as Blackie grasped it. "Don't let the blanket fall off!"

"I do. I've got it, blanket and all!"

"Are you quite sure, my Lord Blackhawke? I mean, you can't even jiggle the bloody thing. Incredibly sensitive detonators."

"Yes, yes, for God's sake! Give it to me!"

Ian held his breath and let the bloody thing go.

When it failed to blow them both to Kingdom Come, Fleming turned and repeated the process three more times.

CHAPTER 55

Dragonfire Club, the Bahamas
Present Day

China, wearing a flowery off-the-shoulder sundress that flattered her glowing sun-bronzed skin and generous figure, reached into the glove box and pulled out a pair of Prada wraparound sunglasses. "Ready to go?" she said, smiling at him from behind the mirrored lenses as she downshifted, going into a tight descending-radius turn.

"Ready. But, China, dear, where, oh, where is that big fat Bentley of yours?"

"Aw, you don't like my little circus car? That Bentley, for your information, belongs to Zhang. She lets me use it whenever I want."

"It's a bloody circus car all right. It's got no doors. It's got wicker seats. It's got bloody fringe on the roof, for heaven's sake! Pink fringe! Is that an option, or did it come standard with the car?"

"Very funny. That Bentley she drives is just one of a whole Tang fleet of Bentleys for clients. She extended one of them to me as a courtesy, given my position as an official representative of our country. My personal car, for your information, happens to be this extremely rare Fiat. What kind of car do you drive these days, by the way? O Lord High and Mighty?"

"A Bentley, actually."

"Ah, of course? Like mine?"

"No. Yours is the latest model. I bought mine used. It's a steel grey nineteen fifty-three Bentley R-Type Continental. Used to belong to the author of the Bond books, Ian Fleming. He drove it all around Cheyne Walk, where he and his wife, Anne, had a splendid flat. Ian did major upgrades under the bonnet, to increase the power. Thing is bad to the bone."

"Pretty good choice. You rather admire this Fleming, don't you?"

"Yes, frankly, I do. He was a great friend of my grandfather's during the war. They were a team, in fact. Engaged in sabotage behind German lines. You have to remember that when the first Bond book to be filmed, *Dr. No*, first hit the international movie theaters, England was deep in a horrific depression, even though they'd managed to beat the bloody Nazis to a pulp.

"And Double-Oh-Seven? Why, he was a great British hero the whole country could root for. He lifted the entire spirit of our nation! I read a book way back then. The title was *How James Bond Saved England*. Enough said."

"Well, Alex, myself being well acquainted with Double-Oh-Seven's exploits, I'd guess he'd rather fancy the little Jolly."

"My dear girl, please don't get me wrong. I believe it to be a fine automobile. But pray tell, I'm curious. Just what is this thing I'm almost sitting in, may I ask?"

"This thing, as you call it, lover boy, happens to be a Fiat Jolly. Based on the famous Fiat Cinquecento. And I love it. It's perfect for Dragonfire Club. I wouldn't want to drive one on the Autostrada around Rome, I'll grant you. But here? *Que bella maccina!* May we proceed, or do you prefer to Uber it? Or, as the Americans say, use your thumb?"

"Uber? Here? You're kidding."

"Kidding, of course," she said, somewhat exasperated. Then she turned the key in the ignition, and Hawke listened appreciatively to the throaty growl of the tiny 1250cc, sixty-eight-horsepower engine. They were off.

"Let's make this trip fun," she said. "It's no distance at all, and I can show you places you've not seen, off-the-beaten-path sorts of places, and it promises to be a lovely evening."

"I'm at your command," Hawke said, trying to get comfortable in the hard wicker seat.

"I like the sound of that!" China said, smiling.

"Just don't get too bloody used to it, darling."

The sun was already setting as they roared out of the club property, following the coastal road in the direction of the undeveloped part of the large island. Hawke had to admit she handled the little micro car expertly, pushing the Jolly upwards of sixty, her hair streaming in the wind as she changed through the four gears with the precision of a brain surgeon.

When they'd reached the end of the headland, she veered left, onto a narrow lane that dropped off steeply with thick jungle crowding in on both sides. Hawke caught a glimpse of water, a secluded bay through the trees ahead. But before they reached the beach, China spun the wheel right and sped through open wrought iron gates that had seen better days.

A moment later, he got his first glimpse of the house, a rather grand white affair perched atop a hilltop that had been cleared of jungle to accommodate it. It was what Hawke liked to call another "faded glory." Quite old, probably late eighteenth century, classic, and really rather stately. It was the work of a gifted architect from the late British Colonial period: a wraparound porch on the second floor that would provide shade from the sun and great views of sunsets over the bay below, French windows on the ground floor, and stately white columns framing the front door.

Faded pink garden walls surrounded the sloping green lawns and opened into a small private garden at the rear with a swimming pool. The pool ran the full length of a higher wall thickly covered in ivy. Not a breath of air back here, just the warm velvet touch of evening, the night filled with the blooming scents of Caribbean flowers. Bougainville, Barbados lilies, orchids, and claw crab. A chorus of cicadas was sawing away, celebrating a darkness punctuated only by a slim sliver of silver moonlight.

"Pol Roger all right with you?" she said, going behind a splendid old bar made of Bermuda cedar.

"Only if you're having one."

"Mais oui, monsieur."

"Il n'y a pas de quoi. Une pour moi."

China, giggling, replied, "You still remember how we used to speak French in restaurants, darling? I mean, when you were telling me all your deepest secrets, eh, *mon ami?*"

"I do. I hope I never told you all my secrets."

"And God knows you've got enough of them."

She had put a record on an old RCA Victrola player—something you never see anymore, more's the pity. The Édith Piaf album *Chansons Parisiennes* filled the room with soft piano and that unmistakable smoky voice singing *"La Vie en Rose."* Then China disappeared into the kitchen, and Hawke was left alone to explore the room. The furniture was English, probably Georgian, as in old, but still comfortable.

There was colorful eclectic art on the walls, and prints of Matisse, Manet, Monet, and Picasso. On another wall, prints of lovely paintings by the American Impressionists Winslow Homer and John Singer Sargent. The place had been carefully furnished with the feminine touch. The choice of a pale white paint on the walls, paint that turned a rosy pink when sunlight filled the room the way it did during the late afternoon and early evenings in Paris flats. Also, ornate gilded mirrors and thick Turkish carpets that he'd helped her choose from a rug merchant in Bodrum.

She was back, an open bottle of champagne and two glasses in her hands.

Hawke took a glass, brimming with Pol Roger, raised it to her, and said, "As my late grandfather, Admiral Hawke, used to say, 'I admire the catholicity of your art collection.'"

"Hardly Catholic, dear. We're all Buddhists under this roof, darling, dogs and servants included. My brilliant housekeeper, Priscilla, even made up a name for my art. She called it Impressionism, meaning it gives one the impression of a scene. An impression that is the result of color forces coming into contact with the retina. If you follow my logic."

"I do. I respect it."

"Yet, I distinctly heard you say the word 'catholicity,' Alex. Nothing at all to do with the Holy See in Rome."

"Yes, I did use that word. Nothing at all to do with the church. It means a collection of someone driven by various tastes and sensibilities. That's all."

"Oh, I see."

"Your house is lovely. China by Limoges. Exquisite even. The Buccellati silver service is an opulent work of artisanal brilliance. Thank you for sharing it with me tonight. It's a far cry from the demented opulence of Dragonfire Club. I much prefer this, to be honest. Why did you buy it?"

"So I can hide from the world. Including this one."

"You? Hiding? I can't imagine you hiding from anything."

"I'm going to serve dinner. I want you to set the table, the one in the rear garden by the pool."

She poured herself another glass of bubbly and returned to the kitchen.

And so they had dinner in the garden with the illuminated swimming pool shimmering behind them and the ice-cold stars crowding the night sky. There was a silence between them, not altogether uncomfortable. Even the cicadas had finally decided that enough was enough.

Hawke saw plainly that it was inevitable that they should become lovers once again. But perhaps he had confused the situation, something he might well come to regret. Putting it bluntly, it was still quite possible that she was his enemy. Perhaps even his deadly enemy. He decided to stay silent. He still needed information from her. He had decided to see this thing through to the bitter end.

As if intuiting his thoughts, she locked eyes with him and said, emotionless, "Do you still want more information, Alex? Do you even believe a word I say?"

"I enjoy hearing more about you. It's been a long time since we've had a chance to simply sit and talk to each other."

"What do you want to know, Alex? My God! Was I responsible for the disappearance of the prince? No. Do I know what actually happened to him? Why should I tell you if I do? You know nothing about my life now, and unless it's connected to your work, you couldn't care less."

"You're wrong on both counts. If we're both on the same side, it seems crazy to have secrets from each other."

"Tell me a secret, then," China said. "Now. Right now."

"Only if you swear to reciprocate in kind."

"I swear."

"China, I've seen things here at Dragonfire Club. Things that go far beyond the possible kidnapping of the Queen's grandson. I think this bloody island is just the tropical tip of an iceberg of a massive criminal international enterprise, based in China, whose tentacles reach all the way around the world and back."

Her eyes snapped into focus, and he knew he'd piqued her curiosity. Easy as she goes, he said to himself, protective barriers going up. Dangerous waters ahead.

"Things? Such as?" she asked.

"Dangerous things. Things that, if they should ever get out, could result in global destabilization or even world war."

"Are you serious?" she asked.

"Quite," Hawke said, and raised his flute of champagne to her.

CHAPTER 56

Dragonfire Club, the Bahamas
Present Day

S o, for fun, tell me, just how big is the Tangs' security force, including all the peripheral islands?"

"I'd say very significant. Extremely well trained and heavily armed with the very latest weapon technology. Don't get anywhere near these guys, Alex. They take no prisoners. Trust me."

"I see. Last thing: What is Zhang's true role in this operation? Is she a coequal partner with the Tang twins? Does she really run the joint? Is she playing me? Does she have any idea what I do for a living?"

China laughed out loud. "Alex, please! Tell me you're kidding! Of course she knows! They don't let anybody set foot in this place until they've been vetted, as you used to say, six ways from Sunday. What does she do here? I'll tell you since you asked. She's a whoremonger. A bloody pimp! On an international scale, of course."

"Tell me."

"She's a human slave trader, on an epic scale. She holds slave auctions, televised live once a month on the dark web. The women are paraded out naked and interviewed live on camera. Zhang is the auctioneer. Then the women are auctioned off to the highest bidders. You have to pay a huge membership fee to even access the website. The men who know about this are sheikhs and swindlers, titans of industry, dukes and earls, captains and kings, movie stars and billionaires, Silicon Valley wonder boys and CEOs of Fortune Five Hundred companies. You remember Jeffrey Epstein, Alex?"

"Who could forget him?"

"Big Jeff was tight with the Tangs, very tight. Had a piece of the action. When he wasn't banging cheerleaders and babysitters on Pedophile Island, his private island in the Caribbean, he was right here at Dragonfire Club, helping Zhang with the auctions."

"How do the women get here?"

"Zhang and the Tangs have scouts who deal in human flesh all over the world. Mostly Russia and Eastern Europe, but everywhere. India, Indonesia, Thailand, Turkey, South America, you name it. Loaded aboard freighters in foreign ports in darkness and stowed down below in the bowels of the ships for the duration of the voyage. Not much water and a minimum of food and medicine. A lot of those poor women don't survive those hellish voyages. Can you even imagine the scandal, the worldwide public outrage lavished on China if all this ever leaked? It would take Beijing decades to recover!"

"No wonder MSS sent you here. This powder keg is just a nightmare waiting to erupt. One that must be keeping President Irby's pal Xi Jinping awake at night."

"Now you're starting to get it. You ever hear of Ellis Island, Your Lordship? I doubt it."

"It was the island in New York Harbor where, between the year eighteen ninety-two and nineteen fifty-four, all the masses of foreign immigrants were processed and interrogated. Either judged disease free and admitted or sent back."

"And?"

"Are you listening to me? Dragonfire Club is the Ellis Island of the twenty-first century, Alex! The women arrive by the boatload at Nassau Harbor every month, unloaded out onto the docks in the dark of night, and bused in vehicles with blacked-out windows to a remote hangar complex located farther inland. There they are processed and interrogated by Zhang and surrogate representatives of Dragonfire Club, LLC. All under the watchful eye of that filthy rich bitch girlfriend of yours."

Hawke said, "Look here, China, pay attention. She's hardly my girl-friend. And besides, I thought you two kissed and made up the other night."

"Look. She's bad news right down to the bone. I'm just waiting for her to fuck up royally so that I can take that fat ass of hers off the chessboard. The Tangs, for all their money and power, are not beyond the reach of the MSS, the Chinese government's secret intelligence network. People like me, for instance.

"Alex, if the Tang brothers didn't pour billions into the Beijing gov-ernment's coffers every year? Believe me, the whole Tang family would end up in reeducation camps somewhere in Western China, maybe even land appropriated from the Russians in southern Siberia."

Hawke looked at her and said, "You know why I'm here, China. So, tell me, why are you here?"

"I'm a paid agent of the Chinese government, MSS. Wherever in the world China has an interest, there go I. I buy houses in these places to secure my personal comfort."

"What's their interest here in the Bahamas?"

"None of your fucking business."

"No secrets, remember?"

"Give me a cigarette," she said. Hawke did, then lit it for her with his old steel-case Zippo.

"Thanks. All right, here you go. Xi Jinping and the government of the People's Republic of China grow weary of the criminal excesses of the Tang Dynasty, at home and abroad. At a time when China is trying to facilitate better trade relationships and political partnerships with the West, the United States, the Tangs continue to give China a black eye everywhere they go. Enough is enough. Should they fall—and they will—I am being groomed to take over the entire enterprise. Clean it up. Take it legit. It will make me my fortune. Happy now?"

"And the twins? When are they coming back?"

"They're not coming back anytime soon, I can tell you that. They've already been— Shall we say, detained?"

"Does Zhang know all this?" Hawke said, lifting his wineglass and swirling the honey-colored liquid in the palm of his hand. Puligny-

Montrachet was one of the few wines that could trace its origins back to Roman times, and he drank it as much for its age and antiquity as for its taste.

"Good?" China asked.

"Quintessentially delicious. Thanks for remembering."

"To answer your question, no, Zhang does not know. But she will when I tell her."

"My God, what have I stumbled into here?"

"A horde of fire-breathing dragons, my boy. Careful you don't get burned!

"Do you burn, China?"

"Yes. But only in your bed, my darling man."

Hawke paused to light another cigarette and gather his thoughts. He felt that she was being at least somewhat honest with him. And he was tempted to ask about the submarine pen. And the POW camp. But he instinctively held back from going there. If he opened that giant can of worms, it could quickly spiral out of control before the United States could confirm what he'd given to Brick. And there could easily be hell to pay on a worldwide scale.

An international crisis, to be sure. Battle of the Titans, Heavyweight Division. America versus China. A bare-knuckle fight that could escalate far beyond the Cuban Missile Crisis in 1962. The world had trembled on the brink of all-out nuclear war with Soviet ships carrying more missiles headed straight into the teeth of the United States naval blockade.

When President Alton Irby and CIA chief Brickhouse Kelly got wind of a secret Chinese nuclear submarine pen located just hours off the coast of Florida, all-out war with China was a distinct possibility, should China refuse to back down and accede to America's demand that they get those three subs out of America's hemisphere. And the equally disturbing news of a reeducation camp for Chinese dissidents, undesirables, and political enemies? Worldwide rage at China's human-rights violations would go through the roof. In short, Hawke had somehow managed to suddenly find himself in a dire situation way over his head with no obvious way of getting out of it!

It was plainly time for him to keep his head down, to keep his mouth shut, and to follow Brick's instructions. Namely to find the prince within three days, free him, and get the hell out of town. Hand this mess off to the Yanks. Aside from the Tangs' kidnapping the prince, Britain clearly had no dog in this fight.

If Hawke were President Irby, he'd have the U.S. Navy sail the world's most technically advanced attack submarine, the USS *South Dakota*, right into the maw of Dragonfire Club and kick the vile Tang Corporation and the Chinese gangsters the hell out of America's backyard.

And while he was at it, he'd get COMPACFLT—the Commander, U.S. Pacific Fleet—to issue orders that a U.S. carrier battle group from the Pacific Fleet would sail directly into the heart of the South China Sea and form an impenetrable naval blockade located the exact same distance from the Chinese coast as their secret sub pen was located from the coast of Florida.

Then he'd go home to England, fly away to that sceptered isle, home to his beloved Cotswolds family estate at Hawkesmoor, and thereupon attend to his beautiful boy, his son, Alexei, and his gardens.

And perhaps a round or two out on the links at Sunningdale with his dearest old friend and the world's best worst golfer, the inimitable Chief Inspector Ambrose Congreve of Scotland Yard!

CHAPTER 57

Dragonfire Club, the Bahamas
Present Day

As the lovely alfresco dinner wound down, Alex Hawke noticed that China was making ever-more-frequent trips out to the kitchen to refill her wineglass. Clearly, she'd been under a good deal of stress, leading what was essentially a double life here at Dragonfire Club. She knew she was always only a whisper away from Zhang and her brothers uncovering the real reason she was living here now. To spy on them. And that would merit a death sentence or a life sentence to a four-by-eight-foot cell deep undergound.

She wasn't exactly drunk, but she was getting there.

Hawke got to his feet and said, "Dear girl, this has been absolutely lovely, a perfect evening. But as I may have mentioned, I promised my friend Stokely Jones that I'd look in on him up in the Castle's nightclub, where he's dining with a friend of ours, chap just arrived tonight from Miami. Would you like to come? I'd love it, but only if you're not too tired. . . ."

"You really think you can be rid of me that easily, Alex?"

"Don't be silly, woman. I never want to be rid of you."

She looked at him, searching his eyes for the lie behind them, but not finding it, and her own eyes glistened with tears that threatened to spill over.

China essayed a cheery smile but didn't quite pull it off. "Oh, Alex, I'd adore to go! I'm not anywhere near calling it a night this early. Let's go. Do you mind driving?"

"I'd kill for the chance to drive that beast of yours. Put it through its paces and see what she can do."

Half an hour later they entered the long driveway that snaked up the hill to the Castle. When he pulled up at the entrance, valet parking boys rushed to welcome China Moon back to the Castle.

"Come here often?" Hawke said, teasing her.

"Oh, do shut up, Alex," she said, and made her way through the milling crowd and inside the Castle's walls. Hawke was right behind her. "I need a drink," she said.

"Coming right up. I'm just trying to see if I can spot my friends. Is there a separate dining room apart from this lounge?"

"Yes, one flight up. See the curving staircase on the far side of the room?"

"I do. All right, let's get you a big fat cocktail, honey. I may even join you. What will you have?"

"A Don Julio margarita, fresh lime juice, salt. Napoleon, the tall Bahamian over there, knows how I like it."

Hawke signaled the barman over and placed their order. When it came, Hawke was surprised, and pleased, to see that she was taking small sips of the concoction, pacing herself. He surmised that the stress of living so much at the edge these last months, sitting atop a time bomb, had caused her nerves to fray. And as he knew all too well, that was when you had to start watching your alcohol intake like a wily fox that's invaded your personal henhouse.

She swiveled her stool so that she could loop her left arm over Hawke's shoulders and draw him nigh.

She leaned her head into him and said very softly, "I've not been completely truthful with you, darling."

"That's all right. At least I know you're trying."

"In the garden, over dinner, I kept seeing the flickering light of the candles in your beautiful blue eyes and wondering, after the life you've led, and all the madness you've had to live through that—"

"That what?" he pressed.

"That all I can see in those eyes of yours is innocence. Maybe not complete innocence, but the vestiges of innocence going back to your boyhood. You've never lost that, Alex. And it's one of the things that made me fall in love with you . . . and why I decided that I had to tell you what I've been hiding ever since you arrived."

"I'm listening. . . . ," he said.

"It's about your godson, Prince Henry. I know where he is. And he's . . . he's not at all well, Alex."

"Tell me."

"Zhang, discovering that I was sleeping with him and in a jealous rage, had him thrown into prison. On an island not far from here. The conditions for the prisoners are not good. And Henry was subjected to endless interrogations and in the beginning beatings, brainwashing, mind control, electrodes attached to his testicles—all those things and worse. I went to visit him two days ago. His condition terrified me. I demanded that he be removed from his cell and transported to the infirmary. He desperately needs medical attention or he'll—"

"Die?"

"Wait. Let me finish. I thought maybe the sick bay at the camp was not sufficiently manned with good doctors and equipment. So, I went straight to the commandant's office and demanded his immediate release."

"And?"

"He said no. He had informed Beijing that a British Royal was near death and that we needed to get him off this island as soon as possible. To that end, a Chinese Army Air Force tactical transport aircraft is en route to Nassau right now. May have already landed. A medically equipped plane will land at the facility and take him to the airport at Nassau and then to Beijing, where he can get the best care possible. Xi Jinping has demanded that he be kept safe and attended to during the long flight. A doctor and a nurse are on board. . . ."

"We cannot let that happen, China. You remember Otto Warmbier, the poor boy who was imprisoned by Kim Jong-un in North Korea?"

"Of course. Our Supreme Leader does not want to see a Chinese repeat of that PR fiasco on the world stage. Not after all I've told you about Xi Jinping's absolute insistence that my country earn a respected seat as a civilized member at the table of nations. . . ."

"And when is the transport flight due to land over in Nassau?"

"Last I heard, sometime around noon tomorrow."

"Tomorrow? My God, China, we've got to get him out of there now!"

"I know, I know! Why do you think I was behaving so abominably? I was getting desperate as to what to do!"

"Listen to me. I've done a ton of hostage rescue work as you can imagine. All over the world. As have my friends Stokely and Harry Brock. If we have to storm the gates and shoot our way out, that's what we'll do."

"Easier said than done."

"At least, on the other hand, we know where to look, don't we?"

"Yes. He was kept in the D building, right behind the security block. But by now, after my temper tantrum with the commandant, they might have moved him to a room at the infirmary. Either way, I'll show you to him."

"Good. Are you carrying, China? Because we could always use an extra shooter if we need one and—"

"I beg your pardon?" a supercilious voice said from right behind them. Hawke looked over his shoulder and saw the imperious little mustachioed French maître d' he'd seen when they first entered.

"Yes?" Hawke said coldly. He'd disliked the man on sight.

"I'm terribly sorry, monsieur. *Je m'excuse.* I'm afraid your guest here is improperly attired for the lounge, and the management has asked that madam leave the premises. Immediately, I'm afraid."

Hawke had to stifle the urge to break the pompous little twit's nose, but one look at China, and he knew that was not the way to go.

Instead Hawke said coolly, "*Vous êtes un cretin, monsieur,* and we'd be happy to leave. Your drinks are badly mixed and your hors d'oeuvres are not fit for human consumption. *Au revoir,* for now, you little toad, but when I see you again, you will require hospitalization. Come on, darling, grab your drink and let's get out of here. It's begun to stink in here. . . ."

Hawke took her hand to direct her back to where they'd entered. She pulled her hand away and said, "No, Alex, we can't leave just yet. Unfinished business, you might call it."

China marched across the dance floor to the gilded staircase she'd pointed out before, the one that led up to the Castle proper and the restaurant. Hawke used the time on the stairs to speed-dial his pilots. Fuel up and be ready to fly by midnight at the latest, he told him.

Hawke spotted Stokely the second he entered the busy restaurant. There were three of them seated on the red leather banquette. Stoke on the left, Brock on the right, and who should be seated between them but his old friend Zhang. She had her arms around both men, squeezed in between them with her breasts yearning to be set free from her plunging décolletage.

Stoke got to his feet, waving at Hawke to come over to the table. Harry was smiling at him but had no interest in waving him over. He was too busy drooling over Zhang to the point where some of his saliva was clearly visible on her silk blouse. She either didn't care or hadn't noticed. Hawke stepped aside and let China lead the way to the table.

Zhang was grinning up at her.

"Well, well, well, if it isn't Dragonfire Bay's own dragon lady. It's China Moon and her terribly misguided boy toy. . . . Slumming, are you, darling?"

China opened her mouth to speak, but Hawke stepped on her line. "Misguided in what way?" he said. Hawke leaned forward so that Zhang's nose and his nose were nearly touching.

Zhang gave him what was likely intended to look like a smile but came out as a nasty snarl. She hissed, "Misguided in so many ways, darling, but most especially in your taste in women. I mean, seriously, look who the boy toy is dragging around tonight! The dragon lady herself!" She sat back and let her response hang there in the air over the table.

Harry saw Stoke remove her arm from around his neck, and Harry wisely did the same.

Hawke saw what was about to happen next before anyone else.

China, smiling at her rival all the while, proceeded to lean across the table and up into her face. She secured Zhang's attention and uttered one single, solitary word: "Bitch!" The word dripped with hateful sarcasm.

And having delivered that verbal blow, she then heaved the entire contents of her cocktail glass into Zhang's face.

Zhang, in a blind rage, screamed something unintelligible. Her carefully coiffed hair was now hanging down to her bare shoulders, thick damp strands over her face. She had sliced limes on her head and shoulders, ice cubes melting into the heat of her imposing cleavage, and worse, the citrus juice was stinging her eyes to the point where she couldn't see at all. She began thrashing about like a madwoman, howling and clawing at the air and hissing like some insane feline creature who'd been mortally offended.

She tried to get to her feet, eager to have a go at China, but Stoke put an iron clamp on her biceps and shoved her back down on the banquette.

Hawke looked at Stoke with an intense focus that spoke volumes to his old friend. Something serious was going on, and Hawke needed his help.

"S'up, boss?" he said.

"Stoke. You need to come with me. Now. You and Brock. Something's come up. A full-blown emergency. Get up. You, too, Harry. We need to go. Now! Leave her there!"

The four of them raced down the staircase and out into the night. There was a long line of cars disappearing down the hill, all waiting to enter the porte cochere at the entrance.

China went immediately to the head valet and said, "Wilson, we're with Zhang. There's an emergency. She wants her black Bentley brought up here immediately. She'll be out in just a moment, so if you value your job, hurry!"

The long black car rolled up moments later. Wilson got out and held the door open for the lady, reaching for his mobile with his other hand. Hawke slid into the passenger seat while Stoke and Harry climbed into the backseat.

After a moment Stoke spoke up. "Boss. You think, in hindsight, we should have called in the Legionnaires? This could spiral up pretty quickly with all the security forces around."

"You mean, the boys from Belize?"

"Uh-huh. I sure do."

Hawke said, "Thunder and Lightning are still on standby, but it's too late now. This thing ends at midnight, when we put Prince Henry on the plane and get the hell out of the Bahamas. I will say one thing and I mean it."

Hawke turned around, looked at Harry Brock and said, "I'm glad as hell you came back, Harry. I sincerely am."

Stoke turned his head to the window and smiled.

And off they went to save the world one more time.

Off into the star-spangled night.

CHAPTER 58

China left two little patches of rubber on the concrete drive as she accelerated the big car, roaring away from the Castle, fishtailing the Bentley a bit upon reaching the bottom of the hill, but instantly and expertly correcting it. Hawke was glad she was driving. She was, in fact, a seriously good driver and knew all the roads and all the shortcuts on the island. She could get them to their destination in a hurry.

"Where to?" she asked, never taking her eyes off the road.

"The marina," Hawke replied.

"Got it," China said. "I know a shortcut. Ten minutes faster than the coast road."

"Good," Hawke said.

"What have we got, boss?" Stoke piped up from the rear.

"Trouble," Hawke said. "I just learned from China that Prince Henry is currently a permanent guest at that little reeducation camp over on Devil's Island. He's been starved and maltreated and is not in good shape at all. Needs emergency medical attention. The Chinese government doesn't want him to die for reasons of bad publicity such as North Korea received in the Otto Warmbier debacle. They've sent a transport plane to pick him up and ferry him back to Beijing. Obviously, we cannot let that happen under any circumstances."

"When's that plane s'posed to land, boss?"

"Around noon tomorrow."

"Better than I thought. We got everything we need to get him out aboard the Wally boat. Since we no longer care if anybody sees us or not, we can probably lean on the throttles and cut the travel time in half."

"Sounds good, Stoke."

"I'm going to need a gun," China said, her eyes unwaveringly on the road. "I usually carry but not tonight."

"Lots to choose from, China," Stoke said. "We got an arsenal on that boat."

"Good," she said.

"Boss, once we exfiltrate the prince, where we going?"

"Pindling Airport in Nassau. Private aviation. Gulfstream will be juiced up and spooled up out on the tarmac waiting for us."

"Where we going next?"

"Miami. I'll let you and Mr. Brock off, then head out to Bermuda to refuel. Having recently been hospitalized there, I know all the doctors at Edward VII Hospital. Good place for Henry to recover, too. Sand, sun, and saltwater treatment. Ambrose Congreve is on the island, too, and would love to debrief him so Scotland Yard can go after these people."

"Love it," Stoke said. "Ambrose is the man!"

"Mr. Brock?" Hawke said, looking at him in the rearview mirror. "Are you still with us?"

"Yes, sir!" Harry said. "No idea what I was in for, but I am ready to rock, sir!"

"Rock?" Hawke said. He and Mr. Brock had never been able to get on the same page. He found the man annoying and prone to profanity.

Hawke thought China, daredevil that she clearly was, was going to put the big Bentley up on two wheels when she swerved into the parking lot at the Dragonfire Club Marina. He looked at his watch. It was almost midnight. Five hours or less of darkness left until dawn. With China showing the way to the building where Prince Henry was confined, and her knowledge of the compound, he felt his odds of success were fairly high. The four of them had not only the element of surprise in their favor, but extremely heavy firepower for such a small hostage rescue team. He would have much preferred to have Thunder and Lightning, his hostage rescue specialists based down in Costa Rica, along for the ride tonight but time and circumstances had not permitted it. Those guys meant business. They were ex–French Foreign Legion or Mossad or British SAS and what have you. He was momentarily glad of Brock. The man could hop and pop with the best of them. A stone killer in a firefight.

The marina was dead quiet.

"Hold on, boys," China said, taking a hard right and aiming the big black Bentley directly at the locked entrance gates of the marina.

"China! What?" Hawke said as she increased her speed.

"Another shortcut," she said calmly and just blew right through the padlocked metal fencing, literally blowing the two gates off their hinges and flying into the water on either side of the big concrete pier.

She slowed slightly now, driving nearly all the way out to the very end of the wide pier where the Wally was moored.

"Alex," she said, suddenly in charge, "you and Stoke go fire the engines and free the mooring lines. I've got one last detail to take care of, and I need Mr. Brock here to give me a hand. Mr. Brock?"

"Sure. What do you need?"

Hawke shrugged his shoulders and looked at Stoke, shaking his head as they walked away. What the hell was she up to now?

China remained behind the wheel, and Harry walked around the front of the car, stepping carefully because there were only a few feet of room between the automobile's chromed radiator and the end of the pier.

"What's up?" Harry said, putting his hand on the driver's-side windowsill.

"Pretty straightforward, actually. I'm going to park Zhang's Bentley out here in the underwater garage."

"The underwater what? Are you sure you—"

"I'm putting it in neutral. Could you pull my door open? Thanks. So, get back there and give me a good push. I'll get out and push, too, from right here while I keep the front wheels straight. When you've got it rolling fast enough to go off the end on its own, just say 'Go!' I'll let go of the steering wheel and jump the hell out of the way." She saw him with both hands on the trunk in the rearview mirror, really leaning into it.

"Okay, Harry?"

"Yep!"

"Okay ... start ... pushing ... *now*!"

"Boss!" Stoke cried out. "You got to see this!"

"See what?" he said, looking over at the far end of the pier where Zhang's precious Bentley was rolling forward toward the end of the pier, clearly about to swim with the fishes. "Bloody hell!" Hawke exploded.

The big Bentley, with China holding the wheel and Harry Brock pushing from behind, looked like it was headed right off the end of the pier!

The car was heavy as hell, but between the two of them, they got enough momentum going. When China abandoned ship and was safely out of the way, Harry really put his shoulder into it. He could not believe what they were doing but the woman clearly had her mind made up.

Hawke and Stoke looked on in shock as the Bentley rolled ... right off the end of the pier! And went straight down about twenty feet before it hit the surface with massive splash. . . . The big Bentley had gone vertical before it hit and now only the back half of the automobile remained sticking up out of the water.

China watched the last of the bubbles of the car reach the surface of the black water, then turned to her audience and bowed deeply in their direction.

"Just taking a bow, boys. What do you think?"

Hawke, shaking his head, said, "Holy God, China, what the hell?"

"That's some crazy shit right there, boss," Stoke said, just on the off chance that he wasn't aware of it.

————

Hawke had slipped aboard and down into the helm seat, leaving Stoke up on the dock to free their lines and push off. Hawke fired the big 650HP outboards, not nearly as concerned about the noise as he'd been in the past. He was well past caring what anybody in this bloody place thought about what he did or did not do anymore.

He had only one thought on his mind now: getting inside that main gate, locating his godson alive, and getting him the hell out of there.

He'd briefly thought about returning to the hotel so he and Stoke and Brock could grab their belongings. But he immediately thought better of it, knowing he'd never be able to forgive himself if he arrived at Prince Henry's bedside too late. They were never coming back to Dragonfire Club, but for the length of his stay, he'd never left anything of real value in the penthouse, or any top secret comms from MI6; those he'd either deleted or burned in the fireplace after reading them.

Stoke jumped down, taking the seat adjacent to the helm, and Harry and China, wearing a big fat smile, both leapt down into the cockpit and seated themselves on the aft banquette.

Hawke swiveled around and looked at China. "What the hell, China?" he said. "I mean, seriously. That's one extaordinarily valuable automobile. What were you thinking?"

"Tell you later, dear. Just tying up some loose ends, that's all."

"Lines free! Hit it, boss!" Stoke said, and Hawke firewalled the two chrome throttles. The pointed bow of the big Wally came up out of the hole in a hurry, and the boat surged forward, picking up massive speed as Hawke put the nose of the bow dead on the breakwater and the harbor mouth leading to open water. At this speed, he put them at Devil's Island sometime just before one o'clock. He'd run bow up on shore, and they'd follow the trail Stoke had hacked through the jungle to the site overlooking the camp.

If it was all quiet, he told his team, China would descend alone to the bottom of the hill, approach the gate, and use the facial ID system. If it worked, she'd give them a high sign, and they'd all descend to meet her, then emerge from the jungle cover and run straight through to where all the red jeeps were parked. In addition to those lovely .50 cal machine guns mounted at the rear, China said the jeeps all had keys in them. They'd split up, two per jeep, and drive straight to the building where she believed the victim still might be.

If he was not, they'd jump back into the jeeps and go straight to the infirmary. The driver of each jeep would be using the light machine gun. The second passenger would be firing the .50 cal.

If the gates wouldn't open, China would come right back up to their hilltop position and grab her AR-15. Then the four of them would get ready to storm the gate and fight their way into the compound.

At that point, Stoke, on Hawke's signal, would use the M203 40mm grenade launcher to take out the two guard towers, one after the other. One RPG fired at each end of the perimeter fencing topped with razor wire would suffice. Then he would blow the main gates off their hinges with another couple of well-placed RPG grenades. Then they'd race down the hill and follow China to get the two jeeps and head to the D building and rescue the prisoner.

That was the plan so far as Hawke had thought it through in his mind. Hawke handed the Zeiss binos to Brock, then cupped his hand around the Zippo and fired up another fag. As China made her stealthy descent down to the compound entrance, he needed to settle himself a bit to prep for what was to come. He kept harkening back to the scene up at the Castle. He had been shocked to learn the truth about Zhang Tang. It had been his intention, prior to tonight, to tell her at some point about their shared history. That both their grandfathers had been lifelong friends! He'd realized that the Chinese ambassador whom he'd met as a boy, his grandfather's close friend, was also Zhang's grandfather!

But that was back when he'd thought she was a harmless person who just happened to have two violent criminal masterminds for brothers.

After all he'd heard of Zhang's true nature from China at dinner that night, he knew he could never feel the same way about her. In his experience, only the truly evil were capable of looking away from their epic crimes against humanity. And here she was, a prime example of the species. Just before they'd left the garden to go to the Castle, he'd asked China about the twins. . . .

"They've been detained, apparently. Guests of the state."

"Why were they detained?" he'd said.

"Fraud against the government. Not the first time, either. The Tang brothers had huge shipbuilding contracts courtesy of the government, and forensic accountants had discovered they had been keeping two discrete sets of books for years, bilking the government of billions." She'd informed her superiors at SHA, the Strategic Huyou Agency, about this and other actions they'd taken that were strictly forbidden.

"What's the penalty?" Hawke had asked.

"Prison time. Some white-collar country club jail or other. I don't know how long they'll get, simply because they annually funnel huge amounts of off-the-books profit into PLA coffers."

"Pity I never got to meet them," Alex Hawke said.

"No, it isn't," was her reply.

"Because?"

"Because while they are very attractive and incredibly charming, they are thoroughly despicable human beings, responsible for decades of incredible human suffering around the world. Why, I'd like nothing better than to see them behind bars for life, not to mention that ghastly beast of a sister of theirs."

Hawke smiled. "Got the picture," he said. "And it ain't pretty. I agree."

CHAPTER 59

Warm Springs, Georgia
February 1942

The Chinese ambassador, accompanied by his ADC, or aide-de-camp, Yang-Tsing, also known as his bower and scraper in chief, his minder, had not yet finished packing his bags. Tiger was planning a long winter weekend down in the heart of the American southland. The White House social secretary, a tallish beauty with snow-white hair always in a chignon, Mary Trice Clewis, had rung up the embassy a few days earlier.

Miss Clewis had informed Tiger's secretary, Kimberly Li, that the president was spending the weekend down at the Little White House in Warm Springs, Georgia. Save for his staff and his beloved Scottie, Fala, FDR would be all alone. Eleanor and her very close companion, the AP reporter Lorena Hickok, whom she called Hick, were traveling together to Appalachia.

And Miss Clewis had informed Miss Li quite frankly, "The president was feeling somewhat down and worn out. He thought it might be cheery to consider this a belated Christmas holiday. The one you both had to skip because you were working so hard."

FDR had asked Miss Clewis to ring up the Chinese Embassy and see if she could not enjoin the ambassador to take the presidential train down to Warm Springs, join him at the Little White House, and keep him company. Tiger was a bit torn. He had been planning to spend the weekend in the country at his beloved Sevenoaks, with his beautiful Spanish countess.

But, of course, Tiger had replied that he'd be delighted to take the train down South for faux Christmas with the president. He'd never spent any time there, but just two years earlier, he'd been a huge fan of David O. Selznick's fabulous Civil War epic, *Gone With the Wind*, and was thrilled to see a bit of Georgia while entertaining the president. FDR had recently purchased a brand-new four-ton blue Packard convertible, and the ambassador was looking forward to chauffeuring him about and exploring the countryside.

"Well, I think that's about it, Mr. Ambassador," Yang-Tsing said, fastening the leather straps on all three pieces of Goyard luggage.

Tiger scratched his chin, considering. "My shaving kit? My sleeping pills? A bottle of Scotch whiskey to give to the president as a present? You sure you haven't forgotten anything?"

Yang-Tsing scratched his balding pate and said, "No, sir, I think we got it all. If we don't want to miss that train, we'd best get downstairs now and get to Union Station, sir. It's raining pretty hard out there right now, and we might hit a lot of traffic."

Tiger paused and took one last look around the room, trying to remember if there was anything he'd forgotten. Satisfied there was not, he said, "Lead on, my good man. I'm right behind you!"

At the elevator, as Yang loaded all the luggage inside, Tiger suddenly turned to his ADC and said, "Go ahead down and help Bobby Ray Beavers get all the luggage inside the car. I'll be right down. I just remembered something I forgot to pack."

"Yessir," Yang said, pushing the button for the main floor. Tiger, as if in some kind of freaky trance, walked quickly back to his quarters and into his bedroom. He walked straight over to his mahogany chest of drawers and pulled open the sock drawer. *Socks? Had he really forgotten his socks?*

In a slow motion, almost dreamlike manner, as if in some kind of sleep walking coma, stuck his right hand inside the drawer, fishing around among all the socks until his fingertips grazed cold metal and he found what he'd come back for. He withdrew his hand and lovingly admired his most-prized possession. The pistol his father had given him during a short and highly unpleasant visit to his country home.

The beautiful but lethal short-barreled Colt .45 revolver with carved ivory handle grips.

He ejected the cylinder and saw that there were six .45 hollow-point caliber slugs inside.

He quickly snapped the action shut and, suddenly wondering what the hell to do with the damn gun, slid it into the right-hand pocket of the handsome new Burberry mackintosh that the countess had given him for Christmas. He'd hated breaking the news to Victoria about his abrupt change of plans. But the Countess de la Maza had been very understanding. It was part of her charm, and he thought the emerald-and-diamond brooch he'd selected for her at Van Cleef & Arpels would salve all wounds until his return.

He caught sight of his face in the dusky mirror above the dresser. He had a strange look in his eyes, one that reflected the almost-surreal trancelike state he found himself in.

Oddly, he seemed at his worst when he was in the company of the little bald-headed ADC. A few weeks earlier, he'd been on the verge of firing the little gnome and had accused him of giving him frequent migraine headaches. It had occurred to him, early on, not unreasonably, that perhaps his father, who had asked a lot of strange questions about his relationship with his minder, was actually in league with the fat little traitor!

And in the wake of the old man's visit to Sevenoaks, there had been a series of late-night phone calls that, despite the lack of a caller on the line, caused him vicious headaches the next morning. Very few people were given his private number in the country. One person who'd always had it? Yang-Tsing.

And then it struck him like a hammer to the gut. Tiger's father had been the one who'd first put the little fellow on his son's embassy staff! To spy on him? Or, worse, to practice his mind-control methods on Tiger in order to get the son to do his father's insane bidding!

He felt almost as if he were walking underwater . . . almost as if, during his brief visit to Sevenoaks, his father, using ancient Chinese mind-control techniques, had somehow hypnotized him. Buried preordained actions deep within his brain! Was that even possible? He'd been reading about recent astounding advances in the science of mind control that Chinese scientists were making. . . .

"Shape up or ship out, mister!" he barked at his reflection in the mirror. Not even remotely sure what he'd meant by that absurd command, he then walked back out into the hallway, pulling the door shut behind him.

It was all a bad dream, he told himself, climbing into the back of the big black Cadillac.

"Union Station and step on it!" he said to Bobby Ray Beavers, his driver.

"You got it, boss. Where you going, you don't mind my asking."

"I don't mind. I'm headed down into the heart of the southland, all the way to Georgia. A small hamlet outside of Atlanta called Warm Springs."

"The Little White House, sir?"

"Bobby Ray, you know that's classified Secret Service information."

"I know, I know. But Georgia? That's the sacred soil, sir! Mr. Ambassador, you best get down on your knees and kiss the ground when you get off that train!"

"Georgia's that good, is it, Bobby Ray?" he said.

"Way better than that. You've never been there before, right?"

"First time."

"You want to hear about it, sir? I was born in a little Georgia town called Lower Bottom."

"Where is that?"

"Well, it's right down the mountain a ways from Upper Bottom."

"Sounds reasonable."

"Makes sense, don't it?" Bobby Ray said with a laugh. "But let me tell you about my hometown, Claxton. You like fruitcake?"

"Never tried it, no."

"Well, sir, Claxton, Georgia, is the undisputed Fruitcake Capital of the World."

"Fancy that."

"You like football?"

"You mean soccer?"

"No, sir. I mean good old-fashioned American football. This year? Well, I'm here to tell you that my team, the Georgia Bulldogs, are going to the Sugar Bowl in New Orleans on New Year's Day, going up against Alabama's Crimson Tide, a six-point favorite."

And for the next fifteen minutes, Bobby Ray Beavers did just that. He delivered an expert tutorial on all things Georgia and points south of the Mason-Dixon Line. And told the ambassador exactly why Bobby Ray Beavers had come to believe with all his heart and soul that the South well and truly would, one fine day, surely rise again.

CHAPTER 60

Union Station, Washington, D.C.
February 1942

Following the traitorous spy Yang-Tsing and the porter with the rolling luggage cart, to the sounds of slamming railway car doors echoing up and down the concrete platform, the ambassador found a string of eight coffee bean green Pullmans. They'd all been built in 1929, and they formed the presidential railroad fleet, Miss Clewis had told Miss Li. Each tipped the scales at more than one hundred forty-two tons and was a literal rolling fortress with the president inside one of them. The trick was that no one besides railway staff and the president's Secret Service knew exactly which car he could be found in. Armor plating and three-inch-thick bulletproof glass added another layer of security.

It was, Tiger thought, a rather inspiring sight to behold. The railway cars were all glistening from a recent bath in the yards. They were lined up in the shadows, waiting for the powerful steam locomotive to arrive, the one that would tug the presidential rail fleet all the way down to, if you could believe Bobby Ray Beavers, the land of hope and glory.

While the interiors were spare compared to the lavish Victorian clutter that ran riot inside the White House, the Pullmans were plenty fancy enough. Entering through the vestibule's heavy door, a traveler would step into an observation lounge packed with stuffed velvety armchairs in shades of rust, green, and blue. Draperies hung from each of the room's eight windows. Gleaming art deco ashtrays sprouted like chromium fountains from the wine red carpeted floor.

The president's guest would be rolling down to the Promised Land on the B&O Line, Tiger had been told by the Baltimore & Ohio's general passenger agent in Washington's Union Station. Despite his odd state of mind, Tiger found that his excitement about a train trip into the heart of the South was growing as departure drew near. The party came to a halt beside a Pullman with the name HILLCREST CLUB emblazoned in gold leaf above the windows, running the entire length of the big wagon.

"All right, suh, I reckon this is us," said the tall, distinguished-looking black porter, a handsome silver-haired gent who had introduced himself as the president's trusted porter, Mr. Fair.

A repository of countless overheard secrets, Fred Fair still remembered how embarrassed FDR had been the day the two had first met, years before, when "the boss"—as almost everyone called FDR, including those who did not work for him—had fished in his pockets for change but come up empty. "I want to tip these people," FDR had whispered to an aide. The leader of the free world who was more concerned about tipping a Pullman porter than boarding his train on time—that was the president that Fred Fair knew and loved.

The Chinese ambassador would be boarding the Pullman known as the Hillcrest Club, Fred informed them, and traveling in enviable quarters, one of the first-class staterooms. In addition to its eight spacious rooms, the club car harbored a lounge at one end with soft low chairs perfect for reading in and wooden tables just big enough for a game of gin rummy or canasta.

The large windows were sparkling in the sunshine now, and Tiger Tang collapsed into the nearest armchair, one right next to a window. He would wait there while his luggage was unpacked and probably for a good time after that. Untold sights lay ahead of him, and he'd be damned if he was going to miss a single solitary one of them!

The light from the windows was marvelous and he pulled out a book he'd bought just for the trip. It was a runaway bestseller written by a Southern author named Margaret Mitchell. The book was called *Gone With the Wind*. He cracked it open and started to read.

The story put him in just the right mood for the trip. He was looking forward to seeing the South. He was especially thrilled at the prospect of seeing the city of Richmond, Jefferson Davis's capital of the Confederacy, which would be coming up about ninety miles south of Washington. He'd been something of a Civil War scholar during his first year at Oxford, and he'd found Robert E. Lee and the underrated Jefferson Davis and General James Longstreet all fascinating players in the tragic drama that split the bitter nation into a war that cruelly pitted brother against brother.

A waiter appeared from the lounge car and asked if he'd like a beverage and at what time he'd like his evening meal served in the dining car.

"Yes, dinner at eight." Tiger smiled up at him. "I certainly would endorse a cocktail notion. A double shot of Mr. Jack Daniel's famous whiskey with a splash of branch water, please, sir!"

"Yes, suh, Mr. Ambassador. Bourbon and branch, yes suh, coming right up! The president, he likes that one, too!"

CHAPTER 61

Devil's Island, the Bahamas
Present Day

By the time the little war party had raced the big Wally boat full throttle across the placid bay, run the bow up on the beach as far as it would go, stowed the boat up inside the mangrove swamp, and made their way through the thick, ropy jungle to their observation point atop the island's only hill, an hour had elapsed since leaving the marina. They had met with no resistance and had observed not a single vessel during their seriously rapid transit.

Hawke had insisted they all smear their faces and hands with black greasepaint and remain completely silent moving through the jungle. He remembered the microphones camouflaged in the trunks of trees that he and Stoke had encountered. Not to mention the three Bahamian guards who'd silently appeared out of nowhere and who would have been only too happy to shoot them on sight or haul them down the hill and into captivity.

At the top of the hill, Hawke was whispering some last-minute instructions to China Moon before she descended the hill to try gain entry to the camp the easy way.

"Take this," he said, giving her his little peashooter, as his boss, Sir David Trulove, called it. It was a Walther PPK, his favorite. Light and small but lethal. She could easily conceal it in the pocket of her black windbreaker. She nodded her approval.

"If it was good enough for 007, it's good enough for me," she said.

"Ready to go?" Hawke asked.

"Ready as I'll ever be."

"Remember, we'll be covering you from up here. We've got the high ground. We've got clear lines of fire inside the compound. If there's trouble, we'll have your back."

She nodded and disappeared down into the jungle on the hillside.

A few long moments later, they saw her emerge from her cover and walk swiftly up to the main gate. All was still quiet, no activity at the two watchtowers, no sign of life in the windows of the darkened security block.

They could see a metal box, mounted on a large post just outside the gates, giving off a dim glow in the darkness. China stepped up to it, leaned her face inside, and waited for the outcome. Hawke, of course, was praying the damn facial recognition thing would let her in and save them all a lot of trouble.

China stepped back, a smile on her face.

Silently, the two heavy gates swung wide. She strode inside, head high, fearless.

She looked back up at her unseen comrades, who were waiting for her signal on top of the hill, and pumped her right fist in the air a couple of times before retreating back into the shadowy structures behind the guard block to wait for their arrival at the jeeps.

It had occurred to Hawke that, based on the island's location, so far off the beaten path, and the incredible defenses it had against intruders, it was highly unlikely the camp had ever suffered an enemy intrusion of any kind.

That would certainly account for the laxity they were so fortunate to now encounter.

That was when four powerful searchlights lit up the night. One atop each watchtower at the corners. China was running from the crisscrossing beams, trying to find shelter among all the darkened buildings just as the two brilliant white beams caught up with her. Machine-gun fire erupted instantly from both towers and stitched a line of small explosions in the dirt that almost reached her heels.

The guards who were firing had seen where she'd disappeared, but they had no idea where she'd be hiding by the time they'd reached her.

"Take those bloody towers out, Stoke!" Hawke said.

The big man already had the M320 44mm grenade launcher up in firing position. Hawke could make out two or three shadowy figures emerge at the top of the closest tower. One of them had his high-power binoculars trained on the top of the hill. "Nearest one first," Hawke said. "Do it now!"

"Tangos out, descending steps. Fire!"

There was a blinding flash of yellow-red flame from the muzzle and a whoosh of sound from the deadly rocket. A second later an explosion obliterated the top of the tower, and Hawke saw three bodies falling to the ground, dead.

Stoke had affixed another grenade to his weapon.

"Guards coming out of the second one, Stoke. Fire!"

The smoke cleared and revealed that the entire watchtower, enveloped in flames, was pitched at an impossible angle, and finally crashing to the ground while still burning. The gates that China had opened with only her pretty face seemed to be stuck in the open position.

Suddenly, powerful searchlights mounted atop the security block rooftop began searching for their position on the hilltop.

"Stoke! Get another round mounted on that damn thing and turn out those bloody lights on the roof." A second later, the lights were suddenly extinguished by a quick volley of RPGs. The roof of the building was now afire.

"Move out!" Hawke said, and the three warriors raced down through the jungle and bolted across the concrete apron and through the gates, heading straight to the battalion of jeeps lined up a couple of hundred yards behind the guardhouse.

As they raced past the concrete building, a door opened on the side of the solid structure that was the security block.

Stokely Jones Jr., the big man who'd once been a heavy-weapons instructor with the SEALs in Afghanistan, was a fearsome enemy when he had an M320 in his hands. He'd taught his young soldiers how to fire the thing with deadly accuracy, even when they were on the run.

He sighted in on the emerging targets, estimated the range, squeezed the trigger, and put a big bad round of death right through that freaking open door! "That damn party is officially over, boss!" he said with a big smile.

CHAPTER 62

Devil's Island, the Bahamas
Present Day

Stoke took dead aim and fired the RPG at a trio of guards racing across the concrete apron toward them, automatic weapons spraying fire in their direction.

Seeing the highly explosive round take those three players off the field, Hawke caught Stoke's attention and gave him a big smile and an "Attaboy, Stoke!"

It was dark again. Hawke saw China dart out of the alley between two bunkhouses and sprint across the open pavement toward the jeeps.

Their luck held. They got into two of the closest jeeps, both with swivel-mounted .50 caliber machine guns bolted down at the rear. Brock took the wheel of the first, and Stoke climbed up into the back and loaded fresh rounds of ammo to both of the guns, the one in his hand and the mounted one.

"You drive," Hawke called to China. "I'll be the backseat shooter."

"Aye-aye, sir!" she said.

"Let's start 'em up, Mr. Brock," he said.

They both started their jeeps up and sped across the wide concrete yard to what was actually a large village of identical buildings. The only difference among them was the large white letters stenciled on the walls and the corrugated tin rooftops. There had to be at least fifty or sixty of the damn things.

Hawke had to shout to be heard over the roaring of the two engines. "China," he called out, "which building was Henry located in?"

"D!" she shouted, and pointed straight ahead to where the undistin-guished building marked D was located. "Something doesn't look right, Alex. I'm not sure this is the same building they took me to that night."

"Might it be?"

"I suppose. It was a moonless night, very dark, and I was very upset. Maybe I just wasn't thinking clearly. Maybe I misunderstood, and it was building B instead."

"Let's just have a quick look," Hawke said, and China was already hit-ting the brakes.

She nodded, and everybody climbed out.

China stuck her face into the ID lens beside the single dooor, and open sesame, they were all inside. This room, China saw, was not at all what she remembered.

Everything was white: the walls, the floors, and the ceiling, all the work surfaces, the porcelain sinks, the white protective clothing and face masks hanging from wall pegs as they came in, the neon lights. And ev-erywhere racks of test tubes and countless Bunsen burners.

Hawke knew what he was looking at. And this was no reeducation camp, at least if all the other buildings where built out like this, Hawke thought. No, what this was, was an extremely sophisticated, spotless lab-oratory. It was a laboratory dedicated to the mass production of extremely high-grade heroin, with an expertise and sophistication such as he'd never seen before.

After all the crappy drug labs he'd seen in Asia, he knew it took twenty-four hours to produce twenty pounds of pure heroin. The process was complicated, fraught with danger. If the morphine mix was over-heated, the explosion would unleash the fires of Hell on everyone inside. The fumes given off would be poisonous enough to knock an elephant off its feet, and a bad leak could very well kill everyone in the room.

What Hawke now beheld took heroin production to an entirely new, perhaps even global, level. He looked around. This one spotless white room, Hawke believed, was just the tip of the iceberg. It was large, filled with equipment that was expensive and brand-new: vacuum pumps, mas-sive stainless steel electric blenders, electric drying ovens, and sophisticated venting and exhaust systems. By the door where China was standing was the very latest reflux condenser, while next to that were gleaming flasks and test tubes ready to be loaded into an autoclave for sterilization.

"This is nuts," China said, suddenly standing beside him.

This was the HQ for a meticulous narcotics operation, the Google, the Amazon, the epicenter of a worldwide narcotics operation.

And Hawke realized just how ingenious the Tang brothers had been. They'd built the mammoth facility to resemble one of the mind-control camps seen all over China, where inmates wandered about in rags and slept in bunkrooms overcrowded with sick and dying Muslims. No one would ever think twice about entering such a pestilential prison.

If he had to bet, he'd bet that perhaps just one of the countless identical buildings here was actually used for such a purpose. And that was the one the commandant had shown China that night. The one where Prince Henry was being held. The rest? They were all smack labs, cranking out enough heroin every day to feed the insatiable worldwide demand and supply the high-quality product the Tang crime family had to keep pumping out, year in, year out.

China had unwittingly led him into the very heart of a Tang criminal operation. She had unmasked a vast criminal enterprise charading as a respectable international business. Resorts, hotels, casinos, feature film production, prostitution, white slavery, the whole enchilada, in fact.

This was where Prince Henry had stuck his nose. Not the sub pen or even the white slavery auctions of women at the Castle, as deeply secret and dark as they both were.

No.

This was why they'd held on to Henry, terrified to let him go.

And why they were now, in all likelihood, slowly poisoning the very life out of him! Hawke squinted, having caught a glimpse of pale pink on the eastern horizon. Dawn was drawing nigh and closer by the minute.

"We're running out of darkness, let's go! We've got to get to that infirmary and get the prince the hell out of there now!" Hawke said, and they raced back outside and into the jeeps. Roaring away, flat out through the narrow streets of the compound.

CHAPTER 63

Devil's Island, the Bahamas
Present Day

How far away is this bleeding infirmary?" Hawke asked China as they came to an intersection. Hawke, who was manning the swivel-mounted .50 cal machine gun in the rear of the jeep, now kept an eye on his watch. He couldn't afford to take it for granted that the Chinese transport flight into Nassau would arrive at the estimated time. It might be a few hours late. Or it might be a few hours early. Speed was of the essence now. It was everything.

China said, "This is the main road off to our left. Leads straight through the middle of the camp all the way to the rear entrance, where the hospital is, maybe four miles from here.

"Take a left here, Harry," she shouted at Brock, tires squealing and smoking, hanging a hard left. "Step on it, Mr. Brock."

Ten minutes later, the two jeeps were speeding at eighty miles an hour on the main road. They needed to arrive now, get inside that infirmary before the guards knew they were coming, before they could mount a defense.

"Next right!" China shouted again to Brock, as she spun the wheel hard over, putting the jeep up on two wheels to make the turn. Hawke found himself holding on to the bolted-down machine gun just to avoid being ejected from the jeep at this speed. A large white structure loomed up ahead. Had to be the sick bay, had to be.

"This is it!" she said as they both pulled up in front of a six-story white building, a lot of glass and steel, very modern compared to the rustic wood-hewn laboratories. The infirmary had a well-marked emergency room, a flashing red neon high up on the entrance at the side blinking ER . . . ER . . . ER. Illuminated high on the wall above the entrance, big letters in polished steel read:

THIS BUILDING IS A GIFT TO THE PEOPLE OF THE BAHAMAS
FROM THE TANG FAMILY, 2014

They all dashed inside the main entrance doors, weapons at the ready.

China coughed loudly to get the attention of the sleepy nurse holding down the fort at the reception desk, at three o'clock in the morning. When the first cough didn't do the trick, she slammed her machine gun down hard onto the granite counter right in front of Nurse Diesel.

"Oh! Can I help you, miss?" the startled woman said.

"I'm here to see one of your patients! Now, lady!"

While Hawke, Stoke, and Harry hung back and kept to the shadows, China flashed her MSS ID and gold-and-red shield inside its leather wallet.

"I'm an official with the Chinese government. My name is not important. What is important is that we're here to pick up one of your patients. British national. His name is Henry."

The nurse, who'd heard that the Chinese Secret Police were en route to the island by medevac chopper to evacuate this patient later on this morning, was doing her best to be polite to this policewoman. She didn't like the look of that badge one bit. She was nearing retirement, and the last thing she needed was to get sideways with the Chinese Secret Police.

"Yes, yes, of course. I think you're a little early, but we've been expecting you. Top floor. There's the elevator over there. Push six. Then go to your right to the VIP critical care ward. The duty nurse will show you to his room. He's in six-oh-two. Don't be shocked. He's very weak. Malnourished. Someone's mistreated him very badly. He'd lost a lot of blood when he arrived here."

"And just who do you think mistreated him, Nurse?" China said.

"I'm just a receptionist," the terrified woman said. "I have no idea who's responsible."

"I just bet you don't," China said in disgust, then turned and walked away.

———————

Hawke pushed six. Once upstairs, they all went right to a pair of double doors with small porthole windows. Clearly, this was the floor where the VIPs got the VIP treatment. The duty nurse clearly had gotten a call from reception and was waiting for them in the corridor, standing by a closed door marked 602.

"He's in there," she whispered, pushing the door open for them.

China grabbed Hawke's hand and silently pulled him over to the young man's bedside. In the dim light, a gaunt, pale figure was snoring raggedly.

"Oh, my God, Alex. It's him all right," she said simply. "Look at him. I cannot believe he's still alive. . . ."

Hawke joined her. "Yes, it's Henry. Looks like we got here not a moment too soon," he said, grateful beyond measure that at least his godson appeared to still be clinging to life. Ever the handsome lad, he was now very thin and grey, with a thin sheen of perspiration on his sallow cheeks and forehead. Hawke checked his pulse. "Sixty-two. Not strong, but just maybe strong enough," he said, laying his hand gently on the young man's forehead and removing it. "No fever," he said quietly.

"Tell me what you need, Chief," Brock said.

"Couple of things, Mr. Brock. First, go down the hall to the nurses' station. We need a couple of orderlies with a stretcher and a gurney," Hawke said. "I saw a few of them parked along the wall to the left of the elevator." He then turned to China, who was holding the boy's hand. "China?" he said.

"What else can I do for him, Alex?" she asked.

"Go to the nurses' station down the hall. Flash your badge. Tell them you need white orderly gowns, four of them, and stethoscopes. Go now! Hurry it up."

Stoke, upon seeing a reddish glow from the window on the ceiling and hearing the swell of voices from the ground below, glanced out the nearest window.

Stoke said, "A whole mess of guards down there, boss. Looks like they've barricaded the rear gate and set our two jeeps on fire. We gotta find ourselves a whole new way outta Dodge!"

When the two orderlies arrived with the stretcher and the gurney, Hawke allowed them to carefully remove Henry from the bed to the stretcher and then secure him to the top of the gurney. He then asked the orderlies if they'd mind bringing a saline drip from the nurses' station and antibiotics as well.

He figured they'd be gone long enough to give them a good ten minutes or so to get the prince out of the building.

As soon as the two orderlies headed left down to the nurses' station, Hawke and party went right. All four had donned the white orderly gowns. Harry Brock and Stokely were wheeling the prince's gurney and wondering what in the hell the boss man was up to now.

"This way," Hawke said. "We're going down to the emergency room on the ground floor."

The wide elevator doors slid open, and they rolled the gurney inside. Hawke pushed the button marked ER, and down they went. Arriving there, all walked straight to the exit, not looking at a soul. Nor did anyone look at them. The ER was dead this time of night, and they barged right through the exit doors and down the ramp to where the ambulances were parked.

Hawke went to the first of the two ambulances and climbed behind the wheel. The key, as he'd prayed, was in the ignition. He twisted the key, and the motor coughed to life. He craned around to see into the darkened rear bay of the vehicle.

China and Brock were carefully loading the sleeping prince into the red-and-white ambulance. Stoke was up front with Hawke, riding shotgun but with the big M-60 7.62mm machine gun in his hands instead of a Purdey twelve bore.

China reached forward and tapped Hawke's shoulder.

"Gurney's secure. We're ready to roll back here, boss," she said, earning a smile from Hawke at that first use of his nickname. "Harry and I will stay back here with Henry and monitor his vitals. I checked his oxygen. Not great, but sustainable. Pulse, seventy-two."

Stoke had also given his M79 rocket launcher to Brock in the rear just in case anyone on Devil's Island thought it might be a really good idea to get on the ambulance's tail and start shooting at them. Hawke told Harry to just blow out the bloody rear window and open fire if anyone got too close for comfort.

"Just put a damn round through it, Mr. Brock, and fire away. Stoke and I will do the same from up front."

CHAPTER 64

Devil's Island, the Bahamas
Present Day

Ten minutes into their escape via ambulance, Brock shouted up to the front seat, "I got three bogies on our six, boss! Motorcycles. Armed guards like the gang who set our jeeps on fire back there!"

Hawke glanced back at the situation. The three bikes were running side by side and gaining. He said, "Lure them in a little closer before you blow the window. Then let it rip! If one manages to get past you to either side, Stoke and I will deal with them. Got it?"

"Aye-aye, Skipper!"

Stoke had turned around in his seat to watch the speeding bikes closing in on them.

He said, "Okay, Harry, doing good, buddy. Let 'em come. The closer, the better. Get them inside fifty yards and then shower those bastards with glass! You go first for the guy in the middle. Then the two on the outside. Like the boss said, if they get past you, we'll deal with it up here."

Five seconds later, the interior of the ambulance was rocked by the massive and deafening concussion of the big gun, and the shattering of the glass window.

The cyclists tried desperately to veer away, but they'd foolishly gotten way too close.

Brock sighted in on the middle rider's collarbone and literally blew him and his bike right off the damn highway and into a deep ditch. Then he swung for the guy on the right and did the same thing. The guy to his left, no fool, had instantly accelerated fiercely ahead. When he got abreast of the passenger-side window and got a good look down the mouth of the big black barrel and the big man with his finger on the trigger, it was the fearsome look in that man's eyes that would be the last thing that went through his mind.

Stoke took the shot, pulled the trigger. The cyclist literally disintegrated before his eyes and then any trace of him vanished.

Ten long minutes passed before Brock shouted from the rear, "Bogie on our six, Stoke! Two cats in one of the fifty-cal jeeps!"

"Lure 'em in, brotha! Then take the mofos out for good!"

"Roger that!" Harry said, and five minutes later the jeep had closed to within twenty-five yards. "Say your prayers, assholes!" Stoke heard Brock say a second before the M79 roared fire and the jeep was lifted into the air by the powerful rocket and began cartwheeling backward end over end into the boggy swamp now on their left. Stoke caught a tangy whiff of salt air wafting up from the swamp. They were getting close. The sea loomed out there in the dark.

An hour later, with no more unpleasant interruptions, they finally reached the bay and turned right onto the sandy path that ran down to the water. Hawke was relieved to see the stern of the Wally boat still sticking out of the thick mangroves. He braked to a stop, and he and Stoke climbed out of the ambulance. Stoke pulled open the wide rear door and peered inside.

"How's he doing?" he asked China.

"Doing pretty well, Stoke, I think, considering all the excitement we had back here on that wild ride. His vitals are all holding steady. He finally said something. He asked for water. He drank a lot. He's terribly dehydrated."

Hawke said, "Let's get him in that boat and get the heck out of here, Harry. I'll help you carry the stretcher. You see that sky out yonder?"

Harry looked up.

Out there on the eastern rim of the world, all along that fine line where sea meets sky, a blazing red-orange disk heralded dawn's imminent arrival. They'd timed it just right. By the time the Chinese PLA soldiers arrived at the infirmary to take the prince, they'd be long gone.

The speeding Wally boat scratched a frothing white wake across the pink mirror of the bay. Hawke was staring at the radar screen, and he didn't like what he saw one bit.

They'd picked up one of the missile frigates, and it was gaining on them. He shoved the throttles forward, firewalling them, and cried out to Stoke, "Battle stations! Stoke, you and Mr. Brock get on the stern and secure yourselves in tight. I might be taking some very high-speed evasion turns here in a few minutes. We've got one of the missile frigates on our ass. Get the M-Sixty and the M-Seventy-nine battle ready. Concentrate your fire on the bridge. They're closing on us now! Fire when ready!"

Geysers of white water began arising all around the speeding Wally. The missile frigate was sighting in on them with the big foredeck cannon. Hawke put the boat into a series of tight turns starboard and port, never staying on either course for longer than fifteen seconds. . . .

He looked over his shoulder and saw how much ground the big cruiser had gained . . . not good.

"Mr. Brock, take out their bridge deck. Pump as many rockets into it as you can before they get lucky and sink us with that bloody bow gun!"

Hawke heard the successions of explosions before he saw them. When he looked over the stern, he saw nothing but flames licking up from the Chinese missile frigate. The ship was not only afire, but wallowing and clearly rudderless now. The bridge and probably all the officers inside were but a memory. The mere idea that a little speedboat might be capable of such withering firepower had clearly never occurred to the Chinese skipper.

Hawke called out, "Good on you, Mr. Brock! Mr. Jones! Nice shooting!"

At the helm, Hawke finally relaxed and allowed himself a private smile. It was time to start thinking about the future. He could see it all now. . . .

As soon as he boarded his plane in Nassau, he'd put a call through to Sir David Trulove at MI6 in London and give him the good news. Sir David in turn would then put a call straight through to Buckingham Palace, thus putting a buoyant smile on the face of the Queen of England.

He could hear the conversation playing in his head.

"Lord Alexander Hawke has just called from Nassau, Your Majesty," Trulove would say to Her Royal Majesty.

"Yes?"

"He has asked me to inform Her Royal Majesty that her grandson Prince Henry is now safe and in Bermuda to recuperate at King Edward VII Hospital for a few days on his way home to his grandmother! He's been dangerously unwell for a time. But the good news is, Hawke got to him in the nick of time. And Hawke assures us that the prince is going to make a speedy recovery now that he's in good hands. He'll be fine."

How did Shakespeare put it? Oh, yes, Hawke remembered:

All's well that ends well.

CHAPTER 65

Meissen, Germany
February 1942

It had begun to snow. Rather heavily, in fact. Ian Fleming was flat on his back on the sharp-edged cinders between the railroad ties and steel rails. He was under the massive locomotive, using his torchlight and peering upward, inspecting the undercarriage, looking for the perfect spot to stow the first of the two A devices. These were the ones that detonated instantly upon contact. It was a tricky business, to be sure.

He had considered stowing them somewhere in the cab, but it quickly became apparent that wouldn't work. Instead he had to find a more suitable placement for the devices. Fortunately, this was hardly the first time he'd placed a bomb in the bowels of an enemy train. He'd become quite adept at this stuff. Just last week he'd blown up a Hamburg bridge just as three Nazi staff cars carrying twelve Waffen-SS officers were fast approaching with their convertible tops down. The drivers had all jammed on the brakes but they were going far too fast, and the trio of big Grosser Mercedes had plunged hundreds of feet down into a rocky gorge.

Their screams had echoed up to him almost all the way down.

Ian had left Hawke up in the cab just in case another rail-yard detective or nosy Nazi showed up and wanted to play cops and robbers. To that end, he'd made sure Hawke had the right weapon for this work. Prior to leaving his flat in Mayfair, he'd chosen his best handgun, the Webley Mk VI, and fitted it out with a sound suppressor. Silent but deadly.

Ian, quite justifiably, was worried that when the railroad guard whom Hawke had shot failed to return from his yard shift, others would come looking for him. Hopefully, the dead man had been on the early part of his shift and not at the tail end of it. If a search party was sent out to find the dead, they'd see the two Norton motorcycles and that would be the end of this mission, not to mention the Grand Finale for him and Commander Hawke.

Hawke lit another cigarette and kept up his pacing inside the cab, his eyes searching the yard for any signs of movement or an approaching automobile. A job made a good deal more difficult because of the thick and all-encompassing ground fog. This kind of fog, a pea-soup fog, had killed people in London in 1814. They had suffocated.

Suddenly, Ian was shouting up to him from beneath the train in muffled tones. "Hawke, can you hear me, old man? Could you come down here for a second if you're not frightfully busy?"

Hawke stuck the Webley into the waistband of his thick gabardine britches and descended the steel steps to the ground. He bent down and saw Fleming with a huge smile on his face.

"Found the perfect place to hide these two little Christmas packages, Commander. Bend down. I'll show you."

Hawke dropped to his knees and bent down to have a look. Ian was at the most forward part of the huge steam engine.

"See this?" Ian said, shining his torch on what, to Hawke's eyes, was just a mechanical jumble.

"Where?" he said.

"Maybe where I'm pointing the torch?"

"Yeah, I see it. Looks like some kind of a shelf."

"Well, it isn't. It's a bloody cowcatcher. Or at least it's the brace for the one mounted at the front of this beast. They're designed to sweep away any stray creatures standing on the track, not at all sure where they are, when suddenly an oncoming train locomotive slams into a small herd of cows from behind. The cowcatcher enables the crew to push cattle or other creatures to either side of the tracks without stopping the train or harming the animals."

"And the reason you're so fascinated with this particular cow-catcher is?"

"It's bloody well perfect! It's the perfect spot to hide our two impact detonator devices. The placement ensures that the first thing the locomotive hits will cause two hellish simultaneous explosions and blow a massive hole in whatever it hits, thus triggering the two secondary devices stowed higher up a few moments afterward. I'm going to place the two secondary devices directly up under the cab's floor. Just for the blunt aftershock it will deliver to our German pals in Berlin."

"You should do this stuff for a living, Fleming," Hawke said mildly.

"I already do." Fleming laughed. "Pity I'm not getting rich. Better get back up in the cab and keep a weather eye out, Alex. This would be a very bad time to be distracted by gunfire and mad Rottweilers gnawing at one's ankles. Oh, and one more thing. I'm done with all the blankets. Wrap yourself up in them and try to find someplace to stay warm and moderately comfortable. I'll take the graveyard shift and wake you when I'm done down here. At least an hour before first light."

"Ian, I'm sure this is a foolish question, but do you know even how to start up one of these iron beasts?"

"Not really. But we'll have an engineer showing up for work soon to handle that. To refresh your memory, here's how I see it. We pull guns on the poor sod when he arrives inside the cab with his lunch pail and you will tell him in German to do exactly what we say. He fires up the steam engine as directed. I tell him to slowly advance the throttle to ten kilometers per hour. That's when, on my signal, you will leap from the cab, using the tuck-and-roll technique I taught you to avoid injury. You'll need to hit the ground running first, as I told you, in order to avoid a face-plant into those jagged cinders. That would play hell with your rosy complexion."

"So far, so bad. Then what, pray tell?"

"Leave that to me. Your job will be over. I'm still searching for a way to advance the throttle wide open after we've both bailed out. But certainly not while I'm still inside the cab. Not until we're both safely on the ground and running for our bikes and racing like two bats out of hell to get back to the barn."

When Fleming had finished mounting all four devices securely beneath the locomotive's undercarriage, he brushed himself off and mounted the steps up into the cab. Hawke had found a fold-down bunk and covered it with the blankets. He was sleeping like a baby, but snoring loudly and mumbling something in his sleep.

Ian bent his head down and put his mouth close to Hawke's right ear so Hawke could hear him.

"Rise and shine, m'lord!" he said brightly.

Hawke's eyes popped open. "Wha? Whassat? No. I don't know! Whass that tuck-and-roll idea again?"

Fleming smiled, plucked the Webley from Hawke's hand, climbed up onto the engineer's stool, lit another cigarette, and struggled to keep his eyes open.

He must not have succeeded.

In what seemed like a split second, Ian sat bolt upright. A tin lunch pail had been flung up into the cab from below and was now rattling around in the small space, bouncing merrily toward his feet and making a racket loud enough to wake the dead. But the noise didn't wake Blackie Hawke, who was probably still having nightmares about tucking and rolling from a speeding locomotive.

Ian had the revolver in the inside pocket of his leather bomber jacket. He kept his hand in his pocket and waited. A second later, he saw a beefy little darling coming up the steps and into the cab, a dead stogie jammed in the left side of his mouth. *"Wie geht's, mein Herr?"* Ian said, completely exhausting his German vocabulary in four words. And then he reached over and shook Hawke awake.

"Wha?" Hawke said, sitting bolt upright and clearly not knowing where he was.

"You've got a visitor, Commander! Sigfried! Say hello to him."

"Who the hell is he?" a drowsy Hawke said, pulling the blankets round his shoulders.

"Damned if I know," Fleming said with a smile. "Limited German vocabulary, you know. But you're fluent in Nazi. Tell him we're not going to hurt him. We just need a favor. It'll be worth a thousand deutschmarks to him if he helps us. Tell him we're the new owners of this locomotive, but we don't know how to start it."

Hawke smiled at the guy and repeated in German what Ian had said. Then the two of them were off to the races in that unlovely language, where even saying "I love you" (*"Ich liebe dich!"*) sounds like "I'm going to kill you!"

"What's he saying now?" Fleming asked.

"Thinking it over. He says he'll help us start the damn thing, but he wants his money first."

"Wouldn't you know it? Son of a bitch," Ian said, pulling out the Webley so Fritzie could get a good look at it. "Tell him this is his money. Tell him he's out of options. He either helps us out, or I pay him in installments, one bullet at a time."

Hawke told the German engineer what Fleming had said, and his eyes went wide.

"Blackie, do you see that metal handhold on the instrument panel, just below the windscreen?"

"Yes. What about it?"

"Here's some rope. Tie his hands with it and then secure the bitter end to the handhold. Give him enough rope that he's able to remain standing no more than a foot from that throttle lever."

After it was done, Hawke said, "Now what?"

"Tell Fritz to fire this monster up. Now, preferably."

Fritz did it without hesitation. He was clearly petrified.

"Okay, done. And next?" Hawke said.

"Tell him to advance the throttle. Slowly. Get this behemoth rolling. No faster than ten kilometers per hour. A fraction more and I put a bullet in the back of his head. Stress that last point."

The big locomotive didn't overcome inertia very easily, but soon they steamed out of the yard proper and proceeded down the tracks in the middle of the high street of the picturesque village. They crossed over an ancient bridge over the Elbe, and suddenly they were in the open with rolling meadows deep with new fallen snow. This had been Ian's late-night brainstorm. Hawke had no idea how to tuck and roll from a moving locomotive. But Ian had informed him that now, the snow all round was so soft and deep, he couldn't possibly hurt himself.

The engineer had his eyes locked on the tracks. He didn't want any trouble with these two English lunatics.

Ian motioned for Blackie to join him seated on the pull-down bunk covered with blankets.

"All right, old chap," Ian said. "All the marbles right now. You ready?"

"I am. But tell me something. You piqued my curiosity. How the hell are you going to get him to increase speed up to a hundred kph with us still aboard?

"We're not going to be aboard. You jettison first. At this speed, around eight kph, and in this freshly fallen snow, you won't need to pull off a perfect tuck and roll, which, by the by, means simply you pretend like you're doing a somersault onto the grass in summertime. . . . Tuck your head down, bend forward, and push yourself over the top in a full rotation. Got it, partner?"

"Oh, yes. Fully briefed. It's something akin to diving off the high board into a swimming pool empty of water."

"No, no, no. The snow is your water. You see that now?"

"Actually, I do now, yes. I was a little worried about that part."

"I know."

"Really? How?"

"You kept talking about it in your sleep. On your feet, buddy. I'll be right behind you soon as I deal with Fritzie."

"What are you going to do to him?"

"You'll see. Go stand at the top of the steps and get ready. I'll signal you when it's your time to jump."

"Fair enough. But just ensure you get yourself off his death train, too. We've got a lot more Germans to kill, Ian."

"Yeah, I know. Go whisper something reassuring to Fritzie. Then go stand at the top of the steps. Hold on to that grab rail at the top of the steps. Things might get a little dicey in here if I don't pull off this crazy scheme of mine. . . ."

Fleming stood up and walked forward until he was about two feet behind Fritzie. Hawke was looking at him, wondering what the hell he was up to.

"Okay, Blackie, on my count. Ready?"

Hawke nodded yes.

"Five! Four! Three! Two . . . and . . . *one*! Go, go!"

On the count of two, Hawke had seen Fleming put a shoulder into the small of Fritzie's back, hitting him hard enough to send him pitching forward and slamming his big beer belly hard into the throttle lever, shoving it all the way forward. Firewalled.

The fire-breathing monster got back on its haunches and roared ahead toward Berlin.

Hawke, lying peacefully buried in the snowbank, saw Fleming come flying out of that speeding locomotive, which was now doing about forty kilometers per hour, and bury himself feetfirst into a large adjacent snowbank. He was only visible from the waist up. Hawke got up and went to his friend, and patted the top of his head. "You quite all right, brother?"

"Never better," Fleming said, watching the train speed away into the distance. The train was now traveling at speeds of more than a hundred miles per hour, so it wouldn't take poor Fritzie very long to get to his appointment in Samarra sometime around midnight.

Hawke dropped to his knees in the soft snow and said, "Question, Fleming. What's to prevent Fritzie from throttling back and hitting the brakes?"

"Oh, that. I considered that, frankly, Blackie. He's been bound hand and foot, gagged, and secured by a chain to his stool at the rear of the cab. Can't get within a foot of the throttle. Or the brakes."

"Glad to hear it. Well, we bloody well did it, didn't we?"

"And, moreover, lived to tell the tale."

They both burst out laughing the joyous laughter of the young, the brave, and the victorious.

As the locomotive disappeared round a bend, Hawke put his hand on Ian Fleming's shoulder and said, "Question."

"Shoot."

"You think they'll let us do this again?"

"Listen. You keep feeding Blinker and Winston more bright ideas like Skyhook and Phantom Locomotive? We'll be doing this until there aren't any more Nazis left worth killing."

"Think of it, Ian," Hawke said. "Right now there are nearly twenty speeding locomotives, all filled to the gills with your cocktails of high-powered explosives, all going a hundred per in the same direction to the same destination. . . ."

"Right. And at the stroke of midnight, when those twenty simultaneous explosions rock Berlin to its core, when those bloody locomotives blow a mile-wide crater in the center of Berlin? Destroy the German rail system in a single blow? They're going to have to take Herr Hitler away in a straitjacket! And you know what else, Hawke?"

"No. What?" Hawke said.

"Jesus. Did you just throw a snowball at me?"

"I did. And your arms are pinned by your side. What are you going to do about it?"

Fleming suddenly stood straight up and reached down for a handful of snow.

It was all-out war after that.

Two grown men, rolling about in the freshly fallen snow, and laughing their fool heads off.

CHAPTER 66

Little White House, Warm Springs, Georgia
February 1942

The Chinese ambassador awoke early on that frosty morning to the music of the rails. The familiar "clickety-clack, clickety-clack, down the track" sounds of steel wheels on mirror-polished steel rails below, and a light tapping at the chamber door to his compartment. He stretched his arms upward, rubbed his belly, and then said, "Yes? Who is it?"

The door was opened just wide enough for the porter to peer in at his passenger, still abed. Tiger was curious about the wide white smile on the old gentleman's lovely nut brown face. He was in an altogether too cheery mood for this time of morning.

"Jes me, suh," Fred Fair said.

"Mr. Fair! Good morning to you, sir! What time is it?"

"Just gone seven. Got some good news for you on this beautiful mawnin', suh! That's for sure!"

"You do, do you, Fred? And what news might that be at this early hour? Wait. Don't tell me. The Japanese have surrendered in the Pacific? Hitler is on the skids in Poland? The French? Marshal Philippe Pétain and the Vichy government have surrendered to Germany again, and Parisians are planting trees on either side of the Champs-Élysées so the invading Nazis can march in the shade?"

"Well, no, suh. I don't rightly know what you're sayin', but may I enter, please?"

"Of course you may enter, sir. This splendid rolling palace is, after all, your sole dominion, not mine! I, good sir, am a mere transient!"

The ambassador was a bit mystified to find that he himself was also in a jolly state and had not the slightest idea as to where that had come from. Possibly—no, certainly—it was the magic of sleeping aboard a train speeding south through the silent night. Roaring past the flashing red railroad-crossing lights as they sped through all and sundry points south on their way to the Promised Land.

The tall porter smiled at that and took three long strides across the deep red carpet to the windows opposite the ambassador's wide berth. He took hold of the window shade's dangling cord and turned to face the ambassador. "Curtain goin' up, suh. Here she comes. . . ."

"On what? Are we there yet?"

"Oh, no, suh. We still 'bout three-quarters of an hour out from the station. Just time for you to shower and have yourself some breakfast. Chef has made up a mess of blueberry griddle cakes got your name on them. No rush. I got you all packed up last evening while you were in the dining car enjoying that delicious quail."

"Well, what is this all about, Fred?"

"Got some very good news for you and the boss, that's what."

"Well, tell me, for goodness' sake! My curiosity is killing me."

"Good news is, looks like you and the boss going to have yourselves a nice, bright . . ."

"A nice, bright—what, exactly?"

"A nice, bright . . . snowy weekend, suh!"

Fred released the cord, and the blackout shade went rattling up, winding itself around the spool with a clatter. Beyond the frosty window was a glorious white wonderland of snow.

"You know, there is just about nothin' but nothin' the boss loves more than a good old white Christmas!"

"It's truly beautiful, Fred," Tiger said, sitting up in his bed to see the white flakes swirling against the windowpanes, the blur of sweet Georgia pine forests racing by, already festooned in white gowns, the ice on the gentle hills beyond, now dazzling in the bright winter sunshine.

"If there's anything that can cheer up the boss, it's this beautiful snowfall, suh. That and, of course, the fact that you came all the way down heah to keep him company. Yessuh. He's always telling me the only companionship he needs is that old hound dog, Fala. But I know him too well. Folks say that he's been powerful lonely down here ever since he arrived."

Tiger looked at him and smiled.

"Fred, where are you up to tomorrow? Are you working?"

"Oh, I dunno, suh. Boss always gives me the Sundays off. But I don't really have any family anymore, so to me, it's just another day on the calendar. I jes' sit by the radio all day. Have me a taste of 'shine ever' now and then, too."

"Well, I probably should clear this with the chief, but how about this? Why don't you come to the Little White House and have supper with the president and me? Would you like that?"

"Oh, yessuh, I truly would. But I wouldn't dream of intruding on the boss's weekend. Just wouldn't be right, suh."

"Well. You wouldn't be intruding at all. I'm inviting you. And I'm telling you, you'd be welcome at the president's table, Fred. You think about it. If you decide to come, just let me know. I'm sure he'd be delighted. . . ."

"Well, let me think on it, suh. But I appreciate the thought, suh. I really do. I'll be back hereabouts to fetch you when we pull into the station."

CHAPTER 67

Warm Springs, Georgia
February 1942

The big black locomotive, huffing, puffing, and tugging the long chain of snow-frosted green Pullman cars, chugged into the little Warm Springs station house at eight-thirty that morning. Fred Fair and a local porter helped the ambassador get all his luggage down onto the platform, where two very sturdy-looking Secret Service agents, coats and ties and raincoats, waited in the swirl of snow.

"Mr. Ambassador," the taller and sturdier of the two agents said, extending his hand. "I'm Special Agent in Charge Alex Griswold. I'm with the president. This is Agent Smithers, sir. Let us be the first to welcome you to the Little White House. The president is very excited at your arrival, sir."

"As am I," Tiger said. "As am I!"

Tiger shook hands with both government men, and they all followed Mr. Fred Fair and his luggage trolley along the platform to the station house and the parking lot adjacent. There was a snow-coated grey government four-door Dodge sedan near the station house door and Fred loaded the luggage into the trunk.

Tiger quickly decided he was going to like this sleepy little town down South and all it stood for: the simple life lived simply and with a strong sense of civic pride and history and good old-fashioned holiday fun. The Chinese ambassador climbed into the rear seat of the car and they were on their merry way.

The little railroad village was picturesque. Every shop window was brightly lit and, despite the snow, shoppers were bustling up and down the sidewalks. The car had just passed a busy little toy shop, and Tiger leaned forward and spoke to the driver.

"Pull over, please, Agent Griswold. Do you mind? I need to run into that shop back there and pick something up. Won't be five minutes!"

Agent Griswold pulled over to the curb and slowed to a stop, and Tiger got out and disappeared into Santa's Workshop, as the place was called.

Tiger had been sitting back there, looking out the window at all the pretty little shops. He'd been feeling perfectly miserable over the meagerness of his poor gift for the president. And then, passing the toy shop, he'd spied something in the front window that would cheer the president up if anything could.

Five minutes later, he emerged with a huge package that was nearly as big as Tiger himself. It was wrapped in green and gold paper with a beautiful Currier and Ives print, and tied up with a big red bow. Smithers popped the trunk, and Tiger placed his prize inside and pulled the door shut.

Now he sat back with a smile on his face, secure that his present was going to light President Roosevelt up like a Christmas tree! Now he could just take in all the charms of the little village without a worry in the world. He'd learned the history of the famous resort last night in the lounge car when he'd gone back there for his nightcap.

While he was sipping his whiskey, Fred Fair had regaled him with tales of old Warm Springs and how it had evolved.

Settlers had first arrived in the late eighteeth century. The population grew with the advancement of the railroad, and by the 1830s, it was the site of a summer resort and thriving village. In 1893, Mr. Charles Davis had constructed the Victorian three-hundred-room Meriwether Inn, with resort pools, a dance pavilion, a bowling alley, tennis courts, and trap shooting. The warm water flowing down from the hillside of Pine Mountain was used to create the resort pools. All very grand in the day, but by the turn of the twentieth century, the town of Warm Springs and the resort were in decline.

Along came George Foster Peabody, a prominent businessman and philanthropist from New York. He purchased the resort property in 1923. Peabody shared the story of a young polio victim's recovery after bathing in the swimming pools at Warm Springs with his good friend Franklin D. Roosevelt, the young politician paralyzed from the waist down in 1921 from polio. FDR arrived at the resort in the fall of 1924, hoping against hope to find a cure in the waters. The next day, he began swimming and immediately felt a noticeable improvement.

For the first time in three years, he was able to move his right leg! Because he was nationally prominent, his successful visit assured publicity for Warm Springs. A syndicated national newspaper supplement featured his experiences, and many flocked there in the hopes of a cure. In 1926, FDR bought the resort property and twelve hundred acres from Peabody for some two hundred thousand dollars. His new house, finished in 1932, was his cherished getaway from war and depression thereafter.

———————

Tiger, staring out his rear window, was remembering his many winters during his school years in England. He'd loved the brisk weather even then. But somehow, it was far more endearing in the little town of Warm Springs though he could not tell you why.

"Here we are, sir," Special Agent Griswold said from up front. "Welcome to the Little White House, Mr. Ambassador!"

They had turned off the highway and climbed the winding drive up the hill to the residence. Tiger had not known what to expect after all the grandeur of Hyde Park, but he found the modest little one-story, six-room cottage very charming. Climbing out of the car, he instantly understood why his friend the president enjoyed the serenity of the views overlooking a heavily wooded ravine and the rolling white hills beyond.

A tiny but pleasingly plump housekeeper in a pink apron came running out of the house to help Agent Smithers gather up the luggage and get it inside. Lugging a bag up the walk, the elderly lady said, "Welcome to the Little White House, sir. My name is Mable, Mr. Ambassador! Praise the Lord, the president has been expecting you, sir, Lawdy me! He's sitting in his study by the fire. You'd best get yo'sef in there and give him a good look at you! Lord knows he ain't talked 'bout nothin' else but you for the last three days! All day long, I swear, I do, 'Tiger said this, and Tiger did that!'"

The ambassador laughed and Mable added, "That's the God's honest truth, Mr. Ambassador! The boss is fit to be tied, I'll tell you that much!"

Mable reminded him of the wonderful actress he'd seen in *Gone With the Wind*, Butterfly McQueen, who'd played Prissy so beautifully. And then, somewhat to his astonishment, he bent down and gave the woman a quick peck on her plump cheek before darting inside.

It felt like the little house was already putting out its own welcome mat. There were the aromatic scents of pinewood-burning fires wafting in from the library and the kitchen. And a fat Virginia ham, studded with cloves and pineapple slices in the oven, and cookies and gingerbread men and mincemeat pies and even Christmas plum pudding. Softly, "Silver Bells" was playing on the wireless down the hall, Bing Crosby in a duet with Rosemary Clooney broadcast from Radio City in New York:

> *City sidewalks, busy sidewalks,*
> *Dressed in holiday style,*
> *In the air there's a feeling of Christmas!*

CHAPTER 68

Little White House, Warm Springs, Georgia
February 1942

A uniformed butler, in a bright red bow tie and a splendid Tyrolean green felt waistcoat with polished sterling silver buttons, met the young ambassador trying to stamp the cold out of his frozen boots on the doorstep, then coming through the doorway. The butler, Jarvis by name, smiled and said, "Welcome to the Little White House, Mr. Ambassador! We are so deeply honored to have you as our guest, sir."

"The honor is all mine," Tiger said generously.

"May I take your coat and hat, sir," Jarvis said with a broad smile, "and that present?"

"I'll keep it. Thank you, Jarvis. I want to give it the president personally. How is he feeling today?"

"Better today, believe me! The president has been all over the place, never sits still, just as restless as a long-tailed cat in a roomful of rocking chairs, sir."

Tiger went to his room and changed into flannel trousers, velvet slippers, and his favorite red flannel Christmas blazer bought back in Oxford days in a shop on Savile Row, London. He headed for the library, already feeling very much at home.

Tiger stopped just short of the door into FDR's library.

When he entered, he was delighted to see that the room was decorated for the belated holiday.

"Merry, Merry Christmas, Mr. President," he said, striding in, hiding his face behind the big gift. "I cannot tell you how honored I am to be here with you and in such a beautiful part of the world. Now I know why you spend as much time as possible down here."

"Tiger, could you possibly put that giant Christmas present down. I can't see your face!"

"Oh, sure! Sorry! Afraid I got a little carried away with my present," he said, placing the package on the floor under the Christmas tree.

He loved the fact that FDR had had the Lionel HO gauge model train set up so he could watch it race around the base of the tree with its whistle tooting and smoke pouring from its stack!

"Merry Christmas, Tiger, my friend," FDR said, putting his hand out. "Cannot tell you how delighted I am to have you here in Georgia. I felt badly that it was such a last-minute invitation! I sincerely hope I didn't interrupt any well-laid plans, old fellow! Sit down! Sit down! Take the other leather armchair closest to the fire. Let me get you a cocktail! I'm sure the sun is well past the yardarm somewhere in the British Empire. We'll drink to your friend Hawke, shall we? I understand from Eleanor that he and Miss Woolworth have announced their engagement."

"Indeed, he has, and indeed, we shall, sir," Tiger said.

"Good, good, I hate to drink alone. Don't you?"

"To be honest, Mr. President, I only drink when I'm alone or with somebody...."

FDR eyed him for a moment and then broke out into his braying laughter. "Sorry ... ahem ... sorry, but that's funniest drinking joke I've ever heard. Where did you pick that up?"

"One of my flatmates at Oxford. Never passed up a chance to use it, either."

Roosevelt reached up and took a silver bell from the tabletop. He shook it three times and then called out, "Jarvis! Jarvis, are you out there lurking about? We need cocktails in here. Urgent! Tiger, perhaps you'd rather have a splash of champagne?"

"No, no, but thanks. I'll just have—"

"Oh, here you are at last, Jarvis. The ambassador would like a cocktail.... Tiger?"

"Yes, I'd like a nice Jack Daniel's bourbon on the rocks with a dash of bitters, please."

"Of course, sir."

"Scotch, please," the president said. "There's an open bottle of Cutty Sark over on the drinks table, Jarvis."

The drinks served, they raised their glasses, and Roosevelt said, "To that brave warrior Blackie Hawke, may God keep him safe over there, rattling Hitler's cage with that naval officer chap of Churchill's, Ian Fleming."

"To Blackie Hawke, may he come home safely once more!" Tiger said, taking a sip. "And to our wives and girlfriends, and never the twain shall meet!"

It was an old joke, to be sure, but the president, who loved a good joke and out of sheer kindness, managed a believable laugh.

The president sipped his whiskey and enjoyed his cigarettes, cajoling the ambassador to tell him tales of his childhood days in China. Tiger, who'd long realized that a guest always had to sing for his supper, didn't disappoint with his stories of childhood pranks and games.

They were called to supper around three. On the large mahogany sideboard in the dining room, in the flickering golden light of the three massive sterling silver candelabra, and beneath an epic oil painting of the Battle of Yorktown, they saw Jarvis carving away at a delectable-looking ham. Mable was there, too, spooning up epic portions of spinach soufflé and au gratin potatoes festooned with parsley.

After the repast, FDR said, "Heavens, tell Cook that was delicious, Mable! But if I have just one more bite, I fear I shall burst my silver buttons! What about you, Tiger? Do you have any spare room for pudding?"

"Is it rude to ask what it is, sir?"

"Hardly. Fool if you don't, my dear boy. Plum pudding with brandied butter, or hard sauce, as we Johnnie Rebs say down here in the good ole southland."

"Perfect."

"Jarvis," FDR said, "the ambassador here is going to have the plum pudding with hard sauce. Could you serve dessert in the library? Then I shall have my glass of port and sit and stare at my beautiful *Tannenbaum.*"

Tiger said, "*Tannenbaum?* Is that what you said, *Tannenbaum?* Not familiar with the term...."

"Yes," the president said with a glint in his eye and a small wisp of a smile that instantly conveyed to Tiger that the man was having him on.

"And what, pray tell," Tiger said, "is a *Tannenbaum?*"

"Someone told me you had a fine English education. I think it was your father, in fact. Cambridge, Oxford, all those la-di-da oh-so-British schools. Was I misinformed?"

"Guilty as charged, Mr. President. So, *Tannenbaum.* It sounds German. Is it? Because if it is, I've yet to learn that guttural language. To my ear, it always sounds as if they're shouting curses at one another. But I'm sure that Herr Hitler will one day have us all yelling at one other."

"Not if Winston and I have a say in the matter, he won't. In the meantime, *Tannenbaum*, as dear Winston informed me on the telephone last evening, is Nazi-speak for Christmas tree. A song or something. Right now that madman is probably by the tree, singing it to his little mistress, Eva Braun."

"Aha! Good one! May I ask you a question, Mr. President?"

"Sure. As long as it's not too personal," he replied with a smile.

"Well. I've long been curious about something. Why is it that your dear friend and ally, Churchill, always pronounces the word 'Nazi' as 'Nar-zi' in all the newsreels at the picture show?"

Roosevelt burst out laughing.

"Why? I'll tell you exactly why. Because he has it on the highest authority that every time Hitler sees those newsreels, Churchill's obviously deliberate mispronunciation of the word drives him stark raving mad! He throws things at the screen and shouts at his staff to fucking do something about it! Of course, they can do nothing and this is, of course, a source of never-ending delight to the prime minister!"

"Marvelous, sir! Absolutely marvelous."

"Yes, quite. One second. Oh, Jarvis, a word if you don't mind! Oh, yes, please serve the dessert and throw a couple of logs onto the fire, will you, please? The ambassador here has a limited constitution and always appears to be shivering in this house."

Tiger found himself wishing this magic day would never end. Sitting there by the crackling fireside, with the icy snow beating against the windowpanes, and the cold winter winds howling round the eaves and down the chimney, the music turned low, just loud enough to provide good cheer in the background, and the company of this truly magnificent man whom he'd come to worship . . . it was all—how to say it?—it was a sense of utter peace and friendship and belonging such as he had never before experienced.

Magic. If that were not too strong a word.

And yet? And yet there was something amiss, something almost but not quite beyond his mental grasp. There was a steady undercurrent flowing along beneath all the peace and fellowship and good cheer. Something hiding in each of the unopened Christmas presents of red and green and silver and gold. . . .

Something inside of him, too, a dark place in his mind that made him afraid of what horror might lie buried inside his mind, or even inside one of those many boxes. Something that, once revealed, could destroy it all in a heartbeat.

He knocked back his glass of aged port, got up, and went to the drinks table to pour himself another. He was not going to let anything intrude into this peaceful scene. He'd keep his demons walled up within the confines of his mind until the danger had passed. And then he'd take whatever action was necessary to be rid of his father and his horrible curse forever.

Feeling a bit better, he leaned back against the cushions and started counting the number of ornaments on the tree, the beautiful tree.

Norwegian spruce, the president had told him. Fifteen feet high and scraping the ceiling, lush green and perfectly shaped. Decorated with silvery tinsel and countless vintage ornaments of gold and silver, red and green. And the garlands of tiny American flags winding their way up the tree to the glorious gold-and-silver angel that perched atop the highest bough.

And so, happily content, the two them remained right where they were. They sat there in the glow of candlelight from the lit tapers on the tree into the wee small hours. Ever jovial and convivial, they gladly sipped their whiskey, talked their talk, and joked their old and oft-told jokes.

There was a word for moments like this, Tiger was thinking, as the president embarked on a story about Blackie Hawke, a guest at Number 10, sipping champagne with a pink and quite nude Churchill in the loo, while in the midst of his nightly bath.

The word rested on the tip of his tongue for a moment, then leapt up into his brain.

Cozy.

Tiger believed that in his later years he would always look back on these few precious hours and days as among the happiest of his lifetime.

But the next day, sadly, would be an entirely different story.

CHAPTER 69

Little White House, Warm Springs, Georgia
February 1942

The butler, Jarvis, stuck his head inside Tiger's room and said that they would not be serving breakfast in the dining room that morning. The president had awakened with a terrible headache, a dry mouth, and a stomach in open revolt against the flood of whiskey and port wine and God knew what else.

Tiger, out of sheer need for survival, had learned the hard lesson of pacing himself. And after all, who was to say how much a man could or should imbibe?

The president, just before turning in, had told Tiger that it was the most enjoyable evening he'd had in months.

Tiger had readily agreed. He felt that his relationship with the American president, while very strong, had deepened since he'd arrived. And then, in the throes of tossing and turning, the dreaded migraine came, like a harbinger of the nightmare voice again, in his brain, not in his ears. His father's voice:

"You will put a bullet in Roosevelt's head, my son. It is your solemn duty to His Excellency."

Tiger swore and snapped back into the moment.

After setting his travel alarm for noon, he fell fast asleep, thinking, as he drifted off, that he'd draw a steaming hot bath and just soak for a while before dressing and reporting for duty as ordered beneath the tree.

What was that infernal sound splitting his brain in two? Ah. Of course, the alarm clock. He swung his long legs out of the bed and stood on the old hooked rug, peering at the pure white brightness streaming into the room. He could hardly credit it.

A blizzard was raging outside when he'd finally gone to bed. And now this: clear blue skies, sun sparkling on the freshly fallen snow, wind way down to a breeze. In short, this crystal-clear white "Christmas" morning would salve a lot of what was ailing his friend. Overworked, battling his crippling illness, frequently confronting life and death global issues of such spectral enormity, Roosevelt was amazing in that he had the capacity to deal with those issues.

And yet he did.

That was Tiger's president, the man who cared about tipping porters at Union Station, despite the crushing weight of the world on his shoulders.

Tiger walked over and had a good look out the windows and saw a beautiful blue automobile coming up the drive.

A big, powerful car, a Packard convertible. And not just any old Packard, oh, no. This majestic and gleaming dark blue beast was the 1938 V12 Convertible Coupe, Model 1607. The bee's knees was what the motoring press had called it upon its debut at the Detroit Auto Show a few years ago. And it surely was. The trunk was full to bursting with presents meant for President Roosevelt that Jarvis had collected from the post office and the railway station in town. Once they were all unloaded and carried inside, Jarvis returned the blue Packard to the heated garages down the hill.

It was quite a scene in the library when Tiger arrived that morning. The entire household staff was in there, as well as the two stalwart Secret Service agents, everyone sipping hot cider and gathered round the tree, round the president. FDR performed his traditional role as White House Santa and also, apparently, also did so down here in Georgia. Fala, his Scottie, was puddled at his feet with yesterday's ham bone for company.

Suddenly the president's big booming voice sounded, magisterial in the small room.

"Oh! I see the Chinese ambassador has honored us with his presence. I believe this is for you, Tiger," he said, and handed him a small book-shaped package. "Whatever do you think it might be, Tiger, old sport? A tie? A comb or a pair of polka dot socks? Ice skates? Sam Snead Golf clubs? No? What, then, my friend?"

Tiger laughed. "Gee whiz, Mr. President, I have no idea. But definitely not golf clubs. May I open it?"

"Of course. By all means, do so. I'm desperate to see what that monstrosity of yours under the tree is, so get on with it!"

Tiger ripped away the paper and looked at it.

It was, he knew, the one book the president had long prized above all others: *Rewards and Fairies* by Rudyard Kipling, wherein the poem "If" could be found. Tiger had read that poem at Cambridge, and he'd loved it so much, he'd committed it to memory. Most especially he loved the stanzas that read:

> *If you can dream—and not make dreams your master;*
> *If you can think—and not make thoughts your aim;*
> *"If you can meet with Triumph and Disaster*
> *And treat those two impostors just the same . . .*
> *Yours is the earth and everything that's in it,*
> *And—which is more—you'll be a Man, my son!*

Tiger bent to pick up FDR's present from 'neath the tree and handed it to the seated president. He said: "Merry Christmas, sir. May Almighty God aid, comfort, defend, and protect our two great nations from overwhelming peril in the days and weeks and months and years to come."

"Fine sentiments indeed, sir," Roosevelt said, smiling up at his friend, "eloquently delivered. Now, what is this monstrous gift you've brought?"

FDR untied the red ribbon and began snatching away, as was his wont when opening presents, and tossing the crumpled paper atop the large pile steadily growing at his side until all was revealed. A huge stuffed Scottie! The spitting image of Roosevelt's beloved hound writ large! He leaned forward and placed the gift on the carpet at his feet and beside his dog.

"Why, bless my soul. It's you, Fala! Look here! It's the spitting image, indeed, wouldn't you agree, Fala?"

Upon hearing his name spoken aloud by his master, the sleeping dog awoke and happily began licking the large stuffed animal's mirror image face.

"Well, Mr. Ambassador, I'd say your delightful present has already brought much joy into this house! Fala and I both thank you from the bottom of our conjoined hearts! We shall treasure it for all time."

After the all and sundry gifts had been opened and admired, after all the fancy wrapping papers had become so much ash and gone up the chimney like so much smoke, after the all the egg nog spiked with Southern Comfort whiskey had been imbibed, and all the last savory bits of turkey with apple-raisin stuffing had been enjoyed, washed down with all the fine Château Margaux, the president announced to Tiger that he'd had his beautiful blue Packard convertible washed and fueled, and it was time for Tiger to get behind the wheel and take the two of them tearing about the rural countryside until it got too dark to see.

"What do you think?" the president said. "Sounds smashing, does it not? Hot stuff in the chill air!"

Tiger agreed. "Oh, indeed it does, sir! It sounds like heaven to me. The air is so clear and bright and refreshing. Yes, sir, a ride in the country in the brisk country air! Just what the doctor ordered, Mr. President!" It's cold, sir. I'm just going to my room to get something. My Navy peacoat, I think."

Then he stood there in the hallway, stock still, staring at the closed bedroom door, unable to remember what he'd returned here for. And there was another problem.

The sudden and overwhelming specter of darkness.

Evil was lurking everywhere; darkness was falling inside his mind, pushing out the light. He saw a thin pale hand with long skinny fingers beckoning to him; it was bedecked with jeweled rings and bracelets like the ones that Tingling Ma, the famous Mandarin warrior, had worn in his childhood history books.

He heard himself say again the words "Sounds like heaven to me!" Then, a deep shudder, along with a profound surge of dark emotions that felt a good deal more like Hell than Heaven, rushed through him. He pulled the door open and stepped inside, gripped with fear of the unknown.

He shook it off, that feeling, and pulled his U.S. Navy peacoat from a hangar in his closet and shouldered into it. It was old and worn, a gift from Blackie Hawke when Tiger had said he admired it. He turned and started to leave the room and then froze in place. He'd forgotten something else, but what? Ah, yes. He went to his dresser and pulled open the top drawer. His fingers touched the heavy Colt revolver and froze. Staring at his oddly mournful eyes in the mirror above his dresser, he slipped the ivory-handled pistol into the jacket's inside pocket.

He did not know it yet. But he was a powerless man walking, going through the motions, inside a preordained and deadly dream.

CHAPTER 70

Little White House, Warm Springs, Georgia
February 1942

The Chinese ambassador volunteered to go down the hill to fetch the Packard from the garages there. He desperately needed some cold fresh air to clear the miasma that clouded his mind. He got a jolt when he hit the ignition button and the massive V12 engine exploded into life. Cheered for some unknown reason, he smiled and pumped the accelerator a couple of times just to get the revs up. It was deafening inside the small wooden building.

It had been bone cold walking down the snowy lane, and he had been glad of his warm peacoat. The temperature was somewhere in the low forties, and as he had hoped, it had been exhilarating to breathe in the cold, cold air.

He'd been delighted with the president's suggestion of exploring the countryside in a top-down car, seeing things through FDR's eyes. The president had outlined this much anticipated outing from start to finish. First, his favorite places: the old swimming hole, the original one-room schoolhouse dating back to the early nineteenth century, the magnificent views from the top of Pine Mountain, source of all the warm springs feeding the healing pools by gravity.

When he crested the hill and rumbled up the paved drive to the house, he saw FDR in his chair, covered with a plaid woolen blanket, waiting under the porte cochere by the front door, chatting amiably with his butler, Jarvis. Tiger, feeling somewhat refreshed and returned to the real world, rolled to a stop a few yards away, smiled at his jovial host, waved his hand, and tooted the loud ah-ooga horn three times. For some reason, the president found all this foolishness somehow amusing, and both Jarvis and the boss broke into wide grins.

"How do you like her, Tiger?" Roosevelt called out. "A beauty, what?"

"Love it, sir! Just a stunning piece of machinery! Listen to that big twelve-cylinder engine roar!"

Vrooom-vrooom went the big V-12 as Tiger pumped the throttle and Jarvis helped the president manage the transfer from his wheelchair to the spacious tufted leather passenger seat.

"She's a stunner, all right," Roosevelt said, getting settled and arranging his furry lap robe over his withered legs. "I have a long-standing habit of naming all the automobiles I love the most. What do you think of Big Bertha?"

Tiger smiled and told the truth. "Sounds like your fat maiden auntie to me, sir."

"I know. How about the Blue Flyer?" Jarvis said.

Roosevelt looked at Tiger. "How about the Blue Torpedo?"

"Pretty good," Tiger said. "How about the P-51?"

"P for Packard?" Roosevelt asked.

"Yes, sir. And P-51 like the Army's new single-seat fighter plane. Hottest thing in the sky these days, Mr. President."

"P-51, it is, then," Roosevelt said. "Good for you, Tiger. I like a young man with a keen imagination. Come on, now. Let's get this P-51 show on the road!

"Where to first, sir?" Tiger said, engaging first gear and overcoming inertia to get the behemoth rolling.

"The ole swimmin' hole, driver!" FDR said. "And step on it, son. Step on it!"

The ambassador had not been quite sure what to expect when he arrived in Warm Springs. But he'd never have guessed what fun it was to be with the American president when he put down his burden and forgot for a while all of his cares and woes: the weight of the entire world on one man's shoulders, the way forward to victory on both fronts, and all the brave young lads who wouldn't be coming home to their mothers, the horrific loss of his Pacific fleet to the treacherous Japanese . . . his endless lists borne with courage and optimism and a bedrock determination to emerge victorious and preserve the precious liberty and freedom and justice for all that his nation had been founded upon.

"Turn right here on the dirt road," Roosevelt said, remembering that Tiger had no earthly idea where they were headed.

The road through the woods was sketchy going for most of the way to the ole swimmin' hole. Tiger was praying to his gods that the tires did not get stuck in this icy muck, and wondering how the hell he would ever be able to get the president of the United States out of these woods and back to safety, should they become stuck in the muck and worst came to worst.

His only comfort was that the president had carefully outlined the order of sites to be visited on this expedition in the company of Special Agent in Charge Griswold and Agent Smithers. If for some reason the two adventurers did not return in a reasonable time, this swimming hole would be the first place they would look.

"Here it is, although in winter you don't really get the charm and beauty of it as you do in summer. Here is where the Roosevelt boys, all four of them, learned how to swim and get in touch with nature. They've always said their fondest memories will be of this holy place and all the good times they enjoyed as the years rolled by. . . . I hope to bring my grandsons here one day . . . when the war is at long last over and all my brood is home safe with me."

"Where are they now, sir?" Tiger said, lighting a cigarette FDR had stuck into his ivory holder.

"My boys?" the president said. "Well, as you might expect, Tiger, young Jimmy, Elliott, Franklin Jr., and Alex, the whole lot of them joined the U.S. Armed Forces and are all now serving overseas. With some distinction, I might add. We're very proud of them, you know, their mother, Eleanor, and I."

"As well you should be, sir. So, what's next on our itinerary?"

"Let's take the P-51 up to the top of Pine Mountain. That's where I want to be as it gets close to sunset. Glorious views from up there. You know, as an old New York Dutchman, I never knew much about the country south of the Mason-Dixon Line. But I have to say, there is much to love down here. And if it hadn't been for my banker friend Peabody, who discovered the springs as a possible cure for my polio, I'd have died all the poorer for not knowing this part of our country."

"It's a delight. It really is. I had no idea. I studied the Civil War, of course, both at Cambridge and then later at Oxford. I always sensed a romantic quality about the old South. Now I know the truth of it. Shall we head up there now?"

"Indeed we shall, my boy. Indeed we shall!" FDR then leaned his noble head of silver hair back against the red seat cushion, took a puff of his cigarette, and exclaimed, "'To the top of the porch, to the top of the wall! Now dash away! Dash away! Dash away all!'"

It was getting on five o'clock, and as the sun dropped, so, too, did the temperature. Tiger could sense that the president was getting uncomfortable in the frigid air, but didn't want to admit it and cut the adventure short. He was having too good a time.

The president touched his shoulder and said, "Look there! There's the original one-room schoolhouse over on the hillside. Dates back to eighteen forty or so. It was falling down, so one summer I convinced my boys to rebuild it. They had no carpentry skills to speak of, but by jiminy, they got the job done, didn't they?"

"Turn here?" Tiger said.

"Yes, that's the road up the mountain. Tiger, I hate to say it, but I'm getting rather cold out in this wind. I have a second fur lap blanket back in the trunk. Would you mind terribly pulling over here and fetching it for me?"

"Not at all, sir, not at all. It's cold enough up here, all right."

He returned with the blanket moments later and helped the president get comfortable. Then he climbed back behind the wheel and chugged up the snow-choked mountain road, which, luckily enough, had recently been plowed.

"All righty, then," FDR said some minutes later, "here's what the park rangers refer to as the scenic overlook. Let's just pull over and watch the sun setting in the western sky, all right?"

"Fine, sir. It's lovely up here."

"Do you mind if we don't speak?" FDR said. "I just want to watch this glorious spectacle in silence. I feel I'm slowly running out of peaceful days like this . . . and I just . . . I just . . ."

But he never finished his thought.

A few minutes of silence passed.

"Mr. President?" Tiger heard himself say, without recalling ever having summoned up the intention to sound those two words aloud.

"Yes?" Franklin said, his pale blue eyes still fixed on the far horizon. An alarm sounded. His friend's voice had sounded exceedingly odd. Stilted. And mechanical. What could be the—

"I have something for you, sir. A gift. Actually from General Chiang Kai-shek himself."

"What in God's name are you talking about, Tiger?" FDR said, instantly sensing that all was not as it should be. When he turned to face the ambassador, the American president truly thought he was losing his own mind.

The handsome young diplomat suddenly had a large pistol in his hand. It was a revolver, a big one, and he was calmly aiming it at close range, point blank, at the head of the United States president. As if he was about to put a bullet in his forehead. Tiger an assassin? God in heaven! Madness! Roosevelt had put every bit of trust he had in this young fellow. And now he was about to die for his mistake? It was sheer insanity.

But Roosevelt never betrayed one iota of fear. Cool, collected, and calm, he was ever the iceberg, people would say, when his emotions were spiraling out of control; his rock steady blue eyes, his facial expressions, all bore no visible trace of whatever fierce turmoil might be raging inside.

His voice was cold and and as steady as was humanly possible. He said, with no discernible trace of emotion:

"Put the gun down, Tiger. Now. You don't want to do this. There's something terribly wrong with you. My sense is that you have no idea what you're doing. It's like you're in some kind of trance. Hypnotized perhaps. Is that what this is about?"

"I'm going to put a bullet in the head of the president of the United States," Tiger said, sounding like a space robot in a Flash Gordon movie.

Every syllable coming out of Tiger's mouth was mechanical. And his eyes were out of focus, glazed over, but then Roosevelt saw the ambassador's trigger finger begin to tighten . . . the knuckles of his finger starting to go white with the mounting pressure. . . .

"Stop this insanity, Tiger! You can't do this! You're not yourself, boy!"

But. You could see in his dead eyes that he was going to fire that gun, Roosevelt realized, and unless he acted, there was not a damn thing he could do about it.

FDR said, in a chillingly cold voice, "Tiger. Is that gun loaded?"

He nodded.

"And you're pointing it at me?"

Another nod of his head.

Tiger then spoke again, a cold, dead, dull monotone that chilled the marrow of a man's poor old bones.

"This is for my father and my country. They have ordained it. I have no choice."

"Tiger! Do not do this!"

The president could see the knuckles of Tiger's gun hand turning white as he gripped the weapon more tightly and applied more and more pressure to the trigger. . . .

Then he saw Tiger's eyes go wide with shock as the president's powerful left hand came out of nowhere and closed like a steel vise around the ambassador's right wrist. . . .

"God help you, son!" Roosevelt said, tightening his grip around Tiger's gun hand. He was not at all surprised to see the ambassador wince in pain. He had, after all, been using all the powerful muscles of his upper body for decades to substitute for the loss of strength in his legs, his lower body. His biceps and forearms bulged beneath his tailored suits. His forearms were long and well-muscled and extraordinarily powerful. And his wrists? His steely grip when shaking a man's hand had often been described as nothing less than viselike.

Tiger, for his part, now began to try to wrench his gun hand away from the iron grip, gritting his teeth in pain as Roosevelt increased the pressure around the fragile bones of his wrist.

Tiger sensed now, and the president well knew, that the small bones of Tiger's wrist were about to be crushed into pieces if the powerful Roosevelt kept up this degree of mounting pressure.

"Nod if you can hear me, Tiger," the president said calmly, and waited coolly for a reaction. Any reaction would do.

Tiger nodded his head mechanically. His eyes were glassy, and he seemed dazed and confused, as if he had no idea where he was or what he was doing.

FDR said, "Now, I want you to look me in the eye but not say a word. Nod if you understand."

Tiger looked over at him, silent, his eyes now full of pain and even remorse.

He gave a brief nod of his head.

"I'm now going to count to five, Tiger. If, at the end of that count, you have not dropped your weapon to the floor, I am going to crush all of the bones in your right wrist, pulverizing them. You'll never have use of your right hand again if you don't drop that weapon. Do you understand me? Nod if you do."

Tiger nodded.

"One," Roosevelt said, increasing the pressure. "Two." He heard a brittle bone crack, and Tiger screamed in pain. "Three," he said, feeling all the compression and destruction of the smaller bones. "Four," he said. "Drop it, Tiger, now! Or I will hurt you like you've never been hurt before! You will never use that hand again. Do as I say. Do it now, I order you!"

The gun fell with a thud to the carpeted transmission hump.

Roosevelt slowly opened his hand, turned his eyes toward Heaven, and breathed a silent prayer of thanks to his Lord.

Tiger, hot tears coursing down his cheeks, seemed to be having a seizure of some sort. He threw his head back and burst out screaming, seeing for perhaps the first time the gun that had been in his hand now lying at the president's feet, and then he was howling and weeping and holding his throbbing right wrist in his left.

Tiger looked skyward and screamed at Heaven, both in pain and despair, so blinded by tears was he that he never noticed Roosevelt leaning over to pick up the revolver. The president started to put it in the glove compartment, then thought better of doing so. He cocked his right arm and flung the pistol away with all his might, as high and as hard as he could, out into space, high in the air before it disappeared from sight, bouncing down the mountainside to the purplish valley below.

"Take me home now, Tiger," the president said. "I think we've both had quite enough adventure for one day. Are you capable of driving, do you think? I mean, with that wrist?"

"Yes, sir," Tiger said, still sobbing, his wrist gone black-and-blue, with what looked like unbearable remorse for what he'd almost done.

"You're sure, son?" Roosevelt said quietly.

"I'm all right now. I'm so, so terribly sorry, sir. I don't know what came over me. I swear it. Of all the people on this earth, you are the man I most revere. . . . You are the father I never had. And pardon me, but I love you like a father! I truly do! I think—I think I need help, sir. Some kind of help, Mr. President. I feel like I'm losing my mind . . . or have already lost it, sir!"

"Yes, I'm quite sure you do. And I shall see that you get help, son. So, as soon as we get home, I am going to have you speak with Special Agent in Charge Griswold and Agent Smithers. I want you to explain to them in great detail every single thing that led up to this wholly bizarre moment. Go back in time as far as you have to. They will be merciless with their questions, as well they should. And then they will put you in a private room at Bethesda Naval Hospital with a battery of senior military psychiatrists for a full analysis. And, perhaps, they will all tell me that the U.S. State Department will have to have you recalled home from your posting so that you are no longer a threat to me."

"I understand," the man sobbed.

"I saw the look in your eyes, Tiger. I heard your voice coming up from Hell itself. You had no idea where you were or what you were doing. I will tell them that. In the end, your future will rest with them alone. I will have no say in the matter, either to defend you or accuse you."

"Yes, sir. I understand exactly. I will tell them about my father's visit and—"

"Stop! I don't want to hear it, Tiger. Not a word of it! You and I will never speak of this again!"

They drove home. The silence now hovering between them was as cruel and as heartbreaking as the death of an unborn child.

Tiger sat there behind the wheel, looking straight ahead, sensing how terribly uncomfortable and saddened the president was feeling. And he wished to Heaven FDR hadn't thrown the goddamn gun away.

Tiger would have returned to China and used it on his father.

And then on himself.

CHAPTER 71

Pindling Airport, Nassau, the Bahamas
Present Day

Hawke's Gulfstream was a G650 airplane with a ceiling of fifty-one thousand feet and a top speed of nearly seven hundred miles per hour. They'd arrive in Miami in well under two hours. Hawke couldn't help but silently worry about Henry's condition. He knew that until he got that boy to the hospital alive, every damn minute counted.

There was, as Hawke well knew, a very comfortable queen-sized berth in the aft owner's cabin aboard his new G650. Prince Henry was still awfully weak, and the comfortable berth would be perfect for this short hop over to Bermuda. Earlier, he'd been on the mobile to Colin Falconer, his new pilot. He'd informed him there'd been a change of plan. They were no longer flying direct to Heathrow.

As per his instructions, Captain Falconer had prepositioned the airplane at a distant location on the far side of the field. Hawke was taking no chances at this point. It was entirely possible that Tang Security had been following them, though keeping back at distance to avoid being spotted. Or, even drones.

That was why, when he finally reached the Nassau airfield, he had driven the overheated ambulance right through a maximum-security gate barrier and taken out a good stretch of hurricane fencing along with it. He was now racing away from the perimeter and out across the grass and the grid of runways.

Hawke had driven the big ambulance at full speed, dodging departing United and JetBlue flights outbound to Miami, and all those aircraft now taxiing out to get in line for takeoff or heading in to the terminal gates with their arriving passengers. Just as he reached his own plane, he saw flashing blue lights in the distance headed this way at speed.

"Welcome aboard, sir," Falconer said as Alex ascended the stairs and entered the cool air of the cabin. "How was your vacation, sir? As peaceful as you hoped?"

Hawke smiled at the handsome six-footer, an ex–Royal Navy airman who, just like Hawke himself, had been in Afghanistan. Hawke said, "Nowhere on earth is ever as peaceful as I hope it will be, Colin. But I cannot complain. Ultimately, we were successful in our efforts to find His Royal Highness and get him safely off that Devil's Island. Nightmare Island. Here he comes now, out of the ambulance. Could you please assist Mr. Brock and Mr. Jones in getting his gurney up the steps? I'd appreciate it. Thanks."

A woman he'd not seen approached him in the aisle.

"Lord Hawke? I'm Nanette. Captain Falconer said you might be needing me." She was dressed in a perfectly tailored powder blue air hostess uniform and seemed qualified enough for what he'd explained to Falconer. And she was quite pretty in that English Rose way he'd always fallen for.

"Welcome aboard, Nanette. And you're a certified nurse—an RN, is that correct?"

"I am indeed, sir," she said with a very posh English accent. "Your captain inspected all my credentials. Would you like to see them?"

"Not at this moment. Maybe later," Hawke said, hopefully.

China Moon suddenly appeared in the open hatchway, heading straight for him, bumping Nanette out of her way.

"We did it, Alex!" China said. "We damn well did it, did we not?"

Hawke said, "We did. And thank you, dear girl, for coming to my rescue. I was sorely afraid I'd arrived at Dragonfire Club with too little too late. Without your help locating him, I really don't think he would have made it out alive."

She smiled, looking around at the extremely luxuriously appointed interior: saddle leather, bespoke, and elegant hardwood paneling and gleaming brass hardware everywhere. She said, "This is one helluva airplane you've got yourself, boss. Stoke and Harry are preparing to bring Henry up now. Where do you suggest we put the young prince?"

"There's an owner's cabin aft. The berth has been made up with fresh linen. And the room is filled, I hope, with the fresh tropical flowers I ordered for when he wakes up."

China said, "Let me go have a quick look. I'll be right back. Where do you want me to sit?"

"Oh, I don't really know, China. . . . Next to me perhaps?"

China laughed and made her way aft to ensure that the cabin was ready. Hawke turned away and looked out over the airfield. Stoke and Harry Brock were just now starting up the staircase. And the racing fleet of security vehicles with the flashing blues was getting dangerously close.

"Nanette, we're bringing my godson aboard. He's been through hell. Malnourished, dehydrated, and tortured. I want you to spend your time aboard attending to him. Not me nor my passengers." He turned away and went to the open door, then leaned out.

"Stoke!" Hawke called to him. "Get a move on! See all those blue lights coming this way? We can't afford to let those guys get any closer! They'll use those vehicles to pin us in!"

"Aw, damn, boss. I didn't even see those guys. Here we come!"

Three minutes later they were coming up the steps and through the door with His Royal Highness Prince Henry. Nanette had gone back to the aft cabin to make sure Henry was comfortable and had what he needed. Hawke had told Falconer to make sure Nanette had the proper medical equipment and medicines. So in her absence, Hawke, who knew this plane inside and out, secured the cabin, got the main door closed and locked, and stuck his head into the cockpit.

"Cabins secure, lads. Everyone's seated and buckled up. Let's get outta town, boys! While we still can."

Hawke looked at his old steel Rolex and smiled. He'd have the boy in a real hospital bed at King Edward VII, surrounded by doctors and nurses, in less than two hours.

And he'd have China by his side. He would have bet a million quid she'd never speak to him again. But he'd have lost. There was something intangible between them; that was all he could think. Not a very astute observation of human behavior, he'd admit. On the other hand, there really was something between a man and a woman that was all about the chemistry. The bloody smell. He'd once been seated next to Carolina Herrera, a famous fashion designer, at a fancy dinner party on the Upper East Side of New York.

"What's that scent, Alex?" she'd asked him early in the party. "Because if I'm right, it's the only scent in the world that I approve of for men, other than my own, of course."

"I buy it in Paris. Have done so for decades or more. I like it because it's stimulating, helps me wake up in the morning and feels good on my face. Citrus, I think, but I'm no expert on fragrances."

She looked at him, then sniffed him, possibly flirting. She was a very talented and good-looking woman, after all. "It's *Eau d'Orange Verte*," she said. "Hermès."

"Yes, the shop on the Faubourg Saint-Honoré."

"*Et voilà!* I knew it!" she said.

Maybe China likes me for my cologne, he thought. That Carolina woman certainly seemed to. Who the hell knows what women like?

———

For the first few days on the sun-kissed isle of Bermuda, Hawke spent most of the time he wasn't swimming six miles out in the open sea, or taking the sun with China by the new pool he'd had built at Teakettle Cottage, sitting by Henry's bedside. He planned to begin reading Sir Arthur Conan Doyle's *A Study in Scarlet* to the prince on the off chance that he might still be able to hear. And there were visitors as well. Congreve, of course, and his wife, Lady Mars, came by daily to check on his progress. Diana Mars had asked Hawke for a favor. Could she and Ambrose hitch a ride to Heathrow three days hence, when he, Pelham, and the prince would fly onward to England?

Of course they could. Ambrose had asked if, en route, he might debrief Prince Henry on the details of everything that had happened or that he had seen while at Dragonfire. It would be vital information for both MI6 and his own Scotland Yard.

Pelham would come to the hospital to relieve Hawke for the evening shift. Then China would come to relieve Pelham and take the graveyard shift. And there was an endless parade of caring visitors from London, all of whom now lived or vacationed at the Coral Beach Club in Bermuda and belonged to the families just like Hawke's that were all lifelong friends of the Royal Family.

One day, Hawke got a call from the prince's doctor, the chief of staff at King Edward VII.

"Come and get him, Lord Hawke. I think your young prince is well enough now that you can care for him at the cottage. All he needs at this point is a day or two of healthy food, a lot of sunshine, and swimming in the ocean to build up his lost strength. There's no reason he cannot expect to have a full recovery."

"I'll be there early tomorrow morning, Doctor. I'll stop by and collect him. A day or two here and then I'm flying Henry direct to London. Back home. And back to his adoring grandmother, the Queen."

Hawke and China had a quiet farewell dinner that night. No one called it a farewell dinner. Both knew exactly what it was.

She wanted just the two of them out on the terrace, with the waves crashing below and Pelham serving spaghetti alle vongole under the star-studded skies.

Then he called Brick Kelly on his encrypted mobile.

"I've got Prince Henry, Brick. We got him out just in time."

"Good news is, he's alive, old boy. You ever figure out why the hell those damn Tang brothers kidnapped him in the first place?"

"Oh, yeah. Henry saw some serious Dragonfire stuff he wasn't supposed to see."

"Like the sub pen? The Chinese missile frigates?"

"Yes. But that wasn't what really did him in. He saw the massive heroin factories the Tangs have built in the jungle. Fifty, maybe sixty identical, fully functional heroin factories operating twenty-four seven to supply worldwide dealers working for Dragonfire, the name the Tangs gave to their entire empire."

"Got that. Thanks. I spent the afternoon at the White House with the president, the secretary of state, and the secretary of defense. I briefed them on the intel you gave me about what you saw. The sub pen, the Chinese Navy missile frigates, the complete enchilada. The president could not believe the Chinese would have the balls to put a sub base so close to American shores, especially during these bloody trade negotiations. But he's taking proper countermeasures, effective immediately."

"What kind of countermeasures?"

"Tomorrow morning, State is going to issue a démarche to the Chinese Embassy here in D.C. They've got seventy-two hours to get those three subs the hell out of here. When the time limit has expired, failing that, the Navy is going to enforce a naval blockade, just like Kennedy did. Commander, Naval Surface Forces Atlantic has been ordered to ring the entrance to that bay where the pen is located with a battle group. Navy fighter jets will commence heavy aerial bombardment to take out the pen and everything around it. Bunker busters, the whole shooting match. And he doesn't give a good shit whether those three subs are there . . . or not."

"Brick, listen, could you call the president and tell him about the bloody heroin factories on Devil's Island? In one blow we could knock hell out of the world's global heroin supply. That's worth some heavy ordnance all by itself."

"Absolutely, buddy! You saw all this yourself? You can verify what Henry is saying? That's a confirm?"

"Saw it with my own baby blues, pal."

"Good enough for me. I'll get that word out now. Sit tight. Our boys will turn that place into a fucking parking lot in about ten minutes. Where are you now?"

"The hell out of there. I'm at my house in Bermuda, acting as my godson's personal fitness instructor."

"Bombs away," Brick said. "Take care of yourself, buddy. And come to Washington sometime, will ya? The president has heard so much about you from me, now he wants to meet you. I think you two would hit it off."

––––––––––

Hawke and China Moon agreed to bed together that night, even though both were sensing it would probably be for the last time. He held her close, thanking her for coming to help in the prince's rescue.

But he made no promises.

And neither did she. China, who'd told Alex she had an apartment on South Beach, would get off the plane in Miami, along with Stoke and Harry Brock. She was headed back to Beijing in a few weeks to brief government officials. Unless, of course, she determined that Zhang had ratted her out regarding her participation in the prince's rescue. Then, she said, she'd have to go on the run for a while until they lost interest in her. He would see her when he saw her, she told him. It had been fun while it lasted. He'd never looked better. And his new interrogation technique was to die for.

Besides, they'd always have Paris, she'd reminded him.

And all that other tommyrot and happy horseshit.

CHAPTER 72

London
Present Day

When Hawke and Prince Henry had boarded the G650 at eight that morning at Bermuda International, Pelham, Chief Inspector Congreve, and his wife, Lady Mars, were already aboard. They were seated comfortably amidships facing one another over the round fruitwood coffee table and sipping tea from William Yeoward Gosford china and the Buccellati silver service on the table.

All three got immediately to their feet when they caught sight of the Queen's grandson Prince Henry coming through the cabin door right behind Alex. The prince, who had heard all about these people, smiled and went over to introduce himself. Lady Mars curtsied, and they shook hands all around. Invited by Ambrose to join them, the prince took a seat.

Hawke, who was leaning casually against the wooden bulkhead outside the cockpit, was having a final word with his captain.

"And the time of arrival at Heathrow?" Hawke said.

"Depending on the tailwind, flying time a wee bit short of seven hours, sir. Somewhere right around three this afternoon, I'd say, sir."

"Good. Good," Hawke said, already thinking about something else. Prince Henry had told him that he didn't want his grandmother the Queen to see him like this. If they were going to Buckingham Palace, he wanted time to get properly attired. He wanted a proper suit, shirt, and tie; he wanted to replace his flip-flops with a pair of brogues from Lobb;

he wanted to get a hot-towel shave and a haircut at Truefitt & Hill's—all that sort of thing.

Hawke agreed. But it would be nearly five before they could get to Savile Row, and that wasn't nearly enough time. He had an idea. He would ask Lady Mars if she could possibly invite the prince to their country estate for the night and make sure he got a good, healthy supper. Then, early the next day, Ambrose could take the prince to Hawke's Savile Row tailor, Anderson & Sheppard, to get kitted out.

And to the Royal-warranted Truefitt & Hill barbers after that!

She readily agreed, saying how charming the prince was and that she and Ambrose would be delighted.

The copilot closed the cockpit door, and Nanette battened all the hatches and secured the cabin for takeoff. Not for the first time did Hawke notice her splendid figure and balletic movements. He smiled inwardly, knowing he'd done the right thing by letting China go. Way past time to move on.

They'd had a thing. It was over and time to move on and let all the bloody chips land where they might.

"I say, Ambrose," Hawke said, "may I have a word?"

"But of course."

"Very good. Let's go back to the banquette aft, shall we?"

When they were seated, and Congreve had got his beloved brier pipe going, Hawke explained the situation regarding the young prince.

"I see, I see," Ambrose said. "He's quite right, you know. God knows he's improved mightily, but he still wants to look the way his grand-mother expects him to look at their reunion."

"Well, you're very kind, Constable. I know I could do it, but as you know, my allegiance is now to my son, Alexei. He's been in Madrid for a month now. He's been the guest at the palace of my good friend the Duke of Alba. I told you about that, of course. Before I was very nearly killed, along with Pelham."

"You did. I'm happy to oblige. I enjoy his company immensely. Great sense of humor, you know. You must be very proud of him, dear boy."

"Oh, I am indeed!" Hawke said.

Lord Hawke and Prince Henry arrived at Buckingham Palace at ten that rainy morning, right on the button.

They were escorted promptly up to the Royal Families' private residence by a footman who had almost literally jumped for joy when he laid eyes on the long-lost prince.

"Home at last, sir. Home at last you are! Her Royal Majesty is beside herself with excitement. Come, come, let's hurry!"

"Where is Her Majesty, Giles?" Henry asked, trying to keep up with the footman racing up the staircase. There were seven hundred seventy-five rooms in Buck House, and even Henry had never seen most of them.

"Sir, she's in the White Room. Breakfast is being served there now, sir."

"I'm famished," the prince said. "Lead on!"

Hawke was thrilled with his mood and his appearance. Congreve had done an excellent job at the tailor's and the barber's and at Lobb's famous shoe emporium.

When they arrived at the White Room, Her Royal Majesty was at her desk, answering Red Box mail, as she did every morning. When they entered and were announced by the footman, she looked up, and there was such joy in her eyes.

Prince Henry went to her side, bent down, and hugged her tightly, his eyes closed, hers wide open and smiling at him.

"Oh, Grandmother," Henry said. "I am so terribly sorry about all this. I knew you were bereft and worried, but there was simply no way they would let me communicate with you. And I will tell you, had not Lord Hawke found me when he did, I would not be here."

"Lord Hawke, Alex, my dear boy," the Queen, who was crying, said, "I will, as long as I live, try to find the right words to thank you for what you've done. Losing Henry would have been the end of me. I don't think I could have soldiered on. I really don't."

Hawke bowed deeply and said, "It was my very great honor to serve you, Your Majesty, I promise you."

"Thank you, Alex. When I think back on all you have done for me, done for this old family. That Christmas at Balmoral? You saved us all, and we all know it. It's why I insisted to Sir David that he send you out to the Bahamas. I knew you were the only man in England who could find Henry and bring him safe home to me. . . ."

"Thank you very much, ma'am," Hawke said with a little bow.

"Henry," Hawke said, turning to the boy, "I'm up to the north of Scotland for the weekend. Do a little shooting. Lots of pheasant this time of year. Want to have a go?"

The prince smiled, his arm still around the Queen. He said, "My Lord Hawke, I cannot think of a single thing I should like better on this earth. Is Alexei coming with?"

"Certainly. I'm teaching him about the dogs and the shooting. He loves it."

"Well, count me in."

"It's done, then. I have a beautiful old place up there. An ancestral home called Castle Hawke. We can go stalking for stags in the Highlands as well. Drink a little whiskey. . . . You know the drill. Ever had haggis, by the way?"

"I think not. I've heard of it, of course, but not a clue as to what's really in it."

"State secret. But it's sheep's liver minced with spices, salt, oatmeal, suet, and onion inside the lining of the animal's stomach. . . ."

"I realized something just now, sir. I have not ever managed to properly thank you for what you've done for my grandmama and myself. I shall never be able to repay you, for I shall forever be in your debt, sir."

"It was your grandmother who saved you, Henry. Never forget that. And with that, I shall take my leave. I'm sure you both have a great deal to talk about. And I've got my son waiting for me at my house in Belgrave Square. I'm taking him to Queen Mary's Rose Garden this morning. With his new puppy, an English springer named Captain."

Hawke bowed again, backed away from the Queen, and left the reunited alone. He hurried back down to have his old Bentley fetched and rushed home to his son.

Alexei had grown a lot in Madrid with the Duke of Alba. He was growing up too fast, and Hawke decided that they needed vastly more time together.

To that end he'd bounced an idea off Sir David.

He was going to build another yacht, this time a sailing yacht. A big one. A two hundred twenty footer, a gleaming white yawl. She would be yar, sleek, and fast. She would be comfortable belowdecks, and seaworthy, and have a certain grace about her under sail.

She would also be, appearances to the contrary, a state-of-the-art warship.

He and his precious ten-year-old son, Alexei, would sail her around the world, across the seven seas to the far-flung ends of the earth. He would teach the boy how to hand, reef, and steer. Teach him about the tides and the currents, celestial navigation, steering by the stars, heeling over, riding hard on the wind. Two adventurous souls bound by blood and love, seeking peace and solace from the sea and all who lived there in her beautiful, bountiful aquatic universe.

And if ever they should perchance encounter a knave or two in Port Royal, Jamaica, or any dastardly pirates out there on the sun-splashed Spanish Main, or any of those fiendish blackguards at Dragonfire Club who'd almost killed poor Henry, they would deal with them, too, and smartly at that. And if fate should turn her back on them, or turn away from them, leaving them to their own devices, and should they find themselves be sore afraid, then they would simply sail away to the other side of the world. They would ride like the wind. They would sail once more into the breach and damn the torpedos!

God save the Queen!

And the devil take the hindmost!

EPILOGUE

Lord Hawke would never see China Moon again. Her instincts about her bitter rival for Hawke's affections, the treacherous Zhang Tang, had been spot-on. When Zhang's twin brothers, fresh out of a Chinese white-collar crime lockdown, arrived at last back at Dragonfire Club, she'd instantly given them a full account of the goings-on in their absence.

The glamorous British lord and his exotic inamorata, China Moon, both of whom had disappeared, had caused no end of trouble for the Tang family. Both had arrived at Dragonfire Club sailing under a false flag. China had claimed she was merely vacationing once more at her beautiful home here on the island. But Zhang had told Tommy and Jackie Tang that China was on a mission, secretly looking for dirt on the brothers' Bahamian operations for the plethora of Tang enemies back in Beijing.

And Lord Hawke, who had claimed to be a wealthy British business-man, had in fact been sent to Dragonfire Club by Scotland Yard. The Queen of England had demanded he continue to search for the missing prince while undercover at the resort.

They had both been very successful.

Hawke had discovered the top secret Chinese submarine base. Not to mention their vast drug operations. Both now destroyed, as her brothers well knew from new reports, by the U.S. Navy.

China, hiding out in Paris at the Ritz for some months, had been walking home on a rainy night from the Place de l'Opéra to the Place

Vendôme when she'd realized she was being followed by two men wearing black fedoras and black trench coats.

She was a little worried. The pit of her stomach felt like a cage full of blind mice. She tried to remain calm. After all, she was a senior officer in the Chinese Secret Police; she was no novice at even the cleverest forms of escape and evasion. To her dismay, she tried every trick in her book and was unable to shake the tail.

She started running, believing that if she could only reach the entrance to the Ritz and dash inside, she'd be safe. Hotel security forces would get rid of them for her.

She darted into an alley behind the hotel proper, the very same one Princess Diana and her erstwhile lover, Dodi Fayed, had used to escape the press waiting for her at the main entrance before she climbed into the Mercedes W140 with her death-crash driver, M. Henri Paul, behind the wheel after he had imbibed a snootful of wine down in the Hemingway Bar that afternoon.

China's Chinese assailants were closing in. She heard the footsteps splashing through the puddles and gaining ground on her. Her stiletto heels weren't helping matters much. She wasn't going to make it. Her only hope was to turn and confront them. She did so out of sheer desperation, and it was a fatal mistake.

The two men kept coming at her, raised their guns, and emptied two 9mm magazines into her spasmic body, which they left twitching on the wet pavement. She wasn't found till next morning when early kitchen staff members were throwing out the previous evening's garbage. She was not a pretty sight. The neighborhood rats had been at her all night.

Since she made it a habit never to carry identification while on the run, no one was ever able to find out who she was. She was buried without ceremony in a paupers' cemetery in the Ninth Arrondissement.

And as for Ambassador Tiger Tang, of whom much has been said here, four long years of world war elapsed after his attempted assassination of the American president. In those bitter days gone by, the ambassador would never have predicted that, on this early spring day filled with sunshine, he would have found himself standing next to Eleanor Roosevelt in the rose garden at Hyde Park, waiting for the president to arrive.

About a grueling month after the near tragic episode up on Pine Mountain in Warm Springs, he'd finally been exonerated, cleared of any wrongdoing by a presidential panel of the most senior military psychiatrists. It was demonstrably proven in a secret military tribunal that the Chinese ambassador had never intended to bring harm to the president. At the time of the attempted murder, he had been a victim himself, acting mindlessly under the control of ancient Chinese mind-control techniques. As the president had written in a letter to the tribunal, he firmly believed that in that moment, Ambassador Tang had not even been aware of any of his actions at the time.

Tiger returned to the embassy and carried out his duties with a vengeance. Because of the near tragedy his father had instigated, he redoubled his efforts to help Roosevelt get critical Chinese support in the war against Japan. And because of his loathing for his father and those in his Beijing crime family, he began a diet of steady political disinformation to his father that continued to the end of the war in the Pacific.

And so, the two men continued their very unique friendship for those years. Afternoons up in the president's study overlooking the Hudson River, Franklin with his stamps and Tiger reading aloud to him, perhaps the latest Hemingway novel. And, of course, the fishing expeditions on the salmon rivers of Montana, the Christmases at the White House, the state dinners. It would all come to a sad end, of course, when Roosevelt, age sixty-three, finally met the Reaper while having his portrait painted by a Russian artist named Madame Shoumatoff at the Little White House, the refuge he had so dearly loved in his lifetime.

He did not live to see the victory he and Churchill had envisaged and enabled. Few had been aware how terribly Roosevelt's health had been deteriorating due to the demands placed on him by the two-front war.

Now Tang was amid the sorrowful weeping of the many gathered at the Hyde Park grave site, including not only heads of state, but also countless victims of polio who had benefitted so greatly from his leadership.

Ambassador Tang, unable to hold back the flood of tears, stood in silence as the procession bearing the casket of the magnificent figure drew nigh: this giant of the twentieth century, a man who had steered the nation through the depths of the Depression, through the grim years of war when no one could have been certain of the outcome.

As the president's casket was about to be lowered into the freshly turned earth in the rose garden of his estate at Hyde Park, there was a prolonged silence. Tiger had to force himself to even watch these events unfolding.

And then he heard these four fateful words that signaled the end and knew he was not dreaming. It was really all over now. His friend was no longer. A handsome young Marine, splendid in his red, white, and blue uniform, saluted and said loudly enough for all to hear....

"Bugler, sound the taps."

POSTSCRIPT

For his part, Commander Hawke had exacted a last-minute measure of revenge on the supremely evil Tang twins. Arriving on *Chop-Chop* at the airport marina with the ailing prince, he saw that an ambulance had been duly summoned out to the main dock by his pilots. There was also a van crammed with all the weapons and unused ammo that was to be ferried across the field to his airplane.

Once it was all stowed in the plane, he asked Stokely Jones to remain on the Wally tender with his RPG weapon a few minutes after everyone else had departed.

"Sure thing, boss," Stoke said. "What's up?"

"Just curious," Hawke said. "We got any of those rocket grenades left? Or did you expend them all in the firefight on the island?"

"Lemme check," he said, digging into his canvas rucksack. "Yeah, we got one. But only one."

"One's all we need."

"Really, boss? What you got in mind? I don't like that evil smile on your face."

"Had an idea, that's all. Think you might find it rather amusing. . . ."

"Talk to me."

"Right, then. So, jump up on the dock and cleat off the bow and stern lines, right?"

"Got ya," Stoke said, and hopped up onto the concrete dock with both lines in his left hand and the M79 grenade launcher in his right.

Hawke smiled up at him. "Okay, so, now, we cleat the lines off. But, I want you to use a whole lot of extra line at both stern and bow. Okay? Like twenty, maybe thirty feet."

"No shit? What if that cold front comes in tonight. This million dollar boy toy'll be blowing all over the place you leave that much slack in the lines. Boat could hit a piling or something, spring a damn leak . . ."

"Not necessarily."

"Really? Why's that?"

Hawke said, "I'll show you. Go ahead and affix the grenade to the muzzle of the launcher."

"Okay . . . done. Now what?"

Hawke reached over and shut down the burbling outboards. "Lemme get off the damn boat and I'll tell you."

"You're acting weird, boss. You ain't going to do anything crazy, are you?"

"Well, I'm not sure. It's either crazy or it's brilliant. It's either sheer insanity or it's pure genius. You be the judge."

"You don't tell me right now, I'm liable to throw *you* in the water!"

"Fine, fine. See that stainless steel screw cap set into the teak deck in the center of the cockpit?"

"Hard to miss it."

"Good. That's your target."

"What? You mean with the RPG?"

"Precisely. I want you to fire the grenade at the screw cap. Then we run like hell for the plane. . . ."

"Boss, get serious man. I do that? I'll blow a hole a foot in diameter in the bottom of the hull! This million dollar baby'll go to the bottom in about twenty seconds!"

"I know. You think the Tang Brothers will be pissed off?"

"Pissed off doesn't even begin to cover it."

"Yeah. I think so, too. But how pissed will they be when they find their big fat Bentley rusting away on the bottom, right beneath their beloved *Chop-Chop?*"

"Oh man, boss, that's just cruelty. But I love it."

"So, let's do this and get the hell out of the bloody Bahamas. I've had enough. Ready?"

"If you say so."

"Aim . . . *fire!*"

The powerful grenade exploded out of the muzzle with a loud bang and a whoosh and blew a huge hole in the deck. Seawater started spouting upward into the cockpit almost instantly. It was a gusher, all right, a bona fide geyser.

"Good shot, brother! Now let's get the hell out of here before the Nassau Constabulary arrives on the scene!"

They ran like hell.

Hawke looked over at Stoke and was startled by his own burst of laughter. He had been right, after all. The sinking of the good ship *Chop-Chop*, or the *Lollipo*, as Stoke had come to call it, with a rocket-powered grenade bore no trace of tragedy. It wasn't tragic at all. It was the pure bliss of unapologetic schadenfreude. It was funny of an order of magnitude that brought forth torrents of explosive laughter and reduced two grown men to tears of joy.

ACKNOWLEDGMENTS

A few kind words, dear readers, about my new editor and good friend, Tom Colgan.

Tom is legendary in this publishing business, justifiably so, for his peerless editorial skills, which are considerably beyond considerable; his many kindnesses, which are lavished upon his colleagues and authors alike, all and sundry; his cheery disposition; his keen wit; and his cherished James Thurber–esque sense of humor. After reading another of his daily "Plague Journal" essays, I called him and said, "Tom, you're too funny. I think you're a cross between Mark Twain and Will Rogers."

"Good cross to be in," he replied. I'd also like to express my gratitude to Team Colgan/Bell at Penguin Random House.

Therefore, a big shout-out to those folks whose fingerprints are all over this book: Loren Jaggers, Fareeda Bullert, and Sareer Khader. Thank you one and all!

And then there is Mr. John Talbot. My new agent, confidante, coconspirator, and oftentimes psychiatrist. John is a singular man. Incredibly wise about this book business, with vast experience as an editor before the career switch, and an uncanny ability to answer any vague and querulous literary or business questions of mine, always succinct, elegant, and articulate. Much like John himself. Thank you, John. I owe you a big fat lunch at 21 Club!

And next, the great Jon Adler. Jon is my business partner in the new film/TV production company we started late last year. It's called El Dorado Entertainment. We already have a signed movie deal with one major Hollywood studio, and an A-list screenwriter who is attached to bringing my young adult/historical/time travel books, *The Time Pirate/Nick of Time* series, o the big screen or streaming. Jon is my number one fan and has been a huge help to us in bringing this new project to life!

Ryan Steck. A name known by any and all who labor in the vineyards of the thriller novel. Besides his encyclopedic knowledge of the genre, Ryan is a book doctor extraordinaire, an editor, and a huge promoter of us pencil pushers. More importantly, I will acknowledge his huge contribution to all of us. When I came of age in this thriller game, there was a pervasive air of competition between all of us writers. A given. But Ryan changed all that single-handedly. He took it upon himself to turn us into a community. A group of people who became friends, not competitors, people who supported the work of their fellow authors and cheered their successes. This is no small thing. It has made our profession much more satisfying and rewarding.

Friends I have made during these years include many people I care about and respect. Daniel Silva, Brad Taylor, Mark Greaney, Nelson De-Mille, Brad Thor, the late Vince Flynn, the late Mary Higgins Clark, the late Dorothea Benton Frank, the late Tom Wolfe . . . and many more.

I also am indebted to the lovely Lady Hornblower, as she's known around here. Cynthia Hornblower manages my website, newsletter, my "Writer's Block" videos, as well as books all my appearances around the world. Thank you, Lady H, for all your help and for putting up with me all this time!

And lastly, a tip of the battered fedora to my three literary heroes. Giants who have provided inspiration and artistic guidance for my own work since I first put pen to paper at age eight . . . with reverence . . . and even love:

Mark Twain. *The Adventures of Huckleberry Finn* is the seminal American novel.

F. Scott Fitzgerald. *The Great Gatsby* is the great American novel.

Ian Fleming. James Bond is the twentieth century's most popular hero.

So we beat on, boats against the current,
borne back cease-lessly into the past.

—Nick Carraway, *The Great Gatsby*

CHARLESTON, SOUTH CAROLINA, APRIL 4TH, 2020